An Economic History of Europe

An Economic History of Europe will provide students with a comprehensive introduction to European economic history from the fifteenth century to the present day. Individual chapters offer brief references to previous historical periods and events, with special attention given to core themes concerning economic development, and an analysis of their change through time and space.

Core themes examined in each period include:

- the increasing prominence of industry
- international trade
- supply and demand dynamics
- agriculture

The unique structure of this text will not only enable students to gain a firm grounding in the long-term evolution of the European economy, but also provide a historical overview of the economic development of individual countries. Individual contributors analyse the shift from the modern to the contemporary period and offer a broad explanation of the historical roots of the problems which face today's economic development.

This key new text will prove indispensable reading for students in economics, economic history, development economics and history.

Antonio Di Vittorio is Professor of Economic History at the University of Bari in Italy and President of the Italian Association of Economic Historians.

An Economic History of Europe

From expansion to development

Edited by Antonio Di Vittorio

Routledge
Taylor & Francis Group
LONDON AND NEW YORK

First published in Italian by G. Giappichelli Editore in 2002
(Dall'espansione allo sviluppo: una storia economica d'Europe)

Published in English in 2006
by Routledge
2 Park Square, Milton Park, Abingdon, Oxon OX14 4RN

Simultaneously published in the USA and Canada
by Routledge
711 Third Avenue, New York, NY 10017

Routledge is an imprint of the Taylor & Francis Group, an informa business

Typeset in Baskerville by
Florence Production Ltd, Stoodleigh, Devon

British Library Cataloguing in Publication Data
A catalogue record for this book is available
from the British Library

Library of Congress Cataloging in Publication Data
A catalog record for this book has been requested.

ISBN10: 0–415–35624–5 ISBN13: 978–0–415–35624–4 (hbk)
ISBN10: 0–415–35625–3 ISBN13: 978–0–415–35625–1 (pbk)
ISBN10: 0–203–00260–1 ISBN13: 978–0–203–00260–5 (ebk)

Translation by Katherine M. Hunt (except Chapter 4 by John A. Davis)

Contents

List of illustrations

Maps

Figures

Tables

List of contributors

Giuseppe Bracco is Professor of Economic History at the University of Turin.

Albert Carreras is Professor of Economic History at Universitat Pompeu Fabra of Barcelona.

John A. Davis is Professor of History at the University of Connecticut, Storrs CT.

Antonio Di Vittorio is Professor of Economic History at the University of Bari and President of the Italian Association of Economic Historians.

Giovanni Luigi Fontana is Professor of Economic History at the University of Padua.

Alberto Guenzi is Professor of Economic History and Dean of the Economics Faculty at the University of Parma.

Paola Massa is Professor of Economic History and Dean of the Economics Faculty at the University of Genoa.

Introduction

This text aims to provide an overall view of European economic history from the sixteenth century – when new horizons were opened up – to the present day. It also seeks to convey, as well as underline, the basic unity of the economic process from the time of the first voyages of discovery, in the late Middle Ages, until now.

The great cycle of European economic growth, which started in the mid-1440s, is first examined in its phase of expansion, during which there was an increase in production but no increase in productivity. Subsequently its development phase is studied, and it was during this period when there was an increase in production, as well as an increase in productivity. The two phases are not separated by the industrial revolutions and the start of the industrialization process but are linked by them. As John A. Davis shows very effectively in Chapter 4, on the eighteenth century, the phases of expansion and development are closely identified in different areas of Europe, often at very different times.

It is necessary to take into account this growth pattern of the European economic process over the centuries. It is especially important at a time when interest, even in the field of economic history, is increasingly focused on the present, and the time scale is continually being reduced.

Another aim of the book, in the light of the creation of a united Europe, is to underline how Europe had already followed a common path once, before taking it up again in the twentieth century, in a different way and in a different form.

A 'module' format has been adopted so that these objectives can be achieved. Each chronological period stands on its own, as far as possible, and each contains ample reference to previous periods, in order to lend continuity to the historical discussion. The repeated reference to institutions and single events further reflects the way the book is to be used. It is hoped that, far from encumbering the text, this will facilitate its 'modular' use. Another way of accentuating its aims is by presenting the book in a 'top-heavy' format, with the earlier periods covered in far less detail than the transition phase from the modern to the contemporary era. The content of the earlier chapters is also articulated differently from that of the contemporary era itself. In this way, the problems of development that are closer to us are approached and opened up gradually, without neglecting the context from which they emerged, and with which they are connected.

Bibliographical references are limited to those that are strictly indispensable for each chapter.

I cannot close without expressing my gratitude and appreciation to my colleagues Paola Massa, Giuseppe Bracco, Alberto Guenzi, John A. Davis, Giovanni Luigi Fontana and Albert Carreras for having agreed to make their own contributions to what has become a common project.

Antonio Di Vittorio

1 The economy in the fifteenth century

Preconditions for European expansion

Paola Massa

An integrated economic system: Europe in the fifteenth century

The geographical background

Geographers describe Europe, or the Old Continent as it is sometimes called, as a large indented peninsula extending for thousands of kilometres seawards. This circumstance has had a decisive effect on Europe's climate and greatly influenced the lives of its people, motivating them to navigate, explore and colonize new lands. Over the course of centuries the internal territorial divisions of Europe have undergone considerable variations as a result of numerous wars and subsequent political changes. However, despite their impact and influence, and despite enduring political divisions, economically we can consider fifteenth-century Europe as a single unit, as a community united by similar, or at least complementary, interests.

The French historian Fernand Braudel identified a process of integration in the economic fabric of Europe, occurring between the Middle Ages and the modern period, and he took the Old Continent as the basis for a model of economic development that he defined as a 'world system' or 'world economy'.[1] In his model, the population was subdivided into different social groups. These had differing demands for goods and manufactured products, and were largely self-sufficient for their requirements; thus they did not recognize any great economic advantage, or chance of enough profit, in exchanges with other groups beyond their boundaries. A further interesting aspect of Braudel's development model of modern Europe is how the territory and economy of the Old Continent ultimately came to include not only the whole Mediterranean area, but also the North African countries that had economic links with it. The waters of the 'internal' sea of the Mediterranean were an important point of intersection for the movement of goods, precious metals and people.

This idea of Europe is one that embraces an economic world with physical boundaries, limited by mountain chains, the North Pole and the African desert. It is a view of Europe that perhaps we can still look to today as we reflect on its political and cultural characteristics and historical traditions.

Urban poles of development and markets

An important aspect of the 'world economy' model in its application to fifteenth century Europe[2] is the way it underlines the dynamic changes that lead to successive and increasingly advanced stages of development. Braudel argued that a number of urban centres emerged, which he defined as 'poles', and which provided 'leadership' at different times. It was under their motivating force that certain sectors of the economy were expanded and formed bodies that, in different periods of history, acted as nuclei attracting greater numbers of productive resources, because of the more advantageous operating conditions.

At least until the mid-fifteenth century, apart from the textile industry (particularly the manufacturing of woollen cloth), it was in commerce where good profits could be made. Commerce, which could be called 'commercial capitalism', had existed since the early thirteenth century. Marco Cattini has described it as 'the merchant acting as middleman between producer and consumer and closing the great gap in time and space that lay between the place where certain goods were acquired and where they were sold'.[3] Merchants were men with considerable financial means and credit, and were considered reliable. They had a close technical knowledge of their wares in addition to being well versed in commerce, law and accounting.

During the fifteenth century two key areas of trade became increasingly important for the whole European economic system. The first coincided with the Italian cities

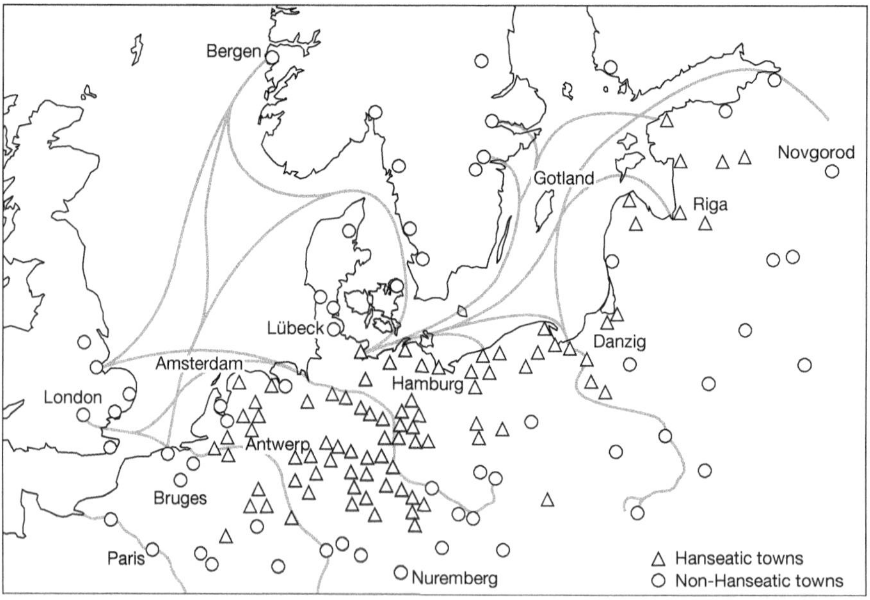

Map 1 Areas of Hanseatic trade around 1400.

Source: F. Braudel, *Civiltà materiale, economia e capitalismo*, III, *I tempi del mondo*, Turin, 1982 [1979], p. 89.

of the Mediterranean including Genoa, Venice, Pisa, Amalfi, Ancona, Naples, Messina and also Sienna and Lucca, which specialized in trade with the East and supplied Europe with indispensable products such as spices.[4] They also engaged in trading primary goods such as cereals and raw materials. The second was in the Baltic Sea area, where as far back as the mid-thirteenth century a group of ports, including Bruges and Antwerp, Hamburg, Danzig, Stettin, and Novgorod on the Russian coast, had joined to form part of the Germanic Hanseatic League. Hansa ships sailed from the Baltic Sea to the North Sea through the Sound, and all the northern European countries, including England, depended on them for their supplies.

Political factors complicated the pre-existing social and economic balances however. Overland trade was made difficult during the Hundred Years War (1337–1453), but it enabled Bruges to succeed in establishing itself as a midway port. When, at the end of the fifteenth century, Bruges fell out of favour with the Habsburg dynasty, its place was taken by the cosmopolitan mercantile centre of Antwerp, which was also the venue for one of the first international commodity exchange markets.

Goods, routes and means of transport

Throughout the fifteenth century, and for much of the sixteenth, the most important economic sector in Europe continued to be the production and trading of textiles. Tens of thousands of lengths of wool and silk cloth were traded and redistributed from Flanders, the Venetian hinterland, Tuscany and the important Italian 'silk cities' such as Lucca, Venice, Florence and Genoa. There was also a significant seaborne trade, involving bulk commodities such as grain, salt and timber. Important raw materials like iron, lead, tin, copper, leather, wax and furs, as well as grains such as rye, oats and barley, were transported to the North Sea ports by the Hanseatic League, while cargoes of Asian and Mediterranean produce such as oil, wine, spices, rice, dried figs, raw wool, dyes, alum[5] and textiles arrived from the opposite direction. Goods with a high unit value and low bulk were exchanged at international trade fairs such as the one in Champagne, which had been taking place since the thirteenth century, or in Geneva and Lyons since the fourteenth century. Every three months these fairs provided important meeting places for merchants, who came from the main countries, both north and south, to exchange goods and conduct their business transactions.[6]

Transporting goods along the various trade routes was not always easy. Mule caravans loaded with goods and people had to cross the Alps over passes that were often deep in snow. In the interior of Europe there were plenty of regular services and shipments along the rivers and canals, but there were still numerous obstacles, such as water mills or fulling works in mid-stream, that made costly transfers necessary. There were also dues and tolls to pay, or services that were under the monopoly of the corporations. The route of choice was therefore the sea; the transport it provided was slow and hazardous, owing to mishaps caused by human error or acts of nature, but it was undoubtedly less costly. Sailings did not usually take place in winter, but this was offset by the greater distances that could be covered and the high profits from the transport of both expensive goods and the relatively cheap bulk commodities. Before the explorations and geographical discoveries at the end of the fifteenth century, ships still sailed within sight of the coast wherever possible, but there was a gradual increase in the tonnage of the vessels. These were now being equipped with a greater number of masts and with stern rudders, and were making better and more rational use of sail power. Alongside the rowing galleys,[7] ships known as carracks, or *navis*, were appearing, and caravels later in the fifteenth century. For coastal navigation smaller boats were used. They were similar one to another but often had very different names. Throughout the century improvements to instruments, and developments in cartography, gradually reduced the margins of error and lowered the risks that were an integral part of navigation.

The gradual development of an efficient money market

In medieval tradition, going back to the time of Charlemagne, the treasury held the right to mint coins. It was a right that the most important cities also claimed for themselves, and when after lengthy and often difficult negotiations they succeeded in winning that right, they guarded it closely. Monarchs resisted this, since coins were seen as a symbol of sovereignty, but also, and perhaps more important, because the mint was a primary source of financial revenue. The revenue was acquired either legally through the right of 'seigniorage'[8] or illegally through gains the treasury could make by issuing coins of increasingly poor quality but whose legal value remained unchanged.

During the early Middle Ages the only coin actually in circulation was the silver *denaro*, whose weight and fineness varied considerably from one mint to another and from one year to the next. However, the general tendency was for these to decrease, one reason being the scarce supply of the metal on the markets. With rare exceptions, gold, as a means of payment, was used in the form of objects or bars whose value was measured by weight, or in the form of Byzantine or Arab coins. The wide availability of these coins delayed monetization in the western areas of Europe even after 1000, which was a period of strong recovery in trade that coincided with the first Crusades, a considerable increase in population and a steady decline in barter.

In the period until the eleventh century, exchanges were typically made using forms of payment that the French historian Frédéric Mauro has defined as 'borderline'. For example a family made use of any surplus goods, produced beyond its own needs, for the purpose, though this arrangement was more common in country areas and generally in closed economies. Barter was widely practised on regional or international markets, and for this purpose salt was one of the most enduring commodities. Another widespread form of 'payment' was the free provision of care and medical treatment for much of the population, by the Church and the monastic orders. Before the spread of printing, parishes and convents provided education and culture. They also organized water supplies in the urban centres.

After the mid-thirteenth century, coin gradually made its way into every field of economic life; even feudal taxes that had been payable in kind were now starting to be paid in money. Some historians maintain that the first gold coin of any importance was the *genovino*, which was coined in Genoa and dated back to the second half of the twelfth century. The *fiorino*, issued in Florence, and the Venetian gold ducat, later called the *zecchino*, belonged to a slightly later period. France followed the example set by the Italian cities and in 1266 issued the *parigino*, while some years later England did the same with the *noble*. However, the development of a money market was delayed because there was insufficient precious metal in circulation suitable for coining. Thus, until the mid-fifteenth century, there was a considerable discrepancy between supply and demand. Only modest quantities of precious metals were being extracted and, in any case, these were only partly used for coinage. Gold, as well as silver, was required for making jewellery and plate, church and convent treasures, which were considered as risk-free investments.

In the second half of the century the bimetallic system developed in Europe, and the search for new deposits of gold and silver produced positive results; meanwhile the increasing price of metal provided a further impetus. The application of new mining techniques that were being developed led to better exploitation of the known deposits. The availability of silver increased with the improved exploitation of German, Austrian and Hungarian mines, and at the end of the century there were increases in the quantities of gold. Two simultaneous circumstances caused an increase in the availability of gold. First there was the exploitation of the gold reserves in Guinea and Senegal, following the Portuguese explorations along the African coasts. These sources boosted the circulation of European money, supplementing the gold supplies that had long been coming from the Sudan, across the Sahara to North Africa, where they were exchanged for Italian and Spanish products. Second there was the result of the early voyages of Columbus that brought the 'gold of the isles' from Santo Domingo, Porto Rico, Cuba and the Antilles into Spain.

However, even this was still very little compared with the growing needs of the economic system of Europe, the development of which was closely linked with variations in the available quantities of precious metals and the instability of their value. Here it should be pointed out that the monetary organization of all states was based on a distinction between real, or coined, money and money of account, between which the state fixed a ratio. Money of account acted as a unit of measure for the currency in circulation,[9] and, at least until the sixteenth century, was rock-solid.

All in all there were many different coins circulating in Europe, yet, at the same time, attempts were being made to bring stability to the international money market. Apart from money of account, there was also a tendency towards trying to keep the exchange ratios constant. Two examples illustrate the efforts that were made to bring order and innovation to a technically archaic system. First there was the formation of the Rhenish Monetary Confederation in the fifteenth century; eleven sovereigns and seventy-four German cities signed an agreement whereby, for a certain period, the Rhenish florin was to act as the only legal currency. Second there was the *scudo di marco*, which had a more sophisticated and significant purpose; this type of money of account had first circulated in the thirteenth century fairs of Champagne, and during the course of almost three centuries had gradually merged in such as way as to meet the needs of merchants from different countries.

It is more difficult to assess how rapidly money circulated in the fifteenth century. Gold was circulating less rapidly than silver (through the effects of Gresham's law[10]); this circumstance was further conditioned by individual territorial circumstances, the role of credit, and the slow recovery of capital invested in commerce and manufacturing. The consequences were to be much greater in the following century, when the first great period of European inflation occurred, and when there was exceptional development in commercial and financial business on an international level. From this point of view the fifteenth century, particularly the second half, was a time when the European economic system was adapting to pressures of all kinds.

The merchant bankers: the first instruments and institutions of credit

While economic activity was still carried on within a feudal framework the lack of money was not seen as an important problem, but the gradual development of trade – which postulates the need for a suitable substitute for money – led to attempts to get round this deficiency. The granting of credit long remained an unregulated and often illegal practice, and as a result, though average rates of interest in western Europe varied between 5 per cent and 10 per cent, merchants and artisans did not acquire the capital they needed for an investment, since its cost would certainly have been greater than any profit from it. Initially the clientele of banker-moneylenders consisted mainly of people requiring money for the purchase of consumer goods. But the fifteenth century was still dominated by the medieval conviction that any payment for the loan of money was immoral, which was the official view of the Church. Even the bill of exchange was viewed with suspicion and considered as a loan in disguise (which indeed it did become), despite its use for a commercial transaction. The only case where it was permissible was if it was negotiated on another market and in a different currency from the drawer's, in which case the interest was camouflaged within the exchange rate.

The leading figures in the sector of credit were the merchant bankers. They were non-specialist financial dealers who opened current accounts and received deposits without, initially, paying any interest, at least not overtly. An account would be opened to facilitate a client's payments, withdrawals and giro operations 'in writing', which meant that the transaction was entered into the merchant banker's account books at his *banco*, or 'bench'. The banker could use the sums he received to carry out his own business, which might be mercantile or entrepreneurial or in the field of insurance, and at the same time gain greater professional and social credibility for himself. When changes in the doctrinal attitudes of the Church allowed greater freedom, it meant that the depositor could now be paid a 'fair' interest rate. Business deals, which were initially negotiated only on the local *piazza*, or market place, gradually moved to other markets, or *fuori piazza*. Venice, Genoa and Barcelona, but especially towns in south Germany and Tuscany,[11] were flourishing centres for this type of activity, which now saw the progressive development of a wide range of instruments of credit, including advance payments on goods and associated banking techniques such as endorsements and cheques.

Apart from the large and dynamic families of merchant bankers, who operated mainly out of Italy with branches and correspondents throughout Europe, there were also a number of public institutions of credit, particularly in Spain and Italy. One of the oldest of these was the Banco di San Giorgio (Bank of St George), which was founded in Genoa in 1408. Other forms of credit also existed, and these would be further refined over the next centuries. They included loans to sovereigns or cities, securities, annuities and investments for partnership in companies. The mid-fifteenth century was especially marked by the spread of pawnbroking under the management of the Monti di Pietà, whose main purpose was to provide charitable aid. These organizations were founded by the Franciscan monks, and the first Monte, in Perugia, dates from 1462. The Monti were an alternative to usury for people who, though poor, were not destitute; the money was required in the short term, and the borrower was confident of soon finding the resources to pay back the debt and redeem the items he had pawned. By the end of the century this typically Italian institution had spread to most of the peninsula. Its strong point lay in the low interest rates, which did not usually exceed 10 per cent and in some cases were much lower. In the case of particularly small amounts they were even zero. The capital the Monti used for their activities initially came from their own sources of revenue, and was not subject to any charges. A century later some of them started gathering deposits, but for a long time no interest was charged.

The supply of and demand for goods: agricultural and manufactured goods

Population patterns

In quantitative terms the major factor conditioning the demand for goods is population. However, no definite or complete data for population patterns and structure between the Middle Ages and the modern period are available, since the first censuses and reasonably accurate figures date only from the early nineteenth century. However, some estimates, especially those concerning urban areas, can provide a certain degree of reliability, and even on a wider territorial scale it is possible to make some statistical observations and hypotheses.

The medieval period was marked by a long-term steady growth in the European population, despite a high mortality rate that could be defined as 'catastrophic' and which was caused by wars, famines and epidemics.[12] There was also the 'normal' mortality rate, which in itself was very high, especially as regards the death of infants and children under the age of ten. Such a mortality rate was a direct consequence of the poverty and hardships that the population endured. Its effect on the demographic structure of the Old Continent was almost paradoxical; it was always a 'young' population, with the average life expectancy calculated by Carlo M. Cipolla as never being more than forty to forty-five years.[13] Cipolla had addressed the immense problem of calculating the overall population of Europe, including European Russia and the Balkans, and concluded that in 1000 it was about 30 million to 35 million inhabitants. He calculated that in the mid-fourteenth century it had grown to 80 million, amounting to almost a third of the total world population of around 300 million. Between 1247 and 1351 the population of Europe was reduced by a third, as a result of the enormously high number of deaths during the great epidemic known as the Black Death, which had started in the East and spread very rapidly.[14] Besides the high number of deaths, there were two further consequences. The first was that, from then on, the plague became endemic in Europe, with scattered focal points and serious outbreaks at regular intervals. The second was that, for over a century, the European population remained at considerably reduced levels compared with the pre-1347 levels. It was not until the end of the fifteenth century that the overall population again reached the 80 million mark, although during the first half of the century there were marked regional imbalances. Growth was slow in France owing to the Hundred Years War (1337–1453), and in Italy the upward trend was also very slow. On the other hand the Iberian peninsula, Germany and England showed much stronger rates of growth. A more generalized upward trend started after 1450 with the recovery of the economic system, which had been heavily affected by the plague. The reduction in population, and hence in demand, increased the availability of resources somewhat, and led to improved living conditions for people for several decades, though it did not activate the economy as a whole.

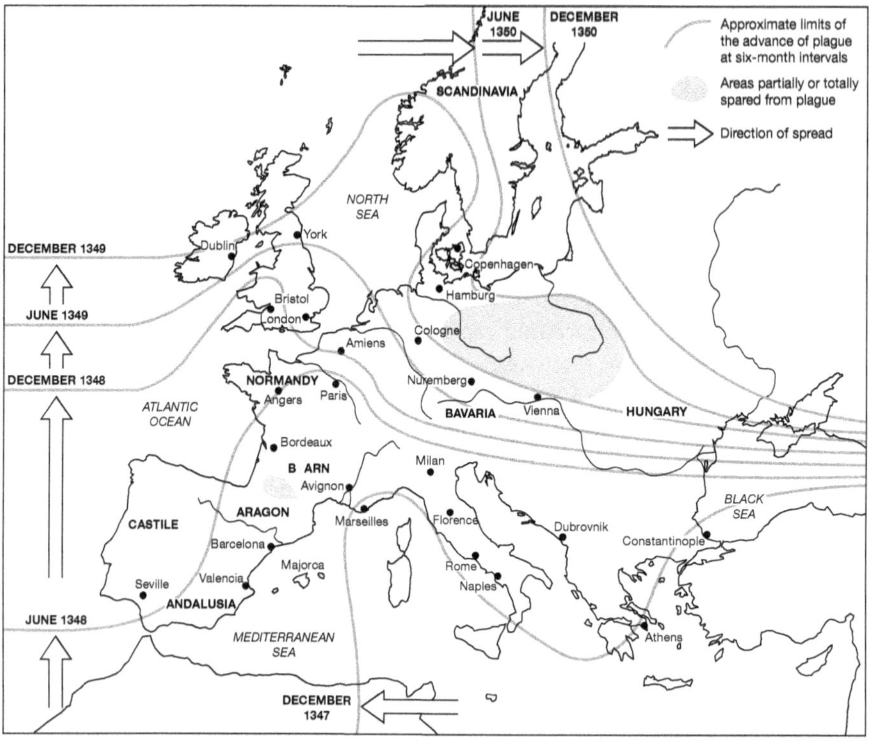

Map 2 The spread of the Black Death in Europe from 1347.

Source: E. Carpenter, 'Autour de la Peste Noire: famines et épidémies dans l'histoire du XVI siècle', *Annales E.S.C.*, 17, 1962.

The European population was also showing a tendency towards concentrating in towns. This was mainly to seek better protection, but also to search for more lucrative employment. It has been calculated that in the pre-industrial period the population living in urban centres averaged 10 per cent, with peaks of 15–20 per cent in some areas.[15] The movement towards the towns usually followed one of two trends; either from rural areas or from smaller to larger towns. In Italy there was a movement of people from Padua and Verona to Venice, while Milan was an important magnet for other Lombard centres. In the early fifteenth century, in Italy alone, there were about ten cities of around 50,000 inhabitants[16] while the rest of Europe had no more than nine.[17] Such movements of people inevitably had consequences for the urban areas, and the greater concentrations of population in the towns obliged the public authorities to provide a more wide-ranging and efficient system for the supply and distribution of primary consumer goods.

Consumption and investment

Expenditure in fifteenth century Europe was primarily on consumption, and largely to meet private demand; the amount of capital invested in manufacturing activities was considerable, but this was more a result of the slow market process than because it was tied up in plant and machinery, and in any case it concerned only a small minority of the population. Public expenditure on goods and services was not very different from private expenditure, except in times of war; investment in the productive sectors was negligible, with the mining industry as practically the only exception. Means of communication were the only infrastructure in which states showed any real interest; there was state involvement in the building of ports, canals, road networks and shipyards as well as civic authority buildings. The Church and the Roman Curia similarly invested in building activities. F. Mauro has debated the question of whether the financing of maritime enterprises in remote countries could also be considered as public investment:[18] the conclusion is probably that it could. This applies not so much to the Spanish conquests, but certainly to the policy of the Portuguese sovereigns who, throughout much of the fifteenth century, financed shipbuilding as well as trading expeditions.

Private individuals, especially from the aristocracy, channelled their profits from land, and other investments, into expenditure on goods such as fine furniture, tapestries, paintings and jewellery, which are not easily separated into luxuries and investments. In any case, the greatest share of individual income was absorbed by primary needs such as food, housing and heating. Even the spiritual relationship a person had with the Church needed to be paid for, not to mention the compulsory payment of tithes. In 'normal' years, around 80 per cent of a person's income went on primary goods, and the demand for these goods was constant even during the frequent agricultural crises. If people ate little and badly an important reason lay in the very low average of individual incomes. Clothing was a further item that involved considerable expense but this increased in relation to income, unlike food.

The staple 'diet' of the poor classes consisted of cereals (which apart from wheat also included rye, barley, oats and spelt), chestnuts and almost a litre per head per day of drinks such as wine and beer (which provided energy). Income levels varied according to wage patterns and price levels and set natural limits to people's wants and needs. Social and economic differences were reflected in calorie intake and diversification of foodstuffs. Apart from differences between rich and poor, there were those between town and country, as well as the different geographical areas of Europe. In the central and eastern parts of Europe the consumption of meat and animal fats needs to be reassessed, and the same applies to vegetable oils in the Mediterranean area. The intake of fish protein in areas by the sea should not be underestimated, and salted or dried fish was also widely consumed, despite its high cost. The demand for salt and spices remained steady though it was limited to small quantities *per capita.*

The primary sector: forms of cultivation and innovations

The primary sector includes industries such as agriculture, forestry and fishing, which involve natural raw materials.[19] Agriculture, in particular, has been the main occupation of populations for centuries, and in the pre-industrial period it engaged over 65 per cent of people. According to some economists,[20] an important indicator of the structural change of an economic system is when the great changes resulting from the industrial revolution lead to equal numbers of workers in both the agricultural and the industrial sectors. Indeed, when a person's income increases, there is a corresponding decrease in the proportion he invests in food resources.

At the end of the Middle Ages land was still the major resource of the European economy in terms of value, what it produced and the labour force it employed. It is difficult to provide a clear, overall picture of agricultural yields, organization and produce, because of the many differences determined by the climate and geography of the continent. In the Mediterranean areas of Europe, cereals were cultivated alongside a number of crops such as vines, olives, mulberries and citrus fruits, in addition to sugar cane and cotton in the most southerly areas. Oats, barley and rye, as well as plants such as flax and hemp used in manufacturing textiles, were grown in the northern and Atlantic areas. Cereal crops, which were also an important source of supplies for the rest of the Old Continent, were cultivated in central and eastern Europe.

The population increases in Europe, which became more generalized from the middle of the fifteenth century, had a number of wider consequences in the long term. One was the gradual break-up of the closed medieval *curtis*[21] of western Europe and its opening up to the market. Another was deforestation, which in the second half of the fifteenth century made new areas available for agriculture, at a time when all usable land was already under cultivation. There were also land reclamation projects, as well as the introduction of new agrarian contracts, such as the *mezzadria* sharecropping system in Tuscany at the end of the century and ricefields in the plains of the Po valley, where pre-capitalist forms of management and large-scale land leases were introduced. These were all indications that the fifteenth century, rather than being a period of crisis, was one of readjustment after violent upheavals, and that the economic system was going through a transitional stage. During the first decades the negative consequences of the wars, famines and epidemics of the previous century were being felt, with serious effects on the economy because of the decrease in population and reduced trade, not to mention the difficulties in organizing production. However, after 1450 the process was reversed and the population once again started to increase, though already there had been signs that wages were increasing and that a new equilibrium between the quantity of cultivable land and the supply of labour was being found.

In agriculture, the most important innovation was the replacement of the classic binary rotation system, in which fields were left fallow every other year, with a three-yearly rotation system. This brought several advantages: soil productivity was improved, since the amount of cultivated land increased by a third; work was more equally distributed throughout the year, since crops were now sown in autumn and spring; in addition, there was less risk of famine. There were also two significant innovations closely linked with the new form of crop rotation. First a new type of heavy wheeled plough was introduced, which was no longer made of wood but of iron, and second draught horses were used, with important changes being made to harnessing and equipment. Contemporary writers calculated that each horse could carry out the work of three or four oxen. However, their maintenance was three times as costly, and they were also required for transport and military operations. The cost effectiveness of adopting horse power thus depended on circumstances and had to be carefully assessed.

The secondary sector

The goods and manufactures required by the population, apart from those produced for its own consumption, gave rise to activities that involved the processing of raw materials, and since they were located in different areas important flows of traffic developed for their redistribution. The fifteenth century was a 'pre-industrial' period, in the sense that it came before the period of industrialization that started with the English industrial revolution in the mid-eighteenth century. However, if the expression is limited to meaning the use of technology appropriate to that particular period, then the fifteenth century can be considered 'industrial'. The raw materials subjected to industrial processes included agricultural products such as cereals, wood for building ships and making tools, plants such as flax for manufacturing textiles, or the mulberry which was important in the production of silk. One extremely important raw material was wool, while leather, used for many different manufactures, was also worked in countries along the Mediterranean coast of Africa. In the second half of the century, paper was produced from rags as well as from fibres containing cellulose. Important centres of paper production in Italy were located in Tuscany and Fabriano, but also in other parts of Europe such as the Vosges and the Dauphine.

The sector that employed by far the greatest number of workers was textile manufacturing, particularly wool products, which had been the case for centuries. England and Spain were the most important areas providing the raw wool, while the manufacturing centres were mainly urban centres such as the cities of Flanders and those of central and northern Italy. Their high quality products were much in demand on the international market and were bought and sold at the fairs and ports.

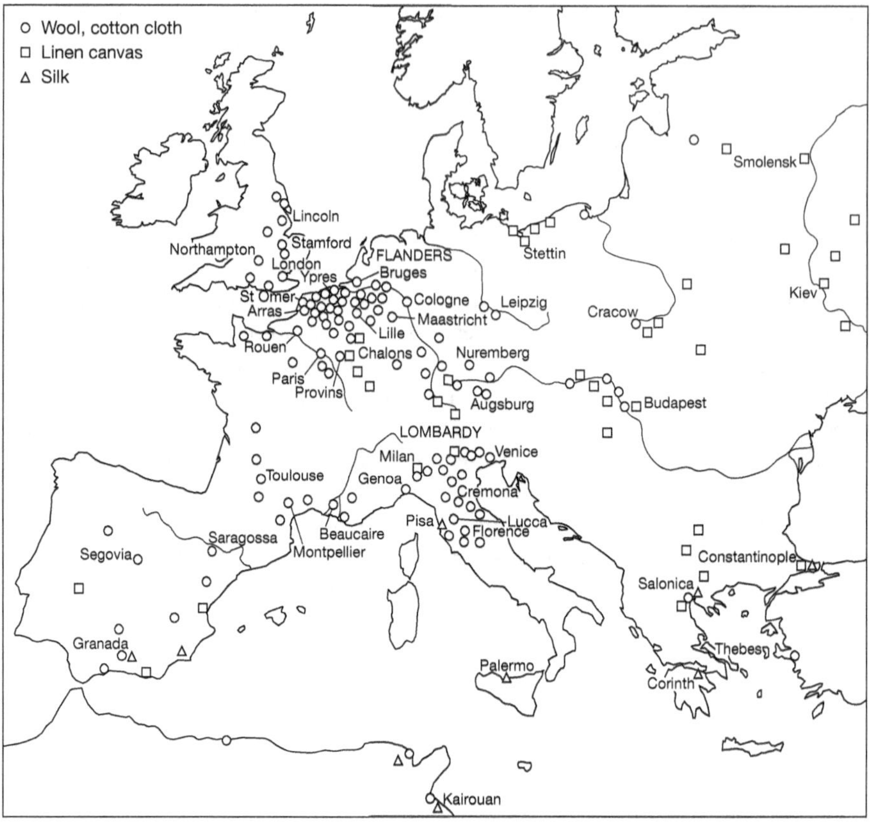

Map 3 Leading centres of the textile industry in twelfth century Europe.
Source: R.S. Lopez, *La rivoluzione commerciale del Medioevo*, Turin, 1974, p. 170.

Associated with this was a heavy demand for dyes and the previously mentioned alum, as well as the manufacture of clothing and other goods in common use.

The mining and metallurgical industries, as well as early attempts at working iron, especially in the central and western areas of Europe, provided tools, ploughs, building materials and arms. A wide range of metals, especially precious metals, became available and their particular locations often meant they had to be transported long distances by sea.[22]

The sea itself provided an abundance of resources such as coral, fish and salt, which were the basis for a variety of manufacturing processes and employed people living in its vicinity. Salt in particular was an important commodity, used not only for everyday purposes but also for salting meat and tanning leather. In the mountain areas it was in great demand from the cattle farmers, who used it for feeding to their animals. In northern Europe, where the seas had a lower salt content, people needed it in order to preserve fish. Indeed, salt was perhaps one of the best examples of long established exchanges between European peoples. The Mediterranean areas produced it from the sea and exported it in considerable

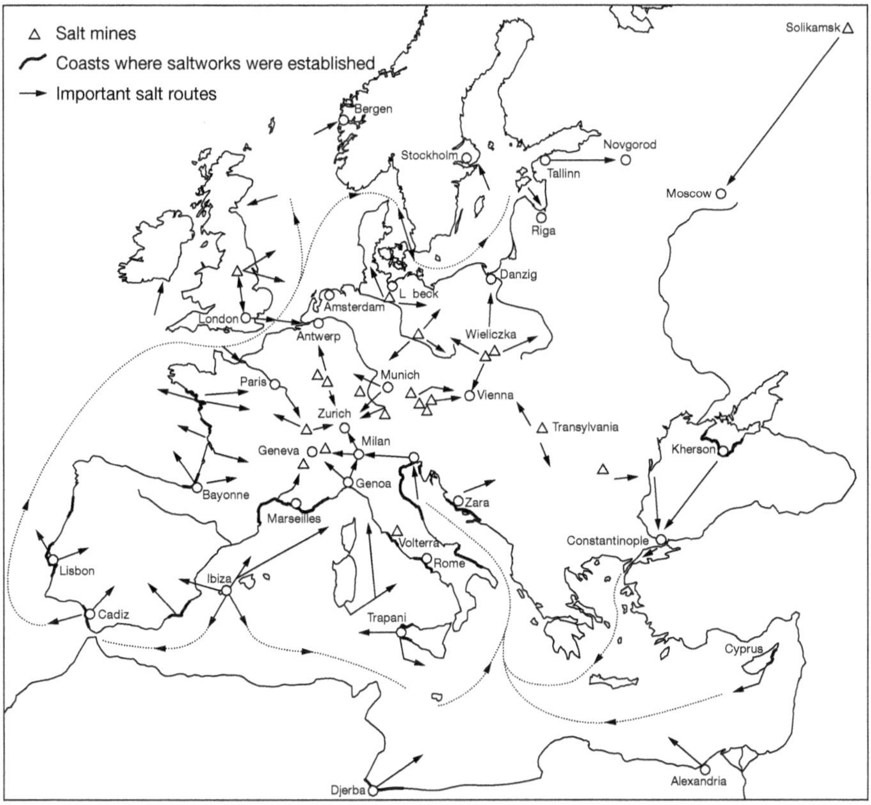

Map 4 The main saltworks and mines in Europe and salt traffic routes, fourteenth to sixteenth centuries.

Source: J.F. Bergier, *Una storia del sale*, Venice, 1984, p. 70.

quantities to northern Europe, while at the same time the countries of central Europe supplied the rock salt they obtained from mines. In their turn, the fishermen in northern Europe sent back the fish they had caught and preserved with the imported salt.

Imports from the Asian continent

In F. Braudel's model of the European economic system, with its self-sufficiency as regards goods,[23] there was one important exception, which was spices. Europeans had depended on imports from the Asian continent for centuries, and since precious metals were the only form of payment accepted on the Eastern markets before the arrival of the Portuguese, the Old World's economic system suffered from a significant and constant trade imbalance.

The trade included spices such as pepper, nutmeg, ginger, cinnamon and cloves but other commodities like perfumes, medicinal herbs and roots, in addition to the dyes, arms, silks, carpets, cotton, precious stones and ivory all gave rise to one of the most flourishing and ancient international trades. There were two phases to the trading operations. First the Eastern merchants, from countries such as Malaysia or India, consigned their products to Arab agents on the shores of the Indian Ocean, at places like Calicut in Malabar. The goods were then transported to the shores of the Mediterranean via sea and/or land, or up the rivers from the Caspian and the Black Sea, even as far as northern Europe. European merchants were involved in the second phase, acting as intermediaries between East and West. In the fifteenth century, the most important merchants in the Mediterranean area were from Venice and Genoa, and, to a lesser extent, from Provence or Catalonia. Throughout the period spanning the twelfth and sixteenth centuries, Venice was the greatest spice market in Europe and attracted large numbers of merchants from the European interior. Other maritime centres also made huge fortunes from this trade in costly luxury goods, which for European society had by now become a 'need', creating a steady demand for them. In order to acquire them, people were prepared even to sacrifice part of their income, though the way they were used determined the level of the demand.

Historians do not all agree as to their uses. Some argue that it was part of a vogue, a longing for an unnecessary extravagance or a way of displaying wealth, in view of their high cost. Others maintain that therapeutic and aphrodisiac properties were attributed to spices, and that they were also used to preserve food, or to camouflage the poor state of the food itself when it was being cooked. Doctors recommended the use of spices, and spice sellers would sell them to the sick at high prices. In food preparation and seasoning they played a comparable role to that of salt. The quantity of pepper that was traded was the same as that of all the other spices put together, and it is calculated that at the end of the fifteenth century Asian production was more than 100,000 cwt, almost all of which found its way into Europe. Other products included betel, rhubarb, opium, amber and musk, sandalwood, incense and camphor, and from the medical point of view were considered to have therapeutic functions.

The enormous profitability of this international traffic continued to attract capital and interest, even in the second half of the fifteenth century in spite of the long depression following the Black Death, and the situation in the Middle East that was becoming increasingly complex, after the fall of Constantinople and the subsequent Turkish conquest of Egypt. But, as Roberto Lopez has stated,[24] the Golden Age of the Mediterranean merchants had ended, and capital and interest no longer came from them but from the sovereigns of the Atlantic states. However, Italian entrepreneurs, for whom the pepper trade had driven the economy for almost two centuries, continued to play a significant role.[25]

Work organization and techniques

The organization of labour

Rural domestic industry

By using raw materials that were easily accessible and did not need to be acquired from the market, farming families had long met their own needs in the way of manufactured goods – especially textiles and utensils made out of wood and iron. These subsistence manufactures were produced when the family nucleus was not occupied in farming activities, and they went a considerable way to meeting the agrarian population's demand for primary goods. This was therefore *rural family* (or *domestic*) *industry* for auto-consumption.

Artisans and corporations

On the other hand, in the urban areas of Europe since the Middle Ages, the main economic activities had been organized into professional or trading associations. These were based on two common principles: equality and solidarity between members, and remaining separate from everybody else. Stipulations regarding the way specific forms of production were co-ordinated went even further: raw materials were to be purchased collectively; inside competition was prohibited and quality standards and common prices for the manufactured goods were expressly laid down. There were set procedures for membership and for learning individual trades. Members of the group, who were united by formal bonds under a specific set of regulations, or statute, enjoyed social benefits and took part in various forms of religious worship, with each trade having its own patron saint and very often its own devotional chapel inside a church. In Italy these groups were known as *corporazioni* or *Arti*, and in other parts of Europe as trade guilds. Their workshops or laboratories, which were often concentrated in a particular area of a city, were owned by master artisans assisted by apprentices and various underlings who were taught the trade but whose entry into the guild was carefully controlled by the ruling elite. The guilds enjoyed a monopoly over specific products and were able to safeguard their positions to a greater or lesser extent depending on the market trends for their goods. Before a guild member was able to become autonomous he had to undergo a tough examination at the end of a lengthy period in the workshop; however, relatives of the master artisan, who was already enrolled or 'matriculated', were exempted.

This system, on which artisan production was based, lasted several centuries and was still the pillar of urban labour organization in the fifteenth century. It was viewed benignly by the town government authorities, who saw in it a means of exercising control and guaranteeing social harmony, as well as securing tax payments. The corporations guaranteed product quality and regarded any innovation with suspicion, so much so that technological development in the sector was delayed and labour negatively affected. They went so far as to demand a ban on the entry of potentially competitive foreign products and thus achieved true customs protectionism. At the same time they were committed to safeguarding their own technical expertise and severely punished members who left the town and the guild and divulged trade secrets to the outside world.

The master artisan's workshop was thus the technical unit of production, but as Carlo M. Cipolla has pointed out, concentration of labour and capital was minimal and waged labour practically non-existent.[26] Tools were personal property, and the working hours were extremely long, extending from dawn to dusk, as many town statutes testify. As a rule the artisan produced goods for the market, which was not just the local one, or on commission, and was unlikely to produce any for stock; nevertheless he still took on a risk, though it was minimal (see Table 1.1). The sectors ranged widely: food, textiles, clothing, building, the working of wood, metal (from iron to precious stones) and leather. It was only when the guilds, instead of being self-governing bodies safeguarding group interests, started to become the means of gaining privileges that their interests clashed with those of society as a whole, and they began to be resented in the towns.

Domestic industry

In many regions of Europe, artisans were sometimes involved in complex production processes where semi-worked products were passed on to other workers with different specific skills. This was especially so with textile manufacturing, but also in other sectors such as metal and leather working. The artisan lost the direct link that he had had with the supply markets and the outlets for his products, and the

Table 1.1 The structure of industry in medieval and modern times

	Artisan industry	*Home industry*	*Capitalistic or manufacturing industry*
A Location	City or town	Countryside	Near source of energy or raw materials
B Workplace	Workshop or laboratory of master artisan	Worker's dwelling	Factory (plant, mill, works, etc.)
C Worker	Master artisan, *garzone* (apprentice) and casual worker	Peasant	Worker
D Work cycle	Continuous	Alternating with agricultural work	Continuous and co-ordinated
E Head of enterprise	Master artisan	Merchant entrepreneur	Capitalist entrepreneur
F Owner of:			
raw materials	Master artisan	Merchant entrepreneur	Capitalist entrepreneur
work tools	Master artisan	Peasant (not always)	Capitalist entrepreneur
finished product	Master artisan	Merchant entrepreneur	Capitalist entrepreneur
G Most widespread industrial sector	Textiles and clothing, manual processing of wood and metals, leather, building, food	Textiles and clothing	Iron foundries, copper works, flourmills, sawmills, fulling mills, papermills, tanning works, glassworks, etc.

Source: G. Felloni, *Profilo di storia economica dell'Europa dal medioevo all'età contemporanea*, 2nd edn, Giappichelli, Turin, 1997, p. 157.

production process became dominated by the merchant-entrepreneur, who owned not only the raw materials and working tools but also the finished product. Under him were the artisans, who only worked on what they were provided with, and had no economic autonomy, and over whom he had technical control.[27] The artisans were paid by the piece, within a system that greatly reduced the risks; they ended up becoming workers in their own homes as part of a network of independent workshops, all co-ordinated and managed by a single individual. It was a relatively flexible system of production. However, since the manufacturing cycle was often quite long (as much as six months in the silk sector), the merchant-entrepreneur needed to have a good knowledge of the markets, which often were international because of the range of his business, so that he could judge the degree of investment he required in raw materials and wages. Wages were paid in advance instalments; on the one hand this meant that the merchant-entrepreneur constantly required available supplies of money, and on the other that the artisan ended up by being a waged worker. This situation was further accentuated in cases where the artisan was categorically prevented from working on his own, and the relationship with the employer became an exclusive one. Conflicts often arose over the amount of pay and became even more acute when an important change in employment conditions was introduced whereby the employed worker could not refuse to be paid in kind. This was the 'truck system', which was still common at the time of the English industrial revolution.

The organization of the cottage industries did not change significantly when they became partly or completely ruralized. In some areas (such as Flanders) this change was already taking place in the fifteenth century, but it became more widespread in the rest of Europe in the following centuries. Textile production carried out in the countryside was a way of supplementing family incomes, but it also meant that supplies of primary goods could be obtained more cheaply and the excessive rigidity of the urban centres and guilds could be eluded. Furthermore, even though it meant relaxing controls on production quality, it did lead to important social changes, since female labour was now introduced into the production process, playing a role that was well defined and by no means marginal.

Technical innovations

In recent centuries the most dynamic factor of economic change and development has been technological innovation. During the fifteenth century there was a flourishing of technical improvements in several significant productive sectors. They affected the various fields of economic activity in different degrees and with different consequences, but were seen mainly in the mining and metallurgical industries, and in a number of manufacturing processes. However, as with agriculture, there was no clear-cut dividing line between the Middle Ages and the modern period.

One of the most important inventions ever, and certainly of the fifteenth century, was the printing press with its movable types, and the techniques of the printing process remained almost unchanged until the eighteenth century. Though there were no immediate consequences as regards the number of workers involved, it unquestionably increased the productivity of the book trade and enormously increased the availability of information, particularly the circulation of technical and economic information. A further consequence was a heavy increase in the demand for paper, the production of which had been an active concern since the fourteenth century and now experienced a boom. The superiority of paper over previous writing materials, such as parchment, lay in its lower cost. The number of readers, both inside and outside the universities, as well as those of the copyists' workshops, had already been increasing in the fourteenth century, and now experienced an upsurge. Only fifty years after the invention of movable type, Europe had 236 cities with printing shops, and around 20 million books, produced with the new technique, were in circulation.

The improvements in the art of navigation and shipbuilding also played a fundamental role in the success of the geographical explorations and discoveries. The introduction of gunpowder and its application to firearms, which were also carried on ships, was likewise important for European overseas conquests. This, together with the use of firearms and artillery in wars, accounts for the greater strategic importance of the metallurgical industries. The application of gunpowder in the mining industry ultimately led to other improvements such as pumps to extract air, and wagons with wooden wheels to transport material, all of which contributed to making it more cost-effective to mine at greater depths. Similarly, the first blast furnaces, which benefited from associated innovations such as hydraulic bellows, mechanical hammers and grinding mills for crushing the ore, first made their appearance in the fifteenth century, especially in Sweden and the southern part of the Low Countries and Luxembourg, but also in some areas of Italy such as Tuscany and Brescia. Methods of textile production and building remained more traditional during this period, but discounting agriculture they were still the sectors with the greatest number of workers overall.

C.M. Cipolla has pointed out that in Europe areas of great innovation (such as fifteenth century Italy) existed alongside others that were less innovative. This resulted in the movement of 'human capital', closely connected with which was the knowledge and spread of new techniques to a greater or lesser degree. It is perhaps too soon to talk of the mobility of labour, but it should be remembered that as early as the fifteenth century, and right up to the industrial revolution, countries were well aware that the emigration of specialist and technical workers could have negative consequences for the economy. The power to control the movement of people nevertheless seems to have been extremely limited at that time.

The development of sources of energy

The scarcity of available energy meant that the known sources had to be rationally exploited, but it also led to experiments in more advanced technologies with the aim of increasing their efficiency. The search for new resources was equally important, but in practice was conditioned by the availability of the land on which they were found.

In the Middle Ages animal power played an important role alongside human energy, as we have seen in relation to agriculture. In transport it was used directly, or for drawing boats along the internal watercourses and canals, and horse power was particularly important in mining. Non-animal power, such as energy from wind and water, involved a different approach. Though cost-free it was discontinuous, and required investment to be exploited by means of mills and waterwheels, that could be used in many manufacturing processes.

Besides being used for heating, wood and charcoal provided over 50 per cent of the energy required for economic activities despite the small size of many workshops, as Paolo Malanima has shown.[28] The example of ironworking is particularly interesting and it has been calculated that at the end of the fifteenth century 2 cwt of mineral ore and 25 m^3 of wood were still required to obtain half a hundredweight of iron. In this period only a few countries had begun to use coal, which had been mined in England and central Europe since as early as the thirteenth century. Its use was limited to a few areas such as Liège where the first blast furnaces were located, and was of no real importance to the economy for at least another two centuries.

Geographical and economic expansion

New horizons

A particularly significant aspect of the second half of the fifteenth century was the widening of geographical horizons, and that the era of the great explorations and territorial discoveries coincided almost exactly with a period of demographic growth. An important consequence was the search for sea routes between Europe and Asia, and the colonization of new lands in the west. Over the next century Europe would benefit from a greatly increased availability of resources of food and precious metals, though at the same time the Mediterranean would lose the central position it had gained in trade, and in particular its monopoly of the spice trade.

Two countries on the Atlantic Ocean, Portugal and Spain, were to play the leading role in this expansion, though ultimately they did not succeed in taking full advantage of the gains they had made, or of the new wealth they had conquered, as we shall see when we examine the sixteenth century. The areas of central, eastern and northern Europe would not be involved to any significant extent in the prosperity of the sixteenth century, partly because the most important trade routes were changing, but also because of the dynastic and religious wars that diverted energy away from economic activities. Only later, in the seventeenth century, would the Low Countries, England and northern France ultimately become the area of Europe deriving the greatest benefit from the economic changes associated with the great discoveries.

Portugal

Portugal was a small and relatively poor country that in due course came to dominate a vast maritime empire in Asia, Africa and America, achieving a considerable feat in the context of European expansion during this period. By 1515 the Portuguese already held sway over the Indian Ocean.

Portugal's territorial borders had become firmly established by the fifteenth century, but the country was still sparsely populated, with a limited number of small towns and a largely subsistence economy, with the main exception of fishing and saltworks in the coastal areas. Despite its sparse population, it was not totally self-sufficient in food products, especially in cereals, and it had to import corn as well as manufactured products. Besides salt and fish it also exported a few Mediterranean products such as oil, wine, fruit, cork and hides.

The explanation for the great Portuguese expansion overseas lay in the knowledge built up from designing ships and developing navigation techniques. These skills were part of the shrewd policy pursued by two members of the reigning family; first the king's younger son, Prince Henry, known as 'the Navigator' (1393–1460), and second King John II, who ascended the throne in 1481. Henry set about encouraging the explorations of the African coast, with the ultimate aim of reaching the Indian Ocean. By 1415 the Portuguese had already ventured ashore in Morocco and occupied Ceuta, a small fortress and important Christian outpost in Arab territory, which acted especially as a strategic base for a country that was aiming at commercial expansion. Henry set up a study centre, as it were, in his castle on the Sagres promontory in the extreme south of Portugal, where he gathered together astronomers, geographers, cartographers and navigators of every nationality. This continued a strong tradition dating back to the previous century, when the Portuguese crown collaborated with Genoan navigators and Italian merchants in several ventures of exploration. Almost every year from 1418 until his death, he organized expeditions during which seamen mapped the coasts and currents with painstaking precision, and updated the already known portolans.[29] They also rediscovered and colonized the Atlantic islands of Madeira and the Azores, as well as the Canaries (later ceded to Spain), established trading relations with the indigenous chiefs along the African coast, and had no qualms about searching for gold and slaves. Henry did not live long enough to realize his greatest ambition, and at his death the Portuguese navigators had sailed only a short way south of Cape Verde. But the scientific and explorative work that had been carried out under his patronage laid the foundations for subsequent discoveries.

After his death the impetus to exploration was lost through lack of royal support, but apart from this there was competition from the lucrative trade in ivory, gold and slaves that Portuguese merchants were carrying on with the indigenous kingdom of Ghana. When King John II came to the throne in 1481 exploration was revived once again, and in the space of a few years his navigators had almost reached the extreme southern tip of Africa. Eventually, in 1488, Bartholomew Diaz sailed round the Cape of Good Hope, which he had named the Cape of Storms. The next year, after crossing the Mediterranean, Pedro de Covilhão reached the Red Sea by land and went on to explore the west coast of India. The next voyage he made paved the way for Vasco da Gama, who reached Calicut by sailing round Africa between 1497 and 1499. Many ships and men were lost during this expedition because of disease, mutiny, storms and other difficulties, but the ships that did come back were laden with spices that more than compensated for the heavy cost of the voyage. Once they had seen the size of the profits, the Portuguese, in as little as ten years, and using military force as necessary, managed to oust the Arabs

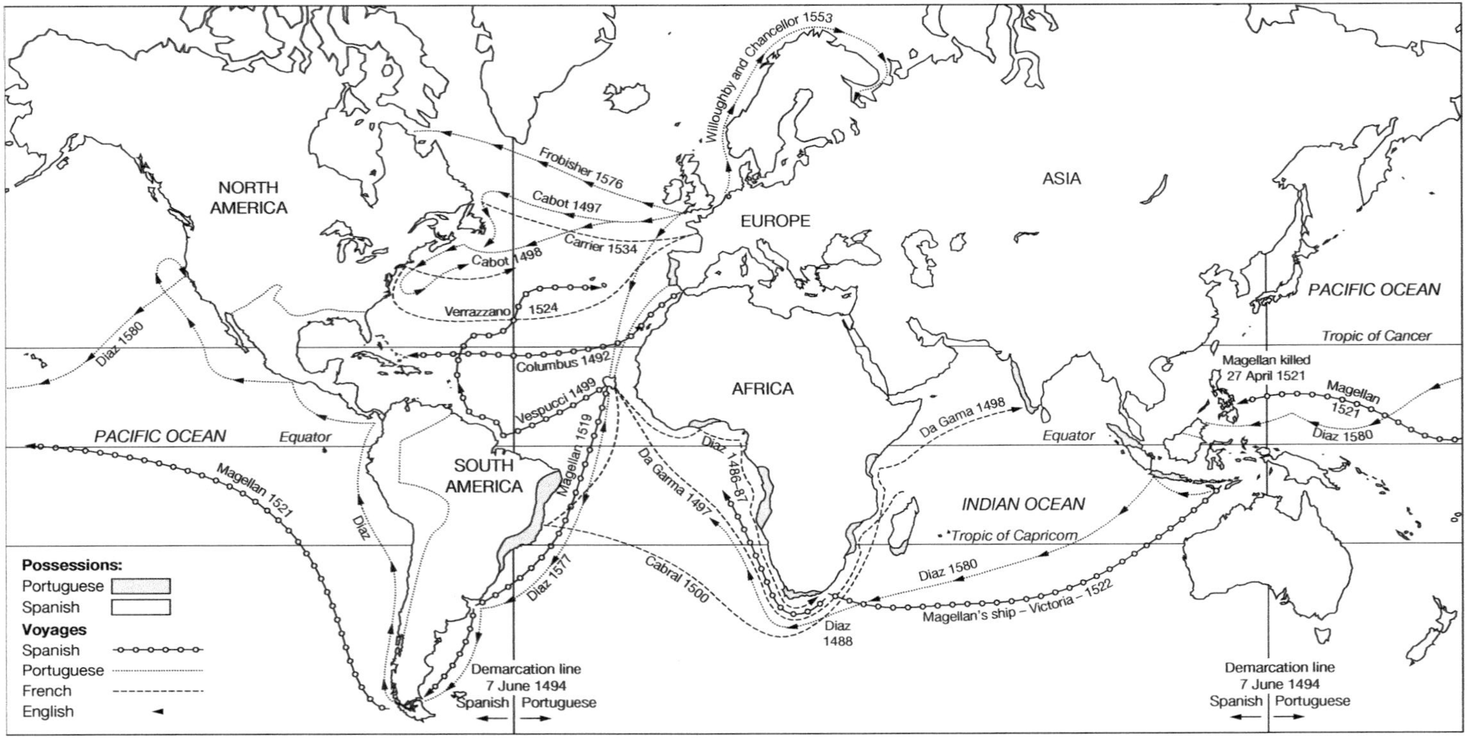

Map 5 Voyages of discovery in the fifteenth and sixteenth centuries.

Source: R. Cameron, *Storia economica del mondo*, Bologna, 1998, p. 164.

from the Indian Ocean and organize fortified trading posts as far afield as the fabulous Spice or Moluccan Islands. In 1513 one of their ships anchored at Canton in southern China, and by the mid-sixteenth century they had also established trade and diplomatic relations with Japan.

During the first decades of the sixteenth century the Portuguese continued to strengthen and expand their settlements in Asia. They did not, however, push towards the interior of these regions, but confined themselves to controlling the sea routes. These routes were already completely transforming the geography of exchange between Europe and Asia, and the limits of the economic interests of the Old Continent were reaching farther and farther eastward.

The Spanish economy and the New World

The other country that played a leading role in European expansion was Spain, but in this case it was westward. Economic conditions in Spain created their own particular problems and there were also serious difficulties relating to internal unity.[30] The varied nature of the territory gave rise to difficulties and conflicts. There were fertile coastal regions to the east and south, mountainous areas to the north and in other parts of the country, and a high plateau area known as the *meseta* that embraced the central part of the peninsula. In the field of agriculture the Arab and Moorish peoples, who had populated Andalusia before the Christian reconquest, had left a considerable heritage. They had been excellent market gardeners and had brought the art of irrigation to a high level, but the religious fervour of the Spanish sovereigns led to this legacy being wasted. At the same time as many Muslims were already leaving the country, and in the same year as the reconquest of the kingdom of Granada and the discovery of America by Columbus, they also ordered the Jews, who were skilled artisans and traders, to be expelled from the kingdom.

The productivity of Spanish agriculture was among the lowest in western Europe. One of its main problems derived from the conflict between the peasants and the large landowners. The land had remained intact as a result of particular property laws such as the *fideicommissum*,[31] and was largely given over to sheep rearing. Wool had a very profitable outlet on the international market, because of the strong demand from the textile centres, especially in the Mediterranean area. The unique practice of transhumance was widespread among shepherds, who moved their flocks between the summer mountain pastures and the winter quarters on the lower plains. It was unique because of the enormous distances that had to be covered, and the way it was organized, not to mention the royal protection it enjoyed. The sheep farmers formed a corporation known as the Company of the Mesta and were a powerful lobby at court. Putting a tax on the migrating flocks at strategically located toll stations was an easy matter. Wool was a valuable goods item that brought money, unlike many agricultural crops, and it could be easily taxed when it was exported. In exchange for paying higher taxes, the Mesta was granted special privileges, including the right to unlimited grazing on common land, to the detriment of agriculture.

Spanish expansion was perhaps more fortuitous, and less concerned with seeking new economic horizons for trade, than that of Portugal. Cameron has succinctly described how in 1483 or 1484, when the ships sent by John II of Portugal were still opening up routes along the African coast, a Genoese named Columbus, who had served in the Portuguese navy and married a Portuguese woman, petitioned the king to finance an expedition over the Atlantic to reach the east by sailing westwards.[32] The proposal was not altogether an unusual one, since there was already a widely held belief that the earth might be spherical. John II had already authorized privately financed expeditions westwards, but resources were being concentrated on the more realistic project of sailing round Africa. Columbus's proposal was consequently rejected. However, Columbus would not admit defeat and turned instead to the Spanish sovereigns Ferdinand and Isabella. However, they were involved in war against the Arabs, and did not think the enterprise was feasible. The English and French sovereigns thought likewise; finally, in 1492, to celebrate the victory over the Moors at Granada, Isabella of Castile agreed to finance his expedition. On 12 October that year, after sailing for over two months, he reached the islands that were to be called the West Indies, since it was thought he had actually reached Asia. Columbus called the indigenous people Indians, though their evident poverty caused him dismay. He sailed back to Spain, and the following year returned with a much larger and better equipped expedition of seventeen ships and 1,500 men, taking cattle and other animals to start the real work of colonization.

New conflicts on the seas and the Treaty of Tordellisas

At the close of the fifteenth century there were thus two states up against each other on the seas. Both were perhaps convinced they had reached the same rich Eastern markets, but by opposite routes.

As soon as Columbus arrived back from the first expedition, Ferdinand and Isabella turned to Pope Alexander VI so that a 'demarcation line' could be drawn confirming Spanish rights over the lands that had just been discovered. This ideal line was to be drawn between the two poles, at a longitude of 100 leagues (about 330 miles) west of the Azores and Cape Verde. It was to divide the non-Christian world into two halves for the purpose of further explorations, with the western part being reserved for the Spaniards, and the eastern part for the Portuguese. A year later, in 1494, when the Treaty of Tordillas was being drawn up, the King of Portugal persuaded the Spaniards to mark out a new line that was to lie about 210 miles farther west of the 1493 line. This seems to point to the fact that the Portuguese already knew of the existence of the New World, since the area of South America bulging eastwards, which would form the bridgehead, and later become Brazil, was in the Portuguese hemisphere in the second treaty. In 1500, during the first great Portuguese trading expedition after the return of Vasco da Gama, Pedro de Cabral headed straight for this area and claimed for Portugal the territory on which he landed, before continuing for India.

In the meantime explorers from other countries were following in the footsteps of Columbus. John Cabot, an Italian at the court of Henry VII of England, undertook a voyage in 1497 with financial backing from a number of Bristol traders, and reached the island of Newfoundland and Nova Scotia. The following year he explored the northern coastline of North America with his brother; but the results were considered so economically insignificant that the king compensated them with a mere £10. At the beginning of the next century, French merchants financed another Italian, Verrazzano, to search for a western route to the Indies. Ten years later the Frenchman Jacques Cartier carried out the first of three voyages that would lead him to discover and explore the St Laurence river. All this marked the beginning of a process of liberation from the restrictions of medieval knowledge towards a new and different geographic and economic outlook.

As Cameron has also observed,[33] the most dramatic and significant aspect of European expansion – the premises of which were laid down in the fifteenth century – was the transfer of European culture, and the way it modified non-Western cultures, even leading to their extinction. The economic changes, whether quantitative in terms of the amount of goods circulating, or qualitative in terms of new products and markets, need to be seen against the cultural, social and political repercussions that these events were to have over the following centuries.

Notes

1 F. Braudel, *Civiltà materiale, economia e capitalismo*, vol. III, *I tempi del mondo*, Turin, 1982, pp. 5–50.

2 Braudel considered that a slightly modified model could also be applied to the next two centuries.

3 'nell'interporsi del mercante tra produttore e consumatore, grazie alla enorme distanza spaziale e temporale che, per certi merci, separava i luoghi di approvvigionamento da quelli di vendita'. M. Cattini, *La genesi della società moderna contemporanea*, Parma, 1992, pp. 170–1.

4 Spices form the great exception to F. Braudel's 'self-sufficiency' model.

5 Phocaea had been the source of this substance until the fall of Constantinople in 1453 when it was replaced by Tolfa, near Rome. Alum was used as a mordant in dyeing textile fibres, and in the tanning of leather.

6 The next section of this chapter explains how, in an economic system based only on metal currency, the possibility of transacting business without it reduced the need to have it in circulation; this was a great advantage, since obtaining the precious metal usually involved long and hazardous journeys. The trade fairs were precisely where the bill of exchange originated; this was an instrument of credit used throughout Europe and acted as a draft in a foreign currency deferring payment in time and space, whether to settle a business deal or grant a loan. It enabled trading houses to expand their range of business and to operate more efficiently.

7 Allowing for defence requirements, in the fifteenth century the average crew-load ratio was one sailor for every four to five tons.

8 The right of a feudal lord. (*Translator's note.*)

9 This was a *lira*, which was made up of twenty *soldi*, each of which consisted of twelve *denari*.

10 The hypothesis formulated by the English financier Thomas Gresham in the sixteenth century that bad money drives good money out of circulation. (*Translator's note.*)

11 Florence had over thirty banking houses in 1470.

12 According to Cipolla, the other two ills became more common or were worsened because of war; famine resulted from the destruction and pillaging of crops and cattle by the passing armies, while epidemics were often the result of the poor state of health and sanitary conditions of the armies, and spread more rapidly among a malnourished population.

13 C.M. Cipolla, *Storia economica dell'età preindustriale*, Bologna, 1990, pp. 13–17 and 171–84.
14 For example, in England the mortality rate was over 20 per cent of the population. In some Italian cities over three-quarters of the inhabitants died. During epidemics and famines, there was an increase in the number of deaths but there was also a decrease in the number of births, so the two results were compounded.
15 P. Malanima, *Economia preindustriale. Mille anni: dal IX al XVIII secolo*, Milan, 1995, pp. 19–20.
16 Genoa, Milan, Venice and Florence had almost 100,000 inhabitants each.
17 Paris (almost 100,000), London, Cologne and Barcelona were among the most important.
18 F. Mauro, *L'Europa del XVI secolo. Aspetti economici*, Milan, 1974, pp. 138–48.
19 There are some anomalies. Mining really belongs to the primary sector, but is normally considered a secondary activity; transport, which is often included in the secondary sector, is a service (considered a tertiary activity).
20 In particular W.W. Rostow, *The World Economy. History and Prospect*, Austin x, 1978, p. 778, and S. Kuznets, *Economic Growth of Nations. Total Output and Production Structure*, Cambridge, 1971, p. 14
21 The heart of a large medieval estate was the interior courtyard, or *curtis*, which by its very nature was 'closed' with respect to the economy of the period. (*Translator's note.*)
22 For instance copper was found only in Sweden and Germany, tin in Cornwall and Ireland, lead in Austria and Hungary.
23 F. Braudel, *Civiltà materiale, III*, pp. 5–50.
24 R.S. Lopez, 'Market expansion: the case of Genoa, *Journal of Economic History*, 24, 1954, pp. 445–54.
25 C.M. Cipolla, *Allegro ma non troppo*, Bologna, 1988.
26 C.M. Cipolla, *Storia economica*, pp. 130–1.
27 It is noteworthy that even in the fifteenth century he was still not specialized: he was a merchant-entrepreneur as regards textiles, but was also banker, insurer, dealer in spices, metals and grains.
28 P. Malanima, *Economia preindustriale*, pp. 84–91.
29 Precise nautical charts of the coasts. (*Translator's note.*)
30 The last Arab territorial outpost, the Caliphate of Granada, fell only in 1492. Though Isabella of Castile and Ferdinand of Aragon had been joined in marriage in 1476 the two kingdoms continued to be ruled separately, sometimes following different policies, until their grandson Charles came to the throne.
31 A type of arrangement in a will whereby the heir was obliged to pass on the entire inherited property, or a part of it. (*Translator's note.*)
32 R. Cameron, *Storia economica del mondo*, Bologna, 1993, pp. 158–65.
33 *Ibid.*, p. 167.

2 European expansion in the sixteenth century

Giuseppe Bracco

Population

European population patterns

In the sixteenth century Europe experienced expansion with regard to practically every economic parameter, and in every sense of the term. Not only did Europeans arrive in all corners of the world, but on the European continent itself the population started to increase steadily at the beginning of the sixteenth century, even though the growth rate differed from one area to another.

Various types of documentary evidence regarding the population is available, but does not include censuses, since only very few of these existed, and where they did exist they were very unsophisticated and basic. Furthermore they were used primarily for fiscal purposes, and their main concern was with particular sections of the population, such as family nuclei, and generally excluded young children. In many areas of Europe records of baptisms, marriages and burials were kept in both Catholic and Protestant parishes, and make up for the lack of public records. The keeping of parish records became firmly established during the sixteenth century in Italy and England. In Italy it came about with the Counter-Reformation, and in England with the rise of the Anglican Church, while other Christian countries with their different denominations were to follow later.

Beyond the strictly demographic data, signs of the expansion of the European population have been found in almost every field of economic life. Studies of specific areas have shown how both the causes and the effects of population expansion differed in different areas but, in any case, confirm the overall pattern. It has been calculated that in the sixteenth century the population of Europe completely recovered from the enormous losses that it had suffered in the pandemics of the fourteenth century, and even surpassed previous levels, reaching a figure of around 100 million inhabitants.

In a century that marked the transition of European society, from the medieval world to the modern era, the territorial distribution of the population was still very similar to that of the previous age. Settlement continued to be mainly scattered, with small centres prevailing, and nothing that could be called a large city, even though it was in the sixteenth century that the future metropolises of the modern era started to develop. It is estimated that, at the beginning of the sixteenth century, there were only four cities with a population of 100,000 inhabitants or over: Milan,

Naples, Venice and Paris. By the end of the century the number had risen to eight: Milan, Venice, Rome, Naples, Palermo, Paris, London and Lisbon. There were estimated to be seven cities with 50,000 inhabitants or over, at the start of the century, rising to thirteen by the end. 5.6 per cent of the European population was calculated as being urban at the beginning of the century, and by the end of the century this figure had reached 7.6 per cent.

The evolution of the population inevitably followed different patterns in different geographical areas, and was affected by the political and military events that troubled the European countries. There was also a fairly clear-cut divide between the two halves of the century, with the treaty of Cateau Cambrésis in 1559 forming a watershed, especially in the areas where the major military actions had taken place.

Birth and death rates both showed very high values, and in normal times such levels would have created a positive balance, but in a particularly difficult period the age-old problems of a pre-industrial society could not be avoided. The three basic ills of famine, war and epidemic continued to exert their dire effects throughout the century, although measures were now starting to be developed to counteract their negative consequences. There were a number of dietary improvements, and the first forms of health regulations started to appear. War itself affected population patterns in further ways, causing people to move from one area to another on a considerable scale.

Migration in the Old and New Worlds

The wide-scale movement of the population of Europe during the sixteenth century followed different patterns.

One direction of population flow was from the country to the town, reflecting the incipient urbanization. One particularly representative case was that of England, with the transformation of the countryside due to the enclosures and the growth of London, whose population grew five times in the course of a century. It has been estimated that the urban population of England rose from 3.1 per cent to 5.8 per cent. In Spain it rose from 6.1 to 11.4 per cent, in Portugal from 3 per cent to 14.1 per cent and in the northern Low Countries from 15.8 per cent to 24.3 per cent. In Italy the situation was different; in the first half of the century the population spread to very small centres, while urbanization itself started again only in the second half of the century.

A phenomenon typical of the agricultural economy was reflected in the movement between town and country. This related to people who had no means of subsistence, and who were generally and indistinctly classified as 'paupers'. Studies on the effects of the different crises on population distribution show that the poor moved from town to country and from country to town, according to the different seasons, which determined the sequence of harvests and the places where food would be stored. In periods of crisis the poor also moved, to some extent, from one town to another, seeking out the places where the scarcity of food was less serious. One measure that was frequently adopted when facing a crisis was to classify and register paupers who had come from another place, and force them to return to where they had come from, or where they normally resided.

The movement of people from one country to another followed different patterns. One of the most remarkable cases during this period was that of the Swiss. Many of them migrated to different countries as soldiers in the service of the European courts, and this migration was organized by what was to all practical purposes a public institution at the canton and federal level. The wars of religion played an important role, causing entire homogeneous groups, like the Walloons, to migrate to the Low Countries, or more mixed groups to England. The imperial armies, and those of the King of Spain, were also involved in similar wide-scale transfers. Furthermore, the mercantilist policies of European states also encouraged the movement of skilled individuals from the guilds and corporations; these people found themselves having to decide between opportunities offered by the host country or punishment in the country of origin.

There was also the movement from one continent to another, which had particular features of its own. Though the new territories available to Europeans held out undeniable attractions, migration to the new countries was not by any means a mass movement; several obstacles were in the way. To start with, there were the objective difficulties of a long, gruelling journey and the inhospitable nature of the places to which Europeans would have to adapt, and live in as pioneers, at least until the new cities were built; this would not happen until the following century. Those who migrated to the Americas were mostly men seeking opportunities in overseas trade, and who exploited the resources that became available as the interior was explored; they did not reflect the whole range of different occupations in Europe. The foundations of European emigration to the Americas were laid by seamen and merchants, who had their own special skills, or by bureaucrats who represented the monarchies in possession of the colonies. A distinction must also be made between permanent and temporary migration. Many of those who had chosen to follow the road to adventure and fortune returned to their original homelands. At the same time, a permanent population very slowly began to develop, with the births that were naturally occurring helping to increase it. Migration between the continents was, in any case, an important contributing factor in the creation of a new class of entrepreneurs, who operated side by side with their traditional counterparts, and eventually even replaced them.

During the sixteenth century there was a further migration to the Americas. This was of people who, though they went with the Europeans, were not of European origin. They were the slaves who were taken, mainly out of Africa, to provide the labour that was required on the new sugar cane plantations. There was no real emigration to either Asia or Africa, in the sense of people going there with the aim of settling permanently. Those who did go to these two continents were the men needed to run the commercial and military bases that the European countries, and Portugal in particular, had set up as centres for trade.

The quality of life

In the fourteenth century Europe had experienced the appalling tragedy of the Black Death, which had decimated its inhabitants in a way that had never been experienced before. During the sixteenth century, however, contagious disease could be considered part of everyday life, since epidemics of plague and other diseases occurred frequently, in different areas. This question has been widely studied and several explanations have been given, which all focus on a number of elements in common. It was clear that the plague had become endemic in Europe, and there were frequent and regular epidemics of it. The most affected areas were the urban centres where people were living in overcrowded and unhealthy conditions, especially in places where the increase in population had not been offset by an increase in the number of dwellings. Thus one of the main causes of the epidemics lay in the unhygienic living conditions; but since these had always existed, there must have been some other cause to trigger epidemics. It has been pointed out that the people who were affected by the epidemics must have been so physically debilitated that their defences had been weakened, and that the likely cause of such debilitation was famine. During the sixteenth century, there was in fact a series of famines that highlighted the problem of corn supplies, which in itself was a further indication of the growing urban population. Over the century towns were forced to set up permanent organizations to tackle the everlasting problem of provisions. State authorities issued regulations that alternated between export bans and other initiatives, in order to guarantee the availability of corn, and generally there was heavy expenditure on the part of public administrations. The corn trade itself was the centre of large-scale commercial operations, with merchants and cargo vessels plying the seas of Europe, from the Baltic to the eastern shores of the Mediterranean. Exceptional efforts were made to transport the corn from the seaports to the cities of the hinterland by mule train. Here was something new in the traffic flows of the Mediterranean area, which in previous centuries had been practically self-sufficient for its requirements.

The famines themselves had different causes. Low productivity of the land was intrinsic to the agriculture of the time, and the seed-to-product ratio was limited. Therefore famine was inevitable every time environmental conditions caused a crisis. Low seed germination, parasites, storage problems and the shortage of fertilizers made it practically impossible to offset the effects of bad weather conditions. Another factor was the wartime destruction of crops and the loss of supplies due to the armies that passed through; not having any provisions of their own, they lived off the resources of the areas they happened to be in, whether it was allied or enemy territory. Furthermore, though hygiene in dwellings and urban centres was poor, it was even worse in the armies engaged in the numerous wars that troubled Europe in the sixteenth century. Military units were the likely cause of the spread of germs and parasites that contributed to the numerous epidemics during the century. The famines and the passing armies started a vicious cycle, in which precisely those people who had already been weakened were particularly badly hit by disease.

Yet another factor in the spread of diseases was the migration of people from Europe to other areas of the globe, as a result of the expansion that was taking place. Diseases started to spread from one continent to another, and the maritime cities experienced epidemics of diseases that were being brought back. Diseases that had been quite unknown on other continents were carried there by Europeans, while at the same time diseases were being brought back to Europe that had not previously existed there.

Agriculture

The land

In the sixteenth century, the world of agriculture was very varied. Not only were there inevitable differences in crops due to different environmental conditions, but many changes were also taking place as regards the use and ownership of the land itself. Any one area could be divided into feudal, ecclesiastical, common or open land, with a wide variety of usages and customs, and the exploitation of the land for farming was affected by factors such as declining feudal power, the crisis of the ecclesiastical institutions, especially the monasteries, as well as the merging of privately owned common land. The confiscation of Catholic Church land in England under Henry VIII was the most far-reaching in extent and importance, and the expropriations carried out by the Vasa in Sweden were a similar case. The process had involved many of the greatest monastic abbeys on the continent since the last quarter of the fifteenth century, with significant effects. There was a move towards separating the monastic lands into two main parts with different functions: these were the cloistral and the *commendam*, or benefice. The monks, whose numbers were now reduced, kept the cloistral areas; since the monks now had fewer requirements, these areas were accordingly reduced in size. The abbot beneficiaries, *abati commendatori*, took over the land i*n commendam*, and the land was now viewed mainly in terms of the revenue that it could yield. Some of the knightly orders were also reorganized and re-established over the century, or even founded *ex novo*. Their original connections with the reconquest of Jerusalem were now lost, but one way of gaining new privileges from the sovereign powers was to develop the organization of farming.

The availability of arable land had been one of the major problems for agriculture before the decline in population caused by the Black Death, in the fourteenth century. Many initiatives had been adopted to reclaim uncultivated land, and attempts had been made to acquire new land outside the traditional areas. With the decrease in population, there was a fall in consumption because of reduced demand. Yields had consequently declined, but when the population started to slowly increase again in the sixteenth century the problem resurfaced, and it was crucial to find ways of achieving greater overall productivity.

In much of Europe, the old feudal pattern had already been broken up, but age-old farming methods were still being used at the beginning of the century. The land supplied the basic food requirements, and raw materials for manufacturing, but there were still no signs of the far-reaching changes in farming techniques that would take place in the next centuries; they would be introduced only very gradually. Nevertheless, crops that had previously received little attention were now being cultivated more widely. This was all taking place within the context of new forms of land tenure; in the overall search for sources of revenue, farming was seen as a means of investment, and the age-old need to provide for subsistence was being superseded. A number of contributing factors lay behind this change. On the one hand, there was the growth of the towns, and their increasing influence over the consumer market for agricultural produce; on the other, there were those with capital, who were seeking opportunities for investment, whether for direct income, or to secure supplies of raw materials for the manufacturing industry. The sixteenth century could well be considered the period when the significance of the land for fiscal purposes was realized. With taxation of the land becoming more widespread, a fiscal struggle between state and town ensued, to gain control over the revenue from it.

Despite the different forms of ownership and contracts, and the changes that were taking place, it should be underlined how much of the land in Europe was split up into very small holdings, because of the way that the work in the fields was carried on. The activity of owners, tenants, peasants and paid workers was limited by considerations of distance and space, since where it was carried out had to be within reach of the dwelling place, and it had to be possible for an entire family to collaborate. The mid-sixteenth century saw the rise of a new form of habitation in farming areas. This was a result of the interest in investment and land improvement, but also of the need to provide for the farm worker's family.

One particular aspect of the search for new arable land in the sixteenth century was land reclamation. In some parts of Europe, land was reclaimed on a considerable scale, and even led to the radical transformation of extensive areas. Important projects were carried out in Italy, France and England, and those carried out in the Low Countries were quite exceptional. Rather than being innovations as such, they developed and utilized known systems, but on a much larger scale, using new methods and energy resources. The ingenious applications of Leonardo da Vinci in Italy, and the role of the windmills in Holland, belong to the great moments of history.

New agricultural products

At the start of the century European farming was still producing the same crops as in previous centuries. There had been no significant innovations, and existing resources were exploited as far as possible. European farmers continued to cultivate a wide variety of plants for food, which included all kinds of cereals and edible fruits. Wheat, rye, barley, oats, spelt, millet, sorghum as well as chestnuts were cultivated, while olives and grapes began to attract the attention of agronomists, who took advantage of the new printing methods to publish their studies. Flax and hemp were cultivated in many areas for textile manufacturing, while cotton was restricted to areas in the south of Europe.

One of the most significant consequences of the geographical explorations was that people discovered new plants. However, these plants were not actually adopted in the sixteenth century, and became part of the European farming tradition only in the following centuries, bringing about profound changes in diet and helping to alleviate the effects of famine. Potatoes, maize, tomatoes, tobacco, tea, coffee and cocoa were only the most significant products of the many that were being brought to Europe during the sixteenth century. At first they were regarded as curiosities and made available to botany enthusiasts, or else they were supplied to meet the demand for unusual luxury consumer goods. Herbs and plants thought to contain medicinal and healing properties aroused greater interest; these plants were not cultivated, but became items for the import trade. The new plants from which dyes could be obtained were a similar case.

New opportunities for agriculture came from plants that had already long been known in Europe but were now being cultivated more widely and could be exported. Rice was a legacy from the Arab occupation of the Iberian peninsula, and spread to northern Italy. It was particularly useful for consumption on ships. Other cereals had created problems on long transoceanic voyages, since their oil content made them more difficult to store, and they were more perishable. Mulberries contributed to the expansion of silkworm rearing, first in Italy and then in France, and laid the foundations for the future development of the silk industry. This period saw the start of the great sugar cane venture; except for a few small areas in the south, cane was hardly grown at all in Europe. Thanks to the Portuguese and Spaniards, sugar cane gradually found its way to central and southern America via Madeira and the Canary Islands, and in the following centuries it became one of the most important crops in the New World. It also involved slavery on a dramatic and huge scale.

Rice, mulberries and sugar cane all required a long period of time before the final product could be obtained, and they also required heavy capital investment. Canals and water mills were needed in the rice plantations; the mulberry plantations had to have rearing grounds for the silkworms, and the silk industry itself needed machinery, such as spinning wheels; large numbers of people were required on the sugar plantations, and producing the sugar involved complicated procedures.

The ships that sailed between America, Asia and Africa were an important means of exchanging and spreading knowledge about plants. Conscious efforts were made to add to those that were already available, but important developments often came about purely by chance. The food provisions that were loaded at different ports round the world for the ships' passengers, who were not only Europeans but also Asians and Africans, included seeds and plants of all types. The attempts at planting them and adapting them to the new environments alternately failed and succeeded. The European ships created specific demands as regards food provisions; this led to a number of consequences on the Old Continent and on those with which people were coming into contact. Europeans wanted to ensure that food from the homeland would also be available overseas. Examples of this were the vine and the olive, which were specifically selected to provide wine and olive oil. Attempts at establishing vineyards and olive groves were not successful, but they did lead to increased production and certain improvements in some areas of Europe itself.

Contact with other continents also led to significant developments in livestock breeding. Large numbers of live animals were carried on the voyages, for two main reasons. First, animals, and particularly horses, were required by men-at-arms for transport and in battle, and second, live animals could provide food. It was not feasible to carry meat on board, since it was difficult, if not impossible, to preserve it; but apart from the meat, live animals could provide other food products such as milk and eggs. Furthermore, one of the aims of colonization was to recreate the same way of life as in the homeland as far as possible. Thus horses, cattle, sheep, pigs, rabbits and poultry travelled with the crews on their voyages, and became established in the new areas of European settlement. They started to multiply, and in many cases their numbers increased considerably. On the other hand, very few animals from other parts of the world were suitable for European farming, apart from the turkey; exotic animals were a source of curiosity or amusement rather than anything else. More significant results were achieved with attempts at cross-breeding between animals of the same species but from different places. Animals with specific characteristics that could be used in specific environments and conditions were also bred. A typical example was the horse, which was being increasingly used in farming for pulling ploughs, as in the Low Countries, or for providing extra power.

Anticipating the new science

Innovations

In the sixteenth century there was very little to show that the results of the scientific revolution had many applications, even though the century was marked by personalities who are universally recognized as the precursors and founders of the new science. Nicolaus Copernicus died in 1543, Galileo Galilei was born in 1564 and Johannes Kepler in 1571; but each encountered difficulties arising from the Counter-Reformation and its attempts to revive former teachings.

The publication of texts on the techniques of metallurgical production perhaps best illustrates the level of knowledge in the sixteenth century, though they probably did not play a very important role in disseminating their subject matter; as Cipolla has argued, this was more the fruit of practical application than of literature.[1] The great interest in metallurgy, resulting from greater market demand, was reflected in books describing techniques and alloys that had been in use for centuries. Important publications were *De la Pirotechnia*, by Vannoccio Biringuccio, printed in Venice in 1540, and *De re metallica*, by Giorgio Agricola, printed in Basle in 1556, and in themselves were great scientific achievements. The need for metals increased with the requirements of war, whether on land or at sea, and these two works gave detailed accounts of techniques for extracting and working minerals, and prepared the way for future industrial processes. Great resources of energy and capital were required to excavate the shafts, ventilate the mines, hoist up the minerals and provide plants for crushing, sorting and roasting. Waterwheels and windmills were utilized to provide mechanical power, but even so wood was still an irreplaceable fuel. Its use ultimately led to the destruction of much of the woodland heritage in the areas close to the centres of production. In England it led to a real supply crisis, and the price of wood more than tripled in the course of the century. But metallurgy also held out attractive opportunities for investment and profit to holders of capital. Many great banks, such as the Fugger in Augsburg, financed and subsidized enterprises in this sector, guaranteeing not only the production, but also the worldwide distribution, of metals and metal products.

The greatest demand for iron and bronze came from military quarters, but bronze was also important for making cannon, bells and statues. In addition to these, other metals contributed to the evolution of metallurgical techniques. There were also attempts at producing steel, but its use was still very limited. Tin, lead and copper, as well as other ores of lesser significance, were used in important alloys, such as pewter. This was of great importance in manufacturing pots and pans, in addition to print types, the production of which was decisive for centres such as Venice, which specialized in publishing. The precious metals such as gold and silver that arrived in large quantities from America and Africa also had important applications at different times, but perhaps the most significant innovation was the development of the amalgam technique for extracting silver.

In the sixteenth century interesting developments were taking place in all types of building, and the adoption of new techniques led to the construction of buildings that were generally larger than in the past. Grand halls in palaces, and high vaults in churches, were the result of new techniques in design and structure. There were innovations in the way bridges were constructed; locks and sluice gates were being built to regulate canals. The latter inventions were first introduced by Leonardo da Vinci in Lombardy, and very soon spread to other European countries, where they contributed to boosting internal navigation. Navigation was one of the sectors most actively engaged in seeking innovations and improvements based on practical experience in the field; developments took place in shipbuilding, armaments, orientation, map making, the measurement of time and space, and in food provisioning. There were many and various problems to solve if the voyages, and supremacy on the seas, were to be guaranteed, and they required a great many human and economic resources.

Improvements in orientation techniques led, among other things, to an exceptional development in cartography. The sixteenth century is rightly the century of the Flemish cartographer Gerardus Mercator, who at the start of the modern era made a greater impact in this field than anyone else. Charts and maps of the new continents became priceless assets for navigators, and were one of the foremost priorities and concerns for those who were the first to reach distant coasts and countries. Other fields, such as land surveying, which was then being developed especially for fiscal purposes, also benefited from all this activity, which was inevitably carried out with measuring instruments. In the later half of the century a large number of texts on geometry and land surveying were published; Luca Pacioli's text entitled *Summa de Arithmetica*, published in 1494, had been the starting point for these books, but attempts were now being made to add more practical solutions to make calculations easier.

In the sixteenth century all types of seagoing vessels existed. The Mediterranean galleys, which had reached a remarkable level of efficiency, were still in use and worthily performed the role for which they had been created. Warships were mainly powered by oars, though they were equipped with a lateen sail for use during moments of peace. Merchant ships were now mainly equipped with sails, though they still had a number of oars which were used when manoeuvring in port or during emergencies. In the fifteenth century the appearance of the new caravels had marked the beginning of different sailing techniques for European sailors; in the sixteenth century there was an exceptional increase in the development of numerous types of sailing ships with different keels and sets of sails. Safe navigation and cost-effective transport were priorities. The tonnage of ships increased, as did the productivity of the vessels; the crew-to-cargo ratio has been calculated as averaging one sailor to every four or five tons in the fifteenth century, and as much as seven tons by the mid-sixteenth century. The Portuguese, Spanish and English were the major builders of large warships, the construction of which was based on a very different model from that of the previous centuries. The galleon is the typical example, and is invariably associated with the Invincible Armada of Philip II or the English fleet of Henry VIII and Elizabeth I. These sixteenth century vessels had a displacement of 1,000 tons.

In the traditional textiles sector there were important developments; those taking place in the wool trade, in particular, were decisive in bringing about important changes in the pattern of production. The traditional centres of the previous centuries were now being overtaken by new centres, and consequently there were both areas of development and areas of crisis. The Low Countries and England exploited their long-standing resources, and managed to conquer the markets traditionally dominated by the Italian medieval cloth merchants. The new, brightly coloured cloths known as short-cloths, though lighter and less durable, were one of the most common items exported from the port of London in the sixteenth century. Yet, at the same time, Europeans from the economically more powerful classes were beginning to show an interest in silk produced on the continent.

The organization of production and labour

With the growth in population, the accessibility of new territories, more abundant raw materials and technological improvements, Europeans, during the sixteenth century, found that they were in a position to provide themselves with the goods and services they needed in order to meet their actual demand. However, traditional occupations in the various economic and social sectors did not suffer during the course of the century; on the contrary, they continued side by side with the long process of transformation that the new prospects brought with them. Some of these had developed almost spontaneously, while others were the result of political, economic and social changes. The sectors of agriculture and mining are a case in point. Over the century, the demand for food products, raw materials, textiles and minerals called for increased production and different ways of organizing labour, both out in the fields and down the mines. Subsistence agriculture was superseded in many places, and farming for the market was being encouraged. The consequence of this was the development of new types of field labour, in the form of waged work. This change was facilitated by the replacement of feudal land tenure systems with the new farms producing for the market, which brought new opportunities for investing capital and making profits.

In the territories of the New World in America, after the first pioneering experiments, field labour created a number of problems, especially in the second half of the century; first there were the intrinsic difficulties of the environment itself, and second there were others relating to the types of crops that could be cultivated. There was no significant emigration of European farmers, and the conditions in which they had to work were very different from those on the European continent, despite the attempts of the Spanish *conquistadors* to reproduce the systems of their homeland, especially as regards land tenure. The local labour force made up of the original inhabitants was soon exhausted. It was not possible to organize a large influx of colonizers from Europe, and as a result African slaves were resorted to; this led to labour relations of a quite exceptional nature. The principle of slave labour seems to have re-emerged in Europe with the Portuguese on the Iberian peninsula itself, following their explorations of Africa in the previous century.

The exploitation of the mines also experienced an analogous process of expansion and was, if anything, even greater. It had already started in the first decades of the century; the increased demand for minerals, especially copper, silver, iron and mercury, as well as rock salt, involved the complex organization of plant and workers, which in their turn required financial resources on a hitherto unknown scale. Opportunities for investment in mining had attracted capital from rich merchants since the late fifteenth century. Mining activity was now being structured into much larger enterprises than previously, and large numbers of waged workers, who formed the first great concentrations of workers in specific areas, were being employed. These trends were particularly marked in the mining areas of central and eastern Europe, from Poland to the Tyrol, financed with capital invested by the great merchant bankers of Augsburg, especially the Fuggers. With the expansion of the markets for mineral supplies, with new mines gradually being discovered and exploited, especially in the second half of the century, and with the possibility of acquiring other mineral ores through the new trade routes, mining, as well as the interest of those holding capital, changed in importance. However, this did not mean that the processing of mineral ores and the use of products obtained from it ceased to develop at a later time; there were signs of the development of a new form of labour that would make headway in the following centuries, carried along on the wave of the technological innovations that were to come. The secondary sector was also very active, and numerous forms of occupation were being exploited in manufacturing during the sixteenth century. There were opportunities for work that lay half-way between the traditional and the innovative, and this was precisely one of the most significant aspects of the economic expansion of Europe. At the same time it marked the transition from the medieval economy to that of the modern era. The artisan workshops, which had sustained the fortunes of the merchants, still played a decisive role; however, the guilds were now experiencing all the risks inherent in their statutory regulations, which had hindered and slowed down the adoption of innovations, especially in the traditional wool textile sector. Some sectors, such as the shipyards and naval arsenals, required considerable numbers of workers. Visible reminders of how huge these workplaces were still stand to this day. All the specialist jobs were carried out under the same roof, and included the preparation of wood and timber, cord, canvas, navigational instruments, cartography and armaments; the list touches on a whole range of economic activities.

The manufacture of consumer goods and semi-finished products was largely carried out using the labour of field workers, who were available in their free time. Being seasonal, farm work left ample periods free for other activities, and this was how employment in the homes of farm workers was able to develop.

Many interpretations have been put forward as to the evolution of the first industrial society and the various phases it went through over the centuries. 'Proto-industry' and 'pre-industry' are terms that have often been used to define the different forms of productive organization that produced the goods needed to meet consumer demand at all levels. It is perhaps safe to say that, in the context of the general expansion taking place in sixteenth century Europe, forms of industrial organization already existed that had developed in previous centuries, but in the sectors of shipbuilding, mining and farming they began to appear on a much larger scale than before. In particular, production processes were being developed in which fixed capital played a greater role than previously. At the same time there was an increased demand for energy, especially from water mills and windmills; they were undergoing mechanical improvements so that the rotation of their axles could be transformed into other forms of motion that were needed for different work processes.

International exchanges

Trade flows

The geographical explorations led to far-reaching changes in international trading patterns, and they affected the volume of trade as well as the trade routes themselves. The old mercantile world that had emerged from the Middle Ages was upset by gradual changes that brought significant consequences. Mediterranean Europe, including Italy, and northern Europe, with the Hanseatic League and the Low Countries, were the two traditionally strong areas of commerce that were forced to reassess their trading activities. Sea routes were increasingly being used to transport goods; the improvements being made to ships now enabled them to carry low cost bulk merchandise that could not previously be transported overland. These developments inevitably led to the creation of new centres and lines of communication, in response to changing requirements in the field of finance and investment. It was natural that the growing population would become urbanized in towns on the seaboard, or in those that were connected to it by navigable rivers or canals.

The Mediterranean basin lost its central role. This was not so much because of a decline in the traditional flows of traffic, as the internal exchange of local products continued to be lively. It was because of the partial loss of goods from Asia and Africa; these could now be transported direct to the central and northern regions of Europe, around the Cape of Good Hope, thus bypassing the Mediterranean.

The polices of the emerging nation states also led to changes in trade patterns and trade routes; in applying what would later be defined as 'mercantilist' policies, they increasingly tried to take over control of economic activities, by applying protectionist policies, which in the search for almost global supremacy even led to violent clashes.

The fifteenth century had ended with the Treaty of Tordesillas of 1494, which divided the world into two zones of influence for the Portuguese and the Spaniards;

but it took a long time before the effects of commercial exchanges with the New World assumed any general significance. In 1503, Spain created the Casa de la Contratación in Seville; the specific aim of this institution was that Spain should have a monopoly over trade with the Americas, and control over whatever came and went across the Atlantic. Seville experienced exceptional development; details of every voyage of the ships arriving there were kept in special *registros*, or registers, containing precise information about the ship's identity, the name of the captain, the armaments on board, the cargo and its value, duties that had been paid, as well as details about the passengers. The Seville *registros* were intended for purposes of taxation, as well as for controlling the flow of precious metals; but they even went beyond that. Spain could keep a careful watch over everything that was transported, and exercised tight political control. Throughout most of the sixteenth century, Spain practically monopolized the official trade and commerce with the Americas; the only exception was the Portuguese trade with Brazil, which however, was less important. For a few decades during the first phase, shipments were mainly from Europe, and consisted largely of manufactures and food products to supply the colonizers in the settlements; but very soon the products that were exchanged were mainly those from America. From the economic point of view, among these the precious metals, especially silver, were particularly important. Initially, the metals were booty from the empires of the *indios*, but later they came from the exploitation of the Mexican silver mines at Zacatecas; in the second half of the century, the Bolivian mines at Potosì were exploited, using a new method of mining based on amalgam with mercury. Later, goods produced *in loco* were exchanged; this was especially the case with sugar cane, brazilwood from Brazil, and cattle hides from the Antilles, where the animals had been previously been imported.

Exports from the Old Continent increased as more and more Europeans settled; they created a demand for textiles, metal tools, armaments and other manufactured products. This was the period when Europeans, especially the Portuguese, who dominated trade with the African Atlantic coast, started to export slaves. Very soon ships of various nationalities, but especially English and Dutch, were becoming involved in the slave trade.

During the sixteenth century, Europe witnessed the loss of its traditional trade and commerce with Asia. The fall of the Roman Empire in the east, the expansion of the Ottoman Empire on the African Mediterranean coasts, and the violent clashes culminating in the battle of Lepanto (1571), almost completely closed the direct routes across the Mediterranean for goods from Asia. After the circumnavigation of Africa by the Portuguese in 1497, and the voyage of Magellan from 1519 to 1521, the old cross-continental routes became less feasible and were replaced by the ocean routes. This further added to modifying the patterns and centres of commerce. A number of Asian products, such as sugar and dyes, were relinquished, and replaced by supplies from America. But spices, silks, pearls, precious stones and cottons continued to arrive; at the end of the fifteenth century, new traders, who were mainly Dutch and English, established great trading companies; these included the English East India Company, and the Dutch companies that were the forerunners of the Vereinigde Oostindische Compagnie (VOC) of the seventeenth century. Also arriving were new products, such as tea. Europe still had a negative trade balance with the East, but American silver could now be used to help clear the deficit.

Currency

Until the fifteenth century, the scarcity of precious metals for coinage had been a considerable obstacle to the creation of an efficient monetary system. In the second half of the fifteenth century, signs were beginning to appear of new adjustments in the various monetary systems, which since the thirteenth century had witnessed the gradual progress of gold and silver bimetallism. Towards the end of the fifteenth century, the new influxes of African gold, brought in by the Portuguese, and the gold that was starting to arrive from Colombia in America, were beginning to make a difference. Apart from the gold, supplies of silver could be obtained from the German, Tyrolean and Hungarian mines, which had been long-established sources on the Old Continent. However, economic development required increasing quantities of money to meet the growth in internal and international exchanges; the various systems that were peculiar to the medieval period were being used less and less for their settlement.

In Europe, the system of coinage and circulation of coins showed great variety. On the one hand, the amount of coin depended on the availability of metal. On the other, it was also an instrument of economic policy, with devaluation or revaluation being exploited as a means to regulate the state's requirements. In such a situation, it was necessary to differentiate between real moneys and moneys of account, with their ratios being fixed accordingly.

In the second half of the sixteenth century, European monetary systems had to deal with the problem of value ratios between gold and silver, and silver and copper. Plenty of opportunity for speculation was provided by the system, and the variations between the ratios; it was possible to take advantage of time lags in adjustment, or the lack of synchronization between the market value and the official ratios. Moreover, precious metals for coinage did not come on to the European markets in an even flow, nor could they have done. An initial imbalance was created by arrivals of gold from Africa, especially in the first half of the sixteenth century; in the second half of the century, silver from America added further to the imbalance. How enormous the quantities were is indicated by the official data on imports to the places officially appointed to receive the cargoes of precious metals from the different countries. But it is also thought likely that further significant amounts of precious metals escaped being included in the official records, since different forms of smuggling, including piracy and corsair warfare, were being organized, precisely in this period.

In the sixteenth century, the coins and precious metals that abounded in Europe certainly aroused the interest of merchants and dealers. Others, ranging from rulers to scholars, also showed interest, and for a variety of reasons now started to devote works to different economic subjects. It was in this period that monetary laws were being formulated, from those of Thomas Gresham to the theory of quantity. The mercantilist polices of states led to heavy intervention in monetary matters, to the extent that some of these policies are expressly defined as 'bullionist'. The quest for the legendary wealth of nations, brought about by the availability of gold and silver, led to the adoption of the technique of over-evaluating coins to attract them, or under-evaluating them to achieve the opposite.

The great variations in the quantities of coined money and the availability of the metal used, not to mention the official price policies, led to consequences that affected everyday transactions at the local level. Even though there was an abundance of coins, they became part of everyday transactions only according to whether they were being overvalued or undervalued. The undervaluation of gold made the use of silver and copper coins more likely; conversely, the scarcity of gold coins at local levels led to difficulties in the circulation of money.

The development of the coin system during the sixteenth century was somewhat chaotic, despite the minting of large coins in both gold and silver. These included the Portuguese cruzado, and the Spanish eight reales piece; they were particularly important, and became standard coins, especially the Spanish coin. Large coins were a guarantee in high finance and in international relations, where a degree of stability was required. Problems arose in more general transactions; the need for money to sustain economic expansion, or to meet extra state expenditure, especially for a war, and during critical moments of famine and epidemic, also meant a need to create liquidity and increased quantities of currency.

Close investigation of the extraordinary events marking European monetary history has given rise to speculation about the inevitably connected question of price trends. It has led to the period of the second half of the sixteenth century being defined as that of the so-called 'price revolution'. In terms of economic models, and with regard to the quantity theory of money, there is no doubt that an increase in the quantity of circulating money can lead to changes in price levels, all else being equal. On the basis of a number of confirmed cases, it has also been suggested that the trend in prices was at variance with the trend in wages. But this did not seem to have affected the whole of Europe at the same time; one reason for this was that the increased quantity of precious metal available for coinage in many places coincided with phases of economic expansion.

Finance

Requirements of the state

In the sixteenth century, the feudal legacy was still reflected in the system of state finance, and was increasingly at odds with the different levels of administration that were becoming established at local level, especially in the towns, but also over wider territorial areas.[2] Thus at the close of the Late Middle Ages there was a considerable disparity between the state finances of the central power and those of the decentralized and local powers, with quite considerable differences in the ways the two different powers raised finance to meet their expenditure requirements. These differences were beginning to emerge out of the long process of development of the absolute state, which had started in the sixteenth century, and which would become more clearly defined in the later centuries of the modern era. Sovereigns obtained their revenue from a number of sources that included taxation, income from Crown tributes, possible alienation of property and privileges, and loans. The sources of revenue of the local authorities were not generally very different in the way they were defined, but were basically differentiated.

Crown taxation was mainly indirect, and took the form of taxes on consumption, customs duties and tariffs on both imports and exports. Direct taxes appeared to be more prevalent at the local level; these could be taxes on personal property, but more often on real property. Extra finances, often levied throughout the century to meet the various requirements as they arose, for war in particular, led to a combination of the two forms of organization. In cases of need, the Crown demanded additional contributions from the local authorities, who officially obliged by making a general contribution, but actually raised the necessary funds through their own taxation schemes, and precisely this system led to many of the fiscal innovations of the century, whether in France, Italy, Spain or the Low Countries. In practice, the procedure started with the Crown informing the state authorities at the local level of its needs; these could either be to meet a common danger, or to provide the pomp required by the state in its attempt to increase its power in the overall struggle for supremacy. A war was declared, or a dynastic marriage made, for the requirements of the Crown, but their effects, hopefully beneficial, would ultimately be for the good of the whole community. The sovereign thus required his subjects to be involved in sharing the burden by making general contributions that could be defined as a subsidy or gift. The subjects were practically compelled to comply, and the burden was shared among them according to a complex system based on time-honoured custom, or on available data that were empirically assessed and agreed upon. This was an extra contribution, and it was met with funds raised locally; it came out of the taxable sources normally used and approved by the members of administrative bodies such as local councils. In practical terms, in the centralized accounts the item was recorded as a subsidy or gift, while at the local level the corresponding tax item appeared in its usual form as an ordinary tax contribution that had been increased. Taxes at local level varied greatly but they were mostly direct taxes, since indirect taxation was primarily the domain of the sovereign. During the sixteenth century, some of the instruments that appeared in this complex transformation of taxation included the French *taille*, the *centesimal* of the Low Countries, the *fondiaria* of Lombardy, and the *tasso* of the Savoy states. Similar measures were adopted in the papal states. Charles V tried to obtain land tax contributions from Flanders, but failed. Contributions to be paid to the central administration of the state were, at the local level, to all intents and purposes direct taxes on real property, with some cases of direct taxes on personal property. Clear evidence of this process is the greater interest in censuses, and assessments of land and goods: whereas previously their supervision had been limited to the local level, now it began to be controlled from the centre. The survey carried out by Charles V in Lombardy is a case in point.

With the development of trade and exchanges, there was a significant increase in revenue from the duties and tolls under the control of the sovereign. England obtained considerable revenue from the movement in its ports, and Elizabeth I gave precise orders to step up measures, particularly in 1564, to combat smuggling, which was always ready to spread whenever taxation could be avoided. Spain and Denmark also obtained considerable revenue from maritime tolls, evidence of which is provided by the Seville *registros*, and the registers of the ships passing through the Sound.

In continental Europe there was a gradual increase in indirect taxes on consumption, and they became the most important source of revenue for the state. Foodstuffs and drink, among other things, were affected by a whole series of fiscal measures that involved different products; sometimes they were short term measures to obtain extra finances, but more often they were applied over the long term, even if their rates varied. The *gabelle*, the long-established and traditional tax on salt, played an important role; besides fixing the price of salt, it also fixed a minimum consumption for people and animals, setting up monopolies on its supply, trade and distribution.

Though there was a considerable increase in fiscal revenue, it was still not sufficient to meet the huge financial requirements of the European states that were engaged in expansion on various fronts, and were in competition against each other. They sought various ways to boost the influx of revenue, and contracted intermediaries to exact the tax payments, so that the money due to enter the state coffers could be exploited in advance, even if part of the revenue had to be relinquished. Furthermore, similarly to the contracts for collecting taxes, the sale of public offices enabled considerable revenue to be raised.

But even these mechanisms were not sufficient to solve the various problems of liquidity, and in the sixteenth century recourse to debt had spread practically all over Europe.

The public debt

Public debt was certainly no innovation, but it became more widespread in the sixteenth century, and in particular it took on more complex and organized forms. It still encountered obstacles due to the canonical ban on granting loans with interest, though this had been gradually lifted after the thirteenth century. However, the increase in so many different types of loans reached such a pitch that the Pope was prompted to intervene and take steps to regulate them.

Public debt in the sixteenth century gave rise to numerous types of loans, that could be subdivided into the two traditional forms of redeemable and irredeemable loans. They included perpetual annuities, life annuities, loans guaranteed against fiscal sources, Crown monopolies, or revenue from Crown assets, loans backed up by saleable bonds, or other types of bonds, such as floating rate or consolidated bonds, short and long term loans. All these provided fertile ground for innovation and development, and involved the great bankers of Florence, Genoa, southern Germany and other European centres. A multitude of savers also found opportunities for investment, and in some areas of Europe they had already experienced similar forms of investment in their own towns, as in the case of Genoa.

The development of public debt in the European states, during the sixteenth century, gave rise to specialized centres where both capital and bankers converged, and to which sovereigns resorted, in conformity with local regulations. In the first half of the century, the main negotiating centre for French public debt securities was Lyons, where its fairs took place and Italian and German bankers gathered; in the second half of the century, Lyons was overtaken by Besançon, at whose fairs the Genoan bankers predominated. The requirements of Charles V were such that a large number of bankers and several centres were involved, covering an area of business that stretched from Antwerp to Medina del Campo, and included Seville. The Genoese and German bankers, among whom were the Fugger and Welser families, controlled a considerable flow of money, making use of the new credit instruments. At times they were successful, while at others they encountered problems with variations in interest rates, and the possibility of financial loss due to the bankruptcies of various states. The resilience of European bankers was put to the test by the financial crises of Spain, France and Portugal in the mid-sixteenth century. The Genoese bankers, who had successfully asserted themselves as intermediaries between investors and public finances, were the ones who came out on top. Their financial predominance was also made possible when Spain shifted its European interests towards the Mediterranean area, where the main Spanish dominions were concentrated. The savings of vast sectors of the Italian and Spanish population were tied up in the *asientos* and *juros de Castilla*, the credit instruments managed by the Genoese.

The level of public debt of a number of European states also led to cases of insolvency, defined as states of bankruptcy, the most conspicuous cases being the bankruptcies declared by Philip II in 1557, 1575 and 1596. In reality, they were moments when sovereigns rescheduled the handling of the debt, and tended to change the terms of the contract, since they could not pay the interest, or pay back the capital that had been loaned. Essentially the dates and terms of payment were changed, if not the actual interest rates themselves. In this way short term loans were transformed into long term loans, or even into irredeemable loans or revenue *tout court*. Moreover, even in the case of irredeemable loans, sovereigns were able to apply the right of redemption clause, which in practical terms meant that the interest rates that had been applied were renegotiated.

Different roles in Europe

The leading areas: Portugal and Spain

Christopher Columbus and Vasco da Gama symbolize the territorial expansion of the Europeans. At the end of the fifteenth century, they carried the flags of Spain and Portugal to America, Africa and Asia, and at the beginning of the new century both Spain and Portugal took every opportunity to develop their economic activities. The Treaty of Tordesillas acknowledged the new circumstances, and paved the way ahead for the two countries; for almost the whole of the sixteenth century, in different ways, they controlled trade and the trade routes, until other European powers intervened to change the balance of power between the countries engaged in world trade.

The Portuguese mainly involved themselves with trade in Africa and Asia, and built up a considerable model of naval activity. In the early years of the century, the entire burden of carrying out naval expeditions was taken on by the Crown.

In order to reach the coasts of East Africa and Asia, great fleets of large ships were assembled, and provided with large numbers of armed men to tackle the conflicts that very soon arose. The voyage round Africa, towards the east, inevitably meant encroaching upon an already well established trading network that brought goods to Europe, over ancient routes through Asia Minor and Africa. The Arabs controlled this network, which was also essential for Mediterranean centres such as Venice; it was only natural that they should challenge any intruders. However, the aim of the Portuguese was not to conquer the countries of the East, or to colonize them, but to guarantee trade for themselves. However, they had to defend their trade, and in doing so they exerted great military effort, which was made all the more difficult by the great distances from the motherland. They set up bases in Africa and Asia; on the one hand, these provided the necessary stop-offs for their ships, and on the other, they were stations for the collection and storage of goods destined for European trade. However, they too had to be defended, and the Portuguese created the ports and settlements that were essential for their supremacy, from Mozambique to Calicut, and from Goa to Macau.

The Portuguese organized the expeditions to the East on an annual basis; the voyages themselves lasted over a year, or even a year and a half. At the start of the century, the ships left with cargoes of minerals and metals, including copper, cinnabar, coral, lead, and above all silver and coins. On their return journey, the holds were packed with pepper and other spices, such as ginger, cinnamon, nutmeg, cloves and camphor, with loads of up to 1,500 metric tons. Two-thirds were calculated to be pepper, and the price of pepper fluctuated considerably all over Europe. With the growth in trade, there was an increase in the types of goods exported and imported. At the end of the golden period of Portuguese trade with the East, and before the union with the Spanish crown, that is, until 1580, Portuguese ships left with cargoes of oils, wines and textiles, and returned to Europe with silks, porcelains, pearls and precious stones, essences for perfume, as well as the usual spices.

Portuguese trade with the East very soon attracted the interest of European merchants and bankers, and they found ways of being included in the expeditions organized by the Crown. Italians were among the first to join the expeditions between 1500 and 1505, and groups were led by Florentines and Genoans; soon afterwards they were followed by Germans. Foreigners who took part in the Portuguese voyages found themselves subjected to a number of regulations imposed by the Crown. Strict controls were in force from the moment the goods were purchased on the oriental market to when they were sold on the European markets; the Crown held an almost exclusive right, which was only occasionally relaxed. The naval expeditions had extremely high costs, one reason for which was the loss of large numbers of vessels during the voyages, though this did give rise to a considerable development in shipbuilding in Lisbon, Oporto, Setubal and the Azores. However, despite the costs, the trade in spices guaranteed huge profits, which were often 100 per cent more than the capital invested. Until 1514, when it held the monopoly for itself, the Crown had a 30 per cent share in the pepper cargo. The fall in prices that inevitably resulted from the arrival of such large quantities led partly to the need for state intervention in the spice trade. The Portuguese crown also tried to develop Lisbon as one of the leading commercial cities in Europe, so that it could compete against Antwerp and London, which were destinations for Portuguese ships. In the last quarter of the century, Portugal was up against risks from English, French and Dutch piracy, and the costs of expeditions to the East became unsustainable for the Portuguese state finances. In 1578 the spice trade was contracted out to Conrad Roth, a German merchant from the Fugger city of Augsburg, who took on the expenses and risks; half the imported goods went to the king, but these were reconsigned to Roth at a predetermined price.

The relationship the Portuguese had with Brazil was quite different. This was the part of America that fell to the Portuguese by the Treaty of Tordesillas. It very soon became clear, from the early expeditions, that Brazil would not offer up any riches comparable to those the Spaniards could gain from the countries they had conquered. Apart from the brazilwood that was widely available for providing dyeing materials, and that gave its name to the region, it was soon obvious that its greatest wealth lay in its environmental characteristics, and in its potential for agricultural exploitation. However, there were numerous problems; one of the first was that the men who had come over the sea from Portugal had no aptitude for agriculture. Besides that, the indigenous population showed no inclination towards farming either. In addition there was the nature of the land itself.

Results were gradually and laboriously achieved through a system of land concessions, which were granted on condition that the land was cultivated, and that imported labour became available. This labour was provided by slaves; for the Portuguese this was less of a problem, since they were already familiar with the use of slaves in the homeland, and for almost a century they had had contacts with the African coasts, where slaves were offered to them just like any other goods coming from the interior. Finally, the production of sugar cane was considered the most suitable crop for the territory; it was later followed by cotton. The trade in African slaves became in itself a source of profits for the Portuguese, who took advantage of their monopoly in the trade with the Atlantic coast of Africa, and became the suppliers of the Spaniards in America.

Events surrounding Spanish expansion in America were very different. It had begun with a vision of conquering trade with the Indies, but it soon became clear that America was not the place that could provide the goods they had expected. However, they did find great riches, as well as great civilizations, and this ultimately led to a long period of conflict and conquest. In Africa and Asia the Portuguese had only built bridgeheads, and this limited any conflict with other long-established interests dealing locally in production and trade. The Spanish, on the other hand, had to conquer and colonize completely new territories, which led them, over the course of the century, to build up an empire that occupied most of the new continent.

The conquest and colonization of the American territories have fascinated scholars, who have analysed causes and effects, and pointed to the many initiatives that were carried out. The organization of the influx of precious metals to Seville certainly left the greatest mark on the sixteenth century, but during that period, colonial policies were developed and pursued that exclusively affected relations between America and Spain; they were later to have consequences for the whole of Europe, reaching far beyond that century. In the early decades, the Spanish put all their efforts into the needs of colonization; products, apart from gold and silver, were initially obtained from the Antilles, the first area of Spanish settlement. During this early period, Spain sent shipments of seeds for cereals and food plants, sugar cane, citrus fruits, olives and vines, tools for working the land, in addition to livestock such as horses, oxen and sheep, which were unknown in America. Farming and animal breeding practices were transferred from the Antilles to the continent. After the traumatic events of the military conquest, the Spaniards now needed to create an organized structure in the new dominions; they appointed two viceroyalties, and established a ruling and administrative class modelled on the one in Spain. This process influenced the type of men who emigrated from Spain and Europe. The Spanish sovereigns were involved in carefully regulating the flows, since they were concerned about ensuring the appropriate development of their dominion. They could not neglect the demands of the Catholic Church, which had also contributed to promoting the discovery and settlement of the new continent.

It is widely believed that the first Europeans to arrive on the Spanish ships were mainly men who were attracted there in the hope of making a quick fortune. They were mainly from Andalusia and Extremadura, and from the leading classes of Castile, a part of Spain that was heavily characterized by large landed properties owned by the crown, the nobility and the clergy. Once the mirage of gold had faded, these men chose to acquire land; they could obtain it through concessions granted by the Spanish crown, which looked upon itself as the owner of the new territories. The Castilian pattern of land ownership, with large estates, was partly reproduced in America, and also determined how labour was employed. Initially labour was to be supplied by the native inhabitants, but was subsequently provided by the African Negroes who were brought in.

Because of the rigid control over trade with the Americas that Spain had set up with the Casa de la Contratación, and the Council of the Indies, merchants were prevented from entering indiscriminately or in great numbers. Instead, individual and temporary trade licences were granted, but only to merchants, such as the Genoans and Germans, who were considered compatible, and who were indispensable for the crown's financial requirements. Controls were also carried out in the American ports of Vera Cruz, Porto Belo and Cartagena, which were the only ones authorized to have dealings with Seville. Spanish intentions were that merchant ships should sail from and to America in convoys under the protection of warships, and follow common routes, even if they were travelling at the expense of their owners. But whatever their intentions, between the two shores of the Atlantic, both smuggling and piracy were rife.

Areas in the balance: the Italian states

Historians commonly divide economic developments on the Italian peninsula during the course of the sixteenth century into two fairly well defined periods. The first was marked by a crisis that followed the wars that were fought on its territory, combined with the destruction, and subsequent decline of production in traditionally strong sectors such as textiles. In the second period, there was a slight recovery, but in the meantime changes had taken place in Europe as a whole, and products that had been taken over from the Italians were now being produced and marketed. This interpretation is adequate as a first impression, but cannot claim to be exhaustive. What is undeniable, however, is that the Italian economy in the sixteenth century was extremely diversified, in much the same way as the different states, among which the peninsula was divided, differed from one another.

Closer examination of the different sectors shows clearly how manufacturing output was negatively affected by wars; there was a general fall in production, especially in the central and northern areas, which in previous centuries had been the strong area. Throughout the whole area, the conflicts had clearly affected the distribution of the population. The population in the town centres showed a lower concentration, and there was a related reduction in the number of centres of production, with fewer specialized workshops; indeed, it became impossible to meet domestic consumer demand, which in itself was on the decline, let alone produce enough to sustain exports. Apart from all the general difficulties, there were all the expenses due to the wars. They had eaten heavily into the public finances and led to increased taxation, which in turn led to an increase in production costs. This triggered off a dangerous cycle as regards the European market, which was now tending towards an increase in competitive production. However, this crisis in the traditional sectors had little effect on the initiative of those who were engaged in commerce; they became significantly involved in the process of European expansion throughout the world. This was quite apart from the fact that some of the greatest European navigators were Italian.

Italian merchants had built up a solid network of interests and enterprise based on their international experience, and this proved extremely useful at a time when the expansion of the markets and opportunities for business across the oceans created a demand for commercial and financial expertise. While Italy itself was being put to fire and sword by foreign armies, and many cities including Brescia, Rome, Pavia and Genoa were being sacked, Italian traders and dealers were operating virtually all over the world, and exploiting their well tried business techniques. At the beginning of the sixteenth century, there was still every reason for people to come to Italy to learn accounting and trading practices.

Italians still played a prominent role in the great European fairs, where goods were exchanged, but that role was especially significant in places where the great financial transactions were negotiated, and where the credit instruments based on public loans of the European states were traded. One after the other, Antwerp, Lyons, Besançon and Piacenza were the places where Italians carried out their financial activities, during the sixteenth century. The Genoese bankers were particularly active at Besançon and Piacenza, and transformed those places practically into exchange fairs. It was in this connection that during the sixteenth century there was a change in the specialization of Italian merchants. Initially they had been trade merchants, but later they started to become involved in activities that were more specifically financial. They took advantage of the changed attitude of the Church towards finance, and offered to intermediate in the investment of public securities, especially those of the Spanish and French crowns; in France, Florentine bankers operating in Lyons played a particularly important role.

During the sixteenth century, the types of goods that passed through the ports and along the routes of the peninsula did not change significantly; what did change were the quantities. In the Mediterranean basin, there was a trade in local products from its shores; these included food products such as cereals, oil and wine. Other products were sea salt from the islands, sugar, raw wool, cotton, alum, dyes and leather hides. In addition there was iron, as well as manufactured goods such as textiles from Tuscany and Lombardy, Lombard armaments, books, Venetian glass and paper. These were only the most important.

In the last quarter of the century, Genoese galleys found themselves controlling a totally new trade. This was the transport of huge quantities of precious metals, especially coined silver, which were being transported from Spain to Italy as part of a complex financial agreement, following the difficulties encountered by the Spanish crown; after a bankruptcy in 1557, it declared bankruptcy a second time in 1575. There was an exceptional increase in the influx of silver from the Americas, far exceeding 100 tons annually between 1570 and 1580, and 200 tons in the following decades. Apart from this, the development and success of the Piacenza exchange fairs, which were controlled by the Genoans, made the port of Genoa the ideal terminus for the fairs.

Venice also experienced fluctuations in its trade, relating to the changing pattern of trade with the East; this was especially the case with spices after the massive intervention of the Portuguese. It suffered a crisis early in the century when it was forced to trade the pepper brought into Europe by the Portuguese, but later resumed direct contacts by way of Egypt. It also traded other products from the European interior, such as minerals from the mines under Fugger control, which were exported from Venice. The considerable quantities of tin and lead that passed through led to the city specializing in the production of printing types, and increasing the number of printing presses.

The southern Sicilian ports, and Ragusa in Dalmatia, had had a long tradition of involvement in the wheat trade, but were now engaged in managing it on a greater scale, in response to increased consumer demand and the search for new sources of supply. It was also in response to the serious famines that occurred during the second half of the century. It was in this particular sector that the English and Dutch navies first came to prominence in the Mediterranean.

In view of the overall variety of the Italian territorial areas, studies on the economy of the sixteenth century have identified areas of crisis, and areas of growth at different times. There is no doubt that in the first half of the century the wars created enormous difficulties for the pre-existing system of production. However, changes were taking place in the institutions as a result of the new Spanish influences and the international relations of the Italian merchants, and they played a fundamental role in bringing about new developments. Visible proof of this has come down to us in the form of the great churches and palaces, with their fine works of art. They are the result of considerable investment, and provide evidence of the existence and vitality of a number of great princely Italian courts. They too were affected by developments in finance, with the deferment of debts and related fiscal and financial instruments. The papal court was a case in point.

Sixteenth century Italy thus saw many changes that affected practically every sector of economic life. They brought about profound changes in the systems that had sustained the development of the economic and social life of previous centuries. The outcome was a changed equilibrium between the different regions. Some, such as those of the central and northern areas, appeared to regress, at least in comparison with other strong European areas; others managed to find room for great development, as in the case of Genoa, and Venice continued to play an important role. However, the south found itself having to pay dear for the burdens that the policies of Philip II had imposed on it. There still remained a traditionally weak area in the north-west, but an embryonic development process started when the Savoy dominions transferred their centre to that part of Italy.

The emerging areas: England and the Low Countries

In the sixteenth century, two areas of Europe showed signs of unique and lasting development which was considerably more advanced than any that had taken place in previous centuries; these were England and the northern Low Countries. Both countries were affected by far-reaching political events: in England the most significant was the reign of the Tudors, while in Flanders it was the wars of religion. Their economic development followed different paths, which cannot be easily or completely outlined.

In the period before the sixteenth century, the area known as the southern Low Countries, which had Bruges as its centre and Antwerp as its port, experienced considerable development; indeed, it was considered one of the hubs of the European economy, comparable to Italy. Furthermore, important commercial centres like Amsterdam, Bremen and Hamburg had made headway in the immediate vicinity. Their position on the North Sea had made it possible to exploit the great lines of communication that linked the sea with the interior regions of central Europe; these were the navigable rivers of the Rhine, the Elbe, the Scheldt and the Moselle. In the North Sea ports, products from the Baltic Sea and England, such as corn, raw wool, linen, hides, wool and salt, were exchanged with products from the interior deriving from mining, industrial and textile activities; the German fairs also provided trading opportunities. This was the case until the era of the geographical discoveries, and the development of ocean-going navigation.

When the Portuguese began their trade in the East, they were compelled to use the North Sea ports, since Lisbon was decentralized with respect to European trade. They found that Antwerp was the most favourable market for produce from the East Indies, especially pepper and spices; they later also used Amsterdam and Hamburg. During the same period of the early sixteenth century, the influx of cloth from England to these ports had by now become quite considerable. Thus a nucleus of centres, with a concentration of almost all the products that were traded internationally, was developing; at the same, it was undermining some of the Baltic and Mediterranean trading bases.

Maritime activity on the seaboard of the Low Countries intensified considerably, and the livelihoods of the inhabitants became increasingly connected with the sea. With the start of the century, the fortunes of the southern Low Countries continued, but the northern Low Countries encountered problems relating to the narrowness of the territory, and the paucity of resources that could be obtained from it. The inhabitants of the northern Low Countries set about regulating the sea waters; they worked intensively, pumping the seawater away, using power from the expanding network of windmills that provided the mechanical motion required for the different operations. Thus they were ultimately able to derive a unique form of economic development from the sea itself. Signs of their enterprise were already in evidence during the struggles to form an independent state of the United Provinces of the Low Countries, between the end of the sixteenth century and the beginning of the seventeenth. This was later to become Holland, whose independence was recognized in 1648 with the Treaty of Westphalia; during the course of the seventeenth century, its economic development would be inexorable.

The last quarter of the sixteenth century thus witnessed the decline of Antwerp and the growth of Amsterdam as the main centre of economic activity in the Low Countries. The administration of Antwerp was based on a centralized system that had the effect of restricting economic activity; the granting of privileges and concessions was not conducive to attracting the new energies that were now emerging. Amsterdam, on the other hand, had a more permissive approach that created more favourable conditions; the arrival of men, enterprise and capital was facilitated, if not actively encouraged.

It has often been suggested that the underlying reason for the economic success of this area is to be found in the Protestant Reformation that took hold in Holland. The break with the past, which resulted from the wars of religion, undoubtedly played a role, since it enabled large numbers of highly skilled and professionally experienced individuals to come to Holland after their expulsion from the Catholic countries. However, perhaps a more plausible reason was that Holland, in the final decades of the sixteenth century, was able to take advantage of a number of objective circumstances.

In particular, the definitive break with Spain and Portugal, and the consequent ban on trading, forced the Dutch to find their own way of obtaining products from the Americas and the Indies. These products had previously arrived mainly through the intermediation of the Iberians, though dealers from other European countries also intermediated. In the final years of the sixteenth century, the Dutch were engaged in organizing major expeditions to the East Indies; this brought them up against the Portuguese, and they were led to seek a new model of economic expansion. The Portuguese expeditions to the East soon came under tight state control, while the Dutch granted greater liberty, so to speak, to private initiative. However, private initiative was organized through companies that were loosely set up for the purpose, which in the early seventeenth century would become more regulated. The direct intervention of the Dutch in the Americas was to come later.

However, in the sixteenth century the main traffic flows for the Dutch were through the Baltic Sea; records for the transits through the Sound, which was the mandatory route connecting the North Sea, show that by the last decades of the century well over 50 per cent of all the ships passing through were Dutch. In the ports and emporiums of Holland it was now possible to find all the goods that were being traded by sea. At the end of the sixteenth century, the Dutch were in a position to trade with the whole of Europe, set up new methods of processing the raw materials that were now available, develop sophisticated commercial and accounting techniques, and generally operate in conditions that were completely innovative; furthermore, they also had access to large amounts of capital.

During the sixteenth century in England, economic developments differed from those in other European countries. Its geographical circumstances, and the organization of the state, brought about particular changes and prospects. Many historians have analysed the case of England and emphasized particular or more general aspects of its economy at different times. During the sixteenth century, a combination of many factors was at work; these included wool production, changes in agriculture, the development of manufacturing, the availability of raw materials, relations with the European continent, maritime transport, absolute monarchy and the participation of the social classes, as well as the Anglican Reformation. All contributed in various ways to building up a general framework that enabled England to face the coming centuries successfully.

English wool had always been one of the main products in the foreign trade of the country; it had been exported in considerable quantities to the European continent, and to the traditional wool textile centres, such as Italy and the Low Countries. Customs duties on wool exports had guaranteed significant revenue since the thirteenth century, but with the help of a protectionist policy, attempts had been made to develop a manufacturing industry *in loco* in order to exploit its inherent advantages. Though this particular policy came up against opposition from the wool producers, who preferred to exploit the advantages of the free market to gain the best prices and conditions, the sector had managed to establish good contacts with European merchants. They supplied the quantities of wool, and at the same time sent to England the high quality products that were in demand. Moreover, the English already had a toehold on the continent; until the sixteenth century, it had continued to exert authority over a number of territories on the continental shore of the English Channel. The official statistics for English exports at the beginning of the century, which thus did not allow for contraband, showed that the quantities of wool cloth had far surpassed those of raw wool in weight. Throughout the century, there was a considerable increase in the quantities of textiles exported, particularly those in the form of short-cloths. Antwerp was the ideal centre for distributing them to the rest of Europe, and the spread of English cloth has been seen as one of the causes, and effects, of the crisis of Italian cloth. The fall in Italian production, in the first part of the century, was a consequence of the destructive wars fought in Italy, but also of the success of the short-cloths themselves. They had come on to the market since not only were they able to take advantage of the scarce supply, but they also had very competitive prices, even though there was a difference in their intrinsic quality.

The increase in wool production in England brought about changes in the structure of agricultural production; pasture land was extended, and there was an increase in the weaving industry, which in its turn led to a demand for labour. These two factors led to consequences that have been the subject of numerous historical interpretations. On the one hand, the demand for pasture accelerated the process of field enclosures, which led to the expulsion of the weaker classes from the countryside. On the other hand, because of the fluctuation of employment in manufacturing activities, more and more people found themselves open to risk. In the countryside, apart from the effects caused by the expansion of sheep rearing, there were also those caused by the suppression of Church property; the expropriations carried out by the Crown led to changes in farm organization, which had negative repercussions for the small farmers. Although these processes undoubtedly took place, they do not seem to have affected the whole country. The increase in population was probably more general, and called for changes in the agricultural sector in order to guarantee supplies of foodstuffs such as corn for the needs of the expanding urban centres.

England had links with the sea, but the country had been excluded from the great geographical discoveries of the Portuguese and Spaniards. In the fourteenth century, a voyage had already been made by English ships to North America, under the command of the Venetian John Cabot; but it did not produce any appreciable results. Owing to circumstances, English sailors had practically no choice but to navigate in the North Sea; however, they finally managed to gain access to other European seas, especially the White Sea, the Baltic and the Mediterranean. Access to these seas, and the possibility of carrying on trade, was gained through the companies; these were organized on similar lines to the Company of Merchant Adventurers, which had already been engaged in managing exports to the European continent since 1467. The new companies that were to operate on these seas were set up in the second half of the sixteenth century, the Moscovy Company in 1554, the Eastland Company in 1579 and the Levant Company in 1592. Towards the end of the sixteenth century, relations were also established with Africa, through the Guinea Company, set up in 1588, and the Morocco Company in 1595.

Organizations for trade with the East, and the Americas, were set up later. In these areas, advantage had to be taken of the difficulties of the Portuguese, and the Spanish had to be besieged. The English seriously embarked on the struggle against Spain during the reign of Elizabeth I. The English naval fleet had grown in the first half of the century, and Henry VIII had already devoted considerable resources to it. This even led to the devaluation of the pound sterling, which suffered a decline. Yet ultimately, this was another factor that brought about benefits for English exports.

In their attempt to acquire territories, the English turned their attention towards the American continent; they acquired the island of Newfoundland, and the region that they named Virginia, to honour the queen who had granted the necessary privileges for the voyages and conquests. However, no immediate advantages were gained from the acquisition of these territories, and the colonization of North America would be taken up again only in the next century. Greater successes were gained from the 'corsair war', during which Spanish ships transporting the American riches were pursued by armed ships operating under licence from the English crown. By the end of the sixteenth century, the English navy had begun to play a fundamental role in practically all the seas of the world, and the navy was now set to become the decisive element in the development of the country. In terms of population, which was estimated at around 250,000 inhabitants, London was the second largest city in Europe; it had started with a population of around 70,000, but experienced exceptional development during the course of the century. It was on the way to becoming the leading city in terms of economic importance.

The seafaring English had behind them a country that was able to undergo a far-reaching transformation. During this period, the entire economic policy of England was aimed at protecting internal production with the application of import duties. In the sixteenth century, the English started to do without the intermediation of foreign merchants, and became increasingly autonomous in guaranteeing trade for themselves.

The events surrounding the wool cloths were perhaps the most conspicuous in the European context; but in the course of the century there were also successful developments in many other products. For example, iron working witnessed a considerable increase. Iron was essential for producing cannon, and was thus of great significance in the supply of artillery for ships, whether they were merchant ships or those engaged in the piracy wars; it partly solved the problem of the scarcity of bronze, due to the lack of copper in England. There was the problem of fuel, because of the shortage of wood on the island, but this was gradually solved with the use of coal. Naval shipbuilding was actively promoted; at the same time there were developments in new sectors that engaged waves of immigrants. They were coming to England as an effect of its international relations, apart from the religious wars. London received an influx of immigrants, who brought with them cultural and technological skills that found fertile ground for development, and among its inhabitants there started a vocation for internationalism. Like Amsterdam, London also witnessed the growth of professional skills connected with trade and commerce; these included management and insurance techniques. The great expansion in population naturally brought with it a development in building and all the other activities associated with it.

The rivalry with Spain culminated in the naval battle against the Spanish Armada in 1588, the great fleet built by Philip II in order to invade England and settle accounts for ever. The victory of the English effectively marked the start of the decline of Spanish sea power. It was also the consecration of the English navy, which was to play a fundamental role in the future political and economic development of the country.

Notes

1 C.M Cipolla, *Storia economica dell'Europa preindustriale*, 5th edn, Bologna, 1994, pp. 179 ff.

2 There has been renewed interest in the study of public finances and the national debt. A considerable bibliography exists for practically all the European states, whether as single publications or in collected works such as *The Rise of the Fiscal State in Europe, c. 1200–1815.* (Oxford, 1999) edited by Richard Bonney. A great deal of quantitative data is also available, which cannot be presented in a general context, but the outline developed is of interest for our present purposes.

3 European expansion in the seventeenth century

Alberto Guenzi

GENERAL TRENDS

Demography: crisis and recovery

Overall patterns

Economic historians have always regarded the seventeenth century as a period of marked demographic stagnation, if not regression. One after the other different regions of Europe suffered serious food crises and epidemics, which arrested the trend towards growth that had started at the end of the Middle Ages. Recent research focusing on particular areas has partly revised this analysis, but it has not completely refuted it.[1]

The seventeenth century was the last in which the demographic patterns of Europe were constrained by practically insurmountable conditions. In the early modern era, population could not increase beyond certain fixed limits, set by the ratio between cultivable land and people's food requirements. During the sixteenth century there had been a steady increase in population, and in order to meet the increased food requirements marginal land was soon turned over to cultivation. Marshland was reclaimed, woods and forests were cut down, and even pastures and stony areas were partly tilled, but ultimately the real capacity for feeding the growing population was at risk. After 1590, for several years in succession, large areas of Europe were afflicted by famines, which proves that agriculture at that time was incapable of sustaining population growth for any length of time. The conjunctural crisis in the last decade of the sixteenth century soon became a structural crisis that changed the economic situation of much of the continent. As had already occurred in the mid-fourteenth century, between the sixteenth and seventeenth centuries a precarious equilibrium had been reached in which the slightest variation could lead to catastrophic consequences. A short drought or the invasion of a parasite was enough to cause a serious subsistence crisis, at least at the local level. A population habitually undernourished was fertile ground for endemic diseases: in chapter XII of *I promessi sposi* Alessandro Manzoni describes how after two years of poor harvests in 1630 the plague spread to the whole Milan area.

What made the pandemics of the seventeenth century less serious than those at the end of the Middle Ages was a new tendency in the population towards later marriage and lower birth rates, which had started practically everywhere and had gradually become established. European people were seeking to prevent the terrible crises that had hit them in the past, and were partly successful. At the beginning of the seventeenth century the European population was in fact lower than it had been in the first half of the fourteenth, and the consequences of the crises that did occur were everywhere less serious. However, in central Europe, and in central and northern Italy, war was a further negative factor to contend with. In the Germanic empire and its neighbouring regions, the armies that had been constantly passing through for thirty years brought death and destruction with them; they also contributed to the spread of contagious diseases, and plundered crops and livestock.

That being the overall picture, we will now examine the different regional situations and see how their particular patterns affected economic trends as a whole.

Regional differences

In a number of regions, growth had already come to a halt before the end of the sixteenth century. Since the 1570s, areas that were very remote from one another, such as the Languedoc, Castile and central Russia, had shown signs of demographic stagnation, if not of actual regression. In the 1590s, on the plains of the river Po valley, many urban centres entered a regressive phase.

According to Michel Morineau, this was only the first phase of the demographic crisis of the seventeenth century.[2] The second phase, which was even more devastating, coincided with the Thirty Years War (1618–1648) and mainly affected central Europe; in the 1620s and 1630s the effects of war came in addition to those of plague. The territories of the empire, and northern Italy in particular, were badly affected. The upheavals due to the war hindered recovery from the loss of population due to the epidemics, and the consequence was lingering economic stagnation. The Po valley was particularly vulnerable. It was the focal point of two different epidemics, one spreading from the Mediterranean area and the other from the eastern plains; it was also the crossing point for armies that had been passing through since 1616. Pierre Chaunu has estimated that the population in the Po area decreased by more than 20 per cent between 1600 and 1650.[3] Even in regions that had not been affected by the war, or only very slightly, the consequences of the plague were no less serious. Lower Normandy, for example, was repeatedly affected by epidemics between 1620 and 1640, with a death rate of between 20 per cent and 25 per cent. In the same period a series of poor harvests claimed many victims in Scotland, where between 1620 and 1623 the death rate almost doubled.

The third phase was geographically more concentrated, but again it involved areas that had already been affected, such as Italy (particularly the south) and Spain. Between 1647 and 1656 the loss of over a million inhabitants (about a fifth of the population) was recorded for the Iberian peninsula, excluding only Catalonia. The south of Italy suffered similar losses. Other epidemics were recorded in Ireland, and in central France in 1652. In the latter area, apart from the effects of the plague, there were those caused by a succession of poor harvests, not to mention

Table 3.1 Death rate in towns of central and northern Italy during the plague epidemic of 1630–1631

Town	*Population*	*Deaths*	*% deaths*
Bergamo	25,000	10,000	40
Bologna	62,000	15,000	24
Brescia	24,000	11,000	45
Como	12,000	5,000	42
Cremona	37,000	17,000	38
Florence	32,000	9,000	12
Milan	130,000	60,000	47
Padua	76,000	19,000	25
Parma	30,000	15,000	50
Verona	54,000	33,000	61
Venice	140,000	46,000	33
Vicenza	32,000	12,000	38

Source: C.M. Cipolla, *Storia economica dell'Europa preindustriale*, Bologna, 1980.

the military operations that took place from May to September. Further peaks in the death rate were recorded in France in 1661–1662, and in England in 1665; these crises did not actually cause a fall in population growth, but did slow it down considerably. In 1690 Finland, Russia and once again France were affected by another agricultural crisis that lasted twenty-five years and was almost exclusively due to the weather. Almost a quarter of the Finnish population died of famine in 1696 after a long succession of poor harvests. The situation was similar in Russia and France, though in France it was more complex since the deaths were caused not so much by the famines as by the wave of epidemics (not plague) that struck between 1692 and 1715.

The overall picture was thus extremely varied and not all Europe was equally affected. At least three regions – the Po valley, the Iberian peninsula and the areas of Germany between the Elbe and the Rhine, and between Bavaria and Westphalia – experienced an actual fall in population. Other regions such as France, Germany east of the Elbe and Russia showed prolonged stagnation. Finally there were areas such as England, the United Provinces and Ireland where the crises only caused a slowing down of growth.

Effects on living standards, consumption and prices

Demographic stagnation had significant economic consequences, which naturally varied from one region to another. A fall in overall numbers generally leads to a fall in demand; this has important repercussions particularly on the market for foodstuffs. In a pre-industrial economy the primary sector is the one that predominates, and is consequently the one mainly affected.

In Germany and northern Italy, the areas worst affected by the demographic crises, there was a very marked fall in cereal prices due to the decline in demand.

If we take 100 as the price of wheat in 1626 (immediately prior to the great catastrophes caused by the epidemics) in Germany in 1651 it fell below 60, while in the Italian Po valley it was constant at just over 60. After 1676 in Germany there was a slight recovery, but in Italy the price of cereals continued to fall until the end of the century and showed no sign of recovery. In 1750 it was still below 60. In France the fall was less marked and more gradual, as was also the case in the Low Countries and Poland, where prices had even tended to rise until 1650.

Perhaps the most interesting case is that of England, where the price of agricultural commodities was related not only to demographic factors, but also to technological and organizational factors. Again taking 100 as the price of cereals in 1626, in 1676 (coinciding with the peak in mortality of the 1660s and 1670s) the price level was 90. The real fall in prices came later, in the very early years of the eighteenth century, and was the result of the extraordinary increase in the productivity of English agriculture, a phenomenon that would be decisive for subsequent developments in the European economy.

In the next chapter we will consider the effects of the fall in prices on the agrarian structure of the continent in more detail, but at this point it is useful to bear in mind that the phenomenon set off far-reaching, interrelated processes. In the first place, the areas under cultivation were greatly reduced to make way for pastureland, and in many regions there was a decline in the value of land and its use. In this situation real salaries tended to increase, partly because the available work force had become scarcer, and partly because prices were tending to fall. The seventeenth century saw an end to the increase in prices that had been going on for so long, and the start of a deflationary phase; this certainly brought about improvements in living conditions for the economically weaker classes. However, ultimately the crisis had different repercussions on different social classes, and in different geographical areas. While there were improvements among agricultural labourers and waged workers generally, living conditions for the small landowners, tenants and sharecroppers considerably worsened. Throughout the previous century these farmers had benefited from the steady increase in cereal prices, and managed to make a profit by selling their surplus produce on the market. But in the seventeenth century markets were less receptive, and with the fall in prices small owners and farmers were often forced into debt and into selling their properties or becoming salaried workers. This process certainly benefited the large landowners and was widespread in the Po area and in France; it also occurred in England, where institutional factors were involved too, as will be seen later. For the poorer classes in the urban areas the fall in the prices of farm produce was an advantage. It was enhanced by the tendency for nominal wages to increase, and thus real salaries went up even higher. This situation was more marked in regions like Germany, where according to Slicher Van Bath, wage levels increased by over 20 per cent between 1650 and 1699, while in the same period cereal prices halved.[4] In England between 1626 and 1726 the real wages of journeymen in the towns almost even doubled. The growth was more limited in France, but over the same hundred-year period it increased by over 50 per cent.

Agriculture and land ownership

Technology and new crops

In some regions of Europe, peasants continued to account for as much as 90 per cent of the population during the seventeenth century, and the primary sector generally engaged over 70 per cent of Europeans, with small landowners, farmers, sharecroppers, farm labourers and, where they still existed, serfs forming a world of great diversity. As we saw in the previous chapter, the different demographic trends had different effects on the various regions and social classes, but it was perhaps in the world of agriculture where these differences were most evident.

The major agricultural product was undoubtedly wheat, the one that determined patterns throughout the whole sector. Providing bread was a categorical imperative and everything had to be subordinated to this essential need. Other cereals, such as oats or rye, were also grown in areas like Germany to meet this need in times of famine, but for the overwhelming majority of European peasants wheat was the only possible crop.

The seventeenth century was not a period of great technological progress, and indeed one is struck by how few writings and studies on agronomy there were compared with the previous century, when practically all over Europe there was a boom in treatises on how to improve the use of the land. This could be merely symptomatic of an agricultural economy that was not very progressive, or not seeking to increase productivity, but simply aimed at upholding revenue from the land. But though superficially agriculture seemed to be going through a static phase, in reality there were glimpses of signs of change. When the serious effects of the demographic crises brought about a lower demand for wheat, a new phase began that marked a change from the previous century. Whereas in the sixteenth century, under pressure from the growth in population, even pasture was cultivated, and new ploughing, fertilizing and sowing techniques were attempted, in the seventeenth century there was renewed interest in stock farming, vine growing and the cultivation of industrial plants, especially for textiles.

Vine growing had always been an important supplement for the income of peasants, and in the modern era the consumption of wine was relatively high, since at that time it was a unique source of calories, mineral salts and vitamins. Over the seventeenth century, there were many indications that vines were being cultivated more extensively. There was a steady increase in exports of wine, at least until the middle of the century, and particularly in France. The quantity of Bordeaux wines exported at the end of the sixteenth century amounted to 30,000 tons, while by 1640 it was 60,000 tons. There was a similar trend in central Italy, while in other areas such as Hungary, the Iberian peninsula and Sicily it was even more marked.

Stock farming and cereal production could be considered as activities in competition with each other. The increased demand for cereals even led to pasture being cultivated, and the possibilities of providing fodder for animals were thus reduced. This started a process that ultimately led to a reduction in the productivity of the land, and jeopardized the prospects of feeding the population as a whole. Cattle were needed for working in the fields as a source of energy, as in the case of oxen, but they were also an important source of manure for the fields themselves. In addition to providing meat, stock farming also produced large quantities of raw materials for the important tanning industry. Any reduction or increase in livestock, particularly cattle, was a crucial aspect of the agrarian history of the seventeenth century. In the regions worst affected by the Thirty Years War, such as Germany, the Po valley and central Europe generally, stocks of cattle were greatly reduced, and it took a very long time before previous levels were recovered; in these areas farming went through a period of great crisis. On the other hand, in areas such as England and the United Provinces, which were less affected by the wars or not at all, there were developments in stock farming with new agricultural methods that involved better systems of rotation and manuring. Furthermore, seventeenth century Holland witnessed the beginnings of a type of intensive stock farming that prevailed over cereal cultivation. The feasibility of the new system was confirmed when wheat started to be imported in order for cattle to be exported. In eastern Europe stock farming remained considerably more widespread than in the western areas; throughout the century the Danube area exported cattle, whose meat and hides were consumed and processed in Italy, France, Germany and Spain.

During the course of the century, very little progress was made from the strictly technological point of view, as already mentioned. The plough was still a rudimentary tool that could not penetrate the soil to any great depth, and its use required a great deal of energy, whether human or animal. Rudimentary and inefficient systems and tools were also used to harvest and thresh cereals. Seed productivity varied greatly, ranging from an excellent seed to yield ratio of 1:9 in some particularly fertile regions of England, the Po valley or Tuscany, to very low ratios of a little over 1:2 in the mountain areas. This naturally applied only to normal years. In unfavourable weather conditions, yields were so low that the chances of cultivating the fields in the following year were put at risk.

While there was a chronic shortage of manure over much of Europe due to the scarcity of livestock, crop yields were negatively affected by backward farming methods. Farming was mainly based on a two-year rotation system, where wheat or another crop alternated with a period of fallow. This limited the area of cultivated land, and did not guarantee good soil regeneration. In the sixteenth and seventeenth centuries, a new three-year rotation scheme for farming was tried out. The cultivable land was divided into three parts: one was sown with wheat, another with a less important cereal or legume, while the third was left to recuperate. The benefits in terms of output were immediately apparent. With the two-yearly rotation system only half the land was cultivated, while with the three-yearly system two-thirds of the available land were sown every year. The new system also brought benefits in terms of productivity. A typical case, especially in France, was to introduce legumes such as broad beans and peas into the rotation system. This option brought with it the dual advantage of enriching the earth as well as providing produce with its own potential market. The fall in cereal prices was a setback to these efforts, which would be resumed only in the next century. To a certain extent the introduction of maize made up for the lack of innovation. This particular cereal caused a minor revolution in the agricultural system of some areas of Europe. Imported from America, it could guarantee far higher yields than wheat, and could be used to feed both animals and humans. It was also useful in the three-year rotation system, since it could be planted between the wheat and fallow. Unfortunately, the plant required particular soil and weather conditions, and it ultimately became restricted to only a few areas, such as France and the Po valley.

The case of England was a separate one. Its experience in the field of agriculture differed from that of the rest of Europe, and it was somewhat complex. The cultivated areas were extended, new agricultural techniques were systematically adopted and all the available knowledge of the time was put to use. Different types of ploughs were adopted according to the terrain, and increasingly effective fertilizers were used, which all led to considerable advances in English agriculture. However, it is quite likely that these procedures were also being adopted in other areas, particularly those that were not suffering losses of population, such as central France, the Low Countries and Scandinavia.

Agriculture provided several raw materials for use in urban manufacturing plants. These included hemp and flax, which were grown especially in western France, Romagna, southern Germany and the Baltic countries. The production of wool was boosted with the extension of pasture to areas already under cultivation, especially in Spain and southern Italy. The rearing of silkworms took place almost exclusively in Italy, and was concentrated in the countryside of Lombardy, Emilia, Tuscany, and more generally in the south. The various phases of silk production such as reeling, twisting and weaving were an important supplement to the income of peasants in these regions. It was also an important manufacturing sector for the urban economy. Over the century silkworm breeding was also introduced into France and Spain, but Italy retained its leading position in this field.

Land ownership

Apart from the technological aspects, factors such as land ownership and systems of land tenure need to be considered in order to understand the transformations in the agricultural sector. In the first place, there were enormous expanses of unproductive or barely productive untillable land that could not even be exploited for gathering and hunting to any great extent. Second, there were areas of land that were used for various purposes by a community such as a village, or the families in a particular parish. This was common land used intermittently mainly for pasture, and was only partly tilled and cultivated. The use of such land was liable to be strictly regulated by laws that were determined more often than not by custom and tradition.

Besides this common land – later to become land to be 'conquered' by new classes of owners – there were the fields under full peasant ownership, or those included under the vast wide-ranging seigniorial system. Those under peasant ownership were particularly widespread in England, southern France and eastern Europe, but the peasant owners were not necessarily prosperous. Indeed, their small farms were often vulnerable to fluctuations in the market or to freakish weather. Falling prices forced many of them into debt, and subsequently into selling their land. Peasants who did not actually own the fields they farmed, but who could pass on the rights of use to their heirs, found themselves in a similar situation. These tenant farmers had to make an annual payment to the landowner, which varied in amount but rarely exceeded a tenth of the yields. They were often subject to the *corvée* system, which meant they had to provide labour for a number of days on the owner's land, and they worked and lived in the part of the property not directly managed by the seignior. Not all peasants were as lucky as those we have mentioned, who lived mostly in the Low Countries and northern France. In many other regions, inheriting the use of property was neither a right nor a custom, but was subject to heavy charges; such was the case in England, central France and southern Germany. In many areas the rights of peasants were highly precarious and there was every chance of being forced to leave the land they worked on; this was the prevailing situation in eastern Europe and southern Italy. The land belonging to the seignior might be farmed by peasants subjected to the *corvée* system, or leased on the basis of more modern systems; these could be fixed rate tenancies that were often paid in money, or a particular type of partial tenancy known as *mezzadria*, or sharecropping. In more advanced areas such as the Po valley and the Low Countries, these types of land tenure were not uncommon, but where large estates predominated they could not develop.

This was the overall picture of the forms of land tenure that the seventeenth century inherited from the previous period. But economic and social upheavals led to rapid evolution in this area too. The fall in prices created difficulties for the small landowners, who were often forced into debt and subsequently into relinquishing their property, as we have said. Those who benefited were the large landowners, whether they were from the nobility, the Church or the bourgeoisie. Land ownership was thus further concentrated in a small number of hands. This was particularly evident in northern Italy, France and Germany east of the Elbe. In England the situation was different in that the appropriation of land by the dominant classes did not affect the small owners so much but mainly involved the open fields, which after the enclosures became part of vast estates. The effects and consequences of the enclosures were first felt in the seventeenth century, but it was especially in the eighteenth century that changes in land ownership and tenure brought about real economic change. Later, when examining the question of the enclosures, it will be seen how the privatization of land led to a cultural revolution of fundamental importance from the social and political point of view.

It may seem strange that the prosperous classes should continue to invest in the acquisition of land at a time when prices and profits from the land tended to decline. But it should be remembered that agriculture was by far the most prevalent activity in pre-industrial societies, and land was in any case the most important economic asset, and the low risk investment *par excellence*. Moreover land ownership secured political and economic dominance, even in the towns. This led to an extremely important evolution in the world of agriculture, especially in the more developed areas. First, land became definitively recognized as a marketable good, and a land market developed that could not have existed in a feudal system. Second, the purchase of land by non-rural classes led to the development of more advanced forms of tenancy.

Refeudalization

What is outlined above applied to western Europe. In Europe east of the Elbe, Prussia, Poland, Hungary, Bohemia and Russia, the fall in prices led to a development that in some respects went in the opposite direction. In order to safeguard their agricultural revenue, the large landowners in these areas greatly extended their properties; but in contrast to their western counterparts, they also pursued a policy of strongly containing labour costs, even going so far as to revive serfdom.

Eastern Europe had for centuries been the 'granary' of the continent. The low population density regularly gave rise to surpluses that were exported to the west. This steady flow was a magnificent source of wealth for the ruling classes, especially those of Poland and Russia, and when they were faced with difficulties in the grain market these ruling classes extended their properties and forced the peasants to remain on their land at all costs. Thus in the mid-seventeenth century Poland, Romania and Russia reinstated serfdom, and in many areas feudal rights that had long fallen into disuse, though never officially abolished, were exercised once again. The situation was fairly similar in a few western areas, especially in southern Italy and southern Europe generally. It was a way of further increasing, or safeguarding, agricultural revenue.

This move was known as 'refeudalization', precisely because it brought back a number of aspects that typified the feudal system. With reference to western Europe the definition may appear far-fetched, but it is certainly appropriate to the eastern areas. The response of the rulers to the crisis in those areas did not lead to any progress in contractual relations in the world of agriculture, as it did in the more advanced areas. But it did mean that living conditions for the peasants only got worse.

Cities, manufacturing, commerce and finance

Corporations and proto-industry

During the course of the seventeenth century, manufacturing activities did not undergo any significant changes from the technological or organizational point of view. But in a number of specific sectors some degree of technological progress did take place. One such case was chemicals. Improvements were made in purifying saltpetre, which was required for producing the gunpowder needed in the numerous wars. The dyeing industry benefited from the introduction of new techniques and the availability of new products from America. But these innovations were of no great importance, especially in comparison with those that were to appear in the following century.

As in the past, manufacturing continued to take place both in the towns and in the country areas. In urban areas work processes were generally carried out by specialized workers in artisan workshops. In the rural areas, when they were not busy in the fields, peasants would work in their own homes performing a number of operations related to textiles in particular. But industrial work in the home was not exclusive to the country areas, and often played a central role in the towns as well. In the seventeenth century, on the initiative of entrepreneurs in the international market, the two forms of industrial production (rural and urban) were combined to form complementary elements within a complete single manufacturing process. A division of labour between town and country was thus established that combined the need to contain production costs with the need to standardize and check the quality of the product. The peasants, who were poorly paid, had the low-skilled laborious jobs, while the artisans, who were well paid, were given the more delicate highly skilled operations. In addition to these two systems, there were the large centralized enterprises such as arsenals and blast furnaces, where as many as several hundred men and women worked. These were generally initiatives promoted by governments, as part either of a social policy to provide work for those in charitable institutions, or of an economic policy to organize the production of goods that were strategic for the economy and defence of the country.

In the towns, the master artisan, assisted in the workshop by a variable number of workers and boy helpers (in Italy called *garzoni*), continued to be part of the corporation or guild made up of all the master artisans carrying on the same activity. The corporations, especially in Italy, but also in Spain, Germany and France, were still important in carrying out tasks such as quality control on manufactured products, safeguarding their members' interests, negotiating with the politically powerful, handing down technical skills, as well as providing members with mutual aid. The corporations were long blamed for being one of the main reasons for the economic decline of the Italian cities in the seventeenth and eighteenth centuries, since their excessive control over production methods and organization forced Italian entrepreneurial merchants into making products that no longer satisfied consumer tastes. Recent studies, however, have shown that the corporations were able to respond flexibly to the challenges of the international market by renewing production methods and products.[5] The artisan's workshop with its structured organization had arisen four centuries earlier with the urban revolution, and had met the requirements of a well defined and protected market within the walls that surrounded each town. During the fourteenth and fifteenth centuries, when this market expanded, at first provincially, then regionally, and finally internationally, the master artisans were no longer able to predict the demand for quantity or quality, and it was out of this context of uncertainty that the merchant-entrepreneur emerged, who was to play a leading role in European history until the industrial revolution. Through the skilful exploitation of his commercial skills and organizational ability he ultimately managed to transform the members of the corporation into qualified workers who were at the same time employees.

The merchant was the 'director' of manufacturing production. He supplied the artisan with the raw materials and very often also with the fixed capital. He decided on the characteristics of the finished product, fixed its price and arranged for its sale on the market. The merchant-entrepreneur, who was often a member of a corporation himself, did not limit his organizational activity to the town, but in seeking to lower production costs he often provided peasant families with work as well. This was the start of the 'putting out' system of production based on work in the home, which was to play such an important role in the economic development of Europe. The artisan's workshop, cottage industry, town and country, were thus all parts of an integrated system at both local and continental level, which would be consolidated and expanded during the course of the seventeenth century.

However, these events and changes were almost exclusively limited to the textile sector. Other production processes did not adapt well to this type of organization, either because of the large amount of fixed capital that was needed, as in mining, shipbuilding and ironworking, or because of the particularly high technical and professional skill that was involved, as in gold working and carpentry. In some areas of the continent, particular forms of land tenure made it very difficult to transfer any type of manufacturing activity to country areas. The *mezzadria* share-cropping contract, for example, committed the peasant family to only working in the fields, and did not allow peasants to engage in spinning or weaving.

There are numerous examples to show that the economic and non-economic functions of the corporations did not end with the success of the putting-out system and rural proto-industry. In the more active centres of the Italian Po valley such as Milan, Bologna and Venice, many corporations, particularly those producing for the international market, formed associations of merchant-entrepreneurs, which in some cases became true cartels that could decide on prices and the quality and quantity of products. In other areas during the seventeenth century, the organization of guilds weakened considerably. In the Low Countries and England their decline was the result of the process of modernization that favoured systems in which capital accumulated from mercantile activity could more easily be invested in manufacturing. In these countries the guilds had also lost their usefulness because manufacturing was now almost entirely carried out in the country areas. In addition there were large concentrations of immigrants from France and the southern Low Countries. These exiles often brought with them new products and techniques, and their success in the markets caused an upheaval. France, where manufacturing was subjected to rigid state control and the corporations were granted special privileges, was a different case. The effects of this system, which gained strength in the second half of the century, will be seen in the pages to follow.

The social and economic changes of the seventeenth century ultimately worked to the advantage of countries like England and France, but especially the Low Countries, whose manufacturing production increased steadily while Italian and Spanish production declined. There were numerous reasons for this success. The low incidence of population crises facilitated the rapid development of internal markets and set limits to wage increases, which resulted in more competitive prices. The success of more efficient farming methods in these areas meant that it was possible to feed a rapidly growing urban population and enable rural families to engage in manufacturing activities in certain periods of the year. Further contributing factors were the successful achievements of these countries in international commerce and the fact that they were on the Atlantic, which was now gaining in importance at a time when the Mediterranean was losing its central role.

These crucial changes altered the hierarchy of the urban economies. The cities that were more dynamic and became strong focus points for the economies both on the continent and beyond, were all located in north-western Europe. Though manufacturing was mainly carried on in the homes of peasants, the business of management, organization and control, and especially trading, was still concentrated in the towns. The coefficient of urbanization was thus a very sensitive indicator of economic development in the pre-industrial period, and in this respect, during the course of the seventeenth century, the Mediterranean lost its central position. At the start of the seventeenth century seven out of twelve cities with over 100,000 inhabitants were in the Mediterranean area. These were Naples, Milan, Rome, Palermo, Messina, Venice and Seville, while the other five were Lisbon, Paris, Antwerp, Amsterdam and London. At the end of the century, the figures for the Mediterranean cities were the same as a hundred years previously or slightly higher, while in the Low Countries and England urban expansion had taken place on an enormous scale. Apart from the spectacular growth of cities like London and Amsterdam, a dense network of medium-size and large towns had developed, which were both cause and effect of the economic development in the two countries.

Markets and trade

The expansion of markets brought about a profound evolution in the way manufacturing was organized. Merchants were now subjecting a production system that had originally been intended to meet the needs of a limited and protected market to the requirements of rapidly growing trade. Owing to the geographical discoveries that had taken place in the previous two centuries, this trend was even more marked during the seventeenth century. As we have seen, the colonization of the new continent and the opening up of new ocean routes brought into Europe unfamiliar products like tobacco, coffee, chocolate and sugar that gradually found favour on the markets. Sugar was not a completely new commodity, but now that the immense productive potential of territories like Brazil and the Antilles could be exploited, its price was considerably reduced, and it became accessible to a much wider section of consumers.

These new trade routes also continued to guarantee a steady stream of precious metals such as gold and silver from America to Europe. Although this traffic had declined considerably since the previous century, it was still extremely important economically. However, the real change in seventeenth century trade with the American colonies came with the enormous growth of traffic going in the opposite direction, that is, from Europe to America. Europeans who had emigrated in order to colonize the new lands now began to demand manufactured products such as textiles, arms and metal utensils, and manufacturing plants on the Old Continent, which had been experiencing a fall in domestic demand, were given a new lease of life.

This lucrative trade became one of the main reasons for the conflicts between the great powers of Spain, Portugal, England, the Low Countries and France. During the seventeenth century, leadership was being taken over by England and the Low Countries. England was slowly breaking into Mediterranean trade, which until then had been under Italian control, while the Low Countries came to exercise virtual control over all the Atlantic routes. The English and Dutch became specialized in the trade of one of the most significant 'products' of the period, which resulted from the need to cultivate the immense American territories and the scarcity of the indigenous population. The colonizers opted for an alternative that would have quite dramatic repercussions from the human point of view, but which proved to be an extremely lucrative business for unscrupulous merchants. During the course of the seventeenth century every year 20,000 Black Africans were taken from their lands and sold to the American colonists to work as slaves on the sugar and cotton plantations.

Such large-scale transoceanic traffic entailed enormous economic outlay and the tying up of capital for long periods, and the different nations and great capitalists found various ways of confronting this problem. In the Iberian countries the state itself sponsored organizations such as the Casa de Contratación in Seville that were in charge of monitoring the entire trade with the New World. Initiatives in England and Holland were almost all in private hands, though they could take advantage of concessions granted by the state, as in the case of the overseas trading companies like the English East Indies Company (1600) and its Dutch equivalent (1602), which were often formed as shareholding companies.

The success of the new trade routes did not mean the end for the existing ones, however. The Mediterranean had lost its central position, but it still continued to be a hugely important market. Italian cities continued to produce silk textiles that were much sought after on the markets of north-western Europe. Sicily and the whole of southern Italy and Spain were still able to export raw silk, corn, oil, sugar and salt, the latter also coming from Cyprus and Crete. Spain was still a great exporter of raw wool that was then processed in Italy, Flanders and England. With the opening of the new ocean routes, the Mediterranean trade in spices and silk with the Levant was greatly reduced, but did not completely disappear. Venice kept its status as one of the world's main commercial ports despite the loss of the leadership it had enjoyed in previous centuries.

The Baltic Sea also continued to play an important role on the great scenario of international trade. Here the Dutch exercised virtual control, and ships from the United Provinces carried corn, salted fish, furs, iron and copper from Poland, Russia and Scandinavia to the west.

American metal and Spanish bankruptcies: monetary and financial difficulties

As we have said, since around 1550, the arrival of American metals had been causing inflation; historians more recently have called this the 'price revolution'. This process continued until around 1630, and its development differed from country to country. It has been calculated that on the continent as a whole, the rate of inflation was around 2–3 per cent annually; today this would be considered low, but for the pre-industrial period it was quite exceptional. In the first chapter it was mentioned that the change, or deflation, started before the middle of the seventeenth century, and a contributing factor, besides population, was the considerable decline in precious metals coming from America.

The dwindling supplies of gold and silver from America had further important economic consequences, particularly in the monetary and financial fields. Large amounts of American metal reached Spain, partly as taxation but mainly in exchange for goods, since the colonists were theoretically allowed to trade only with the mother country. The problem was that Spain was not able to meet the demands of the colonies. Other nations thus took advantage, and very soon American gold and silver found its way to Amsterdam, Florence, Milan and Lyons. The situation was further aggravated by the revolts in the Low Countries that had forced the Habsburgs to greatly increase their war expenditure. In order to meet this expenditure, debts were incurred with the major European bankers from 1568 until the middle of the next century. Banking families such as the Fuggers in Germany, the Diazes in Portugal, but especially the Dorias, Spinolas and Centuriones in Genoa paid the Spanish king advance sums of money to pay the wages of the mercenary troops fighting in Flanders, and the bankers were repaid with proceeds from various taxes. However, by 1609 80 per cent of the Spanish tax revenue had been mortgaged, and when he ascended the throne ten years later Philip IV discovered that the taxes were all in the hands of foreign bankers. This way of managing public finance was the result of extravagant foreign policies, and could not be kept up for very long; the King of Spain was periodically forced to declare bankruptcy, which was in fact a way of renegotiating the interest on debts. The bankruptcies clearly had serious repercussions on the financial system of Europe, which were further aggravated by the policy of gradually debasing the currency, especially the fractional currency, of Spain and other areas under Habsburg rule (Germany and Milan).

Non-Habsburg Europe did not experience the same ruinous situations. Indeed, in addition to benefiting from improved financial techniques, many areas also benefited from the large amounts of liquidity coming from America, and enjoyed very low interest rates. In Holland and England the interest rate on public debt bonds over the whole century fluctuated between 4 per cent and 6 per cent. These two countries were unquestionably the most advanced from the financial point of view, though interest rates in France and the Venetian Republic were also tending to decrease.

NEW POWERS

Mercantilism and the formation of the modern state

What we know today as national states slowly and laboriously began to take shape during the course of the seventeenth century. The wide-ranging scope of the functions that these new entities took on immediately posed economic, financial and administrative problems. It was one thing to organize the defence of a small regional state in the Italian Po valley, or a feudal estate in central France, but it was quite another to equip an army that could sustain the foreign policy of a great monarchy like France, or the fleet of a world power like England.

When Louis XII asked Trivulzio what was the secret of conquering Milan, the great *condottiere* replied that three things were required: 'money, money and more money'. In fact, political development went hand in hand with economic and administrative development. The steep rise in military expenditure forced countries to seek new revenue, and new territories were often subjugated for this purpose. The bureaucratic structure had to be expanded so they could be administered, which in turn led to increased expenditure, and so it went on. Only countries with territories of sufficient size could afford the luxury of maintaining a stable bureaucracy to administer the state, and especially to levy taxes; only countries with sufficient revenue could maintain armies and fleets that were increasing in size and becoming more and more costly. Hence the great nation states arose in order to meet increased expenditure, but as they made headway their expenditure increased even further. Until the industrial revolution, sovereigns constantly had to face enormous financial difficulties. The unending search for new sources of revenue made it essential to develop better economic policies, and the seventeenth century marked the ultimate triumph of mercantilism.

Aware that increased private income could help to increase revenue from taxation, those who were in charge of state finances were prompted to deal with economic matters more systematically. The national balance of payments and military expenses were thus decisive factors in the formation and structuring of nation states, and the mercantilist policies were in a sense the most efficient tool for meeting these needs. But nation states also arose and became consolidated for reasons that had little to do with war administration and expenditure, and were linked with religious, cultural, linguistic and other aspects. Mercantilism did not only reflect the need for ever greater monetary resources on the part of central governments, it was also an economic policy that had the strong support of the urban and rural middle classes, the landed aristocracy, the financial sectors and more generally the rising social classes. What shaped the different economic policies adopted by the different states, and ultimately determined what forms the nation states of western Europe would take, was the compromise between the will of the central government, with its embryonic state apparatus, and the demands or opposition of the different social classes.

Out of this overall situation emerged three countries: Holland, England and France. Their institutional and economic evolution showed three different approaches to the problems connected with the formation of the modern state. Their economies went in the opposite direction to those of the rest of the continent. They were the first countries to attempt new forms of public administration and ways of representing different interests. They also tried new types of state intervention in the economy. The three experiences correspond to three different models of state and three different levels of economic performance.

Holland

From independence to leadership in international trade

Historians have long been fascinated by the extraordinary development of the United Provinces in the seventeenth century. Scholars have not exaggerated when they refer to the Dutch 'miracle'.[6] Since the late Middle Ages, the Low Countries had already experienced very strong economic growth. However at the forefront of this development was the area, in the south, roughly corresponding to modern Belgium and Luxembourg, while the northern provinces, the modern Netherlands, had remained backward. Until the fifteenth century the most important financial and manufacturing centre had been Bruges, but in the next century the leadership passed to Antwerp. The main cities in the northern provinces had been part of the Hanseatic League but were excluded from it during the fifteenth century. However, in 1471 freedom of trade in the Baltic Sea was also extended to Dutch ships. This was to be crucial for the future development of Holland, since trade with the Baltic was still of utmost importance for the economy of the country.

The economy of the Low Countries in the seventeenth century developed a dualistic system. On the one hand Antwerp acted as the financial capital and the main trading centre for valuable products such as spices, silk, silver and English wools; on the other Amsterdam had taken over absolute control over the Baltic area, where the trade in corn, fish, salt and timber was of considerable importance. In addition, in the limited Dutch countryside, a highly evolved form of farming had made headway, in which contracts of tenancy predominated. Peasant farmers were often engaged in manufacturing activities, in keeping with the classical model of rural proto-industry.

In the second half of the sixteenth century the Low Countries began a long struggle for independence. After Charles V renounced the imperial throne, they formed part of the immense Spanish empire of the staunchly Catholic Philip II. The war had several causes that were primarily religious; but they also involved protecting ancient town liberties against Spanish *dirigisme*. The struggle was made even more bitter by the increasingly harsh repression, which led numerous hitherto Catholic nobles, such as William of Orange, to support the Protestant cause and ultimately, in 1581, it brought about the division of the Low Countries. The southern region remained under Spanish control while the northern area, now called the United Provinces, declared its independence in July 1581.

Various factors determined the successful outcome of the struggle for independence of the United Provinces, among which were the crucial support of England, and their own supremacy on the seas. The war in the Low Countries was a decisive turning point in European history, since it marked the beginning of Spanish decline. The prolonged conflict was an extremely costly one, especially for Spain, and the first truce was only signed in 1609, when Spain granted *de facto* recognition of the United Provinces as an autonomous national entity, but they were not formally recognized until 1648.

After the end of the struggle against Spain, the economy of the northern Low Countries appeared to be more vigorous and dynamic than ever. Even after forty years of war this young nation was the most highly developed in Europe. One of the contributing factors to this success was the mass migration to the northern provinces of Protestants from the southern provinces, which were still under Spanish and Catholic control. This forced migration was a particularly important factor for social and economic change and many Walloons, who had come from the south, were among the great capitalists of Amsterdam. The whole area of Holland, with Amsterdam at its centre, became the hub of development and soon the United Provinces themselves were known simply as Holland. At the same time it benefited from the decline of Antwerp, which was actually the outcome of a deliberate policy, on the part of the Dutch rulers, to block the port of Antwerp during the conflict against Spain, and even after the truce in 1609 this block was continued.

The war against Spain prompted further improvements in the already powerful Dutch navy. The fleet of this small nation was qualitatively and quantitatively superior to those of Spain and France, and competed on a par with England's. Dutch shipbuilding was at the forefront because of its ability to build ships that were better from every point of view and at costs that were as much as 50 per cent lower than those of its English and Spanish rivals. The distinctive Dutch merchant ships of the seventeenth century, the *fluytschips*, had a higher capacity (from 200 tons to 500 tons) than other vessels of the time, and with far lower running costs. With these technological advantages and their advanced financial and commercial expertise, the Dutch took control of international trade and became involved in all types of trade. Amsterdam itself became the centre of the widest trading network the world had yet seen.

Exchanges now included Italian silks, French wines, American coffee, cocoa, sugar and silver in addition to the usual trade with the Baltic and the North Sea. Hides and timber were arriving from North America, but the real step forwards was when the Dutch became involved in trade with the East. In 1602, once these rich markets had been penetrated and Portuguese power had been weakened, the Dutch East India Company was established. For the rest of the century the trade in spices, silks, carpets and all the other Eastern products that were highly sought after on the European markets was in Dutch hands.

Dutch success was not only due to trade but also owed much to the great development of manufacturing in towns such as Leiden and Rotterdam, and farming in the areas of Holland and Zeeland. The Low Countries were successful at diversification and were able to cover a wide market. The cities became successfully involved in the production of carded wool textiles, satins and mixed textiles, while the country areas specialized in the production of lower quality textiles, which was a sector where low labour costs were a decisive factor in success on the market. The expansion of the market due to the growth in exchanges with the colonies, combined with increased internal demand, was what enabled Dutch manufacturing to flourish. One figure is sufficient to indicate how strong the growth process was: the number of pieces of wool cloth produced in Leiden in 1585 was 30,000, while by 1664 it had soared to 140,000. Besides the important textile industry, there were great developments in other manufacturing activities such as shipbuilding and sugar works, sugar being one of the products most in demand throughout the seventeenth century.

Highly advanced farming methods based on efficient canal and irrigation systems, as well as sound manuring and crop rotation techniques, were further contributing factors to Dutch supremacy, and attracted the admiration and envy of other nations. In addition to this was Dutch skill in claiming land from the sea by means of an ambitious system of dykes and drainage pumps, which considerably extended the cultivable land area, and ultimately resulted in productivity far exceeding the European average, as well as providing the possibility of employing peasant labour in manufacturing activities.

Supremacy on the seas and a new type of colonialism

The Dutch miracle has attracted the attention of historians, who have put forward numerous interpretations. One enduring hypothesis was that the great economic dynamism of the United Provinces sprang from the capitalist spirit that lay deep in the Protestant ethic.[7] In more recent times attention has been concentrated on the decisive role played by natural resources and technological factors. For example, heat could be produced from peat at a much lower cost than from wood, and energy could be provided by the technique of harnessing the wind. Holland was the land of windmills *par excellence*. The Low Countries thus gained competitive advantages in terms of production and manufacturing costs. In the case of the shipbuilding industry one can only conclude that Holland possessed the most advanced technology of the period. Other scholars maintain that the astonishing aptitude for creating wealth lay in the fact that there were no juridical and institutional impediments such as existed in other areas. New activities could develop freely because of the absence of a central authority, and because the influence of the guilds was negligible, unlike France that was governed by mercantilism, or Italy that was suffocated by the corporations.

But any single interpretation contains strong limitations. There were many reasons for development and each was important. Religion, technology and the form of government undoubtedly contributed to the development process but what seems to have been more important is the continuity of that process, and the way it was able to sustain itself uninterrupted for 150 years. Over such a length of time competing countries would have had the chance to close the technological gap, or adapt their political institutions to the new economic challenges. But they did not, and until the start of the industrial revolution Holland's role did not decline.

Other circumstances also helped to give stability to Dutch development. These were connected with its strategically located position between the Baltic Sea, North Sea and Atlantic Ocean and with the capacity for creating institutions that were able to circulate a great part of the national wealth on a long term basis. Trade with the Baltic was almost entirely in the hands of the Dutch and, in some years, 85 per cent of the exchanges were handled by Dutch intermediaries. It provided a solid foundation for the economy of the Low Countries, but the war with Spain meant that it was no longer possible to rely on Portuguese salt, to preserve the fish from the north which was transported all over Europe. However, the Dutch wasted no time in launching into colonial ventures, and in 1598 reached Venezuela. Their commercial activities were not limited to the salt trade but, very soon, extended to a vast number of other products, particularly tobacco and pearls. This early experience at the turn of the seventeenth century, was the starting point for a new type of colonialism that the Dutch invented for themselves and which would find its greatest expression in Asia. The first Dutch expeditions to the East were made during the last decade of the sixteenth century. By 1600 the number of ships that regularly sailed the Indian Ocean, flying the flag of Orange, already equalled those of the Portuguese. Ten years later the ratio was four to one.

In order to understand how such spectacular expansion could occur, the Dutch 'system' needs to be analysed in more detail. Portuguese ships would be practically empty when they left Lisbon, and carried only the silver required for purchasing the products such as spices, silks and carpets that were going to be resold in Europe. The Dutch ships, on the other hand, were always fully loaded, whether on the outward or on the homeward voyage. As the Venetians had done in previous centuries in the Mediterranean, as well as precious metals the Dutch also used manufactures as goods for exchange. Like the Venetians, besides exporting their own manufactures, they also acquired products from neighbouring areas such as Germany, from where they imported arms and textiles, for example. Amsterdam thus became a great centre for re-exports, where many of the goods that arrived would leave almost immediately, in the search for a more lucrative exchange. Such an important role in transoceanic traffic could only be carried on if there was a framework through which to co-ordinate it. It had to be strongly rooted in Dutch society and at the same time capable of controlling trading posts on the Asian continent, at a distance of tens of thousands of kilometres. From the early seventeenth century the Dutch Company of the East Indies provided Holland with such a resource. It was thanks to this remarkable economic and commercial institution that Holland had access to more money and more ships to carry out its foreign policy and international trade than both Portugal and England together.

The VOC was set up in 1602. It was formed by merging existing companies that had been engaged in trade with Asia since 1594. It had a somewhat complex structure and was divided into six chambers representing Amsterdam, Zeeland, Rotterdam, Delft, Hoorne and Enkhuizen. Each chamber had a share in the company's capital, to a variable amount that was predetermined in the company's statute. Amsterdam alone contributed half the amount. Each chamber issued par-value shares until its quota was reached. The equivalent English company that had been founded in 1600 had already been splitting up the capital into shares and putting them on offer, but now the main innovation lay in the length of time the capital was tied up. Until then, shareholding in a commercial enterprise had been limited to a single voyage. Now, for the first time, shares in the East India Company committed investors to the overall activity of the company for a period of ten years. In short, the new model brought stability to the company by guaranteeing the continuity of its activities over time. A share market was immediately created, since shares were in the holder's name and an investor might want to free up his capital before expiry, while another might be willing to pay more than the nominal value for shares that were likely to bring in a good return. After the ten years had expired, with full support from the national government, the company refused to liquidate the shares, whose nominal value had by now already doubled. The VOC had to all intents and purposes become a share company in the modern sense, its capital no longer subject to an expiry date, and negotiable on the Amsterdam stock exchange.

The company was thus responsible only to its own shareholders, and the sort of bureaucratic restrictions that had permeated Spanish and French colonialism, to give two significant examples, did not affect Dutch trading. Dutch colonialism was based on creating, or conquering, coastal trading bases from which to control the economy of the neighbouring territories. Some historians consider that Dutch policy in the colonies was feudal.[8] The production of spices was controlled by the company through its own representatives; output was regulated in such a way as to meet actual European demand and avert any supply crises. It required manual labour from the indigenous population, for which the Dutch assured the local princes of their military support. However, the Dutch never engaged in military campaigns of conquest or penetration of the interior. The company, naturally, imposed its own conditions on the local authorities and ensured that the prices for colonial products, which were fixed over several years, were favourable to the Dutch. In this way Dutch colonialism was able to maintain a balance between maximum profits and maximum containment of management costs. It was also made possible thanks to the great flexibility in organization. The VOC representatives in the colonies – the governors – were given great autonomy, and though this gave rise to misdoings and the personal accumulation of wealth to the detriment of the company's accounts, it did not jeopardize the basic soundness of the VOC, except only very marginally, since the profit margins were so high.

The example of the VOC was very soon copied, not only in Holland, but also in England and France, albeit with different economic results. The Dutch Company of the West Indies was set up in 1621. It differed almost immediately from its eastern counterpart since it sought to establish well rooted and sizeable colonies in Brazil, Guyana, the Antilles, and at the mouth of the Hudson river. The latter colony, New Holland, grew considerably and by 1660 already had 10,000 inhabitants but four years later its capital, New Amsterdam, had to be ceded to the English, who renamed it New York. The result of this defeat was to prompt Holland to resume its former strategy, and it started to play a prominent role in Atlantic trade as well.

The development of Dutch manufacturing has long been interpreted as the triumph of individual freedom over control from the guilds and there is no doubt that numerous activities sprang up and became successful outside the sphere of guild control. These activities were connected with trade and navigation and included the production of vinegar, brandy, soap, tar, rope, sugar and tobacco. However, the traditional textile activities, which were also largely destined for international trade, experienced astonishing growth during the same period, even though they remained under the aegis of the town guilds; it was with the endorsement of the guilds themselves that these textile activities were transferred *en masse* into the country areas.

Great innovations: the stock market and companies

The previous section described the role of the companies in Dutch colonialism, and it was pointed out that they could not have developed their full potential without an evolved stock exchange. In the early decades of the seventeenth century the Amsterdam stock exchange perfected its regulations, services and products to make it one of the driving forces of the Dutch economy. Each day, from midday until two in the afternoon, 4,000 investors, speculators, merchants and middlemen crowded together in the courtyard of the stock exchange to carry out their business. It is significant that on Saturdays only 2,000 people were at the stock exchange, that being the day the Jews did not work. The Dutch financial system was very flexible and dynamic, and it was much easier for Dutch entrepreneurs to acquire the necessary capital for some new enterprise, or trade, than it was for their counterparts in any other country.

High profits could be made from trade, and the Amsterdam stock exchange attracted capital from all over Europe. There was always an abundance of currency circulating in Holland and as a result interest rates were consistently lower than elsewhere. But, for all its exuberance, the financial system was accountable to a set of stringent norms. The stock exchange had developed operating methods that could guarantee transparency in its dealings, and it gave wide sections of the population access to investment in securities. For instance, shares in the VOC could be bought through investment companies that could deal on the market only with the approval of the States General. Even the particular form of investment that so astonished contemporaries, and which today we would call 'futures', was the responsibility of stock exchange dealers and subject to a stringent system of checks and guarantees.

The methods of the stock exchange so permeated Dutch society that they were even reflected in forms of commerce that developed completely outside the institution itself. One case was the tulip trade, which experienced astonishing growth between 1636 and 1637, largely thanks to speculation. It also experienced an equally astonishing collapse that reduced hundreds of investors to poverty. Although it was carried on in taverns and beer parlours, the process was able to thrive because of the rigidly regulated system of exchange, and a goods evaluation system that derived from the gold trade. The regulations were clear and the procedures safe, and these were indispensable factors in the success of activities with high speculative risk.

The steady growth of the securities market led to the circulation of increasing numbers of shares and different forms of non-metallic currency. The Dutch authorities were fully aware that the situation was potentially unstable – and one just needs to remember what was to happen in France in the early eighteenth century when John Law put forward proposals based on the Low Countries' system. With the agreement of the national government, the great capitalists once again created an institution that was able to bring equilibrium and soundness to the whole economy, and at its centre was the Bank of Amsterdam. The primary task of this institution was to guarantee instruments of credit, and it did not hesitate to slow down the economy if that was necessary. At a time when every other country was wondering how to attract as much currency as possible Holland had quite different problems of economic policy to deal with.

This was the overall framework within which the companies operated. They were the most striking demonstration of the superiority of the Dutch institutional and economic system. Control of the VOC was entirely in the hands of sixty managers called *Bewindhebbers*, who represented the most important shareholders and formed a sort of board of directors. The appointment of the managers was based on the balance of power between the various chambers, but the unity of the company was never questioned. The general assembly of managers was made up of seventeen members delegated by the managers themselves and selected for their commercial skills. The organization worked smoothly and could make rapid decisions. All administrative questions were settled on behalf of the shareholders. Meetings were not limited to discussing purely technical questions, such as what type and quantity of goods to purchase in Asia, but also involved possible ways of influencing the economic or foreign policy of the Union and, in practice, the VOC acted as a lobby. The other companies acted in a similar way, though they had fewer resources. All this made Dutch institutions particularly responsive to economic and commercial circumstances, and they were permeated with a sense of pragmatism that was unthinkable in the context of French absolutism, or the still chaotic English parliamentarianism.

Modern capitalism made headway in a country whose framework of norms and institutions derived from a typically medieval concept of 'freedom' based on particularisms[9] and the pre-eminence of town autonomy over central authority. Two bodies of medieval origin, the Provincial States and the States General, were central to the political system of the United Provinces, and the way they functioned was particularly unwieldy. Yet precisely this unwieldiness created a certain constancy in national politics that could easily be turned to the advantage of the merchant and entrepreneurial class.

France

From continental power to transoceanic enterprises

Events in France in the seventeenth century were somewhat complex and contradictory. France did not experience economic growth comparable to that of England, let alone that of Holland, but it did play a central role in political, military and economic events at world level. The great religious struggles that had begun in the previous century continued in the seventeenth, and they also had repercussions on the country's economic and social situation. A large number of Protestants left France in search of greater tolerance, prior to the revocation of the Edict of Nantes in 1685. From the strictly economic point of view, until the middle of the century France lived in a state of stasis, or at most of very slight progress. After 1660, its growth, albeit of a quite particular sort, was steadier and will be discussed in more detail further on.

The France of the modern era, and to a certain degree even the France of today, was marked by scarce urbanization and generally by a low density of population. There were no cities of any great size, with the exception of Paris, which was a case apart, Marseilles and Lyons. Even at the end of the seventeenth century, important urban centres like Bordeaux, Strasbourg or Toulouse did not even have 40,000 inhabitants. The vast majority of the French population lived in country areas, and the percentage of peasants was much higher than the west European average.

An analysis of the economic evolution of France in the seventeenth century must therefore start from the world of agriculture. From the strictly productive point of view, historians generally agree that the seventeenth century was one of stagnation, or even slight regression, in much of France. Obviously there were great regional differences, but overall the available data seem to confirm the image of centuries-old inertia. Frequent population crises and particularly adverse weather conditions caused a sharp fall in the production of cereals, and a decrease in other produce like vines and olives, though this was less accentuated. Such a pattern has to be seen in the context of an agrarian system in which the feudal seigniory still prevailed, at least in the central and southern regions. A slightly different model of land ownership, in which censual lands were alienable, had already taken hold in the previous century in the areas north of Paris. As a result, an embryonic land market had been able to develop, though even in these areas the rights of the seigniorial landowner were restricted by custom. Thus the image of heavily concentrated land ownership needs to be partly revised, because in reality the owner had very little opportunity to make any great profits from his lands.

Over the century this structure changed. As was happening in northern Italy, and in England but in a different form, a large class of *nouveaux riches* such as merchants, doctors, bankers and jurisconsults[10] was appearing, who were all ready to invest in land. As we have already seen, land was a safer investment, especially during a recession, and was a prerequisite for the social promotion of the new economically successful classes. This process put large areas of land into the hands of essentially urban social groups, and overturned a long-standing system of equilibrium. It led to a tendency among landowners, who were members of the bourgeoisie, the nobility and the clergy, to increase revenue from the land by raising the dues payable by the peasants. The outcome of this evolution was new types of contracts, such as sharecropping and short term leases, which meant that the land had to be more intensively exploited. But increased taxation by the state also made the situation of the peasants precarious. The increase in taxes and taxation limited the accumulation of capital and thus prevented the full development of modern agriculture, which required heavy investment but which was taking place in England and Holland. Significant progress was recorded only on the seigniorial lands, and only where the lords were particularly 'enlightened'. Regardless of which regime they lived under, the majority of peasants found themselves having to cope with steadily growing indebtedness throughout the century, and in the long term were forced to give up both property and rights.

Signs of the changes occurring in the middle of the century were most evident in the manufacturing sector. Until 1630 the textile industry in Picardy, Normandy and Brittany, which specialized in wool processing, showed steady if limited growth, but after the first serious population crisis at continental level, these manufactures went into a deep recession that lasted until at least mid-century. Even centres like Amiens, Beauvais and Rheims, which specialized in producing higher quality textiles, were affected by the mid-century crisis. But from 1660 the trend was reversed, and the main regions and cities experienced a phase of expansion, largely due to public commissions and demand in the colonies. It should be emphasized that textile production was carried on both in the towns and in the country areas, and engaged peasants in the spinning and weaving processes, especially in central and northern France.

The Lyons silk industry was a case apart. Silk manufacturing had been developing continuously since 1620, and in thirty years the number of looms had doubled from 1,600 to 3,200. There was a similar increase over the next forty years, bringing the number of looms to 5,000 by the end of the century. Steady demand from the court undoubtedly had a positive effect on this particular product. The silks from Lyons were mainly aimed at meeting the demand for luxury goods that few centres could create on a level comparable with Versailles. After 1660 the French production of luxury items such as porcelain, mirrors and glass, and war manufactures connected with the iron industry and shipbuilding, was given a boost by strong backing from the state as well as by extremely protective customs duties that formed part of a precise economic and social policy. The development of important manufactures, largely with royal capital, was undoubtedly aimed at increasing the country's productive capacity, but its purpose was also to achieve greater social peace. The Gobelins' factory, founded in 1662, which produced numerous types of luxury articles, was perhaps the most famous and emblematic case, but it was not the only one. Royal manufacturing plants multiplied during the reign of Louis XIV, and French industry reached the highest pinnacles in the world production of luxury goods.

On several occasions during the Valois reign, France gave clear proof of its expansionist and hegemonic ambitions on the European continent, particularly on the Italian peninsula and in a number of areas of central Europe. French foreign policy found a natural outlet in colonial expansion, but the French kingdom was in fact the last to systematically engage in transoceanic enterprises. As regards the American continent, the first attempts at colonization and penetration date back to the later half of the sixteenth century, while the first voyages to the East started in the early years of the seventeenth century, with the French Company of the East Indies being founded in 1604. But these can be considered isolated episodes and not the results of a far-reaching trading strategy. Even the colonization of Canada by Samuel Champlain in the first years of the century suffered the consequences of an almost total lack of capital due to limited commitment on the part of the state.

It was Cardinal Richelieu, the prime minister, who first realized the great importance of colonial development. He saw colonial enterprise as an important means of weakening Spanish influence, and in order to upset the balance of power in Europe made overseas expansion a state priority. In 1626 the French created a number of settlements in Guyana and the Antilles, and in 1628 the Company of One Hundred Associates was founded to provide Champlain with the capital required for continuing the colonization of Canada. In Canada, where Montreal was founded in 1641, French penetration came up against many obstacles, not least the strong resistance of the Iroquois, backed by the English.

In other areas colonization was more successful. In Africa numerous settlements were established in Guinea, Senegal, Gambia, Sierra Leone and Mauritania between 1633 and 1635, all with the aim of acquiring slaves, gold and ivory. Again helped by generous contributions from the Crown, the Company of the East Indies founded colonies in Madagascar with the particular purpose of practising trade warfare. However, this early colonialism achieved only marginal objectives, and proved incapable of endangering the solidity of the Spanish empire, or even making the slightest impression on the positions conquered by Holland and England.

A new stimulus to colonization came with Colbert, who was chief minister to Louis XIV. After 1664 he had the two main Companies of the East Indies and the West Indies radically restructured. They were practically refounded, with new members and new administrators that were chosen by the government. They received fresh capital mainly from the state, as well as ships supplied almost exclusively by the royal navy; the results were more enduring. In North America the fur trade was expanded, causing a worsening of the conflict with the indigenous peoples. A new colony, Louisiana, connecting the Gulf of Mexico with French possessions in Canada, was founded in 1682. In the East, results were less spectacular because of tough competition from the Dutch and English. It was very difficult, if not impossible, to establish a firm foothold in these markets, and in 1682 the ships of the Company of the East Indies were finally let out to a private company.

Considering its late start, all in all, the French colonial venture produced important results. Overseas expansion stimulated a heavy demand in shipbuilding, metallurgical and war industries, as well as in trading, which until then had not experienced any considerable development. French colonialism would reach its peak only in the next two centuries, but the foundations that Richelieu and Colbert laid in Africa and the Far East during the seventeenth century were its starting point.

The homeland of mercantilism

French economic development was not as rapid as the Dutch nor as strong as the English; it also differed in that the state played an important role. The government not only promoted important initiatives such as the royal factories and the colonial companies, but it also pursued a consistent policy of customs protection for internal products. All these initiatives went under the name of 'mercantilism'. This word needs to be considered for a moment. It has long been used as a derogatory term to indicate an economic policy whose main objective was to achieve an active trade balance. In other words, exports needed to exceed imports, as that was the only way to increase the supply of money in a country where there were no mines yielding precious metal ores. Thus the basic principles of mercantilism were very simple: it was crucial to increase the productive capacity of the country, encourage the production of goods for export, make it easier to put them on the foreign market, and finally discourage the importation of foreign goods, with the exception of the raw materials required for local production.

There were certain corollaries to these general principles. Since the purpose was to be successful in foreign markets, trade was encouraged. Manufacturing was boosted in every way to ensure that national manufactures would find a successful outlet in foreign markets. This also involved a policy of increasing the population, since a numerous population provided a labour market in which salaries tended to decrease, to the benefit of manufacturing companies. Mercantilism generally showed little concern for agriculture; it was not considered suited to producing wealth in the same way as trade and industry were, since the yields it could offer were conditioned by natural forces.

We mentioned the negative verdict that historians and economists often expressed for this type of policy. Advocates of free trade, from Adam Smith onwards, denied that it could have any real efficacy, practically concluding that it could not even be regarded as a true economic policy. Today opinions on mercantilism are less negative, and there is more emphasis on its capacity for analysing the underlying economic situation. The economists of the sixteenth and seventeenth century had quite rightly seen that international trade was one of the main factors in the process of capitalist accumulation, and instinctively understood the validity of the quantity theory of money. This, combined with a strong determination to increase the power, especially the military power, of the great nation states that were being shaped, was what lay behind the attempts of economists and rulers to develop their countries' trade and production at all costs.

France was probably the nation that pursued these policies most systematically. Especially in the second half of the seventeenth century French mercantilism consisted of a number of disparate measures, and attempts were being made to give them continuity and coherence. Jean-Baptiste Colbert (1619–1683), Louis XIV's minister of finance from 1661, was the prominent figure of French mercantilism, and the economic policy pursued by France in the last decades of the seventeenth century became known as 'Colbertism'.

Colbert was up against two opposing problems. On the one hand there was the need to remove the huge deficit in public finances that had resulted from the numerous wars fought in the first half of the century. On the other it was essential to provide France with a manufacturing sector and navy capable of competing in international trade and in the colonial struggle. In dealing with the first problem, Colbert did not hesitate to use radical methods such as the establishment of a Chambre de Justice, whose aim was to put a stop to the network of financiers who speculated on the Crown's debt and covered up what was in actual fact a real state of bankruptcy. Besides inflicting enormous fines and arbitrarily lowering interest rates on loans, the Chambre even went so far as to condemn a number of speculators to death, and the former finance minister Fouquet to life imprisonment. Only an absolute power of the sort introduced by Louis XIV could implement such drastic methods, thanks to which the annual interest on debts decreased from 27 million livres to less than 8 million between 1661 and 1683. At the same time, Colbert radically reorganized the administrative bodies that were responsible for levying land taxes, of which the most important was the notorious *taille*. The aim of the reform was to prevent bullying, fraud and embezzlement on the part of the tax collectors, and it was certainly one of Colbert's greatest successes. Whereas previously over 25 per cent of the revenue from taxes had ended up in the pockets of the collectors, after the reform the proportion decreased to below 4 per cent. Moreover, preconditions for lowering taxation were created, which did in fact decrease by about 20 per cent in less than ten years. In addition to this there were periodic purges of the registers of the nobility, and the number of those exempt from paying taxes was considerably reduced. Even though the complexity of the French taxation system remained an unresolved problem, in the space of ten years the net amount of tax revenue increased from 31 million livres to 75 million livres. With these financial resources, vigorous public intervention in the economic sphere became possible.

Colbert encouraged intervention in all areas of production. These included shipbuilding, the war industry, haberdashery, hosiery, silk, luxury draperies, light draperies, glass manufacturing and lace. Incentives varied greatly and ranged from simple tax exemption to the granting of temporary or perpetual monopolies, loans on favourable terms, public contracts, and even money prizes and honorary titles for those producing manufactures that were in the national interest. The enterprises known as 'Royal Factories' were a typical case; initially only factories under royal ownership were granted the privilege, but it was subsequently extended to enterprises that distinguished themselves for the quality of their products.

All the measures were an integral part of a highly protectionist system of customs duties. In order to be able to benefit from the incentives, the factories had to be subjected to strict controls on the quality of their products. On his appointment as minister, Colbert promoted a wide-ranging survey on the state of the French economy. It was known as the *enquête*, and was completed in less than three years. The results of the survey showed how behind the country was, especially compared with Holland, and Colbert opted for quality of production rather than containment of costs. On an international market dominated by other nations, this decision seemed to be the only one possible. If any success was to be achieved, it was necessary to target the upper range of consumers who were less affected by price increases, and guarantee that what was ordered was actually delivered.

The factories were inspected by the same network of authorized inspectors and intendants as those who had conducted the *enquête*; the corporate guilds were also involved. Colbert created a bureaucratic system whose special purpose was to constantly monitor the national economy. At the same time he made use of the existing system of corporate guilds, and their privileges and powers were actually widened. The vigorous development of the Lyons silk factories, for example, was also an outcome of the many privileges granted to the city's corporate guilds. The guilds in their turn were committed to adhering to strict regulations regarding the width and length of the textiles, the colours, the numbers of threads used in the warp and even the size of the looms. The immigration of skilled workers from other countries was also encouraged in the effort to improve the quality of national products.

The *enquête* also showed that France was lagging behind in the field of trade. In this respect one of the main problems was the weakness of its fleet, which was mainly made up of ageing ships. However, as a result of the system of incentives and awards for naval shipbuilding, and the increase in duties that foreign ships docking in French ports had to pay, in less than twenty years the tonnage of the merchant navy doubled. Yet these robust developments in shipbuilding did not lead to analogous results in international trade. The exploitation of the colonies of Martinique, Guadaloupe and Santo Domingo in the Antilles, brought about an increase in the sugar trade, and trade with the East also increased to some extent, but on the main routes the Dutch and English were too far ahead for the gap to be closed in such a short time. Moreover the French nobility and upper classes showed little inclination to invest in colonial and trading enterprise, and even the huge profits accumulated by the great merchants were invested in land, the public debt or the acquisition of some lucrative public office.

'Colbertism' certainly appeared to produce brilliant results from the quantitative point of view, and there were developments in manufacturing, foreign trade and in France's role as a colonial country. But growth was more limited, and the enormous effort that had been made did not create that particular resource that distinguished Holland and England, which was a numerous and articulate group of entrepreneurs capable of taking on the responsibility of leading and carrying on the industrial development of the nation.

Costs and benefits of bureaucratization

The results of Colbertism were largely nullified between the end of the seventeenth century and the first decades of the eighteenth when Louis XIV once again launched into costly wars in Europe and America. A financial and fiscal system that had been in a state of precarious equilibrium was upset by the extra increases in military spending. The French public debt reached the astronomical figure of 2 billion livres in 1710, and created the premises for yet another colossal bankruptcy. However, Colbert's reforms did have long-lasting effects, as did to a certain extent those of his predecessors, from Richelieu to Mazarin.

The far-reaching measures adopted in manufacturing industry, and in the system of taxation and finance, required the creation of a means of control that was as efficient and ramified as possible. The intendants whose task this was played a leading role in the administrative and bureaucratic reorganization of the country. They were part of a network of information that was present in every province; at the same time they acted as agents for the central government in the peripheral areas. This was perhaps the first attempt at centralization of administrative authority, taking account of specific local conditions; it was no accident that the *enquête* was carried out by intendants who, though they were royal agents, were closely involved in regional affairs, though at times Colbert allowed them to override the local parliaments. This type of centrally controlled administration, which enjoyed very wide powers and prestige, for a long time remained one of the distinctive features of French institutional organization, and is still discernible even today in the organization of the prefectures. A two-way information channel between the centre and the periphery had been created whereby administrative decisions taken in Paris could be enforced, and at the same time local petitions could be presented to the central government. In addition to this was the role played by the Conseil d'Etat, which was the highest body of administrative justice for controversies between taxpayers and collectors. This particular body brought bureaucracy a step nearer to becoming impersonal, and paved the way for the administrative reforms that would later take place in many European states.

However, Colbert's system was fundamentally extremely *dirigiste*, to the extent that local and individual liberties in the economic field were greatly limited. Local and national representational bodies similarly found themselves being practically ineffectual. This showed the 'pathological' side of a determination to intervene that was dictated more by financial and fiscal requirements than anything else. The outcome was that entrepreneurial and organizational initiative was stifled, and likewise there were no incentives to participation in building up the state or in developing its military, commercial and economic power. The next chapter will show how different the situation was in England, and how the institutions there ultimately succeeded in creating a unity of purpose among the national government and different interest groups.

Another problem was customs protection; this excluded from international competition the few centres that could engage on equal terms in the contest with the great world powers. To the merchants in the main French ports of Rouen, Saint-Malo and Nantes this effect of Colbertian mercantilism was only too plain, but their protests went unheeded. The same thing applied to those whose income came from agriculture, who found themselves being subjected to heavy taxation, with the revenue only going to the benefit of manufacturing and commerce. Indeed, unequal development was a further negative effect of interventionism during Louis XIV's reign.

At the end of the day, the problem of taxation was not a specifically French one, but in the second half of the century in France it was taken to extremes, because of balance of payment requirements. Taxation levels and methods were out of all proportion to the productive capacity of the country, despite the attempts that Colbert made to rationalize them, and despite the creation of the system of intendants. The ambitions of Louis XIV were greater than the capacity of the economic structure to sustain them, and consequently the system of taxation was too onerous and perennially unstable.

But perhaps the limitations of Colbertian mercantilism lay more in its motivation than in its results or methods. Its final aim was not the creation of a well organized state in which citizens were encouraged to take part in political decision making: it was quite simply to finance the wars of Louis XIV. Instead of a state founded on juridical principles, Colbert created a 'financial' state, and any form of representation or autonomy was considered a hindrance to it, and had to be removed in any way that was necessary. The institutional evolution of France went in the opposite direction from that of England. The positive aspects of Colbertian centralism would take effect only in the next century. Only after the Napoleonic experience could a juridical and institutional system be consolidated that went beyond absolutism, and could endow the state with a modern organization based on the system of government that had been created by Colbert. In conclusion, Colbertian *dirigisme* brought about only limited effects from the economic point of view. But it did provide France with the bureaucratic system of prefects, and an early form of administrative justice, which formed the basis for the future evolution of the national economy on capitalist lines.

England

From revolutions to economic expansion

The seventeenth century was a century of bitter strife in English history, with two civil wars in the space of fifty years. But it also brought a new constitutional framework, with new social classes taking over the reins of national economics and politics. The background of religious conflict acted as a catalyst for all the internal struggles. What is extraordinary is that, as in the case of Holland, the economic growth that had started in the previous century was not held back by the great turmoil. Indeed, it might even be said that the upheavals of this century were symptomatic of the great metamorphoses that had been taking place in the economy and society of England ever since the previous century. The sixteenth century was in fact the period when England changed from being an exporter of raw wool to an exporter of finished wool products. This evolution was no small achievement, as it was a sign that the economy of the country had made a qualitative leap forwards, since finished products clearly had a greater value than raw materials.

The consequences of these increased exports, and especially the fact that they had now changed, were decisive for the social and economic situation of England and its subsequent development. The wool industry demanded increasing supplies of raw materials, and as a result there was an increase in the area of land given over to sheep grazing. As often happened, manufacturing was transferred to the country areas, especially now that the 'new draperies' had proved successful. Though they were less prized they were much sought after, and these particular textiles became increasingly successful on new markets like the American one. But more important, these textiles also opened up the markets of northern Europe to English producers. Between 1630 and 1640 the number of pieces exported each year to these markets rose from 3,000 to 13,500. The new draperies were also exported to the Mediterranean market, and though English penetration of this market was slower throughout the whole of the seventeenth century, it was steady. During the same period there was an impressive expansion of the English navy, which was second only to Holland's, thanks to the increase in trade, as well as to the conflict with Spain. Thus in the first half of the seventeenth century, England already had a solid manufacturing industry that had partly changed the agricultural landscape, in addition to a navy capable of sustaining a rapidly evolving trade network.

Another of the leading sectors of the English economy at the beginning of the seventeenth century was the iron industry. This activity had not had a long history in the British Isles, but since the second half of the sixteenth century it had experienced spectacular growth. The exploitation of iron ore, which was a widely available raw material, led to the production of cast iron almost doubling between 1575 and 1600, and over the next fifty years this trend continued. According to Carlo M. Cipolla, such a huge increase took place because the English were able to overcome the scarcity of the then available fuel by replacing it in the seventeenth century with coal, which was a cheap and widely available source of energy in the ground.[11] English production of coal rose from 210,000 tons in 1550 to 1.5 million tons in 1630.

But trade, and particularly international trade, was the sector that experienced the fastest growth, and carried the whole English economy of the seventeenth century with it. In this respect England was similar to Holland. As we have seen, the English navy was one of the most powerful in the world, and by the end of the century it was by far the greatest. Its growth was concentrated in the second half of the century; in less than fifty years its overall tonnage rose from 90,000 tons in 1660 to 260,000 at the end of the century. England had solid foundations from which it could launch into the colonial venture. The East India Company was set up in 1602, and it very soon became the only one capable of competing with the Dutch VOC. By 1609 the English had already achieved supremacy in India, leaving only Goa to the Portuguese, and India remained the heart of English colonial expansion in Asia.

The position of the Dutch on the Asian continent was weakened only in the following century; perhaps the English could not outdo them there, but in northern America things were very different. In 1610 tobacco cultivation was started in Virginia, which almost immediately became the main supplier of this important product for the mother country. Because of the success of the American plantations, no fewer than 80,000 English people reached the shores of the New World between 1620 and 1640. They were attracted by the enormous potential of this land, which produced not only tobacco and sugar, but also cotton, which was becoming increasingly important to the English economy. English colonialism in northern America was different from both Spanish and Dutch colonialism. The colonization of northern America was organized by the Virginia Company, which brought mainly farmers and traders overseas, and the transportation of the goods produced in the new colonies was what ultimately became the real cause of conflict with the other continental powers. However, the English monopoly of this trade was never seriously called into question, and it was one of the main strengths of the British economy.

The English came up against greater difficulties and opposition when they tried to penetrate central and south America. Nevertheless they achieved important successes, especially in the Caribbean, where they occupied the Bermudas, Barbados and Jamaica. Smugglers operating with Spanish America, as well as privateers, used these places as their starting out bases, and smuggling and piracy became two very important items in the English economy. On the Atlantic, the English navy also succeeded in gaining the lead position in the sugar and slave trades, which of all the trades were the two most lucrative. In 1631 the first colony was founded in Africa. This was in Gambia, which acted as a departure point for the slaves being sent to the sugar plantations in the Caribbean and south America. London consequently became the 'managing centre' of an extensive trade network, and like Amsterdam the English capital specialized in the re-export trade. Tropical products from the colonies were exchanged in England for large quantities of economically important European goods such as iron, hemp, silk and wine. The population of London grew at a spectacular rate, and in the space of a century it tripled, rising from 200,000 inhabitants in 1600 to 600,000 in 1700.

However, underlying English economic growth was also considerable progress in agriculture. One of the first important moves was to increase the surface area given over to cultivation. This process had begun in the second half of the sixteenth century, but went through a period of stagnation in the first decades of the seventeenth century owing to the population crisis. It steadily picked up again after 1630–1631 as the growing urban population brought about an increased and diversified demand for agricultural products. The more widespread use of fertilizers such as marl and ashes made it possible to develop the cultivation for the market of vegetables such as turnips, cabbages, cauliflowers and peas; potatoes were yet to become fully established. The gradual reduction of common land meant there could be further developments in producing for the market, and this question will be discussed in the following pages.

Changes that would be decisive for the future development of the country also took place in the credit sector. This was a sector where England was at a definite disadvantage compared with areas such as the Low Countries or Italy. The two classic operations were still land mortgaging and pawnbroking, which indicated an economic system that had evolved very little. However, steady improvement in services and techniques was recorded over the century, and was accompanied by a steady drop in interest rates, which naturally had important repercussions on the manufacturing and trade sectors. Added to this was the policy of the English authorities to penalize moneylenders, and though this did not actually discourage the practice it ultimately made contracts more advantageous to debtors, and encouraged English entrepreneurs to take greater risks. In terms of volume the London stock exchange could not yet compare with that of Amsterdam, but it was fast increasing.

In short, English economic growth in the seventeenth century did not experience the same strong rates as the Dutch, but it did create the preconditions for the huge expansion that was to take place in the next century.

The enclosures and Navigation Acts

The economic development of England in the seventeenth century perhaps poses fewer problems of interpretation than that of Holland. A number of objective circumstances, such as the lower incidence of population crises, and the lack of involvement in the wars of the first half of the century, may lead to oversimplification; but these circumstances certainly had an influence on English economic trends, and created an advantageous situation. But the real problem of interpretation is not so much linked with the sustained economic growth that undoubtedly took place, as with the fact that by the end of the seventeenth century the social, economic and institutional state of England was such that it was ready for the great enterprise of industrialization. What is more, compared with other European nations, it started out at quite a considerable disadvantage.

As already mentioned, from the technological and organizational point of view, the agricultural sector went through a radical evolution that brought profound changes to the social and economic relations of the rural world. A process of land concentration that was without equal in Europe started in the sixteenth century in England, but especially in the next century; however, in the main, this process was still not as great as it would be in the eighteenth century. Whether their wealth came from agriculture or commerce, the more prosperous classes increased their ownership of land in three ways. The first was to transform long-term inheritable lease contracts into short-term non-inheritable leases; the second was for small owners who had been hit by the fall in agricultural prices to purchase plots of land; the third was to buy up open fields that had been used as common land. The greatest upheaval from the social point of view was undoubtedly caused by the latter, though its effects were not fully felt until the eighteenth century.

The first system transformed leaseholders into tenants, and marked the end of the feudal system, as well as the gradual disappearance of the common land. Feudal revenue became land revenue and land could be used more freely by the owner. The second system was much more closely related to the economic situation. Like those on the continent, peasants in England could not contend with the fall in agricultural prices; they were forced into debt and had to sell their small farms, which were over-dependent on trends in the market. The third system severed the last feudal links of English agriculture. Its original intention was to join up properties that in the open-field system had been scattered, by changing the boundaries. This process naturally led to a reduction in the areas used as common land, and peasants could no longer graze their cattle or cultivate small vegetable plots there; consequently they had fewer opportunities for supplementing their income. At the same time, the large landowner could use these fields for grazing sheep, whose numbers were rapidly increasing thanks to the development of the wool trade, or for cultivating crops for which there was rising demand. A typical case was malt; as a consequence of the rise in beer consumption, its cultivation was rapidly increasing.

The process was accompanied – supported, even – by a simultaneous increase in agricultural productivity. While the transition from feudal to land revenue did mean increased taxation for peasants, the brunt of the increase could be borne better than in other places, thanks to the innovations in technology and management. Those in charge of managing the properties, who often employed waged labour made up of former small owners or leaseholders, were convinced of the need to diversify produce, invest in fertilizers and develop stock farming, and the market outlet became a decisive factor for the new farming methods and the new class of agricultural entrepreneurs. Thus in seventeenth century England, land came to be one possible investment, not only for the long-established large landowners but also for the rising urban middle classes, and after 1662 the enclosures were approved by a Parliament largely made up of traditional and new landowners.

The governments that succeeded one another in the course of the century all seemed to direct their policies towards increasing national wealth and power. It is remarkable that these policies coincided perfectly with the interests of broad sections of the English population, and thus met with wide approval, especially among the more active classes of society. English mercantilism developed both from above and from below, and it was very different from the French version both in theory and in the results it achieved.

The Navigation Acts were a typical example of English mercantilism. Their aim was to reserve trade in the ports of the mother country and the colonies only to English ships. Control over traffic in the ports of an island was clearly synonymous with political security, and naval development could guarantee independence and the expansion of trade without having to be subject to foreign merchants. The first detailed Navigation Act that applied to the nation as a whole was in 1651. There had been a series of partial and less systematic measures during the first half of the century that enshrined the main principles of future decrees, but the ban on unloading goods from ships not carrying the British flag was extended to all the English ports in 1651. The 1651 Act was approved during the revolutionary government of Oliver Cromwell, and denied access to all foreign ships; the real target was the Dutch, however, who wasted no time in responding. The war that took place from 1652 to 1653 did not change English attitudes, and British ports were definitively closed to foreign ships and merchants, at least from the formal point of view. Numerous cases of fraud led to a decree in 1660, issued by the restored government of Charles II, that all English ships built overseas were to be registered, and had to have a captain who was English and a crew that was at least three-quarters English. The Staple Act of 1663 closed the loop by stipulating that the colonies were permitted to buy only from England the products they needed. England and its colonies now formed a closed and impenetrable system that could guarantee a huge market for the manufactures of the mother country. The English navy and merchants were free to expand their activities without having to face any competition. In being able to maximize their profits from the trade with the colonies, British merchants were in a strong position to compete against the Dutch, French, Spanish and Portuguese.

The results were evident. In the second half of the seventeenth century, the tonnage of the English merchant navy doubled, and a fifth of the non-agricultural labour force was engaged on ships or in the ports. By enforcing trade with the colonies, the Navigation Acts also had the effect of guaranteeing the expansion of the domestic market, since prices for such significant products as silk, tea, sugar and spices were invariably lower than outside England. There were also indirect results. The expansion of trade, for example, led to great progress in finance. In practice the traditional English companies were unions between merchants, but without any company capital, while the new joint stock companies were organized on the lines of the Dutch companies. The East India Company and the Africa Company were stock companies that brought profits to investors from many different social groups that included shopkeepers, traders, nobles, agricultural entrepreneurs and even members of the royal family.

It is worth emphasizing once again the importance of the re-export trade, which could perhaps be regarded as one of the surest indicators of economic development in the pre-industrial era. At the end of the seventeenth century, England re-exported to Europe two-thirds of the tobacco from central and northern America, a third of the sugar, and two-thirds of the silk and spices from India. Practically all the cod caught by the English in Newfoundland was sent to the Mediterranean area; meanwhile the role of the English slave ships was also becoming increasingly significant.

Farming and commercial capitalism; the success of individualism

The age of the Stuarts, in whose hands England's destiny lay between 1603 and 1714, is defined by English historians themselves as a decisive period in the country's history, despite the great upheavals.[12] There were turbulent political changes that affected the monarchy, which became something very different from what it had been until the early seventeenth century. The powers that Parliament succeeded in gaining for itself meant that that institution had a totally new status, and it acquired wide-ranging powers in economic and fiscal matters. But that was not all. The kingdom's debt could be guaranteed to a greater extent than ever before, or than in any European nation, and this encouraged people to loan money to the Crown. The availability of huge financial resources enabled England to build up and pursue an expansionist foreign policy, an aspect of considerable importance. The aggressive policy and powers of the English rulers, both Crown and Parliament, had the wide consent of much of the population. The defeat of Spain, between the sixteenth and seventeenth centuries, was of economic and religious significance, but also of great national significance. By reducing royal prerogatives to the advantage of Parliament, a situation was created in which the interests of the nation were closely linked with those of the rising classes.

Who were these rising classes? Starting with the rural world, the new tenant farmers were undoubtedly among them. The far-reaching changes that were taking place in the world of agriculture had, in fact, turned many peasant farmers into tenant farmers. Peasant families often remained on the properties to which they had been granted special concessions indefinitely, or almost indefinitely; but now they had to pay the landowner a much higher rent. Thus instead of a real exodus, a profound cultural transformation took place. Whereas previously the objective each season had been to produce enough for own consumption, now there was a prime need to increase production in order to create a surplus for the town market. But because of the constantly expanding market, a vicious cycle started – tenant farmers increased their profits, but thanks to the new contracts, landowners promptly raised the rent. Thus, though the term is not quite accurate, the rising classes also included landowners. Among these were noblemen of ancient lineage, but also merchants and citizens such as lawyers and doctors who held their own professions. For both the latter and the former, one possible form of investment was in land, and large sums of money might be utilized not only for purchasing it but also for improving it. Indeed, the English nobles differed from most of their continental counterparts in that they were not averse to investing capital in productive and commercial activities. Hence the aristocracy played a very significant role in the progress of agriculture; but it was also equally significant in other fields. Noble families loaned money to shipbuilders, entrepreneurs and merchants, or even acquired shares in the companies themselves. They frequently gave their backing to commercial and manufacturing enterprises, or undertook banking activities at the local level, and those who invested in mining were often nobles. All this, in addition to the activity of the urban and rural middle classes, contributed to making the English economic system more vigorous than the pretentious continental systems.

The other great opening for investment was in trade, both domestic and international. In this case the risks were far higher, but the margins of profit were also correspondingly higher. Thus a very extensive group of capitalists was created who drew their wealth from the expansion of trade, and as in the case of agriculture, all types of potential investors were represented. When the companies were transformed into shareholding companies, small shopkeepers, country traders and potentially anybody who had managed to accumulate any money also began to invest in international trade.

The worlds of both agriculture and trade were widely represented in Parliament, which had been gaining considerable powers since the second half of the century. No representative institution in Europe could compare with the House of Commons as regards political and economic prerogatives. Within Parliament itself there were deep divisions over religion, but there was overall agreement as regards the prerogatives of the Crown in the field of the economy. Despite the numerous vicissitudes and changes it went through, the parliamentary system never once relaxed its policies on trade, naval expansion or land privatization.

The assurance that they would not have to suffer the consequences of the legislative whims of a reckless king was probably one of the decisive factors in strengthening the class of agricultural entrepreneurs and capitalists engaged in trade and manufacturing. These classes existed all over Europe, but it was only in England after the seventeenth century that they could count on a form of government that represented them in some way, and that protected them from a higher power.

One final aspect that needs emphasizing is the receptivity of English society. Where religion was concerned it was perhaps not so receptive, and many fled to America as exiles so they could profess their faith. But from the economic point of view, the English were always quick to learn anything that could be turned to their advantage, especially from the Dutch. With manufacturing protected, a powerful navy and highly advanced agriculture, any progress made in management only multiplied English efficiency. At the end of the century, in 1694, the Bank of England was established; the idea was not an original one, but this was the only country that knew how to fully exploit the potential of a well regulated national debt for development and investment.

AN OVERALL VIEW

By examining the dynamics of supply and demand, and studying the profiles of three countries whose experience perhaps indicates elements that typify the century, I have attempted to focus on a number of aspects of the seventeenth century. In conclusion, I would like to take up two questions that in my view play a central role in understanding the seventeenth century from the economic point of view. In the first place there was the function performed by mercantilism. The fact that it was adopted as government practice brings us to the essential issues of this century. If one looks beyond all the different arguments relating to the crises affecting the seventeenth century, the century was one that experienced the process of leaving the medieval legacy behind. People reasoned along different lines and on a much wider scale, markets were national and international, institutions reached beyond the urban and regional scale, and states with strong central powers were becoming established. As regards the outside world, this new conception was reflected in mercantilism, with increased power on the seas and in non-European territories and the aim of achieving a positive trade balance. In the domestic sphere greater authority was exerted over production costs, with control over prices, wages and labour, and even over consumption. By affirming the principle that wealth deriving from the power and influence of the state meant wealth for the whole national community, mercantilism ultimately set up a new system of values and principles in which different social classes became mutually dependent and complementary. Thus in order to enrich the state, the rich had to be consumers, merchants had to provide goods for the foreign market so that gold would enter the country, the nobility had to develop the land so that people could be fed and the national economy supplied with industrial raw materials. In short, while on the one hand mercantilism exaggerated the role of the state and advocated an idea of wealth in terms of the availability of gold and silver, on the other it was positive in that it reasoned in terms of the international market and pointed to the strategic role of manufacturing output.

The second question that strikes me as being particularly interesting regards the process of selection that was triggered by the crisis of the seventeenth century. The economies of the European countries were affected by plagues, wars and poor harvests to different degrees and with different consequences. By the middle of the century the geography, but especially the hierarchy, of the countries of Europe had changed profoundly. Against the background of overall decline, the Mediterranean countries and Germany emerge as the 'losers', and Holland and England as the 'winners'. If we examine it from a different point of view, this indisputable result can provide us with a new line of interpretation. Since the period of the communes until the present day, one area in particular has played a leading role in the European economic system. This area includes northern Italy, Switzerland, part of southern Germany, the Rhineland and Holland, while on the other side of the North Sea it even reaches as far as London and south-eastern England. The particular shape of the area has led economists and geographers to refer to it as the 'blue banana'; historians talk of the 'central band', the 'central belt' or even the 'urban column'.[13] Whatever the case, for eight centuries this area has formed the background of the most important financial markets, for the cities that at different times dominated the European and then the international markets, and also for the main 'multinational firms'. In other words, during the entire pre-capitalist and capitalist period Europe had an area of excellence to which the capitals of the economic system have belonged at different times (Venice, Genoa, Antwerp, Amsterdam, London). The trend over many centuries has been for the centre of this area to gradually shift from south to north: in the period of the communes its heart was in Italy, and its centre of gravity was the Mediterranean area, while during the modern period its centre shifted first to Holland and then to England.

From the economic and social point of view, the events of the seventeenth century were certainly negative, and at times even dramatic, but they accelerated, facilitated and perhaps confirmed a process that had been under way, and was consistent with the underlying economic structure of the continent.

Notes

1 M.W. Flinn, *Il sistema demografico europeo*, Bologna, 1983, provides a thorough, though not quite updated, review of demographic studies on the various European regions in the modern era.

2 M. Morineau, '*Il secolo*', in P. Leon (ed.), *Storia economica e sociale del mondo*, vol. II, Part.1, Rome and Bari, 1980, pp. 59–108.
3 P. Chaunu, *L'Histoire, science sociale. La durée, l'espace et l'homme à l'époque moderne*, Paris, 1974, pp. 44–5.
4 B.H. Slicher Van Bath, *Storia agraria dell'Europa occidentale*, 500–1850, Turin, 1972, pp. 291–3.
5 A. Guenzi, P. Massa and F. Piola Caselli (eds), *Guilds, Markets and Work Regulations in Italy, Sixteenth to Nineteenth Centuries*, Aldershot, 1998.
6 Cf. C.M. Cipolla, *Storia economica dell'Europa preindustriale*, Bologna, 1980, pp. 264–74.
7 A clear reference to M. Weber, *L'etica protestante e lo spirito del capitalismo*, Florence, 1945.
8 Cf. M. Morineau, *La sfida Europa–Asia*, in P. Leon (ed.), *Storia economica*, vol. I, pp. 605–13.
9 Principle whereby, in a federation, each state or minority has a right to further its own interests or retain its own laws and traditions. (*Translator's note.*)
10 People who were qualified to advise on legal matters. (*Translator's note.*)
11 Cf. C.M. Cipolla, *Storia economica*, pp. 281–83.
12 Cf. C. Hill, *La formazione della potenza inglese*, Turin, 1977, pp. 10–12; M. Kishlansky, *L'età degli Stuart*, Bologna, 1999, pp. 41–2.
13 Cf. K. Davids and J. Lucassen (eds), *A Miracle Mirrored. The Dutch Republic in European Perspective*, Cambridge, 1995, pp. 21–2.

4 The European economies in the eighteenth century

John A. Davis

New perspectives on economic modernization and Europe's many paths to the twentieth century

In contrast with the centuries that preceded and followed, the distinctive themes in the economic history of Europe in the eighteenth century seem at first sight more difficult to define. Whereas the economic history of seventeenth century Europe is still dominated by the debates on the nature and significance of the great economic and demographic crises of the era, the economic history of the eighteenth century has long been overshadowed by the search for the origins of the industrial revolutions that in the following century would transform first the European economies and then those of the entire planet.

As a result, the European eighteenth century is more quickly identified with political and cultural events, with the Enlightenment, the American War of Independence, the French Revolution and the crisis of the European *ancien régime* monarchies. Its economic history, by contrast, has been approached mainly with an eye on what would follow. In the last few decades, however, economic historians have heavily revised the ways in which the questions posed by the industrial revolution had been approached since the Second World War, as we shall explore in more detail below. The principal outcome of this revision has been an awareness that the different European economies made the difficult and often painful path to the twentieth century in a variety of different ways and at a variety of different speeds. Above all it has led to a significant revision of the idea that there was a single model for the modernization of the Western economies that was pioneered first by Great Britain in the late eighteenth century, and then imitated in one form or another by all the other countries that successfully industrialized in the course of the nineteenth century.

That paradigmatic model of modern economic development was made famous in the now classic study of the first industrial revolution in England by the American economic historian, W.W. Rostow. In numerous studies, but especially in his *Stages of Economic Growth* (1957), Rostow took the English industrial revolution as the empirical base for a general model of modern economic development which the author believed to be applicable to all economies in all places and at all times.

For Rostow, industrialization constituted the definitive moment of economic transformation from the pre-modern to the modern, and to underline the qualitative nature of this transformation he used the aeronautic metaphor of the 'take-off' into self-sustained economic growth. It was the new capacity for self-sustained and infinite growth that distinguished the new industrial economies from all previous forms of economic activity and production. The industrial 'take-off' was, therefore, an epochal and fundamental event in world history in which technology and machinery provided human societies with hitherto unattainable increases in productivity.

The causes and origins of this 'industrial revolution' and the reasons why it occurred first in England in the closing decades of the eighteenth century were none the less complex. An inherent part of Rostow's 'model' was the notion that industrial 'take-off' occurred as the result of a series of prior changes or 'revolutions' that established the economic, institutional and cultural pre-conditions for industrialization which at a certain moment converged to provide the impetus that energized the definitive break with the past. According to this interpretation, the 'industrial revolution' was the necessary culmination and point of arrival of all prior economic and institutional change. These prior changes included an 'agricultural revolution', which through increasing the productivity of agriculture enabled increased quantities of labour to be released from the primary sector of the pre-industrial economies, hence creating the basis of a new industrial labour force. Improved agricultural productivity came from the adoption of new methods of farming, new crop rotations, the introduction of nitrogen-fixing crops to reduce fallow and provide animal feed as well as new forms of farm management, and was essential if the growing numbers of individuals engaged in industrial activities were to be fed. No less important in that respect too was a 'demographic revolution' that would increase the supply of labour and demand; a transport revolution that would increase mobility and make possible the expansion of local and inter-regional trade; a credit revolution that through the development of new banking institutions would make flows of investment available for commercial and industrial ventures; and last but not least a commercial revolution that could generate new wealth, new entrepreneurial attitudes, new patterns of demand and consumption, and push out the frontiers of trade on an international as well as a national or local basis.

Rostow's model had strong ideological overtones and can be read now as an early Cold War hymn to the virtues of free enterprise capitalism. But it also reflected a wider consensus among economic historians, and in its broad outlines the model was accepted even by its strongest opponents. Karl Marx's classical analysis of the nineteenth century capitalist revolutions had followed a very similar model, which again emphasized the cumulative nature of the process of modern economic growth and the decisive, qualitative discontinuity represented by the emergence in the late eighteenth century of the first examples of mechanized and steam-powered industrial production. Rostow's Marxist critics in the 1960s did not challenge the concept of a sequential series of economic, institutional and social 'revolutions', even though they did follow Marx in emphasizing the exploitative character of bourgeois capitalism. In fact, where Rostow and his Marxist critics differed most was not in their analysis of the origins of the industrial revolution but in their interpretation of the nature of industrial capitalism. For Rostow, industrial capitalism was the product of free enterprise, which had been able to prise open hitherto hidden technological capacity that made the generation of wealth potentially infinite and unending: for Rostow's Marxist critics, industrial capitalism was based on a system of exploitation in which the wealth of the rich derived from the labour and expropriation of the poor, a system which would inevitably become increasingly contradictory and unsustainable as it evolved.

The research inspired by Rostow's thesis has in the intervening decades shown this paradigmatic model to be both inadequate and in many respects inaccurate and distorting of economic realities. The critique of Rostow's single model of economic modernization has been developed as strongly by liberal historians as by Marxists. Indeed, one of Rostow's earliest and most perceptive critics was the Russian-born American economic historian Alexander Gerschenkron, who insisted that the patterns of modern industrial development in each country have been very different, and that those differences owed much to the specific timing of industrialization.

It is now also clear that a central weakness of Rostow's model lies in the difficulty of measuring or dating the precise moment of industrial 'take-off' in the different European countries. In fact, the great volume of new research inspired by Rostow's study and the debates it inspired have revealed that the 'stage theory' of modern economic growth does not fit the historical reality of the eighteenth and nineteenth century European economies. The validity of the concept of an 'industrial revolution' in the eighteenth century has as a result been questioned, since it is now clear that even in the most advanced economies the elements of continuity with the past were as evident as those of innovation until well into the nineteenth century.

This has not caused economic historians to lessen the profound and unique character of the 'industrial revolutions' in the process of modern economic development first in Europe and North America and then in the rest of the globe. But it has led them to interpret the 'industrial revolutions' as broader structural processes, in which the establishment of the early industrial sectors was as much a consequence of deeper structural change as its cause, and in which mechanization and the use of steam power were in the earliest phases only one aspect of broader structural changes. Without denying the importance of the new industries that came into being in the late eighteenth and early nineteenth centuries, economic historians now prefer to approach the origins of industrialization in the context of broader processes of economic change and modernization that were taking place at a transnational level.

But Rostow's paradigmatic model has been revised in other important ways too. Economic historians are now increasingly aware that before the nineteenth century the most obvious signs of economic growth were to be found at a regional rather than a national level. Indeed, it is in many respects quite artificial and anachronistic to speak – as Rostow did – of economic growth in terms of 'national economies', since these would be the products of modern economic development and not its starting point. 'National' economies, like the 'nation state', were only just beginning to take shape in the eighteenth century, a century still dominated (at least in Europe) by the politics of the dynastic, not the 'nation', state. The elements of economic unity in the Habsburg monarchy before 1800, for example, were weak to the point of being non-existent, but even much more centralized states like

Great Britain and France consisted of many different economies, most of which were highly localized in structure and organization.

These means too that Rostow's insistence on the specific qualities present in individual European societies that promoted, or failed to promote, modern economic growth has become less convincing. Economic historians have become wary of arguments that seek to link the timing of the early industrial revolutions with the structure of different eighteenth century European societies, and a sociological interpretation of industrialization now looks unconvincing for at least three reasons. First, these explanations imply that 'national' societies already existed in Europe in the eighteenth century, which is anachronistic. Second, research since the 1970s has shown that the distinct social and cultural attributes which Rostow and others ascribed exclusively to the English were to be found in many other parts of Europe in the same period: eighteenth century England and Scotland did not enjoy a monopoly of 'modern' values, forms of social organization or the freedom from 'pre-modern' constraints on economic development. Third, many parts of France and the southern Netherlands (nineteenth century Belgium) experienced forms of economic growth at least as dynamic as Great Britain's in the eighteenth century, but with a lesser propensity towards mechanization.

These shifts reflect a more general crisis of the historical sociologies of modernization that took shape in the decades after the Second World War, to which Rostow's study made an important contribution. These have now given way to forms of analysis and interpretation that are more sensitive to economic and structural forces. Economic historians now focus on the broader processes of economic growth in Europe and the whole economic area that the European economies had come to dominate by the early eighteenth century (the Americas, and especially the rapidly expanding Atlantic economies, Africa, the Indian subcontinent, and Asia). Taking economic growth as a phenomenon that was much more generalized throughout Europe in the eighteenth century, the questions that economic historians now pose seek to explain not only why in some cases economic growth gave rise to industrialization but not in others, but also the effects of economic growth more generally on all eighteenth century European societies and economies. In that perspective, industrialization is no longer seen as the inevitable culmination of all previous forms of economic growth, but as something that was originally rooted more closely in the particular circumstances and contexts of economic growth in eighteenth century England. That means that the chronological gap between England and its European competitors is better understood as evidence of different patterns of economic growth than as a sign of the social or economic 'backwardness' of England's European economic competitors and trade partners. Indeed, many historians have argued that both the southern Netherlands and France experienced more dynamic economic growth in the eighteenth century than Britain, and that the innovations that led to the development of the first industrial sectors in the English economy were driven in large part by the need to catch up with or move ahead of these dynamic continental neighbours.

These new approaches to the study of the emergence of the contemporary European economies reflect a more general reaction against normative models generally in the social sciences and humanities. But they have resulted in shifts of perspective that have quite radically reformulated the central issues that face the economic historian of eighteenth century Europe. The most important shift has been to relate the process of industrialization that begins at the end of the eighteenth century to the broader processes and more general processes of economic growth that were experienced throughout Europe as a whole. At least in its earliest stages, mechanization and industrialization were not necessarily the only or even the best ways of achieving economic growth, and it was only later as the industrial economies grew in substance and power that industrialization became synonymous with modern economic growth, and indeed an indispensable part of it.

In the eighteenth century, however, this was not the case, and economic historians now look to locate early industrialization more concretely in the context of the diversified and diversifying impact of the forces of change and modernization on the European continent as a whole in the eighteenth century. Behind this shift lies an awareness that the experience of modern economic growth in Europe, as in the rest of the world, has been varied and complex. Different European societies have experienced the impact of broader structural changes taking place in the international economies with varying degrees of intensity, varying degrees of speed and also with different timing. In place of Rostow's single path to the twentieth century, European societies have travelled many different paths to achieve economic modernity. By emancipating the economic history of Europe's long eighteenth century from the shadow of the industrial revolutions, the central focus of the economic historian is to explain the nature of the changes that were taking place in this period which would within a relatively short period bring into crisis the whole economic, social, cultural and political fabric of what by the end of the century was dismissively termed the *ancien régime*. If that more general experience was shared by the countries of the European continent as a whole, these new approaches have also placed new emphasis on the important changes that were taking place in the seventeenth and eighteenth centuries in the economic relations between Europe and the rest of the world. The 'global economy' would be a product of the nineteenth and twentieth centuries, but a 'world economy' had existed from much earlier and its structure and organization underwent important changes in the period covered in this chapter. The changes taking place within the European economies necessarily had important consequences for the emerging 'world economy', but those changes were in themselves at least in part driven by European economic expansion in the non-European world.

European economic development in the eighteenth century: the central themes

In the context of these new perspectives, the eighteenth century not only retains but even regains its importance and fascination for the economic historian. Although the periodization of economic history does not conform neatly to that of the calendar century, the period running from the late seventeenth century to the early nineteenth witnessed changes that marked a fundamental divide between medieval and early modern Europe, on one hand, and contemporary Europe on the other. The central theme, the central process, throughout Europe in the eighteenth century was the crisis and ultimate collapse of the institutional, cultural, political and economic fabric of what became known as the world of the *ancien régime.*

A term invented after 1789 by the supporters of the revolution to consign to the dustbin of history the centuries of ignorance and superstition that had preceded the advent of 'enlightenment', the idea of the *ancien régime* was always polemical and reductionist. In reality, the revolution constituted less of a break with the past than its most enthusiastic champions were able to admit, continuities that lay at the heart of Alex de Tocqueville's later analysis of the political and economic significance of the revolution. But this sense of change and innovation was also inseparable from the culture of the eighteenth century. This does not mean that the eighteenth century really was an 'Age of Enlightenment': those writers who consciously appealed to the principles of 'enlightenment' and deliberately asserted the primacy of reason over faith and tradition knew themselves to be a beleaguered minority, even though their influence was greatly enhanced by the sympathetic audience they found among the rulers of the era. The Enlightenment was in part heir of the great 'scientific revolution' of the previous century, but it was also a sign of a new cosmopolitanism that brought Europeans into contact with one another, from St Petersburg to Edinburgh, from Oslo to Rome, from Madrid to Warsaw, from London to Naples, from Paris to Berlin: it also brought the Old European World into closer contact with both the Orient and the newly emergent New World, especially in the decades before and after the American War of Independence.

Both the Enlightenment and the rationalist spirit to which it gave expression were products of many different things, but not least the changing relations between the European continent and the rest of the world. The rapid expansion of the colonial plantation economies in South and Central America, in the Caribbean and in the European colonies in Louisiana, Maryland, Georgia, the Carolinas and Virginia as well as new commercial and territorial rivalries in the Far East, in India, Asia, the China seas and Japan all demonstrated the strength and impact of the European presence overseas, as did the rivalries that accompanied this process of expansion. With Spain's hold over its American empire failing rapidly, first the Dutch then the British and the French pressed to establish their own commercial presences and where necessary to drive out their competitors by force. This was in part a continuation of an older process of European expansion overseas that had been pioneered by Spain and Portugal in the fifteenth and sixteenth centuries, following in the earlier paths set by the great early modern commercial empires of the republics of Venice and Genoa and then challenged by the rise of the Dutch maritime empire in the seventeenth century.

The economic history of Europe in the eighteenth century was marked by a new phase of colonial expansion that brought Europeans in increasing numbers not only to the unexploited lands of the North American continent but also to the East, and especially to the Indian subcontinent. This expansion was accompanied by intense rivalries among the European colonizers, which provided an extension to the dynastic rivalries that in the seventeenth century had made Europe a theatre of almost constant warfare. In the eighteenth century these struggles continued, and in particular locked the rival monarchies of France, Spain and Great Britain in an almost unrelenting struggle for naval and commercial hegemony both in the

Atlantic and in India, but in Europe itself the incidence of warfare relented especially after the mid-century, creating new possibilities for the expansion of trade and production.

While there is now a considerable body of literature on the complex question of what if anything the colonial empires contributed to economic growth in Europe itself in this period, much less attention has been paid in the past to the impact of economic change in those European countries and regions that were not the epicentres of innovation and expansion. What are often referred to as the European 'peripheries', following the term used by Emanuel Wallerstein, were until quite recently treated as regions that failed or were unable to respond to the stimulus of change and modernization. Such a view consigned a vast part of the European continent – most of the German states except for those in the Rhineland or with access to the Baltic, the whole of eastern and central Europe from the Baltic to the Balkans – as well as Mediterranean Europe – the Italian peninsula and islands, the Iberian peninsula – to stagnation.

Geographically the centre-periphery analogy has always been difficult to apply, and in the case of Europe in the eighteenth century quickly breaks down. From the very beginning the so-called peripheries were no less directly caught up in the new processes of economic transformation than the so-called 'centres'. Indeed, the impact of increased demand for agricultural products and of new incentives for market production had far-reaching economic and social consequences that brought upheaval and conflict to many parts of rural Europe long before the industrial revolutions gave rise to those urban proletariats that would trouble the slumbers of bourgeois Europe in the nineteenth century.

Even though both the roots and the consequences of economic change and economic expansion in Europe in the eighteenth century varied enormously, it was the processes of change that gave Europe's economic history in the 'long' eighteenth century an underlying thematic unity. The rapidly growing numbers of wealthy northern Europeans who began to follow the itineraries of what was termed the 'Grand Tour' to rediscover the classical sites of antiquity were to provide a very important indicator of these new European realities. Although the Grand Tour was essentially a journey of education, like contemporary tourism it often served to narrow rather than broaden the mind and reinforce prejudices rather than dispel them. But it was a phenomenon that revealed many features that were essentially new in the economic as well as the social and cultural history of Europe. It revealed first new forms of wealth, and even if these were located primarily within the aristocracies the social background of the participants in the Grand Tour began to broaden as the century advanced. The first travellers were mainly English and French, but they were joined by Scandinavians, Germans, Russians, as well as subjects of the sprawling Habsburg monarchy.

The ability to travel was in itself an important indication of new forms of wealth. When the Duke of Kingston completed an eighteen month 'tour' accompanied by members of his family, servants, carriages and an immense amount of baggage he had spent a total of £20,000 sterling, a huge figure for the time – yet no more than a single item in an increasingly costly and ostentatious aristocratic life style. The ability and the desire to travel was also closely linked to the birth of what would today be called a 'consumer culture', whose origins we can now date precisely to the eighteenth century. It also reflected the increased political stability of the European continent that made travel possible and relatively safe, even though travellers were eager to enliven their reminiscences with accounts of uncomfortable roads, even more uncomfortable and insect-ridden inns, as well as spine-chilling encounters with brigands and highwaymen (most of which were probably fictional).

These individual travels were also part of a broader process of internal exploration and discovery of the European continent and the different European societies that was no less important than the better-known saga of the discovery of the non-European world by Europeans. But this was not the work of travellers alone but also of rulers, who were responsible for the first systematic attempts at administrative reorganization. The Enlightenment idea that public administration should be based on the principles of reason found its way into the administrative practices first of the Austrian Habsburgs with the reforms of Maria Theresa and Joseph II, then of the French monarchy following the appointment of Turgot. The principle drew fresh force from the example of the American Declaration of Independence (1776) that was explicitly grounded in the rational ideas of the European Enlightenment, and in the decades before the revolution in France administrative reform became the order of the day for European courts from Madrid to St Petersburg and from Naples to Berlin. Even though the practical outcome of these reforms was often modest, they established the critical premise that rational government was possible only when public administration possessed accurate knowledge about the conditions of society, of agriculture, trade and manufactures. To achieve this, governments began to collect and collate data and information on an unprecedented scale, and were assisted in this by the contemporary developments in mathematics that gave rise to the new science of statistics, the inseparable partner of the rise of modern administration. Similarly the new science of 'political economy' that developed from the writers of the Scottish Enlightenment and found its most classic statement in Adam Smith's *Wealth of Nations* (Edinburgh, 1776), illustrated the growing importance that governments attached to the promotion of economic growth. Together with the French 'Physiocrats', the English and Scottish political economists provided administrators with new principles on which to base their economic policies, at the heart of which was the idea of the creative force of free enterprise. But free enterprise could take root and flourish, they argued, only when the traditional constraints and restrictions that hindered and encumbered the use of land as private property (free, that is, from the constraints of feudal rights or customary collective usages) had been removed, and once the corporate privileges and monopolies traditionally exercised by the urban guilds and the different taxes and *gabelles* exacted on internal trade had been dismantled.

Such principles, however, came into sharp collision with the older realities of the European economies, whose organization and institutions (except in the cases of Great Britain and the Dutch Republic) still bore the deep imprints of feudal institutions, corporate monopolies and collective use rights. In the following sections of this chapter we will examine how the forces of change were undermining and transforming the fabric of the European *ancien régime*. That process had not reached completion by the end of the eighteenth century, but by 1800 the crisis of the Old

European Order was irreversible: the reasons for that had as much to do with economic change as with cultural and political innovation, even though all three were closely interrelated.

Agrarian Europe, 1700–1800

It is right to underline the profound and irreversible economic changes that took place across the European continent in the course of the eighteenth century, but that does not alter the fact that in most respects European societies and the European economies in 1800 were much closer to those of 1700 than to those of 1900. In 1800 the overwhelming majority of Europeans were still engaged in agriculture, the majority as landless labourers or impoverished peasants who owned or leased some parcel of land. While much of European agriculture was still dedicated to meeting the subsistence needs of peasant cultivators and their families, this did not preclude important changes. Although often technically quite simple – the adoption of improved ploughs or new forms of scythes – these could considerably improve productivity. More important, however, was the steady diffusion of new subsistence crops like the potato and maize that were more abundant and reliable than cereals.

There were also, as there always had been, regions where commercially oriented agriculture was more fully established, even when it was conducted primarily by peasant farmers. Grain for export was grown on large estates in eastern Germany and Poland, while large farms dominated France's northern provinces as well as in the Loire, Saône and southern Languedoc. Highly commercialized and intensive mixed farming (arable, livestock and dairy farming) was practised on the Dutch polders reclaimed from the sea in the previous century, while the rich soils and pastures of the southern Netherlands provinces of Brabant and Flanders also sustained highly intensive farming and animal husbandry. At the end of the century the English agronomist Arthur Young expressed his admiration for the livestock rearing and dairy farming practised on rich meadows created on the complex of irrigated land in lower Lombardy to the south of the Po, which he ranked as one of the richest and most fertile agricultural regions in the whole of Europe.

In most parts of Europe, and especially in the uplands and in the arid regions of southern and Mediterranean Europe, agricultural yields were low, however, and farmers were vulnerable to natural disasters, disease and the weather. But during the second half of the century prices began to rise generally, encouraging production to increase. This provided strong new incentives for those regions where intensive agriculture was already practised, but also had important consequences for regions that hitherto had been less closely involved in production for local or intra-regional trade. In the absence of new methods of farming, increased production in these regions was generally achieved by adopting new crops and by bringing new land under cultivation. The diffusion of the cultivation of the potato that had begun in the previous century expanded rapidly, especially in northern Europe, and was followed by the adoption in large areas of southern Europe of maize that offered a more reliable subsistence crop for peasant farmers than wheat. But these changes carried heavy costs. Ireland would reveal the dangers of over-dependence on the potato, while a diet based exclusively on maize brought with it the terrible disease of pellagra resulting from critical vitamin deficiencies.

The expansion of cultivated land in its turn led to the destruction of woodland, often causing serious problems of soil erosion and environmental damage. In many areas, the expansion of cultivation was accompanied by the enclosure of land on which the local communities had formerly exercised collective rights and by encroachments on the common land on which the livelihood of many rural communities depended.

The economic geography of eighteenth century Europe was made up of a mosaic of local, regional, and intra-regional commercial systems, in which typically agriculture supplied the subsistence needs of the rural population and also the needs of neighbouring urban centres. Agriculture and the pastoral economy also provided the principal supplies of raw materials for manufacturing, most obviously textile fibres (wool, flax, linen, hemp, silk yarns). The structure of regional and local economic systems was shaped primarily by geography, and even in the most prosperous eighteenth century states, economic geography rarely coincided with political geography. At least three distinct economic systems coexisted in France, for example: one that was southern and predominantly Mediterranean, another that was northern and oriented towards manufactures and a third that was western and Atlantic. Similarly in Spain the great commercial towns of Cadiz and Seville, that vied for primacy in the trade with the Americas, contrasted with the Mediterranean vocation of Catalonia and with the more closed circuits of the interior and the Castilian plateau which fragmented into a mass of local economies. The territories ruled by the Habsburg monarchy had even less cohesion: the southern Netherlands (modern Belgium) were completely cut off from the rest of the Austrian empire, but there was no greater contact between the central and eastern provinces of the Monarchy: Galicia and Bukovina looked eastwards; Vorarlberg supplied raw materials to the textile industries of the Swiss cantons and Swabia; Lombardy, the richest and most fertile Habsburg possession, was also mainly landlocked and had few commercial contacts north of the Alps. By contrast, the network of waterways around the confluence of the Meuse and Scheldt rivers gave rise to a genuine 'economic region' that ran across many different political frontiers. The Baltic Sea was also the hub for networks of inter-regional and trans-regional trade that connected the economies of the Scandinavian countries and the northern states to the rest of Europe by sea, river and land, reaching as far as southern Germany, the Mediterranean and (via the Black Sea) the Middle East.

But geography also left other regions cut off from all but the most local contacts. The most isolated were the mountain communities, whose inhabitants were accustomed to migrate over long distances to supplement seasonal labour elsewhere, or earn a lean existence by peddling the products of the pastoral and forest industries of the mountains. Even settlements on the plains were easily isolated, however, if they were cut off from contact with other centres by the lack of roads that were passable at all times of year. But even where roads were good, which was always an exception, terrestrial transport costs were high – particularly for bulk goods like grain. This was one reason why peasant farmers in parts of Scotland and Ireland chose to distil their grain to make whisky, which although it could be sold only on contraband markets, had a much higher value added than grain and was less costly to transport than grain.

Rivers, waterways and the sea provided the fastest, most secure and extensive networks of communications in pre-modern Europe. The Italian city of Bologna remained a major exporter of silk textiles, for example, long after other north Italian towns that had been major centres of textile manufacturing in earlier centuries had gone into decline, largely because proximity to the river Po enabled it to maintain contacts with markets and customers in France, central Europe and even farther away. But in many parts of Europe in the eighteenth century, towns that had formally been major centres of manufacturing were in decline. One reason was the monopolist privileges that they had enjoyed in earlier periods, which now made their products over-expensive and restricted their ability to adapt to new demand.

In many parts of Europe towns also exercised extensive privileges over agricultural producers. These had originated in attempts by the rulers to insure against food shortages in major urban centres. Urban guilds and corporations often enjoyed the right to purchase prime necessities from rural producers at fixed prices, while strict controls over manufactures meant that in most areas the towns also enjoyed a strict monopoly over most forms of artisan production. In the course of the eighteenth century these *ancien régime* institutions came under increasing pressure. They were the target of contemporary economic writers, who rightly argued that such privileges subordinated the interests of rural producers to urban consumers and inhibited the development of agriculture and industry.

Urban privileges also came under scrutiny from the rulers because the privileged status of the towns made them a magnet for migration from rural areas in search of work and food. If the flow of rural migrants towards the cities was a constant feature of the eighteenth century, in time of famine or harvest failure those flows became almost uncontrollable. In response to the growing problems posed by the urban poor, many eighteenth century rulers built magnificent poorhouses which remain to this day eloquent testimony to the rise of urban poverty, in the seventeenth and eighteenth centuries. But these institutions are more significant as monuments to the paternal benevolence of the rulers than as effective responses to the growing problem of urban poverty and the reformers were quick to urge the rulers to strike at the root of the problem and strip away the privileges that benefited urban corporate interests and urban consumers to the detriment of agriculture and hence of society as a whole. In place of the monopolies and internal constraints on trade that typified *ancien régime* Europe, the reformers pressed for the freeing of internal trade, especially in prime necessities. In 1754 the French monarchy accepted the logic of these arguments and issued the first decrees designed to free internal commerce, but many obstacles remained.

The campaign for the freedom of internal trade was also accompanied in the 1760s and 1770s by increasingly vocal denunciation of the constraints imposed on agriculture by custom and feudal privilege, and indeed on all those institutions that infringed the free use of land as private property. Throughout many parts of continental Europe much of the rural population was subject to the institutions of feudalism, although the meaning of feudalism varied enormously from one country to another and from one region to another. In Poland and other parts of eastern Europe feudalism had been reinvented in the late seventeenth century by landowners in an attempt to offset the impact of falling prices for grain exports by increasing the yield of feudal exactions and obligations. The belated eastern European *servitù della gleba* bound the peasants to the land and made them subject to forced labour and would persist into the nineteenth century. These changes were directly linked to the opportunities created by increased demand for grain imports in countries like England, which continued to encourage the expansion of cereal-producing *latifondia* that relied on serf labour in the Polish territories in the eighteenth century. But in many other parts of western and southern Europe feudalism survived in the form of monopolies and taxes rather than servitude, although in others it either never existed (as in Tuscany) or else had disappeared altogether (as in Lombardy). But if eighteenth century Poland offers a classical case of a belated 'feudal reaction', it was by no means unique, and it has often been argued – and was indeed also argued by contemporaries – that an important cause of the rural tensions that exploded in France after 1789 lay in the attempt by French landlords to prop up falling rent rolls by exacting feudal levies, many of which had become almost nominal, with new rigour.

For the thinkers and writers of the Enlightenment, feudalism symbolized all the defects of an irrational and reactionary European *ancien régime*. During the course of the century 'feudalism' became a term of invective and many institutions that had quite different historical and juridical origins were simply lumped together as aspects of 'feudalism'. This inevitably resulted in simplifications, and in particular lost sight of the fact that in many cases agrarian feudalism – indeed, feudalism *tout court* – had originated from institutions that had been designed to balance and reconcile different social and economic interests in rural society. In political terms feudalism had originated as a means to regulate the conflicting interests of rulers and their magnates: but in economic terms the collective rights exercised on feudal land, for example, had originally provided the rural populations with recourse against the power of the great landowners. An inherent feature of feudalism was the notion that the rights of property were not absolute and that all feudal property was subject at specific times to a variety of collective uses. In France, feudal landowners had by the eighteenth century in most cases successfully put an end to those collective use rights, although the rural communities continued to exercise them on the village common land. But these too were often the target of ambitious landowners who were keen to acquire and enclose land that had formerly belonged to the local community. In many parts of Mediterranean Europe collective use rights on feudal land and the public nature of the common land belonging to each village played an especially critical role in the rural economy. But here too increasing incentives to commercial production in the second half of the century encouraged landowners legally or illegally to expropriate and if possible enclose public land.

Collective use rights were also of critical importance for the transhumant economies that dominated much of central and southern Spain and Italy down to the nineteenth century. The regulations that made possible seasonal migrations of flocks of millions of sheep and other animals as they made their way every spring from the winter grazing on the lowlands or the coastal plains to the rich pastures in the mountains after the snows had melted, which would be repeated in the reverse direction again in the autumn. These regulations were not feudal in origin, but shared the same essential principles. Both in Spain and southern Italy, the regulation of transhumant grazing was modelled on the *Mesta* created in Spain by Alfonso the Great in the fifteenth century: as well as establishing a royal administration that levied taxes on the graziers, these regulations ensured that the migrant flocks were assured passage on their biannual migrations from the uplands to the lowlands as they passed over private and feudal property.

For the reformers of the eighteenth century, any form of collective use was offensive because it infringed the principle that ownership rights should be absolute so that the landowner was free to use his land as he thought fit. When governments began to support that principle and encouraged the process of privatization and enclosure it not only brought the interests of settled farmers and graziers into conflict but also threatened delicate ecological balances that had been preserved in earlier centuries. The biannual movements of livestock from mountain to plain created important linkages between the economies of the highland and lowland communities, but also played an important role in making cultivation possible on infertile soils. In southern Spain and Italy, for example, annual rainfall was low and soils were thin and arid. The natural fertility of the land was as a result poor, but the presence of the grazing flocks on the lowland plains during the winter months provided a unique source of natural enrichment on the barren soils, and the manure left by the sheep made the cultivation of wheat possible in the months after the flocks had made their way back up to the mountains. When the routes of seasonal migration were closed or reduced, the entire system was thrown into crisis.

One of the most critical signs of change in the rural economies of eighteenth century Europe was the steady growth of private and enclosed land at the expense of the land that had formerly been subject to some form of collective use. That process was most fully and precociously developed in England, where privatization and enclosure had been actively encouraged by Parliament in the second half of the seventeenth century. That momentum was maintained during the eighteenth century, and was driven by the growing commercial demand for agricultural products and the development of new principles of farming and farm management. The result was that in the more fertile agricultural regions of England, the small landowning peasant class that was typical of much of the rest of Europe began to be replaced by a class of wealthier 'tenant farmers' and by farm labourers who neither owned nor rented land of their own but depended on the wages they earned working on the farms of the bigger landowners or the middling tenant farmers. Even in the poorer hill country of northern England, as well as in the Scottish highlands and Welsh hill country, the rural poor lived a more isolated and independent life than their European counterparts.

Together with the rise of what was known as 'high farming', that is to say, the development of large farm enterprises entrusted to professional administrators designed to maximize production for the market, the absence of an extensive class of peasant farmers was a distinctive feature of English agriculture in the eighteenth century. However, historical research does not corroborate Karl Marx's apocalyptic depiction of this process as the forced expulsion of the English peasantry, who became converted into the new factory proletariat of the industrial revolution. The process was more gradual and nuanced, and resulted in the restructuring of rural society as a relatively stable class of tenant farmers replaced the more precarious peasant properties typical of many parts of continental Europe. But it remains true that in much of England – as in the northern Netherlands – the rural poor had no customary right to the land and new methods of farming were more easily introduced than elsewhere. In contrast to the rest of Europe (and Ireland) where the increased rural population remained in rural areas, thereby increasing pressure on resources and exacerbating the demand for land, in England intensive farming and enclosures meant that the surplus rural population moved instead to the rapidly expanding provincial towns and cities.

As in the Dutch Republic, the absence of a peasantry tied to or dependent on the land gave English landlords much greater freedom than most of their continental counterparts to use their land as they chose. It is still not clear how much impact on agricultural productivity the famous experiments in improving animal breeding, in introducing new forms of nitrogen-fixing crops (clover) or animal feed (the famous 'turnip'), the development of more intensive crop rotations and new techniques for enriching the soil may have had. The pioneers of these innovations, like 'Turnip' Townshend and Thomas Coke of Holkham, won international fame for their innovative and progressive approach to farming, and throughout Europe long-established associations of gentleman farmers like the Georgofili of Florence began to discuss the new developments. But even in England few had the means to copy these examples, while much of the increase in productivity in cereal farming in East Anglia (which together with the 'high farming' counties of the Midlands were the epicentre of the eighteenth century 'agricultural revolution') was a result of the massive land reclamation projects carried out in the previous century with public funds by Dutch engineers.

England's enclosures, improving landlords (in fact more often improving administrators) and the champions of the new science of agronomy were clear signs of the spread of new methods and principles of capitalist farming, but improvements in agricultural productivity were occurring elsewhere too. The southern Netherlands had one of the most intensive farming systems in Europe, combining livestock rearing and dairy production with extensive arable. For France, Michel Morineau has challenged the views of Braudel, Leroy Ladurie and Chaunu, who argued that the persistence of small peasant farms in much of France preserved a 'Malthusian' constraint on increased agricultural productivity down to and beyond the revolution. But if the peasant sector proved more adaptive than was previously thought, the extensive farms of Normandy, the Isle-de-France and the northern provinces kept pace with developments in the southern Netherlands.

For agriculture as well, therefore, eighteenth century Europe was once again a mosaic of contrasting regional realities. The Netherlands with their polders reclaimed from the sea, the Isle-de-France and Normandy, the irrigated central Po valley in northern Italy all provided examples of highly productive agricultural regions, while the expansion of domestic and foreign trade was encouraging the development of commercially oriented agricultural production in other areas too: the expansion of vines and viticulture in southern France and Catalonia, the production of flax and hemp in Ulster and the northern German states, increasing production of silkworms and raw silk on peasant farms in the hill country of northern Lombardy and the Veneto were all signs of these changes. Growing demand for naval supplies also encouraged the production of timber, linen, hemp and pitch and other naval materials in all the regions that had access to the ports of the southern Baltic. Behind the outward appearance of immobility, all kinds of changes were taking place in the complex mosaic of Europe's varied agrarian economies in the course of the eighteenth century. If these changes were in most cases less than revolutionary, the gaps separating the regions of more intensive agriculture and productivity from the rest were growing, while at the same time the regional responses to the growing impact of a market economy were highly differentiated. Yet the impact of those forces was being felt throughout agrarian Europe.

The enigma of the eighteenth century: the demographic revolution

But what was the source of the new demand that was encouraging the spread of commercial production throughout many different parts of rural Europe in the eighteenth century? One of the most enigmatic problems facing the economic and social historian of eighteenth century Europe is the break that occurred during the course of the century with all previous patterns of demographic development. This occurred with different timing in different parts of Europe, but it was a European and then a global phenomenon that has never been reversed. (See Table 4.1).

The first sign of this change came from the fact that during the first half of the century grain prices continued to fall despite the steady recovery of population levels from the terrible demographic crisis of the previous century. This signalled that agricultural production was able not only to keep up but to exceed demand even if this was achieved through more extensive production rather than increases in agricultural productivity. Population expansion, in other words, did not provoke the 'Malthusian crisis' typical of previous centuries. But what caused European populations to expand in the eighteenth century remains one of the great unsolved puzzles of contemporary European economic and social history. Population

Table 4.1 The European population, 1700–1800 (million)

Country	*1700*	*1750*	*1800*
Europe	132.00	156.00	204.00
France	21.50		29.10
United Kingdom	5.06		8.66
Sweden	1.37		2.35
German states	14.50		20.70

Sources: E.A.Wrigley, *People, Cities and Wealth. The Transformation of Traditional Society*, Oxford, 1987, p. 272: J-P. Bardet and J. Dupaquier, *Histoire des populations de l'Europe, vol. II: La révolution démographique, 1750–1914*, Paris, 1998, p. 196.

expansion in early modern Europe had followed what demographers call a saw-edged graph: no sooner did the population begin to rise than it would become the victim of subsistence crises, famine, disease and dearth. In the eighteenth century there were many major subsistence crises, yet recovery was rapid and overall the population began to embark on the long curve of expansion that has not only remained unbroken but has accelerated subsequently with unprecedented geometric speed.

Demographic historians continue to debate why this change occurred in the eighteenth century. There is no conclusive evidence that people were living longer or that more children were surviving: in fact, infant mortality throughout the eighteenth century and much of the nineteenth remained extremely high, and death was an ever-present reality for even the wealthiest Europeans at all ages and especially among infants, as the literature of the period eloquently bears witness.

The new patterns of population expansion that originated in the eighteenth century have to be explained in terms of clusters of different developments that affected different regions at differing times and with differing intensity. Among these contemporaries would certainly have pointed to the apparent disappearance, or weakening, of the great epidemics that had devastated previous generations of Europeans. Disease obviously did not loosen its hold on the European populations, the greater part of whom were chronically impoverished and undernourished, and hence prey to all manner of ills and ailments. But although the last outbreaks of the Black Death may have continued down to the twentieth century, eighteenth century Europe experienced a brief respite from the plagues of the medieval and early modern world, and were spared the new epidemics like cholera that would afflict their nineteenth century successors.

Why this should have happened is unclear, but it was certainly not the result of improved hygiene or medicine. The development of Jenner's famous vaccine against smallpox improved the appearance of Europeans but it did not offer them longer lives. Indeed, the impact of medical science on human life expectancy remained negligible down to the early twentieth century. Many historians have argued that, in the absence of evidence that European were living longer, a lowering of the age at which people were marrying provides a better explanation of the increase in population, since this would have raised fertility and reproduction rates even if mortality rates did not decline. But demographic historians have shown that a trend towards earlier marriage can be the result of very different circumstances, and that it was often the poorest, whose children had the lowest chances of survival, who married youngest and produced most children. Earlier marriages might easily result in unsustainable levels of population increase, as occurred in Ireland, for example, in the early nineteenth century. The Irish case also points to the importance of the introduction of new food crops like the potato (and in southern Europe maize), which at least initially provided more reliable subsistence crops that helped support the expanding rural populations, albeit in the long run at high cost. However, in the absence of improvements in their health or life expectancy the most likely explanation for the expansion of the European populations in the eighteenth century was a tendency to younger marriage and hence higher birth rates among the intermediary social classes.

The growth of trade

Internal

The steady, often unspectacular and largely unmeasurable expansion of local and intra-regional trade was one of the most general signs of the economic expansion in eighteenth century Europe. Part of it was due to the fact that increasing numbers of Europeans were living in towns, meaning that throughout Europe farms had to supply the needs of growing numbers of people who were not directly engaged in agriculture. Indeed, the stimulus to economic growth was in almost direct proportion to the vitality of urban centres. In the German states there were only two cities with a population over 100,000 – Berlin and Hamburg. In most German states, except for Lower Saxony and the lower Rhineland, economic life revolved around small and fairly static urban centres, and even the demand generated by the numerous administrative centres and capital cities (for example, Munich, Stuttgart, Würzburg, Ansbach, Bamberg, Erlanger, Dresden, Kassel, Hanover) was met by foreign rather than local products. On the other hand, fewer than 4 per cent of the population of the Habsburg monarchy lived in towns with more than 10,000 inhabitants at the end of the eighteenth century. The situation in Spain was similar, except for Cadiz, Seville, Madrid and Barcelona. Despite northern Italy's famed 'hundred cities', population expansion was stronger in rural than in urban centres in the eighteenth century, with the partial exception of Milan. In the south, on the other hand, the elephantine size of Naples (around 400,000 inhabitants in the mid-eighteenth century) was a consequence of its privileged status, not of economic vitality: nevertheless the city provided a major opportunity for commercial production for the agriculture of the rest of southern Italy (see Table 4.2).

Table 4.2 European urbanization, 1700–1800 (million)

Population	*1700*	*1750*	*1800*
1 Europe			
Total population	132.0	156.0	204.0
Urban population (towns over 5,000 inhabitants)	14.5	18.1	23.5
Towns with over 2,000 inhabitants	18.8	23.4	29.8
2 Urban population of towns with over 5,000 inhabitants			
North-west Europe	6.2	7.9	10.8
Southern Europe	6.0	7.1	8.2
Eastern Europe	2.2	3.1	4.3
Continental Europe	13.5	16.3	20.1
3 Rate of urbanization (per 100 inhabitants)			
North-west Europe	12.0	13.1	13.9
United Kingdom	11.8	17.3	20.8
Rest of north-west Europe	12.1	12.2	12.0
Southern Europe	19.4	19.7	18.3
Eastern Europe	4.6	5.2	5.3
Continental Europe (excluding Russia)	12.9	13.8	13.8

Source: J.P. Bardet and J. Dupaquier, *Histoire des populations de l'Europe*, vol. II, p. 196.

The fastest rates of urban expansion were found in those regions where economic growth was also most dynamic – the southern Netherlands, to a lesser extent the Dutch Republic, numerous French regions, the lower Rhineland but above all the United Kingdom. Once again geography and politics had important roles to play in this, particularly geography. Many European rulers attempted to promote internal trade by improving communications, and in France this led to a notable extension of the canal system. But in this case the principal beneficiary was the Paris region, and more extensive improvements in communications were ruled out by high cost.

It was only in Britain that an effective system for engaging private investment for building roads developed through the system of turnpike trusts, associations created by landowners under licence from Parliament to build highways and then recover the cost through tolls on traffic. But for most European regions before the Age of the Railway, poor communications and isolation from local markets were a vicious circle that could not easily or cheaply be broken. Most European commercial circuits, therefore, remained local, with little possibility of expansion, while growing commercial demand privileged those that were blessed by geography with access to seaports or inland waterways. An important part in this expansion was undoubtedly also played by the rapid expansion of coastal shipping and short-distance seaborne trade. This expansion is impossible to measure, but it was by sea rather than by land that increasing quantities of agricultural products and industrial raw materials began to find their way to foreign markets. From the Baltic to the Mediterranean, small coastal craft played an unheroic and unsung but critical role in channelling a vast range of commodities towards the main entrepôts of longer-distance or international trade, and were often the only means by which local producers could reach extra-regional markets. These activities also provided the foundations for the emergence of numerous small ports specializing in local coastal trade, providing a base for groups of local merchants, ship brokers and financiers who played a critical function in linking demand to production in even the remotest corners of the continent, contributing in turn to the gradual penetration of market forces into previously isolated economic circuits.

International trade

Although long-distance maritime trade has attracted much greater attention from economic historians, it constituted a much smaller proportion of European trade than that carried by humbler coastal craft. Down to 1800, the great bulk of European trade took place within European boundaries, even though the dramatic expansion of overseas, and especially transatlantic, trade was one of the most striking indicators of the vitality of European economic expansion.

Even before Karl Marx, it was often assumed that the profits that the leading European powers acquired from trade with the non-European world had made a critical contribution to the process of capital accumulation that made possible Europe's subsequent economic expansion and industrialization. That thesis has more recently been revised and reproposed by Immanuel Wallerstein, who has argued that the great discoveries of the late fifteenth century gave rise to a world economic system whose original axis was the Spanish empire and which brought the Old and the New Worlds together.

As Fernand Braudel noted, neither Spain nor any other European power had the resources or the manpower to monopolize the vast territories and resources of the New World. Commercial ventures backed by other European rulers, particularly the Dutch, the British and the French, together with the religious emigrations of the seventeenth century, also brought European settlers to North America. At the start of the eighteenth century these new European colonies were still huddled precariously along the Atlantic seaboard, penetrating inland only where – as in the case of Canada and New England – there were navigable inland waterways. Farther south, the cultivation of tobacco made possible the development of plantation economies in the Carolinas, Maryland, Georgia and Louisiana on the model of the sugar plantations in the Caribbean.

In all these regions, and farther south in the Caribbean and in South America, England, the Dutch Republic, France and Spain jockeyed continuously for position throughout the century. But despite the geographical immensity of the American territories, their populations were scant and commercial needs few. For European merchants they offered many valuable raw materials, but their commercial opportunities were limited, with the result that until the later decades of the century – indeed, until after the American colonists gained their independence from the British crown – the Atlantic trade was much less rewarding for European merchants than its European counterparts. At the end of the seventeenth century, non-European trade accounted for less than 10 per cent of London's rapidly increasing commercial turnover, and much the same was true of Amsterdam. Even by the 1720s, when the Atlantic trade was booming, English exports to the American colonies accounted for less than 50 per cent of the value of exports to the Mediterranean region.

As R.T. Rapp has argued, the competitiveness of English and Dutch merchants in international trade in the seventeenth and eighteenth centuries was in any case a consequence of their ability to outrun their commercial rivals on European markets. In the case of the Dutch, this owed much to the technical capacity of the Dutch *fluitshipt* that carried larger cargoes faster than the ships of any of Holland's commercial rivals. As a result, navigation was a key factor in the emergence of the Dutch commercial empire, and by the 1670s the Dutch commercial fleet equalled in tonnage the combined merchant fleets of England, Portugal, France, Spain and Germany. But the superiority of Dutch shipping was also reinforced by the capacity of Dutch manufacturers to produce commodities that were more competitive than those of their rivals. In 1700 Amsterdam was still the most important commercial city and financial centre in the world, providing the organizational and institutional links between long-distance trade with the Orient, with the Americas and with the Baltic.

The Dutch and, following hard on their heels, the British and French, commercial empires of the seventeenth and eighteenth centuries were then very different from the earlier Spanish and Portuguese commercial empires, which had relied primarily on extracting raw materials and precious metals from dependent colonies. The structure of Dutch, British and French international trade was more complex and more dynamic, and involved the development of new triangular commercial systems, combined with dominance of the lucrative maritime carrying trade.

By the end of the seventeenth century the British and the French were beginning to oust the Dutch from trade with north America. This was partly because both countries had adopted monopolist legislation (England's Navigation Acts of 1651, revised in 1721: Colbert's protectionist measures in France) to exclude foreigners from their own colonial trade and requiring that all goods landed in colonial ports were carried on metropolitan vessels and loaded from metropolitan ports. It was also partly because the Dutch domestic economy began to lose impetus. Its principal manufacturing centres, especially the woollen industries of Leyden, failed to adapt to the demand for lighter cotton cloths in the eighteenth century, mainly because domestic demand in Holland remained buoyant. The heavy investment costs of land reclamation and defence in the seventeenth century also caused inflationary problems and lessened the Dutch government's capacity to defend the republic's commercial interests overseas.

The gradual comparative marginalization of Dutch international trade in the eighteenth century (although the scale of the republic's international trade still remained substantial down to the end of the century) illustrates how the vitality of the internal domestic economy was a critical condition for the expansion of international trade. Spain offers a similar example. After 1720, Spain's trade with its American and Caribbean colonies was controlled by Cadiz, which took over the administrative monopoly previously held by Seville. During the course of the century Spanish trade with its American colonies continued to expand in volume, yet this gave rise to no new ancillary economic activities in Cadiz or Andalusia. Cadiz grew rich and became the first city of Spain, yet when war with Britain at the end of the century deprived Spain of its colonies the prosperity of Cadiz quickly disappeared, leaving very little behind. The colonial trade had not acted as a stimulus to the development or specialization of agriculture in Andalusia, or for the development of new processing industries or even to significant new tertiary activities. When the Andalusian economy was no longer able to provide commodities to meet American demand, Cadiz merchants turned to Catalonia and to other European markets to supply what they needed.

The French west coast ports, Bordeaux, Nantes, Rochefort, which expanded dramatically in the eighteenth century in response to the expansion of France's Atlantic trade, were also important centres for the development of new manufacturing and processing industries. Commercial demand did in this case stimulate specialization in agriculture (and especially viticulture), but as happened in Andalusia, once France lost its colonial empire as a consequence of Napoleon's wars, the whole of the western seaboard was caught in a spiral of prolonged economic recession and decline from which recovery was slow and partial.

Commercial rivalry between Britain and France in the eighteenth century extended to the Indian subcontinent, but its primary focus was the Atlantic and it was here that the major commercial and political battles were fought out. There were important structural differences in the long-distance trade of the two countries, however. Just as the Dutch had relied on innovative nautical design to outstrip their competitors in the previous century, English merchants relied heavily on new commodities and products and succeeded in developing complex but effective networks that linked the expanding new American trade with older European markets. One unspectacular but none the less important example was the growing importance of exports of dried and salted fish from Newfoundland to the Iberian and Mediterranean countries, where the expansion of British trade had been blocked by lack of alternative export commodities to English manufactures (mainly textiles) that were subject to heavy import duties. Growing exports of salt cod enabled the British merchants to increase their purchases of Mediterranean agricultural products without having to pay for them in cash.

The structure of British overseas trade was determined above all by the need to balance Britain's permanent trade deficit with the Baltic countries. This was caused by Britain's dependence on the Baltic countries for supplies of timber and materials required in shipbuilding (such as tar, caulk, sailcloth, hemp) as well as for grain. As the system took shape, the Baltic deficit was offset by positive balances accruing from trade with the rest of Europe and the Mediterranean countries in particular, and with the Atlantic colonies and plantations. The original destination of the inhumane trade in African slaves was to provide labour on the Portuguese plantations in Brazil and in the Spanish, British, Dutch and French colonies in the Caribbean. But the narrow opportunities presented by trade with the colonies and plantations encouraged the development of the trade in African slaves to the new colonies in the North America, albeit in smaller numbers. The trade in slaves purchased from the coastal regions of West Africa and transhipped to the plantations of the Caribbean and North America was known as the 'Middle Passage' because it completed the missing 'leg' in a complex triangular commercial system. When the ships bound from Africa had discharged their human cargoes they took on consignments of colonial goods (sugar, tobacco, dyes, coffee) which were carried back to English or European ports, where fresh cargoes of manufactured goods and prime necessities were loaded for sale on colonial markets. The return journey might take a ship first to Boston or Baltimore, then on south to Barbados to unload any remaining cargo (mainly cheap cotton clothing for the plantation slaves and European luxury products for the plantation owners and administrators). The ships then sailed in ballast to Africa to return with a fresh consignment of slaves, and so recommence the whole commercial mechanism.

The system became more dynamic in part because the imports of colonial goods (sugar and molasses, and tobacco) provided the basis of new processing and re-export industries (sugar milling and distilling, preparation of tobacco for smoking, chewing or snuff) in the ports of Bristol, Liverpool, Glasgow, Bordeaux and Nantes. These new commercial systems showed a strong capacity for expansion, but they were also subject to frequent ups and downs as a result of natural disaster (shipwrecks), temporary situations of over-supply on metropolitan markets resulting from the landing of too many colonial cargoes at a given time or from a decline in the interest of consumers.

The most important, but also most problematic, new dynamic came from the gradual expansion of the European settler economies. As the European colonial markets grew in importance and economic vitality they increased the complexity and value of the trade relations between the Old and the New World. But as the

British discovered, it also proved difficult to force the settlers to continue to accept restrictive regulations designed to prevent them developing their own manufactures and subjecting them to taxation whose proceeds went entirely to the metropolitan exchequer. But although these resentments contributed to the rebellion of the north American colonists against British rule, in the final decades of the century after the wars of independence trade between Britain and its former American colonies grew even faster than before. It was also in these years that the American plantations became important suppliers of what was to be the principal raw material for Britain's new mechanized textile industries: cotton.

Even in Britain's case, however, the importance of the Atlantic trade in the eighteenth century must not be exaggerated. It played an even smaller part in France's foreign trade, which was nevertheless larger than that of Britain and expanded equally rapidly in the course of the eighteenth century. This was partly a factor of geographical size and population: France's population in 1700 was around 19.3 million, compared with Britain's 6.8 million. According to François Crouzet, the output of commodities in France in 1700 was two and half times greater than that of Britain, and by the end of the century France had achieved an even greater lead.

The long-standing Marxist argument that foreign trade provided the wealth, and hence the capital accumulation, needed for European industrialization has not withstood the test of historical research. According to the data on European foreign trade at the close of the eighteenth century elaborated by Paul Bairoch, 79 per cent of all European extra-regional trade took place across European borders and did not go outside Europe: 10 per cent of the total went across the Atlantic; 8 per cent to Latin and South America and the Caribbean; 5 per cent to Asia and less than 1 per cent to Africa. Using those figures, Patrick O'Brien has calculated that the countries that Wallerstein describes as the 'periphery' absorbed around 20–25 per cent of Europe's extra-European exports: in total those exports represented only 4 per cent of the combined gross national product of the European states, meaning that less than 1 per cent was destined for the 'periphery'.[1]

Nor is there any evidence, if we take just the English case, that profits from international trade were reinvested in manufacturing enterprises. Indeed, quite the reverse. Those fortunes that were not burned out in failed ventures were more likely to be invested in land or in building sumptuous new town houses or country villas than in manufacturing ventures, whose capital requirements in the early phases of industrialization were in any case not great. Wealth from trade went to bolster more lavish styles of urban consumption and living, helped develop new tastes and forms of recreation, new fashions for clothing for men and women and so forth. It also contributed to the development and expansion of a new commercial culture and new commercial institutions, commercial and maritime insurance, the expansion of credit and the rise of commodity and investment markets – although as John Law's South Sea Company of the 1720s indicated, these were notoriously speculative and unsafe. Colonial trade also encouraged the expansion of a variety of traditional consumer good industries, and perhaps indirectly some important new industries – especially brewing. More directly it also stimulated expansion of shipbuilding: between 1700 and 1763 the British merchant fleet grew from 323,000 to 496,000 tons and virtually doubled again by the end of the century.

Although this expansion occurred without bringing changes to traditional methods and techniques of construction, it did result in decisive improvements in techniques of maritime navigation such as the development of the seaborne chronometer that finally made possible the accurate calculation of degrees of longitude as well as the massive operation of accurate mapping and charting. Most important of all, however, was the dramatic decrease in the cost of long-distance transport.

Foreign trade in general and colonial trade in particular therefore played an important part in expanding the capacity of the market to supply consumer goods, but cannot in itself explain why the demand for consumer goods was growing at the same time. The Atlantic trade gave rise to the rapid growth of Britain's west coast ports: Bristol grew from 48,000 inhabitants in 1700 to 100,000 by 1800: Liverpool from 6,000 to 35,000 in the same period, but many other provincial towns that were not connected with the Atlantic trade were growing equally rapidly in the same period.

It seems that the contribution of the expansion of extra-European trade to the economic growth of Europe in the eighteenth century is still best defined by Carlo M. Cipolla's famous dictum that foreign trade was a 'necessary but not sufficient condition for economic growth'. The same point was made in slightly different terms by two leading American historians of European industrialization, K.P. Thomas and Donald McCloskey, who have argued that 'the most important effect of foreign trade on internal industries came from industrialization to trade, and not vice versa'. However, if there were no direct links between the expansion of foreign trade and European industrialization, the rapid growth of new consumer markets was an important reflection of the spread of new forms of wealth among ever larger sections of the European elites. With the growth of the new consumer economy came new cultural ideas and attitudes, and the new forms of physical mobility evident in the growing numbers of wealthy persons who travelled the itineraries of the Grand Tour to admire the wonders of nature and the remains of antiquity. Contact with the non-European world gave rise to a new fascination with oriental art and design, but also encouraged a desire for greater knowledge of the older European worlds, and as people moved so did ideas and comparisons. None of these things are easily measured in economic terms, but there can be no doubt that they played an important and indeed critical role in undermining the more closed worlds of the European *ancien régime.*

Industries and manufactures

The nature and scale of the changes that were beginning to erode the institutions and fabric of the *ancien régime* were no less evident when we take an overview of industrial and manufacturing activities, the ways in which these changed during the course of the century, where, why and with what effects. It is best to start with a general panorama that leaves until last the two countries whose industrial and manufacturing development has been most fully studied – the United Kingdom and France. The reason for this is partly methodological, because by starting with a more general picture it becomes clear how much of the literature devoted to the origins of the first industrial revolution has failed to pay sufficient attention to the broader changes taking place in Europe as a whole.

The southern Netherlands (Belgium)

It is now generally acknowledged by economic historians that the European region that experienced the most dynamic and sustained economic growth in the course of the eighteenth century coincides roughly with modern Belgium – in other words, the southern Netherlands provinces that after the revolt of the Dutch provinces in 1580 were part of the Habsburg monarchy and remained under Austrian administration until they were invaded and annexed by France in 1797.

The southern Netherlands formed an economic region that was rich in natural resources, with one of the most advanced agricultural economies in Europe. It was a region blessed by networks of waterways that were extended in the eighteenth century by canals and roads that gave it one of the best systems of communications in Europe. In the words of Voltaire: 'among the modern nations, it is only France and the little country of Belgium which have roads worthy of Antiquity'.[2] Indeed, as late as 1850, the Belgian network of canals and roads was three times greater than that of England.

From the earliest times many of the most important centres of metalworking and textile production had been located in these provinces. Hainault had long been one of the principal producers of worked metals in Europe, thanks to rich deposits of mineral ores and coal. The first Newcomen steam pumps were being used near Charleroi as early as 1737, although the use of steam power in mining remained quite limited thereafter because the Belgian mines did not present particular problems of drainage (unlike their English counterparts, which tended to be much deeper). Hence the uptake of steam power in mining came later, and was used after 1800 primarily to power winding gear to bring the coal to the surface.

The output of coal and worked metals in the Borinage expanded rapidly during the course of the eighteenth century without major recourse to mechanization. The tendency for early co-operative mining ventures to give way to new commercial associations formed by groups of entrepreneurs was an indication of this expansion, which did not need to abandon traditional techniques. But structural changes were also taking place. The small forges and primarily family-based metalworking industries that had formerly clustered round the valleys of the rivers Sambre and Meuse rivers began to move, or were replaced by others that moved closer to the cities of Liège and Charleroi, where there was better access to local and extra-regional markets and new opportunities for specialization and adaptation.

The cities of Brussels and Antwerp also began to take on new roles. While Brussels was primarily an administrative centre it began to assume new importance as a financial and commercial centre as well. Antwerp had until the time of the Dutch revolt been the principal port of the Netherlands. Its commercial decline thereafter seemed irreversible when in 1648 the Dutch unilaterally closed the Scheldt to Belgian vessels. But even though the Scheldt remained closed until the time of the French invasion and annexation of the Netherlands at the end of the eighteenth century, Antwerp's importance as a financial and commercial centre and as a rival to Amsterdam continued to increase.

As well as the ironworks and coal mines of the Borinage, the southern Netherlands provinces included many important centres of the European textile industry. Here too important changes were taking place. Verviers remained a major centre for the production of woollen cloth, and it was here that the English entrepreneur William Cockerill introduced the first steam-power machines in 1799. In the following years Cockerill worked with other Belgian entrepreneurs to set up their own machine-building enterprises, so that the spinning mules and jennies that had been in use in England for barely two decades spread rapidly among Belgian textile manufacturers in the first years of the new century. In 1807 Cockerill was a partner in a similar venture at Liège, where in 1813 he began building the first Belgian steam engines.

The other major textile centre in Flanders was the city of Ghent, which was famed for its fine wool and linen fabrics. During the course of the eighteenth century the Ghent manufactures underwent a change that was typical of the direction in which the new economies were moving. Ghent's traditional high quality fabrics were quickly replaced by new, lighter and cheap cotton fabrics which (via Cadiz) found ready markets in South America. However, this process of conversion and the expansion of output was not accompanied until the beginning of the following century by the assimilation of the new technologies that accelerated output and reduced the cost of spinning.

This in itself is a good example of the principle that in the eighteenth century economic growth and industrialization were neither synonymous nor necessary partners. As would be demonstrated in the early nineteenth century, Belgium enjoyed all the material resources and infrastructural conditions to sustain industrialization but in functional terms the pressure to replace manpower by machines in the eighteenth century was not felt very strongly. The reason was the abundant supply of labour, which was adequate to meet the needs of both industry and agriculture (although the two were frequently combined as a result of the spread of domestic industries) and of manufactures. Labour costs in Belgium in the second half of the eighteenth century were 60–70 per cent lower than in England: because labour was relatively cheap the incentive to mechanize was correspondingly weak too and the cost-benefit analysis of replacing men with machines was less persuasive. Similarly the ease with which coal could be removed from the ground lessened the need to invest in expensive steam pumps when natural drainage could serve the same purpose.

By contrast, the Dutch provinces experienced much less change. They did not enjoy the same natural industrial resources, and much of the land reclaimed from the sea by dikes and polders was devoted to intensive farming. In contrast to the southern Netherlands, where the population was abundant, the reclaimed lands of the Dutch countryside were scarcely populated, and the majority of Dutch industries remained urban. Relying on the domestic market, the woollen manufacturers of Leyden felt little pressure to change their methods of production, even though competition from their southern neighbours, from the French and the British drove them out of the foreign markets they had conquered in the previous century. Holland's other great industry, shipbuilding, was based in Amsterdam, and as in England and France continued to thrive without bringing, or requiring, significant technological changes.

Proto-industrialization

There was one important innovation in the expansion of manufacturing production in Flanders in the eighteenth century that was being replicated in many other European regions in the same period: the spread of industries outside the towns and in primarily agricultural regions. The American economic historian and demographer Franklin Mendels coined the rather awkward term 'proto-industrialization' to describe this process, which has long been familiar to economic historians either as domestic outputting or as the *Verlagssystem*.

These terms all refer to the system of pre-industrial production in which merchant-manufacturers supplied raw materials to domestic workers who engaged in a variety of manufacturing operations (but especially textile spinning and in some cases also weaving) in their own households. Sometime this was done on an urban basis, but at other times it employed rural workers who combined domestic manufacturing with agricultural labour or working their own small plot of land.

Mendels drew attention to the fact that during the eighteenth century many different forms of domestic outputting were expanding in many different parts of Europe, but primarily in rural areas and above all in rural areas where farming conditions were poor. His own examples were drawn from the expansion of rural manufacturing in the poorer regions of Flanders, but similar trends were evident in the upland districts of Yorkshire in England, in the upland valleys of many Swiss cantons, in Germany, France, Italy and elsewhere.

This phenomenon attracted a great deal of attention from economic historians in the 1970s, not least because it seemed to indicate an alternative path to economic modernization, in which modern manufacturing production could be integrated with agriculture and remain under the control of primarily peasant or proto-industrial families. 'Proto-industrialization', in short, had strong 'green' overtones and appealed especially to those who believed that 'small is beautiful'.

These concerns have tended to divert attention away from the important insights present in Franklin Mendels's original formulation of the question of 'proto-industrialization'. In the first place, this formulation drew attention to the scale and importance of the ruralization of manufacturing in the course of the eighteenth century, and the relative novelty of a process that marked a decisive move away from the monopolies over manufacturing that had been exercised by towns in most parts of Europe in previous centuries. Peasant families had of course always engaged in a variety of forms of handicraft production both for their own needs and to meet local demand, but the innovation of 'proto-industrialization' lay in the fact that it was organized by urban merchants with a view to production exclusively for the market. By using rural labour, which was cheaper than urban labour, urban merchants could reduced production costs and therefore increase the competitiveness of their products on local and external markets.

These systems of rural manufacturing could develop only where there was already some surplus of rural labour. From the perspective of the peasant households, manufacturing provided a supplementary source of income, which could be combined with agricultural work by reorganizing the labour supply available within each household or peasant family. Much of this additional labour was carried out by women and children, and it was frequently the women who effectively took control and organized the inputs and tasks of the different members of the family.

The phenomenon of 'proto-industrialization' also had a bearing on the broader question of demographic expansion. In rural communities where proto-industrial activities were predominant there were strong incentives for the birthrate to increase. The need for additional labour within the family unit, together with the increased earnings derived from manufacturing, encouraged earlier marriage and the establishment of independent households by young married couples at an earlier age. If that contributed to demographic expansion, it also in the course of a few generations began to put great pressure on the 'proto-industrial family economy', which now had more mouths to feed. As proto-industrial production expanded and became more widespread, the increase in textile production also caused prices to fall and reduced the level of profitability for both the peasant producers and the merchant capitalists. The latter began to find this form of production increasingly difficult to control, since production was carried on within the peasant households without supervision, and unduly lengthy, since there were long delays before the merchant finally received and sold the finished products and so recovered the initial capital invested in raw materials and production. In technical terms, by contrast, the centralized factory system that replaced domestic production offered economies of scale, more rapid production cycles, greater control over quality and quantity, faster returns on capital outlays and not least greater flexibility on the part of the entrepreneur in responding to changing market conditions. The cost was born, however, by the new factory labour force, which no longer had any direct contact with the land and so had nothing on which to fall back when market conditions caused the employer to cut back production and lay workers off.

None the less, the spread of new manufactures outside the old urban centres marked another profound challenge to the economic fabric of the European *ancien régime*, and illustrated the strength of the tendencies that were encouraging new forms of regional specialization. This was often evident in towns that had not previously been centres of manufacturing where guild or other regulations were weak. Krefeld, for example, which had been a possession of the house of Orange before passing in 1702 to the kingdom of Prussia, became a major silk weaving centre in the eighteenth century. By 1790 40 per cent of the households in Krefeld were engaged in silk weaving, of which over 75 per cent of the output was sold outside the city.

At the same time, the decline of the older-established textile towns throughout Europe accelerated. From England to northern Italy new and cheaper fabrics were displacing the older draperies and the heavy luxury cloths on which the early modern textile industries had been based. Their decline was a consequence not only of price competition, but also of changing tastes and of the disappearance of the traditional elites. Changing tastes and styles in clothing, the development of a new market in clothing 'fashion', were all further symptoms of a new consumer economy in the making. This meant that even among the elites, the eighteenth century offered producers much greater opportunities than in the past, while the social composition of the consumers of these products was also changing and expanding. But the really powerful innovation was the development of New

Economy textile markets that finally began to make inroads into the vast worlds of rural self-sufficiency that still dominated much of Europe. These new markets were based on the growing urban populations in Europe itself, but they were also augmented by the needs of the colonial plantations, where food and clothing were the principal items of expense in the maintenance of large armies of slave labour. From that basis, European merchants also found their way to supply the vast markets of South America, India and Asia, where they had to be competitive in cost with local industries and local producers to succeed. It was for that reason that the Indian subcontinent changed within barely a century from being one of the biggest textile producers in the world to become a net importer of Western textiles and yarn while its own industries went into rapid decline.

Other European centres of pre-industrial manufacturing

In addition to the southern Netherlands, eighteenth century Europe was a patchwork of new and old manufacturing regions, many of which showed signs of rapid expansion and dynamism during the course of the eighteenth century. The Rhineland was dotted with centres of manufacturing, metalworking and mining of varying degrees of intensity, especially the lower Rhine, the southern Ruhr and Lower Saxony (where less than 20 per cent of the population were still engaged in agriculture at the end of the eighteenth century). There was an important silk industry in Berlin, extensive linen production in Silesia and woollen production in Bamberg and in Württemberg, but in all these cases production was almost entirely craft and family-based. There were important textile industries in Swabia and in the Swiss cantons.

In the Habsburg lands, other than the southern Netherlands, there were numerous mining, metalworking and textile industries in the Alpine (Austria and Vorarlberg) and the Carst (Slovenia) provinces, and many textile centres in Austrian Lombardy. But the highest levels of manufacturing and industrial activity were found in Bohemia and Moravia, and in Silesia, which in 1764 passed to Prussia and deprived the Habsburg monarchy of a major manufacturing area.

In 1789 over 400,000 workers (mainly domestic workers) were engaged in wool, cotton and linen spinning in Bohemia, with another 125,000 working in centralized factories: together they constituted around 17.5 per cent of the total population of 3 million. In Moravia and the Czech-speaking part of Silesia there were a further 100,000 textile spinners and weavers. Bohemia also had fifty-nine ironworks, 179 forges, as well as a new but important and expanding glass industry. The new technologies that mechanized spinning were also brought to Bohemia very quickly in the late eighteenth century by Belgian and English engineers, although their diffusion was quite slow because of the continuing prevalence of domestic outputting. Indeed, both Bohemia and Moravia enjoyed extensive natural resources and a good supply of labour that would have facilitated early industrialization. They were also the only part of the Habsburg monarchy (other than the southern Netherlands) that enjoyed access to external markets via the river Elbe. The northern and eastern provinces of the monarchy were almost completely cut off from the south, and the Alpine chain made Trieste inaccessible to internal trade.

But via the Elbe, producers in Bohemia and Moravia could reach the markets of northern Europe and looked to Hamburg as their principal external entrepôt. However, the expansion of trade was severely limited by the proetctionist policies adopted by both the Habsburg and the German rulers. Despite the fact that one English traveller in the early nineteenth century commented, 'Bohemia can feel flattered that it can be for the Continent a little England,' the expansion of its manufactures was severely limited by narrow domestic markets and limited access to external markets.

Another area of significant manufacturing development in the eighteenth century was Catalonia. In contrast to the western provinces that continued to monopolize Spain's trade with the American colonies, Catalonia developed a thriving new manufacturing sector in the course of the eighteenth century that was based on the printing and dyeing of imported calico cloth. By 1780 there were eighty factories producing printed calicoes in Barcelona that employed over 800 workers, in contrast to London, which in the same period had only twenty-three workshops engaged in calico printing which employed around 600 workers. The Catalan calicoes were re-exported to the Americas via Cadiz and to other parts of Europe and the Mediterranean, and provide a further illustration both of the expansion and of the increased regional specialization of manufacturing output in pre-industrial Europe.

This brief and far from comprehensive survey of manufacturing activities (for the moment deliberately omitting the cases of Great Britain and France, to which we shall turn shortly) serves to demonstrate not only the European scale of the changes that were taking place, but also the fact that even in the absence of the diffusion of new technologies important structural changes were taking place in the European economies in the course of the eighteenth century. The expansion of new and old manufactures reflects the growing importance of both internal and external markets, and in many cases the absence of buoyant or accessible markets was one of the most critical obstacles to expansion. The shift from the production of the heavier traditional cloths to new light and more economical fabrics also illustrates a capacity both for adaptation and for creating new markets. New forms of organization of production were also beginning to emerge, although in probably the majority of cases increased output was achieved using well tried methods and long-established techniques.

France and the United Kingdom

The debates on why the critical innovations that established the basis of a new industrial economy occurred first in England are best considered in the context of this broader European panorama of growth and expansion. From what has already been said, it is evident that innovations like the Newcomen steam pump were being imitated in other parts of Europe very soon after they were invented. Despite the efforts of governments to prevent technologies travelling across borders, they travelled with little difficulty. What was exceptional about England was the take-up, practical application and rapid diffusion of new inventions and new machines, a process which in turn stimulated the search for ways to substitute machinery for labour in other processes of production.

To explain why this happened we should start from a comparison of economic conditions in England and in the two other European countries where economic expansion was most rapid in the eighteenth century: France and Belgium. Economic historians are now agreed that in *per capita* terms the expansion of both the commercial and the manufacturing sectors in Britain and France was roughly comparable during the course of the century, and that France may even have moved a little further ahead of its rival by the close of the century. In 1800 France's population was still greater than that of England by at least one-third (approximately 30 million), although it had expanded more slowly over the previous century. France had extensive and highly specialized textile industries in a large number of different regions. As in Flanders and in England, textile production in France made the same shift away from established woollen cloths to the production of lighter cotton and mixed fabrics. The new cotton and linen industries were concentrated in Normandy, Picardy and Alsace, but many towns that had previously specialized in woollen cloths like Troyes followed the new trend and converted to cotton. The main centres of cotton production by the end of the century were Rouen, Lille and Mulhouse, and it was here that the new English innovations (and especially the self-acting mule-jenny for cotton spinning) were taken up most rapidly at the turn of the century. The expansion of cotton spinning in Alsace resulted from the emigration of workers from Neuchâtel. At the same time Lyons was emerging as one of the principal centres in Europe for the production of silk fabrics, effectively displacing the Venetian towns of northern Italy that had previously dominated the production of quality silk fabrics.

These were all signs of the capacity of French industries to respond to changing market forces. France in addition, like the southern Netherlands, possessed a rich patrimony of natural economic resources. In the Pas de Calais, in the territories running eastwards from France's borders towards the Netherlands through the forests of the Ardennes to Alsace and Lorraine there were rich deposits of minerals and coal, while virtually everywhere there were abundant supplies of timber for construction and for industrial purposes, as well as abundant rivers and waterways. Labour was also plentiful and above all cheap.

Taken together these factors explain why the propensity towards mechanization was much less strongly felt in French industries and manufactures (as was the case in Belgium as well) than in England. As M. Levy Leboyer has commented, 'La mécanization n'était donc indispensable pour accrître le produit industrielle'.[3] Abundant supplies of raw materials, no shortages of timber for fuel and cheap labour enabled French industries to expand without difficulty, unlike their English counterparts, which in the same period were faced with numerous bottlenecks. Of these, the one felt earliest in England was the acute shortage and hence high price of timber and charcoal. The shortage of trees was partly historical, and reflected the intensity of English farming methods, but had been exacerbated in the seventeenth and eighteenth centuries by urban expansion and construction and by the equally rapid expansion of the merchant fleet and navy. In the case of house building, bricks came to replace timber, but for shipbuilding the British became increasingly dependent on supplies obtained from the Baltic countries.

Hence the critical importance of Abraham Darby's success in developing a process for smelting iron that substituted coke for charcoal. This breakthrough came early – in 1709 – and was followed later by Henry Cort's new process for 'puddling', which made it possible to use coal in the finishing stages of iron production as well. As a result, by 1800 England was producing 200,000 tons of pig iron a year – a really massive quantity by contemporary standards: by 1870 it had risen to 6 million tons, over half the total world production of pig iron.

These technological innovations were revolutionary in their impact, even if this was gradual rather than immediate. The capacity for producing pigiron of ever improving quality in ever greater and cheaper quantities made available for the first time a manufactured material that would lend its name to the first Age of Industrialization and whose uses were almost infinite. But no less important was the emancipation of the extensive metalworking industries sited around the main mineral deposits in the English Midlands from dependence on timber and charcoal. This encouraged both the expansion of metalwork manufactures and the development of new mining industries as the demand for coal began to rise. It also made possible the development of new industries like glass making (in Stourbridge, Dudley and Birmingham) and ceramic making in the Potteries of Staffordshire. This also encouraged the working of mineral seams in other regions like County Durham, where plentiful deposits of coal in turn gave rise to the development of new industries. Between 1680 and 1780 coal production in England increased by 300 per cent. As new mineral and coal deposits began to be worked, the geography of production expanded and stimulated the expansion of the already extensive network of communications, and after the 1750s especially canals.[4]

Developments in the textile sector initially followed a different pattern. The first cotton fabrics had been imported from India, and met with immediate success on both internal and foreign markets. While the cheapest end of the market was for workers on slave plantations in the Caribbean and America, and for poor overseas consumers, the introduction of light cotton and linen fabrics brought about an important revolution in western European tastes. Thanks to the development of new techniques for printing and dyeing, the new fabrics made possible the development of rich and colourful new designs that were sought after as much by the rich as by the poor. Whereas fashion and taste had formerly been determined by the courts and courtiers, with a preference for heavy opulent fabrics (which European producers now found had few markets, except among the nobility of eastern Europe and Russia and for ceremonial wear – specially for prelates), the new fabrics revolutionized the possibilities of clothing design. The new fabrics also, as the American economic historian David Landes has pointed out, marked a major advance in standards of personal hygiene among Europeans, since they were more easily and more frequently washed than woollen garments.

The development of the cotton industry in Lancashire in the first half of the eighteenth century was linked, like similar developments in Flanders and northern France, to a strategy of important substitution designed to reduce dependence on imports from India. But the strength of demand for the new textiles brought English cotton textile producers up against a series of important constraints: the slowness of the production of yarn using traditional domestic labour, the high cost of labour, the constraints on adapting to rapidly changing market demand imposed by the system of domestic outputting. These constraints were largely overcome by the mechanization of spinning through the use of innovations like the spinning jenny and the cotton mule, which together with the concentration of spinning and printing and dyeing operations in centralized 'factories' made possible the decisive breakthrough in the mechanization of textile production, although the mechanization of weaving would of course follow only much later – in the English case not until the 1830s.

The rapid spread of the new spinning technologies had a variety of knock-on effects that transmitted stimuli to other branches of industry and trade. The demand for steam power was initially quite small, and the great Age of Steam would come only with the Railway Age in the early 1830s. But the expansion of the output of cotton yarns created demand for new machine-building workshops, for improved means of transport. It also brought into being the rise of new 'industrial' towns like Manchester and Oldham that quickly became notorious synonyms for the new Industrial Age.

The mechanization of cotton spinning would in a relatively short space of time prove to be revolutionary in its impact, and enable producers to overcome both the shortage of the supply of yarn and the high cost of pre-mechanized labour. But the cost-effectiveness of those innovations was possible only because of the buoyancy of both internal and external demand. Here we come up against what was probably the decisive difference between eighteenth century England and its European neighbours. Despite the breadth of economic expansion in both France and the southern Netherlands, levels of demand in both cases were more limited. In the case of Belgium this was partly a consequence of Austrian commercial policies and the Dutch blockade of the Scheldt. In the case of France there were many factors to consider: the relatively lower pace of population expansion, the persistence of a large and largely self-providing peasant population, the relatively small size of most provincial towns, and the persisting obstacles to more intense intra-regional trade caused by poor communications, internal tariffs and – not least – France's greater geographical size.

By contrast, eighteenth century England offered easier communications, which enabled producers of manufactured goods in the central counties to reach both the eastern and western seaports without difficulty. Urban expansion was not only more dynamic and rapid, but also geographically more widely distributed than in France. The result was an urban consumer demand that had a range and vitality that could not be found at that time anywhere else in Europe. This was evident in the development of a whole range of new consumer goods industries in addition to textiles. Among these, the new ceramic industries pioneered by men like Josiah Wedgwood were of great significance. Like other manufacturers, Wedgwood looked for new techniques of ceramic making that would enable him to imitate classic styles like the porcelain of Meissen or the cheaper Dutch 'Delft ware' that was still very fashionable in England at lower cost. The technological innovations made in the production process enabled Wedgwood to produce high quality products with innovative designs at low cost, thereby creating new consumer markets. Wedgwood's particular success also owed much to his ability to give his products a distinctive style that also reflected contemporary tastes, a good example being his adoption of the Roman designs discovered in the recently excavated villas of Pompeii for tableware. But these innovations were being taken up by other ceramic makers concentrated in the area that became known as the Potteries, which, as well as dominating domestic markets, quickly acquired expanding export markets as well.

Import substitution and the creation of new markets lay at the heart of many other critical English innovations in this period. In what the Italian economic historian Carlo Poni has described as one of the first major examples of industrial espionage, an Englishman named John Lombe founded a new silk industry in Derby in the early 1720s. Lombe had travelled first to Italy, where he had studied the Bologna silk industry at length, before returning to Derby to put what he had seen in Italy into practice. But in place of the complex system of workshops, skilled artisans and rigid guild regulations of Bologna, Lombe's Derby factory specialized in the production of silk organzine and employed 300 women who worked continuously in two twelve-hour shifts, undercutting the cost of Bolognese organzines by 30 per cent.[5]

The rapid expansion of the English brewing industry in the eighteenth century was another indication of the buoyancy of England's urban markets, even when catering for the needs of the poorest social classes. The industrial production of beer (formerly home or locally brewed as in the rest of Europe) dated from the late seventeenth century, and was in part a response to the growing popular taste for imported products like tea and coffee, but also for gin (which enabled landowners to find an alternative market at a time – the first half of the eighteenth century – when grain prices were falling). The brewing industry was the creation of men like Samuel Whitbread, Benjamin Truman, Samuel Barclay and Henry Worthington, and was probably the first industry to cater for a genuinely mass market. The development of the industry depended on the development of complex methods of storage and transport in order to supply markets that were distant from the point of production. One of the brewing industry's earliest and principal centres was Burton on Trent in the Midlands, from where beers were dispatched by canal and road not only to the towns and cities of the Midlands but also to London, Liverpool and farther north.

The vitality of both domestic and external markets therefore gave the process of economic growth in England particular vigour and set English industrial enterprises on a different path from their French or Belgian counterparts. In both cases the domestic market played the most important role (in 1800 only 18 per cent of French textiles were exported, in contrast to 41 per cent in the English case), but increased demand on internal markets seems to have been the most important factor. The result was distinctive patterns of economic growth, which in the French case led to the expansion of specialized industries that were capable of dominating important market sectors, especially where the emphasis was on quality. The underlying tendencies in the two economies moved, therefore, in quite opposite directions: English industries catered primarily for large volume and low cost markets and supplied goods that not only in France but in much of the rest of Europe as well were still produced by peasant families for their own use; French manufacturers by contrast looked to retain the quality markets where lower volumes of output were compensated by higher value added. And they could continue to do this for some time without the aid of mechanization so long as skilled labour could be found at wages that did not reduce profits.

Even in England the diffusion of mechanized production and the use of steam power was in fact quite gradual, and much slower than has often been assumed. But probably of greater importance were the new ways in which production was organized. Matthew Boulton's famous Soho works in Birmingham had by the 1770s become an object of admiration because of the complex division of labour and production on which it was based. These new forms of production embodied the more general economic principles advanced by the new economic theorists like Adam Smith, and were tangible examples of the values that would inspire the Age of Industrial Capitalism: the central and guiding role of the entrepreneur, together with his absolute power as factory master: the physical transfer of production from the artisan workshop to a centralized 'factory'; the transformation of the independent skilled worker into a simple unit in an interlocking process of production. Older realities survived well into the following century, however, and down to the mid-nineteenth century there were more industrial workers in small artisan workshops in England than in the new mass factories: but Boulton's Soho works remained the epitome of the principles and values that underpinned the new Age of Industrial Capitalism and was quickly imitated by entrepreneurs operating in other national economies.

The role of the state

One of the central themes in the earlier historiography on the origins of the industrial revolutions linked England's precocious industrial development with the presence of a free enterprise culture. This idea has long been at the heart of the different sociological theories of modernization that have been advanced since Max Weber's classic analysis of the links between modern capitalism and the 'Protestant ethic'. While more recent studies have tended instead to emphasize the importance of the specific structural and market conditions that encouraged the use of machinery in England earlier than elsewhere, it is often argued that one of the major constraints on comparable development elsewhere in Europe derived from the intervention of the state.

The role of the state in economic development in the eighteenth century remains extremely difficult to measure, not least because 'the state' is far from easy to define. As a broad generalization, all European states – including Great Britain – continued with varying degrees of commitment to follow the mercantilist commercial and economic policies first elaborated in the second half of the seventeenth century. Mercantilism was based on the premise that the volume of trade was finite, and that each state should adopt protective measures to ensure that its share of trade did not decline, that imports were kept to a minimum and that domestic industries were shielded from competition from foreign imports.

As far as foreign trade was concerned, those principles were never seriously challenged in the eighteenth century, even when pressure grew for the liberalization of domestic trade. The English Navigation Acts of the seventeenth century excluded the merchants of all other countries from trade with British colonies in North America and required that all goods landed in colonial ports must be transhipped from metropolitan British ports. The trade regulations introduced in France by Colbert had a similar function, while Spain's colonial trade was similarly subject to close monopolistic control and was channelled exclusively through the port of Cadiz after 1720.

Changes in commercial policies during the eighteenth century were influenced less by new economic theories than by the material needs facing European rulers. If one of the principal themes in the political history of Europe in the eighteenth century was the attempt by the European dynastic rulers to create absolutist and bureaucratic autocracies, the principal motive for this lay in the rapidly escalating costs of government and the need to increase revenues. Throughout Europe in the eighteenth century, the costs of government and public administration began to escalate without precedent. A major factor in this escalation was the rapidly rising cost of maintaining and equipping the armies and navies on which dynastic autonomy ultimately depended. This required heavier and heavier commitments of public revenues in even the smallest dynastic states, creating the need to maximize existing revenues and find new ones. These pressures encouraged European dynastic rulers to attempt to transform themselves into absolutist rulers and to develop new forms of centralized and bureaucratic administration. In both France and the Habsburg monarchy this would precipitate the political and institutional crisis of the *ancien régime* state. In both cases it was marked by a series of ultimately unsuccessful attempts to create forms of bureaucratic autocracy within the framework of *ancien régime* monarchies, in which power was effectively shared with the privileged orders: the nobility, the Church and the privileged corporations. A critical factor in these conflicts was, of course, the fiscal privileges enjoyed by the privileged orders, which severely limited the tax base of virtually all the continental monarchies and principalities.

The experiments in what used to be known as 'enlightened absolutism' were driven by the rulers' desire to enhance the limited powers of the *ancien régime* monarchies, which in turn required the reorganization of public administration to promote national wealth as a means of enhancing public revenues. State policy, in other words, was driven not by an overall view of the economy, but more immediately by the escalating fiscal needs of the dynastic rulers. These objectives might, but equally might not, coincide with a broader programme aimed at encouraging economic development. Indeed, in many cases this was quite explicitly not sought. In many of the German principalities before 1800, for example, the landed classes were extremely hostile to any expansion of traditional manufacturing or commercial operations on the grounds that these might reduce (and hence make more expensive) the supply of agricultural labour. In the case of the Habsburg monarchy, that broader concern was combined with the concern not to assert the primacy of the hereditary Habsburg lands at the expense of other parts of the monarchy. As a result, not only Lombardy and Slovenia but also Bohemia, Moravia and Hungary were subject to commercial restrictions and fiscal burdens designed primarily to support the centralized administration of the empire and its capital,

Vienna. In the case of Prussia, the monarchy's fixation with the expansion of its army meant that between 1740 and 1780 between 70 per cent and 80 per cent of total state revenues were devoted to military expenditures, resulting in high levels of taxation that restricted the expansion of domestic consumption and non-agricultural production.

This did not prevent either Maria Theresa or Joseph II of Austria from experimenting with administrative and bureaucratic reforms, while Austrian administration in the southern Netherlands and in Lombardy was enlightened and active in promoting not only agricultural improvements and new industries but also popular education and improved civic administration. But those positive effects have to be offset against the protectionist and fiscal aims of Habsburg policy that severely limited external trade opportunities. In France too, despite the alliance between the monarchy and those sections of enlightened opinion represented by the ministers who followed Turgot, mercantilist and free trade principles continued to exist side by side. The measures to relax controls on the internal trade in grain dating from 1754 were an acknowledgement of the proposals put forward by the French school of political economists known as the Physiocrats who advocated greater internal freedom of trade as a means to encourage the expansion of agricultural production. But these liberalizing measures ran up against both fundamental political obstacles and economic and fiscal problems. However convincing in theory the principles of domestic free trade were, the practical problem lay in finding some way of replacing the public and private revenues that would be lost when internal tolls and *gabelles* were lifted, and in any cases it was only in certain places that the ruler – as opposed to the feudal landowners – had the jurisdiction necessary to impose such changes.

In the case of foreign trade, the principles of liberalization were even more difficult, not least because it was evident that even the most powerful commercial nations like the United Kingdom continued to deploy a battery of restrictions and monopolies. European rulers also looked warily at a power that in 1703 had imposed on Portugal a commercial treaty (the Treaty of Methuen) that the Portuguese minister, the Marchese of Pombal, later claimed had enabled the English to take complete control of Portugal's trade with Brazil. The alternative, on which Pombal renegotiated the Anglo-Portuguese treaty in 1754, was based on the reciprocity of concessions on specified goods, and this provided the basis for subsequent commercial negotiations with Spain and France. These concluded with the Eden Treaty of 1786 between Britain and France, which marked an extremely short-lived breach in French protectionist policies that were immediately reimposed after the revolution despite the Constituent Assembly's simultaneous proclamation of the freedom of enterprise and internal trade together with the abolition of the guilds and former royal manufactures on 2 March 1791. The combination of economic liberalism for internal trade with protectionism in foreign trade would continue throughout the Directory and the Consulate, and would remain the essential economic policy of the Napoleonic empire after 1805.

Much of the debate on industrial protectionism has focused on the numerous 'royal manufactories' promoted by European rulers during the eighteenth century. The most famous of these was the Meissen porcelain factory that was built and operated under terms of strict secrecy by Elector Augustus of Saxony. Many other European rulers imitated this model, including King Carlo III of Naples, who married the daughter of the King of Saxony and established his own porcelain factory on the Meissen model in the royal palace at Capodimonte. In the German states, nearly all the first technological innovations were the product of intervention by the rulers: the first spinning jenny at Ratingen, the first steam engine in the mines of Mansfeld in 1795, the first coal-fired blast furnace at Gleiwitz in Upper Silesia in 1794 which was imitated at Königshütte in 1799. These were simply exercises in regal splendour whose purpose was to reflect the glory and creativity of the ruler rather than to make any more significant economic contribution and their influence on the economic process remained limited.

The French historians P. Deyon and P. Guignet have argued convincingly, however, that this was not always the case. In France after the mid-century, the royal patents and privileges awarded to French entrepreneurs formed part of a coherent project aimed at import substitution through the imitation and adoption of new British technologies. Government intervention also proved crucial for the successful development of the Catalan cotton printing industry in the eighteenth century.

The role of the state in economic development has to be set in a much broader context, however. The ability of eighteenth century states to protect and promote economic interests in terms of creating an environment of stability and order in which enterprise and trade could thrive varied enormously. The weakness of the Spanish and Portuguese monarchies was clearly a factor in the growing vulnerability of their foreign trade. In particular, the financial problems facing the Spanish monarchy made the formation of any form of coherent economic or commercial policy increasingly difficult. But this was also true, albeit with differing degrees of severity, of the Bourbon monarchy in France, the Habsburg monarchy and the Dutch Republic. On the other hand there were also many regions of Europe (including the southern Netherlands) that had no voice whatsoever in their economic or political destiny.

Both France and Britain were, by contrast, prepared to act vigorously to protect and extend their commercial interests. Great Britain, for example, made no fewer than nine military and naval interventions in the Baltic between 1715 and 1727 to defend its commercial interests. The most costly war of the eighteenth century, the Seven Years War, was fought between Britain and France for what the British prime minister William Pitt defined as explicitly commercial motives: to prevent France from attempting to unite Louisiana and Quebec and hence forming a colonial system to rival that of the British in North America. In parallel with the wars with France, Britain also repeatedly resorted to force to impose its commercial interests on Spain.

While commercial interests were never the only factor in these conflicts, the struggle for control over Atlantic trade and the American colonies was at the heart of what a recent American economic historian has called the 'Two Hundred Years War' between France and Britain that started in the seventeenth century and concluded only with the defeat of Napoleon's bid to create a Continental economic system on the battlefield of Waterloo in 1815. Britain emerged as the victor in that contest in large part because the British state had succeeded in converting itself into what one Italian contemporary (Luigi Blanch) described as 'una macchina per fare la guerra'. But the key to this success derived mainly from the capacity of the English state to raise taxes and loans without falling into the financial crises that overwhelmed not only the French Bourbons but all the other major European monarchies.

This was possible mainly because of the very different fiscal structures that had emerged from the conflict between the English monarchy and Parliament in the early seventeenth century. But the financial stability of the English state was also enhanced by the foundation in 1694 of the Bank of England, which enabled the British government to raise secured loans and created a foundation of financial stability that had no parallel elsewhere in Europe. The Bank of England had no European counterparts until much later in the nineteenth century, nor could it have because it was answerable not to the king but to Parliament. This institutional independence from the monarchy gave investors in the English public debt a sense of security, while the underlying stability of public finances played a part in the relatively precocious development of provincial deposit and savings banks in England. In contrast to continental Europe, where taxes were farmed out to groups of private investors, in eighteenth century England it was the provincial banks that raised taxes for the Crown.

All these factors enabled British governments to confront military and naval expenditures that proved crippling for their competitors. The clearest example of this was that the British government succeeded in settling the huge debts incurred by the American War of Independence through consolidated loans in the space of two decades, whereas the much smaller debts incurred by France in the same war provoked the final crisis of the finances of the French monarchy that was the direct cause of the events that led to the revolution of 1789.

The greater financial capacity of the British state not only enabled it to wage war more effectively, but meant that British trade could rely on what was by the end of the century the largest and most powerful navy in the world. At the same time, the relative soundness of public finances in Britain assisted the development of wider financial and commodity markets, although as John Law's 'South Sea Bubble' of the 1720s demonstrated, these were never without risk. Nevertheless, new banking operations both in London and the provinces, together with a range of ancillary services from maritime insurance to commercial brokerage enabled London and the leading British ports to replace Amsterdam as the principal centres of international commercial and financial operations. While the state played no direct or indirect role in the development of the new industrial sectors that were established in England in the 1770s, its relative financial stability – together with the relative orderliness of English society, the absence of warfare, major political or civil turmoil – offered an advantageous context for economic growth.

The Napoleonic era

The French Revolution and the wars that followed, culminating in Napoleon's bid to create a continental European empire to rival Britain's maritime empire, brought

Europe's long eighteenth century to a close in economic as well as political terms. The revolutionary wars that began in 1792 initially followed the well established strategic logic of earlier eighteenth century political conflicts. British intervention was initially motivated by strategic rather than ideological or commercial considerations: the need to ensure that the Belgian coast did not fall into enemy hands following the French invasion of the Low Countries in 1796, and the need to maintain the European 'balance of power' following Bonaparte's invasion of Italy and defeat of Austria in 1797 (Peace of Campoformio).

Following Bonaparte's *coup* of 1799 the old commercial and economic rivalries between France and Britain came increasingly to the fore. This was already evident before the declaration of the new French Empire in 1805, which was explicitly inspired by the idea of creating a continental economic system under French suzerainty. But both that project and the empire were in turn reactions to the destruction of the Spanish and French Atlantic fleets at the battle of Trafalgar, which after two centuries of contention finally assured Britain's maritime hegemony. The British victory deprived both Spain and France of their Atlantic colonies, and encouraged Napoleon to create a European colonial system instead.

The logic of colonial subordination had been present in the organization of the French satellite republics after Napoleon's second major victory over the Austrians at Marengo (1800) which led to the occupation of northern Italy and the creation of the Italian Republic. As French armies gained control of ever wider European territories, from the Netherlands to Italy, from the Rhineland to the Elbe, and then Spain too, the continental economic project aimed at excluding Britain permanently from trade with the continental European states. This was in many ways the fundamental purpose of the empire, which involved the occupation of states of no strategic importance like the Kingdom of Naples, the Papal States and the Grand Duchy of Tuscany, and even Spain, primarily to ensure that their ports were not accessible to British ships.

The exclusion of British commerce went hand in hand with the subordination of the satellite economies to the needs of the French economy. The commercial treaties that the emperor imposed on the French satellite states were designed to guarantee supplies of raw materials and in return provide markets for French manufactures. The French economic historian Louis Bergeron has described the Continental Blockade 'as a particular way of waging war but at the same time a quite new way of conceiving France's economic development, which was henceforth to be founded on France's economic domination of the European continent, which would be fiercely defended by force'.[6]

In reality, the continental project proved impossible to realize. This was partly because it encouraged a massive growth in contraband trade in English goods, which reached European destinations via Italy, Spain, the Baltic, the Low Countries and even through French ports. But it was also due to the resistance that these measures provoked in the satellite states, and to the very contradictory consequence of Napoleon's economic policies within France itself. Napoleon's attempts to make the terms of the blockade more severe through the measures imposed by the Berlin Decrees (21 November 1806) through to the Trianon Decrees (July 1810) were in effect an acknowledgement of the impossibility of enforcing the system.

Although the Continental System proved ultimately unworkable – and that failure undermined the Napoleonic imperial enterprise in many other respects too – the Napoleonic episode had important consequences for the economic development of Europe. The most positive feature of the Napoleonic legacy came with the reforming agenda that the imperial armies and administrators spread through Europe. In those countries that came under direct French rule, feudalism was finally abolished and the state reorganized around the principles that had emerged from the revolution in France. The limited monarchies of the *ancien régime* gave way to new administrative autocracies modelled on the Napoleonic regime in France, while former Crown and ecclesiastical lands were sold off to finance the conversion and consolidation of the debts of the former monarchies. The state regained full sovereignty and all private jurisdictions were abolished. Taxes were reorganized to maintain new administrative bureaucracies that looked to implement new administrative mentalities – and in particular to promote the principles that private property and individual enterprise were the keys to economic development. The new bureaucratic states now assumed responsibility for education, for promoting knowledge about farming and manufactures, for maintaining and building adequate infrastructures – roads, canals, land reclamation projects.

As in France, the new roles assumed by the state were in sharp contrast to the theory and practice of the *ancien régime*. Even in those states that did not come under direct French rule, the impetus to reform was felt. In the German confederation the reforms introduced by Von Stein and Von Hardenburg were designed to free the land market in the eastern provinces and to start the work of emancipation of the peasants in the regions of the Gutsherrenschaft, even though in practice this proved to be a slow process. In the Habsburg monarchy too the experience of defeat and the final demise of the Holy Roman Empire founded by Charlemagne was a strong incentive to administrative reform, but in the Habsburg case the issue of feudalism and the emancipation of the peasantry was deferred until the revolutions of 1848.

The adverse side of the French administrative and juridical reforms was of course that the limited monarchies of the *ancien régime* were replaced by new forms of bureaucratic absolutism. But there were also economic costs, and especially in the poorer parts of Europe the fiscal burdens required to support the new bureaucracies were often out of all proportion to economic resources.

In economic and commercial terms, the impact of Napoleonic rule was very mixed. The consequences of Napoleon's economic polices were by no means always negative even in the satellite states. In northern Italy the period of French domination coincided with the massive expansion of the production of silkworms and raw or spun silk to meet the growing demand of the silk textile industry of Lyons. This in fact created the basis of what would remain the most valuable export commodity of the Italian peninsula – and of the unified Italian state after 1860 – down to the First World War. But if the Napoleonic era marked the beginning of the exploitation of raw silk as Italy's principal export commodity, that in itself also embodied the transformation of a region that had traditionally been one of the principal producers of silk cloth and fabric into a supplier of raw materials, a transformation that resulted in the loss of finishing industries and the relegation of northern Italy to the role of supplier of raw materials, no matter how lucrative that trade might prove to be.

Throughout French-dominated Europe the Continental Blockade encouraged new experiments in import substitution. By depriving European manufacturers of supplies of cotton cloth, this encouraged the rapid expansion of mechanized cotton spinning in the southern Netherlands and in the French textile industries. But the lack of imported cotton fabric also brought ruin to other cotton manufacturers, notably in the Rhineland and Switzerland. Many entrepreneurs from these regions moved to other parts of the empire like the Kingdom of Naples where French satellite rulers were eager to establish local textile industries and were encouraging the cultivation of cotton. Along the Rhineland merchants and manufacturers were suddenly cut off from their markets in the east and had to seek to establish new ones in the west and in France. But the terms of commercial treaties carefully protected the interests of French manufacturers.

Gains and losses varied very much from one area to another. In the southern Netherlands annexation by France gave a major stimulus to mechanization in the textile industry and to coal production: between 1800 and 1815 75 per cent of France's total coal consumption was met by the Belgian Borinage. The Ghent textile industry was badly damaged, however, by the shortage of cotton yarn and cotton fabrics as a result of the blockade.

Imperial economic and commercial policies created both disruption and new opportunities, but neither of these was long-lasting except perhaps in the case of France itself. Here the central and fundamental change derived from the loss of France's Atlantic colonies and hence the rapid decline of the cities – Bordeaux, Nantes, Rouen – which had been the most dynamic centres of growth in the eighteenth century. As Louis Bergeron again has argued, France emerged from the Napoleonic episode with a radically transformed economic geography. The western provinces now slipped back into a quieter agricultural existence, while France's industrial centres were consolidated in the north and in Alsace and Lorraine. The decline of the western ports was in part compensated by the growing importance of Marseilles as France's principal Mediterranean port, accompanied by the expansion of commercial wine growing in Languedoc. But it was also significant that even the most advanced sectors of the French economy had not benefited greatly from the privileges that the emperor's commercial policies had showered on them. Their increased ability to produce had simply resulted in many cases in oversupplied markets, and in both northern France and Belgium entrepreneurs complained about the static and inelastic nature of internal markets – an inelasticity that reflected the continuing predominance of peasant households in rural society. The weakness of the Napoleonic formula was that it had been addressed exclusively to the problem of supply and had done nothing, even in France, to strengthen demand.

After 1815 France's economy, deprived of its overseas colonial markets, became more inward-looking and more enclosed within its own frontiers. That was true of Europe as a whole, where the collapse of the Napoleonic empire was followed by a massive return to the protectionist policies of the previous century. In the meantime, the gap between the European and the British economies in terms of industrialization and growth had increased massively. According to the French economic historian François Crouzet, Britain's new commercial and industrial might at the close of the wars with France threatened the whole of Europe with the fate that had already befallen the Indian subcontinent – the threat, that is, of becoming the supplier of raw materials to an ever more industrialized Great Britain. But economic historians have subsequently shown this to be an exaggeration. The process of industrialization was in many respects one that was complementary and promoted growth and new industrial development as it progressed. Sidney Pollard, who described the relations between industrial Britain and industrializing Europe as a 'pacific conquest', has emphasized the complementary nature of the process. After 1815, for example, massive exports of British cotton yarn made possible the rapid expansion of the Saxon cotton textile industry, which developed its own markets in eastern Europe. As in the previous century, Britain's specialization in high volume production encouraged the French preference for high value added quality products such as those of the Lyons silk industry. It was also evident from the example of Belgium that neither government policies nor war were ever sufficient to prevent the rapid diffusion of new technologies where demand existed.

Europe entered the post-Napoleonic century still as an economic patchwork of more and less developed regions. Despite Napoleon's attempts to integrate and unify the European economies around those of metropolitan France, the continuing variations in prices remained an important indicator of the lack of economic unity within the European continent. The contours of the European economic patchwork had not changed significantly, nor would they change until the railway boom of the 1830s marked the beginning of a new phase of dynamic growth in which the Rhineland would be one of the principal protagonists. The two decades that followed Waterloo were a period of falling agricultural prices, static or shrinking demand and scant progress, however. But this could not hide the significance of the changes that had occurred in the previous half-century. The new industrial economies were now a reality, and the new forms of production were spreading rapidly from textiles and machine building to metalworking and chemicals, to the extractive industries and to steam locomotion. The rules of the game of economic growth had been fundamentally transformed: if in the eighteenth century industrialization was still only one among many means of achieving economic growth, the existence of the industrial economies in the nineteenth century made industrialization an obligatory component of economic modernization. Rather than unifying the European economies, however, these developments gave rise to new national rivalries. But despite these internal divisions, the new commercial and industrial capacity of the European economies had fundamentally shifted the economic and political relations between Europe (soon to be followed by North America) and the rest of the world.

Notes

1 P. O'Brien, 'European Economic Development. The Contribution of the Periphery', *Economic History Review*, 35 (1), 1982, pp. 1–18.

2 Cited in C. Vandenbroeke 'The regional economy of Flanders and industrial modernization in the eighteenth century', in *Journal of European Economic History* 16 (1), 1987, pp. 161–2.

3 M. Levy Leboyer, 'Le processus d'industrialisation. Le cas de l'Angleterre et de la France', *Revue historique*, 239, 1968, p. 286.
4 C. Wilson, *England's Apprenticeship*, 1603–1763, London, 1965, p. 300.
5 *Ibid.*, p. 299.
6 L. Bergeron, *L'Episode napoléonien. Aspects intérieurs, 1799–1815*, Paris, 1972, p. 190.

5 The economic development of Europe in the nineteenth century (I)

Growth and transformation of the economy

Giovanni Luigi Fontana[*]

A century of continuous growth

In the long term, economic growth is never a uniform process. Changes first take place, or have greater impact, in 'leader' areas, and are then taken up in 'follower' areas. According to Maddison, a 'leader' economy is one that is closest to the technical frontier; that is, it makes the most efficient use of the available technical knowledge and thus achieves greater productivity of natural resources, capital and labour.[1] To be able to do this, its work force has to be capable of adopting innovations or new technology, and thus its rate of growth depends on the availability of human capital; the countries at an advantage as regards cumulative mechanisms for the research and development of innovations are the developed ones.[2] This hypothesis seems to be confirmed by the history of the world economy from the Middle Ages to the present day. Maddison's reconstruction shows that there have been four consecutive phases, during which different economies were in the lead: the period between the twelfth century and the sixteenth, in central and northern Italy, and Flanders; between 1600 and 1750 in the northern Low Countries; between 1750 and 1890 in England; finally from 1890 to the present day in the United States.

England took over this role with the industrial revolution, thanks to its rapid technical progress in textile production, the iron industry, machinery, and especially in the widespread exploitation of coal as an energy resource; for a long time it enjoyed a monopoly of world trade, which went hand in hand with its industrial power. Between 1820 and 1890, labour productivity increased by 1.2 per cent annually; employment in industry and services rose from 44 per cent in 1700 to 60 per cent in 1820, and to 84 per cent in 1890.

Parts of continental Europe also experienced far-reaching transformations in production, living standards and ways of life during the nineteenth century. There was a decline in the number of agricultural workers between the nineteenth century and the first decades of the twentieth, which took place in all the main European countries and in North America. In England the rate was more rapid; at the start of the century, two-thirds of the population had been actively engaged in agriculture, but this decreased to 8.8 per cent in 1910, compared with 51.6 per cent in the secondary and 39.6 per cent in the tertiary sectors. The main source of wealth and employment was now industry. This marked a crucially important break with the past; thanks to the combined contribution of the revolutions in agriculture, industry and transport, Europe was able to free itself from the limitations that population and the limited resources of the soil had imposed on it. The switch from animal sources of energy, such as the horse and ox, to non-animal sources, such as coal or electricity, made it possible to achieve levels of economic growth that had been unthinkable in previous centuries.

The growth of Europe in the nineteenth century was extraordinary in comparison with that of the preceding century, though compared with figures for the twentieth century, its mean annual growth in GNP of 1–2 per cent may seem slow and irregular. However, most important, the aggregate view of economic development over the century shows that, unlike preceding periods, the nineteenth century experienced only economic growth; the main feature of the economic development of Europe in the nineteenth century was thus its continuity. Although the annual increase varied considerably in different decades, because of short-term economic conjunctures, over the long term it showed a cumulative process with none of the negative figures that had been common until the end of the eighteenth century. If we take 100 as the GNP for 1800, we can see from Bairoch's calculations that a century later it had increased almost five times, and by the eve of the First World War as much as six times (Table 5.1).

The ratio of development to population indicates that the transformations were subject to very complex processes. Table 5.1 shows that economic growth in nineteenth century Europe was much lower *per capita*; taking 100 as the *per capita* GNP for 1800, by 1900 it had multiplied only 2.29 times, and by the eve of the First World War 2.68 times. This indicates that the beneficial effects of sustained economic growth were partly annulled, owing to a considerable increase in the European population.

Table 5.1 The growth of gross national product in Europe (1800–1913)

	Total		*Per capita*	
Year	*1800 = 100*	*Annual increase (%)*	*1800 = 100*	*Annual increase (%)*
1800	100	–	100	–
1830	142	1.18	121	0.63
1840	164	1.43	131	0.81
1850	191	1.52	142	0.86
1860	223	1.57	156	0.90
1870	281	2.36	180	1.50
1880	311	1.00	184	0.18
1890	359	1.46	195	0.59
1900	461	2.54	229	1.61
1910	567	2.08	251	0.92
1913	628	3.52	268	2.29

Source: P. Bairoch, 'Europe's gross national product: 1800–1975', *Journal of European Economic History*, 5, 1976, p. 276.

Table 5.2 Annual growth rates of *per capita* GDP, 1820–1913 (%)

Country	*1820–1870*	*1870–1913*
Austria [a]	0.72	1.30
Belgium	1.94	1.19
France	1.02	1.53
Germany [b]	1.10	1.72
Italy	0.86	0.74–1.30
Great Britain	1.53	1.19
Netherlands	1.47	1.02
Spain	0.35	0.45–1.20
Portugal	0.75	0.72
Russia [c]	0.60	0.90
United States	1.45	1.77

Source: A. Maddison, *Monitoring the World Economy*, Paris, 1995, table. 3.2; L.A. Craig, *The Integration of the European Economy, 1850–1913*, New York, 1997, 9.44.

Notes:
[a] Borders of today's Austrian Republic.
[b] Borders of Federal Germany.
[c] Borders of the USSR.

Reconstructions of the national account series for the two main countries, Great Britain and the United States, show that between 1820 and 1870 there was annual growth of 2 per cent and 4.4 per cent respectively. The *per capita* rates, however, indicate a narrowing of the gap; this is an outcome of the greatly increased American population, following the large-scale influx of immigrants (Table 5.2).[3]

Economic growth and national accounts

Modern economic growth is related to the quantity of goods produced by a country. It is calculated by totalling the value added at each stage of their production; in other words, it is the difference between the value of the finished product and the value of the intermediate products that have been utilized. By definition, this figure corresponds to the sum cost of the factors of production involved; total production thus approximately equals income. Growth is normally measured on the basis of variation in gross domestic product (GDP) at constant prices over time. GDP is the measure of the total value of all goods and services produced within a country by its inhabitants, including the foreigners actively engaged there, over a particular period. Gross national product (GNP) expresses the value of the goods and services produced by a nation, plus those produced overseas in a set period, for example a year. In order to obtain data on changes in GDP over time, it has to be measured at constant prices, to avoid the distortion from the effects of price variations. If one wants to compare the absolute income levels of various countries, a different problem arises. For an exact comparison, it is not enough to convert data expressed in national currencies (e.g. the euro) into that of a single country (e.g. sterling or the dollar) at the average exchange rate for that year. A special exchange rate, the purchasing power parity (PPP), needs to be used to take into account the different price levels. The PPP is unfortunately very difficult to calculate, and only one complete set of data exists, which relates to 1985. Estimates for the income of previous years can be extrapolated from the growth rate given in the national statistics.

National accounts data are irreplaceable as indicators of growth, but they camouflage the performance of developing areas; since growth is initially located in areas where there are more favourable conditions for its development, all countries have regional differences as regards levels and rates of income growth. The case of Italy is emblematic in this respect. Vera Zamagni (1993) has estimated that in 1911 income for the 'industrial triangle' (the area between Turin, Milan and Genoa) was a third higher than the Italian national average, and even surpassed the German or French national average (though for similar reasons it was probably lower than in the leading regions of these two countries). A more precise comparison should therefore be based on estimates for 'regional' income. These are very difficult to obtain, however, because of the lack of data on this scale, and also because of frequent changes in political and administrative boundaries.

Furthermore, figures relating to national income are of little use in understanding the origins and internal dynamics of growth processes, since these are shown as 'an aggregation of discontinuities that show up at local level, but which gradually fade away into uniformity at national level'.[4] Even the dynamics of sectorial change can be camouflaged by national aggregates. An aggregate dominated by a backward primary sector not generally linked to the market (as in the case of Russia) will make agricultural progress in specific regions imperceptible. So too within the secondary sector, new industries, or divisions of old industries undergoing technological innovation, with high levels of productivity and rapid growth rates (as in the case of the Lancashire cotton industry) may continue to have a limited incidence on total industrial production for a time. This is why there is a need for an approach that is at once macro and micro-analytical to interpret economic and social change.

Structural changes

In the European economy, continual growth went hand in hand with structural changes. The most marked change was in the activity ratio, or the ratio between active population and total population, and the distribution of the active population by sector (Table 5.3). Since it is extremely difficult to calculate the active population (those in employment and those seeking employment), the figures are only approximate. Regardless of different criteria for gathering data, all countries, with the exception of Italy and Japan (though figures are unreliable), show an increase in the activity ratio, especially as a result of the increased female activity ratio, while variations for males are less marked. Figures relating to female occupation are affected by the transition from household work to industrial work in the home, or to full employment outside the home.

The transition from a rural and agricultural society to an industrial and urban culture involved profound changes in the occupational structure of the population. Despite the different statistical systems adopted by each country, and the diversity

Table 5.3 Composition of GDP and active population, by sector

	GDP (%)			*Active population (%)*		
Year	*Primary*	*Secondary*	*Tertiary*	*Primary*	*Secondary*	*Tertiary*
Great Britain						
1788	40.0	21.0	39.0	–	–	–
1841	22.0	35.0	43.0	22.3	44.3	33.4
1871	15.0	40.0	45.0	15.3	47.1	37.6
1891	9.0	41.0	50.0	10.7	48.8	40.5
1910[a]	6.0	34.0	60.0	8.8	51.6	39.6
France						
1820	45.7	37.6	16.7	–	–	–
1856	41.9	35.5	22.6	48.9	25.6	25.5
1896	33.6	39.9	26.5	43.4	27.0	29.7
1911	31.7	39.3	29.0	42.0	32.4	25.6
Germany						
1850	47.0	21.0	32.0	–	–	–
1882	36.0	32.0	32.0	46.7	35.5	17.8
1895	31.0	38.0	31.0	39.9	39.0	21.1
1907	25.0	43.0	32.0	36.8	40.9	22.2
Italy						
1869	59.0	17.0	24.0	–	–	–
1881	51.0	18.0	31.0	61.8	20.5	17.7
1911	46.0	21.0	33.0	59.1	23.6	17.3
United States						
1840	–	–	–	63.5	14.5	22.0
1869/70	22.2	21.8	56.0	52.7	26.5	20.7
1889/90	14.2	27.0	58.8	43.0	27.2	29.8
1910/11	18.9	27.5	53.6	31.4	30.3	38.3
Japan						
1872	–	–	–	73.5	26.5	
1885	45.2	14.7	40.1	–	–	–
1890	–	–	–	67.2	32.8	
1895	42.7	18.1	39.2	–	–	–
1911	36.7	23.4	39.9	65.4	14.9	19.8

Sources: adapted from P.A. Toninelli (ed.), *Lo sviluppo economico moderno dalla rivoluzione industriale alla crisi energetica, 1750–1973*, Venice, 1997, pp. 600–1 (on Lebergot, 1966, p. 510; Lévy-Leboyer-Bourguignon, 1985, table A1; Mitchell, 1981, table C1 and K2; Okhawa-Shinohara, 1979, table A12 and A53–4; US Bureau of Census, 1975, series F131–41 and 251–D260; Zamagni,1986, table A1).

Notes:
[a] 1907 GDP figures.

from one census to another, there was a definite trend towards absolute and relative decline in the primary sector (agriculture, hunting and fishing). At the same time there was growth in the secondary sector (mining and manufacturing), and the tertiary sector (all other activities, especially the more modern ones such as public administration, banking, professional activities and public utility services). Hence the concepts of industrialization and modern economic development overlap.

Figures are only indicative, since in traditional societies many people carried out several jobs at the same time; the process, however, shows different rates. In some countries it was more marked; in Germany, from 1882 to 1907, the population engaged in the primary sector decreased from 46.7 per cent to 36.8 per cent, while in the secondary sector it rose from 35.5 per cent to 40.9 per cent. In others it was more moderate; in France, from 1856 to 1911, the population engaged in the primary sector fell from 48.9 per cent to 42 per cent, while in industry it went from 25.6 per cent to 32.4 per cent. In Italy, from 1881 to 1911, there was only a small decrease from 61.8 per cent to 59.1 per cent in the primary sector; in the secondary sector there was an increase from 20.5 per cent to 23.6 per cent, while the tertiary sector remained practically unchanged.

As a rule, where growth was rapid, the decline in agriculture was faster. The transition of the work force to industry and the services may have directly contributed to growth in income, if labour productivity in these sectors was greater than in agriculture. Growth in *per capita* income matched a decline in fertility (i.e. the number of children per woman), in the birth rate and in the overall death rate (especially infant mortality), and a growth in urbanization, literacy and education. There was also growth in the ratio of savings, investment and public consumption to income, at the expense of private consumption; finally there was an increase in international trade, generally accompanied by changes in the composition of trade flows. Many of these changes will be analysed more closely in the following chapters, but here it is worth pointing out that at least half of them took place in the first phase of growth, when income was below $3,000–$4,000 dollars (the 1920s level in Italy), and four-fifths when income was below $8,000 (the 1960s Italian level).

How did growth affect the distribution of income? Kuznets argued that in the initial phases there was greater disparity; this was due to considerable differences in productivity between the different sectors, since the small number of new workers in the 'modern' sectors would earn far more than those in traditional activities. However, this hypothesis has not been convincingly demonstrated. Kuznets's second hypothesis, however, has been confirmed in the light of experience in more advanced countries, such as Great Britain in the 1860s and the United States in the 1920s. He argued that at a certain point in the development process, the trend was inverted, since there was a growth in the percentage of people employed in the new sectors; consequently there was a reduction in the disparity between them and the rest of the economy.

Rates, phases and models of growth: theories and interpretations

England and other countries

Per capita GDP at 1985 US prices, as estimated by Maddison (Table 5.4), enables us to compare different growth rates in the advanced countries. Great Britain dominated the scene until 1890, when it was overtaken by the United States. But by this time all the countries of the Western world were on the path to industrialization (see also Table 5.5). In both the historical and economic analysis, industrialization and development increasingly overlapped.

The growth of Great Britain and the Western world was the focus of the analyses of all the founders of the classical school of political economics, from Adam Smith (1723–1790) to John Stuart Mill (1806–1873), as well as of the initiator of the school of scientific socialism, Karl Marx (1818–1883). Marx established a clear-cut separation between pre-capitalist and capitalist societies; the agrarian world had the features of pre-capitalist society (though Marx did not exclude capitalist developments in agriculture), while industrial production provided the basis for the process of accumulation. But various forms of economic development in different countries of Europe were, in some cases, based on an agricultural system that was anything but closed and backward; in other cases it did not necessarily create a complete break between traditional agrarian structures and the newly emerging capitalist industrial society.

Table 5.4 Per capita GDP, selected countries, 1820–1913 (1985 $)

Country	*1820*	*1870*	*1890*	*1913*
Great Britain	1,405	2,610	3,279	4,024
France	1,052	1,571	1,941	2,734
Germany	0,937	1,300	1,727	2,606
Italy	0,960	1,210	1,355	2,087
United States	1,048	2,247	3,106	4,854
Japan	0,588	0,620	0,813	1,114
Canada	–	1,347	1,662	3,560

Source: adapted from A. Maddison, Dynamic Forces in *Capitalist Development. A Long-run Comparative View*, Oxford, 1991, table 1.

Table 5.5 Per capita income, 1820–1913 (Great Britain = 100)

Country	*1820*	*1870*	*1913*
Austria [a]	74	57	69
Belgium	74	81	82
France	69	57	69
Germany [b]	63	59	76
Italy	62	45	50
Great Britain	100	100	100
Spain	61	42	45
Russia [c]	43	31	30
United States	73	75	105
Japan	40	23	27

Source: A. Maddison, *Monitoring the World Economy*, Paris, 1995, table 3.1.

Notes:

[a] Borders of Austrian Republic today.

[b] Borders of Federal Germany.

[c] Borders of Soviet Union.

Philosophers, historians and economists attempted to identify phases of growth, and to break up the historical process of development into stages or economic systems, each with specific economic, social and institutional structural features. The German 'historical school', the group of scholars considered as the founders of economic history, denied the existence of universal laws in economic development, since each country followed a very different path to progress. In this case the immediate reference was to Germany, and its administrative and territorial fragmentation, as well as its late development, compared with England and France. They argued that economic laws are relative, since they are linked to specific historical circumstances and particular geographical, environmental and institutional conditions, which are limited in time and space; thus they ended by separating economic history into periods, with the theory of 'development stages' as its maximum expression.[5]

The different schools concentrated on problems of economic development; the study of economic equilibrium and the cyclical crises that upset the system of equilibrium, became central arguments for further theories, which ranged from those of the marginalists to those of the different branches of neoclassical orthodoxy that came to dominate much nineteenth century economic thought.

Cycles, fluctuations and innovative activity

As we have said, growth has never been a linear process. Indeed, it has often been marked by temporary variations or fluctuations that normally last for short periods and reflect a particular conjuncture, without changing the overall structure to any significant degree. Countless theories have been formulated to understand what causes the crises, and how they can be avoided. In attempting to find regular patterns in their duration that could help to predict future developments, scholars have repeatedly resorted to history. The subject is a highly complex one, and actual proof of any regularity in fluctuations is still open to debate, but the ideas of Joseph Schumpeter (1883–1950) on this subject have been very influential; in *Business Cycles* (1939) he subjected the existence of three main cycles to empirical investigation. The 'greater', or 'Juglar cycle', named after the French economist who first analysed the notion of the cycle itself in 1860, lasted from seven to eleven years; it was later separated into four phases of 'recession', 'depression', 'recovery' and 'boom', with the classic crises of overproduction generally breaking out half-way through. Next was the 'shorter' or 'Kitchin cycle', named after the American who discovered it in 1923; this was a conjunctural cycle, and it followed a pattern that was basically very similar to that of a stock of finished products. Finally, there were the 'long-period Kondratieff movements' or 'long waves', first detected by the Russian Nikolai Kondratieff in 1922; they lasted for forty-five to fifty years and were made up of two phases of similar length, one ascending and the other descending.

In Schumpeter's view, the cyclic pattern lies at the heart of the capitalist development process. He explains fluctuations in strongly dynamic terms, and emphasizes that development generated by the economic system is by its nature 'cyclical', since progress brings instability into the economic world.[6] Fluctuations are therefore the necessary consequence of the break in stationary equilibrium, and represent the form that development assumes in the capitalist era.[7] According to Schumpeter, 'innovative activity' is a determining factor in development, and therefore in fluctuations. In his analysis he distances himself from the classical school by making a distinction between 'inventions' and 'innovations'. Inventions occur autonomously and often have a scientific origin; since the knowledge gained from them does not depend on a concrete need, they are not important in the analysis of economic development. On the other hand, innovations are developed within the economic system in response to specific needs; they generate 'new combinations' of productive factors, often enabling the results of the inventions to be exploited economically, and for this reason they are fundamental in the economic history of capitalist societies.[8]

Innovations are generated on the initiative of 'innovatory entrepreneurs', who are the true motors of the development process; not only do they introduce new products or new processes, but they also bring about improvements in the organization of enterprises, conquer new markets and find new sources for the supply of raw materials. The initial risk is rewarded with greater profit resulting from the monopolistic position that the innovation temporarily holds; it is only temporarily, because very soon the innovation will be imitated by competitors, the differential gain will be gradually eliminated, and the system will return to a state of equilibrium, until a new innovation reopens the cycle. Innovations are rarely isolated or evenly distributed in time; they tend to come in clusters, and are concentrated in specific sectors. This was the case of the improvements made in the textile industry at the time of the English industrial revolution. It is due to forces set in motion by the first innovation, which other enterprises start to imitate, and is how the cyclical and fluctuating nature of the capitalist growth process comes about.

In the second post-war period, questions of growth and economic development became topical once again, but their objectives differed from those set out in classical theory. In addressing issues of material progress, classical theory was particularly concerned with the problems of the Western world and the capitalist system, while attention was now turning principally to the urgent problem of the economic development of underdeveloped countries.[9] The notion of development had thus come to be defined especially in relation to its opposite, which was underdevelopment. The question that economists, historians and opinion makers asked themselves was how in the past rich countries with a high standard of living had emerged from their underdevelopment.

There was thus a return to speculating about stages of development, and Great Britain was taken as the exemplary case, largely because during the first half of the twentieth century European industrialization had been studied in relation to a diffusive model of the British case. Although important continental experience such as that of Belgium, France and Germany had been studied, European industrialization was generally represented as a development path with 'followers' coming behind 'first movers' and with continental Europe simply confirming the success of the British 'formula'. The 'followers' merely used the new technologies available after they had imported them. However, this interpretation was much questioned and criticized. Authors such as Landes (1978) and Rosenberg (1988) emphasized the existence of a creative process in adopting technologies, and were opposed to pure 'imitation' theories. The identification of precise moments when the continental economies were supposed to have started following behind Britain was also challenged. Furthermore, it was argued that the 'diffusive model' could not explain what happened in the United States, and the conclusion was that Britain was a separate and specific case in the course of European industrialization. The fact that for generations Britain was taken as the model country in the economic field led to a belief that there was a set path to development. Development thus ended by being 'nationalized', and its 'multi-polarity' and 'multi-linearity' were not considered.

Theories of economic history: Rostow's stages and take-off

The study of development phases and dynamics thus experienced a shift in viewpoint; the idea that the British model was imitated wholesale changed to one that acknowledged important differences, and attempts were made to provide general explanations.[10] The aim was to find a common denominator for economic change in contemporary Europe by making a comparative analysis, and showing that no country was unique, but had its place within a model, or was part of a growth theory. During the 1960s, Walter Rostow (1916–2003) and Alexander Gerschenkron (1904–1978) distinguished themselves by constructing models of this type. Taking problems of economic growth as their starting point, they attempted to build up a true theory of economic history. They rejected the use of cyclical models, and instead proposed incremental interpretations of development. Though they conceived it differently, another point they had in common was to emphasize the aspect of discontinuity that characterized the initial phase of the economic growth processes.

In his *Stages of Economic Growth* (1960), W.W. Rostow put forward the first important systematic theorization of economic history. His 'theory of stages', already mentioned in Chapter 4, suggested there was a growth process based on five stages which each country went through before it achieved complete economic development. The five stages were the traditional society, the development of pre-conditions for take-off, take-off, a drive to maturity, and finally the era of mass consumption. Each will be examined in turn.

The point of departure is a traditional pre-industrial society marked by low productivity of human labour, the overriding predominance of agriculture, a close correlation between population and resources, and a self-contained society exposed to the risks of epidemic and famine. In traditional societies the rate of investment is the same as that of demographic growth, where *per capita* income cannot increase, and indeed often decreases. If this type of society is to evolve, it is necessary to create the conditions for an increase in investment; part of production must go on infrastructure and not on consumption.

In the transition period the pre-conditions for take-off are created; it is a period of change, creation of enterprise and accumulation of capital, in which transformation takes place. There is increased production and productivity in agriculture, or mining, so that labour and capital can be channelled into industrial activities. A process of accumulation of economic capital takes place; infrastructures and markets are created, human capital is formed through the provision of formal education, knowledge and skilled labour; enterprise and the acceptance of risk is encouraged. The state plays an essential role in creating infrastructure, especially for transport in the form of roads, canals and railways, since private enterprise cannot provide the quantities of capital required; moreover, their profitability is deferred and is often indirect. There is development of the service industries, and in particular of an efficient banking system. Raw materials are used efficiently if they are available locally, otherwise they are imported; manufactured products are exported.

Take-off is the process of spontaneous or induced economic acceleration which permanently transforms the economy over two or three decades, by bringing it to a stable level of much higher production than at the start. A self-sustaining process of capital accumulation and increase in productivity begins, with growth rates in production and income that have not been previously experienced. There is a rapid and decisive change in economic structures, which is marked by a rise in productive investment to a level of around 10 per cent of net national product. A political, social and institutional framework is created that takes full advantage of the drive towards expansion, so that economic acceleration can be transformed into a process of general and cumulative development, ultimately leading to a steady increase in individual income. Since innovations do not affect the economic system uniformly, there is a development of leading sectors and leading sector industries that influence the whole economy with backward and lateral linkages; because the process generates imbalances, it requires some time for the entire economic system to be involved. Subsidiary industries, such as the mining or the machinery sector, are developed, and industry takes over from agriculture as the chief sector of economic growth.

In the maturity phase, the process of industrial growth is extended, technological and organizational innovations spread to more and more sectors, new leading industries become more dynamic as growth in the leading sectors of the previous period slows down. Investment now accounts for between 10 per cent and 20 per cent of national income. Production far outstrips population growth, and the steady increase in *per capita* income is without precedent. Steady growth transforms the economy structurally. When requirements and opportunities for investment decrease, and the rate of technological innovation slows down, greater resources begin to be allocated to consumption.

Of all the stages, the Age of Mass Consumption is the one that least lends itself to analytical description. It is a conclusion that conforms to the American development model. During this phase the greater distribution of purchasing power for consumption leads producers to invest in product standardization processes in order to lower costs and widen the market for consumer goods, which is essential if the growth rate of the system is to be sustained.

Rostow's model has met with as much favour as it has criticism. It presented an all-round vision of the European economy, analysed its growth, created important concepts such as take-off, or the era of mass consumption, illustrated the stages towards industrial modernization, and showed the experience of different countries at various stages. In the same way as the 'pre-condition' stage resembled the proto-industrialization phase, so take-off for Great Britain was identified with the onset of the industrial revolution; for Belgium and France it coincided with the industrial development of the 1830s to 1860s, for Germany with the period 1850–1873, for Sweden with 1868–1890, and for Russia with 1890–1914. But these periods are not the same if the scale of analysis is applied to regional, rather than national, dimensions. The concept of take-off remains open to question. The fact is that growth is a slow process. Rostow set investment of 10 per cent of net domestic product in productive activities as the threshold for take-off, but this figure has not been confirmed in history. Even where the share of the formation of fixed capital in GDP rose steeply compared with previous decades, as in France in the 1840s,[11] in terms of the net internal product it went up only from 5 per cent to 7 per cent; this percentage includes investment in building activity, much of which does not contribute to production. Thus in Rostow's model conditions were assumed that have not been demonstrated in history. It proposed a growth process taking place through gradual stages immediately following on from each other; but it only partly explained the mechanisms of the transition from one stage to another. For example, what causes the lead-up to the transition, or how are essential agents such as entrepreneurs created? In order to explain something as complex and diversified as economic development, he attributed excessive importance to certain driving sectors. He did not take into consideration any interaction between the different dimensions (i.e. international, national or regional) in which economic development takes place.

In short, his theory was an 'imitation without variants'; it presumed that all economies have to pass through the various phases, and at the same time imposed a unilateral model on all European economies. None the less, Rostow's model enabled a number of scholars to understand the different stages in the development of individual countries. For example, in the case of France, M. Lévy-Leboyer and F. Burguignon recognized an initial period (1825–1859) when the country benefited from the onset of industrialization, from the development of an internal market to absorb agricultural products and consumer goods to a greater degree, and from dynamic foreign trade. They identified a second period of deceleration (1860–1885), when other competing countries were showing progress. Finally they observed a third period from the mid-1850s to the early 1900s when growth resumed once again under the stimulus of industrial modernization

Gerschenkron and the advantages of backwardness

The observation that countries such as France, Scandinavia, Holland and Switzerland experienced analogous growth, but that the analogies were matched by as many differences, led a number of theorists to try to explain the differences in the imitation processes. In Rostow's model, the fact that the factors or determinants of each stage of development were fixed led Alexander Gerschenkron to formulate a new theory in the 1960s. Gerschenkron was a scholar of Russian origin, but was later a professor at Harvard and an expert on the European economies that were not part of the English-speaking world. At the centre of his theory, rather than long-term dynamics, he placed the two most important stages in Rostow's theory, namely pre-conditions for take-off and take-off. Gerschenkron focused his analysis on the mechanisms that enabled late-developing countries to start a process of development. Underlying his analysis was the concept of backwardness relative to the leader country, Great Britain. Different countries were ranked according to a comparison with the number and significance of the prerequisites for development that were present in Great Britain. The degree to which they approximated the conditions existing in English society determined how likely, how rapidly and how closely they would imitate it themselves. Where these prerequisites were lacking, these countries could attempt to close the gap or catch up by other means. Backward areas needed to catch up so as to ease the tension between different countries, or even within a single country. Since there were different degrees of relative backwardness, the alternative factors and economic policies that had to be applied would be different too; that is why European countries experienced different paths to industrialization. In the opinion of Gerschenkron, it was necessary to give a boost to the processes that were normally present in order to close the gap more rapidly. In this respect Gerschenkron's model resembled Rostow's, since it predicated a take-off stage, or 'big spurt'. Gerschenkron argued that the rapid industrialization in the countries that lagged behind Great Britain stemmed from the 'advantages of backwardness'. Latecomers could imitate the technology of others without the need to go through a process of refinements, or to invest financial resources in research and development. In theory, the greater the level of backwardness then the more likely it would be for the following to occur: industrial development would be more rapid, there would be greater development of large-scale industry, and greater concentration of production on intermediate rather than on consumer goods. Furthermore institutions actively engaged in accelerating the industrialization process would play a greater role, agricultural growth would be lower, and more foreign expertise and capital would be imported.

But the country that starts first, or gains the leading position, cannot be sure of keeping it, as the decline of Great Britain in the second half of the nineteenth century, and the change in economic leadership between the Middle Ages and the contemporary era both show. Those that are closest to the leader can take over its leadership, as England did from Holland, while those who have fallen behind can recover leading positions, as in the case of Italy.

A further important element that emerged from Gerschenkron's analysis was that the sectors driving development in the more backward countries were not the same as those that drove the British industrial revolution, since both the contexts and the periods differed. However, Gerschenkron concentrated on the take-off phase and its pre-conditions, and did not draw all the implications. In later phases of development differences continued, 'forming different versions of industrial capitalism, which have shown they can compete not only as regards prices, quality and type of product and services, but also as regards the different institutions governing the production process'.[12]

The investigations of Barsby, Gregory and Crafts showed empirically how the correlations between backwardness and development, although difficult to measure, could be explained differently in different national contexts. The theories of Gerschenkron were extended to different national experiences beyond the restricted nucleus of nations that had been at the centre of attention of historians until the 1960s, and involved England, France and Germany in particular. As will be seen when the experience of individual countries is analysed, Gerschenkron's model pointed to Italian industrialization as a case where the state and the banking system were key substitutes in the catching-up process. The experience of Germany and that of Russia were similarly explained, with the points they had in common as well as specific aspects being underlined.

However, by taking the case of Britain as the 'natural' paradigm, rather than other 'artificial' paths, Gerschenkron left himself open to a conceptual problem. Research into the industrial revolution has underlined the significance of state intervention in creating infrastructures or the system of finance; similar factors were involved to those that Gerschenkron considered typical of backward countries, thus weakening his argument for a clear-cut division between an 'original case' and 'subsequent cases'. Further comparisons between the different paths to development in European countries have been motivated by the application and refinement of Gerschenkron's theories. However, they have either led to the rejection of a single (British) model of industrial revolution, which was R. Cameron's view, or to considering British development as an exceptional case, and not as a model that could be imitated, which was the view of N. Crafts.

The problem of the unit of analysis: Pollard and the economic region

In the 1970s, more and more historians became dissatisfied with these deterministic sequences, and with univocal and linear models of interpretation. There was a growing need for broader and more detailed comparisons of the specific aspects of each case; but there was the problem of which basic unit of analysis and comparison to select. The unit of analysis commonly adopted by historians had been the national one, since statistics gathered from central authorities could be used, and states themselves played a particular role. However, other historians began to think differently and suggested using other units, such as regions; though they did not necessarily coincide with political and administrative units, to a certain degree regions were homogeneous as regards their socio-economic circumstances and interests.

Sidney Pollard (1925–1998) first led this revised historiographical approach; in his fundamental book *The Peaceful Conquest*[13] he showed how the notion of take-off, and to a wider extent the origins of development, should more correctly be applied to the regional and not the national dimension. This even applied to Great Britain itself, since during the industrial revolution it benefited from numerous regions taking off simultaneously. There was even a quite marked disparity in the conditions in different regions or territorial areas within the same country. The national dimension was of little use in analysing the original phases of the industrialization process or even later, since the contributions of the more dynamic areas were 'submerged' in the uniformity of the national aggregates. According to Pollard, European industrialization took place in each country on a regional basis, and an interpretation based on regions could provide more information than one based on broader national aggregates.[14] Pollard has provided numerous cases for reinterpreting the industrialization process at regional level; however the regional dimension was to be considered complementary to the national and international dimension, and not in competition with it. The other fundamental contribution that Pollard made to the debate on how the industrial revolution came about was related precisely to the international dimension. Gerschenkron had argued that the international context acted as the background for the late-developing country; in Pollard's view, developments in the international economy directly affected decisions taken in individual countries, whether positively or negatively. This is the 'differential of contemporaneity' concept; a typical example is the construction of the railways, and the different role it played in the economies of different countries, depending on the particular international circumstances at a particular moment. The concept can be applied to other factors of interference, one of the most important of which was war, especially the First World War; in one way or another it directly affected the development of many European countries.

Path dependence, institutions and economic development; the role of the state

Economic historians have continued to expand on these debates in their search for original pathways and concepts, in relation not only to economic theory but also to other domains. The concept of path dependence, developed by Paul David in particular, has been one of the most significant.[15] In this concept, the explanation for technological and institutional changes does not lie in universal economic laws. Instead, it lies in the actual historical path that the changes took; chains of events, even chance events, in the end ruled out initially possible alternatives, and confined the field of choice to the one that actually won through. This was further confirmation that the path taken by the first comers could not be pedantically followed by those who were starting out on the process of development.

In Gerschenkron's theories the role of the state as a 'replacement agent' in the development process of 'latecomer' countries had already been underlined. In their analysis of the dynamics of development, economic historians have increasingly focused on the role of institutions, or the bodies that regulate economic co-operation and competition between groups and individuals. Competition between different regions took place in the sphere of technologies and production methods. But it also took place in the field of regulatory systems and their capacity to boost development by lowering transaction costs; these included costs for research, the organization and spread of information, implementing innovations[16] and generally making the economy more efficient. 'For this reason, anyone who invents an institution that proves to be more "efficient" for any given historical moment, will be imitated, just as more efficient technology is imitated.'[17] There will be a transition from one institution to the next, according to how economic conditions change.

Douglass North was the scholar who, more incisively than anybody, hypothesized that economic change was the result of institutional change in response to specific needs of production.[18] He argued, for example, that even in Great Britain, the country that most strongly defended *laissez-faire*, the state itself played a fundamental role in creating an efficient national market and revitalizing institutions. According to North, the improved definition and application of ownership rights benefited factory organization, and this in its turn led to the adoption of new technologies and the specialization of labour.[19] Conversely, one of the explanations for England's decline, in the late nineteenth century, was the state's inability to interpret the needs of the market and the world of enterprise.[20] This theory has been criticized as being too exclusive and mechanistic; but it has led to several important developments in the closer investigation of the relationship between institutions and economic development. For example the role of state intervention was justifiable because of transaction costs; intermediate institutions, such as economic regions, local productive systems, and old-established and newly formed industrial areas, also played a role in previous and more recent processes of localized development.

We have already seen the importance of active state intervention in the development of progressive capitalism, in the way it created favourable conditions for freedom of enterprise and the production of public utility goods. The quantity and quality of state involvement in the economic sphere have been the subject of debate ever since. The origins of the debate go back to the first centuries of the modern era: the doctrines of mercantilism, Colbertism, *Cameralwissenschaft*,[21] and later even Physiocracy,[22] in their practical application were to all intents and purposes true economic policies, in which the scope and limits of state intervention were increasingly defined. During the industrial revolution, and later, the debate continued along the lines of *laissez-faire*; the limits of state intervention were fixed, so that market mechanisms could be left to themselves to function harmoniously. However, even Smith and Ricardo highlighted the importance of the state in promoting international exchanges, developing infrastructure and public education, and in combating monopolies and parasitic income. On the opposing front the 'interventionist' doctrine was evolving; this was based on the conviction that the state should actively intervene in economic affairs, since if it was left to itself the market could not guarantee adequate industrial development.

The political, economic and ideological premises for a different approach to relations between state and market, and between public and private sectors, were already being laid down in the early nineteenth century in Belgium, France and Germany. This was also happening in the United States, where Alexander Hamilton, secretary of state for George Washington, first defended these positions. During the twentieth century they were to become fully realized. Though their political and institutional structures differed, all these countries shared a growing belief that the state could play a significant role in the industrialization process. A good example was the Zollverein, the customs union created between German states in 1833 on the initiative of Friedrich List, who attributed an important role to the state. Measures adopted in the development of the railways were a further example. The United States, Belgium, Germany and Italy were countries that had recently been formed, where a more active role of the state was seen to contribute to their successful political and social unification.

However, in the second half of the nineteenth century, theory and practice started to diverge. On the other side of the Atlantic, in the United States, a type of state began to take shape that still prevails today. In Europe, especially on the continent, a different model of relations between state and economy gained ground; in many respects it anticipated a 'strong' state model, as opposed to an American 'weak' state model. During the course of the twentieth century, belief in 'big government' would take hold, albeit with profoundly different experiences. There were the *dirigiste* policies of a number of central European countries during the inter-war period, the formation of socialist states, the start of the first processes of nationalization, and after the Second World War the success of mixed economies.

Regardless of the different ideologies that have always strongly influenced the debate, the role of the state in the economy, with the complex interplay between politics and economics, has been steadily increasing. It ranges from state expenditure[23] to various degrees of state intervention in institutional and legislative policy, infrastructure such as roads, canals, ports and railways, education, control over currency and exchange rates, protectionism, subsidies and incentives, rescue operations, direct management of enterprises and banks, anticyclical measures, and social policy. The reason for this is that industrial capitalist systems

> cannot function adequately without a minimum level of state intervention to guarantee defence and law and order. This means legislation to fix the rules of the market, especially to safeguard competition, and ensure these rules are observed through the administration of justice. The public goods considered essential at various historical moments also need to be provided.[24]

Goods of public utility include the currency and the central bank that administrates it, the postal services, education, infrastructure, transport and health. In addition to these, other types of 'supplementary' intervention in the market have led modern states away from the minimal interventionism conceived by advocates of the free market, and towards variously articulated and extensive forms of mixed economy. However none has gone so far as to reject the market outright, unlike the twentieth century Soviet economy with its central planning.

In conclusion, the variety of approaches and interpretations is none other than a reflection of the extreme complexity and variety of the different pathways to development.

> If certain phenomena show similarity, this does not automatically mean that the various mechanisms of development followed a similar time sequence, nor that the final results were identical. Thus the general models of interpretation that have been put forward at different times can be used as a stimulus for the questions they might raise for critical thought and scientific research, but certainly not to establish definitive explanations once and for all.[25]

Acknowledgement

With the collaboration of Giorgio Riello, whom I thank for his suggestions and additional material for Chapters 5 to 9.

Notes

1 A. Maddison, *Dynamic Forces in Capitalist Development. A Long-run Comparative View*, Oxford, 1991, pp. 30 ff.
2 G. Federico, 'Crescita e trasformazione delle economie', in P.A. Toninelli (ed.), *Lo sviluppo economico moderno dalla rivoluzione industriale alla crisi energetica, 1750–1973*, Venice, 1997, pp. 61–2.
3 *Ibid.*, pp. 57.
4 'un 'aggregazione di discontinuità che risaltano a livello locale, ma sfumano in un gradualismo uniforme a livello nazionale.' P. Mathias, 'Reflessioni sul processo di industrializzazione in Europa', in G.L. Fontana (ed.), *Le vie dell'industrializzazione europea. Sistemi a confronto*, Bologna, 1997, pp. 36–7.
5 G. Di Taranto, 'Introduzione alla storia economica', in F. Assante, M. Colonna, G. Di Taranto and G. Lo Giudice, *Storia dell'economia mondiale*, Bologna, 2001.
6 J.A. Schumpeter, *Business Cycles. A Theoretical, Historical and Statistical Analysis of the Capitalist Process*, New York, 1939, p. 238.
7 T. Cozzi, 'Cicli economici', in *Enciclopedia delle scienze sociali*, vol. IV, Rome, 1994, p. 729.
8 P.A. Toninelli, *Progresso, sviluppo e ciclo nel pensiero economico contemporaneo. Un'introduzione*, in id. (ed.), *Lo sviluppo economico moderno*, pp. 49–50.
9 H.W. Arndt, *Lo sviluppo economico. Storia di un'idea*, Bologna, 1990, p. 71.
10 P.K. O'Brien, 'Do we have a typology for the study of European industrialization in the nineteenth century?' In *Journal of European Economic History*, 15 (2), 1986.
11 M. Levy-Leboyer, 'Investimenti e sviluppo economico in Francia, 1820–1930', in M.M. Postan and P. Mathias (eds), *Storia economica Cambridge*, vol. VII: *L'età del capitale*, Turin, 1979–80.
12 'configurando varie versioni di capitalismo industriale, che hanno mostrato di competere non solo sui prezzi, la qualità e i tipi di prodotti e servizi, ma anche sulle diverse istituzioni che governano i processi di produzione'. V. Zamagni, *Dalla rivoluzione industriale all'integrazione europea*, Bologna, 1999, p. 34.
13 Italian edition 1989.
14 *Ibid.*, p. 6.
15 P. David, 'Comprendere l'economia del sistema QWERTY. La necessità della storia', in W.N. Parker (ed.), *Economia e storia*, Rome and Bari, 1988 (original edn. 1985).
16 D.C. North and R. Thomas, *L'evoluzione economica del mondo occidentale*, Milan, 1976, p. 117.
17 'Per questo motivo, chi inventa un'istituzione che si rivela più "efficiente" per un dato momento storico, si vedrà imitato, così come si imita la tecnologia più efficiente.' V. Zamagni, *Dalla rivoluzione industriale all'integrazione europea*, p. 37.
18 D.C. North, *Structure and Change in Economic History*, New York, 1981; *id.*, 'Transaction costs in economic history', *Journal of European Economic History*, 14, 1985.
19 D.C. North and R. Thomas, *L'evoluzione economica del mondo occidentale*; D.C. North, *Structure and Change in Economic History*; D. North and B. Weingast, 'Constitution and commitment. Evolution of institutions governing public choice in seventeenth century England', *Journal of European Economic History*, 49, 1989; P. Hudson, *La rivoluzione industriale*, Bologna, 1995.
20 B. Elbaum and W. Lazonick (eds), *The Decline of the British Economy*, Oxford, 1986; W.P. Kennedy, *Industrial Structure, Capital Markets and the Origins of British Industrial Decline*, Cambridge, 1987; S. Pollard, *British Prime and British Decline. The British Economy*, London, 1989.
21 The science of economic administration (*Translator's note.*)
22 Based on a doctrine of government of Quesnay, stating that the natural order underlying society was based on land and its natural products, which were the only true form of wealth (*Translator's note.*)
23 G. Brosio and C. Marchese, *Il potere di spendere. Economia e storia della spesa pubblica dall'Unificazione ad oggi*, Bologna, 1986.

24 'non possono funzionare adeguatamente senza un livello minimo di Stato che garantisca difesa e law and order (ossia una legislazione che stabilisca le regole del mercato, fra cui in prima linea la difesa della concorrenza, e le faccia osservare attraverso l'amministrazione della giustizia) e fornisca qualche bene pubblico ritenuto essenziale nei vari momenti storici.' V. Zamagni, *Dalla rivoluzione industriale all'integrazione europea*, pp. 40–1.

25 'Alla similarità di un certo numero di fenomeni non corrisponde automaticamente né uno stesso ordine di successione temporale fra i vari meccanismi di sviluppo, né un identico ventaglio di risultati finali. Perciò i modelli interpretativi di carattere generale che sono stati via via proposti possono essere utilizzati unicamente per gli stimoli e gli interrogativi che essi forniscono alla riflessione critica e alla ricerca scientifica, e non già per stabilire dei canoni esplicativi definiti una volta per tutte'. V. Castronovo, 'Introduzione' L. Segreto (ed.), *La rivoluzione industriale tra il Settecento e l'Ottocento*, Milan, 1984, pp. ix–x.

6 The economic development of Europe in the nineteenth century (II)

Demographic dynamics and social change; the role of agriculture

Giovanni Luigi Fontana

The European demographic revolution

The variable of population dynamics is of prime importance in understanding the economic and social changes of the nineteenth century. Production and consumption are correlated to the increase in the population and the way it is distributed geographically, socially and by age group. Despite the importance of demographic data, and although statistics and social sciences were originally developed during the nineteenth century, the available documentary evidence is fragmentary and sometimes based on conjecture, even for important countries.[1] Though the figures cannot be considered as in any way precise, they help us to make useful approximations for outlining the general picture and understanding the underlying ratios and trends.

According to some estimates, the European population, which between 1600 and 1800 had grown at a modest rate of 0.42 per cent annually, between 1800 and 1914 increased at the rate of 0.93 per cent annually. Over the century, many European countries experienced annual population increases of between 0.5 per cent and 1.5 per cent.[2] This was a true demographic revolution, which led to changes in structures, and different patterns of behaviour and settlement.

Britain anticipated the trends that would subsequently involve all the other countries. A large increase in the population after the 1740s meant there was an increase in the labour force in country areas, as well as for putting-out systems, or for urban activities. By the second half of the seventeenth century demographic pressure had already made wide sections of the population available for employment in new manufacturing sectors, such as the cotton industry. Similar, if not higher, increases to those in Britain also took place in other areas of Europe, for example in the Austro-Germanic area. This was the beginning of the 'demographic transition', or the transition phase from the 'demographic model of the *ancien régime*' to the 'new demography'.

The former model, in line with Malthusian theories, was marked by a combination of a high birth rate and a high death rate, which created self-balancing mechanisms between population and resources. Coming up against a rigid system of agricultural production, any growth in population would lead to a reduction in the availability of food, and the already meagre diet of the population would be further reduced. This could trigger a rapid increase in mortality through famine and disease and thus bring the population back to previous levels.[3] According to recent studies, the demography of the *ancien régime* was characterized by a combination of practices and behaviour in individuals and families that tended to reduce female fertility, which however affected the birth rate to only a limited extent. These included remaining unmarried, or systematically delaying the age of marriage. It is estimated that the number of unmarried European women remained constant at around 15–20 per cent, and that on average men married around the age of thirty and women around twenty-five or twenty-six, thus 'reducing' female fertility by a decade. Late marriage, and widespread non-marriage, was precisely what mainly differentiated the Western demographic experience from the rest of the world, where hardly any women over the age of twenty-five were still unmarried.[4]

All these generalizations need to be qualified somewhat. Social differences, for example, are a primary determining factor in demographic behaviour patterns. In any case, from the nineteenth century onwards, the 'Malthusian trap' was no longer in operation; the stability model was supplanted by the development model. For the first time in the history of mankind, an increase in the population did not create a crisis in the available resources. Thanks to parallel changes in production systems, the possibility of expanding the overall economic system increased. The change lay not so much in the intensity of the demographic growth as in the fact that for the next two centuries, and until the present day, it was uninterrupted and showed no regression.[5]

Between 1800 and 1900 the world population increased by 70 per cent, rising from 978 million to 1,650 million (Table 6.1). The number of inhabitants in Asia and Africa increased by a third and a quarter respectively. In Asia it increased from 630 million to 925 million and in Africa from 107 million to 133 million, while in Europe, Russia included, it more than doubled, rising from 208 million to 430

Table 6.1 Evolution of the world population, 1750–1900 (million)

	1750		*1800*		*1850*		*1900*	
Area	*No.*	*%*	*No.*	*%*	*No.*	*%*	*No.*	*%*
Europe (excluding Russia)	125	15.8	152	15.5	208	16.5	296	18.0
Russia	42	5.3	56	5.7	76	6.0	134	8.1
North America	2	0.3	7	0.8	26	2.1	82	4.9
South and Central America	16	2.0	24	2.5	38	3.0	74	4.4
Africa	106	13.4	107	10.9	111	8.8	133	8.1
Asia	498	62.9	630	64.4	801	63.4	925	56.1
China	200	25.2	323	33.0	430	34.1	436	26.4
India and Pakistan	190	24.0	195	19.9	233	18.5	285	17.3
Australia and Oceania	2	0.3	2	0.2	2	0.2	6	0.4
Total	791	100.0	978	100.0	1,262	100.0	1,650	100.0

Sources: adapted from E.A. Wrigley. *Demografia e storia*, Milan, 1969; P.A. Toninelli (ed.). *Lo sviluppo economico moderno dalla rivoluzione industriale alla crisi energetica, 1750–1973*, Venice, 1997, p. 602.

million inhabitants. Between the nineteenth century and the present day it has more than tripled, reaching 650 million. In the same period, the Asian and African share of the total world population decreased from 64.4 per cent to 56.1 per cent and from 10.9 per cent to 8.1 per cent respectively; the European share increased from 21.2 per cent to 26 per cent. Furthermore, with the mass migrations that marked the century, Europeans contributed heavily to tripling the number of inhabitants of Latin America, Australia and Oceania, and to multiplying that of North America thirteen times. On the eve of the First World War, Europe had 480 million inhabitants, three times the population of 1750. At the start of the nineteenth century, one person in five was European; by the end, it was one in four. If the Europeans and their descendants who settled on other continents are added to those in Europe itself, then it was almost one in three.

A comparison of densities (the number of inhabitants per square kilometre) shows that the greatest population concentration was on the least extensive continent (Table 6.2). In 1800 Europe, with 18.7 inhabitants/km^2 compared with 13.7 in Asia, was already at the top of the table. At the start of the twentieth century it had a density of 40.1 inhabitants/km^2, almost double that of Asia (21.3 inhabitants/km^2) and ten times that of Africa (4.0 inhabitants/km^2).

The population in different European countries increased at different rates, at different times and with different degrees of intensity. In the first half of the century, the areas of north-western Europe grew more rapidly, while in the second half it was the south and east of the continent that showed particularly high rates of population growth (Table 6.3). In Italy, the population grew steadily throughout the century, with different growth patterns for birth and death rates according to the different regions; some regions, especially the south, experienced massive emigration, with important economic consequences in the short and long term between the 1880s and the First World War (Table 6.4).

Table 6.3 shows how, in the second half of the nineteenth century, the growth rate of France slowed down considerably, owing to the birth rate declining more rapidly than in other countries. Elsewhere, a continuing high birth rate, together with an overall decrease in the death rate, brought about marked increases. However, even here national figures can conceal significant local or regional differences. At the end of the nineteenth century, for instance, Italy was characterized

Table 6.2 Population density by continent, 1800–1900 (inhabitants/km^2)

Areas	*1800*	*1850*	*1900*
Europe	18.7	26.6	40.1
Asia	13.7	17.0	21.3
Africa	3.0	3.1	4.0
North America	0.2	1.1	3.4
Central and South America	1.0	1.2	3.4

Source: J. Heffer and W. Serman. *Il XIX secolo, 1815–1914: dalle rivoluzioni agli imperialismi.* Italian edn. ed. by S. Zaninelli, Milan, 1998, p. 19.

Table 6.3 European population in the nineteenth century (million)

Country	*1800*	*1820*	*1830*	*1840*	*1850*	*1860*	*1870*	*1880*	*1890*	*1900*	*1910*
Austria	–	13.5	15.5	16.6	17.5	18.2	20.2	22.1	23.7	25.9	28.6
France	27.3	30.5	32.6	34.2	35.8	37.4	36.1	37.4	38.1	38.4	39.2
Germany	–	25.0	28.2	31.4	33.4	35.6	41.0	45.2	49.4	56.4	64.9
Ireland	4.8	6.8	7.8	8.2	6.6	5.8	5.4	5.2	4.7	4.5	4.4
Italy	17.2	19.7	201.2	22.9	24.3	25.0	26.8	28.8	28.4	30.1	32.4
Norway	0.9	1.0	1.1	1.2	1.3	1.5	1.7	1.8	2.0	2.2	2.3
Portugal	2.9	–	–	3.7	3.5	3.6	–	4.2	4.7	5.0	5.5
Russia[a]	40.0	48.6	56.1	62.4	68.5	74.1	84.5	97.7	117.8	132.9	160.7
Spain	10.5	–	–	–	–	15.6	–	16.6	17.5	18.6	19.9
Sweden	2.3	2.6	2.9	3.1	3.5	3.9	4.2	4.6	4.8	5.1	5.5
Great Britain	14.1	16.3	18.5	20.8	23.1	26.1	26.1	29.7	33.1	37.0	40.8
Europe Total	205.0				275.0		320.0			414.0	450.0

Sources: adapted from: B.R. Mitchell, 'Statistical appendix', in C.M. Cipolla (ed.), *The Fontana Economic History of Europe. The Emergence of Industrial Societies, Part 2*, London, 1973, pp. 747–8; B.R. Mitchell, *International Historical Statistics. Europe, 1750–1988*, Basingstoke, 1992. pp. 1–5; S. Pollard. *La conquista pacifica. L'industrializzazione in Europa dal 1760 al 1970*, Bologna, 1981, p. 148.

Note:
[a] Estimated figures for Russia.

Table 6.4 Evolution of the Italian population, 1791–1911 (1914 borders)

Year	*Population (in 000)*	*Annual increase per 1,000 inhabitants over previous decade*
1791	17,479	–
1801	17,860	2.2
1811	18,257	2.2
1821	19,000	4.0
1831	21,088	10.5
1841	22,355	5.9
1851	24,162	7.8
1861	25,017	3.5
1871	26,801	6.9
1881	28,460	6.0
1901	32,475	6.6
1911	34,671	6.6

Source: J. Heffer and W. Serman, *Il XIX secolo, 1815–1914: dalle rivoluzioni agli imperialismi*, ed. S. Zaninelli, Milan, 1998, p. 29.

by a relatively homogeneous growth in population over the whole country. Yet socio-economic differences in different parts of the country were matched by fundamentally different demographic mechanisms. The north of Italy had both a low death rate and low birth rate, while the south of Italy showed a high mortality rate and a high birth rate (Figure 6.1 and Table 6.5).

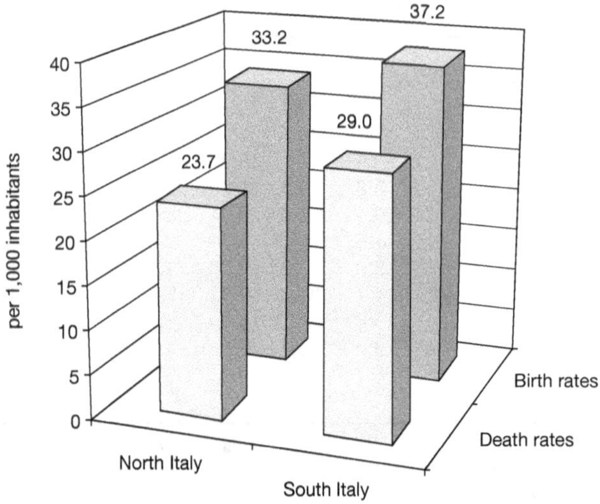

Figure 6.1 Mortality and birth rates in Italy in 1895.

Source: adapted from C. Trebilcock, *The Industrialization of the Continental Powers, 1780–1914*, Harlow, 1981.

Table 6.5 Trends in the Italian population from 1862 to 1911 (annual average per thousand inhabitants)

Period	*Birth rate*	*Mortality*	*Natural increase*	*Net migration*
1862–1871	37.4	30.3	7.1	–0.3
1872–1881	36.9	29.6	7.3	–1.3
1882–1891	37.2	26.9	10.3	–2.8
1892–1901	34.2	23.7	10.5	–4.2
1902–1911	32.2	21.3	10.9	–4.1

Source: J. Heffer and W. Serman. *Il XIX secolo. 1815–1914: dalle rivoluzioni agli imperialismi*, ed. S. Zaninelli, Milan, 1998, p. 30.

The 'new demographic model'

The new European demography that developed with the industrial revolution hinged on a fall in the death rate, and a decline in the birth rate.

> The average fertility and high mortality that had marked the demographic development of pre-industrial Europe – a variation of the high fertility and high mortality that would be the model for the evolution of the whole world population until the 1940s – was thus replaced by the drastic reduction of both parameters. In any case, there was rapid growth in the short term, due to the fall in the death rate rather than to any increase in fertility. In the next phase, there was a marked decline in fertility, and the subsequent increase in

population did not depend on the increased number of births, but mainly on longer life expectancy.[6]

Thus demographic variables, economic indicators and social circumstances were brought into relation with each other.

Death and birth rates, which are the components of population balance, underwent a structural change. In the first place, the great mortality crises that had been a feature of the pre-industrial period were becoming scarcer, thanks to the combined effect of two factors: the disappearance of the great epidemics, and the decrease in the cycles of famine that had previously been a feature of agricultural production patterns. People became more resistant to disease, thanks to the combined effect of improvements in both diet and hygiene. Considerable progress was made in public hygiene as a result of sanitation measures and the modernization of towns. The new industrial technologies that were beginning to be applied reduced the number of harmful risk factors for health in the cities; sewer systems were being laid down and modernized, open sewers eliminated, streets widened, water piped, and urban amenities generally being developed. The overall decline in epidemics, bacterial infections and infectious diseases was made possible by the extraordinary progress in medical science, from the smallpox vaccination of Jenner (1796) to the 'microbe revolution' carried out by Pasteur (1822–1895) and Koch (1843–1910). During the course of the century, disinfection led to aseptic hospitals, and aspirin to anaesthetics. Epidemics claimed fewer victims and became less frequent, though they did not disappear completely, or immediately, as the European cholera epidemic of the 1930s demonstrated.

A comparison with other parts of the world shows more clearly what changes took place in Europe. After 1848 there were no further outbreaks of famine in Europe, although it seriously affected Ireland, where the potato crisis (1845–1850) caused the death of over half a million people and acted as a strong stimulus to migration. In India, famine claimed 30 million victims between 1860 and 1900; in China droughts and floods continued to produce real demographic catastrophes. The same contrasts were seen in sanitation. Cholera, which in India claimed 6 per cent of the population between 1882 and 1890, remained endemic for the whole century, spreading to the Turkish and Russian empires in 1817 and to the whole of Europe between 1831 and 1834, where in France there were 100,000 victims. It reappeared in 1847–1849, with 23,000 deaths in Belgium and 600,000 in Russia, and later in 1855 in the western Mediterranean and the Crimea, before disappearing in the second part of the century, except for an outbreak in Spain.[7] Typhoid fever also decreased during the second half of the century in north-western Europe. Smallpox, plague and leprosy, common in Asia and Africa, decreased all over the European continent: the plague disappeared in the eighteenth century and smallpox declined during the nineteenth. Two great endemic diseases remained – tuberculosis, and malaria in the Mediterranean area – yet they would no longer be the cause of a mortality crisis.[8] Mortality due to war also decreased, in comparison with the high number of deaths caused in other parts of the world, especially in civil wars, like the Civil War in the United States or the Taiping Rebellion in China. Thus, the great losses in population no longer had to be offset by the birth rate.

The nineteenth century marked a fundamental change. Neither the fertility nor the mortality of the European population depended any longer on the availability of food, and there was a positive balance between resources and population. In England in the eighteenth and nineteenth centuries, the increase in population speeded up the modernization of agricultural production methods, which would enable the additional demand for resources to be met. Population increase and technological innovation went hand in hand. The 'agricultural revolution', already under way with more efficient crop rotation, stock farming, manuring and the first agricultural machines, brought about a sharp rise in the productivity of the land, making it possible to produce more with fewer workers. Given the increased productivity, it now became possible to meet the new requirements and at the same time 'free' a certain number of agricultural workers for industrial and commercial activities in the towns. 'The outcome of the process was therefore the opposite of what took place in the *ancien régime*: demographic growth stimulated productive growth and this caused further demographic growth.'[9] The revolution in agriculture and industry made it possible to improve the quantity and quality of food. The revolution in transport and the progressive expansion of markets broke the isolation of many areas, alleviating the effects of any subsistence crises; falls in production could be offset by imports.

As a consequence of improvements in diet, hygiene, health and medical care, life was prolonged and life expectancy at birth increased. The average life span of Western people, which for countless centuries had remained steady at around thirty years, rapidly rose to forty during the course of the nineteenth century and reached fifty in the early twentieth century; in Sweden it would reach seventy by 1965, and eighty at the present day. The increase in average life expectation occurred mainly in the countries and social classes that benefited most from material and scientific progress. The natural mortality rate decreased, especially the infant mortality rate. In England, between 1780 and 1820 the rate fell from 16 per cent to 12 per cent. Infant mortality decreased slowly, because of limited progress in paediatrics and child care. In France, it went down from 187 per thousand in 1810 to 126 per thousand in 1906. In Russia in the same period the rate was still 250 per thousand.

Generally speaking, throughout the nineteenth century there was no marked change in mortality during the first year of life, or in older age groups, but there was a considerable increase in the life expectancy of the young and middle sections of the population. The increased number in the middle section, which included those with reproductive potential, were reflected in the general fertility rate, causing a further increase.[10]

Another important factor concerned the social distribution of mortality. In a comparison of social classes and professional categories, there was a clear disparity as regards death. Life expectancy varied considerably depending on occupation or social status. It was precisely in the cities of the more advanced industrial regions where this phenomenon was most evident. In the mid-nineteenth century, the life expectancy of the English had reached an average of around forty years, but in some of the poor areas of Manchester it remained steady at twenty.[11] At the end of the nineteenth century, infant mortality in the working class areas of York was three times that of affluent families. Around 1885 the mortality rate in the prosperous quarters of Paris was fourteen per thousand, compared with thirty per thousand in working class areas.[12] Malnutrition, poor hygiene in the home or workplace and lack of medical care weakened the physical resistance of the lower classes, especially of the town workers, but also of the agricultural workers, leaving them more vulnerable to the calamities which continued to strike during part of the nineteenth century, though they were less devastating than previously.

In France and England, countries for which we possess statistics covering centuries, mortality decreased rapidly in the first two decades of the nineteenth century, then remained stable for some time, before falling again towards the end of the period. Unlike mortality, in the new European model the birth rate decreased very slowly, before showing an upward trend starting in the 1880s; but it was not very marked or linear. At the start of the demographic change, economic development boosted the birth rate. Results of the historical reconstruction of the English population between the sixteenth and the nineteenth centuries, by the Cambridge Group of Historical Demography, have shown how only a third of the growth in the population of England and Wales in the eighteenth and nineteenth centuries could be explained by a decrease in the death rate. A marked increase in the birth rate seemed to be more significant. The younger age groups, which were more numerous, had the ultimate effect of increasing the number of births, especially in the areas most affected by industrialization. Opportunities for work were increasing, child labour meant that having children became more remunerative, and the greater availability of food was an incentive to marry and procreate. The lower age of marriage has been seen as the stimulus to a marked increase in female fertility. Some scholars have even suggested that there was a decrease in contraceptive measures within the new family and social structures; it did not last long, however. Apart from some quite marked regional variations, it seems that the break with the pre-industrial demographic model did not bring about a substantial change in the European model as regards the age of marriage.[13]

In the medium term, the trend was towards a gradual and overall decline in birth rates. The phenomenon, recorded in France from the early nineteenth century, was soon seen in the United States as well. Towards the end of the century this same tendency affected the whole of western and north-western Europe, ultimately extending to eastern and southern Europe in the course of the twentieth century. In short, the case of Europe shows different demographic mechanisms at work, even in areas adjacent to each other geographically. In the second half of the nineteenth century, the advanced countries witnessed the spread of family planning and birth control – overcoming cultural and religious resistance – which gradually weakened the traditional close correlation between marriage and fertility. The number of children became increasingly related to questions of consumption and social status. The great diversity between social classes, due to socio-economic differences and the influence of mental attitudes to the family and sexual behaviour, needs to be constantly kept in mind. In England in the 1880s, the fertility rate was inversely proportional to social level. In general, the decline in births reflected the desire of families to maintain or improve their standard of living. In nineteenth century bourgeois society, the new social levels were no longer based on birth, but on income and consumption. Fewer children meant a better chance of fulfilling their needs, achieving a better education and a more agreeable and better-paid occupation. Religious convictions could not change a trend that saw the more affluent, and better-educated, classes being the first to practise birth control. Meanwhile, in 1900, birth rates remained high among the lower classes, as well as in the countries on the fringes of the industrial revolution, or that were only partly affected by it. Familiarity with birth control later extended to the lower classes generally; but this did not occur until the First World War, when peasants and workers were given instruction in the use of contraceptives, in this case to prevent the spread of venereal diseases.

In conclusion, despite some religious resistance, the Western demographic model showed that the ratio of economic development to population growth could be gradually improved through non-traumatic birth control methods and the free choice of individuals and families.

Urbanization, migration and colonization

The combination of population explosion and economic transformations brought about a redistribution of the population, on geographical and occupational lines. Industrialization and urbanization proceeded at the same rate. Demographic stagnation in the cities meant that the growing demand for labour from industry could be met only if the rural population became urbanized. At first, the move to the towns was gradual and only temporary; but because of the changes taking place in the country areas with the declining work force, and because of the crisis in the rural cottage industries due to competition from factories, it gradually gathered strength. Weavers, agricultural, domestic, seasonal and migrant workers were all attracted to the towns, and converged on the factories. The railway boosted a mass movement towards the urban conglomerations, which swelled with hundreds of thousands of migrants. The urbanization of wide areas of the continent was the clearest evidence of the transformation taking place in ways of life.

In Great Britain, the proportion of town dwellers to the total population rose from 48 per cent to 73 per cent between 1851 and 1910–1914; in France it went from 25.5 per cent to 44.2 per cent, and in Russia from 7.8 per cent to 19.6 per cent. In 1800, Europe had twenty-three cities with more than 100,000 inhabitants, but a century later there were 135; altogether this was 46 million people, compared with the 5.5 million of a century earlier, that is, 11 per cent of the total population as against 3 per cent previously.

In Renaissance Italy, towns and urban centres had flourished, and many of these still had a considerable number of inhabitants. With the industrial revolution, other European areas similarly flourished, and took on new features. What happened in England after the second half of the eighteenth century was without precedent, particularly with regard to its intensity. In the half-century between the first census of 1801 and the Great Exhibition of 1851 alone, the number of inhabitants in Liverpool multiplied four times, and in Manchester no less than five. But it did not only affect the new industrial towns. The number of inhabitants in Brighton, for example, rose from 7,000 to over 65,000; in Oxford from 12,000 to 27,000, and in a county town like Hereford from 7,000 to 12,000.

As industrialization proceeded, other European countries experienced the same trend. In Germany and Austria in 1800 there were only three cities with more than 100,000 inhabitants: Berlin, Vienna and Hamburg, to which were added Munich and Breslau, fifty years later. The fourteen cities with over 50,000 inhabitants had fewer than 2 million inhabitants altogether. Yet, following rapid industrial growth in the second half of the century, by the beginning of the twentieth there were already seventy-six centres with more than 50,000 inhabitants, containing 13,650,000 people altogether. Berlin and Vienna had over 2 million; Hamburg had 1.1 million inhabitants, and Leipzig, Dresden, Cologne and Munich over half a million. In the small centres of the Ruhr basin, growth was even more spectacular: Essen grew from 9,000 to 295,000 inhabitants; Düsseldorf from 27,000 to 359,000; Dortmund, which in the mid-nineteenth century was still a small village, grew to 214,000 inhabitants in the space of a few decades.[14]

Economies of conurbation, and heavy dependence on local mineral resources, led to the development of urban areas with a high industrial concentration. As Table 6.6 shows, between 1800 and 1910 the number of cities with over half a

Table 6.6 Population of the principal European cities in the nineteenth century (000)[a]

City	*1800*	*1850*	*1880*	*1910*
Hamburg	130	132	290	931
Amsterdam	217	224	326	574
Barcelona	115	175	346	587
Berlin	172	419	1,122	2,071
Birmingham	74	233	437	840
Brussels	66	251	421	720
Budapest	54	178	371	880
Constantinople	600	–	–	1,200
Dresden	60	97	221	548
Glasgow	77	357	587	1,000
Leipzig	30	63	149	590
Liverpool	80	376	553	753
London	1,117	2,685	4,770	7,256
Madrid	160	281	398	600
Manchester	90	303	462	714
Marseilles	111	194	360	551
Milan	135	242	322	579
Munich	40	110	230	596
Moscow	250	365	748	1,533
Naples	327	449	494	723
Paris	587	1,053	2,269	2,888
Rome	163	175	300	542
St. Petersburg	336	485	877	1,962
Warsaw	100	160	339	872
Vienna	247	444	1,104	2,030

Source: B.R. Mitchell, *International Historical Statistics, Europe, 1750–1988*, Basingstoke, 1992, pp. 73–4.

Note:
[a] With at least 500,000 inhabitants in 1910.

million inhabitants rose from three to twenty-five. Driven by industrialization and the revolution in transport, there was a rapid development of both small centres and of important cities, but above all, there was a growth of great metropolises that had long been at the centre of their respective national economies. London grew from 1,117,000 inhabitants in 1800 to 2,685,000 in 1850, from 4,770,00 in 1880 to 7,256,000 in 1910; Paris from 587,000 in 1800 to 1,053,000 in 1850, to 2,269,000 in 1880, and to 2,888,000 in 1910. Industrialization meant new prospects for the management and organization of huge population masses. One needs only to think of the improvements in water supply systems, or gas pipelines for urban lighting. Large cities sprawled into suburban areas; in their centres multi-storey buildings were constructed, with building techniques and materials being adopted in order to optimize the available space.

Thus huge numbers of workers found employment in new production sectors; but they also had to physically move to the cities. The social implications of these astonishing events have been the subject of a great deal of debate among historiographers. During the 1960s there were at least two opposing viewpoints. One Marxist line of interpretation, headed by Eric Hobsbawm, pointed to a worsening standard of living in the transition from the pre-industrial to the industrial period. On the other hand, a neo-liberalist line of thinking, headed by Max Hartwell, emphasized the positive effects on living standards of industrialization and urbanization. There is no doubt that industrialization led to the development of dormitory areas without water, street lighting or sanitation systems, and also imposed extremely harsh working conditions and hours on men, women and children, mostly in promiscuous and unhealthy environments. But, on the other hand, it also brought freedom from hunger and poverty, and new opportunities for social and cultural improvement.

The transition from a rural and agricultural society to an industrial and urban one involved profound changes in the occupational structure of the population. Disregarding the different statistical classifications adopted by each country, and differences between one census and another, a definite evolutionary trend could be distinguished: regression in the primary sector of agriculture, fishing and forestry; expansion in the secondary sector of industry, and also in the tertiary sector of transport, commerce, public and private services, and professional jobs. In some countries the trend was more marked; in Germany, the number of people engaged in the primary sector fell from 42.5 per cent to 28.6 per cent between 1882 and 1907, while those engaged in the secondary sector increased from 35.5 per cent to 42.8 per cent. In other countries it was less so; in France, between 1866 and 1906, those engaged in the primary sector decreased only from 49.8 per cent to 42.7 per cent, while the proportions of those engaged in industry rose only very slightly, from 29.0 per cent to 30.6 per cent.

Despite this, for a good part of the nineteenth century, societies remained largely rural, with the exception of Great Britain. The population of hamlets and villages immediately before the First World War was still more numerous than that of the towns in France, Russia, Italy and even in the United States. However, the relative decline in the rural population did not prevent an absolute increase in countries with a mainly agricultural economy, such as those of eastern Europe.

Various forms of contact with the urban world were regularly kept up by sections of the rural population. Ever since the Middle Ages, relations between town and country had been much closer than is normally thought. They were related to the mobility that affected whole professional categories, or geographical areas, in different ways. One illustration is the Alpine macro-region, where groups of people, or even whole villages, would seasonally move to the plains and the towns, even covering enormous distances, for different reasons. They travelled in order to peddle their trade and crafts, to work on the construction of the railways and other infrastructure, to take on domestic work or other business in the towns, and were continental and temporary migrants. Another reason for emigration was to escape religious persecution, which was often the case; many Russian Jews emigrated for this reason, first to England and France in western Europe, and later to the United States. Important political conflicts might also bring about forced migration, as in the case of the 'deportation' of rebels to Algeria in June 1848, or the settlement after 1871 of German-speaking people in Alsace-Lorraine, which was striving to remain French.

After the mid-nineteenth century, however, because of population pressure and adverse circumstances, rural populations were involved in wide-scale migrations that had unprecedented and far-reaching implications. It did not happen only in Europe. The mid-century marked the start of the greatest migration of people in history.[15] Mass internal movements took place in India and China, after the imperialist powers had created new administrative and commercial centres. There were other migratory flows, from Asia towards the developed areas, as in the case of the Chinese to the Californian coast at the time of the Gold Rush. But the huge territorial redistribution of world population that took place in the nineteenth and twentieth centuries unquestionably involved mainly Europeans. 'In a certain way, the populating and colonizing of the nineteenth century marked the high point of the economic, political, military and cultural strength of the West.'[16] Europeans, who on their own continent inhabited about 700,000 square miles, in the course of the nineteenth century ended up by colonizing and controlling no less than 8 million square miles, multiplying the surface area in use nine times. In previous centuries, the greatest movements of people to destinations outside Europe had been those of English emigrants to the colonies of North America, or the traffic in slaves to the plantations of Central and North America. Africa experienced French immigration in the west Mediterranean area, after the Dutch colonization of its southernmost regions. In their efforts to prevent overcrowding in prisons in the mother country, the British changed the demography of distant Australia.

The general increase in the European population could be absorbed, without trauma, only by the more advanced countries. However, it should not be forgotten that strong imbalances had been created between different areas within the same country. Europe by now was an arrangement of areas of emigration and areas of population absorption. Areas that were not very dynamic economically, such as southern Germany, Ireland, Scotland, Scandinavia and parts of the Habsburg Empire, created emigration to adjacent areas that were very dynamic, such as Alsace, northern France, Saxony and the Rhine valley. Internal migrations within Europe overlapped with increasing wide-scale migration to the temperate and sparsely populated areas of North and South America. Driven by increasing population pressure, and the structural changes and crises that periodically affected economic life, the predominant form of emigration was extra-continental and permanent. Furthermore, the new countries held out a great many attractions. There were the prospects, whether real or promoted by propaganda, of enormous expansion; people were motivated by a taste for adventure, and the hope of making a fortune; there were the aspirations of the middle classes with their spirit of conquest, who saw a world waiting to be improved or exploited.

Between 1821 and 1914 a figure estimated at between 46 million and 51 million people left Europe for other continents. The majority emigrated to the United States, which between 1821 and 1880 received two-thirds of the European emigrants. Besides the United States, Australia and New Zealand, Europeans, especially from northern Italy, emigrated to Canada, Brazil and Argentina. Between 1896 and 1914, 3.5 milion Russians emigrated to Siberia. By the mid-nineteenth century the migration had become considerable (Table 6.7), boosted by the revolution in maritime transport and its greater accessibility.[17] Group voyages were organized under the auspices of the navigation companies, as well as voyages encouraged by governments or even by professional organizations, as in the case of British trade unions, in order to help alleviate the national labour market and guarantee wage levels. The English government actively encouraged emigration by providing almost £5 million sterling for the emigration of 39,000 people to Australia in 1869.

At the beginning of the nineteenth century, the majority of emigrants came from England, while from the 1840s onwards the phenomenon also affected other areas. The famine that struck Ireland in 1847 led to a flow of emigrants from the island and caused the population to decline from over 8 million in 1840 to 4.5 million in 1900. The economic crisis of 1848, and revolutions throughout Europe in the same year, led to particularly heavy emigration from Germany and Scandinavia, and from central and southern Europe. Difficulties in the German economy brought about heavy migration between 1880 and 1885. Greater population pressure in

Table 6.7 Transatlantic emigration from Europe, 1851–1920 (000)

Country	*1851–60*	*1861–70*	*1871–80*	*1881–90*	*1891–1900*	*1901–10*	*1911–20*	*Total*
Austria and Hungary	31	40	46	248	440	1,111	418	2,334
France	27	36	66	119	51	53	32	385
Germany	671	779	626	1,342	527	274	91	4,310
Italy	5	27	168	992	1,580	3,615	2,194	8,581
Norway	36	98	85	187	95	191	62	754
Portugal	45	79	131	185	266	324	402	1,432
Russia	–	–	58	288	481	911	420	2,158
Spain	3	7	13	572	791	1,091	1,306	3,783
Sweden	17	122	103	327	205	324	86	1,184
UK and Ireland	1,313	1,572	1,849	3,259	2,149	3,150	2,587	15,879

Source: W. Woodruff, *Impact of Western Men*, London, 1966.

the poorly developed countries of eastern and Mediterranean Europe led to the emigration of Slav and Latin people, which continued to increase until 1914. Through emigration, Spain lost a third of its natural increase in population. The Habsburg Empire lost about a sixth and Italy more than half. Between 1850 and 1910 about 62 per cent of the over 6 million Italian emigrants came from regions of the south, and 32 per cent from the north. To appreciate the extent of these emigrations, it only needs to be remembered that the number of emigrants between 1870 and 1910 was 12.3 per cent of the population of Spain in 1910, 3.7 per cent of that of Austria and 18.3 per cent of that of Italy.

Movements on such a huge scale had far-reaching effects on the sending countries, as well as on the destinations. Migrations of peasants, farm workers, hired labourers and craftsmen profoundly changed the labour market on both sides. Italian emigration, which exploded at the end of the nineteenth century (Table 6.8) with the agrarian crisis, became a way to alleviate overcrowding in the countryside, especially in the south; it also brought in a flow of new financial resources in the form of remittances from the peasants who had emigrated. These remittances contributed significantly to balancing Italy's account with foreign countries, and the drive towards industrialization, in the nineteenth and twentieth centuries, took place in this context. 'One of the characteristic features of Italian dualism – the extreme poverty of the south – thus became an organic component in the development process that took place between 1896 and 1913.'[18]

Conversely, the economies of the New World gained benefits from the exodus from the Old.[19] The social and economic, as well as demographic, make-up of the

Table 6.8 Average annual expatriations from Italian regions per 1,000 inhabitants, 1881–1910

1881–1890		*1891–1900*		*1901–1910*	
Veneto and Friuli	20.31	Veneto and Friuli	33.85	Abruzzi and Molise	33.70
Basilicata	16.52	Basilicata	18.11	Calabria	31.66
Piedmont e Valle d'Aosta	9.94	Calabria	12.12	Basilicata	29.76
		Abruzzi and Molise	10.69	Veneto and Friuli	29.47
Calabria	7.95	Campania	10.61	Campania	21.63
Abruzzi and Molise	6.52	Piedmont and Valle d'Aosta	7.98	Sicily	21.50
Liguria	6.05			Marches	20.57
Lombardy	5.77	Tuscany	5.86	Piedmont and Valle d'Aosta	16.50
Campania	5.50	Emilia Romagna	5.59		
Tuscany	4.79	Sicily	5.05	Umbria	14.96
Emilia Romagna	3.00	Lombardy	5.03	Emilia Romagna	12.94
Marches	2.00	Marches	4.77	Tuscany	11.90
Sicily	1.66	Liguria	3.78	Lombardy	11.33
Apulia	0.80	Apulia	1.85	Apulia	10.71
Sardinia	0.20	Lazio	1.36	Lazio	9.83
Umbria	0.15	Umbria	1.22	Sardinia	6.88
Lazio	0.02	Sardinia	0.86	Liguria	6.10

Source: J. Heffer and W. Serman. *Il XIX secolo. 1815–1914: dalle rivoluzioni agli imperialismi*, ed. S. Zaninelli, Milan, 1998, p. 31.

American continent came to develop original features.[20] The departure of younger and more enterprising people left demographic gaps in the homeland that would only later be filled. In the recipient countries, the prevalence of a younger, more fertile age group in the population led to an increase in the birth rate, which had already been boosted by the lower age of marriage. A comparison of the 1900 and 1940 age tables for the United States[21] shows that the 1900 table resembles the typical age composition of pre-industrial societies; there is an overwhelming majority of inhabitants under the age of forty. The 1940 population, on the other hand shows a general rebalancing of the age groups, most likely due to the effects of family planning and the population living to a greater age. Between 1861 and 1920, which was immediately before immigration was restricted, over 28 million Europeans emigrated to the United States. They helped decisively in urbanizing and industrializing the country; and at the same time they changed its social and cultural character, founding communities based on ethnic and national groups, such as 'little Italy' and 'little Ireland', that would play an important role in the history of North America. Germans and Scandinavians formed communities in the Mid West, while Italians, Russians, Poles and Austro-Hungarians settled on the north Atlantic coast. These communities gradually melted into the mass. The inflow of Slavs and Mediterranean people, Catholics, Orthodox Greeks and Russians, and Jews at the end of the century, caused concern to the supporters of a White Anglo-Saxon and Protestant (WASP) America; measures taken against Chinese immigration in 1882, and in 1907 against the Japanese, prefigured the 1921 and 1924 quota laws against eastern and southern Europeans.

For tens of millions of European peasants the difficult and painful decision to emigrate meant contact with other cultures, and learning about other systems of values and behaviour, and adopting new codes of life and work. The 'melting pot' proved to be one of the keys in the development of the United States. The concentration of large numbers of immigrants in sectors with specialized activities led to forms of 'ethnic enterprise'; a typical case is Italian enterprise, which in its development and interaction with economic expansion in the mother country in the second half of the twentieth century would gradually build up the Italian business community throughout the world. In short, the most important and dramatic demographic events in the history of the European population became a fundamental component of modernization.

Changes in the agricultural sector

The progressive cutback of employment in the agricultural sector is one of the most conspicuous aspects of the economic development of Europe. Although the economies of different countries have been affected at different rates and to different degrees by the cutback, agriculture has continued to play a fundamental role in the process of modern economic growth. The changes in the agricultural sector that preceded and accompanied the advent of industrial societies made it possible for an increasingly urbanized population to be fed; it also provided capital and labour for other sectors of the economy, and created export flows and market demand for industrial products and services. All this was possible thanks to increased agricultural production, productivity of labour and productivity of the agents of production.[22]

Contrary to Malthusian forecasts, the increase in European agricultural production in the relatively long term enabled the population of the continent to grow without its living standards becoming significantly lowered, and without imports of food products from countries outside Europe being significantly increased. Estimates of that increase, however, are still uncertain; until the mid-nineteenth century they fluctuated widely. More abundant data are available for the second half of the nineteenth century, though they are not always reliable. Table 6.9 gives the growth rates of agricultural production for the four most important countries of western Europe compared with those for the United States and Japan.

Regardless of the fact that they are clearly lower than for the economy as a whole, it will be seen that the growth rates are always positive, except for Great Britain in the period 1870–1912, and are definitely higher in the United States. The table also shows a steady decline in growth rates in all the countries. A correct assessment of these figures needs to take into account that the growth of demand for agricultural products is structurally lower than that for manufactured products and services. Since the end of the nineteenth century the demand for industrial raw materials, such as wool and cotton, had grown less than relative consumption, because of the use of synthetic substitutes. The consumption of foodstuffs was affected by the slowing down of population growth, since the *per capita* increase in consumption is subject to natural limits. Ever since the initial phases of economic growth, changes in food consumption had been taking place; for example, there was a transition from a diet based on cereals and vegetables to one based on meat and animal products.[23]

Since the decline in demand made it superfluous to greatly increase overall production, it seems more appropriate to assess the performance of agriculture in relation to the growth rate of labour productivity or, preferably, of all the factors. Once again calculations are affected by the limited availability and reliability of data, especially up to the mid-nineteenth century. In any case, the productivity of labour apparently grew almost as much as overall production.[24] Agricultural production increased considerably; growth was both extensive[25] and intensive.[26]

Table 6.9 Growth rates of agricultural production, 1800–1912

Periods	*Great Britain*	*France*	*Germany*	*Italy*	*United States*	*Japan*
1800–1850					3.00	
1816–1850		1.42				
1850–1870		0.78	1.50		2.84	
1856–1870	0.59					
1870–1912	–0.13	0.49	1.49	0.84	2.34	
1886–1912						1.38

Source: P.A. Toninelli (ed.), *Lo sviluppo economico moderno dalla rivoluzione industriale alla crisi energetica, 1750–1973*, Venice, 1997, p. 624.

Note: Moving three-yearly averages (excepting the United States in 1850–1870).

Extensive growth, with land, labour and capital growing simultaneously, came about where land was available at a low or negligible cost. In the nineteenth century, in the countries where land had been exploited for a long time, the cultivated areas were not very extensive. But in countries on the margins of continental Europe, such as northern Scandinavia, the Hungarian plains, Prussia east of the Elbe, and Russia, where the cultivated surface area doubled between 1860 and 1880, they were more extensive. However, in the immense spaces of American virgin land, in Canada, Brazil, Uruguay and Argentina, Australia and New Zealand, and even Siberia, they were particularly extensive; in the United States the cultivated land area tripled between 1850 and 1910. The revolution in maritime and land transport brought these land areas into the circuit of international exchanges. They could benefit from low production costs, because of the low relative land value and extensive cultivation; in the overall context of the international division of labour they could take on the role of providing food products and raw materials for the urban and industrial regions. Reduced transport costs boosted the flow of European emigrants to these regions.

On the other hand, in a great many European countries, a significant increase in agricultural land area was possible only with complex land reclamation schemes; Italy distinguished itself in this field, not to mention the immense operations carried out by the Dutch to reclaim land from the sea. However, the difficult and onerous reclamation of land for agriculture was offset by the loss of land to urbanization. Reclamation of land was an example of extensive growth in Europe; it differed from the extensive growth in the American or Australian areas, since it was based on an increase in the quantity of capital and/or labour per unit of land. Productivity was also increased through projects for the irrigation of arid land and the alkalization of acid land.

The increase in overall productivity of the factors was the result of innovations that were both land-saving and labour-saving; the former were aimed at increasing yields from the land, while the latter aimed at increasing labour productivity. Since land was the scarcest factor, the first innovations were in land saving. During the English agrarian revolution of the eighteenth century, the continuous rotation system was perfected, and became more widespread; it became known as 'high farming', and had been carried out in the Po valley since the late Middle Ages, and in Holland in the modern era. During the agrarian revolution, new fodder plants were introduced so that the practice could be extended to all types of land.[27] Continuous rotation increased the cultivated surface area by a third, or even half, thanks to the elimination of the period of fallow, when the land was left to rest in order to restore its fertility. Fallow land areas were planted with nitrogen-fixing leguminous vegetables, which were subsequently used as cattle feed. The increased numbers of cattle also increased the quantity of fertilizing manure.

Further changes took place in the varieties of plants that were cultivated and the breeds of livestock that were raised. Species were introduced that were more suited to the different types of weather and soil conditions. Among the species already introduced, maize was increasingly used to feed livestock; the potato, which supplied two or even three times more calories per unit of land than wheat, became the staple diet of the population of north-western Europe. Over the nineteenth century, the quality of cultivated crops steadily improved. Beet was cultivated more extensively; it was used for producing sugar and feeding to livestock, and like the leguminous plants, aerated and replenished the soil, making it possible at the same time to feed greater numbers of stabled animals. There were increased yields per unit of product; this objective was also achieved by selecting varieties that were less susceptible to parasites, and/or were more suitable for specific environmental conditions. In order to restock the vineyards which were destroyed by phylloxera between 1870 and 1880, grafts from American plants were used. There were also significant changes in stockbreeding, and dairy cows and beef cattle were being raised in order to adapt to new demands. Another great land-saving innovation was the introduction of chemical products for use as fertilizers and insecticides. Fertilizers of animal origin, such as manure, and Peruvian guano, and of artificial origin, such as phosphates, Chilean nitrates, potassium salts and superphosphates, were used in combination with fertilizers of vegetable origin. The production of perphosphates started around the middle of the nineteenth century. The massive use of fertilizers, and increased mixed cultivation, led to the fallow land being rapidly eliminated and the land being cultivated continuously, with increasingly complex rotations.

The labour-saving innovations mainly consisted in perfecting equipment such as sickles, ploughs and harrows made of iron; this continued throughout the nineteenth century, and contributed considerably to an increase in productivity. At the end of the eighteenth century and in the first decades of the nineteenth, machines started to replace human labour; these included wheat threshers, cotton pickers, and wheat harvesters, and the end of the nineteenth century saw the appearance of the combine harvester. In some situations, there were serious technical problems to overcome before machines could be used; such was the case with the milking machine, which was introduced only in 1895. The increase in the size of farms led to greater mechanization; farms were now increasing in size as a result of a policy being carried out to reduce excessive parcelling of the land. In numerous areas of the continent, it also came about as a response to labour strikes. The invention of the tractor, the first of which were built in the 1890s, meant that the mechanization of farming could be speeded up and extended.

Technical progress increased yields and productivity per worker. On the plains of Hungary, for example, the number of days required for harvesting and threshing wheat was reduced from 130 working days in 1872 to only thirty-three in 1914. In 1914 a 'map' showing the modernization of European farming could be superimposed on to one showing the geographical distribution of yields. In north-western Europe, yields of wheat per hectare ranged from 33 cwt in Denmark to 21 cwt in Germany and Great Britain; this differed greatly from southern Europe, where the figures were 13.2 cwt for France, 10.5 cwt for Italy and 12.6 cwt for the Danube area of Hungary.

The spread of progress in farming depended on the willingness, and possibility, of farmers or landowners to adopt new techniques. Where farm labour was scarce, and therefore costly, there was an incentive for farmers to cultivate the land by increasing the working capital; but where rural population pressure was strong and farm wages were low, farmers had far less interest in increasing their capital. Moreover, appropriate investment skills were needed, a consideration which was related to the technical and organizational environment in which the landowner lived; modernization took place more rapidly where the class of large landowners was open to technical progress. It did not matter whether they exploited the land directly, as in the Prussia of the Junkers, or divided their property into large farms and entrusted the management to tenants with sufficient capital, as in the case of English landlords.

In contrast, the small peasant properties were where innovations were adopted more slowly; neither the resources for investment nor adequate technical training were available. There was a tendency to freeze savings unproductively in the purchase of very costly land, rather than invest it in modernizing equipment; this was the case in numerous regions of France, in the south-west, the east, and in Brittany. The medium-size farm was a more favourable environment for technical change; this was especially the case if it was well integrated in a network of co-operatives for buying and selling, or if it benefited from state aid in the field of agricultural training, as in Denmark or Holland.[28] Co-operatives made it possible to overcome the disadvantages of small farms. The development of the co-operative movement is considered the decisive element in the great success of Danish agriculture, which reached maximum levels of land and labour productivity.

Adopting innovations was, however, a complex process and conditioned by environmental considerations. In Mediterranean regions high farming was not possible, since fodder plants could not withstand the long summer droughts.[29] Soil characteristics determined the different types of equipment and machinery. Research and agricultural experimentation had low 'appropriability',[30] and state intervention was required, the first public experimental station being created in Germany in 1852. The system was later imitated in many countries, so much so that if state commitment had been different it 'would have affected the capacity for developing techniques suited for each specific environment, and thus in the final analysis the rate of technical progress'.[31] The state created research institutions and specialized organizations; in Italy, for example, it promoted agrarian meetings, and formed a network of travelling schools of agriculture, which saw their greatest expansion under the Giolitti government.

Journals on agronomy experienced a real boom throughout the nineteenth century, and played an important role in promoting innovations; this was especially the case in areas where the majority of people were able to read, and income was sufficiently high to allow the purchase of a journal.[32] Innovations often spread by being imitated, or through the direct exchange of information; it was therefore a slow process. There was also the subjective perception of risk and its acceptance; this depended on factors such as information about the new techniques, or the availability of credit.[33] It was one thing to face it by relying only on the resources of an individual farm, as in Italy; it was quite another to face it with the technical and financial support of a co-operative, as in Denmark.

The greatest agricultural development was in north-western Europe, in England and in the area between the Paris basin and east Prussia, where both types of improvement complemented each other. In any case, the extension of farmland, technical progress and intensification of cultivation considerably increased overall agricultural production. Its growth rate was higher than that of the population;

the revolution in transport made it possible to avoid subsistence crises and improve the diet of the masses in industrialized countries. It also led to changes in the agricultural geography of the world and the system of prices.

Because of the effects of weather conditions on farming production, agricultural prices fluctuated more markedly than prices for industrial products; moreover, producers were too numerous to have any control over the market. Despite this, even agricultural prices, like industrial prices, showed long-term trends; between 1815 and 1845 prices fell, and were at the centre of measures such as the Corn Laws and quasi-prohibitionist systems. During this period of depression, the well drained limestone areas adapted better to the complex practice of mixed or high farming with corn, barley, rape and livestock, while in the heavy clay areas investment was needed to improve the land, which reduced the farmer's net revenue.[34]

From the 1840s to the end of the 1860s, agriculture benefited from a number of positive circumstances. The price of corn rose; there was little competition from the new countries, or from Russia, since the transport revolution still had only limited effects; internal demand, especially for animal products, increased, and prices remained high until 1883. In addition, in the system of mixed farming greater prominence was given to stock farming, which was more profitable; it developed as an activity in its own right, and was no longer merely a supplement to cereal farming. Transformations in land use intensified, with the canalization and drainage of wetland; but the agricultural system still hinged on wheat farming, for technical as well as psychological reasons. Farming traditions, insufficient knowledge and unwise investment worsened the impact of the 'great depression' of 1877–1896 on European agriculture; the effects of the transport revolution were now being felt, with competition from the animal and vegetable produce arriving from the virgin lands. The agricultural crisis of the last quarter of the nineteenth century was, above all, a cereals crisis, and of wheat in particular. The immediate response was to implement protectionist policies, and a series of tariffs were imposed in Germany, France, Italy, Austria-Hungary and Spain during the 1880s; England did not follow suit and remained committed to free trade, but considerably reduced the area devoted to cereals. The west and north of England, which had long since turned to stock farming, were not affected by the crisis, which hit arable farming particularly badly. The development of stock farming in various European countries was one of the more positive consequences of the great agricultural crisis (Table 6.10).

Table 6.10 Composition of agricultural production around 1910 (%)

Produce	*Britain*	*France*	*Germany*	*Italy*	*Spain*
Cereals	11.0	22.2	18.6	20.9	31.4
Seed produce	10.3	9.0	13.1	14.3	18.5
Tree produce	5.7	24.4	2.7	36.0	19.8
Animal produce	73.0	44.1	65.6	28.8	30.3
Total	100.0	100.0	100.0	100.0	100.0

Source: adapted from: P.K. O'Brien and L. Prados de la Escosura, 'Agriculture and European Industrializaton, 1890–1980', *Economic History Review*, 44, 1992, pp. 514–36.

The responses and effects differed widely, in view of the variety of agricultural systems, which in themselves reflected the great variety of terrain and climate.

Notes

1 The lack of systematic surveys for a part, or the whole, of the period for many countries explains the discrepancies in the tables drawn up by different authors.
2 With an annual growth rate of 1.5 per cent a population doubles in fifty years and increases four times in a century.
3 M.W. Flinn, *Il sistema demografico europeo*, Bologna, 1983.
4 J. Hajnal, *Modelli europei di matrimonio in prospettiva*, in M. Barbagli (ed.), *Famiglia e mutamento sociale*, Bologna, 1977, pp. 267 and 274.
5 P. Macry, *La società contemporanea*, Bologna, 1992, pp. 99–105.
6 'Il regime a fecondità media e ad alta mortalità, che aveva caratterizzato lo sviluppo demografico dell'Europa preindustriale – una variante di quello ad alta fecondità e alta mortalità che guiderà l'evoluzione dell'intera popolazione mondiale fino agli anni Quaranta del Novecento – fu dunque sostituito da un regime caratterizzato dalla drastica riduzione di entrambi i parametri. Sul breve periodo si produsse comunque una crescita impetuosa, dovuta al calo della mortalità più che all'aumento della fecondità. In una seconda fase. la fertilità declinò in misura vistosa e il successivo aumento della popolazione non dipese dal maggior numero di nascite, ma essenzialmente dal crescente allungamento della vita'. L. Allegra, 'La dinamica demografica', in P.A. Toninelli (ed.), *Lo sviluppo economico moderno dalla rivoluzione industriale alla crisi energetica, 1750–1973*, Venice, 1997, p. 87.
7 J. Heffer and W. Serman, *Il XIX secolo, 1815–1914. Dalle rivoluzioni agli imperialismi*, Milan, 1998, p. 22.
8 M.W. Flinn, *Il sistema demografico europeo*, p. 143.
9 'L'esito del processo è dunque l'opposto di quanto si verifica in Antico Regime: la crescita demografica stimola la crescita produttiva e questa provoca ulteriore crescita demografica.' P. Macry, *La società contemporanea*, p. 100.
10 E.A. Wrigley, *Demografia e storia*, Milan, 1969.
11 A. Briggs, *L'Inghilterra vittoriana*, Rome, 1978, p. 391.
12 J. Heffer and W. Serman, *Il XIX secolo*, p. 21.
13 L. Allegra, *La dinamica demografica*, p. 85.
14 M. Reinhard, A. Armengaud and J. Dupaquier, *Storia della populazione mondiale*, Rome and Bari, 1971.
15 E.J. Hobsbawm, *Il trionfo della borghesia, 1848–1875*, Rome and Bari, 1976, p. 237.
16 'Popolamenti e colonizzazioni ottocentesche segnarono, in qualche modo, il punto più alto della forza economica, politico-militare e culturale dell'Occidente.' P. Macry, *La società contemporanea*, p. 106.
17 S. Collison, *Le migrazioni internazionali e l'Europa. Un profilo storico comparato*, Bologna, 1994.
18 'Uno dei tratti caratteristici del dualismo italiano – la estrema povertà del Mezzogiorno – entrò così come componente organico nella struttura del processo di sviluppo che si manifestò tra il 1896 e il 1913.' L. Cafagna, *Dualismo e sviluppo*, Venice, 1989, p. 322.
19 E.J. Hobsbawm, *Il trionfo della borghesia*, p. 245.
20 L. Allegra, *La dinamica demografica*, p. 99.
21 M. Reinhard, A. Armengaud and J. Dupaquier, *Storia della popolazione mondiale*, p. 780.
22 Cf. G. Federico, 'Agricoltura e crescita moderna', in P.A. Toninelli (ed.), *Lo sviluppo economico moderno*, pp. 380–1. The productivity of a factor is given by the ratio between total production and the quantity of the factor. Overall productivity is the average productivity of each factor in relation to its share in the overall product.
23 *Ibid.*, pp. 390–1.
24 For further specifications, *ibid.*, pp. 392–3
25 Because of the increased number of the factors of land, labour and capital.

26 Because of increased productivity of the factors
27 *Ibid.*, p. 396.
28 J. Heffer and W. Serman, *Il XIX secolo*, p. 101.
29 F. Galassi, 'Stasi e sviluppo nell'agricoltura Toscana. Primi risultati di uno studio aziendale', *Rivista di storia economica*, 3, 1986, pp. 304–57.
30 The possibility of the inventor enjoying the fruits of his own invention. G. Federico, *Agricoltura e crescita economica*, p. 399.
31 'avrebbe influenzato la capacità di sviluppare tecniche adatte a ciascun ambiente specifico, e quindi in ultima analisi il ritmo del progresso tecnico'. *Ibid.*, p. 400.
32 This was the case of England. Cf. D. Grigg, *La dinamica del mutamento in agricoltura*, Bologna, 1994.
33 G. Federico, *Agricoltura e crescita economica*, p. 400.
34 J. Heffer and W. Serman, *Il XIX secolo*, p. 105.

7 The economic development of Europe in the nineteenth century (III)

The process of industrialization

Giovanni Luigi Fontana

Great Britain and continental Europe

Between the mid-eighteenth century and the first decades of the nineteenth century, the industrial revolution marked the opening of a new era in the history of mankind. It was the outcome of a number of innovations that were made simultaneously in agriculture, trade, transport and especially industry, and its cumulative effect was felt in Britain before anywhere else.[1] The critical factor of discontinuity was the rapid growth in production capacity due to the use of greatly improved techniques, as well as the exploitation of new sources of energy. The quantity of goods and services available to Europeans grew at hitherto unthinkable rates. Before the industrial revolution, the very slow increase in productivity had conditioned population growth. With industrialization, goods multiplied faster than men, standards of living constantly improved, and economic life experienced continual transformations and accelerations that continue to this day.

Between 1820 and 1980, the gross product of the now industrialized countries grew sixty times; population grew four times, *per capita* product thirteen times, and work productivity at least twenty times.[2] Since the second half of the nineteenth century, industrialization has established itself as a necessary condition for growth, and industrialization and development have ultimately become identified with each other. But this applies only to a limited area of the globe. Wealth has grown in the countries involved in the industrial revolution, but for the majority of the earth's inhabitants there have been no great changes. Income gaps have widened in a way that had not been experienced in previous centuries; in the past, the differences in living standards between distant countries were largely limited.

But nobody can doubt that the industrial revolution was 'the most extraordinary adventure that humanity has known in the course of its history'.[3] Historiographers are still debating the sequence of changes and the way they took place; between the end of the eighteenth century and the first half of the nineteenth, a number of west European countries were totally transformed, and a society arose that was increasingly dominated by progress in industry, science and technology. As a result of this revolution the population of Europe doubled in 150 years. Europe became a highly energy-intensive world; it increased industrial production to unforeseen levels, greatly increased exchanges between the countries of the continent and beyond it, introduced new ways of organizing production, and radically changed the living conditions of entire populations.

The different factors that determined these epoch-making transformations and their relative influence are the subject of a huge mass of literature and endless debate; they start with the experience of Britain, the country that was the driving force behind the breakthrough and subsequent dominance of industry, and with the dynamics of industrialization in other advanced economies. Our concern here is with European economies with all their complexities and different experiences. It has already been underlined how many different paths to industrialization there have been,[4] whether because of the impact of preceding developments, or because of profound changes in the overall framework, as a consequence of British industrialization. For this reason, it is argued that the term 'industrial revolution' should be used only when referring to the British experience, while the term 'industrialization' is preferable for the other regions of Europe and the world.

The exceptional combination of changes first took place in Britain, as we have said; it was also on a much greater scale than anywhere else, and as Phyllis Deane has written, the first industrial revolution was at the same time a revolution in demography, agriculture, trade and transport.[5] This growth is summarized in Table 7.1.

Many scholars have attempted to understand what the decisive element was. According to E.A. Wrigley, at the centre of this long succession of developments that ended in industrialization was the use of energy from coal; he pointed out how the growth of important sectors of the British economy depended on the use of cheap energy on a vast scale.[6] If it had not found a fruitful context for maximizing its profitability, this 'unexpected miracle', in the form of abundant coal that could be exploited, might make the industrial revolution appear to be a 'gift of destiny'. The context was one where there was an opportunity to 'make profits, by selling more at lower prices, which provided a strong incentive to seek increasingly powerful sources of energy, and increasingly automated machines, in order to increase the flow of available products and to contain costs'.[7] In their turn the markets had grown, for Europe, and for Great Britain in particular, because of all these developments.[8] The process was thus a self-sustaining one.

The importance of the overall framework is reflected in the fact that the industrial revolution did not affect Britain alone: it very soon extended to many other regions of the continent, where earlier long-term developments had prepared the terrain. Pollard described industrialization as a 'rash of red spots' crossing frontiers,

Table 7.1 Estimates of the growth of English industrial production, 1700–1830 (%)

	1700–1760	*1760–1780*	*1780–1801*	*1801–1830*
Deane and Cole (1962)	1.0	0.5	3.4	4.4
Jackson (1992)	–	1.3	2.1	2.9
Crafts (1992)	0.7	1.3	2.0	2.8
Cuenca Esteban (1994)	0.7	1.7	2.8	3.2

Source: C. Bardini, in P. Hudson, *La rivoluzione industriale*, Bologna, 1995, table 1, p. 22.

avoiding vast areas of the same country, changing from pale pink to bright pink, and so on until it became bright red.[9] Favourable conditions therefore also existed in other areas of Europe. The industrial revolution was:

> the offspring of a long series of changes that had been taking place in the European economy and society since the middle centuries of the Middle Ages. There had been slow progress in agriculture, more rapid changes in industry, extension of commercial relations within the continent and beyond, and greater attention to the problem of technical solutions in economic activities.[10]

If the start of industrialization 'was only the phase during which a number of slow quantitative transformations caused a real qualitative leap forward',[11] then its continuation was a single process, and 'the plants had common roots and were subject to the same climate'.[12] Thus we should talk about a European industrial revolution (see Table 7.2); however, for different reasons this process is normally described country by country, with 'each country as a plant in a separate pot, growing independently until it becomes a society that can be defined as industrialized, obeying a genetic code fully contained within its seed'. In actual fact, despite the importance of organizational and governmental factors, it had little regard for political boundaries. Concentration of industry and commerce had already transformed the economy and society of a number of areas to a certain degree, long before its effects radiated over the country as a whole. The development and chronology of the industrial revolution in each area were influenced by whether the area had already been more advanced, or were carried along during the general development.[13]

Table 7.2 Four indicators of European economic development, 1800–1913

Year	*Production of iron and cast iron (million tons)*	*Consumption of cotton (million tons)*	*Production of coal (million tons)*	*Railway network (km)*
1800	(0.6)	(0.04)	(12.9)	–
1830	1.5	0.17	29.3	175
1840	2.6	0.31	45.1	2,925
1850	3.9	0.47	67.2	23,500
1860	6.5	0.73	114.6	51,850
1870	10.5	0.86	180.2	104,900
1880	13.9	1.14	216.7	169,100
1890	17.5	1.56	328.3	225,200
1900	25.5	1.99	437.8	292,200
1910	36.9	2.49	573.9	351,000
1913	45.9	2.79	646.8	362,200

Source: P. Bairoch, *Commerce extérieur et développement économique de l'Europe au XIX siècle*, Paris and The Hague, 1976, p. 129.

The age of machines, coal and steam

Convergence and accumulation: textiles

Between 1730 and 1830, the technology associated with the exploitation of new sources of energy became the key factor in the exceptional changes in Europe. However, many important innovations had already been made earlier in the traditional industries of continental Europe. Among these were the production of porcelain in the ceramics industry, chlorine bleaching and Nicholas Leblanc's soda manufacturing process in the sector of chemicals. The Italian silk industry created the first automated spinning machines powered by water mills, and the organization of centralized labour was first attempted at the Bologna silk mill.[14] Initially, it was often the British who successfully imitated technologies that had been introduced in other countries, while the new technologies that marked the British industrial revolution were introduced into other parts of Europe, and later into the United States.

After the mid-eighteenth century, the technological superiority of Europe was consolidated. The oriental empires from the Bosphorus to Japan were beginning to isolate themselves from the rest of the world, and experienced a marked decline in their technological capacities; other parts of the world, like India, were already under Western influence. In some sectors enormous changes took place in production techniques, but benefits in terms of *per capita* income growth came about only when technical progress spread to all sectors. Many of these changes had their roots in the past, but what really changed from now on was the continuity and speed of growth. However, what marked the industrial revolution in Britain was not so much the rapidity of the changes as their duration. Factory production did not replace the cottage industry system, which for centuries had been the basis of the British manufacturing system. Machines like the 'spinning jennies' or looms were used in the home and provided traditional occupations with technological support. A close investigation of English censuses until at least the mid nineteenth century gives clear evidence of a state of 'proto-industrialization' and production based on small enterprises and workshops. The development of Britain should not, therefore, be considered an exceptional case, but one out of the many possible cases that taken together could be called the modernization of European economies.

Machines played a key role, and brought about a considerable increase in productivity, namely the amount produced per worker per unit of time. They were constantly being improved and their use created an avalanche effect. Improvements made to a highly productive machine in a particular sector might cause a bottleneck in production in another sector above or below; the problem would engage engineers, technicians or simple artisans, and this convergence of effort generally ended with a practical solution being discovered, which often created fresh problems in its turn. In this way, progress could be virtually unlimited. This explains why innovations appeared, or were adopted, only at certain moments in an age when scientific and technical knowledge could, in theory, have enabled them to be made earlier.

Technological innovation was thus the result of the convergent and cumulative effort of several innovators,[15] who, during this phase, were mostly skilled artisans endowed with a good knowledge of mechanics. The textile sector was a good example of this process; another was the case of energy sources. Technological innovation reached a critical point with the mechanization of spinning; the first patent for spools to replace human fingers was held by Paul Lewis (1738), but Richard Arkwright was thought to be the inventor of the mechanical spinning machine (water frame) thirty years later (1769), and who actually made it work with the use of two pairs of spools. His machine was accompanied by a further innovation, which was the 'spinning jenny', patented by James Hargreaves in 1766. The next innovation was the 'mule', a spinning machine patented by Samuel Crompton in 1779; this combined the best features of the previous spinning machines, namely the carriage of the jenny and the spools of the water-powered spinning machine. In the mid-1780s, the steam engine was added to the mule, and further increased its productivity. Whereas previously it had taken 5,000 hours of human labour to spin 100 lb of cotton, now it took only 300. The machines were very costly, however, and many entrepreneurs simply could not afford them. Spinning did not really become mechanized until 1815.

In textile weaving the hand loom of the cottage industry remained in use for a long time. Cartwright's loom, which was improved in 1785, spread only after 1815, when the developments in spinning required that weaving be mechanized as well. There was a series of technical improvements throughout the whole century; the self-acting mule of 1830 automated spinning completely, while the mechanical loom considerably increased production. Cotton owed its spectacular success (Table 7.3) to a number of factors: it was easy to dye and wash, flexible supplies of the raw material were available, and the fibre adapted well to the mechanization processes. Wool was more delicate to work than cotton, and once the raw material had been carded and combed the mechanization process was slower. In England, the mule became established in the woollen industry only in the 1830s, and the mechanical loom after 1840; on the continent, they were introduced into wool industries almost at the same time.

Table 7.3 Average annual consumption of raw cotton in the nineteenth century (000 tons)

Period	*Great Britain*	*France*	*Germany*	*Italy*	*Belgium*	*Switzerland*	*United States*
1803–1812	25.7	8.0	–	–	–	–	–
1815–1824	46.0	19.0	–	–	–	–	–
1835–1839	165.8	43.6	8.9	–	5.9	–	–
1850–1854	320.0	67.2	26.0	–	10.8	–	–
1860–1864	327.0	70.8	51.2	–	9.4	–	111.4
1866–1875	498.8	85.4	92.4	17.5	18.5	31.2	205.5
1880–1889	662.0	108.1	166.2	75.5	22.3	24.7	422.7
1900–1909	790.8	205.4	380.4	167.8	48.7	26.0	950.4

Source: P.A. Toninelli (ed.), *Lo sviluppo economico moderno dalla rivoluzione industriale alla crisi energetica, 1750–1973*, Venice, 1997, p. 629.

Coal

The 'Age of Change' was marked by the transition to another energy paradigm.[16] There was a transition from the 'civilization of wood' to the 'coal paradigm'. One of the underlying reasons for European power had been the widespread distribution of forest areas.[17] At the time of the French Revolution about 200 million tons of wood were consumed each year in Europe. Industrial activities, such as the production of bricks, glass and steel, used heat energy sources and devoured forests on a huge scale. An average foundry, working in alternate years, consumed the equivalent of 2,000 ha of forest. At the end of the eighteenth century, in some industrial regions of France, there were extremely high levels of deforestation; they had serious repercussions on the water regimes and geological structures, and also caused heavy increases in the cost of fuel.[18]

In Britain, as far back as the seventeenth century, the high cost of wood, the increase in population, and the fact that coal happened to be available, led to coal being gradually adopted in manufacturing processes that required energy from heat; it was adopted in glass factories, breweries, furnaces, salt refineries and laundries, but not in the iron industry. During the eighteenth century, the proximity of coal deposits to the sea, the navigable waterways and the network of canals, which were extended in order to transport coal, combined to make its distribution relatively straightforward.[19] By 1700, the coal extracted amounted to 3 million tons, compared with 600,000 tons in the rest of the world. By 1800, these figures had increased fourfold, and the energy from British coal was equivalent to the energy obtained each year from 6 million ha of forest.[20]

The growth in demand made it necessary to obtain coal from increasingly deep seams, from which water had to be pumped. In 1698, Thomas Savery patented a device, known as the 'miner's friend', for removing water from the mines. In 1705, the artisan Thomas Newcomen conceived a steam machine that used atmospheric pressure to create a vacuum in a cylinder that was alternately heated and cooled, and was initially used to pump water from the mines in Cornwall and northern England. It was a great commercial success, and in the space of only a few years had spread to France, Germany, Belgium and Italy and later to Sweden and the United States. Shortly afterwards, in 1709 Abraham Darby, who owned an ironworks, managed to produce good quality cast iron; he used coal heated at a high temperature in the absence of air, and thus liberated most of the impurities in gaseous form to leave a light porous product, known as coke. The use of carbon coke, and other refinements, in ironworking made it possible to produce cast iron, and later steel, by means of the puddling process; thus there was no longer any need to depend on increasingly scarce supplies of charcoal. At the same time a more reliable and durable product could be produced.

These two innovations were to be decisive for the role of coal in economic development.

> They triggered off a unique 'virtuous cycle' between expansion in coal consumption, the development of machinery, the take-off of the iron industry, mechanization of transport and the further spread and diversification of the

demand for coal, which thanks to continual innovations, would drive the economic system forwards relentlessly and only run down towards the end of the nineteenth century.[21]

Although much of the textile industry continued to use water power, coal was what sustained development, and facilitated the industrialization of the regions that had an abundance of mines. In 1913, 88.5 per cent of the energy consumed worldwide was still supplied by coal.

Improvements made to the original innovations gave them a new lease of life. James Watt, the University of Glasgow laboratory technician, universally known as the father of the steam engine, enormously improved the energy efficiency of Newcomen's machine between 1769 and 1775. He separated the condenser from the cylinder-piston block, so that this could be kept constantly heated; the steam passed from the cylinder to the condenser, and created the vacuum that generated the movement. In the 1880s, Watt, together with Matthew Boulton, continued to make further innovations that guaranteed the success of the steam engine, 2,500 units of which were being built by the end of the eighteenth century. Watt's steam engine was adopted in mines, iron foundries and cotton mills, and came to symbolize the technologies of the British industrial revolution (Table 7.4).

The steam engine exemplifies how the basic innovations of the early industrial revolution grew out of a combination of creative genius, often of artisans, and the need to reduce costs; they were 'the fruit of rationality and technical ability at the same time'.[22] Sometimes they worked on physical principles that had still not even been formulated. Their success also depended on complementary innovations being available. Watt's engine could take advantage of Wilkinson's drilling machines, which made it possible to create cylinders of greater accuracy and durability; problems of safety could be resolved, thanks to Richard Trevithick, who in 1802 succeeded in making the engine work at a pressure of ten atmospheres. This in turn

Table 7.4 Overall power of steam engines, 1840–1896 (000 h.p.)

Country	*1840*	*1850*	*1860*	*1870*	*1880*	*1888*	*1896*
Great Britain	620	1,290	2,450	4,040	7,600	9,200	13,700
Germany	40	260	850	2,480	5,120	6,200	8,080
France	90	370	1,120	1,850	3,070	4,520	5,920
Austria	20	100	330	800	1,560	2,150	2,520
Belgium	40	70	160	350	610	810	1,180
Russia	20	70	200	920	1,740	2,240	3,100
Italy	10	40	50	330	500	830	1,520
Spain	10	20	100	210	470	740	1,180
Sweden	–	–	20	100	220	300	510
Holland	–	10	30	130	250	340	600
Europe	860	2,240	5,540	11,570	22,000	28,630	40,300
United States	760	1,680	3,470	5,590	9,110	14,400	18,060
World	1,650	3,980	9,380	18,460	34,150	50,150	66,100

Source: D. Landes, *Prometeo liberato*, Turin, 1978, p. 288, and W. Minchinton, 'Patterns of demand, 1750–1914', in C.M. Cipolla (ed.), *The Fontana Economic History of Europe*, Glasgow, 1973, p. 165.

made it possible to increase the power of engines, reduce their size and fuel consumption and mount them on ships and carriages. We will see further on how the mechanization of transport opened up a new phase in civilization; but it also initiated a new chapter in the history of the spread of energy. Steamboats and railways transported coal to areas where sufficient quantities of it were not available; thus in the nineteenth century, for the first time, an integrated system for producing and distributing energy was established, which in its turn became a great consumer.

Improvements in the steam engine also led to innovations in the sources of primary energy that steam was replacing. Between 1750 and 1850, the use of water power brought about significant innovations, such as John Smeaton's cutting wheel, wheels made of iron, the Poncelet wheel and the Furneyron turbine, in areas where there was an abundance of water; this delayed the spread of steam energy, or limited its use to periods of low rainfall. However, throughout the eighteenth century, the driving force *par excellence* was still water power, even in Britain; in 1830, when steam was about to triumph in British industry, water power still accounted for a quarter of the energy used in the cotton sector. This decreased to a seventh only in 1850, but in the wool industry it still provided a third of energy requirements. The definitive breakthrough for the steam engine came between 1800 and 1850, thanks to a number of innovations and improvements that had been made in the field of machinery and ironworking in the meantime. During those fifty years, the engine did more for science than science did for it;[23] it led to the science of thermodynamics, and made an important contribution to formulating the concept of energy.

Meanwhile, between 1760 and 1790, coke had replaced charcoal, first in Great Britain and later on the European continent, thanks to the refinement and wider use of the Darby process. By 1790 in Great Britain there were eighty-one coke ovens, and twenty-five charcoal ovens; over 85 per cent of all production was concentrated in the coal basins. Fifty years later, almost 2 million tons of cast iron were being smelted, more than in the whole of the rest of the world. Throughout the entire period of the industrial revolution there was a predominance of iron. Producing steel was a difficult and costly operation, despite the new process of smelting and forging at high temperatures that had been adopted in the seventeenth century, and the use of coke-fired reverberatory furnaces that could bring steel to fusing point, introduced by Huntsman in 1740.[24]

As a result of continual technical improvements and greater integration between the stages of production, large-scale heavy industry became successfully established; between 1790 and 1840 coal consumption per ton of cast iron was halved, making it possible to achieve economies of scale. But none of this would have been possible without the use of steam power; initially it had been used to activate bellows, but later it was used to operate hammers, lathes and other types of machines.

Resources and energy

During the period of industrialization England had a unique energy model based on the country's available resources. Water power was relatively widespread, but provided only small amounts of energy, but there was an abundance of fossil fuels that could be converted into mechanical energy using the appropriate means. Water power was used for operating textile machinery, while the mines and iron-works required much greater energy. Steam power became more cost-effective thanks to the improvements made in the first thirty years of the nineteenth century, and it was adopted in a variety of production process. Coal and steam did not, therefore, 'make' the industrial revolution, but enabled it to develop and spread.[25] British technology was not slavishly imitated by others: only the technologies that were more suited to the available resources were adopted, or modified according to specific requirements or circumstances. This was especially so in the case of sources of energy: the energy requirements of different countries and regions were met by combining the use of water, wood, coal, charcoal and coke in various ways. Countries starting out later on the path to industrialization could benefit from the 'advantages of the latecomer', and immediately adopt technologies that had taken over a century to reach satisfactory levels.[26]

Belgium, which was close to England, was the first country to start this process; it was well provided with coal, and its geomorphology resembled that of England. In Belgium, as in England, textile activities initially ran on water power, with steam being used in the mines and ironworks. During the first half of the nineteenth century, the textile industry and water power went together; this was the case almost everywhere, including France, Germany, Switzerland and northern Italy. Only where coal was more abundant, as in Belgium, or when important deposits were discovered, as in Germany and the United States, did steam rapidly replace the waterwheel. The predominance of water power went unchallenged throughout the whole Alpine area from the Dauphine to Baden, from Bavaria to northern Italy; it also enabled the great development of the textile industry in Switzerland to take place.

The combination of coal and heavy industry developed its full potential in Germany. The key to the process was the rapid development of the coal-bearing basin of the Ruhr; in the space of twenty years, a pleasant farming valley was transformed into the region with the highest concentration of heavy industry in the world. In 1850, once the exploitation of the deeper seams had begun, 1.6 million tons of coal were mined, and by 1870 this had risen to 12 million tons. A modern iron industry based on coke was established, which became the driving force behind the whole industrialization of the *Reich*, and the area of Rhineland-Westphalia was later to lead the world in the field of carbon chemistry.[27]

Germany and the United States both developed very rapidly with the discovery of vast deposits of coal. After a slow start due to the massive use of wood to make up the energy balance, the output of the United States surpassed that of Britain, after 1900. By the 1850s and 1860s, Britain, Belgium, France and Germany had doubled, then tripled and even sextupled, their production (Table 7.5). Other countries without coal reserves had to wait until the transport revolution before they could have available supplies for the domestic market; Italy could only develop a national iron industry after technologies using less coal, such as the Siemens-Martin furnace, had been developed. A definitive solution to the problem was to come at the end of the century, when electric technologies could exploit the enormous internal water resources.

Table 7.5 Annual coal production, 1820–1910 (000 tons)

Year	*Great Britain*	*France*	*Germany*	*Belgium*	*Russia*	*United States*	*Japan*
1820	17,700	1,094	1,300	–	–	303	–
1830	22,800	1,863	1,800	2,305	–	799	–
1840	34,200	3,003	3,200	3,930	–	2,244	–
1850	50,200	4,434	5,100	5,821	–	7,580	–
1860	81,327	8,304	12,348	9,611	300	18,181	–
1870	112,203	13,330	34,003	13,697	690	36,667	–
1880	149,327	19,362	59,119	16,867	3,290	72,037	882
1890	184,528	26,083	89,351	20,360	6,010	143,148	2,608
1900	222,794	33,404	149,569	23,463	16,160	244,653	7,429
1910	268,676	38,350	222,302	25,523	25,430	455,041	15,681

Source: Adapted from B.R. Mitchell, *European Historical Statistics*, London, 1981, pp. 418–25.

Machine tools and the 'American system' of manufacturing

These innovations were also made possible by important parallel improvements and developments in the sector of machine tools, such as lathes, cutters, files, planes and rectifiers. Metal parts could be made with the exact mechanical properties and design for machines to function perfectly, and standardized objects could be manufactured; with the use of machine tools operations were rapid and precise. Those who worked in this field were part of a closed professional elite, and passed the technology down through a sort of lineage; after Joseph Bramah came Henry Maudslay, who later set up on his own and trained another three innovators, James Nasmyth, Joseph Whitworth and Richard Roberts. Among the many innovations that could be mentioned were Whitworth's standardization of the screw thread, James Nasmyth's refinement of the steam hammer, and Roberts's invention of a multiple perforator, controlled by a mechanism based on binary logic; it was very similar to the Jacquard loom, and led to the self-acting mule.

In the United States, Eli Whitney, John Hall, Simon North and Thomas Blanchard established the preconditions for the 'American system' of manufacturing; this was the name given during the Great Exhibition of 1851 to the system based on product standardization and interchangeability of parts. Mechanisms with adaptable and interacting parts were produced, and were so precise that a component from one could be used in another similar one, without any adjustment being needed. In order to achieve greater operating speeds and movement of materials, specialized machine tools were used for a sequence of operations.[28] Interchangeable pieces were first adopted in the manufacture of arms (Colt, Remington), agricultural machinery (McCormick), sewing machines (Singer, around 1850), pots and pans (Waltham) and locks (Yale), though initially very tentatively on account of the difficulties. After the Civil War, mass-production methods rapidly spread, first to the production of arms, later to many other manufactured products. They did not spread so rapidly to Europe, since the quality of US goods was lower than those produced with traditional European methods; besides, it involved reducing the number of specialized workers from the production processes. The spread of mass-production methods in Europe was also delayed by a preference for higher quality, sophisticated consumer demand and worker resistance, until the First World War.[29]

International co-operation between the French, English and Germans led to the introduction of gas lighting, one of the most socially significant innovations. The need for it was dictated by the requirements of urban life, as well as by the need to illuminate the large centralized factories, so that work could also be carried on at night time. The British were the first to use gas lighting extensively; the cotton mills of Manchester were illuminated, but so was Pall Mall in 1807. The air balloon was a French invention; the Montgolfier brothers had tested it for the first time on 21 November 1783, and the legend of the 'new technological Prometheus' that accompanied the industrial revolution spread among the masses.[30]

The 'second industrial revolution': the Age of Steel, Chemicals and Electricity

Science and industry: steel

The link between science and industry became even more marked with the second industrial revolution. But until the mid-nineteenth century, and even later, most inventions were the work of ingenious technicians or artisans who had no specific scientific training, but were fully aware of the functional aspects of an innovation. Puddling and smelting with coke owed no debt to the science of chemistry; if anything, before 1850, the scientist's job had been to show what could not work. After 1850 science played a more important role in producing the technological innovations of the period usually defined as the Age of Steel, Electricity and Chemicals. Technical progress owed more and more to discoveries in the laboratory: the electrical and chemical industries increasingly employed research scientists trained in universities or technical schools. Economies of scale, training processes, externalities[31] and network technologies[32] became increasingly significant.

Of all the new products of the nineteenth century, none was more important than steel; it combined the advantages of iron and cast iron, which were plasticity, elasticity and hardness. Steel was the basic product of heavy industry for capital goods, such as machine tools, ships, rails, armaments, bridges and buildings, in addition to numerous consumer goods. The importance was now felt of building machines in a material that had greater strength and elasticity than iron, and was above all less costly. The cost of steel production started to decrease only in 1880, after which it could compete with iron. Production costs were greatly reduced in 1856 when Henry Bessemer introduced his converter. Previously it had taken twenty-four hours to decarbonize three tons of cast iron using the traditional puddling process, but now, with the refinement of cast iron by directly insufflating hot air into the metal being smelted, this was reduced to ten to twenty minutes (Table 7.6). However, the process worked only for ores with a low phosphorus content, like the Swedish and Spanish ores, and excluded whole iron ore deposits, like those in England, because of their chemical composition. This hindered its adoption, until Gilchrist and Thomas discovered a procedure for eliminating phosphorus in 1878–1879, enabling the iron ores of Lorraine, Sweden and other countries to be exploited for the manufacture of basic steel (Table 7.7). The Siemens-Martin furnace (1864–1865) made it possible to use scrap and fuels with a low energy yield; though it required longer, it was able to control fusion better, and also produced a more homogeneous product. It likewise helped in lowering steel prices, and by 1914 it had superseded the Gilchrist-Thomas converters in Britain and the United States.

Table 7.6 Annual production of cast iron, 1788–1914 (000 tons)

Years	*Great Britain*	*France*	*Germany*	*Belgium*	*Russia*	*United States*
1788	69	–	–	–	125	–
1796	127	–	–	–	123	–
1806	248	–	–	–	146	–
1819	330	113	–	–	132	20
1830	688	266	110	90	187	168
1835	1,016	295	155	115	175	203
1845–49	1,785	488	210	177	191	766
1855–59	3,583	900	484	312	254	727
1865–69	4,980	1,262	1,099	496	310	1,317
1870–74	6,480	1,211	1,634	594	375	2,212
1875–79	6,483	1,462	1,791	484	424	2,232
1880–84	8,395	1,918	2,892	699	478	4,327
1885–89	7,784	1,627	3,540	766	616	6,145
1890–94	7,401	1,998	4,335	758	1,098	8,214
1895–99	8,777	2,386	5,974	966	1,982	10,794
1900–04	8,778	2,664	7,925	1,070	2,775	16,662
1905–09	9,854	3,391	10,665	1,388	2,801	23,534
1910–14	9,647	4,278	14,360	2,028	3,840	25,429

Source: B.R. Mitchell, *European Historical Statistics*, London, 1981; *i.d.*, *International Historical Statistics*. The Americas, New York, 1993.

Table 7.7 Production of steel (five-yearly averages), 1880–1914 (000 tons)

Years	*Great Britain*	*France*	*Germany*	*Italy*	*Belgium*	*Russia*	*United States*
1880–1884	1,822	459	972	5	164	255	1,584
1890–1894	3,194	762	2,778	73	276	532	4,378
1900–1904	5,039	1,699	7,412	154	798	2,366	13,616
1905–1909	6,091	2,647	10,846	458	1,373	2,632	21,289
1910–1914	7,141	3,834	15,035	846	2,045	4,093	27,603

Source: B.R. Mitchell, *European Historical Statistics*, London, 1981; *i.d.*, *International Historical Statistics, Africa and Asia*, London, 1982, *i.d.*, *International Historical Statistics. The Americas*, New York, 1993.

Chemicals and electricity

The era of steel was also the era of chemicals, and chemical products multiplied with progress in laboratory research, first in pure chemistry with the work of Ernest Solvay in 1861 on sulphuric acid, and later in organic chemistry with the production of aniline or alizarin, based on artificial colourings, and fertilizers among others. The impact of scientific research was greater in this sector than in any other; its driving centre was in Germany, the country that had the longest tradition of research based on formal scientific teaching and technical training. In 1880 Adolf von Bayer succeeded in synthesizing indigo, which was still very costly; in 1897 the breakage of a thermometer led to the chance discovery that mercury sulphate was the appropriate catalyser for producing it synthetically. The Germans soon surpassed the British in this field, and became the uncontested leaders in synthesizing products such as ammoniac (Fritz Haber in 1904) and nitrates (Carl Bosch in 1913).

In the field of electricity, there had been experiments for commercial purposes in the early years of the nineteenth century; proof of its potential for lighting was provided by Humphrey Davy in 1808, by the electric motor (1821) and by Michael Faraday's dynamo. Its main application in this period was in the field of telegraphy, as we will see later. However, if electrical energy was to become widely used, problems of co-ordinating production, distance transmission and its use for producing light or motor energy had to be solved. In the mid-1860s, C. F. Varley and Werner von Siemens discovered the self-exciting principle and in 1870 Pacinotti and Gramme built the dynamo based on the ring armature. Electrical power transformed the daily lives of city dwellers, changed the structures of workshops, and brought about the appearance of new products like aluminium. Bergès's insights paved the way for hydro-electric power stations. Urban areas were provided with electricity from power stations generated by heat. Thomas A. Edison and Joseph Swan made the first modern light bulbs around 1880, and made it possible to provide lighting in homes; the first lighting network was built in the suburbs of New York. More rapid urban transport, in the form of trams and the underground railway, led to the great spread of urban areas. The electricity installation industry became one of the leading sectors of the industrial world. Chemicals and electricity were the fields where there was the greatest connection between science and industry, while many of the innovations that were made between 1830 and 1914 were the result of improvements in existing knowledge. The experience of the transport sector is a case in point, and will be discussed separately further on.

In the field of energy there was a further 'paradigmatic' transition. This was the start of the oil era, though oil was not a real competitor of coal until 1914. After its discovery in Pennsylvania in 1859, it was used particularly for lighting and lubrication. After 1900, naphtha started to be burned in ships' boilers, but compared with coal the quantities consumed were still very small.

From freezers to typewriters

Important innovations also appeared in other sectors. Because of the nature of European farming, it benefited greatly from fertilizers such as nitrates, potassium, phosphates and fungicides but not so much from the machines that were introduced into the United States by McCormick. Until the internal combustion engine was invented, mechanization was used only where crops could be taken to the machine or energy source, such as the thresher, to be processed. The discoveries of Louis Pasteur (1822–1895) on the origin of bacteria led to important innovations, such as milk sterilization, in the preparation and conservation of food. The centrifuge made it possible to separate whey from milk, and brought about the development of dairy products in Denmark, Holland and Ireland. Refrigeration techniques made it possible to transport frozen meat from the United States to Britain, and after the 1880s, meat could be transported from all over the world to the centres of European consumption. The social and political impact of these innovations was immense. European farmers suffered the effects of such competition, and reacted by adopting protectionist measures; but competition also stimulated the development of policies for innovation in the main countries of continental Europe.

The world of information, which was rapidly growing, was also affected by important changes. The most famous innovation was the typewriter; the arrangement of the first six letters of the QWERTY keyboard provided the solution to the problem of overlapping keys, and led to a real revolution in the way offices were organized and managed.[33] The rotary press was invented in 1846, while a decisive innovation in typesetting was the Linotype created by Ottmar Mergenthaler, a German immigrant to the United States. Innovations such as photography, which were to characterize the twentieth century, were introduced in the nineteenth century. In 1839, Josef Niépce and Louis Daguerre invented the daguerreotype, and 1883 was the year George Eastman invented the Kodak camera.

Apart from economic factors, how a particular social system and its institutions and values worked as a whole affected how soon, and how, the new technologies were adopted. Thus they were part of wider issues concerning the relationship between social change and economic development, and gave rise to a great deal of debate on questions that remain open. In the words of Nathan Rosenberg, technology is not a freely accessible 'black box'. [34] Technological change is closely linked with enterprises, institutions and networks, and is the result of the combined action of different agents, that include enterprises with their strategies and specific organizational structures; it is also the outcome of the institutional environment in which the innovation is created. For this reason, national or specific local factors 'can directly influence technical change and imbue technologies with national traits, or indirectly favour or hinder technical change via the presence or absence of "social capacities" such as educational level, political and commercial organization and financial institutions'.[35]

Agents of industrialization

Entrepreneurs and enterprises

The real driving force behind the capitalist system is the entrepreneur, the individual, or individuals, with the means of production; this is the 'fixed capital', or the machinery and factories, and the 'circulating capital' or the raw materials, stock and financial resources. The entrepreneur organizes production, and decides whether to invest in innovating a technology, a product or a method of managing the production process. If he does not have sufficient financial resources, he can take out a loan in order to purchase the equipment he needs. He hires paid workers and foremen, and sells the product under his own responsibility. In doing so, he takes on an 'entrepreneurial risk', since he has no control over the market. The entrepreneur is remunerated by 'profit' for the active role he has played in the production process; this includes 'interest' on the capital he has invested in the production process and 'reward' for the economic risk involved in managing the enterprise. Profit reinvested in the enterprise can help it to develop or lead to the 'accumulation of capital', which is a source of growth and further profit.

The question of the origins of the capital used by entrepreneurs has been much debated. During the early stages of industrialization, the capital used to finance the development of industrial enterprises came from the entrepreneur himself, rather than from the capital market. In this period the entrepreneur set out to gain the highest possible return from the capital he invested, rather than to achieve a specific volume of production.[36] At that time an infinite number of small independent units, which had no significant influence over prices, were in competition against each other, and were a case of 'perfect competition'. During the nineteenth century, large enterprises gradually started to appear that tended to conquer dominant positions, and were able to enforce their decisions; this was a state of imperfect competition. Pricing later tended to become less spontaneous and was increasingly controlled, depending on whether the market was dominated by a small number of enterprises, known as an 'oligopoly', or a single one, known as a 'monopoly'.

Until the 1860s, most industrial production lay with small or medium-size enterprises, whose capital belonged to a sole trader or a 'partnership'. A partnership was a group of people, or a 'company', each member of which had 'joint unlimited responsibility'. The entrepreneurs might be traders or merchant-entrepreneurs, who had become entrepreneurs to all effects when production was transferred from the home to the factory system. They might also be artisans who had managed to make good profits out of their workshop activity. Or again, they might be inventors with a good head for business, who had set up their own productive activity in order to develop their patents. They owed their success to good luck, but also to enterprise, to their capacity for adapting to changes in the market and to the reinvestment of profits. For every new enterprise that was set up, many failed. A large number of successful entrepreneurs endured extremely difficult periods, which they endeavoured to overcome with all the means at their disposal, which might even be a marriage alliance.

The combination of family and enterprise was a constant feature of the nineteenth century. Though they were the overwhelming majority, family firms could not afford the financial investment required for new technologies or for expansion. The number of joint stock companies gradually increased. Towards the end of the nineteenth century, companies of this type became increasingly important even though at first they were held back by legal failings or restrictions. Since shareholders were liable only for the sums that they had underwritten, and not for the whole of their assets, the state required the companies to be set up under administrative authorization. In 1856, Parliament agreed to the principle of the limited liability company; in 1863 Napoleon III followed suit, and around 1870 the *Gewerbefreiheit* entered German law. In the more advanced areas of northern Italy, initially there were administrative restrictions on the development of small shareholding companies, to be followed later by inadequacies in the legislation of the unified state. After the first timid attempts at relaxing restrictions around 1870, the new trade code, the Mancini Code of 1882, led to greater freedom from restrictions. Although a growing amount of capitalization came from shares traded on the stock exchange, self-financing continued to play a greater role than did the financial market.

The development of shareholding companies was matched by a growth in industrial concentrations. With the advance of new sectors, production lay more and more with a small number of enterprises; in some sectors with a high concentration of capital, this number decreased proportionally as the volume of business turnover increased. Expansion in order to achieve greater economies of scale[37] also took place in traditional sectors, as in the case of the huge cotton mills in Lancashire as early as 1860, or the great industrial wool complexes in Belgium in the same period, and in other industrial areas of Europe. In 1840–1845, the top ten ironworks in France accounted for 14 per cent of national iron and steel production; by 1869 11 per cent was produced by de Wendel alone.[38]

During the 1870s, the fall in prices accelerated horizontal and vertical concentrations, with the aim of securing profits. Since high fixed costs such as debenture interest, interest rates, and taxes, were greater than the variable costs of raw materials, energy, salaries and wages, large companies, despite their losses, had an interest in continuing to produce until the unit sale price fell below the fixed cost per unit produced. Competition from lower-priced goods depressed the market, and threatened the financial solidity of better-managed enterprises,[39] hence the reaction against anarchic competition. The number of 'pools', German *Kartelle* or French *comptoirs* increased; they were bound by agreements to fix the volume of production, selling prices, and conditions for sharing out profits; this was especially the case in Germany in the coal and metal industries. They were less widespread in the electrical and chemical industries, and in these particular sectors there was a prevalence of company mergers, such as the German vertically integrated *Konzerne* (Krupp, Thyssen, Stinnes), the British 'amalgamations' and the American 'trusts'. This type of initiative was especially common in the US oil industry, where a ruthless tariff war was fought in which the Standard Oil Company of William Rockefeller and Henry Flager played a leading role. In 1880, Standard Oil controlled as much as 90 per cent of the refining capacity of the United States; the enormous level of concentration between 1898 and 1906 upset the rules of the economic game by undermining the foundations of the free enterprise economy. The consequence was antitrust legislation in the form of the 1890 Sherman Law, which was however rendered almost ineffective by court rulings. There continued to be a conflict between two differing standpoints: one advocated regulation of monopolies by the state, and the other, adopted by Woodrow Wilson, aimed at restoring competition.[40]

Banks

At the start of the industrial revolution, banks played a rather modest role. In the first half of the nineteenth century they mainly financed international trade and the investment of government loans. The banking system was founded on central banks such as the Bank of England and the Bank of France, and on private banks. The central banks were controlled by a small number of wealthy shareholders; they practised rediscounting, acted as the 'bank of banks', loaned money to the state through the privilege of the issue of banknotes, over a limited area and with the amount limited to a ceiling. The private provincial banks discounted bills for traders and small industrialists, while the large private banks in London and Paris were less attracted to commercial credit, and were involved in the acceptance of bills of exchange and in underwriting public loans; they did not grant long-term loans to industrialists. In the France of Louis Philippe (1830–1848) an attempt was made by Jacques Laffitte to support enterprise, but it met with little success.

As industrialization progressed, this type of system was no longer sufficient to meet the growing need for commercial and industrial credit. New banking institutions arose that accepted capital from small investors; new collecting techniques such as sight deposits, term deposits and current accounts were adopted and money was loaned at a higher interest rate than the rate granted to the depositor. Deposit banks such as the Crédit Lyonnais, and investment banks such as the Banque de Paris et des Pays-Bas, were among the different types of joint stock banks that began to encroach upon the large private banks. The deposit banks had huge resources, or liabilities, in the form of sight and short-term deposits, as well as a network of branches. The investment banks did not have branches, and their resources came from the medium and long-term deposits of wealthy capitalists or companies; a greater proportion of their resources was in the form of paid-up capital and reserves. Their operations, or assets, were even more differentiated: the deposit banks dealt mainly with ordinary transactions such as discounting, advances against securities and overdrafts on current accounts, while the investment banks took on far greater risks by dealing almost exclusively with operations such as long-term investments, capital stock and loans to governments.

Different banking systems evolved in different countries. Britain, for example, had few investment banks; the strength of its banking and financial market lay in its increasingly specialized functions, which included acceptance houses, discount houses and deposit banks, all concentrated in a particular area which was familiar to them. After 1826, joint stock banks were created that developed the use of the cheque, which was able to remedy the Bank of England's 'non-elastic' supply of fiduciary money. The private banks were gradually absorbed by the joint stock banks, or merged with each other. By 1914, most of the financial systems were controlled by five London banks, known as the 'Big Five', some of which had originated in the provinces.

In France, specialization was less marked. The Second Empire saw the development of deposit banks. After a number of failures in granting credit to industry, the Crédit Lyonnais adopted more prudent managing practices, and like the private banks and the investment banks, limited itself to granting short-term credit and underwriting government loans. The Pereire brothers, who founded the Crédit mobilier, aimed at forming a company in limited partnership with industry; the aim was to control all the capital invested in specific sectors such as the railways, shipping companies, mining and heavy industry. However, the plan failed; during the 1866–1867 crisis, short-term debts could not be settled, since its capital was heavily tied up in long-term operations.

In Germany, the link between banks and industry was a very close one. The *Kreditbanken*, such as the Disconto Gesellschaft of Berlin (1851), the Berliner Handelsgesellschaft (1856) and especially the Deutsche Bank (1870) and the Dresdner Bank (1882) were investment banks loaning short-term credit; at the same time they acted as investment banks that channelled their own capital, as well as part of their clients' deposits, towards long-term credit. Thus they went beyond the specialized English forms of credit. 'Mixed banks' helped to finance industrial companies when they were setting up, and helped to place their shares and bonds on the market if they were able to increase their capital.[41] They intervened in the rescue of enterprises, and held a parcel of shares so they could control developments in the enterprises from the inside, though without being major shareholders. In order to reduce risk to themselves, they even advocated protection of the home market and the formation of cartels between companies. In a country with relatively little capital, it was the banks that acted as the principal 'agent' of transformation. The German way of banking was imitated not only in other countries of central Europe, but also in Switzerland, northern Italy and even in Spain and Sweden.

Public institutions

Economic growth in the nineteenth century was largely based on the initiative of single individuals, but among the 'agents' of growth the state and local collective bodies also played a role. The subject of state intervention has already been examined, but here it is worth highlighting the different measures carried out by public bodies at different periods and in different countries. Countries with a strong tradition of local autonomy, like Great Britain or the United States, relied to a greater extent on the spirit of individual enterprise. Larger countries, like France or Prussia, where a more powerful state apparatus had long developed, experienced more articulated state intervention. In countries that began their development later, like tsarist Russia (or Japan), the state was essentially a 'substitute agent' which made up for a weak middle class and a scarcity of capital.

In general, state expenditure tended to be limited by 'orthodox' considerations of the balance of payments. Fiscal policies were more concerned with indirect taxation on consumption than with direct taxation. Income tax was still an exception and had a low incidence. Inheritances were not affected by hereditary taxes, and great fortunes could still be made and handed down to heirs, thus increasing social inequality. Since the marginal propensity to save increases with income, the taxation system encouraged investment, and led to a reduction in expenditure on consumption, which was hit by indirect taxes.

The state exerted its influence by legislating in various ways; it promoted free enterprise by eliminating ancient restrictions such as the guilds and tolls, and it protected inventions with a system of patents. It controlled fraud by regulating the banks and the railways, limiting their harmful effects; it even promoted social legislation, especially after 1880. The state sometimes intervened to help industries in difficulty, as in the case of Napoleon III after the treaty of 1860; it might become an entrepreneur itself, as it did in France after 1811 with the Régie des tabacs. Town councils increasingly took on urbanization projects and contributed to the formation of fixed capital, such as aqueducts, route ways, sewer systems, transport and lighting. At the end of the nineteenth century, some cities municipalized the distribution of gas and electricity, as well as urban transport. Thus it could be said that the absolute *laissez-faire* described by the classical economists never really existed, and that there had always been a sort of mixed economy even in liberal countries, including the United States.[42]

The greatest contribution to development made by public authorities was undoubtedly in the field of education and training, namely the development of human capital, and they have been associated with at least three different aspects.

1. *Education and development.* After the 1860s, the idea of growth, and later of economic development, implied technological innovation that required investment in the technical and cultural fields. Industrialization therefore went hand in hand with the creation of a basic education system, as well as with specialist training at a higher level, and, depending on the country, this took place rapidly or slowly. The United States distinguished itself for the rapidity with which training establishments were set up. In France, institutions such as the Ecole des mines and the Ecole Politecnique, Ponts et Chaussées played a very important role; they also provided the state with a training ground for its own leaders. Schools of engineering were also founded, and several local administrations opened specialist training schools, but at the basic level French technical training was inadequate. In Germany the *Realschulen*, which had already been created under Prussian rule between 1850–1870, were attended by a third of pupils in secondary education. At the higher level, the *Technische Hochschulen* trained the industrial elite. In England, teaching did not become free of charge until 1891; here technical education was provided less through formalized structures than through skills and abilities being learnt 'on the floor'. In the mid-nineteenth century, with technological complexity growing, England was unable to set up an efficient educational system to sustain its position. The primary school system sought to integrate children from the working classes into the social system, rather than spread knowledge and this is seen as one of the reasons why, at the end of the nineteenth century, Germany managed to overtake England.

2. *Education and decline.* The English experience points to the strong connection between education and development, and that a failing in education can lead to loss of the economic position that has been reached. In particular, it seems that a social structure in which there is no investment or active participation in the culture of industry is an impediment to development, precisely because of misguided decisions in education. While technical and scientific training in engineering was being neglected, in universities like Oxford and Cambridge humanistic training was experiencing an upsurge. In England, the problem was not so much the quantity of education that the upper classes were receiving as the type of education.

3. *Education and change.* More recently, educational and technical training has been associated with the concept of economic change. A qualitative view of European industrialization has always considered that the concepts of 'human capital' and 'social capital' are more significant. Thus, teaching and reproducing knowledge and skills that are not only specific, but also highly innovative, were among the fundamental factors of development. School, as an educational institution, needs to be considered within a wider context that includes whole families, communities, organizations, as well as social practices and values. In regional development models, for example, skills and knowledge are created and disseminated in an informal and non-codified way, and education is not simply a question of levels of literacy.

National pathways

Great Britain and the United States

During the nineteenth century, industrial development was seen as underpinning the political and military power of nations, and the number of tons of cast iron and steel that were produced counted more than people.[43] Between 1815 and 1914 the hierarchy of power changed significantly, Great Britain firmly maintained its position at the top until the 1880s, when it began to fall back, and by 1914 it was in third place. At this time world industry was still concentrated geographically: 72 per cent of manufacturing production came from four countries: the United States (35.8 per cent), Germany (14.3 per cent), the United Kingdom (14.1 per cent) and France (7 per cent). With the rise of Belgium, Switzerland, Sweden, Russia, Italy, Japan and Spain (Table 7.8), from the 78 per cent of 1870 they showed an overall drop in their share.

During the first half of the century, Britain had enjoyed overwhelming supremacy. Its technical development ensured low prices for cottons produced in large quantities. In the general climate of *laissez-faire*, there was also an abundance of raw materials and coal, as well as a dynamic domestic market. Entrepreneurs were able

Table 7.8 Distribution of world manufacturing production, 1870–1911 (%)

Country	*1870*	*1881–1885*	*1896–1900*	*1906–1910*	*1913*
Great Britain	31.8	26.6	19.5	14.7	14.0
France	10.3	8.6	7.1	6.4	6.4
Germany	13.2	13.9	16.6	15.9	15.7
Italy	2.4	2.4	2.7	3.1	2.7
Belgium	2.9	2.5	2.2	2.0	2.1
Russia	3.7	3.4	5.0	5.0	5.5
United States	23.3	28.6	30.1	35.3	35.8
Japan	–	–	0.6	1.0	1.2
Others	12.4	14.0	16.2	16.6	16.6
World	100.0	100.0	100.0	100.0	100.0

Source: *League of Nations*, 1945, p. 13.

to accumulate capital and adopt more modern machinery. However, British supremacy declined in the last quarter of the nineteenth century (Table 7.9). The *per capita* industrial output of the United States had caught up with that of the United Kingdom by 1900, but in absolute values American industry was already in first position by the 1880s owing to a number of factors. These included an abundance of well located and easily exploited natural resources, customs protection that kept the most dynamic internal market in the world for American entrepreneurs, demographic growth following the great migrations, and a social environment that was particularly favourable to the accumulation of material wealth and the adoption of more modern techniques. Moreover, there was a good balance between productive sectors and different areas of the country, as well as the growth of large enterprises in strategic sectors of development. In the meantime, thanks to its very rapid progress, Germany had become the second industrial power in the world.

The relative decline of British industry underlined its overall image of an economy on the wane. In reality it was the inevitable slowing down of an economy that had reached its full maturity ahead of its time, and having exploited all its own resources had reached the limits of technology. The causes of this decline have given rise to much debate, and two main types of cause have emerged. On the one hand there are objective economic reasons, such as the difference in the cost of the factors of production, labour and capital, between the United States and Great Britain. On the other side of the Atlantic the relative lack of manpower meant a rise in the cost of American labour that led industrialists to invest in machinery, despite the higher interest rates. On the other hand there were social factors, with English industrialists hanging on to old forms of production and technology; their attitude of self-satisfied superiority contrasted with that of the German entrepreneur, who was more innovative and managerial.[44] English education did not much concern itself with basic training or technical management; the 'cult of practical experience'

Table 7.9 Comparative indicators of production around 1911

Countries	*Population (millions)*	*Steel produced (million tons)*	*Electrical energy produced (billion kWh)*[a]	*Sulphuric acid (000 tons)*
Great Britain	41	7.8	3.0	1,082[b]
France[c]	39	4.7	2.1	900[b]
Germany	65	17.6	8.8	1,500
Hapsburg Empire	65	2.6	1.0	350
Italy	35	0.9	2.2	596
Russia	122[d]	4.9	2.0	275
United States	98	30.0	43.4	2,500
Japan	52	–	1.5	–

Source: V. Zamagni, *Dalla rivoluzione industriale all'integrazione europea*, Bologna, 1999, p. 55.

Notes:

[a] Figures for 1914.

[b] Figures for 1913.

[c] Excluding Alsace and Lorraine.

[d] With the Asiatic provinces: 165.

as the source of success hindered the development of new industries, while in Germany these were based on laboratory work in the field of electricity and chemicals. In England, enterprises continued to remain within the family, while in Germany a very close relationship between banks and industry was established. The Germans, like the Americans, were more interested in technical efficiency, and in the long run overtook the British, who were more interested in immediate financial returns.

Belgium

England's most immediate competitors on the European continent emerged from the Napoleonic wars with the need to catch up and overcome considerable disadvantages. They had less favourable natural conditions, and lacked the type of coal that was easy to mine or transform into coke; they had less abundant capital, more elaborate, and therefore more costly machinery, and a mentality that was less interested in profit and more attached to the family business; there was also a shortage of technicians and skilled workers. English law did not relax restrictions on the transfer abroad of staff and machine designs until 1825, but on the continent industrial espionage was fairly common, and workers and technicians were being enticed with good salaries or favourable conditions to set up new activities. A good example was the case of John Cockerill in the Walloon area; in the space of a few decades he was to set up a company that would become the largest Belgian enterprise.

In the mid-nineteenth century, the new industrial geography of the European continent was being shaped in areas where there was an abundance of coking coal and where heavy industry and production could be developed. These areas were the Black Country of England, South Wales and south-west Scotland, the departments of the Loire, the Nord-Pas de Calais in France, and the Belgian Walloon area. Another area was the Ruhr in Prussia; its development between 1850 and 1870 underpinned the kingdom's military power and formed the material foundations of German unity.[45] Even outside the coal centres there were strong industrial areas. This was especially the case where existing industry was newly developed, where there was an abundant and skilled work force, or where transport was convenient, as in the great cities of London and Paris, in the textile regions of the Walloon areas, Alsace, Switzerland or in the pre-Alpine belt of north Italy.

The Belgian area was the one that conformed most closely to the English model; it had the advantage of possessing similar natural resources, it had the long maritime, trading and manufacturing tradition of Flanders, and it was close to England. Its model for development was typical of a 'small country', and in 1913 its population was 7.7 million. During the Napoleonic period it had benefited from its inclusion in the vast French market, and later with the Restoration it was incorporated into the Netherlands. After independence in 1830, Belgium continued to cultivate its own economic interests. It built up a strong industrial system out of its mining and metalworking activities, the Verviers wool industry (which was the strongest on the continent), the mechanization of its traditional linen trade, the cotton industry of the Ghent area, and the engineering and iron industry; it later incorporated sugar refineries, glassworks, shipyards and factories for railway and tramway material. Finally, by exploiting the discovery of sodium bicarbonate by Solvay in 1862, it also developed a chemical industry.

In addition, Belgium set up an original financial institution for sustaining industrial activities that England did not have; this was the Société générale pour favoriser l'industrie nationale des Pay Bas, and it was established with the support of King William I of Holland in 1822. After 1830 it was known as the Société générale de Belgique; it was an investment bank that held shares in the companies which it had set up, and followed their interests very closely. The Banque de Belgique was founded in 1835, and in less than four years it set up or took over twenty-four industrial firms. The state was particularly active in the construction of railways, which boosted the engineering and coal industries. By 1840 Belgium was the most industrialized country on the continent, and in relative terms remained such until the First World War.[46]

France

France, unlike Belgium, followed a different development from the English model. It was at a disadvantage compared with England, since its institutions were less suited to industrial development, it had a different entrepreneurial outlook, and its coal was scarce. During the first half of the nineteenth century, it continued to concentrate on agriculture, and in 1856, 49 per cent of the population was still engaged in farming, as against 22 per cent in Great Britain. This was despite significant developments in the sectors of cotton, ironworking, with the great industrial complex of the Schneiders at Le Creusot,[47] and engineering industries. Sugar refineries, papermaking and rubber processing were also important. The manufacture of luxury goods with high added value by artisans and domiciled workers accounted for three-quarters of industrial output, and still enjoyed great prestige and deep-rooted traditions under the direction of the Paris fashion centres. In his letters on the Great Exhibition of London in 1851, Adolphe Blanqui wrote that 'the true prosperity of our country lies in the progressive development of its natural industries, that is to say, all the arts in which the ability of the hands and the purity of taste can exert an influence'.[48] These were its 'natural industries', which helped to make France the second commercial power in the world, thanks to the high volume of exports.

The country started to grow at an excellent rate during the Second Empire. Apart from the potential for very diversified growth, a decisive contribution was the construction of a railway and telegraph network by the state, which had a considerable impact on the economy.[49] Napoleon III also actively promoted the setting up of Crédit mobilier by the Pereire brothers; it was intended to function on the Belgian model, but its outcome was bankruptcy. French industrial development was negatively affected by a number of factors. France was defeated in the Franco-Prussian War and lost Alsace-Lorraine; the recession of the 1880s, which was made worse by epidemics that hit the important silk and wine sectors, had particularly damaging effects; the trade wars with Italy and more generally the protectionism of the period penalized a country that relied heavily on exports. Furthermore, the internal market slowed down owing to the negative conjuncture, and the population showed only a modest growth rate. Thus a number of structural weaknesses emerged; among them were the features and small size of enterprises, whether they were agricultural or manufacturing; then there was the marked dualism of French industry, which was divided equally between a large sector of artisan niche production, and modern industrial areas that were generally localized near the small number of large urban centres. Furthermore, there was over-dependence on water power for energy. At the start of the new century, electricity brought about a recovery, which had its driving sector in the car industry, and France became the first country in Europe to channel its developing car industry towards the assembly belt and American technology.

Germany

Thus the most formidable continental rival of Britain was Germany. After the process of aggregation started by Prussia with the Zollverein, the real take-off came immediately after unification in 1871. The process of development in Germany differed even more from that of Britain than did the development of France. Its basis was the active participation of the state, the close relationship between banks and enterprises, and particularly the driving role assumed by the mixed banks. First there was the financing of railway construction, which was further stimulated by the payment of 5 billion gold French francs after the defeat of France; it then extended to sectors upwards of it, such as mining, iron and heavy machinery. Ultimately it involved almost the whole of German industry, especially the leading chemical and electromechanical sectors, where Germany achieved, and maintained, European and world leadership. The chemical giants Bayer, BASF and Hoechst brought about the development of carbon chemicals, from which artificial dyes were derived, and a large quantity of pharmaceutical products, including aspirin in 1899, and explosives. In its own way the German 'model' was unique, like that of England. After the 1860s, it was described as 'organized capitalism'[50] or 'co-operative managerial capitalism'.[51]

Between 1873 and 1913, growth rates for the German economy were extraordinary (Table 7.10). Thanks to industry, its GDP tripled, forging ahead at an average annual rate of 3.4 per cent during its least brilliant decade during the 1880s, after a steady 3.8 per cent in the previous decade; it reached 5 per cent annually in the five-year period 1908–1913.[52] The most significant aspects of the German industrialization model included the tendency towards concentrating plants, which reinforced the role of the large enterprise; co-operation between enterprises operating in the same sector by means of cartel agreements; strong links between science and industry. These aspects were particularly evident in the three leading sectors of heavy industrial machinery, metallurgy and chemicals. These sectors produced capital goods rather than consumer goods, and were successful thanks to aggressive marketing policies on the international markets. They required heavy initial investment (hence the strong link with the banks), and during their growth they exploited the advantages deriving from economies of diversification (as in chemicals and machinery) or the cost benefits deriving from economies of scale (as in metallurgy).

Table 7.10 German economic development, 1850–1913 (1913 = 100)

Years	*Textiles*	*Food*	*Metals*	*Building*	*Coal*	*Transport*	*Industrial production*	*Total production*
1850	17.7	20.4	1.5	14.7	2.7	1.7	9.5	19.5
1860	25.7	25.3	3.2	16.0	6.5	3.8	12.7	23.9
1870	31.9	30.9	7.5	20.1	13.9	8.9	18.8	29.2
1880	40.1	41.6	13.9	29.0	24.7	16.1	26.1	36.5
1890	65.0	53.3	23.8	45.6	36.9	27.9	39.9	48.7
1900	72.8	74.6	47.5	61.0	57.5	50.1	61.4	68.4
1913	100.0	100.0	100.0	100.0	100.0	100.0	100.0	100.0

Source: M. Cattini, *La genesi della società contemporanea europea. Lineamenti di storia economica e sociale dal XVIII secolo alla prima guerra mondiale*, Modena, 1994, p. 372.

Germany and the United States shared a tendency towards big business. They differed, however, in the different institutional and legislative attitudes to agreements between enterprises.[53] The cartels, whose aim was to limit competition, fix prices and profits and gain monopolistic control over the market, were recognized as legitimate, and in 1897 were protected by the state. From four in 1875 their number rose to 106 in 1890, and to 385 in 1905.[54] After the early twentieth century, forms of closer and formalized co-operation were established; these were the *Konzerne* and the *Interessen-Gemeinschaft*, or 'community of common interests', which were to develop in the period between the two wars. On the eve of the First World War, Germany accounted for three-quarters of the world's chemical exports. In electricity, Siemens and AEG competed directly with two great American companies, General Electric and Westinghouse, while Krupp and Thyssen dominated the steel sector. As in the United States, there was an exchange of technicians and research workers between the research laboratories of the universities and the great enterprises. Finally, as early as the 1880s, Germany introduced a system of social security run by the state and extending to all workers, and was the first European nation to do so.

The Habsburg Empire, Russia and Spain

The German financial system was imitated in the Habsburg Empire with the Viennese Creditanstalt (1855), and the Wiener Bankverein. The Creditanstalt was involved in the sectors of armaments, steel and machinery, petroleum, sugar and other foodstuffs. The system of cartels was also imitated, and on the eve of the war they numbered almost 200. However, the situation of the economy was very different; in the first half of the nineteenth century the Habsburg Empire had not taken part in the modernization process started by Prussia. It was not a very open economy and its international trade was lower than Belgium's; light industry such as food, textiles, glass and paper predominated. Within its vast borders it had very different economic and cultural situations to deal with, apart from infrastructure. The most advanced areas were Austria, Bohemia and the Italian regions.

Slovakia, Hungary and Slovenia lagged behind, while the rest of the empire was among the most backward parts of Europe, despite growth in the period between 1870 and 1910.[55]

Russia and Spain also showed strong regional imbalances that were the result of past legacies. Owing to its enormous territorial extension the significance of the considerable industrial progress that Russia had achieved was 'swamped' in a vast sea of backwardness. On the eve of the First World War, Russia had the greatest number of kilometres of railway in Europe, and produced more or less the same quantity of steel and electricity as France. However, its *per capita* income was a third that of Britain; 75 per cent of its work force was engaged in agriculture (in Italy it was 59 per cent); there was a 72 per cent illiteracy rate (in Italy it was 48 per cent), and only 15 per cent of the population lived in urban areas.[56] Tsar Alexander II finally abolished serfdom in 1861; however, the cultivation of land was not liberalized, nor were peasants allowed any mobility, but were transferred to peasant communes.

Land privatization really took place only with the reforms of the Stolypin ministry in 1907. The Tsar himself had encouraged the construction of railways and the reorganization of banks. The state played a very active role as a Gerschenkron-type 'replacement agent' for private channels of investment. It introduced the gold standard to attract foreign investment, protected strategic industries, commissioned armaments and granted generous subsidies to enterprises, especially foreign ones. Foreign capital in fact played a fundamental role; it financed half the Russian debt, which was mostly used for the railways, and 40 per cent of the capital of all share-holding companies. But to meet this, the Russian state levied a tax on income that was already low, thus further restricting private demand and penalizing industries that produced consumer goods such as textiles and food. After the 1880s, the demands of the state brought about the take-off of heavy industry, such as coal, steel and machinery, associated with the railways and armaments. It made very rapid progress, not only in the industrial areas of Moscow and St Petersburg, but also in the Urals, the Ukraine and the Polish areas.

The economy of Spain was affected by strong dualism, conditioned as it was by a generally backward agricultural system and very low educational levels. However, two areas stood out in considerable contrast. First, there was Catalonia, which had cotton industries in particular, but also machinery, transport, and later electricity and public services. Second, there was the Basque country, which had developed its iron industry since as far back as the end of the eighteenth century, exploiting the mines from where iron ores had previously been extracted for export.[57] Throughout the nineteenth century, the growth of Spain was slow and limited to only a few areas.

Italy

The towns and rich historical and artistic heritage of Italy bear witness to its heyday in the Middle Ages and Renaissance; at that time Italy played a leading role in trade, manufacturing and banking, thanks to important innovations that preceded the industrial revolution. Its industrial activities were concentrated in the central and northern areas, and especially in the belt between the high plains of the Po valley and the pre-Alpine valleys; in these areas there was an abundance of water power, and traditional manufactures benefited from a variety of raw materials, even if they were not abundant. These were textile activities, of which the most important was the production of raw and semi-worked silk; though backward compared with the flourishing manufactures of the modern era, the silk industry was important because of its prime significance for exports. The cotton industry was gradually growing, and despite their traditional importance in a number of Alpine valleys, the iron and engineering industries were backward technically and in their management. In an overwhelmingly agricultural context, there was a prevalence of small production units and artisan production, and modern factories were an exception.

This area had always had strong links with Europe, but during the first half of the nineteenth century it had been affected by the political and territorial consequences not only of the Napoleonic period, but also of Austrian domination, and the fragmentation of states prior to unification. Among these only the Kingdom of Sardinia, especially under Cavour, resolutely set out to modernize its institutions and economy; agriculture was developed, canals and railways were built, and textile manufactures, machinery, shipbuilding and banking were all encouraged. During the pre-unification period, the profound differences between the various parts of the peninsula were further increased; these differences lay in the economic structures, the state of the infrastructure, educational levels and socio-cultural conditions. The task of governments involved in laying the foundations of the newly unified state was made even more difficult while the political unification of the country was still being completed. Although they were weighed down by a very large public debt, which was largely a legacy of the pre-unification states, these governments carried out impressive projects to modernize institutions and infrastructure. They adopted liberal trade laws and some of the most advanced education laws in Europe, such as the Casati Law; they developed the railway network, roads and ports, extended education facilities, confiscated Church and common land and made wide use of fiscal legislation, which included the notorious 'grain law', in order to procure the necessary resources. The currency was linked to the gold standard. Despite the pre-eminence of the former national bank of the Sardinian states, the Banca nazionale degli Stati Sardi, which now became the Banca nazionale nel Regno d'Italia (National Bank of the Kingdom of Italy), the issuing banks of some pre-unification states remained active. Only a few of them were transformed into shareholding companies with the purpose of financing industrial development; among these, the two most important were the Credito mobiliare, founded in 1863, and the Banca generale, founded in 1870. Both were investment banks along French lines.

From the industrial point of view, Italy was penalized by a number of factors; these included a lack of coal, a limited internal market, insufficient accumulation of capital and financing systems, a low educational level and a cultural framework that was not receptive to structural changes in the economic system. From the start, the state played a particularly significant role in preparing the preconditions for development. But governments paid special attention to agricultural, commercial and financial interests that were already consolidated and widely represented by the post-unification ruling class itself. A small, but combative, group of industrialists led a tenacious battle against this situation, and their strength grew with the birth of important companies at the end of the 1870s. In the decade 1870–1880 secondary activities gradually developed, with greater backing from the government during a transition from the historical right to the left. These included the modernization of the navy, and support for the creation of the first Italian steelworks at Terni. The effects of the agrarian crisis of the 1880s (Table 7.11) led to the adoption of a protectionist policy in 1887, and also gave a more decisive thrust to the process of industrialization that was already under way, and which was accelerated during the period of the so-called 'take-off', or *decollo*, between 1896 and 1913 (Table 7.12). The serious bank crisis of the 1890s, with the bankruptcy of the Credito mobiliare and the Banca generale, caused by speculation in the building industry, led to the establishment of the Banca d'Italia (Bank of Italy) in 1893. This bank continued to share the power of issue with another two banks, the Banco di Napoli (Bank of Naples) and the Banco di Sicilia (Bank of Sicily). The role of mixed banks along German lines, such as the Banca commerciale italiana (Comit) and the Credito italiano (Credit), played a greater role in the Italian banking system; another addition to these banks was the Banco di Roma, when it was converted towards the end of the century. Small local enterprises could obtain loans from savings banks and pawnbrokers, but especially from the network of people's banks and rural savings banks set up by liberal and Catholic bodies.

In the final twenty years of the century, all industrial sectors experienced take-off; textile industries such as the Lanifici Rossi, founded in 1817, and Marzotto, founded in 1836, predominated, but there were also important developments in shipbuilding, ironworks, the production of railway material and armaments. There were promising initiatives in the field of chemicals, while the hydro-electric power industry brought independence from coal. On the eve of the First World War, Italy was producing as much electricity as France and Russia, and twice that of the Habsburg Empire. In the meantime, the car industry (Fiat, 1899) and the rubber industry (Pirelli, 1872, which became the first Italian multinational company) made headway. However, the productive power of Italy was concentrated in the regions of the 'industrial triangle' (Piedmont – Liguria – Lombardy), in parts of the Veneto and central Italy, with some isolated areas in a small number of other Italian regions. The performance of Italy thus remained strongly conditioned by permanent regional imbalances,[58] which, despite a number of special measures like the Law for Naples in 1904, would continue to weigh heavily on the development of the country.

Table 7.11 Different estimates of the value of Italian agricultural production

	Vaccaro (1)				*Vaccaro (2)*				*Valentini-Gini*		*Zattini*		*Zamagni*		*Federico*	
	1876–1881		*1890–1994*		*1876–1881*		*1890–1894*		*1909*		*1910–1923*		*1909–1913*		*1911*	
Region	*Lira/ha*	*Index*	*Lira/ha*	*Index*	*Lira/ha*	*Index*	*Lira/ha*	*Index*	*Lira/ha*	*Index*	*Lira/ha*	*Index*	*Lira/ha*	*Index*	*Lira/ha*	*Index*
Piedmont	155	92	145	115	194	98	212	124	319	122	414	137	345	116	342	109
Lombardy	245	145	211	147	288	145	258	150	504	192	494	164	460	154	430	137
Liguria	247	145	109	76	415	209	174	101	344	131	242	80	278	93	442	141
Veneto	196	115	160	111	222	112	184	107	370	141	367	122	361	121	373	119
Emilia	247	145	226	157	282	142	263	153	361	138	493	163	441	148	461	147
Tuscany	**171**	**101**	129	90	252	127	201	117	**227**	**87**	**285**	**94**	**252**	**85**	270	86
Marches	**208**	**123**	190	132	233	117	213	124	**205**	**78**	**316**	**105**	**322**	**108**	332	106
Umbria	**173**	**102**	126	88	227	115	167	97	**218**	**83**	**235**	**78**	**206**	**69**	230	73
Lazio	98	58	95	66	118	60	115	67	206	79	262	87	275	92	312	99
Abruzzi and Molise	177	104	95	66	203	103	113	66	125	48	198	66	234	79	223	71
Campania	246	145	150	104	298	150	183	107	343	131	373	123	441	148	380	121
Apulia	136	80	153	106	142	71	159	93	217	83	266	88	299	100	305	97
Basilicata	86	51	74	51	107	54	92	54	77	29	110	36	124	42	118	38
Calabria	152	90	124	86	193	97	159	93	157	60	157	52	211	71	274	87
Sicily	174	102	159	111	181	91	165	96	259	99	292	97	300	101	370	118
Sardinia	44	26	58	47	47	24	61	36	107	41	91	30	89	30	117	37
Centre-North	192	113	165	115	236	119	209	122	–	–	373	123	343	115	357	114
South	143	84	119	82	158	158	80	77	–	–	218	72	245	82	263	84
Italy	170	100	144	100	198	100	171	100	262	100	302	100	298	100	314	100

Source: J. Heffer and W. Serman, *Il XIX secolo. 1815–1914: dalle rivoluzioni agli imperialismi*, (ed.) S. Zaninelli, Milan, 1998, p. 120.

Table 7.12 Distribution of industrial enterprises in Italy, 1876–1911 (%)

	No. of enterprises			*Workers*			*Installed capacity*		
Region	*1876*	*1903*	*1911*	*1876*	*1903*	*1911*	*1876*	*1903*	*1911*
Piedmont	14.9	8.2	10.8	19.8	13.0	14.9	29.1	16.4	16.4
Lombardy	29.4	14.7	16.8	42.2	27.9	28.5	29.9	23.7	25.0
Liguria	4.2	2.5	4.7	3.4	4.0	5.8	5.8	6.9	7.7
Veneto	13.9	6.8	8.6	9.6	8.4	8.6	12.2	7.8	8.5
Emilia Romagna	5.0	5.8	8.3	3.1	3.9	6.3	2.9	5.0	5.9
Tuscany	7.6	11.2	9.2	6.2	10.5	8.2	3.7	7.6	7.6
Marches	2.6	3.5	3.1	2.5	2.4	2.1	1.8	2.3	2.5
Umbria	1.3	1.8	1.9	0.6	1.5	1.4	1.2	7.9	4.1
Lazio	2.6	3.4	4.1	1.1	2.4	3.1	1.4	2.6	2.9
Abruzzi and Molise	1.1	4.9	3.7	0.2	1.5	1.6	–	2.5	2.5
Campania	5.9	8.7	7.9	7.5	8.3	6.9	11.0	8.9	8.8
Apulia	3.0	5.4	6.0	0.6	2.9	3.6	0.2	1.8	2.4
Basilicata	0.2	1.6	1.1	0.03	0.4	0.5	0.01	0.5	0.3
Calabria	2.6	5.8	3.9	1.1	2.2	1.7	0.4	1.3	1.0
Sicily	5.1	13.8	8.0	1.8	8.8	5.2	0.2	3.8	3.4
Sardinia	0.5	1.7	1.6	0.2	1.9	1.5	0.1	0.9	0.8
Centre-North	81.5	88.6	88.1	88.6	74.1	79.0	88.1	80.3	80.6
South	18.5	11.4	11.9	11.4	25.9	21.0	11.9	19.7	19.4
Italy	100.0	100.0	100.0	100.0	100.0	100.0	100.0	100.0	100.0

Source: J. Heffer and W. Serman, *Il XIX secolo. 1815–1914: dalle rivoluzioni agli imperialismi*, (ed.) S. Zaninelli, Milan, 1998, p. 83.

Notes

1 P. Malanima, *Economia preindutriale*, Milan, 2000, pp. 327–30.
2 A. Maddison, *Phases of Capitalism Development*, Oxford, 1982, p. 4.
3 'la più straordinaria avventura che l'umanità ha conosciuto nel corso della sua storia.' V. Castronovo, 'Introduzione' L. Segreto (ed.), *La rivoluzione industriale tra il Settecento e l'Ottocento*, Milan, 1984, p. ix.
4 P. Mathias, *Riflessioni sul processo di industrializzazione in Europa*, in G.L. Fontana, (ed.), *Le vie dell'industrializzazione europea. Sistemi a confronto*, Bologna, 1997, pp. 35–63. Cf. also Chapter 4 of this book.
5 P. Deane, *La prima rivoluzione industriale*, Bologna, 1973 (original edition 1967).
6 E.A. Wrigley, *La rivoluzione industriale in Inghilterra. Continuità, caso e cambiamento*, Bologna, 1992 (original edition 1988).
7 'di fare profitti vendendo di più a prezzi più bassi, il che forniva un forte incentivo a cercare fonti di energia sempre più potenti e macchine sempre più automatizzate per aumentare il flusso dei prodotti disponibili e contenerne i costi.' V. Zamagni, *Dalla rivoluzione industriale all'integrazione europea*, Bologna, 1999, pp. 24–5.
8 Cf. in particular this volume Chapter 4 (under 'The growth of trade').
9 S. Pollard, 'Processo di industrializzazione ed economia europea', in G. Mori (ed.), *L'industrializzazione in Italia*, (*1861–1900*), Bologna 1981, p. 76.
10 'figlia di una lunga serie di cambiamenti intervenuti nell'economia europea e nella società a partire dai secoli centrali del Medioevo: lenti progressi in agricoltura, più rapidi cambiamenti nell'industria, allargamento delle relazioni commerciali all'interno e fuori del continente, attenzione crescente al problema delle soluzioni tecniche nelle attività economiche.' P. Malanima, *Economia preindustriale*, p. 330.

11 'fu solo la fase in cui tante trasformazioni quantitative lente provocarono un vero salto di qualità.' *Ibid.*

12 S. Pollard, 'Processo di industrializzazione', p. 76.

13 *Ibid.*

14 C. Poni, 'All'origine del sistema di fabbrica. Tecnologia e organizzazione produttiva dei mulini da seta nell'Italia settentrionale', *Rivista storica italiana*, 88, 1976; *id.*, 'Per la storia del distretto industriale serico di Bologna', *Quaderni storici*, 25, 1990.

15 R. Giannetti, 'Tecnologia e sviluppo tecnologico', in P.A. Toninelli (ed.), *Lo sviluppo economico moderno dalla rivoluzione industriale alla crisi energetica, 1750–1973*, Venice, 1996, p. 260.

16 The period in which a particular energy source predominates.

17 F. Braudel, *Civiltà materiale, economica e capitalismo*, Turin, 1992 (original edition 1979).

18 C. Pavese, 'L'energia, le risorse, l'ambiente', in P.A. Toninelli (ed.), *Lo sviluppo economico moderno*, p. 116

19 D.S. Landes, *Prometeo liberato*, Turin, 1978.

20 C. Pavese, 'L'energia, le risorse, l'ambiente', p. 116.

21 'Esse innescarono un singolare "circolo virtuoso" tra espansione del consumo di fossile, sviluppo della meccanica, decollo della siderurgia, meccanizzazione dei trasporti e ulteriore diffusione e diversificazione della domanda di carbone che, grazie a continue innovazioni, avrebbe impresso al sistema economico una ininterrotta spinta propulsiva destinata ad esaurirsi solo verso fine Ottocento.' *Ibid.*, p. 117.

22 'erano insieme il frutto di rationalità ed abilità tecnica.' R. Giannetti, '*Tecnologia e sviluppo tecnologico*', pp. 256–7

23 R. J. Forbes, L'energia fino al 1850, in C. Singer (editor), *Storia della tecnologia*, vol. IV, Turin, 1964.

24 However, the cementation process had been known since the first millennium BC.

25 D.S. Landes, *Prometeo liberato.*

26 C. Pavese, '*L'energia, le risorse, l'ambiente*', p. 123.

27 *Ibid.*, p. 125.

28 J. Mokyr, *Twenty-five Centuries of Technological Change*, New York, 1993.

29 R. Giannetti, 'Tecnologia e sviluppo tecnologico', p. 272.

30 'la leggenda del nuovo Prometeo tecnologico che accompagnava la revoluzione industriale.' *Ibid.*, p. 264.

31 The combination of positive or negative effects that a producer's activity can have over other economic agents.

32 *Ibid.*, p. 265.

33 P.A. David, 'Comprendere l'economia del sistema QWERTY. La necessità della storia', in W.N. Parker (ed.), *Economia e storia*, Rome and Bari, 1988 (original edition 1985).

34 N. Rosenberg and L.B. Birdzell, *Come l'occidente è diventato ricco. Le trasformazioni economiche del mondo industriale*, Bologna, 1988; N. Rosenberg, 'Scienze e tecnologia nel ventesimo secolo', in R. Giannetti and P. A. Toninelli (eds), *Innovazione, impresa e sviluppo economico*, Bologna, 1991; *id.*, *Dentro la scatola nera*, Bologna, 1992.

35 'possono influenzare direttamente il cambiamento tecnico dando alle tecnologie tratti nazionali, oppure favorire o ostacolare indirettamente il cambiamento tecnico attraverso la presenza o l'assenza di "capacità sociali" come il livello dell'educazione, l'organizzazione politica e commerciale, le istituzioni finanziarie.' R. Giannetti, '*Tecnologia e sviluppo tecnologico*', p. 299.

36 J. Heffer and W. Serman, *Il XIX secolo, 1815–1914. Dalle rivoluzioni agli imperialismi*, ed. S. Zaninelli, Milan, 1998, p. 87.

37 Reduction of the average cost of production made possible by increasing the size of a company.

38 J. Heffer and W. Serman, *Il XIX secolo*,p. 88.

39 *Ibid.*, p. 89.

40 The 1914 Clayton Antitrust Act.

41 R. Tilly, 'La banca universale in una prospettiva storica. L'esperienza tedesca', in *Banca Impresa Società*, 1, 1990.
42 J. Heffer and W. Serman, *Il XIX secolo*, p. 94.
43 J. Heffer and W. Serman, *Il XIX secolo*, p. 79.
44 *Ibid.*, p. 80.
45 R. Leboutte, *Vie et mort des basins industriels en Europe, 1750–2000*, Paris, 1997.
46 V. Zamagni, *Dalla rivoluzione industriale all'integrazione europea*, pp. 46–8.
47 D. Woronoff, *Histoire de l'industrie en France du XVI siècle a nos jours*, Paris, 1994.
48 L. Bergeron, 'La via francese all'industrializzazione. Studi, ipotesi, prospettive', in G.L. Fontana (ed.), *Le vie dell'industrializzazione europea*, pp. 257–8.
49 M. Levy-Leboyer and M. Lescure, 'France', in R. Sylla and G. Toniolo (eds), *Patterns of European Industrialization. The Nineteenth Century*, London, 1991, p. 154.
50 J. Kocka, 'Impresa e organizzazione manageriale nell'industrializzazione tedesca', in M.M. Postan, P. Mathias (ed.), *Storia Economica Cambridge*, VII, *L'età del capitale*, Turin, 1979.
51 A.D. Chandler, *Dimensione e diversificazione. Le dinamiche del capitalismo industriale*, Bologna, 1994.
52 R. Tilly, 'Germany', in R. Sylla and G. Toniolo (eds), *Patterns of European Industrialization*, p. 180; J. Kocka, *Impresa e organizzazione manageriale nell'industrializzazione tedesca*, p. 726.
53 P.A. Toninelli, 'Il processo di industrializzazione. Tipologie e modelli, in *id.*, *Lo sviluppo economico moderno*, pp. 459–64.
54 J. Kocka, *Impresa e organizzazione manageriale nell'industrializzazione tedesca*, p. 735.
55 V. Zamagni, *Dalla rivoluzione industriale all'integrazione europea*, p. 64.
56 *Ibid.*, p. 65.
57 G. Tortella, *El desarrollo de la España contemporanea. Historia economica de los siglos XIX y XX*, Madrid, 1994.
58 L. Cafagna, *Dualismo e sviluppo nella storia d'Italia*, Venice, 1989, pp. 319–22.

8 The economic development of Europe in the nineteenth century (IV)

The revolution in transport and communications

Giovanni Luigi Fontana

Roads and canals

Important technical discoveries that could be qualified as true inventions, and a combination of innovations that improved their performance revolutionized the ways in which goods, people and information travelled, over short and long distances. At the end of the eighteenth century, the speed of travel was still conditioned by the use of animal power or by navigation along rivers, canals and coasts. This limited the chances of extending productive activities and increasing exchanges. The railway, the steamship and telegraphy opened up a new era, as much in transport over land and sea as in communications. The new means of transport did not bring about the industrial revolution, which had begun before they appeared, but they had the effect of considerably speeding it up and continually expanding it. In 1815, it took forty hours to travel from Paris to Calais in a stagecoach; in 1914, a fast train took three hours and fifteen minutes. Heavy sailing ships, which were conditioned by wind directions and strengths, and sailed only when the captain thought fit, were replaced, in the second half of the nineteenth century, by regular steam services that transported people and valuable goods to different continents at much higher speeds. Thanks to telegraphy and a network of underwater cables, people in business and commerce could communicate almost in 'real time', from one hemisphere of the earth to the other. After the triumph of the train and the establishment of steamships, in the nineteenth and twentieth centuries, the automobile was to herald the revival of the high road, while in 1914 aviation was preparing to become more than just a sports feat.[1] Since it enabled the factors of production to be transferred, and the finished products to be distributed practically anywhere, transport was not only a commercial means of exchange, but itself also became part, and an important part, of the means of production.[2]

Numerous connections can be established between the transformation of transport and economic development. The theory that the market was the driving factor and regulator of the economic system 'began to be developed just when the revolution in transport and communications was taking place, which in the middle decades of the nineteenth century, transformed the traditional relationship of man with space and the very dimensions of the planet'.[3] However, right from the very start of the industrial revolution, the changes taking place in the sector were being felt. Indeed, one of the main prerequisites of the British industrial revolution was the construction of a dense network of canals that made it possible to cut the cost of transporting raw materials and finished products by about three-quarters of the cost of transporting them overland. Until the 1840s the main investments were channelled into canals and the road network. In England the road network, with all its branches, reached even the remotest village. After the end of the seventeenth century, road maintenance was transferred from the parishes, which made use of the *corvée* system, to toll trusts. By the mid-eighteenth century, 3,400 miles of turnpike roads were in the care of trusts. Capital was private and the revenue from the local trusts was often insufficient to cover expenses. By the early nineteenth century only 6 per cent of the roads were in good condition. At any rate, 3,873 trusts managed 20,000 miles of turnpike roads in 1829 and in 1836 they reached their maximum extent of 22,000 miles, by which time the railways were beginning to compete with the roads and canals.

In many parts of Europe, only the major roads were kept in good condition, primarily to make it easier to move troops. The rest of the road system was given over to local authorities for their maintenance; but the local authorities had neither the financial resources nor the technical expertise required for keeping this up. France was the European country with the best network of communications. Finance came from public sources, and in the second half of the eighteenth century, although the network was particularly extensive, considerable progress was made in building new roads. Improvement in the road networks owed much to new systems of construction, such as those of the Corps des Ponts et Chaussées; this was set up in 1716 by the French to train engineers and manage road works, and was followed thirty years later by the Ecole of the same name. The Telford and McAdam techniques of construction also gradually spread all over Europe. In France, in the early nineteenth century, much of the 33,000 km network of trunk roads was started. The continual movement of troops made it necessary to build *routes impériales*, not only in France, but also in the north of Italy, Belgium and Germany.

Road building continued from 1815 to the middle of the century. Except in the northern states, Italy had to wait until unification before the road network was improved. Investment in road infrastructure came to a stop after the 1850s, and only when the automobile was invented did a new phase of investment guarantee the construction of a basic system for the mass transport of the twentieth century. The cost of overland transport decreased two to four times as a result of doubling the draught power of the horse: its performance increased even further with the construction of lighter carriages to replace the heavy coaches. With the advent of the railway, horse transport fell into disuse for long distances, while for short journeys it continued to be the main means until the early twentieth century.

Rivers and internal waterways had always been the most convenient, and least costly, route for trade, despite the difficulties of transport upstream, which was often very erratic and inconsistent. Barges took three to six days to go down the Rhine, from Strasbourg to Mainz, a distance of 220 km, but a month in the opposite direction. There was a great need for internal transport to be developed and modernized. On the one hand, this was because of the increase in maritime traffic, resulting from reduced transport costs and greater safety on the routes, and on the other hand, because of the increase in population, especially the urban population, that created a greater demand for inexpensive bulk goods. This demand could be met only by improving inland navigation. During the mercantilist period, great canals had been constructed in France, such as the one linking the Loire and the Seine, or the Languedoc canal that linked the Atlantic with the Mediterranean. They were also built in Spain, the Netherlands, Germany and Sweden, but especially in Britain, where river navigation was the natural complement not only to road, but also to coastal, transport. Between 1669 and 1749, more than 200 parliamentary measures were passed for improving internal communications, and over the next seventy years, £17 million were spent on building 2,000 miles of navigable waterways.[4] These were spontaneous initiatives promoted by local entrepreneurs. In Britain, during the first forty years of the nineteenth century, the construction of canals intensified. In continental Europe, canal construction was developed to a lesser degree than in Britain and the United States.

In 1812, the first European steamship, the *Comet*, made its appearance on the Clyde. By 1830, there were 315 British steamships with an overall capacity of 33,500 tons. British-built steamboats, with iron hulls to reduce the risk of fire, had already been at work on the Seine, the Rhône, the Loire and the Rhine for some time. To prevent the performance of the new boats from being affected by the seasonal variation in water level, impressive works to reconstruct the riverbanks were carried out, among which the most challenging project was to regulate the course of the Rhine. In France, especially in the thirty-five years between the fall of Napoleon and the Second Empire, the areas that were mainly involved were the industrial areas; new canals, such as the Saint-Quentin, built in 1810, were dug to link the coal-bearing regions to the urban markets, or to connect waterways carrying heavy traffic, like the Rhône–Rhine in 1834. Germany was behind with the building of canals, and 6,600 km of canal were built between 1873 and the First World War. The canals generally experienced growing competition from the railways, but the ultimate triumph of the railways was due not to any advantages in costs, but to better organization, to speed and to the versatility of the service, except in a few areas like the Rhine valley, which had the advantage of an abundance of waterways. On the other hand, dry countries like Spain gained great advantages from the railway, and for all these reasons, no other innovation of the nineteenth century was so successful.

The advent and development of the railways

The railway was the outcome of a combination of factors that had already existed before the nineteenth century: the rails used in mine galleries and ports, and to supplement canals in the British coal-bearing basins, trolleys and steam-powered machines. It became autonomous with the invention of the locomotive (1825), which was the most important invention in nineteenth century transport. After the introduction of the tubular boiler, the engineer George Stephenson (1781–1848) developed the Liverpool to Manchester line (1826–1829) in the heart of a great industrial area; it demonstrated the cost-effectiveness of the railway for the transport of both goods and passengers, with most of the technical problems being empirically solved at the same time. Subsequently, technical development followed two directions: seeking to achieve high speeds, and seeking to obtain the maximum energy to enable mass transport.

The first objective was achieved very rapidly and in 1835 a locomotive exceeded 100 kph. By the end of the century, journey speeds (excluding stops) had risen from 60 kph to 75 kph for French expresses, 40–55 kph for ordinary trains, while goods trains made do with a speed of 20–30 kph, which, however, was five to seven times faster than that of the horse-drawn wagon. In order to achieve the second objective, the weight and adhesion of locomotives was increased, the number of axles was doubled, and rolling stock, mounted on bogies, became longer. By 1865, a train could transport 200 tons and by 1900 as much as 2,500 tons.[5] Steel replaced iron and cast iron, and in the 1860s rail strength and wagon capacity increased. Continual refinements improved the performance of the railway. These included fuel economies made possible by compound boilers in 1876, and superheating; better safety with the compressed air brake of 1868; gauge standardization and progress in management techniques. Natural obstacles were also surmounted: bridges, viaducts and tunnels enabled the railways to go across rivers, valleys and through mountains. In order to exploit traffic in northern Italy to their advantage, the German railways financed the boring of the St. Gotthard tunnel through the Alps (1872–1882), while their French competitors did likewise with the Simplon tunnel (1898–1906).

The expansion of the railways was exceptional: the 7,200 km that existed throughout the world in 1840 had risen to 925,000 km by 1906. Until then, the problem of having to finance projects on such a huge scale had never arisen, hence the diversity of solutions that were adopted, which ranged from private and public initiatives, to a combination of both. At the beginning of the twentieth century, 70 per cent of the railway lines in the world belonged to private capitalist firms, the remaining 30 per cent to the state. However, by 1914 the capitalist model that regarded the railways as a wholly private concern and that predominated in the nineteenth century was to be found in only a few countries.[6] In Europe branch lines considerably reduced the profitability of investment, and thus at the start of the century, state ownership of the railways was preferred.

The railways reached their maximum density in the North Atlantic area. As Table 8.1 shows, it was in Great Britain that the railway system was conceived and adopted relatively quickly, in order to free traffic from the monopolistic exploitation of the canal owners. In 1835 alone, Parliament authorized investments of £15 million, more than had been spent on all the canals. This was a new, high-technology sector and it attracted investors. In England, it did not represent a factor for future economic development so much as an essential tool for sustaining the industrialization that was already under way. In short, the railways were a consequence of development, rather than a cause. There were thus no problems of finance or inadequacies in the mechanical and metallurgical industry to contend with. The British state could assume a marginal role in financing and constructing the network, even though changes in the laws on capital companies (1825) enabled

Table 8.1 Construction cost of the railway network between 1830 and 1906

Country	*Cost (£ millions)*
United States	3,036
Great Britain	1,294
Germany	740
France	707
Russia	626
Habsburg Empire	468
India	266
Canada	262
Italy	205
Argentina	139
Australia	137
Belgium	87
Switzerland	59
Sweden	51

Source: J. Heffer and W. Serman, *Il XIX secolo. 1815–1914: dalle rivoluzioni agli imperialismi*, (ed.) S. Zaninelli, Milan, 1998, p. 54.

large enterprises to be set up with extensive share ownership. Similarly to what happened with the canals, the privately financed railways increased throughout the country without any co-ordination, until a special body was set up to co-ordinate the traffic in 1842.

In Britain, the railway spread to meet the demand for transport in a country that was already industrial. In the United States, which was second in the race to build railways, it spread to meet the demands of agriculture, which in its turn brought about rapid industrialization.[7] In short, instead of being a mere complement to the economic development already under way, as in Great Britain, in the United States, Belgium, France and Germany the construction of the railway network took on an important modernizing role. It motivated the engineering industry, stimulated *ad hoc* financing systems, and in the case of the United States – given the colossal size of the network – large-scale management systems; it heralded the subsequent development of the scientific organization of labour.

Belgium had always been one of the first to adopt British innovations, but being a country of limited size, the state took on the initiative of creating continental Europe's first network. The decision was also intended to underline the advantages of the country's newly won independence (1830), as was also the case with Italy later. Instead of the spontaneous development that took place in England, an organic system of transport was planned through state intervention, which provided the capital for its construction. The development of national ironworks and heavy engineering industries soon provided the materials to replace imports from Britain; between 1835 and 1842, 559 km of railway lines were built that linked the kingdom's wealthiest provinces together. The task of completing the secondary lines was left to private companies; these were initially British (900 km between 1845 and 1846) then Belgian, but they were successful only where the state could act as guarantor. The average cost of construction per mile (£16,500) was about half the British cost.

In 1870, Belgium had about 3,000 km of railways (Table 8.2). Starting from this period, the state began buying back the private network at a low price, and by 1914 it owned 95 per cent of the total network. It could thus charge very low fares, and grant workers special season tickets, but it did not earn any great revenue. A similar model of development took place in Germany, and later in Russia.

Germany invested heavily in building and developing its railway network. The German states, and France, were the only other European areas involved in the pioneering stages of railway building (pre-1850). Around 1840, in the German areas, as well as in France, there were about 450 km each of lines in the mining districts and suburbs. Ten years later, Germany had 5,856 km of railway while France had only 2,915. In France the real take-off came during the Second Empire (1852), once the hostility of those advocating the completion of the canals had been overcome. In the German areas, steam navigation on the Rhine and the rivers west of the Elbe delayed the start of the railway, but in 1839 the Leipzig to Dresden line was opened, followed by lines transversely connecting the north-south navigable river valleys. By 1847, the Rhine and Berlin lines already reflected the supremacy of Prussia.

The construction of the German railway system did not follow a standard formula. It relied on government and private initiative, as well as on the heavy investment of foreign capital. Like the American railways, those in Germany were built on 'spartan' lines, with average costs of only £11,000 per mile, to which the lower cost of land also contributed. Locomotives initially came from the United States and Britain, but by 1843 domestic production already accounted for over half the demand. Initially governments avoided investing in railways, but since they could not fail to notice their military and political role, they took advantage of loans and bonds, in order to take control of a large number of companies. By 1860, the state was running 55 per cent of the Prussian network (see Table 8.1).[8]

In France before 1850, investment in the railway system was limited. Because it was impossible to finance it publicly in such a large country, the prevailing

Table 8.2 Extent of the railway network, 1840–1913 (km)

Year	*Great Britain*	*France*	*Belgium*	*Germany*	*Italy*	*Habsburg Empire*	*Russia*	*Europe*	*United States*	*World*
1840	2,390	410	334	469	20	144	0	2,700	4,500	7,200
1850	9,757	2,915	854	5,856	620	1,357	501	23,100	14,400	37,600
1860	14,603	9,167	1,729	11,089	2,404	2,927	1,626	51,000	49,000	106,000
1870	20,000	15,544	2,897	18,876	6,429	6,112	10,731	101,300	85,400	205,200
1880	25,060	23,089	4,112	33,838	9,290	11,429	22,865	162,700	149,900	365,500
1890	27,820	33,280	4,526	42,869	13,629	15,523	30,595	208,000	249,700	566,900
1900	30,070	38,109	4,562	51,678	16,429	19,229	53,234	257,900	292,200	707,500
1910	32,184	40,484	4,679	61,209	18,090	22,642	66,581	321,600	358,400	925,300
1913	32,623	40,770	4,776	63,378	18,873	44,800	70,156	–	400,197	–

Source: adapted from J. Heffer and W. Serman, *Il XIX secolo. 1815–1914: dalle rivoluzioni agli imperialismi*, (ed.) S. Zaninelli, Milan, 1998, p. 54; P. Toninelli, *Lo sviluppo economico moderno dalla rivoluzione industriale alla crisi energetica, 1750–1973*. Venice, 1996, p. 612; V. Zamagni. *Dalla rivoluzione industriale all'integrazione europea*, Bologna, 1999, p. 51.

system was to grant temporary concessions to private industry, under state control. A law in 1842 provided for roles to be shared. The government would decide on the structure of the network, and assume responsibility for the purchase of land and infrastructure, including ballast, bridges, tunnels and stations; concessionary companies were responsible for the rolling stock, work force and organization of services under a system of contracts that were revised several times because of deficits in the running costs. British and French capital only gradually came to be invested in what seemed to be a sector too closely controlled by government policies and requirements. In 1848, France had only 1,800 km of railway, but by 1870 over 15,000 km. In 1878, the state bought back 2,600 km, but by 1908 the whole western network was in deficit.

In the first half of the nineteenth century, in other countries, there was no lack of isolated initiatives; often the railway had been limited to connecting the capital with the sovereign's summer residence.

The twenty-year period between 1850 and 1870, which saw the construction of the European continental and North American networks, has been defined as the 'Golden Age of the railway'. In Europe 50,000 miles of new lines were built, compared with the 15,000 that had been operating in mid-century. The greatest development was in France, with 9,300 miles at an investment of 7 billion francs, thanks to capital being raised by the Crédit Mobilier, owned by the Pereire brothers. State guarantees to pay the interest on railway company bonds enabled it to catch up with Germany – in 1869 both had about 17,000 miles of track – and to rival Britain as regards quality of equipment and rolling stock. The lower availability of coal stimulated French engineers to adopt energy-saving solutions, such as double expansion locomotives, which placed their railways at the cutting edge in Europe.

In the Baltic area, in eastern and Mediterranean Europe, the railway era really started only after 1850. In Italy, the railway system was developed on the initiative of the government in the period after unification. Before unification, projects were very limited and mainly concentrated in the north of the country. The most important line was from Milan to Venice. The ruling class of the new kingdom of Italy saw the construction of a railway system as a fundamentally important condition for the consolidation of national unity, and the modernization of the country. However, because of the poor state of Italian industry, construction was achieved only by depending heavily on foreign countries for capital, as well as for fixed and rolling stock. Its meagre commercial success was moreover a heavy burden on the country's balance of payments.[9] In 1865, the network was privatized and concentrated in four mixed groups, with the intervention of foreign companies. The difficulties in this arrangement created a crisis in the system and, under the 1885 convention, led to a reorganization on French lines, whereby the national network was shared between three companies. From this period, better links with the iron and engineering sectors were created, which reduced the need for foreign help. The network continued to be extended; at the same time it created even greater disparity between the areas that were linked to it and those that were not. In 1905, the whole system was finally nationalized.[10] Other countries' experiences reflected their own particular political and financial circumstances. In the Austro-Hungarian Empire, the state set up partnerships with foreign investors, while in Spain and Russia, foreign investment was seen as the best way to acquire new technologies.

The railways revolutionized the transport system: they caused the disappearance of the stagecoach, and limited traffic on the roads to the short hauls, and thus formed a complement to the railroads. The waterways were still used for heavy bulk goods, but no longer for transporting passengers and mail. The railways could reach areas that the waterways could not. In the last twenty years of the century – the third phase of railway building – the branch network in Europe was completed; the great international connections in Europe were created by means of the Alpine tunnels. Meanwhile transcontinental lines were also being built in North America, Asia and Latin America. By 1890, there were 208,000 km of track in Europe, compared with 51,000 km in 1860. The number of passengers had risen from 340 million to 1,750 million annually. In the United States there were 1,750 railway companies; thirty of them ran 66 per cent of the network of 167,000 miles, which exceeded the European network by 25 per cent.

Between 1883 and 1893, in the United States, the first coast-to-coast line was followed by another three, and by one in Canada. They were the main means of opening up the North American continent. The colonization of new territories, and the consolidation of anti-Chinese tsarist influence in Asia and the north Pacific, were made possible by over 6,000 km of the Trans-Siberian line (1891–1903). In the wave of European colonial, and imperial, expansion and with the support of British, French and German capital and technology, railways started to traverse Latin America, China, Africa and the Middle East. They were part of a whole network, which was connected to Europe by means of the ports. 'In the nineteenth-century collective imagination, when compared to the means of transport of seventy years earlier, the powerful and fast locomotives of the end of the century gave the measure of the break with the previous world.'[11]

Maritime transport

The application of steel and iron, as well as technological improvements in the use of steam engines, also enabled great progress to be made in maritime transport. But the breakthrough for the steamship was more gradual than for the railways. The reason for this was not only the slow development of new technology for reducing fuel consumption and weight, but also competition from the sailing ships, which during the eighteenth century and the first half of the nineteenth, had greatly increased their speed and manoeuvrability. The four-masted clipper had evolved from the schooner, and was the pinnacle of sailing technology. It had a lower tonnage (3,000–5,000 tons) than other sailing ships, but it was faster, since it could reach fifteen knots, 300 nautical miles a day, and thus was very useful over long distances. Between 1849 and 1875, it was used on the routes to India, the Pacific and Australia, without fear of competition from the steamship. By 1860, it was taking twelve to fourteen days to cross the Atlantic and about eighty from Liverpool to Melbourne, from Canton to New York and from San Francisco to New York. In 1869, the clipper was affected by the opening of the Suez Canal. This shortened journeys to India and Oceania, and changed the routes to the less windy inland seas. A number of sailing ships then started to adopt innovations that had been introduced on steamships: an iron hull and small steam engines to mechanize various operations such as the windlass, winch and capstan.

Until 1850, steam power brought progress to river rather than sea navigation. Initially, the steamship was in operation on the short sea routes. In 1818, the first sea connections were made on the Irish Sea and in 1821 between Dover and Calais. In the 1820s, they were started across the North Sea, the Baltic and the Mediterranean, with the transport of mail and passengers. From London to Calais it took twelve hours, and from Naples to Leghorn thirty-six. In 1838, the *Sirius*, a steamship with side paddle wheels and boilers working on distilled water, made the first crossing of the Atlantic entirely by steam. In 1840, the *Great Western* began regular mail steamer services, using mixed propulsion; in 1843, the *Great Britain* adopted the propeller, which required the use of gears to multiply the low number of revolutions of the engines.

In the middle of the century, the steamship still had sail rigging and resorted to mixed propulsion, to navigate in the event of engine failure. It was around 1860 that significant progress was made. Iron, and steel after 1879, was used to replace wood in the construction of the hulls, and reduced expenses for maintenance and wear. The propeller eventually replaced the paddle wheel. Double, and later triple, expansion compound engines (in 1869 and 1874 respectively) drastically reduced the working costs and the amount of coal that needed to be stored in the holds, while the amount of space for passengers and goods increased. Around 1880, auxiliary sails disappeared. Boilers with triple, and later quadruple, expansion led to greater cost-effectiveness, and enabled the tonnage and average speed of iron ships to be increased. Furthermore, steam was a labour-saving innovation, since crew numbers could be reduced.

In the 1890s, the tonnage of steamships ultimately surpassed that of sailing ships, but between 1860 and 1865 the sailing ships had a monopoly of traffic in passengers and emigrants to the United States, as well as the carriage of luxury goods. At the beginning of the twentieth century, steamships finally achieved supremacy. The first ones were built for the mixed transport of both goods and passengers, but later they became specialized. Merchant ships started to specialize even further, with vessels being dedicated to specific forms of transport, such as petroleum or frozen meat. In 1870, the first oil tankers connected the United States and Europe, and subsequently came to play an increasingly important role in international traffic.

Parallel to all these transformations, the maritime trade experienced unexpected rates of growth during the nineteenth century, initially with the construction of clippers, then of steamships. Predominance in shipbuilding, and sea power, remained a key element in British economic supremacy, at least until the First World War. In 1914, despite German and French competition, the merchant fleet was still one of the main sources of revenue for the United Kingdom. Whereas, at the end of the eighteenth century, Great Britain had a quarter of European shipbuilding capacity, a century later it was building more than half the ships in Europe. In 1875, the British had 1.9 million tons of steamships, against 4.2 million tons of sailing ships. In 1885, when the capacity of a single steamship equalled that of six sailing ships, Britain had 4 million tons of steamships, against 3.4 million tons of sailing ships. By 1890, the British had 5 million tons of steamships, which was 73 per cent of world tonnage; in Germany, 1.3 million tons of ships, out of 1.9 million tons, were of steel. Conversely, Norway, which like Canada and Italy had a large fleet of wooden ships, still had 1 million tons of sailing ships out of the total of 1.5 million tons.[12]

The new enterprises, based on the management of steamship lines, specialized in transport. Before the nineteenth century, there had been no regular ocean-going navigation service. In 1818, for the first time, American ship owners started a line with sailing ships setting sail from New York and Liverpool on fixed days, introducing a regular and punctual service that reduced uncertainty in the business field. This system was imitated by the steamship companies. They were subsidized by the government for postal services, and thus secured more profitable traffic.

Maritime navigation immobilized less capital than the railways, but it gave rise to significant investments in rebuilding ports and opening inter-oceanic canals. One of the most important projects of the whole nineteenth century was the opening of the Suez Canal, linking the Mediterranean with the Red Sea. 162 km long, and planned by Ferdinand de Lesseps, it was built between 1859 and 1869, after numerous technical, financial and diplomatic problems had been overcome. The duration of journeys between the countries of the North Atlantic, South East Asia and the Far East was considerably shortened. De Lesseps also planned a canal across the isthmus of Panama, but a combination of setbacks brought the enterprise (1881–1889) to a standstill. It was taken up again by the United States, with financial backing from the government, and finally completed in 1914.

The economic consequences

Means of transport can carry out a 'passive' function, namely the movement of goods and people, and an 'active' one, which is the promotion and multiplication of development.[13] By reducing costs, they free resources that can be channelled towards other consumer products, and sustain economic growth.[14] The cost of transport can determine whether the movement of goods is hindered or boosted. One of the greatest economic outcomes of the transport revolution was the fall in maritime freight costs, and the steady reduction of railway tariffs. Lower freight costs came about because of increased competition; they seem to have been more a feature of the first half of the nineteenth century than the second, and therefore applied to sailing ships rather than steamships. But by 1910, freight tariffs were on average eight times lower than in 1820. Railway tariffs also decreased throughout the century. Lower transport costs made it much easier for people to travel; they greatly facilitated contacts and exchanges, as well as economic and social relations. The market for agricultural products could be opened up to a larger extent, and become more specialized. Manufacturing industries could obtain supplies of raw materials and essential intermediate goods more regularly and more cheaply, and could send their products everywhere. Cities could receive food produce, consumer goods and fuel more easily.

Economic geography was transformed. In the last twenty-five years of the nineteenth century, thanks to regular low-cost sea transport, the flow of American corn to Europe upset the cereal-producing economy of Europe. Marginal units of production, once protected by distance and geographical circumstances, were critically affected. Separate and exclusive economies increasingly lost the advantages deriving from their position. Furthermore, modern transport methods were an essential means not only for the rapid colonization of the American west, and the Argentinean pampas, but also for the opening up of Eurasian Siberia.

In general, the railways facilitated the integration of national and international markets, and the more rational allocation of economic resources. The construction of national railway networks triggered off a chain of transformations thanks to backward and forward linkages with other sectors of the economic system. Among the backward linkages was the mobilization of credit for financing investment. Since the railway sector was highly capital-intensive, it boosted forms of international co-operation between bankers and financiers; this was the case with the construction of the skeleton Italian railway system between 1860 and 1870, where English and French capital and technology predominated. The stock markets carried on a lively trade in railway bonds and shares, which were the principal shares of the time. During the Second Empire, the Paris market became the major centre for investment in the railways. Intense rivalry between the Pereire brothers and the Rothschilds over the financing of railway construction in the Mediterranean and Danube areas further enlivened the Paris market. In the face of competition from the financiers of Paris, Brussels and Vienna, London turned its attention to frontier countries, such as Australia, South Africa, India and Egypt, where the interests of the British Empire were considerable.

Though to different degrees, and at different times, the railways played a driving role in economic development, since they involved a whole series of industries upstream in the production cycle. In particular, thanks to the multiplier effect of the investments, they propelled the construction industry, the iron and engineering industries (for infrastructure), and the services sector (for overall management). The forward linkages included market expansion, growth in the agricultural and food sectors, and the greater mobility of raw materials. But the labour market, company organization and the mechanization of office work also experienced far-reaching innovations thanks to the railways. Hundreds of thousands of people worked on building the national railway lines. They were the first great capitalist enterprises, with many delicate and complicated problems to solve; complex management techniques were developed, and the railways provided one of the earliest areas of employment for professional managers. The American railways were the first great enterprises with a multi-divisional structure, in which an articulated managerial hierarchy planned and co-ordinated the movement of trains; it also organized the traffic between the different operating units, and created a separation between company ownership and management. Innovative accounting techniques were adopted to deal with accounts relating to passengers, goods, fares, routes, timetables and cost effectiveness. By the end of the nineteenth century, new mechanical punch card systems were being used that were capable of rapidly processing enormous quantities of data.

The telegraph and the globalization of information

Finally, the nineteenth century also saw important improvements in systems for spreading news and information. For over three centuries, the descendants of Francesco Tasso from Bergamo, who had run the postal services for the Venetian Republic and later the Habsburg Empire, had gradually extended the network to all the countries of the continent, by establishing themselves at the main courts of Europe. At the end of the eighteenth century, regular stagecoach services linked the main cities of Europe. In 1830, it took forty-five hours to get from London to Edinburgh at an average speed of 14 kph. French stagecoaches covered 200 km in a day, with 1.4 tons of goods and sixteen passengers and their luggage. In Prussia, it took forty hours to go from Berlin to Breslau, a distance of 300km.[15]

At that time, information travelled at the speed of horses. During the French Revolution (1792), the physicist Claude Chappe introduced the optic telegraph. By sending signals between positions that were visible to the eye, it was possible to send 8,464 words in code form; when visibility was good, a signal took twelve minutes to travel 300 km. Initially it was used for military purposes and by the police, but from 1830 its use was extended to business communications. Between 1830 and 1840, in Britain and France, the first lines serving the railways and the stock exchange were started, and later direct connections between the lines helped to spread a network of systems.

With the advent of fast transport systems like the railways, the information required for managing them needed to travel at even faster speeds. Several researchers devoted their energies to this, working independently. Cooke and Wheatstone developed discoveries that had been made earlier. The most original contribution, however, was made by Samuel Morse, an American, in 1835, who made a series of improvements to his telegraphic apparatus. His relay system sent back a signal automatically, by means of a code with a maximum of four impulses to distinguish each letter, which greatly extended its range and achieved high speeds of transmission. After 1843, different cities and continents were able to communicate with each other almost in 'real time', which meant hours and minutes rather than months and days, and once cables had been laid across the sea bed the world market was unified. British enterprises played a decisive role in laying the cables; in 1851 the first one was laid under the Channel, in 1866 cables crossed the North Atlantic, in 1872 they reached the Far East, and in 1874 Latin America. By 1902, when the two coasts either side of the Pacific were joined, the round-the-world network was complete. In 1914, 280,000 km out of the 516,000 km of underwater cables that had been laid down were controlled by British companies, both private and public. This was a powerful factor in confirming London, the capital of England, as the centre of the world market.

The effects of the symbiosis between telegraph and railway were thus extended to the financial market, and the 'railway mania' of 1840–1850 enormously extended the activities of the London stock exchange, giving rise to a dozen exchanges in the provinces that were linked to each other thanks to the telegraph'.[16] In the 1860s, in the main European countries, despatches from the stock exchange were far ahead of any others. The international telegraphic communication service called for measures to harmonize regulations and standardize technology, and was the first to do so, even preceding the railways and postal service. The first interconnections (Prussia–Austria, in 1849; France–Belgium in 1850) were followed in 1855 by the West European Telegraphic Union (between France, Belgium, Switzerland, the Kingdom of Sardinia and Spain). Ten years later, once the Morse code had been universally adopted in 1858, this led to the International Telegraphic Union, the first supranational administrative and technical organization. As regards the telegraph, in certain cases, finance first came from public sources and then passed into private hands (the United States) or vice versa. In Britain, in order to make up deficiencies and keep tariffs down the domestic network passed to the state; in Europe, it was the first case of the nationalization of a public service aimed at correcting distortions in the market.

Half a century after the appearance of the telegraph, the advent of the telephone, an invention of uncertain paternity, speeded up and intensified the spread of information even further. Its appearance on the economic scene came about in 1877 because of the initiative of Bell. In 1879, the telephone transmitted 100 to 200 words a minute, instead of the fifteen to twenty of the telegraph, without any need for an operator. For the whole of the nineteenth century, it remained an eminently American innovation, limited to the world of business, 'since the usefulness of an apparatus within a network is based on the number and type of other users connected'.[17] Its use did not extend to private communication until the end of the century. By 1900 it served 6 per cent of households in the United States, but its main application was still limited to business. Finally, the way was paved for the invention of the radio and the creation of a system of mass communication by the first radio transmissions made by Guglielmo Marconi (1874–1937), in 1896.[18]

Notes

1 J. Heffer and W. Serman, *Il XIX secolo 1815–1914. Dalle rivoluzioni agli imperialismi*, p. 51.
2 C. Wilson, 'Transport as a factor in the history of economic development', in A. Vannini Marx (ed.), *Trasporti e sviluppo economico. Secoli XII–XVIII, Florence*, 1973, pp. 313–21.
3 'cominciò ad essere elaborata proprio quando si compiva quella rivoluzione dei trasporti e delle comunicazioni che nei decenni centrali dell'Ottocento trasformò il tradizionale rapporto dell'uomo con lo spazio e le dimensioni stesso del pianeta'. C. Pavese, 'I trasporti e le comunicazioni', in P. Toninelli (ed.), *Lo sviluppo economico moderno*, p. 301.
4 *Ibid.*, p. 306.
5 J. Heffer and W. Serman, *Il XIX secolo 1815–1914*, p. 52.
6 *Ibid.*, p. 55.
7 L. Girard, 'Trasporti', in H.J. Habakkuk and M. Postan (eds), *Storia economica Cambridge*, vol. VI, *La rivoluzione industriale e i suoi sviluppi*, Turin, 1974.
8 C. Pavese, *I trasporti e le comunicazioni*, p. 318.
9 G. Guderzo, 'A proposito dello sviluppo ferroviario in Italia dal 1850 al 1914. Aspetti geografici. economici e sociologici', *Bollettino della Società pavese di storia patria*, I–IV, 1972–1973, pp. 1–34.
10 V. Zamagni, 'Ferrovie e integrazione del mercato nazionale nell'Italia postunitaria', in *Studi in onore di G. Barbieri*, vol. III, Pisa, 1983, pp. 1635–49; S. Fenoaltea, 'Le costruzioni ferroviarie in Italia, 1861–1913', *Rivista di storia economica*, n.s., I, 1984, I, pp. 61–94;

R. Lorenzetti (ed.), *La questione ferroviaria nella storia d'Italia. Problemi economici, sociali, politici e urbanistici*, Rome, 1989; A. Giuntini, *Contributo alla formazione di una bibliografia storica sulle ferrovie in Italia*, Milan, 1989.

11 'Nell'immaginario collettivo ottocentesco le potenti e veloci locomotive di fine secolo, raffrontate ai mezzi di trasporto di settant'anni prima, fornivano la misura della rottura con il mondo precedente'. C. Pavese, *I trasporti e le comunicazioni*, pp. 320–1.

12 *Ibid.*, p. 326.

13 F.O. Voight, 'I compiti della moderna scienza dei trasporti', *Rivista internazionale di economia dei trasporti*, I, 1974, pp. 263 ff.

14 P.L. Spaggiari, *Trasporti, mobilità e sviluppo*, Parma, 1985; C. Pavese, *I trasporti e le comunicazioni*, p. 302.

15 C. Pavese, *I trasporti e le comunicazioni*, p. 310.

16 'la railway mania degli anni 1840–1850 ampliò enormemente l'attività della Borsa di Londra facendo sorgere una dozzina di borse in provincia che comunicavano grazie al telegrafo'. *Ibid.*, p. 326.

17 'perché un apparecchio in rete è utile in ragione del numero della tipologia degli altri utenti collegati'. *Ibid.*, p. 329.

18 These were sent from Poldhu, in Cornwall, England. (*Translator's note.*)

9 The economic development of Europe in the nineteenth century (V)

International exchanges and monetary systems

Giovanni Luigi Fontana

Europe and the world economy

The network of international exchanges played a fundamental role in European economic development. By the start of the modern era, the European continent (particularly the Atlantic powers of Spain, Portugal, England and Holland) was at the centre of a dense network of international trade with the Americas, Asia and the coastal areas of Africa, and during the nineteenth century international trade experienced prodigious growth. With the revolution in transport, the entire world became a single market, where men, goods, capital and ideas became more mobile than they had ever been before. By 1913, the value of the international trade in goods was twenty-five times greater than it had been in 1820, and Europe dominated international exchange; more than three-fifths of world trade was carried out by eight nations. By far the greatest role was played by Great Britain, which in 1800 controlled 36 per cent of world trade, 27 per cent in 1840, and 23 per cent in 1873; even in 1914 it still controlled about 14 per cent. Until the 1880s, France was in second place, though a long way behind the leading country; however, at the beginning of the twentieth century, it was overtaken by Germany and the United States.

The development of exchange, which continued even during the protectionist period, but at a slower rate, led to an increasingly complex international economy, which remained firmly linked to the gold standard, because of the predominance of British trade and the stability of the pound sterling. During the nineteenth century, trade relations that already existed were further consolidated, while in other areas new links and balances were being formed. In the period between 1815 and the First World War, international trade and financial relations were intensified as a result of a number of factors which had a decisive influence.[1]

First, there was the technological progress that went with the British industrial revolution and the industrialization of the continent. The British cotton sector, for example, became totally dependent on imports of the raw material from Asia and the Americas, while, in the opposite direction, textile products, iron, steel, chemical and engineering products found new markets outside Europe. However, while on the one hand, technological innovation led to an increase in the international trade for low cost manufactured products, on the other, it led to production being imitated, with imported goods being replaced by goods produced domestically.

Second, there was a heavy increase in the natural resources used in manufacturing processes, and the flows of imports and exports within Europe, as well as to North America and the Third World areas increased considerably. Next, there was the revolution in transport and communications, which we have already analysed. In 1873, 27 million tons of goods were transported by steamship, but by 1898 this had increased to over 63 million tons. Commercial relations and political links were further consolidated by a series of projects like the Suez Canal (1869), the canal linking Rotterdam and the North Sea (1872), and the Panama Canal (1914), which also drastically reduced the cost of transporting goods to and from transoceanic destinations.

A further factor was the marked growth in world population. As we have already seen, the population of the planet rose from 900 million in 1800 to around 1.6 billion in 1900. European population growth led to unprecedented movements of people, which strengthened the economic, social and cultural links between different continents. There was greater mobility of labour than previously. Emigration caused salaries and incomes in the countries of emigration and immigration to converge.[2] Demand for consumer goods increased, as did the trade in products manufactured in Europe. The Old Continent increasingly came to depend for its food on produce from outside Europe. Imports of wheat are a case in point, and this will be discussed later in connection with European trade policies.

Finally there was the accumulation of capital. While England was largely self-sufficient as regards its supply of capital, the same could not be said of other European, or non-European, economies. The process of capital accumulation by the 'follower' countries was rapid, and large amounts of foreign investment were attracted by high growth performance.

The triumph of free trade and the development of international trade

The development of international trade had been limited by high transport costs, by people's low purchasing power and by the poor variety of goods, but in the course of the nineteenth century it experienced an exceptional increase. Between 1820 and 1913, world exports increased thirty-three times,[3] and the period of free exchange between 1842 and 1873 was when the highest rate of growth was recorded. From the 1870s until the First World War, when protectionism increased, the volume of international trade continued to rise, but more slowly. Its impact on GDP was greater in smaller countries with more specialized products; in larger countries its impact was weaker. Furthermore trade became more multilateral. 'Countries did not need to balance exports and imports with each trading partner, because balance could be achieved in the aggregate, thus allowing greater flexibility in the use of world resources.'[4]

Fluctuations in trade are normally conjunctural, or related to the customs policies of different countries. Britain was the first country to break with the mercantilist tradition contested by the classical school, and by David Ricardo in particular.

Nineteenth century liberal economic thought argued that after the natural barriers to trade and commerce between countries had been removed, it then became necessary to eliminate the artificial barriers, in other words the duties and prohibitions on imported and exported goods. International free trade allowed the principle of the specialization of labour to be extended, which increased the overall productivity of the international economic system and brought about a more efficient use of resources. It was also a powerful factor for modernization, since on the one hand, strategic raw materials and advanced technology could be imported, and on the other, manufactured products, even of inferior quality, could be exported to neighbouring areas, enabling the industries in the follower countries to become consolidated.

Economic change in the nineteenth century took place against a background of constant debate between free trade supporters, who rejected customs barriers, and protectionists, who argued in favour of the need for them, if only for a certain period. The advantages and disadvantages of protectionism have been one of the most debated and controversial issues among economists and economic historians ever since. There is, however, general agreement 'that excessive protectionism has only negative effects, while more modern theories of commercial strategy justify a moderate degree of temporary protection combined with stronger competitivity'.[5] The fact remains that no country, not even Great Britain, achieved industrial development where there was complete freedom of trade. The countries that were more favourable towards free trade were smaller ones like Holland and Denmark that gained greater benefits from international trade. During the nineteenth and twentieth centuries, the largest countries, like the United States and Russia, were also the most protectionist; like the newly unified Germany, they sought to promote the development of industrial sectors that were still in an embryonic state by focusing on the potential of the domestic market.

During the seventeenth and eighteenth centuries, most European countries, as we have seen, embraced mercantilist theories; trade relations with other states were based on a positive trade balance, and, for the economy to prosper, exports had to exceed imports. This meant that the state had to intervene to provide protection from the influx of foreign goods, and subsidize exports of national products. Fiscal motives went hand in hand with economic concerns, and in many European countries, customs and excise duties accounted for an important percentage of the total revenue from taxation.

In Britain during the second half of the eighteenth century, new ideas about the economic and commercial relations between states started to be formulated. The intellectual climate of the Enlightenment and the industrial revolution led to a general review of the trading policies that had hitherto been pursued. Three important works laid down the theoretical foundations of free trade: *The Wealth of Nations* by Adam Smith (1776), *On the Principles of Political Economy and Taxation* by David Ricardo (1819) and *Principles of Political Economy* by John Stuart Mill (1848). Adam Smith argued that the wealth of nations could be increased through the more efficient allocation of resources. Ricardo formulated the 'law of comparative costs', and demonstrated the advantages of specialization and the 'international division of labour', whose aim was to optimize resources. Another argument in common was that optimization could be achieved only by abolishing artificial barriers, since the 'invisible hand' of the market brought about the optimal allocation of factors and production.

However, in international competition the state only apparently adopted a stance of non-intervention, and the various governments attempted to achieve a 'natural equilibrium' of economies by means of trade agreements. Free trade was conceived and embraced particularly by strong economies, like that of Britain, while countries that were becoming industrialized adopted protectionism. During the upheavals of the French Revolution, the application of free trade theories met with considerable difficulties. Although the 1786 Eden Treaty between France and England, for the abolition of a number of customs duties, is considered the first step towards free trade, war expenses led to an increase in customs tariffs in line with mercantilist theories. Strong sectors, protected by these barriers, gained positions of privilege, which they were reluctant to lose when peace returned, and after 1815 protectionism increased once more. Manifestoes in support of protectionism included the *Report on the Subject of Manufactures* by the American Alexander Hamilton (1791) and *Das nationale System der politischen Oekonomie* by the German Friedrich List (1837). These writers questioned whether free trade could be adopted as an absolute principle; whether or not it was appropriate to apply protectionism had to be evaluated according to a country's level of economic development. List argued that free trade benefited countries that were already developed, while it prevented others from becoming industrialized. Thus the transition from an agricultural economy to a new industrial one could occur only with the aid of a protectionist system. These theories, which were also supported by the American Henry Charles Carey (1793–1879), gained particular acceptance in the United States. On the New Continent protectionism continued to be applied in association with the political theories of Monroe. Protectionism was adopted by the United States during the Civil War, and until 1913 its industry was among the best protected from competition. In 1833, Germany adopted the Zollverein, a customs union that formed a type of common market, with customs duties between the German principalities being abolished in favour of a common tariff for foreign countries. The Zollverein was created under the auspices of Prussia, and initially linked twenty-five of the thirty-nine confederate states. In 1851–1852 the North Sea principalities became part of it, but Austria remained excluded. The customs unification of 'Little Germany' was the forerunner of the solution that was adopted in 1871 with political unification.

The fall in prices caused an increase in duties on specific products. Governments were preoccupied with lowering direct taxation, and thus tended towards raising customs duties on consumer goods. A typical case of this type of legislation was the Corn Laws; they were a complicated system of duties on imported corn that the British introduced during the Napoleonic Wars, when the price of corn had risen rapidly. In order to protect home producers, a duty system was imposed, with duties varying according to the home price of corn. This helped to protect the interests of the large landowners, who saw to it that prices were kept high. The economic and social costs fell on the less prosperous classes; but they also indirectly affected the industrial interests of the nation, through higher wages. The Corn Laws made it almost impossible to import cereals from abroad because of the imposition of customs duties, and led to increases in bread prices during the subsistence crises that were triggered off. Partial attempts to attenuate them, such as the sliding scale (1824–1826), made practically no impact on the protectionist system. In 1839 the Manchester industrialist Richard Cobden (1804–1865) formed the Anti-Corn Law League, and organized campaigns against the government for the repeal of the Corn Laws. Cobden argued how British industry depended on weather conditions that affected harvests; a poor harvest led to an increase in the price of bread, which brought about a decrease in the consumption of other products, and this resulted in unemployment, as well as a fall in British imports and exports. In dealing with the economic crisis of 1839–1842 and the Chartist revolt, Robert Peel (1789–1850) sided with the Manchester programme; in his government's budget of 1842, he reduced customs duties and reintroduced income tax. The 1846 subsistence crisis in Ireland led him to finally repeal the Corn Laws; it was a victory for industrial interests over protectionism, particularly of the agricultural classes. The Whigs continued to dismantle the mercantilist system until the ultimate triumph of free trade in 1860. The fact that Britain was at the peak of its economic power and political prestige led others to follow its example, and the first to do so was the France of Napoleon III.

Changes to the economic situation could come about only if the whole context of exchange regulations could be redefined, and the 1860 Cobden–Chevalier trade agreement between Great Britain and France is to be understood in this light. The agreement stipulated that Britain should remove all customs tariffs on imports of French goods, with the exception of wine and brandy, which were considered luxury goods; France was committed to reducing tariffs on British goods, and 30 per cent was to be the maximum rate that could be imposed. The significance of this agreement extended far beyond the two nations directly involved. It was an innovation that had exceptionally far-reaching consequences for the future of European trade relations. The so-called 'most favoured nation' clause meant that the effects of the agreement could be extended to other countries by only one of the two signatory nations. France, for example, negotiated a series of agreements with Belgium (1862), the *Zollverein* (1862), Italy (1864), Switzerland (1864), Spain (1865), Holland (1865), Scandinavia (1865) and Austria (1866). As a result of the most favoured nation clause, Great Britain came to enjoy the benefits of special privileges that France negotiated with the states with which it had signed a trade agreement. This meant that during the twenty years after 1860, free trade experienced a chain development that involved the majority of European nations.

Return to protectionism

After the 1870s, in several countries there was a return to protectionism. To understand this change it is necessary to consider a number of factors that transformed the economic and political landscape of Europe in the last quarter of the century:

1 The achievement of considerable levels of industrial development led the entrepreneurial classes in several European countries to seek protection from increasing competition.

2 In the field of agriculture, imports of low-priced corn, especially from the United States and Russia, caused large landowners to advocate protectionism.
3 The economic crisis that affected the whole of Europe from 1873 made competition on the national and international markets considerably more difficult, and even many industrialists favoured a move towards protectionism.
4 The triumph of nationalism and imperialism changed the climate of international relations. The Austro-Prussian and Franco-Prussian Wars of 1866 and 1870 created a series of political conflicts that led to the First World War. In the complex interaction of politics and economics, there was an increasingly close connection between protectionism and policies of 'international prestige'.
5 Colonial enterprise led to a series of diplomatic clashes over the division of territory, especially in Africa. Territorial expansion outside Europe became a burden on the taxation systems of the majority of European nations.
6 With important nations abandoning free trade positions, chain reactions were created and led to a general drive towards protectionism.

All these factors breathed new life into protectionist interests that had never fully disappeared. After the 1870s, other European countries were led to adopt protectionism by the agricultural crisis that had developed because of competition from American and Russian grain; its arrival on the European markets was an effect of the increase in steamship navigation. The conditions were created for a coalition of interests between landowners, who were penalized by lower agricultural prices, and industrialists, who were affected by falls in consumption. This was the case in Germany, where tariffs on national products were adopted by Bismarck between 1879 and 1881; the decision was also dictated by political and fiscal advantages, and the system was developed, in a more moderate form, under Kaiser Wilhelm II (1888–1918). Trade agreements ensured the economic predominance of Germany over the agricultural countries of central and eastern Europe. Italy followed a similar route. In the pre-unification period, exports of agricultural raw materials and semi-finished products (especially silk) had been outweighed by imports of industrial manufactures, thus creating an adverse trade balance. Protectionism was applied in all the states, with the exceptions of the Grand Duchy of Tuscany, and the Kingdom of Sardinia from 1834.[6] The free trade position of the ruling class of the new Kingdom of Italy was closely linked with its foreign policy, as the 1863 Italo-French trade agreement showed. The transition to protectionism was gradual and not without difficulties; conflicts arose between ideologies, in international relations, and in differing interests in different sectors of the national economies. The post-unification ruling class in Italy held that some European countries should develop the primary sector, while others should maintain, or achieve, dominant positions in the secondary sector, in accordance with the theory of international specialization. Between 1861 and 1876, the historical right wing governments applied free trade policies; however, the new left wing government saw the need to accelerate industrialization through a more active role of the state with a 'semi-protectionist' policy, such as the 1878 customs tariff.[7] In 1887 came the turning point as regards tariffs (the *svolta tariffaria*),[8] though they were applied only in trade agreements with individual foreign countries. They were tenaciously supported by an agrarian-industrialist coalition led by the foremost industrialist of the day, the wool entrepreneur and senator Alessandro Rossi of Schio.[9] The Italian case is interesting because of its international repercussions. Hitherto France had been the trading partner of Italy *par excellence*, exporting industrial products and importing citrus fruits, silkworms and a range of fruit and vegetable produce. During the four years between 1888 and 1892, there was a 'tariff war' between France and Italy, during which tariffs were continually being raised. France did not stabilize its tariffs until 1892, when the Tariffe Méline was applied. However, they were still lower than they had been in the first half of the century, since the most favoured nation clause set them at the lowest rate and eliminated any discrimination.

By 1914 the whole of Europe had returned to varying degrees of protectionism. The free trade group was reduced to the nations of north-western Europe with the most developed trade. Great Britain's economic interests worldwide enabled it to remain particularly open to free trade; the British economy thus became the pivot on which the whole economic system of international exchange turned.

Colonialism

The return to protectionism came at the same time as important political changes. Countries like Britain had considerable colonial experience; with its maritime development in the seventeenth and eighteenth centuries, Britain had created a series of areas of influence, free ports, and possessions, particularly in America and Asia. On the other hand, for France, the eighteenth century had marked the loss of its overseas possessions to Britain, and in the first decades of the nineteenth century Spain and Portugal had lost their colonies in South America. Meanwhile, industrialization in Europe brought about the need to expand markets for both finished products and raw materials, and Britain had started a new type of imperialism based on the occupation of vast areas of the globe. At the end of the nineteenth century, its empire stretched from Nigeria to South Africa, from India, Burma and Australia to Canada. Other European nations also set out on the same path; between 1830 and the end of the nineteenth century, France occupied part of Saharan Africa (initially Algeria, Tunisia, Morocco), equatorial Africa, Madagascar and Indochina. Since German interests were more focused on Europe, German colonialism was more restricted, and it was purely for political reasons that Bismarck launched into colonial enterprises. Belgian colonialism was also restricted, while Portuguese and Spanish colonialism was on the decline. Italian colonialism, with the occupation of Eritrea (1885), Somalia (1887–89) and later Libya (1912), was ultimately to fail.

Colonialism was a complex phenomenon and in the long term had many different aspects. From the economic point of view, which was not always uppermost, the colonies were markets for goods, capital and raw materials, and also as an outlet for growing populations, but these elements did not always equally apply to all the European colonies. There was as much difference in their political and economic links as there was in the types of colonies. Great Britain was the only European country that had close economic ties with its colonies. In 1854, about 55 per cent of British foreign investment was in continental Europe, in 1870 it was no more than 30 per cent, and in 1914 barely 8 per cent. On the other hand, in 1854, investments in the colonies and dominions, including India, accounted for no more than 20 per cent of total foreign investment, in 1870 it amounted to 45 per cent, and by 1914 as much as 65 per cent. These figures appear all the more astonishing in view of the fact that in the same period French investment in the colonies amounted to 4–9 per cent of all foreign investment. These figures perhaps substantiate the opinion that there was a connection between British 'economic decline' and over-commitment to typical products of the first industrial revolution. Since such products could be absorbed by colonial markets, Britain had less interest in converting to products that were typical of the second industrial revolution. In the long run, capital that could be used for important processes of technological innovation at home went to the colonies; but it also created a state of immobility in production because of its unsophisticated markets.[10]

The international economy

With the expansion of European international trade, the international economic situation was taking shape. Taking 100 as the total volume of exports from European countries in 1913, in 1820 the index was barely 5, and in 1870 it was about 30. European trade thus witnessed unprecedented development both in developed countries and in those outside Europe. Table 9.1 shows Britain's clear supremacy throughout the nineteenth century. Although new powers like Germany and the United States had achieved considerable levels of industrialization by the end of the century (with Germany even surpassing Great Britain), the role of British trade still predominated. In 1914, Great Britain still controlled about 14 per cent of world trade. These were unparalleled results. Between 1840 and 1860, there was a threefold increase in the quantity of cotton traded worldwide, while that of sugar doubled in the thirty years between 1840 and 1870. Wool, cocoa, indigo, wood, corn, rubber, seed and even guano were at the centre of a dense network of worldwide trade.

Table 9.1 Value of exports, 1820–1913 ($ million at 1913 prices)

Country	*1820*	*1840*	*1860*	*1880*	*1900*	*1913*	*Exports as % of GDP in 1913*
Great Britain	73	189	579	1,052	1,497	2,555	20.9
Germany	–	106	240	549	1,097	2,454	17.5
France	56	86	260	578	818	1,328	13.9
Italy	35	–	–	251	312	485	12.0
Belgium	16	29	87	224	386	717	50.9
Holland	–	–	–	166	267	413	38.2
United States	31	97	229	833	1,733	2,380	6.1
Japan	–	–	–	22	92	315	12.3

Source: adapted from A. Maddison, *Dynamic Forces in Capitalist Development. A Long-run Comparative View*, Oxford, 1991, pp. 311–15. 324–6.

Europe was at the centre of the world system, with about two-thirds of all exports and imports of raw materials and finished products (Tables 9.2 and 9.3). Table 9.2 shows how Great Britain accounted for a decreasing influx of raw materials, while Table 9.3 shows a decrease in the UK share of finished products. A new non-European producer, the United States, was becoming more and more important. However, the industrial role of the United States, which in the twentieth century was to be fundamental, was still not apparent; in 1880, around 80 per cent of its exports went to Europe, and in 1913 Europe still accounted for about 60 per cent of exports from the United States. Yet developments in America were being closely watched, and there were those who predicted its future role on the world scene.[11]

The system of international relations just described can be seen in terms of a 'core–periphery' model in which Europe at its centre firmly controlled the whole system, but saw most of its trade being carried on within its own boundaries. Indeed, it has been observed that the importance of the 'periphery' in the development of the 'core' of the system should not be overestimated. Between 1830 and 1910 (Table 9.4), about 80 per cent of the exports from European countries found buyers' markets within Europe itself. Although this percentage was considerably lower for Great Britain (about 40 per cent), the fact remains that Europe was the centre of production and consumption regardless of economic events in

Table 9.2 Distribution of world trade in raw materials, by continent, 1876–1913 (%)

	1876–1880		*1896–1900*		*1913*	
Area	*Areas*	*Exports*	*Imports*	*Exports*	*Imports*	*Exports*
Great Britain	30	3	26	4	19	6
Continental Europe	50	43	55	46	55	40
North America	7	16	8	19	11	17
Rest of world	13	38	10	32	14	37
World	100	100	100	100	100	100

Source: A.G. Kenwood and A.L. Lougheed, *The Growth of the International Economy, 1820–1990*. London and New York, 1992, p. 86.

Table 9.3 Distribution of world trade in finished products, by continent, 1876–1913 (%)

	1876–80		*1896–1900*		*1913*	
Area	*Imports*	*Exports*	*Imports*	*Exports*	*Imports*	*Exports*
Great Britain	9	38	10	31	8	25
Continental Europe	31	57	33	57	40	56
North America	8	4	10	7	12	11
Rest of world	52	1	47	5	40	8
World	100	100	100	100	100	100

Source: A.G. Kenwood and A.L. Lougheed, *The Growth of the International Economy, 1820–1990*, London and New York, 1992. p. 86.

Table 9.4 Changes in the structure of foreign trade (%)

Great Britain

	Raw materials		*Foodstuffs*		*Manufactures*	
Years	*Imports*	*Exports*	*Imports*	*Exports*	*Imports*	*Exports*
1854–56	53.7	7.1	39.1	6.8	7.1	86.1
1890–92	40.2	14.1	43.0	4.9	16.8	80.9
1911–13	42.5	17.6	37.7	6.4	19.9	76.1

France (exports)

Years	*Raw materials*	*Agric. products*	*Manufactures*
1837–46	4.3	21.8	73.9
1867–76	10.0	38.0	52.0
1887–96	11.9	33.9	54.3
1907–13	14.6	27.4	58.1

Germany

	Raw materials		*Foodstuffs*		*Semi-finished*		*Manufactures*	
Years	*Imports*	*Exports*	*Imports*	*Exports*	*Imports*	*Exports*	*Imports*	*Exports*
1880–82	35.2	14.5	33.6	21.1	19.1	16.0	12.1	48.5
1890–92	36.6	15.8	37.0	14.6	16.5	15.6	10.0	54.0
1911–13	42.5	15.4	34.0	10.1	14.8	21.1	8.7	53.4

Italy

	Raw materials		*Foodstuffs*		*Semi-finished*		*Manufactures*	
Years	*Imports*	*Exports*	*Imports*	*Exports*	*Imports*	*Exports*	*Imports*	*Exports*
1881–83	12.7	12.7	20.6	32.5	29.5	29.5	15.4	15.4
1890–92	32.4	16.1	24.6	28.5	22.2	42.2	20.8	13.2
1911–13	37.2	14.3	19.7	29.3	19.9	24.9	23.2	31.5

United States

	Raw materials		*Foodstuffs*		*Semi-finished*		*Manufactures*	
Years	*Imports*	*Exports*	*Imports*	*Exports*	*Imports*	*Exports*	*Imports*	*Exports*
1821	5.5	60.8	10.9	3.9	7.3	9.8	56.4	5.9
1858–60	12.4	66.2	13.8	4.8	8.3	4.0	47.8	11.9
1890–92	23.1	36.1	18.4	17.9	14.9	5.3	26.6	15.0
1911–13	35.0	33.3	12.5	5.7	18.6	16.1	22.7	30.9

Japan (exports)

Years	*Primary products*	*Light industry*	*Heavy industry*
1874–80	47.1	45.3	7.6
1901–10	14.4	70.7	14.9

Source: P.A. Toninelli. (ed.) *Lo sviluppo economico moderno dalla rivoluzione industriale alla crisi energetica, 1750–1973*. Venice, 1997, pp. 620–1.

other countries. In this case, it was the periphery that needed Europe, in order to start commercial and industrial development.

The growing European industrial powers created financial relations that appeared to be just as complex. Until 1850, as in the case of the construction of the railway system, the foreign investment of most European countries was on the continent itself, while in the second half of the century, capital was increasingly exported on a world scale. European industrialization had created wealth that was destined to find new uses. Great Britain, especially, had had trading and financial links with different trading partners, at least since the end of the seventeenth century, which led, on the one hand, to the investment of surplus capital abroad, and on the other to the refinement of various financial mechanisms for the efficient circulation and use of capital. The great expansion in international trade, with Great Britain as the uncontested leader, could not have taken place without the development of systems of financing.

The whole world market came to be regulated from London, which was the chief port and depot for raw materials and goods. Share and bond markets, foreign currency markets, central banks, private and commercial banks, brokers and other financial agents were the instruments of unprecedented financial expansion; at the heart of the system was the City. In the eighteenth century, about three-quarters of its operators, who were initially merchants and later merchant bankers, were already of foreign origin. London established its financial role with the nineteenth century, and with British industrial development, not only in Europe but also in the world. Bills of exchange were settled through the intermediation of merchant bankers; these were private bankers such as Baring, Rothschild, Schroeder, Hambro, Lazard and Peabody, who granted credit for short-term acceptance. The discount bankers intermediated between the banks holding credit and those seeking to place their assets. Neither Paris nor Berlin had such a specialized and well informed financial market. The supremacy of the pound sterling reinforced the efficiency of the London market; the quality of its services played a fundamental role in the equilibrium of the British balance of payments.

However, it was difficult to find a clear distinction between short and long-term transactions. Profits from trading activities might remain abroad in countries that were becoming industrialized as investments in the form of production activities, normally with higher returns than in the already industrialized countries; they could also be invested in the national debt, as for example in American government bonds. Such mechanisms help to explain the phenomenal growth of foreign investment during the nineteenth century. In 1855, foreign investment worldwide was £420 million; fifteen years later it had reached £1.3 billion, increasing to £4.7 billion in 1900; by 1914, it was £9.5 billion. On the eve of the First World War, Great Britain still accounted for 43 per cent of world investment, and was investing the equivalent of 7–9 per cent of its GDP overseas. Following some way behind was France, with 20 per cent, then Germany, with 13 per cent, and Belgium, Holland and Switzerland with 12 per cent. Foreign investment of the United States was still very modest, at only 7 per cent (Figure 9.1).[12]

Europe was thus not only the world's greatest investor, but of all the continents it was also the greatest recipient of investments (Figure 9.2). Throughout the century,

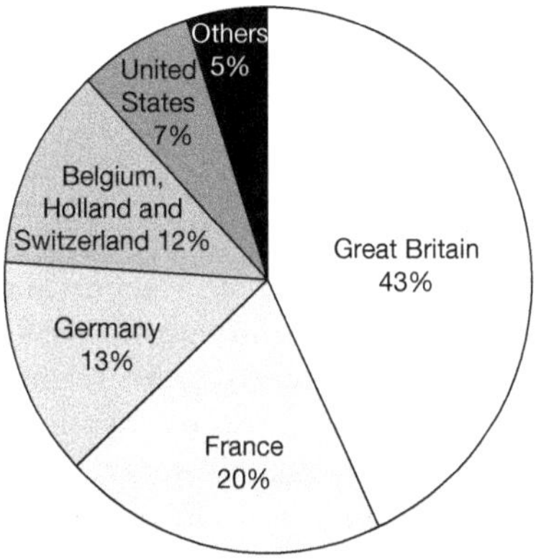

Figure 9.1 Foreign investment in 1914: investor countries.

Source: R. Cameron, *A Concise Economic History of the World*, 3rd edn, Oxford, 1997, p. 311.

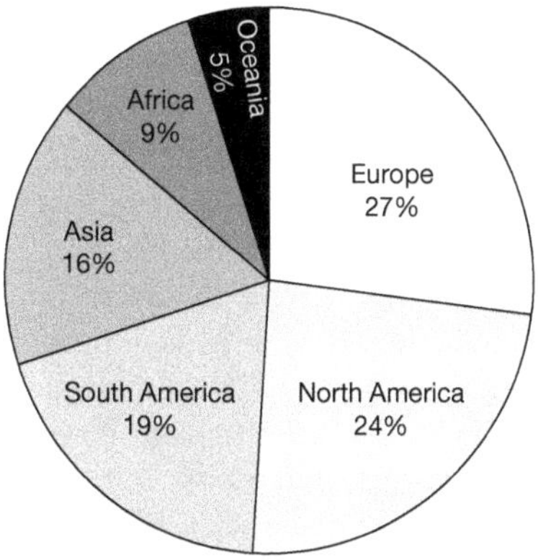

Figure 9.2 Foreign investment in 1914: recipient areas.

Source: R. Cameron, *A Concise Economic History of the World*, 3rd edn, Oxford, 1997, p. 311.

almost all the countries of Europe depended on investment from other European countries to a greater or lesser degree. In 1914, the Balkan countries of Russia and Turkey were the greatest recipients of capital in Europe; it came especially from France, Germany and Holland. For Russia, foreign capital was fundamental in the construction of the railway system, but also for financing the military and naval policies of the tsarist government. Foreign investment in Scandinavia was important for the renewal of its economies and the development of industrialization.

There were different reasons for the outflow of capital to non-European countries. Canada, Australia and New Zealand were seen as new centres for the development of European-style social and cultural models, but especially as models of production and consumption. Investment, particularly of British capital, in Latin America was channelled towards Argentina, Brazil and in part Mexico. On the

Asian continent, China, Japan and especially India, at the time part of the British Empire, received substantial investments, while most foreign investment in Africa was concentrated in South Africa.

The balance of payments and the gold standard

With the aggressive expansion of international markets for goods, labour and finance, a true international economy took shape, and each country was forced to focus on its balance of payments account. This was the means whereby records of all payments made abroad could be matched against all payments received from abroad. Depending on their stage of development, countries had different types of balances of payment. By definition, the balance of payments is in a state of balance; if there is an imbalance, whether it is a surplus or a deficit, this is indicated in the balance on current account. It is an algebraic calculation of the visible trade balance (imports and exports of goods), the invisible trade balance (services, freight, insurance, tourism, banking), remittances from emigrants, and finally interest and dividends. A surplus is offset by exporting capital, in order to restore balance, and adjustments do not generally produce negative effects on the domestic economy. If there is a deficit, the country has to restore balance, either by drawing on reserves in the interim, by borrowing, or by intervening on internal economic variables. This is where one has to start in order to understand how the first successful international system of payments in history actually worked. First, the balance of payments of the predominant country, Great Britain, will be examined (Tables 9.5–6).

In the nineteenth century, the trade balance of the United Kingdom was constantly in deficit. Thus, the exportation of manufactures did not make it possible to accumulate capital that had been exported overseas. Emigrants transferred more capital abroad than they remitted to their families in Europe. Invisible services, such as revenue from the merchant fleet, banking, insurance and transport, enabled a surplus on the balance of trade in goods and services to be made (as in 1815–1835, 1855–1875, 1910–1914), as well as a decrease in the deficit (1835–1855, 1890–1905), in the years when the export of goods was held back by protectionism or competition. The steady growth in foreign investments considerably increased the

Table 9.5 International trade balance of Great Britain, 1816–1850 (£ million, period values)

Period	*Imports*	*Exports*	*Import/export balance*	*Services*	*Capital*	*Overall balance*
1816–20	49.3	40.3	–9.0	14.5	1.7	7.2
1821–25	45.4	37.3	–8.1	14.2	4.2	10.3
1826–30	48.7	35.9	–12.8	10.6	4.6	2.4
1831–35	53.6	40.5	–13.1	14.1	5.4	6.4
1836–40	73.6	49.6	–24.0	18.6	8.0	2.6
1841–45	71.0	54.0	–17.0	15.4	7.5	5.9
1846–50	87.7	60.9	–26.8	22.0	9.5	4.7

Source: A.H. Imlah, *Economic Elements in the Pax Britannica. Studies in British Foreign Trade in the Nineteenth Century*, New York, 1969.

Table 9.6 Industrial income, investments and public expenditure, England and continental Europe, 1800–1910

	Income produced by industrial sector (as % of GDP)		*Investments (as % of national expenditure)*		*State expenditure (as % of total expenditure)*	
Year	*England*	*Europe*	*England*	*Europe*	*England*	*Europe*
1800	19.8	22.0	7.9	12.6	15.3	7.4
1840	31.5	25.2	10.5	14.4	7.9	7.0
1870	33.5	31.3	8.5	17.2	4.8	6.3
1890	33.6	32.8	7.3	18.6	5.9	5.9
1910	31.8	34.4	7.0	19.5	8.2	5.7

Source: N.F.R. Crafts, 'La recente storia quantitativa della rivoluzione industriale', *Rivista di Storia Economica*, 3 (1989).

surplus of revenue from interest and dividends; it even sufficed to bring about a permanent surplus in the balance of payments. Thus during the nineteenth century, the British balance of payments was never in deficit.[13] This was one of the main strengths of the pound sterling, and it became the benchmark currency in the international monetary system. The 'gold standard', as it was known, was created in order to cope with the great increase in commercial and financial relations between different states. Where several different currencies were involved, an efficient currency exchange market needed to be created, and the solution was found in a monetary system that could provide a unit of account into which all the currencies could be converted.

During the nineteenth century, for internal exchanges there was a gradual move towards replacing metal money with banknotes. The use of gold and silver coins had meant that the nominal value of the coin was also a real value, and with the expansion of banking practices, the growing use of banknotes had caused a discrepancy between nominal and real value. Banknotes did not hold real value, but the bank that had issued them was committed to converting the nominal value into gold or silver. The issuing bank therefore had to hold a quantity of precious metal as a sufficient reserve to ensure convertibility of the paper money into precious metal at a fixed parity; this had to be kept equal to a specific amount of the reserve of precious metal, initially established by usage, and later by law. This link between precious metal and circulating paper money meant that, in order to increase the amount of money in circulation, new reserves had to be acquired; at the same time, if there was a decrease in precious metal the amount of circulating paper money had to be reduced. Since at any one time, the reserve of metal was not sufficient to convert all the banknotes in circulation, it was a fiduciary system, based on proper adherence to the rules of the game. If not, there could have been a rush on the banks to convert the notes; this would have led to the collapse of the system, and to a state of forced circulation of the banknotes. The system thus required strict discipline, in the issue of fiduciary money, as well as in the balance of payments. If a country was in deficit, and had to pay its deficit in gold, it needed to restrict growth, or decrease its money supply, so that internal prices would fall and demand would slow down. Imports would thus decrease, but exports could be increased, since they regained their competitiveness. In this way balance was restored 'automatically'. In a situation where there was a surplus on the balance of payments, the reverse happened. However, it could happen that countries with a surplus preferred to increase their reserves and not obey the rules of the game; in that case there was an increase in the amount of money in circulation, with the consequent 'sterilization' of gold. The whole burden of re-adjusting fell on the country with a deficit, sometimes forcing it to leave the gold standard and let its own currency fluctuate.

Observing that the system was thrown into crisis by wars and by the internal difficulties of individual countries, some scholars have argued that the gold standard was what made periods of great international stability possible, and not the gold standard that generated stability, even though that was one of its strengths.[14] Moreover, a fixed exchange system indissolubly links the monetary and fiscal policies of member countries to those of the leader country through the complex interplay of action and reaction, and if it is to function well, the entire international monetary system requires stable and secure leadership. The pound sterling was synonymous with stability, while the franc experienced two periods of forced circulation, between 1848 and 1850 and from 1870 to 1877, while the dollar fluctuated between 1862 and 1878. The nineteenth century showed remarkable monetary stability and the major currencies did not suffer any permanent loss of their purchasing power. However, it was the pound sterling that inspired unconditional confidence; nobody anywhere else had been able to secure such absolute convertibility. The only great market for international credit was the City, and bills of exchange could be transacted there at the best conditions possible. This is why, after 1880, states increasingly included foreign currency in their exchange reserves; this was essentially the pound sterling, which was preferred to gold, since it also guaranteed interest.

In the nineteenth century, the monetary base on which the exchange value of products was fixed was normally a precious metal. Some countries adopted bimetallism, using gold and silver; others adopted monometallism, either only silver or only gold. Until the 1870s, these systems meant that the world could be divided into three monetary zones. The first included countries that had adopted gold monometallism, and their systems were based solely on gold; of these countries Great Britain was the most important. In 1821, Parliament re-established the free convertibility of banknotes, which had been in forced circulation during the war against France; notes issued by the Bank of England were unlimited legal tender and until 1914 could be freely exchanged for gold. The second monetary zone was made up of countries using the silver standard, mainly countries lying on the shores of the Pacific and Indian Oceans. The third zone comprised the countries that had adopted bimetallism. Their system was based on gold and silver, and a ratio between the two metals was fixed by law; in France the ratio had been 1:15.5 since 1803. Bimetallism was inconvenient with regard to one aspect in particular: if there was variation in the price ratio between the two metals, the higher-priced metal had to be sold, and quantities of the lower priced one bought until parity of price between the two metals was re-established. This was the aim of the Latin Monetary Union. The Union had been set up by France in the 1860s and 1870s, and apart from France, also involved Belgium, Switzerland, Italy (between 1865 and 1866) and later Spain, Serbia and Romania. But it was doomed to fail because of the influx of silver after the discovery of new deposits.

Great Britain, on the other hand, had preferred monometallism. In 1717 it had already been established that a golden guinea was worth 21*s*; in 1774, payments in silver coin had been limited to a maximum value of £25, and in 1816 to only £2. After 1821, when the Bank of England resumed conversion of banknotes into precious metal, gold effectively became a standard for the currency. Problems with using a system of bimetallism, and continual fluctuations in the value of silver, ultimately led to silver being excluded as a measure of account; since both gold and silver are also raw materials, their prices are determined by supply and demand. Until around 1870 there was no variation in either the mint ratio or the trading ratio, but then they started increasingly to diverge, to the disadvantage of silver. Between 1860 and 1890, the production of silver increased as normal in the United States and Mexico, while the production of gold, which had increased enormously after the discoveries in California (1848) and Australia (1851), slowly started to dwindle.

In 1873, the new country of Germany decided to put a new coin into circulation; this was the gold mark, and it replaced the silver thaler. The reason for the decision was compatibility with the pound sterling. However, this alignment of gold reserves created an imbalance in trade relations, and the bimetallism countries gradually adopted gold monometallism, so that they would not lose their gold reserves, or be swamped with silver, which was considered poor coin. This was the case of France and the Latin Monetary Union after 1876, and the United States in 1900; it came after long and vexed political debate. Very soon the majority of European and non-European nations adopted the gold standard following recommendations laid down at the Monetary Congress of Paris in 1876. When it became part of the gold system, Italy gained an acceptable level of monetary tranquillity, and it reinforced the basis for development at the end of the century; this was an important result after the monetary crisis that had hit the country in 1866. The negative results of the war against Austria had led the government to stop converting banknotes into precious metal, in order to meet unavoidable state expenditure.

At the start of the twentieth century, gold finally ousted silver, despite the fact that the production of silver was rapidly increasing, with the discovery of new mines after 1890 in the Transvaal, Australia, the Klondike and Siberia. The adoption of the gold standard was associated with British supremacy in international trade, and for the whole of the nineteenth century, because of British predominance in trade, international exchanges were based on the gold standard. Not only was it used for fixing the value of all currencies to gold, but it put British sterling at the centre of the system, and effectively made it a unit of international conversion.

Notes

1 A.G. Kenwood and A.L. Lougheed, *The Growth of the International Economy, 1820–1990*, London and New York, 1992.

2 A.M. Taylor and J.G. Williamson, 'Convergence in the Age of Mass Migration', *European Review of Economic History*, 2, pp. 1977, 27–63; T.J. Hatton and J.G. Williamson, 'What drove the mass migrations from Europe in the late nineteenth century?', *Population and Development Review*, 1994, pp. 1–27.
3 They were to increase a further sixteen times between 1913 and 1992.
4 'I paesi, cioè, non avevano bisogno di bilanciare esportazioni e importazioni con ogni singolo partner commerciale, perché le compensazioni si potevano effettuare sull'aggregato, permettendo in questo modo maggiore flessibilità di uso delle risorse mondiali.' V. Zamagni, *Dalla rivoluzione industriale all'integrazione europea*, Bologna, 1999, p. 117.
5 'sul fatto che un protezionismo troppo elevato ha effetti solo negativi, mentre le più moderne teorie del commercio strategico danno qualche giustificazione a una moderata protezione temporanea accompagnata da un rafforzamento delle capacità competitive'. *Ibid.*, p. 118.
6 L. Trezzi, 'I modi del coinvolgimento nello sviluppo economico europeo', in S. Zaninelli (ed.), *L'Ottocento economico italiano*, Bologna, 1993.
7 P. Pecorari, *Il protezionismo imperfetto. Luigi Luzzatti e la tariffa doganale del 1878*, Venice, 1989.
8 E. Del Vecchio, *La via italiana al protezionismo*, 5 vols, Rome, 1979–1980; A. Cardini, *Stato liberale e protezionismo in Italia*, Bologna, 1981.
9 Among others: S. Lanaro, 'Nazionalismo e ideologia del blocco corporativo-protezionista in Italia', *Ideologie*, 2, 1967; *id.*, 'Mercantilismo agrario e formazione del capitale nel pensiero di Alessandro Rossi', *Quaderni storici*, 5, 1971; L. Avagliano, *Alessandro Rossi e le origini dell'Italia industriale*, Naples, 1970; G. Are, *Alle origini dell'Italia industriale*, Naples, 1974; G. L. Fontana (ed.), *Schio e Alessandro Rossi. Imprenditorialità, politica, cultura e paesaggi sociali del secondo Ottocento*, 2 vols, Rome, 1985–1986
10 L.E. Davis and R.A. *Huttenback, Mammon and the Pursuit of Empire. The Economics of British Imperialism*, Cambridge, 1988.
11 E. Rossi, *Gli Stati Uniti e la concorrenza Americana*, Florence, 1884.
12 See also C. H. Feinstein, P. Temin and G. Toniolo, *The European Economy between the Wars*, Oxford, 1998.
13 J. Heffer and W. Serman, *Il XIX secolo, 1815–1914. Dalle revoluzioni agli imperialismi*, ed. S. Zaninelli, Milan, 1998, pp. 65–6.
14 B. Eichengreen (ed.), *The Gold Standard in Theory and History*, London, 1985; V. Zamagni, *Dalla rivoluzione industriale*, pp. 124–6.

10 The twentieth century – from break with the past to prosperity (I)

Growth and transformation of the economy

Albert Carreras

Introduction to Chapters 10–12

The starting point

The period from around 1900 until the summer of 1914 was one of great prosperity for the world economy. They were the years of the *Belle Époque* and of Edwardian England. From 1900, and even as far back as the mid-nineteenth century, the world economy was a global one. Means of transport, such as overland railways and seagoing ships, and modern means of communication, such as the press, the telegraph and increasingly the telephone, made practically the whole globe accessible. Information, money, goods and people circulated reasonably quickly and surprisingly regularly, and with very little interference from states. Anyone with an interest in economic matters, whether individuals, enterprises or governments, were well aware of what was happening in other parts of the world. If a family had a relative working in another country, its members would be kept in touch with the fortunes of their next of kin, and if things looked positive, they had no hesitation in following suit. If a trade union called a strike to proclaim a forty-eight-hour week, the call would be immediately taken up in neighbouring cities and towns. If the bank rate at the Bank of England was particularly favourable, people would rush to borrow in sterling. If a new mineral ore deposit was discovered, or a new product developed, people and capital would soon converge to exploit the new business opportunities it offered. It is also worth mentioning that passports were the exception, rather than the rule. People were free to emigrate, and millions of Europeans, especially peasants, would leave their lands in the north, south, east and west of Europe in search of a better livelihood in the Americas. There were no exchange controls, no controls on the movement of capital, and no obstacles to trade except for limited tariffs, and these would often be negligible. On account of all this, prosperity spread throughout the world, slowly but steadily.

Indeed, seen from the perspective of the new millennium, what was particularly striking about the world economy at the start of the twentieth century was the convergence of *per capita* income. Despite being subjected to colonial domination, the agricultural regions of the world showed uninterrupted progress. In the advanced countries the poorer social classes increased their income without the impoverished peasants in the rest of the world suffering any negative effects. In the industrialized countries, socialists talked of a 'workers' aristocracy', made up of highly skilled, well paid workers, who earned twice, or even three or four times, as much as unskilled workers. But nothing in that period could compare with the 'aristocratism' of the present-day working classes in the developed world, whose incomes are a hundred times greater than those in poorer countries. In 1900, the poorest social classes went to America in search of higher wages and were free to enter the United States or Argentina once they had been through health checks. Today's poor enjoy no such opportunities, and are barred from entering the countries of the European Union, with no chance of emigrating there.

It has often been pointed out that such miraculous progress could be explained only by a combination of extremely favourable circumstances: the absolute hegemony of London as the centre of the stock market, of finance, trade and services, and the overall predominance of the economy of the British Empire. Britain's outright leadership made the world simpler and facilitated exchanges, and the model collapsed only when other countries started to challenge it, as in the case of Germany and the 1914 war, Russia and the 1917 revolution, and the United States with its isolationism in 1919.

Whatever the reasons were for the equilibrium in the world economy at the beginning of the century, it is towards such a global scenario that our own future is headed. The endless debate about the current process of globalization would be more useful, and less doom-laden, if it started by reflecting on the scope and limits of the phenomenon itself. It is worth noting that only very recently (in some cases around 1970 and in others around 1990) has the degree of commercial and financial internationalization that existed before the European war been surpassed. Likewise, the pursuit of monetary stability is nothing less than a search for the economic remedy (price stability) that had been the main issue during the period of the gold standard. Nor is entrepreneurial dynamism only a thing of today. Indeed, the origins of the major multinational companies can be traced back to the early twentieth century.

All in all, it has taken a century ('short' maybe, but bristling with adversity) to return to the point of departure. Of course, this can never be quite the same as it once was, which is why it is worth investigating what has changed along the way.

Century-long growth

According to the most recent and complete estimates, between 1913 and 1998 the GDP of Europe (including the Asian part of Russia, the Soviet Union and the former Soviet republics) increased almost sevenfold (6.95), with an annual increase of 2.31 per cent. This was even more than in the 1820–1913 period, when it increased 5.61 times (1.87 per cent per year) and almost exactly the same as during the *Belle Époque*, from 1900 to 1913 when it was 2.36 per cent. Is this a large or a small increase? It is undoubtedly large, since it was the greatest century-long increase ever experienced in Europe. But it is small in comparison with the rest of the world. Between 1913 and 1998, the GDP of the great countries of North America and Oceania that had once been colonized by the British, increased more than fourteen times. The same applies to the African continent. Asia increased its economy nineteen times, and Latin America no less than twenty-four. Overall, the economy of the world grew more than twelve times. The lower figure for European growth is conspicuous. In 1913, Europe accounted for 47 per cent of world GDP, but in 1998 for only 26 per cent. In short, contrary to what happened in the nineteenth century, when Europe gained a position of world economic hegemony (from 32 per cent in 1820, to 47 per cent in 1913), in the twentieth century European growth gradually decreased, and shows no signs of changing.

As will be shown later, the explanation for this can be found in the demographic evolution. The fact that the European population increased at half the rate of the world population goes a long way to explain the overall reason for the economic decline in Europe. But the relative improvement in European prosperity *per capita*, offsets the decline to a certain extent – by 15 per cent. In 1820, Europe accounted for 32.3 per cent of world GDP and 21.5 per cent of the world population. Both figures reflect the very significant fact that most of the European population lived at levels of material prosperity that were 50 per cent higher than the world average. In 1913, on the other hand, with 27.7 per cent of the world population, Europe had reached 47 per cent of world GDP, and thus, in terms of individual prosperity, was 70 per cent above the world average. In 1998, this trend had become more marked. Although only 13.5 per cent of the world population lived in Europe, and its GDP was only 26.5 per cent, these two percentages show that European prosperity was almost double the world average. There were proportionally fewer Europeans than before the First World War, but they were relatively more prosperous. Thus, in terms of *per capita* income, Europe managed to improve its own relative position, despite the demographic changes. Indeed, during the twentieth century, European affluence (measured by *per capita* GDP) not only increased, but also grew faster than that of the world as a whole. European GDP increased 4.3 times, while that of the world as a whole increased 3.7 times. From being 70 per cent higher than the average, its affluence rose to almost double. This was a great achievement for the population of the European continent.

The demographic evolution

Over the century, the number of inhabitants in the European countries as a whole increased by around 300 million, rising from almost 500 million to 800 million, or by just over 60 per cent. Table 10.1 shows the situation in 1913, with the then existing frontiers (after the Balkan wars and before the outbreak of the Great War). The bulk of the European population was concentrated in only a small number of countries. The most heavily populated countries accounted for 88 per cent of the total population, while the rest was divided among another fifteen countries. This was also the period of the great powers from the demographic point of view.

If we take the 1998 population figures for the main countries (with current borders matched up with previous ones), even at the end of the century demographic trends could be classified according to annual growth rates: from 1913 to 1950 (which allow for the impact of two world wars) and from 1950 to 1998 (Table 10.2).

Table 10.1 European population in 1913 (millions)

Country	*No. of inhabitants*
Russia	165.7
Germany	67.0
Austria-Hungary	50.5
United Kingdom	45.9
France	39.8
Italy	35.2
Spain	20.3
Belgium	7.6
Romania	7.4
Holland	6.1
Portugal	6.0
Sweden	5.6
Greece	4.8
Bulgaria	4.5
Switzerland	3.9
Serbia and Montenegro	3.0
Denmark	2.8
Norway	2.4
Bosnia-Herzegovina	1.9
Albania	0.8
Montenegro	0.3
Luxembourg	0.3
Total	481.8

Source: B.R. Mitchell, 'Statistical appendix', in C.M. Cipolla (ed.), *The Fontana Economic History of Europe*, London, vol. 4.2, 1973, pp. 738–820; A. Maddison, 'Economic policy and performance in Europe, 1913–1970', in C.M. Cipolla, *Fontana Economic History of Europe*, vol. 5.2, 1976, pp. 442–508; N.J.G. Pounds, *An Historical Geography of Europe, 1800–1914*, Cambridge, 1985. Excludes the small countries with fewer than 100,000 inhabitants or the population of the European part of the Ottoman Empire, already reduced to its present size.

A good point of comparison is the rate of demographic growth in Europe from 1900 to 1913: 1.11 per cent. Nowadays this rate would seem high. In the 'trans-war' years from 1913 to 1950, the population of Europe grew much more slowly. A number of countries suffered significant losses of population; these were countries such as Poland and Czechoslovakia, which had a particularly unfavourable political and military record. Others, particularly France, entered a phase of total stagnation. Germany, Austria and Ireland were very similar. The fringe areas of Mediterranean and northern Europe experienced greater increases. Scandinavian dynamism is an interesting case; it cannot be explained by a belated demographic transition phase, but by a combination of high growth and policies for increasing the birth rate. In terms of 'demographic optimism' the exception is Holland, which heads the table for population increase.

After 1950, and until 1998, there was an increase in the world growth rate, mainly as a result of greater optimism in all countries after the war. Some Soviet bloc countries, like Hungary and Bulgaria, are exceptions, though a number of Western countries also show very low growth rates of between 0.3 per cent and 0.4 per cent.

Table 10.2 European population in 1998 and growth from 1913 to 1998

Country	*Population 1998 (millions)*	*Annual growth 1913–1950 (%)*	*Annual growth 1950–1998 (%)*
Ex-soviet Union	290.9 [a]	0.38	1.00
Germany	82.0	0.13	0.38
United Kingdom	59.2	0.45	0.34
France	58.8	0.02	0.71
Italy	57.6	0.64	0.42
Spain	39.4	0.87	0.72
Poland	38.6	−0.20	0.92
Ex-Yugoslavia	22.5 [b]	0.43	0.72
Romania	22.4	0.72	0.66
Holland	15.7	1.35	0.92
Ex-Czechoslovakia	15.7 [c]	−0.18	0.49
Greece	10.5	0.90	0.69
Hungary	10.2	0.47	0.19
Belgium	10.1	0.32	0.35
Portugal	10.0	0.95	0.33
Sweden	8.9	0.60	0.49
Bulgaria	8.2	1.12	0.27
Austria	8.1	0.07	0.32
Switzerland	7.1	0.53	0.87
Denmark	5.3	0.97	0.45
Finland	5.2	0.76	0.52
Norway	4.4	0.78	0.64
Ireland	3.7	−0.11	0.46
Albania	3.3	0.85	2.10
Others	2.3	. . .	0.89
Total	800.3	0.38	0.70

Source: own adaptation of figures in A. Maddison, *The World Economy. A Millennial Perspective*, Paris, 2001.

Notes:
[a] Russian Federation, 146.9; Ukraine, 50.3; Uzbekistan, 24.1; Kazakhstan, 15.6; Belarus, 10.2; Azerbaijan, 7.7; Tajikistan, 6.1; Georgia, 5.4; Turkmenistan, 4.8; Kyrgizstan, 4.7; Armenia, 3.8; Lithuania, 3.7; Moldavia, 3.6; Latvia, 2.4; Estonia, 1.4.
[b] Serbia and Montenegro, 10.5; Croatia, 4.7; Bosnia, 3.5; Macedonia, 2.0; Slovenia, 2.0.
[c] Czech Republic, 10.3; Slovakia, 5.4.
. . . No data.

The high growth in the second half of the twentieth century was concentrated in the third quarter of the century. From 1950 to 1973 the population of Europe grew by 1 per cent annually. From 1973 to 1990 it grew at half that rate (0.5 per cent), and from 1990 to 1998 by only 0.2 per cent. Furthermore, during the last decade of the century, demographic trends in eastern Europe, including the CIS (Community of Independent States) recorded total stagnation (and even a slight fall, if the Asian republics of the former Soviet Union are excluded). On the other hand, western Europe showed greater capacity for growth, with rates between 0.3 per cent and 0.4 per cent.

The mortality rate, especially the infant mortality death rate, declined sharply, and the most significant effect was a steady increase in life expectancy at birth.

Around 1900, those living beyond the age of fifty – as in Holland (fifty-two) and Sweden (fifty-six) – were the exception. The Italian figure of forty-three years was more common, while in Russia it was as low as thirty-two. A century later, practically all the western European countries had a life expectancy of between seventy-seven and seventy-nine. The Soviet bloc countries had started to approach these levels but then entered a decline; life expectancy in the Russia of today is sixty-seven. Overall, the European continent has completed its demographic transition, and has reached a situation of absolute equilibrium between mortality and birth rates; both rates remain roughly stable, at around ten per thousand. Some countries in the eastern areas are undergoing population losses of around five per thousand (not counting emigration). Such is the case of White Russia, Bulgaria, Estonia, the Russian Federation, Hungary, Latvia and Ukraine. Around 1999, another group of countries undergoing a less marked decline in population (between one and two per thousand) included Germany, Croatia, the Czech Republic, Slovenia, Spain, Greece, Italy, Lithuania, Romania and Sweden. On the other hand, at the opposite end of the table, Ireland, France, Holland and Norway recorded a population increase of three per thousand or more.

We should not forget that, throughout the nineteenth century, Europe was a continent from which people emigrated. Such a tendency could not easily be reversed, so deep-rooted was it in the European collective consciousness. But during the inter-war years the countries of western Europe, which were no longer areas of emigration, began to attract immigration. Workers from southern and eastern Europe responded to a need for labour that had been created by the enormous loss of life and the large number of wounded and handicapped during the Great War. Poles and Italians, in particular, responded rapidly to the opportunities, and moved to Great Britain, Belgium and France. Western Europe as a whole began to be a net destination for immigrants. The Mediterranean and eastern fringes, which had contributed significantly to emigration to America, continued to do so as far as possible, but after the war there was a considerable tightening up of North American immigration policies. European destinations were a new phenomenon, but as a whole the European panorama was still overwhelmingly dominated by loss of population.

After the Second World War, western Europe became attractive for immigration; again this was due to reconstruction, but increasingly because of the high growth in the more developed European countries. Throughout the 1950s, net immigration to this area already exceeded 3 million people, who came from southern and eastern Europe, and from the former colonies. However, transoceanic emigration from the poorer regions still dominated, and it was only during the 1960s that Europe became a continent of net immigration. Western Europe attracted practically all the emigrants from southern and eastern Europe, as well as immigrants from the former colonies. From then on, this new trend became more rapid, coinciding with conjunctural crises and slower growth in the European economy. In recent years, a clear dividing line has appeared between the tendency towards emigration that has once again become established in eastern Europe in its transition to a market economy and the steady attraction that western Europe holds for immigrants.

Economic potential

The quickest way to measure economic potential is through GDP. In his great work *The Rise and Fall of the Great Powers*, Paul Kennedy explained competition between the great powers by examining the development of their GDP. Table 10.3 shows the great European powers in 1913 in terms of their GDP. The six largest powers – which fought against each other in 1914 – between them accounted for around 85 per cent of GDP.

But we shall refer to economic potential as including the imperial components, beyond Europe, of the European powers and not only to the gross domestic product. The GDP – the first and best indicator of economic power – is obtained by multiplying the population by *per capita* income. If we are interested in the progress, prosperity and the well-being of the population, *per capita* income is the best quantitative index. If we are interested in its economic power, namely the overall capacity to mobilize resources of every type, including military resources, then it is the total GDP that counts. In the Europe of 1914, not only was the GDP of the mother country important, but account also had to be taken of the colonial GDP. In purely demographic terms, the impact of the colonial population varied greatly, depending on the empire, as the classification in Table 10.4 shows.

Maddison's most recent analyses enable us to assign *per capita* income levels to the populations in the colonies. Though they are much lower than in the mother country (except in the case of the British dominions), there is no doubt that the importance of the British colonial empire continued to be strongly reflected in terms of economic potential. After making the appropriate calculations and estimates, we can obtain a better idea of the economic importance of the empires from the data in Table 10.5. Using these figures, we can return to the GDP table for 1913 and reclassify the economic potential of the great European powers (Table 10.6). The result is strikingly clear. British potential is much higher than that of the mother country alone, and the United Kingdom is now the uncontested leader

Table 10.3 GDP of the great European powers in 1913

Power	*US $ (1960 value)*	*% of European total* [a]
Russia	52,420	20.4
Germany	49,760	19.4
United Kingdom	44,074	17.2
France	27,401	10.7
Austria-Hungary	26,050	10.1
Italy	15,624	6.1
Spain	7,450	2.9
Belgium	6,794	2.6
Holland	4,660	1.8
Remainder (nine countries)	22,612	8.8

Source: Partial own adapation based on data in P. Bairoch, 'Europe's gross national product, 1800–1975', *Journal of European Economic History*, 5, 1976, pp. 273–340.

Notes:

[a] Excluding the Ottoman Empire.

Table 10.4 Importance of colonial empires in 1913

Empire	*Size of colonial population relative to that of mother country (%)*	*Colonial population (million)*
British	865.6 [a]	394.5
Dutch	804.0	49.9
Belgian	144.7	11.1
French	120.6	48.2
Portuguese	94.0	5.5
German	18.6	12.2
Italian	5.4	1.7
Spanish	4.6	1.1

Source: own adaptation of figures in B. Etemad, 'Ritmi, e ampiezza della colonizzazione contemporanea, secoli XVIII–XX'. *Un approccio quantitativo*, in P. Bairoch and E. Hobsbawm (eds), *Storia d'Europa*, vol. V, Turin, 1996, pp. 1269–86.

Note:
[a] Including dominions.

Table 10.5 GDP of colonies (and dominions) compared with GDP of mother country around 1913 (%)

Holland	181
Great Britain	146
Portugal	43
France	23
Belgium	20
Germany	3
Spain	1
Italy	1

Source: own adaptation of figures in Table 10.4 and in A. Maddison, *The World Economy*, 2001.

Table 10.6 Economic potential of the European empires in 1913

Power	*GDP ($ millions 1960)*	*% of European total*
United Kingdom	108,245	31.9
Russia	52,420	15.5
Germany	51,253	15.1
France	33,703	9.9
Austria-Hungary	26,050	7.7
Italy	15,780	4.7
Holland	13,095	3.9
Belgium	8,153	2.4
Spain	7,525	2.2
Sweden	3,824	1.1
Rest	18,788	5.5
Total	338,836	100

Source: own calculations.

of all the great European powers. Holland is also more important, but without overtaking Italy. The importance of the other countries, on the other hand, does not change significantly.

The situation at the end of the twentieth century was totally different from 1913. The great colonial empires had vanished, the central and eastern empires had fallen apart after the First World War, and a century of differentiated growth ended by considerably changing the ranking of the economic powers. At the end of the century, there was no longer any sense in including the colonies when measuring the economic importance of the different countries, and classification was made much easier (Table 10.7). Little needs to be added to these particular figures. At the top of the table we find the great enemies from the two wars. The United Kingdom and Italy are practically at the same level, with the relative position of France to those two countries changing slightly each year. What is left of the Soviet Union is far less important than any Russia of the past. The former countries of the Soviet bloc have less impact than would be expected relative to their population, and they are a long way behind the small countries of western Europe (excluding the very small ones). What were once Yugoslavia and Albania, both recently involved in devastating conflicts both within and between their borders, lie right at the bottom of the table.

***Per capita* income**

Throughout the twentieth century, *per capita* GDP grew by an average 1.73 per cent annually for the whole population of Europe (Table 10.8). Depending on the period and area, the figures conceal very different patterns. Overall, the prosperity

Table 10.7 GDP classification of European countries in 1998 (international $ billion)

Country	*GDP*	*Country*	*GDP*
Germany	1,460	Ireland	67
France	1,150	Hungary	66
United Kindom	1,109	Romania	65
Italy	1,023	Belarus	59
Russian Federation	664	Slovakia	42
Spain	560	Bulgaria	38
Holland	318	Serbia-Montenegro	29
Poland	258	Croatia	28
Belgium	198	Slovenia	24
Sweden	165	Lithuania	22
Austria	153	Latvia	16
Switzerland	152	Estonia	15
Portugal	129	Luxembourg	13
Ukraine	127	Bosnia	9
Greece	118	Moldavia	9
Denmark	117	Cyprus	9
Norway	105	Albania	8
Finland	94	Macedonia	6
Czech Republic	89	Iceland	6

Source: A. Maddison, *The World Economy*, 2001.

Table 10.8 Growth of *per capita* GDP, 1900–1998 (%)

Area	*1900–1913*	*1913–1950*	*1950–1973*	*1973–1998*	*1913–1998*
Europe	1.25	1.00	3.79	0.96	1.73
West Europe	1.34	0.76	4.08	1.78	1.95
East Europe	1.52	1.50	3.49	−1.09	1.26

Source: own adaptation of figures in A. Maddison, *The World Economy*, 2001.

of Europe grew moderately, at an annual rate of 1 per cent between 1913 and 1950, which is similar to the growth experienced between 1973 and 1998. For almost a quarter of a century, during the so-called 'Golden Age', between 1950 and 1973, growth was almost four times as much. This pattern applies to western Europe (including Greece); growth after 1973 was more than double the pre-1950 growth, and less than half that for the 1950–1973 period. There is a clear bearing between these three phases. The pattern for eastern Europe (including the Soviet Union and subsequent states) is reversed. Despite the wars, things are better between 1913 and 1950 than after 1973. For eastern Europe the 1990s were particularly catastrophic. The first column of Table 10.8 (for 1900–1913), hints at historical measures adopted during a period of prosperity and normality. The figures for this period are better than those for 1913–1950, particularly for western Europe. In any case, for Europe as a whole, and especially for eastern Europe (but not for western Europe), they are better than those for 1973–1998.

If only the years at the start and end of the century (1913 and 1998) are compared, the classification by material level of prosperity speaks for itself (Table 10.9). Around 1913, the richest country in Europe was, logically, the United Kingdom, followed by the small, but very prosperous, countries that had strong trading relations with the United Kingdom, or whose forms of industrial specialization were similar. A good third of the way below Great Britain were the enemies of the Great War: Germany, France and Austria. The great continental powers had very similar income levels. Italy, on the other hand, was slightly lower and only slightly over half the British average but, even so, still surpassed the countries of the peripheral Mediterranean area, eastern and central Europe and Scandinavia (with the exception of Sweden). Russia, with less than a third of Britain's prosperity, was at the bottom of the list of great powers. Its greatness derived from its extensive size and population, not from its prosperity.

Compared with 1913, the 1998 situation is more irregular, with the gap between the countries at the top and the bottom having increased from five to eight times. On the other hand, there is no doubt that the western European countries have largely converged. In 1913, the ratio of difference between the United Kingdom and Portugal was 4:1, but in 1998 it had decreased to 1.5:1. Furthermore, the ratio with Norway, the richest western country, is less than 2:1. It is with regard to eastern Europe that there is renewed disparity, while differences between the western European countries are limited. The four largest countries, Germany, France, Great Britain and Italy, show a difference of no more than 10 per cent between them, while the former Soviet Union has plummeted, and is now relatively poorer than it was in 1913.

Table 10.9 GDP of European countries *per capita* in 1913 and 1998 (international $, 1990)

Country	*1913*	*Country*	*1998*
United Kingdom	4,921	Norway	23,660
Switzerland	4,266	Denmark	22,123
Belgium	4,220	Switzerland	21,367
Holland	4,049	Holland	20,224
Denmark	3,912	France	19,558
Germany	3,648	Belgium	19,442
France	3,485	Austria	18,905
Austria	3,465	United Kingdom	18,714
Sweden	3,096	Sweden	18,685
Italy	2,564	Finland	18,324
Norway	2,501	Ireland	18,183
Spain	2,255	Germany	17,799
Finland	2,111	Italy	17,759
Hungary	2,098	Spain	14,227
Czechoslovakia	2,096	Portugal	12,929
Greece	1,592	Greece	11,268
Russia	1,488	Czech Republic	8,643
Portugal	1,244	Slovakia	7,754
Yugoslavia	1,029	Poland	6,688
		Hungary	6,474
		Bulgaria	4,586
		Ex-Yugoslavia	4,229
		Ex-Soviet Union	3,893
		Romania	2,890

Source: own adaptation of figures in A. Maddison, *The World Economy*, 2001.

There has been much debate over the question of whether there has been convergence or not. For the 1913–1950 period, it is apparent that growth rates were not inversely related to initial GDP *per capita* rates. There was no convergence, with the exception of a good result for the Soviet Union. Between 1950 and 1973, convergence was particularly marked in the case of the poorer western European countries. But it also occurred in eastern Europe (in the Balkans), though less markedly. The most atypical case is that of Ireland, which did not benefit from the wave of prosperity the world was experiencing, and remained anchored to Great Britain, in an unproductive relationship. After 1973, two 'clubs' can be distinguished. On the one hand, forces leading to convergence started to take effect again in the western countries, to the advantage of peripheral countries; this time the country that benefited most was Ireland. On the other hand, the eastern countries declined irremediably; for them, there was only divergence, and considerable divergence at that.

Societies with a high level of consumption

Increased *per capita* income has led to steady improvements in consumption levels. Private consumption has been characterized by a number of elements, one of the most important being food. Two of the main indicators of improvements in consumption are an increased intake of calories and greater dietary diversification. The replacement of cereals and root plants with dairy products, meat protein and fruit has been the element associated with improved living standards. Clothing and housing are other traditional components of consumer expenditure. Clothing has remained at fairly stable rates, while housing has increased significantly over the century, due in part to the heating factor, with which it is usually linked. The areas of consumption that have shown most growth are transport expenses, in particular consumption for individual transport (the car and its maintenance, petrol costs and so on), leisure pursuits, health and education.

Motorization has been the great process of technological socialization of the century. The figures in Table 10.10 are a perfect illustration of the spread of the consumer society. In the period between the two wars, the most advanced countries of Europe were France and Britain – a long way behind the United States. Indices for Denmark, Sweden, Belgium and Switzerland were slightly lower, but still some way ahead of the other European countries. As in many other cases, the greater prosperity of Great Britain, half-way through the century (1950), is accounted for by its leading position in Europe with respect to the use of the car, though during the second half of the century it would gradually lose this position, as we shall see when we consider the role of television. Towards 1970 many western countries had surpassed the United Kingdom, with Sweden in the lead. In 1998, Italy was the country with the highest number of cars. The British levels of 1970 had already been surpassed almost all over Europe, with the exception of Romania, Yugoslavia, Albania and the former Soviet Union republics (excluding the Baltic republics). During the 1960s and 1970s, the spread of the car showed a considerable increase in the southern fringe areas, and also spread in the eastern countries (except the Soviet Union), albeit a decade or two later than in the southern areas. In any case, throughout Europe the car had become the durable consumer good that was in greatest demand.

Among other goods that have successfully represented models of consumption and changes in tastes, we will mention only two: the television set and the personal computer. Their spread is linked with two distinct waves of technological change.

In western Europe, the spread of television sets resembled that of the car in some respects. Since Great Britain was the country in which television was invented, the similarity was even more marked. Broadcasts had begun before the war, but were interrupted because of the conflict, and did not start again until 1947. In 1950, the United Kingdom was in fact practically the only European country that had television; the Soviet Union had begun broadcasts, but had only a limited number of receivers. In 1955, when only in the British Isles could it be said that receiving sets were widespread, the hegemony of the English world was even more evident. The British already had more than a 100 sets per 1,000 inhabitants, at a time when no other country on the continent had even ten; moreover many countries were completely without any television at all. It is interesting to note that, although their income levels were very different, the new invention had not yet arrived in the peripheral areas of Europe (Spain, Bulgaria, Greece, Ireland, Norway, Portugal and Yugoslavia); this indicates that a certain amount of 'osmosis' was involved in its spread. Despite this, and contrary to what happened with the car,

Table 10.10 The spread of the automobile, 1922–1999 (units per thousand inhabitants)

Country	*1922*	*1930*	*1950*	*1970*	*1999*
Italy	1.0	5	7	192	591
France	5.0	26	37 [c]	252	564
Austria	. . .	. . .	7	162	536
Germany[a]	1.0	8	13	227	529
Germany (GDR)			. . .	73	
Switzerland	. . .	12 [b]	31	221	527
Norway	. . .	8 [b]	20	193	505
Belgium	4.0	13	32	213	497
Sweden	4.0	17	36	285	478
Spain	. . .	. . .	3	70	472
Finland	. . .	6 [b]	7	152	462
Slovenia	0.2	1			455
Holland	3.0	9	14	192	427
United Kingdom	7.0	25	46	209	418
Denmark	5.0	22	28	218	411
Estonia	. . .	. . .	. . .		378
Czech Republic	1.0	4	. . .	57	363
Greece	. . .	. . .	1	26	348
Portugal	2.0	4	7	60	348
Lithuania	. . .	. . .	. . .		322
Ireland	. . .	11 [b]	31	134	305
Poland	0.1	1	2 [d]	15	286
Hungary	0.4	2	. . .	24	272
Bulgaria	. . .	. . .	. . .	. . .	266
Slovakia	1.0	4	. . .	57	260
Latvia		. . .	. . .	. . .	258
Yugoslavia	0.2	1	1[d]	35	190
Romania	0.3	2	. . .	2	154
Russian Federation	. . .	. . .	. . .	. . .	153
Belarus	. . .	. . .	. . .	. . .	136
Ukraine	. . .	. . .	. . .	. . .	93
Moldavia	. . .	. . .	. . .	. . .	70
Albania	. . .	. . .	. . .	. . .	44
Bosnia-Herzegovina	0.2	1	1[d]	35	30

Sources: Up to 1970, A. Deaton, 'The structure of demand 1920–1970', in C.M. Cipolla (ed.), *The Fontana Economic History of Europe*, London, vol. 5.1, 1976, pp. 89–131, completed with G. Ambrosius and W.H. Hubbard, *Sozial- und Wirtschaftgeschichte Europes im 20. Jahrhundert*, Munich, 1986. For 1999: World Bank, *World Development Indicators, 2001*, Washington DC, 2001.

Notes:
[a] In 1950 and in 1970, Federal Republic of Germany.
[b] 1928.
[c] 1948.
[d] 1955.
. . . No data.
Blank: not applicable.
Countries that have divided are represented by a single figure before division.

imitation was very rapid, and took place regardless of blocs. The eastern countries were involved in the frenetic spread of television just as much as the western countries. Centralized and controllable broadcasting could, clearly, transform television into a very useful tool for dictatorships. Competition between the systems soon got under way. In 1960, though only Sweden and Denmark, with more than one set per every ten inhabitants, were able to emulate Britain's 1955 achievement, it was clear that the new invention had already caught on all over Europe (except Greece). The 1965 figures for the German Democratic Republic and Czechoslovakia are the most significant element in Table 10.11. The GDR had as many sets per inhabitant as the German Federal Republic, and Czechoslovakia had more than its rich western neighbours, not to mention the other Comecon members (with the exception of the GDR). Five years later, when Greece had already started broadcasts but was still bottom of the list as regards number of sets, almost the whole of Europe (except Portugal, Yugoslavia and Romania) had over 100 receivers per 1,000 inhabitants. It is as well to emphasize that, during this period, there was convergence in consumption levels, with no great disparities with regard to income levels. It could be said that television has had an equalizing effect on Europeans. It is a relatively cheap product, providing a wide range of entertainment services.

Thirty years later, the 1999 figures are interesting for different reasons. There is no question that the use of television has spread on a massive scale, but there are a number of disparities that can be explained only historically. One of these is its low incidence in Yugoslavia, which had already been apparent in the early decades. On the other hand, Greece and Portugal, latecomers as regards television broadcasting, have caught up. Some eastern countries are in top positions (the country with the most is Latvia) and one is inclined to think that the Nordic countries, probably on account of their climate, are favourably inclined to the use of television.

It makes sense to compare the spread of television with that of the personal computer (PC): they are two very different technologies, and of different generations, but they are similar in that they both have screens (Table 10.12).

Table 10.12 is very interesting, since it shows the spread of a new technology throughout Europe. In contrast to what happens with other technologies that are strongly linked to *per capita* GDP, the new information technologies have a very high component of cultural inertia. Thus, geographical proximity overlaps with factors of technological dynamism. The Scandinavian countries are in the lead, as so often; they already lead in many other fields, as they did at the beginning of the century with the telephone. In the cold, northern climate and in countries with a very strong educational substrate, the new information technologies (IT) have spread very rapidly. However, the country at the top of the table is Switzerland, a long way ahead of its neighbours. Ireland's strong position is surprising, and does not correspond to its *per capita* income. This is easily explained by its recent vigorous growth, and by its having become the European location of numerous factories and branches of the great multinational IT companies. There is also a surprising result for Slovenia, with an income a third lower but with a take-up rate on a par with Austria. In relation to their *per capita* income, the Latin countries lag behind, and their use of new technologies reflects their traditionally more limited use of information technologies. On the other hand, some central and eastern European countries show good results: Estonia (more than Spain), Slovakia, the Czech Republic (more than Portugal), Latvia, Hungary, Croatia and Poland (more than

Table 10.11 The spread of television, 1950–1999, (television sets per thousand inhabitants)

Country	*1950*	*1955*	*1960*	*1965*	*1970*	*1999*
Latvia	0.08	4.00	22.0	68	143	741
United Kingdom	11.00	105.00	211.0	248	293	652
Norway	——	——	13.0	131	220	648
Finland	——	0.02	21.0	159	221	643
France	——	6.00	41.0	131	201 [b]	623
Denmark	——	2.00	119.0	228	266	621
Holland	——	7.00	43.0	172	223 [b]	600
Germany-GFR[a]	——	5.00	83.0	200	272	580
Germany-GDR[a]	——	0.80	60.0	201	282	——
Portugal	——	——	5.0	20	38	560
Estonia	0.08	4.00	22.0	68	143	555
Spain	——	——	8.0	55	174	547
Sweden	——	1.00	156.0	270	312	531
Belgium	——	8.00	68.0	163	216	523
Switzerland	——	2.00	24.0	104	203	518
Austria	——	0.20	27.0	98	192	516
Italy	——	4.00	43.0	117	181	488
Czech Republic	——	2.00	58.0	149	214	487
Greece	——	——	——	——	10	480
Hungary	——	0.05	10.0	82	171	448
Russian Federation	0.08	4.00	22.0	68	143	421
Lithuania	0.08	4.00	22.0	68	143	420
Slovakia	——	2.00	58.0	149	214	417
Ukraine	0.08	4.00	22.0	68	143	413
Bulgaria	——	——	0.6	23	121	408
Ireland	——	——	17.0	89	172	406
Poland	——	0.01	14	66	129	387
Slovenia	——	——	1.4	30	88	356
Belarus	0.08	4.00	22.0	68	143	322
Romania	——	0.01	3.0	26	73	312
Moldavia	0.08	4.00	22.0	68	143	297
Croatia	——	——	1.4	30	88	279
Serbia and Montenegro	——	——	1.4	30	88	273
Macedonia	——	——	1.4	30	88	250
Albania	...	...	...	...	...	117
Bosnia-Herzegovina	——	——	1.4	30	88	112

Sources: 1950–70, A. Deaton, 'The structure of demands'; 1999, World Bank, *World Development Indicators.*

Notes:
[a] Germany, unified in 1999, is included with FRG.
[b] 1969.
... No data.
—— Not applicable.
Countries that have divided are represented by a single figure before division.

Greece). The bottom of the table clearly indicates that within Europe there is a strong disparity as regards the spread of the new IT. The countries ranking lowest are also those with enormous problems of growth; these are the Balkan area and a large part of the former Soviet Union (except the Baltic countries).

Table 10.12 The spread of the personal computer in 1999 (PCs per 000 inhabitants)

Switzerland	461.9	Slovenia	251.4	Poland	62.0
Sweden	451.4	France	221.8	Greece	60.2
Norway	446.6	Italy	191.8	Lithuania	59.5
Denmark	414.0	Estonia	135.2	Russian Federation	37.4
Ireland	404.9	Spain	119.4	Romania	26.8
Finland	360.1	Slovakia	109.7	Bulgaria	26.6
Holland	359.9	Czech Republic	107.2	Yugoslavia	20.7
Belgium	315.2	Portugal	93.0	Ukraine	15.8
Great Britain	302.5	Latvia	82.0	Moldavia	8.0
Germany	297.0	Hungary	74.7	Albania	5.2
Austria	256.8	Croatia	67.0		

Source: World Bank, *World Development Indicators*, 2001.

Many of these factors can be understood even better if the number of television sets *per capita* is related to the number of PCs *per capita* (in 1999). The TV:PC ratio gives an idea of the relative distribution of the two technologies, and how the eastern countries have generally caught up. The classification is headed by Ireland, where the spread of the PC has equalled that of the television, in a 1:1 ratio. Moreover, it is interesting that Slovenia is fourth, with a ratio of 1:4 and that Slovakia, Estonia, Croatia and the Czech Republic have a better ratio than Spain. By analogy, countries with a ratio of less than 1:10 are the same as those that were very behind as regards technology: the Russian Federation, Romania, Serbia and Montenegro, Bulgaria, Albania and Moldavia (and other former Soviet republics for which we have no data – in itself a bad sign in a world of IT).

The driving role of technological progress

Before the Great War the world was dominated by the great technologies of the first industrial revolution, based on coal: the iron industry, the steam engine, the railway and the steamship. In the quarter-century before the Great War broke out, the world had witnessed the astonishingly rapid rise of new technologies: electricity, the internal combustion engine and the chemical industry. In the field of communications, the telegraph, which during the second half of the nineteenth century was so distinctive, was enhanced by the addition of the telephone. The new technologies were still far from dominating the industrial and technological scene, but already completely dominated the sector of new investments and new trade. After the massive destruction wrought by the war, rather than accelerating technological change, reconstruction held it back. The mines, furnaces, railways, ships and factories that had been destroyed were repaired as quickly as possible, and thus tended to consolidate the old technologies. On the other hand, technological changes arriving from the United States clearly showed up how antiquated Europe's technology was by comparison. When economic activity had returned to normal, the new technologies re-emerged with enormous vigour and started to become a driving force. Electrification, and the mass spread of the car, were the two most significant technological phenomena of the period between the two wars.

Electrification was already at an advanced stage before the war, and was considered a symbol of modernity. Lenin himself defined the sort of communism that he was trying to achieve in the Soviet Union as 'soviets plus electrification'. During the 1920s and 1930s, there was a considerable deployment of investment in new uses for electricity, but the most significant factor of the period was the spread of the use of electricity to an ever wider range of economic activities: industry, transport, services and domestic life. By 1914, the spread of the car was already under way in Europe. Owing to the high cost of cars, it was limited, but during the war they acquired considerable significance. Great innovations were introduced from the United States, where the conveyor belt system had been created and refined, and which enabled the cost of cars to be drastically reduced, and hence made affordable to wider sections of the population. The Ford Model T was the embodiment of the new car model, and flooded post-war Europe.

The application of science to industry had achieved its first great successes in the chemical industry, which, at the end of the nineteenth century, was the great German speciality. The development of large laboratories that worked on the discovery and development of new products would cease to be a rarity limited to the genius of a few, as in the time of Edison. Instead it became a form of investment that could be perfectly well managed, and provide increasingly predictable results. Chemistry achieved great success in applications aimed at creating new artificial, and later synthetic, fibres. It also entered the field of pure chemistry – which would subsequently develop into the pharmaceutical industry.

During the Second World War, all these technologies, as well as a number of others, were exploited to the full. The radio – which started as wireless telegraphy – was one of the most important. It revolutionized mass communications and political propaganda, besides reducing communication costs and those for mass entertainment, in particular.

Once the Second World War was over, Europe found that a number of technologies had become greatly transformed. Since the war had not affected the United States directly on its own territory, that country had been able to concentrate on rapid technological development – with the aim of producing superior armaments to those of the Germans. Aviation and rocket technology were, consequently, developed to unprecedented levels. Applications for laser beams were discovered, and new materials such as plastic made their appearance, and were starting to be used on a massive scale. Atomic energy, unthinkable before the war, was rapidly developed and channelled into productive uses, in a little less than twenty years. More than in the first, in the second post-war period, Europe benefited from the application of technologies that had been developed in the United States, as a means of its own growth. The technological gap between Europe and the United States had greatly increased and, indeed, Europe had never lagged so far behind the United States as it did between 1945 and 1950.

The systematic application of the conveyor belt – know later as Fordism – was the technological and organizational nucleus that Europe imported from the United States. This system dominated European reconstruction, and the whole of the Golden Age (1950–1973). Europe gradually began to stand out for its capacity to imitate American technologies, and industrially was able to challenge the United

States on its own ground. European enterprises, with European technology, began to enter the international markets in the car, chemical and mechanical construction industries. The mass spread of the car was, without doubt, the most important phenomenon. Others, such as the development of atomic energy, or the incipient IT revolution, overlapped with these, but the prevailing technological paradigm was wholly centred on the car industry. It continued that way until 1973, when the oil crisis, which would be repeated in 1979–1980, destroyed the energy base of this model. Costly energy meant having to scale down the Fordist system. It took time to restructure and adapt it to the new circumstances, and for years no new technologies with the same driving capacity as the previous ones were found that could replace them.

In the 1980s, and particularly in the second half of the decade, personal computers (PCs) started to appear as goods capable of generating an almost inexhaustible demand. The perception of the computer as an element that could be useful for everyone's work, stimulated research, investment and private demand. As early as the 1990s, and contemporaneous with the liberalization of telecommunications, the interconnection of PCs, by means of the protocol known as the World Wide Web, started the Internet revolution. The automated processing of data, combined with their long-distance transmission – in other words the combination of information and telephone technology – was the nucleus of this technological paradigm. It is now generating huge investment, entrepreneurial reorganization on a planetary scale – as well as the occasional case of bankruptcy. Behind the dynamism of the new information and communication technologies lies another no less important revolution, which is still at the stage of scientific development and preliminary industrial application. We are referring, of course, to biotechnology.

All the recent analyses of economic growth factors have highlighted the importance of research and technological development. In the course of time, the developed economies are able to further improve their already very high productivity, mainly through technological progress. In the previous phases, capital had played a fundamental role. Today it has been replaced by human capital – not labour.

In fact, the ready availability of real capital, traditionally recognized as a critical component of economic development, in addition to ever increasing quantities of human capital, makes the European economies highly capital-intensive. The availability of capital *per capita* continues to increase, and this normally runs parallel with growth in production. The development of technologies, like electricity or the motor car industry, has called for huge investments, and in both cases it has been necessary to invest in the search for sources of energy. In itself, this has involved gigantic exploration efforts on a planetary scale, and necessitated the development of specific technologies; large enterprises have been created with that aim. The transport of energy or fuel has demanded a titanic effort. The creation of infrastructure for the use of the new technologies has meant the involvement of public administrations, as well as private enterprise, and heavy investments have been made. The manufacture of tools or products that exploit the new technologies – be they light bulbs, machines or cars – has stimulated the creation of large-scale enterprises devoted specifically to that end. The upkeep of these types of previously unknown products, which are somewhat complicated to use, has involved the wide-scale instruction of people in their use, and has also generated new, mainly small, enterprises that deal with their repair and maintenance; the list is endless.

The main part of real capital that has a multiplier effect on the economy is what is known as non-residential capital. Buildings used as dwellings are, from a somewhat radical point of view, durable consumer goods. The amount of capital that is actually productive relative to GDP indicates the degree to which the economy is 'capitalist'.

The available figures (Table 10.13) show that at the beginning of the nineteenth century the amount of productive capital in the more developed economies was below unity. By the beginning of the twentieth century, Great Britain had increased the ratio of its non-residential capital requirements, but only moderately; only after the Second World War would the ratio increase to any great extent. Around 1950, the economies of the other European countries, for which data are available, were more capital-intensive than the British. This apparent paradox cannot be explained without taking into account the difference between the relative price of capital goods in Great Britain and in the other continental countries. Great Britain, which traditionally exported machinery and transport equipment, benefited from lower-cost capital than other countries. As the changed economic situation, brought about by the loss of British leadership and continental recovery, gradually brought France, Germany and Holland closer to Great Britain, so the gap between the ratios steadily narrowed, with a tendency towards strong growth. Non-residential real capital currently accounts for roughly double the GDP of the advanced European countries.

Growing complexity in science and technology, on which the economic growth of the twentieth century has been based, has required heavy investment in the training of human capital. A widely accepted method of defining this elusive concept is to determine the average number of years of schooling in each country. For some countries (those in Table 10.13), there are sound estimates that confirm a steady trend towards longer periods of schooling (Table 10.14). Societies in which schooling lasted an average of six to nine years (corresponding to a period of primary education – normally already compulsory in the more advanced countries – and some secondary education) have become societies where schooling lasts from twelve to sixteen years, where both primary and secondary education are compulsory, and where post-secondary school or university education is prevalent.

Table 10.13 Ratio of gross stock of 'non-residential capital' to GDP, 1820–1991

Country	*1820*	*1913*	*1950*	*1973*	*1991*
Great Britain	0.68	0.87	0.81	1.32	1.74
Germany	...	...	1.81	1.94	2.32
France	...	...	1.63	1.55	2.22
Holland	...	...	2.06	1.98	2.25

Source: A. Maddison, *Monitoring the World Economy*, 1820–1992, Paris, 1995.

Note: ... No data.

Table 10.14 Duration (in years) of schooling of the population from fifteen to sixty-four years, 1913–1992

Countries	*1913*	*1950*	*1973*	*1992*
Germany	8.37	10.40	11.55	12.17
France	6.99	9.58	11.69	15.96
Holland	6.42	8.12	10.27	13.34
United Kingdom	8.82	10.60	11.66	14.09

Source: A. Maddison, *Monitoring the World Economy*, 1995.

Structural change: the decline of agriculture

Throughout Europe, economic growth and structural change went together. As GDP grew, the contribution of agriculture tended to decrease, while that of industry, which grew more rapidly, continued to make relative gains. The tertiary sector gradually replaced both agriculture and industry and, by the end of the twentieth century had come to be the dominant sector almost everywhere. The decline in the population actively engaged in agriculture was the overriding feature of the century (see Table 10.15).

It can be inferred from Table 10.15 that, around 1910, there were four distinct Europes. In the lead by a long way was Great Britain, which had already almost eliminated its agrarian activity. Only 9 per cent of its active population was engaged in agriculture. A long way behind was a group of countries, from Belgium to France, whose work force had gradually shifted from agriculture to industry. Belgium, Switzerland and Holland were the furthest ahead in emulating the British experience (confirmed by all other indicators). Then came most of central and western Europe, including Austria, Denmark, the German empire, Norway, Czechoslovakia and France following close behind each other. Slightly lower, at between 49 per cent and 58 per cent, came countries that had started out on the path to industrialization, and hence outgrown the agricultural structure, but only to a limited extent: Sweden, Greece, Ireland, Italy, Spain, Portugal and Hungary. Sweden's proximity to Greece, Portugal or Ireland may seem rather paradoxical, but it reflects the fact that Sweden still had the best years of its industrial growth ahead of it, that Greece already had a strong tertiary sector, and Ireland and Portugal were not exclusively agrarian societies, although subsequently they appeared to be more so. The last group corresponds to countries that remained almost exclusively agrarian: these areas, which would later become Poland, Romania, Finland, Bulgaria and Yugoslavia, had percentages of the population actively engaged in agriculture that characterize traditional societies. They varied between 77 per cent and 82 per cent.

In 1950 there was a general tendency towards decrease. Sweden with twenty-eight, and Finland with thirty-three percentage points fewer, are particularly significant cases. Poland, which had started much higher, dropped by twenty-three points. Sweden, however, was undoubtedly the most complete example of a European country becoming industrialized in the inter-war period. None of the other countries with comparable levels in 1913 was to experience such a striking change. Conversely, there were cases like Austria and Czechoslovakia that showed total

Table 10.15 Percentage of the population engaged in agriculture, 1910–1998

1910		*1950*		*1980*		*1998*	
Great Britain	9	Great Britain	5	Belgium	3	Belgium	...
Belgium	23	Belgium	13	Great Britain	3	Great Britain	2
Switzerland	27	Switzerland	17	Germany	3	Germany	3
Holland	29	Holland	20	Sweden	5	Holland	3
Austria	32	Sweden	21	Switzerland	5	Sweden	3
Denmark	36	FRG	23	Holland	6	Denmark	4
Germany	37	Denmark	25	Denmark	7	France	...
Norway	39	Norway	26	Norway	7	Norway	5
Czechoslovakia	40	France	27	France	8	Switzerland	5
France	41	GDR	27	Austria	9	Finland	6
Sweden	49	Austria	33	GDR	10	Austria	7
Greece	50	Czechoslovakia	39	Czechoslovakia	11	Czechoslovakia	7
Ireland	51	Ireland	40	Finland	11	Italy	7
Italy	55	Italy	42	Italy	11	Spain	8
Spain	56	Soviet Union	46	Spain	14	Hungary	8
Portugal	57	Finland	47	Ireland	18	Ireland	9
Hungary	58	Portugal	49	Hungary	20	Portugal	14
Russia (1913)	70	Spain	50			CIS (1992)	17
Poland	77	Greece	51	Portugal	28	Poland	19
Finland	80	Hungary	51	Romania	29	Greece	20
Romania	80	Poland	54	Yugoslavia	29	Bulgaria	26
Bulgaria	82	Bulgaria	65	Poland	31	Yugoslavia	...
Yugoslavia	82	Yugoslavia	71	Bulgaria	37	Romania	40
		Romania	74	Greece	37		

Source: 1910, 1950 and 1980: G. Ambrosius and W.B. Hubbard, *Sozial- und Wirtschaftgeschichte Europes*, 1998: World Bank, *World Development Indicators*, Russia, Soviet Union and CIS: A. Maddison, *Monitoring the World Economy*. The examples with no data in the last column (1998) have been placed near other related cases, where it seemed most rational.

Note: . . . No data.

stagnation – confirming their GDP pattern for those years – and others (Greece, for example) that remained in what seemed to be an apparently transitory situation. The rest (most of Europe) saw the proportion of the population actively engaged in agriculture drop by an average of ten percentage points. All that can be observed is only very limited convergence.

Around 1980 the relative positions were not very different, but there was a strong downward convergence, with decreases usually of the order of twenty percentage points. The whole of central and north-eastern Europe ranged between the 3 per cent of Belgium and Britain and the 11 per cent of Czechoslovakia, Finland and Italy. Czechoslovakia's position reflects its historical inertia, while Finland's is a sign of the degree of change experienced in that country in less than a century. The countries of eastern Europe are at the bottom of the table, but the previous gap is much reduced. Generally speaking, the eastern bloc countries have followed the same pattern of agricultural decline as Europe overall. The decline has been enormous. The agricultural populations of Romania and Yugoslavia have decreased by more than forty percentage points. In the peripheral areas of western

Europe, Spain and Finland have lost a good thirty-six percentage points. In contrast to Finland are Portugal and especially Greece. Portugal has reduced its agricultural share only by half, while the vast majority have reduced it to a third, a quarter or a fifth of the previous level. Greece, however, has reduced it only by a third, and forms the main exception; it is the extreme opposite of Finland.

In western European countries the evolution up to 1980 is perfectly predictable: fewer and fewer agricultural workers in relation to the total active population. Romania is one notable exception, and shows a reverse trend, growing from 29 per cent to 40 per cent. However, it is not the only one, and the countries for which there are no data usually show analogous patterns. With figures for 1980 and 1998 from the World Bank (which do not always match the historical series that we have given), it is possible to have some indication of the extent of the phenomenon, which probably involves Bulgaria, Albania and some of the former Soviet republics, like Latvia, Moldavia and Ukraine. No figures are available for the other republics of the CIS, or for the countries that were formed after the break-up of Yugoslavia. There are indications, however, that lead one to infer that in the Balkan area and the neighbouring areas of the former Soviet Union, there has been a 'return to agriculture', as an effect of the great struggle for survival that is being fought by countries that have largely failed in the transition to capitalism and the market economy.

The century-long decline in the importance of agriculture has coincided with increased agricultural output. It has not been a linear process. During the First World War, there was an enormous reduction in agricultural output, because of the devastation of huge land areas, the massive mobilization of the peasant population, the destruction of cattle barns (with the consequent loss of potential organic manure) and the reduction in the productive capacity (or importation) of organic and inorganic fertilizers. The result was food scarcity on a wide scale, and starvation for millions of people. After the war production picked up considerably. But agricultural production is less flexible than industrial production, and a whole decade went by before the pre-war production levels could be once more recovered. Fortunately for the European food level, agricultural imports from overseas were able to offset the delay in European recovery. Because of the Second World War agricultural production plummeted once again. As after the Great War, but now with even greater urgency, the overriding concern of all public administrators was to guarantee food supplies. In the 1930s and early 1940s, it was hoped that autarkic-style policies would provide a convenient way of ensuring food supplies, and at the same time guarantee national independence if conflict broke out again. The outcome was that European agriculture, which at the end of the nineteenth century had reacted with restrictive measures during the agricultural depression, and after 1918 had intensified this reaction, strongly opposed the application of any free trade principle. The spectre of food shortages was the dominant factor behind policy making and, in fact, agricultural products were not included in the free trade 'rounds'. Nobody seriously attempted to restructure agricultural production, or the agricultural work force, though it was quite clear that agriculture was undergoing an unparalleled and spontaneous decline. During the 1950s, 1960s and 1970s, the farmers who were still actively engaged in agriculture joined in the move towards technological modernization and capitalization of their activities. The green revolution amounted to simply increasing productivity, with the use of tractors, fertilizers and all types of electrical apparatus and machinery, bringing about a steady increase in productivity. The agricultural sector is, currently, no different from any other sector of the European Union, but it is the one that receives the most subsidies from funds made available through Community agricultural policies, and the greatest customs protection from the rest of the world. Pressure group action, combined with historical tradition, has given it infinitely greater bargaining power than any other sector.

Structural change: industrialization and deindustrialization

Until about thirty years ago, European growth was a question of industrialization, and the twentieth century was dominated by industrialization policies. Industrial output grew enormously, but was affected by two world wars, the depression of the 1930s and, from 1975, the most serious industrial crisis of the century, culminating in the deindustrialization process that prevailed in the last quarter of the century. An issue of great importance is the changed localization of industry, as well as competition in Europe; on the one hand between East and West, and on the other between North and South.

Table 10.16 shows how the ranking of countries by percentage of the population actively engaged in industry in 1910 tediously resembles that for agriculture. The only difference is that the latter goes from least to most, while the former goes from most to least. Yet both reflect the same phenomenon: industrialization at the expense of agricultural activity. There are nuances: Germany and Czechoslovakia stand out more for their industrial profiles than for their decline in agriculture. This implies there is a smaller services sector.

Half a century later, in 1960, once the wars, the inter-war period and the post-war period were over, there was a general trend towards net growth in the percentage of the population actively engaged in industry. In countries with less advanced industrialization at the start of the century, the leap forward was spectacular, and countries like Finland and Poland gained twenty points. Several other countries, in the south and east of Europe, gained between twelve and seventeen points, with the exceptions of Greece, Romania and Yugoslavia, which, like the more industrialized countries, did not grow more than seven points. Among these, the decline of Great Britain needs to be underlined. With its decrease of four points (a relative rather than an absolute decrease), it was the only European country tending towards deindustrialization. Austria, Italy, Norway and Sweden, which already showed significant levels of industrialization, gained between twelve and thirteen points, with an equivalent share to that of the more peripheral countries. The countries of the industrial nucleus – from Belgium to Czechoslovakia and from France to Denmark – increased four to nine points. The result was that an intensely industrial area in the heart of Europe was created, with percentages of the population engaged in industry approaching 50 per cent.

Table 10.16 Percentage of the population engaged in industry, 1910–1989

1910		*1960*		*1980*		*1988/89*	
Great Britain	52	Switzerland	50	GDR	49	GDR	50
Switzerland	46	Belgium	48	Czechoslovakia	48	Czechoslovakia	48
Belgium	45	Great Britain	48	FRG	46	Bulgaria	47
Germany	41	GDR	48	Switzerland	46	Romania	45
Czechoslovakia	37	FRG	48	Holland	45	FRG	40
Austria	33	Austria	46	Italy	45	Soviet Union	39
France	33	Czechoslovakia	46	Hungary	43	Hungary	38
Holland	33	Sweden	45	Great Britain	42	Austria	37
Sweden	32	Holland	42	Belgium	41	Poland	37
Denmark	28	Italy	40	Spain	40	Portugal	35
Italy	27	France	39	Bulgaria	39	Switzerland	35
Norway	25	Denmark	37	France	39	Spain	33
Portugal	22	Norway	37	Poland	39	Italy	32
Hungary	20	Hungary	35	Austria	37	Finland	31
Greece	16	Finland	32	Ireland	37	Yugoslavia	31
Ireland	15	Spain	31	Norway	37	France	30
Spain	14	Poland	29	Romania	36	Belgium	29
Finland	12	Portugal	29	Denmark	35	Great Britain	29
Yugoslavia	11	Bulgaria	25	Finland	35	Sweden	29
Poland	9	Ireland	25	Portugal	35	Greece	28
Bulgaria	8	Greece	20	Yugoslavia	35	Ireland	28
Romania	8	Yugoslavia	18	Sweden	34	Denmark	27
		Romania	15	Greece	28	Holland	27
						Norway	25

Sources: 1910, 1960 and 1980: G. Ambrosius and W.B. Hubbard, *Sozial- und Wirtschaftgeschichte Europes*, 1988/89; 1988, countries of the east, É. Ehrlich and G. Révész, 'Tendenze economiche dell'est European', in P. Anderson *et al.* (ed.), *Storia d'Europe*, vol. I, Turin, 1993, pp. 221–309; 1989, countries of the west, G. Therborn, 'Modernità sociale in Europe, 1950–1992', in P. Anderson *et al.* (eds), *Storia d'Europe*, pp. 459–613.

Progress towards industrial specialization would not be an indefinite process. Indeed, the experience of Great Britain, which in 1911 had reached its industrial 'peak' with 52 per cent, would not be repeated. Belgium, the second industrial country of Europe, was to reach its maximum (49 per cent) in the post-war recovery years, around 1947. In fact, all the other countries in Table 10.16 completed their industrialization processes between 1960 and 1980. The most industrialized western countries did so during the 1960s (Switzerland, Holland, Sweden, Denmark) or during the early 1970s (Germany, Italy, Norway); others, in the years of the first oil crisis (Austria, Ireland, France, Spain), Greece and Portugal a little later, between 1980 and 1982. Even some eastern countries followed the same pattern: the GDR, Czechoslovakia and Poland around 1978; Hungary and Yugoslavia a little earlier owing to the fatigue after forced industrialization, which had taken place more rapidly. These differences in the industrialization cycle explain a number of the surprising figures for 1980.

In fact, the eastern countries rank better in 1980, which is underlined by the much lower impact of services in their occupational structure. In 1980, the countries of central Europe formed the industrial nucleus of Europe (the two Germanies, Czechoslovakia and Switzerland, as well as Holland, Italy and Hungary). The two former great industrial powers, Great Britain and Belgium, were already a long way from the top, half-way down the table. The Scandinavian countries, which are known to have the most advanced aggregate indicators of GDP *per capita* on the continent, were suspiciously near the bottom of the table; it can be deduced from this that they were generally heading in the direction of services, and industrial specialization was no longer a guarantee of potential future development. Greece, once again, lagged a long way behind, appearing to hover between two worlds, seemingly neither western nor eastern. Between 1960 and 1980, the other formerly socialist Balkan countries went through a frenzy of industrialization. Romania increased its ratio by twenty-one points, Yugoslavia by seventeen, Bulgaria by fourteen. Among the countries of the capitalist area, only Ireland, with twelve points, shared this degree of intensity.

The 'wind of change' was not generally to be felt by countries under Soviet influence, and around 1988–1989 they would be in top position in terms of industrial specialization. The wealthiest economies of Europe were to be found at the bottom of Table 10.16, with the exception of Greece, which had still not completed its industrial cycle. The vigour and duration of the forced industrialization policies would be in sharp contrast to the transition to the market economy. Under the shock of the accelerated transition, from autarkic and planned economies to open market economies, the industrial specializations were to collapse. Table 10.17 illustrates the phenomenon in all its intensity. All the decreases of over six points in less than a decade correspond to countries undergoing transition. Falls of over fifteen points in nine years indicate a true economic revolution.

Inter-industrial composition: from textiles to electronics

Industry is made up of a combination of very different activities. It is usually held that manufacturing forms the central nucleus of industrial activity. In the broadest

Table 10.17 Decreases in the proportion of industrial value added in overall GDP, 1990–1999 (percentage points)

Slovakia	–27	Slovenia	–8	Holland	–4
Estonia	–24	Ukraine	–7	Belgium	–3
Bulgaria	–22	Czech Republic	–6	Austria	–2
Romania	–21	Greece	–6	Croatia	–2
Albania	–18	United Kingdom	–6	Portugal	–2
Latvia	–18	Germany	–5	Finland	–1
Poland	–17	Belarus	–5	Norway	–0
Macedonia	–12	Hungary	–5	Lithuania	+1
Moldavia	–11	Italy	–5	Ireland	+2
Russian Federation	–10	France	–4		

Source: World Bank, *World Development Indicators*, There are no data for Bosnia and Herzegovina, Spain, Sweden, Switzerland or the former Yugoslavia.

sense, the following are also part of industry: the extraction of mineral ores, the production and distribution of water, gas and electricity and the building industry. Because it is more exclusively technological, it is appropriate to concentrate on manufacturing industry. This is not because the mining sector, or the electrical industry, do not entail advanced technologies, but rather because part of their activity lies outside the sphere of industrial transformation. In the mining sector, part of the value added is land rent, and in the great public services part of the value added is connected more with transport and trade than with industry. These exceptions having been made, the most frequent subdivision of manufacturing industry is into six sectors: food, drinks and tobacco; textiles and clothing; metal production; metal product processing (including transport equipment); chemicals (in the broadest sense) and other sectors. Table 10.18 illustrates the evolution of the relative importance of the industrial sectors during the period of increasing industrialization.

The conclusion is clear, until 1975. The sector in greatest relative decline is textiles, followed by food, and finally the production of metals. On the other hand, the processing of metal products and chemicals has experienced a boom. The remaining sectors have followed an ambiguous trajectory. With a few temporary upsets, caused by differences in development levels, the model is still valid for all countries, and also reflects patterns of consumer demand. The emerging industrial countries tend to specialize in the more mature manufacturing sectors, where the application of new technology has little impact on production costs, and where the primary competitive factor is salaries. The advanced countries tend to be occupied in more progressive sectors, where the human capital component is crucial. In between are the countries that have more balanced resources, and which usually focus on intermediate technologies, and on sectors with high intensity of capital, which is more accessible than human capital. This pattern applied to almost the whole century. The countries undergoing forced industrialization (the east European countries) made huge efforts, after the Second World War, to provide themselves with all the manufacturing sectors, showing a preference for the more advanced technology sectors over the traditional ones, so that, around 1973, there was little difference between the industrial structure of western and eastern Europe. The difference was more marked between north and south. The fall of the Soviet

Table 10.18 Evolution of manufacturing industry in western Europe, by sector, 1913–1975 (as a percentage of the internal product of industry)

Sector	*1913*	*1953*	*1975*
Food	19	14	12
Textiles	18	9	5
Production of metals	10	8	8
Processing of metal products	24	33	38
Chemicals	6	10	15
Other sectors	24	26	22

Source: G. Ambrosius and W.B. Hubbard, *Sozial- und Wirtschaftgeschichte Europes*.

Table 10.19 Changes in the structure of manufacturing industry, 1990–1998 (percentage of added value of industry)

	Food, drinks and tobacco		*Machinery and transport material*	
Countries	*1990*	*1998*	*1990*	*1998*
Western and southern Europe				
Austria	15	15	28	31
Denmark	22	20	24	25
France	13	14	31	30
Greece	22	26	12	14
Holland	21	25	25	25
Ireland	27	20	29	34
Portugal	15	14	13	15
Sweden	10	8	32	39
United Kingdom	13	12	32	32
Eastern Europe				
Bulgaria	22	20	19	5
Hungary	14	19	26	25
Macedonia	20	32	14	15
Poland	21	29	26	23
Serbia and Montenegro	21	29	22	16

Source: World Bank, *World Development Indicators*, 2001. For many countries there are no data.

bloc has totally upset this situation. Although the information available is incomplete, in the poorer eastern countries, in a context of rapid industrial reconversion, it can be seen how in manufacturing there is a trend towards non-skilled labour-intensive activities, and away from capital-intensive and human-capital-intensive activities. This is clearly shown in Table 10.19.

In the countries of western and southern Europe, the normally low-skilled and labour-intensive food, drinks and tobacco sector shows a decline in relation to manufacturing industry as a whole, while in the countries of eastern Europe, for which figures are available, it is experiencing big increases. On the other hand, the machinery and transport equipment sectors, which are more capital-intensive and skilled-labour-intensive, continue to grow in the west, but show marked decreases in the east. The contrast would be even greater if data for the electronic and pharmaceutical industries could be obtained.

The rise of large-scale enterprise

The most dynamic manufacturing sectors were also those in which, during the course of the century, the largest and most successful enterprises appeared. Table 10.20 shows the situation at the starting point. There is no question about North American leadership (there was a total of fifty-four North American enterprises of equivalent size); however, the United Kingdom and Germany both had the same number of industrial giants. Other countries with large-scale enterprises, besides France, were Russia, Belgium and Luxembourg.

Table 10.20 Large-scale European industrial enterprises in 1912

Nationality of head office	*No. of cases*	*Sector of activity*	*No. of cases*
United Kingdom	14	Ironworks	13
Germany	14	Coal mining sector	6
France	6	Chemicals	6
Russia	3	Food, drinks and tobacco	5
Belgium	2	Petroleum	3
Luxembourg	1	Machinery construction	2
Holland–United Kingdom	1	Electrical material	2
		Non-ferrous metals	2
		Textiles and leather	2
Total	41	Total	41

Source: L. Hannah, 'La evolución de las grandes empresas en el siglo XX. Un análisis comparativo', *Revista de Historia Industrial*, 10, 1996, pp. 93–125. The enterprises are classified according to their stock market capitalization or, failing that, according to the book value of their assets.

Among British enterprises there were two textile firms (one of which was Coats, the largest textile multinational in the world), two very large tobacco firms, a beer producer (Guinness), a food company (Lever), two non-ferrous mining concerns, three heavy industry companies (iron and machinery, in variable proportions), a chemical company and an oil company. This was a very varied assortment, and a long way from the beginnings of the industrial revolution. Some brand names are still recognizable even today. The large German companies were concentrated in four sectors: seven in steel and associated heavy industry (often the armaments industry), three in chemicals, two in the coal mining sector and two in electronic materials. A number of the brand names still exist (AEG, Siemens, BASF, Mannesmann), while others have disappeared for ever (many of the iron and coal companies). Among the French companies mining concerns prevailed, and included the four largest. Nationalization, in 1945, led to their disappearance, all of them being absorbed by Charbonnages de France. The Russian companies were dominated by foreign capital and, with the 1917 revolution, were all nationalized. The multinational Anglo-Dutch oil company Royal Dutch Shell, the fifth largest in the world, the second in Europe and still today somewhat ahead of the others, is worth a special mention. Despite the success of new technologies (chemicals, electric materials and oil) there is a prevalence of typically nineteenth century companies, or those of the first period of industrialization. These include textiles, mining, iron and metallurgy, and machine construction linked with the railways and steam navigation. A glance at the fifteen largest enterprises (the fifteen industrial giants of the European economy) shows the weight of industrial tradition even more clearly (see Table 10.21). Only the German companies producing electric goods (AEG and Siemens) were associated with the new technologies. Furthermore, some enterprises, all connected with the food, drinks and tobacco sector and the affluent British market, all inclined towards new competitive strategies based on economies of scale and diversification.

Table 10.21 The fifteen largest European industrial enterprises, 1912–1998

	1912 [a]	*1937* [b]	*1958* [c]	*1973* [c]	*1998* [b]
1	J. & P. Coats (UK)	Royal Dutch/Shell (NL-UK)	Royal Dutch/Shell (NL-UK)	Royal Dutch/Shell (NL-UK)	Royal Dutch/Shell Group (NL-UK)
2	British-American Tobacco (UK-USA)	Imperial Tobacco (UK)	Unilever (NL-UK)	British Petroleum (UK)	Novartis (CH)
3	Rio Tinto (UK)	Vereinigte Stahlwerke (D)	ICI (UK)	ENI (I)	Roche Holding (CH)
4	Krupp (D)	British-American Tobacco (UK-USA)	British Petroleum (UK)	Philips (NL)	Glaxo Wellcome (UK)
5	Imperial Tobacco (UK)	IG Farben (D)	FIAT (I)	ICI (UK)	Unilever (NL-UK)
6	Guinness (UK)	ICI (UK)	Philips (NL)	Siemens (D)	British Petroleum (UK)
7	Mines de Lens (F)	Anglo-Iranian (UK)	British-American Tobacco (UK)	Hoechst D)	Nestlé (CH)
8	AEG (D)	Lever Bros and Unilever (UK)	Imperial Tobacco (UK)	Montedison (I)	Smithkline Beecham (UK)
9	Lever Bros (UK)	Guinness (UK)	Mannesmann (D)	Unilever (UK-NL)	ENI (I)
10	Mines de Bruay (F)	Courtauld's (UK)	Petrofina (B)	Cie Française des Pétroles (F)	L.M. Ericsson (S)
11	Gelsenkirchener (D)	Siemens (D)	Siemens (D)	Bayer (D)	Daimler-Benz (D)
12	Phoenix (D)	Distillers' (UK)	Gelsenkirchener Bergwerks (D)	BASF (D)	Diageo (UK)
13	Siemens (D)	Burmah Oil (UK)	Courtauld's (UK)	Italsider (I)	Nokia (SF)
14	Mines de Courrières (F)	Unilever NV (NL)	Dunlop (UK)	Volkswagenwerk (D)	Zeneca Group (UK)
15	Deutsch-Luxemburg (D)	J. & P. Coats (UK)	Montecatini (I)	Péchiney Ugne Kuhlmann (F)	ELF Aquitaine (F)

Sources: 1912: L. Hannah, *La evolución de la grandes*; 1937: C. Schmitz, *The Growth of Big Business in the United States and Western Europe, 1850–1939*, London, 1993; 1958: *Fortune*, August 1959; 1973: *Fortune*, August 1974; 1998: *Business Week*, 13 July 1998.

Notes:
[a] Stock market capitalization otherwise total assets.
[b] Stock market capitalization.
[c] Assets.

The entrepreneurial importance of the new technologies was already a fact in 1937. Large chemical companies were emerging, and oil companies even more so, while textile industries and ironworks, and especially mining companies, were disappearing from the top of the table. This process considerably intensified in 1958. The strong link between the giant enterprises and the car industry (petroleum extraction, refining and distribution, car production and tyre manufacturing) was already important (five out of fifteen).

Chemicals and electrical goods completed the triad of enterprises using the new technologies. Around 1973, a group of enterprises engaged in pure chemistry (the pharmaceutical companies) entered the scene. The oil companies were more important than ever, and were followed by the chemical, iron metallurgy and machine construction firms. Twenty-five years later, the pharmaceutical companies had multiplied and were the technological and industrial might of Europe, though they had not overtaken the century-old lead position held by Royal Dutch Shell. Notable for their absence are enterprises in the IT sector, whether hardware or software, while large enterprises producing material for telecommunications have appeared.

From Table 10.22 it can be seen that, in 1988, the number of countries represented among the forty-one largest industrial enterprises was more varied than in 1912. Russia, Belgium and Luxembourg have disappeared and Sweden, Switzerland, Holland, Italy, Spain and Finland have appeared. The traditional sectors (textiles, coal, iron) were no longer given, while pharmaceutical and personal care products formed the largest group, followed by electrical and (mainly) electronic goods, oil companies, car companies, food and household goods, drinks and tobacco. The predominant group was focused on chemicals and drugs, followed by enterprises connected with internal combustion engine technology, and then electronic materials. Changes in countries, and changes in sectors, were related to each other: countries with plentiful resources of coal and iron ore had lost their advantage in

Table 10.22 Large-scale European industrial enterprises in 1998

Nationality of head office	*No. of cases*	*Sector of activity*	*No. of cases*
United Kingdom	10	Pharmaceutical and beauty products	9
France	9	Electrical and electronic material	6
Germany	7	Petroleum	6
Sweden	3	Food, home products, drinks and tobacco	5
Switzerland	3	Cars	5
Holland	2	Chemicals	5
Holland–United Kingdom	2	Aeronautical	1
Italy	2	Glass	1
Spain	1	Others	2
Finland	1		
Sweden–Switzerland	1		
Total	41	Total	41

Source: *Business Week*, 13 July 1998.

the sphere of large-scale industrial enterprise. Only those that had succeeded in developing new technologies, and which had a far lower intensity of natural resources, had adapted to the new circumstances of the world market.

Divsification of services

Clark's law, whereby industrial growth is followed by the growth of services, has been realized with astonishing precision. Similarly, it has been possible to record how, increasingly, the rise in services implied the rise of modern services with a high degree of technology and information. The process has had various phases. The first involved the development of services that were modern for the nineteenth century: transport and communications, financial and insurance services. The rise of the modern enterprise, with the growing demand for administrative services, and the opening up of new types of occupation for women, completed the growth pattern of the services sector in the first half of the twentieth century, particularly between 1913 and 1950. During the 1950s and 1960s, the process was inexorable, further driven by the second significant factor: the growth of the welfare state, with its great demand for workers in advanced personal services, particularly in the health and education sectors. The third phase originated in the 1980s, when the IT revolution started to take shape, and then rapidly expanded in the following decade, with the combination of information and telecommunications. The result has been extremely vigorous development in tertiary services. The countries with the highest *per capita* income are, predictably, those that are further ahead in the development of tertiary services, as Table 10.23 shows.

The rise in the development of tertiary services has, ultimately, had a great impact on service enterprises. During much of the century, there was little similarity between industrial and service industries. In company rankings, so much in vogue since the middle of the century, they did not appear together, nor even did different types of service enterprises. Commercial banks were distinguishable from insurance companies, transport companies from electrical companies, those devoted

Table 10.23 Proportion of the population engaged in services, 1998 (%)

Holland	73	Austria [a]	63	Czech Republic	53
Norway	72	Germany	63	Slovakia	53
Sweden	72	Ireland	62	Lithuania	52
United Kingdom	71	Spain	62	Portugal	51
Denmark	70	Italy [a]	59	Poland	49
Switzerland [a]	69	Hungary	58	Slovenia	48
France [b]	69	Greece	58	Ukraine	47
Luxembourg	66	Estonia[d]	57	Bulgaria	44
Finland	66	Latvia	55	Belarus	40
Belgium	66	Russian Federation	54	Moldavia	40
Iceland [c]	66	Croatia	53	Romania	31

Source: The Economist, *The Economist Pocket Book*, London, 2000.

Notes: [a] 1997; [b] 1995; [c] 1994; [d] 1990.

to wholesale trade from all the former ones, and even nationalized companies were classified separately. Now a unified vision of the world of enterprise has been created. This is the result of technological convergence between the different sectors; it has come about because of the transformation of industrial companies and service industries into tertiary services, technical progress in services and the integrating effect of the new IT, the development of the stock markets, the universal tendency to privatize public companies. It is no coincidence that 1988 was the first year that *Business Week* published an integrated classification of companies from all sectors.

Figures for 1998, partially gathered in Table 10.24, correspond to non-industrial enterprises that could appear among the top fifteen industrial companies of Europe. It is interesting to note that the top European service enterprise at the time would come only eighth if it were classified together with the industrial enterprises. On the other hand, sixteen service enterprises appear ahead of ELF-Aquitaine (the fifteenth industrial company). The financial sector predominates, with six banks, two insurance companies and one for other financial services. British and Swiss banks account for the largest share among the banks. The remainder are six telecommunications companies and one for services to enterprise. It is noteworthy that there is not one single transport enterprise. A similar classification for the early twentieth century would have been dominated by railway companies. To a certain extent, the current telecommunications enterprises have replaced the former great transport companies (from the technological, entrepreneurial and financial points of view). Just as the services sector had been traditionally protected from international competition, so there are sub-sectors with companies of very different countries, the heritage of former public enterprises. This is particularly the case with telecommunications. The large European countries are the ones that have

Table 10.24 Large European service companies in 1998 (by stock market capitalization)

Company	*Country*	*Sector*
Lloyds TSB Group	UK	Banking
Allianz	Germany	Insurance
Deutsche Telekom	Germany	Telecommunications
HSBC Holdings	UK	Banking
British Telecommunications	UK	Telecommunications
ING Groep	Netherlands	Financial services
Crédit Suisse Group	Switzerland	Banking
France Télecom	France	Telecommunications
SAP	Gemany	Company services
Telecom Italia	Italy	Telecommunications
AEGON	Netherlands	Insurance
Deutsche Banking	Germany	Banking
Telefónica	Spain	Telecommunications
TIM	Italy	Telecommunications
UBS	Switzerland	Banking
Barclay's Banking	UK	Banking

Source: adapted from *Business Week*, 13 July 1998, pp. 54 ff.

large telecommunications companies. The presence of Italy in the classification with two companies is exceptional. It is reasonable to think that the spread of privatization will ultimately bring about international mergers. However, if this is plausible in theory, it is showing itself to be more complicated in practice. Finally, as regards distribution by country, it is worth noting that German companies, which continued to lose ground in the industrial field, occupy a very good position in the services sector, while the French do not. Furthermore, some of the small countries, like Sweden, which excel in the field of industry, are not equally successful in the field of services.

National growth models

So far, we have examined the growth pattern of the European economy during the twentieth century, and we have seen how the different national economies have acquired increasingly diverse profiles. Now we will outline the more significant trends over the century for the different national economies. As before, far more information is available for the western countries than for the eastern ones. Table 10.25 gives the growth rates for their *per capita* GDP, classified in descending order.

As we have seen in discussing *per capita* income, the results indicate that there are two different sides to the story – two 'clubs' to use the jargon of growth economists. On the one hand, there are the western countries; generally, the poorer they were at the beginning of the century, the more they have grown. On the other hand, the eastern countries have only grown slightly, despite being poor. In effect, the top countries in the table for growth rates over the century correspond to cases of low or low to average *per capita* income. Among the western countries,

Table 10.25 Growth rates of *per capita* GDP, 1913–1998 (%)

Country	*Growth rate*	*Country*	*Growth rate*
Portugal	2.79	Switzerland	1.91
Norway	2.68	Germany	1.88
Denmark	2.60	Belgium	1.81
Finland	2.58	Czech Republic	1.68
Greece	2.33	Ex-Yugoslavia	1.68
Italy	2.30	Poland [a]	1.64
Ireland	2.20	United Kingdom	1.58
Spain	2.19	Slovakia	1.55
Sweden	2.14	Hungary	1.33
France	2.05	Ex-Soviet Union	1.14
Austria	2.02	Bulgaria	1.13
Holland	1.91	Romania [b]	1.03

Source: A. Maddison, *Monitoring the World Economy*, 1995, and *The World Economy*, 2001.

Notes:
Indexes presuppose stable borders. Rates reflect transformations only in economic activity and not in territorial extent.
[a] 1929–1998.
[b] 1926–1998.

the United Kingdom occupies the appropriate position: in 1913, it was the richest country and is the one that over the century grew the least. It is interesting to see that other western countries that had precociously emulated the British industrialization process (Belgium), or that were already very rich (Holland), or that had rapidly adapted to industrialization (Switzerland, Germany, Austria, France), are placed ahead of Great Britain. However, they are below countries that were on the least industrialized fringes of western Europe. These countries are at the top of the table. They include the Scandinavian countries, which had strong growth during the twentieth century, and the western and southern peripheral areas: Ireland, Portugal, Greece, Italy and Spain. On the other hand, all the countries of central and eastern Europe are at the bottom of the table, showing how they have failed to converge towards the prosperity levels of the richer countries.

Countries of the first industrialization

Among the western countries, the British economy was the one with the slowest growth (see Figure 10.1), on account of its leading position at the start; however, over the century it lost its pre-eminence, and became just another western economy as regards its income levels. It had responded very well to the challenge of the two world wars; in both cases it considerably increased its output, and thus found itself in a position to get the better of its enemies. On the other hand, the return to peace was not managed so successfully, and the two post-war periods were marked by economic stagnation. There were important adjustments in the social, political and cultural spheres, one example being decolonization, with all it entailed for what had once been the greatest world empire, and it has to be admitted that Great Britain managed this successfully. But economic issues lost priority. Its

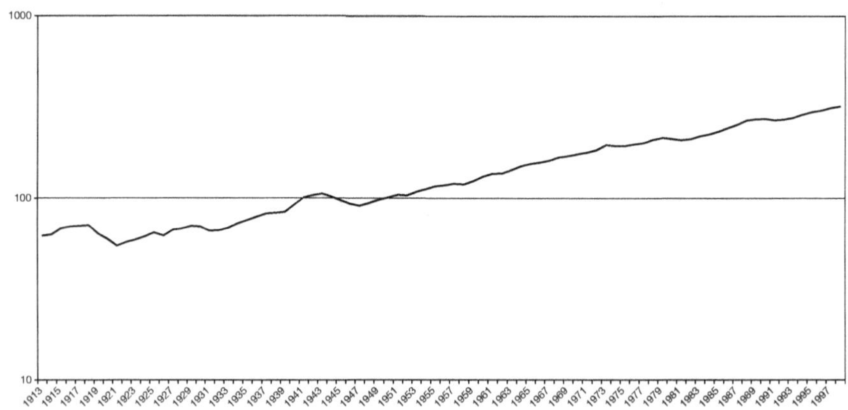

Figure 10.1 British GDP, 1913–1998 (1950 = 100). The indices for Figures 10.1–13 presuppose unchanged borders. The rates reflect only economic transformation and not extent of territory.

Source: A. Maddison, *Monitoring the World Economy*, Paris, 1995, and *The World Economy. A Millennial Perspective*, Paris, 2001.

particular evolution, with wartime acceleration and post-war slowdown, indicates how the great economic crises of the century were felt less in Great Britain; they had, in part, already been predicted. The 1929 crisis was not too serious, nor was the one in 1973. The latter coincided with delayed British entry into the EEC, and it could not benefit from membership as much as the six countries that had created it in 1957. The evolution after 1979 was relatively better than prior to 1973. Great Britain responded to the second energy crisis with a capacity for innovation and a package of measures against government intervention, in favour of the free market, that amounted to an original solution. The price of change was high, but it undoubtedly brought about an injection of economic dynamism into the British economy so that, although between 1979 and 1998 growth was lower than during the Golden Age (1950–1973), compared with other western countries, its trajectory was better. It is also true that in 1945 the United Kingdom was still by far the wealthiest large country in Europe (far ahead of the impoverished Germany, France and Italy and the ruined Soviet Union). But by 1979 it had already experienced a number of years of decline, which continued until the famous moment when it was 'overtaken' by Italy at the beginning of the 1980s.

Belgium, one of the oldest industrialized nations, and undoubtedly the oldest outside the United Kingdom, shows a slightly better performance than Great Britain (see Figure 10.2) but follows quite different paths. It suffered considerably during the world wars, but on both occasions managed to recover fairly rapidly. It was only slightly affected by the Great Depression, but its being linked to the gold standard meant that, like France, it took longer to recover, and between 1929 and 1939 suffered stagnation. In this respect, its evolution differed greatly from Holland's, which benefited from this particular period. As in all countries under German occupation, Belgian GDP declined considerably during the Second World War, but did not suffer the same widespread destruction of capital as during the First World War. The good state of maintenance of its production apparatus

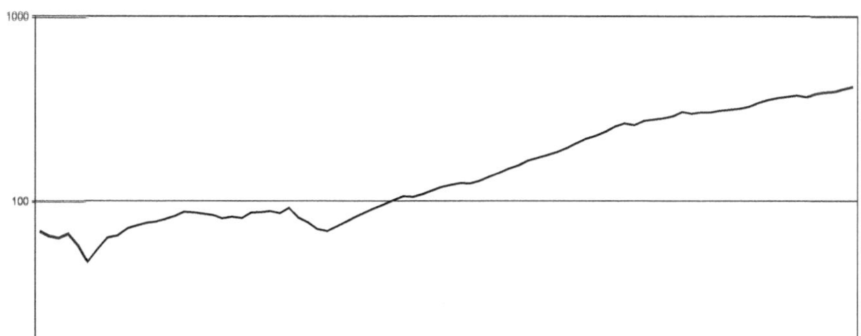

Figure 10.2 Belgian GDP, 1913–1998 (1950 = 100).

Source: A. Maddison, *Monitoring the World Economy*, Paris, 1995, and *The World Economy. A Millennial Perspective*, Paris, 2001.

enabled Belgium to play a very dynamic role in the years of post-war reconstruction. It was able to supply coal, iron, steel and machinery to other European countries. However, for this very reason, it did not benefit from the Marshall Plan to rebuild its production equipment, with the result that by the 1950s Belgian industry was noticeably outdated. In this respect, Belgium's evolution was very similar to Britain's, and Belgian growth was similarly very slow in the European context. But, unlike the United Kingdom, initial integration into the EEC was very beneficial for Belgium. It was hit badly by the oil crisis, as were all countries. Belgium's growth did not enable it to catch up with its pre-1973 trend. Its mining and industrial base, concentrated in the Walloon area and the oldest in continental Europe, with its great coal mines and steel plants, has had to undergo reconversion procedures, ranging from company closures to large-scale subsidies for workers who have been affected. To offset the fall in employment, Belgium, like many others, has resorted to increased public sector employment. The failure of this strategy, in a small country traditionally open to the outside world, involved a search for more beneficial solutions for the Belgian economy. These include granting extremely favourable conditions for setting up, on Belgian territory, industrial plants and headquarters in Europe for all types of multinational companies. In this way, Belgium has been able to attract strong investment and relaunch its economy. Territorially, the new activities have been located in the Flemish rather than in the Walloon area. In the last quarter of the twentieth century, the nineteenth century economic thrust typical of the French-speaking area was thus completely replaced by Flemish dynamism.

In the seventeenth century, Holland was the most prosperous economy in Europe. Despite its political decline during the eighteenth century and much of the nineteenth, at the end of the latter period it started to recover its dynamism, thanks to the systematic deployment of technologies of the second industrial revolution. These freed the Dutch economy from its dependence on coal. During the First World War, Holland remained neutral, and during the conflict, and particularly after it, was able to benefit from its position (see Figure 10.3). Compared with 1913, in 1929 no other western country had grown so much: 77 per cent. In this period, Holland grew faster than the United States and all the other countries that had remained neutral. The Dutch success was due to many factors, one of which was neutrality. The country's role as a maritime port for Germany meant it had privileged access to the whole German market, and Dutch entrepreneurs used this to their advantage on numerous occasions. They were the ones who controlled the German oil market – imports, refining and distribution – thanks to which they developed Royal Dutch. This was to subsequently merge with British Shell Transport & Trading to form Royal Dutch Shell, one of the consistently most important multinational companies during the whole century. In the field of domestic electrical goods, it was again the Dutch who exploited the whole central European market through the technological and commercial leadership of Philips, which was able to triumph where other well placed competitors, like AEG and Siemens, failed. Dutch neutrality, and German downfall, played an important part in this outcome. The second key to Dutch success were good relations and strong trading traditions with Great Britain, with the result that Unilever, one of the

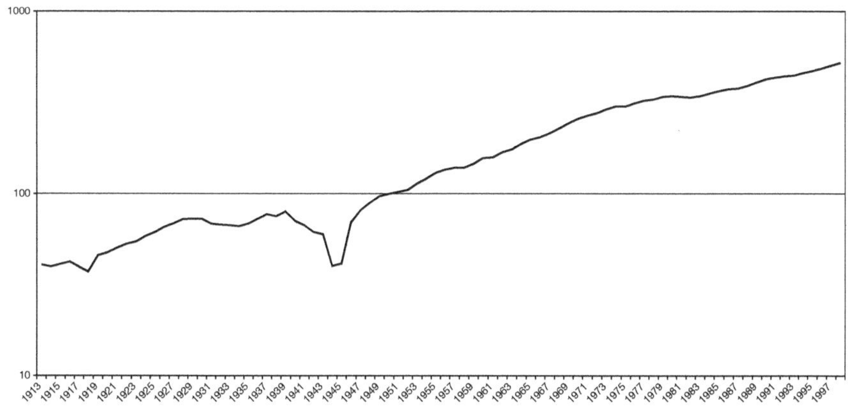

Figure 10.3 Dutch GDP, 1913–1998 (1950 = 100).

Source: A. Maddison, *Monitoring the World Economy*, Paris, 1995, and *The World Economy. A Millennial Perspective*, Paris, 2001.

entrepreneurial giants in the food sector, became part Dutch. Trading has always been an essential ingredient in Dutch success. When, during the 1970s, Holland was to enjoy a much appreciated natural resource (natural gas), the Dutch were tempted to live off the revenue. This was the Dutch disease from which they finally freed themselves at the end of the 1980s, making their welfare state appropriately flexible, and deploying their organizational, entrepreneurial and technological abilities to the full.

The economic evolution of Switzerland is particularly interesting (see Figure 10.4). Like Holland, Switzerland knew how to create wealth for itself, despite not having the natural resources required for the first industrialization. Like Holland, it had been held back somewhat by the European war, and took full advantage of the ruin of Germany and the opportunities that came with it to transform itself into the location for many originally German initiatives, or to provide refuge for industrial activities and services which would otherwise have been realized in Germany. Thus, like Holland, Switzerland gained great benefit from the problems of Germany. It is not surprising that its economic life should always have depended on the ups and downs of its powerful northern neighbour, and on its potential for international intermediation. However, the 1929 crisis had an almost 'French' effect on Switzerland. Its impact was slight, but it generated prolonged stagnation, not only during the 1930s, but also during the whole of the Second World War. Switzerland's big moment came with the end of the war; while everywhere else there was chaos, disorder and confusion, in Switzerland there was tranquillity. Here the wealth accumulated by the Nazis (especially gold, but also currency) lay unused. The massive influx of these treasures suddenly modified the standard of living in Switzerland. From 1944 to 1945, its GDP grew by a spectacular 29 per cent, and from 1945 to 1947 by a further 20 per cent. Such increases did not start from a destructured economy, but rather from a situation of stability. The Swiss economy also had its 'Golden Age' and benefited from high growth, interrupted

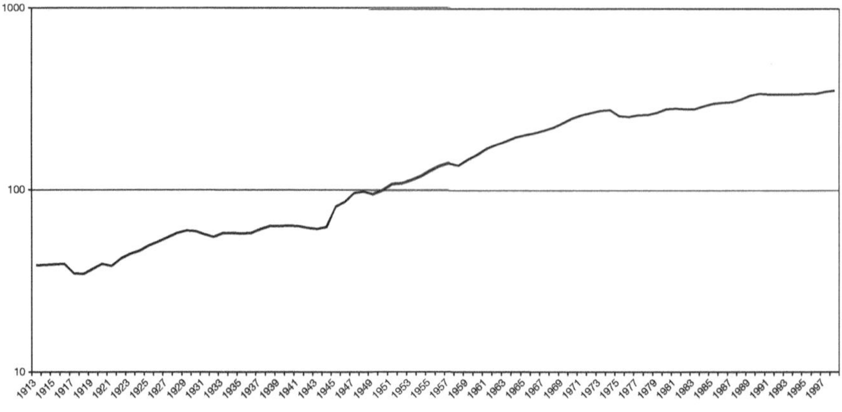

Figure 10.4 Swiss GDP, 1913–1998 (1950 = 100).

Source: A. Maddison, *Monitoring the World Economy*, Paris, 1995, and *The World Economy. A Millennial Perspective*, Paris, 2001.

only in 1949 and 1958, when turmoil in the monetary system affected it for a short time. The oil crisis affected it more than it did any other western European country. Two other phenomena caused stagnation in the Swiss economy between 1990 and 1996: financial deregulation, which turned out to be advantageous to London, and the fall of the Berlin Wall, with the subsequent diversion of German resources to the former GDR. As in the nineteenth century, Switzerland returned to an economy based on industrial enterprises, a 'tiny branch' of top-level multinational pharmaceutical companies.

The role of 'second comers'

Throughout the whole century, the true protagonists of the European economy were countries that in the nineteenth century had responded to the British industrial challenge and turned into industrial powers. In the first place, these were Germany and France, and to a lesser extent Italy; finally, there was Russia.

The twentieth century was certainly not a peaceful one for the German economy (see Figure 10.5). As a consequence of the two world wars, Germany experienced great territorial changes. During both wars, its surface area increased enormously, since it occupied and administered territories of other countries, and its defeat brought about heavy penalties in terms of territory. After the First World War, territorial losses were significant, although the reparations seemed much heavier; those that came after the Second World War were even more radical. At first, this meant the subdivision of German territory into four zones of military occupation under the chief allied countries, as well as heavy territorial cessions to Poland. From 1949 onwards, the establishment of the Federal German Republic and the German Democratic Republic created a division that was to last for forty years; the two parts were not reunited until 1990. The wars, and the great crisis of 1929–1932, dominate the evolution and pattern of the German economy. The first

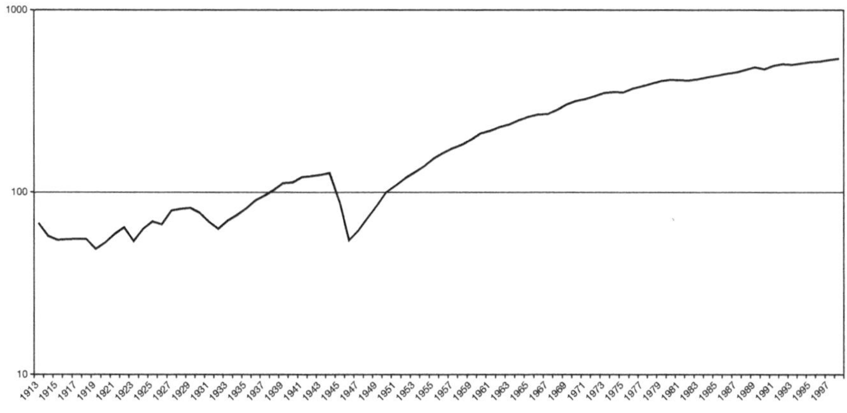

Figure 10.5 German GDP, 1913–1998 (1950 = 100).

Source: A. Maddison, *Monitoring the World Economy*, Paris, 1995, and *The World Economy. A Millennial Perspective*, Paris, 2001.

post-war period was one of great misery, while the second, after a start that had been even worse, eventually ended particularly well. The pattern of German GDP reflected all the hardships of the second post-war period. The First World War, the 1919 crisis, the 1923 crisis or even that of 1929–1932, were nothing compared with the total collapse of 1945 and 1946. A number of authors have interpreted the subsequent economic boom as a specific consequence of the intensity of the collapse and the opportunities for recovery for a country with a suitably skilled population and infrastructure, which could be made productive as soon as it was repaired. During the 1950s, German industry recovered its traditional dynamism and, once again, transformed itself into a provider of machinery and transport equipment for its neighbours. The growing trade links strengthened the case for joining the European Common Market; once good relations with its French neighbour had been endorsed, this was realized in 1957 with the Treaty of Rome. The fall of the Berlin Wall, in 1989, opened the way to the reunification of the FRG and the GDR, which took place in 1990 (in reality, the GDR being absorbed by the FRG). This change in the frontiers of the German nation led to the German economy being the largest in Europe at the end of the twentieth century.

As in Germany, the French economy in the twentieth century (see Figure 10.6) was marked by wars. Despite two victories, the two wars had devastating effects on France, since they were fought on its own territory. The inter-war period was dominated by the spectre of demographic stagnation and economic backwardness. France perceived itself as an economy with no future. A comparison between the German and French evolution in the 1930s shows that the difference could hardly have been greater. From 1929 to 1939, the German economy grew by 37 per cent, the French by 3 per cent. If we look at 1944 and draw a comparison with 1929, the contrast is even more dramatic. The former grew by 55 per cent, while the latter contracted by 51 per cent. The second post-war period was very different from the first, and France started a long phase of growth that banished the spectre

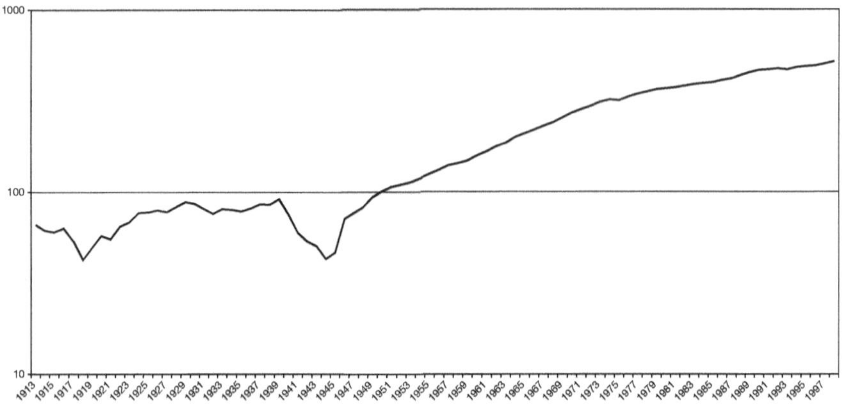

Figure 10.6 French GDP, 1913–1998 (1950 = 100).

Source: A. Maddison, *Monitoring the World Economy*, Paris, 1995, and *The World Economy. A Millennial Perspective*, Paris, 2001.

of stagnation: after 1945 its performance was that of a very dynamic economy. It made the most of post-war reconstruction to renew its transport infrastructure and industrial machinery. Through its political and commercial gamble with the EEC, France was able to expand its markets and eliminate the risk of conflict with Germany, its neighbour and long-standing enemy. The continuity and rapidity of growth, during the period between 1945 and 1974, radically changed the traditional image of a backward and outdated French economy. With good restructuring, and an excellent supply of human capital, it was able to transform itself into a dynamic economy in the sphere of technology and enterprise. With the oil crises, particularly the second, France continued a strategy of increasing demand. In 1981, the difficult international economic conjuncture that coincided with a left-wing majority taking over government brought about negative effects that ultimately caused the franc to be devalued against the mark. The politically negative impact of this situation was such that no French government, since 1981, has dared to detach itself from parity with the mark, considered the touchstone for the adjustment of French economic policy. In 2000, in terms of GDP, the French economy was the second largest in Europe, surpassed only by Germany.

Of all the large European countries that fought during the Great War, Italy was the one that enjoyed the highest growth rates over the century (see Figure 10.7). The successes achieved between the end of the nineteenth century and the outbreak of the First World War did not occur again until the period after the Second World War. However, the overall result was very positive, and can be considered a complete success in terms of convergence. Tangible proof of this was the overtaking, or *sorpasso*, of Great Britain in the 1980s. On the other hand, curiously enough, Italian evolution over the century is reminiscent of Britain's. Apart from the major exception of the 1943–1945 period, Italy also experienced the events of the two wars, mostly from a distance. Its initial neutrality in the First War, and its distance from the war fronts, enabled the Italian economy to prosper during

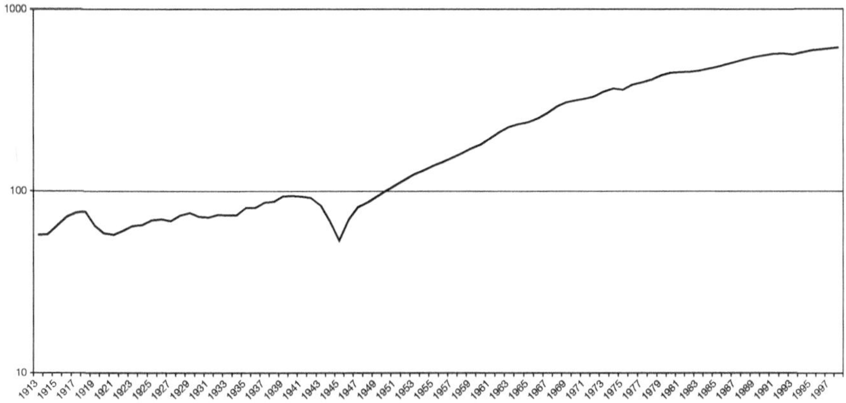

Figure 10.7 Italian GDP, 1913–1998 (1950 = 100).

Source: A. Maddison, *Monitoring the World Economy*, Paris, 1995, and *The World Economy. A Millennial Perspective*, Paris, 2001.

the years of the conflict. The post-war period, on the other hand, was very difficult. The crises of overproduction and the conflicts over redistribution were a fatal combination, and ended up with the emergence of Fascism. Italy's inter-war period was unique, because from 1922 it was practically dominated throughout by the Fascist regime. The first decade was, economically, generally liberal in the macroeconomic field, with the occasional injection of state intervention. The second decade was marked by decidedly more autarkic aspirations, which became steadily stronger until the end of Fascism. Involvement in the Second World War turned out to be fatal for Mussolini, and in 1943 his regime collapsed dramatically. The two final years of the war were chaotic. Reconstruction, on the other hand, was a complete success – one of the post-war miracles. Italy, like Germany and France, made good use of the Marshall Plan to reconstruct its industry and transport networks. It also managed to become part of the inter-European trading network, which eventually led to the EEC. Italy took full advantage of this, both to widen its markets, and to provide new labour prospects for its population. The miracle began to dissolve fairly soon after 1962, but still continued with a certain vigour for eleven years. As we shall see when dealing with economic policies, Italy was the home of some of the most original policies of the century, again in the field of state intervention. This was the case with the rescue operations for banks and industries, as well as regional development policies. In the 1980s and 1990s, Italy attracted attention because of its success with small enterprises and industrial areas, and has been held up as a model for industrial policy makers, especially with regard to its export achievements.

From whatever point of view, the twentieth century is largely the century of the Soviet Union. Its origin in 1917 and its death in 1991 mark the culminating moments of the century. The birth of the USSR was perceived for a long time, mainly thanks to the success of Soviet or pro-Soviet propaganda, as an inevitable result of the failure of tsarism. Nowadays, we know that the tsarist economy was dynamic, but that the structure of power under tsarism changed very slowly, creating the conditions for increasingly strong challenges to the autocracy that held sway. The extreme conditions of the European war brought about political revolution, but they also stretched economic conditions to the utmost, facilitating the birth of progressively more radical alternatives. The Bolsheviks saw their opportunity in October 1917, and seized it. For almost three-quarters of a century they would not relinquish their hold, for whatever reason. However, as in the Buddenbrook syndrome, three generations later the targets that had once seemed interesting were now very different, and to general astonishment, in 1991 the Soviet Union broke up, like a lump of sugar in a cup of hot coffee.

The great stages of the Soviet economy are by now sufficiently well known. The first period, known as wartime communism, was from 1917 to 1921. It was followed by the New Economic Policy (NEP), which continued until just before 1927. In that year the first five-year plan was launched, which meant that there was a clean break in Soviet economic policy, and in the world as a whole. Central planning was to be the official policy for as long as the Soviet Union existed. However, two separate phases need to be distinguished. The first plans, until the Second World War, were wholly aimed at industrialization, and in particular at creating large-scale heavy industry. Then there was the post-war reconstruction effort, which lasted almost a decade. It was followed by attempts at reform following the death of Stalin (1953), and these continued for a further decade. Finally, once reformism had been abandoned, we see the start of the Brezhnev period, marked by a continuing decline. This inertia was to last almost two decades. At the beginning of the 1980s, there were renewed efforts at reform, which were to gather momentum under Gorbachev and his *perestroika* (reconstruction).

The incomplete series for Russian GDP, both Soviet and post-Soviet, reflects the discontinuous nature of Russian economic life in the twentieth century (see Figure 10.8). The First World War must have involved a significant fall in GDP, which continued until 1921 as a result of the world war extending into civil war. The NEP had already been a true economic recovery. After strong growth linked with the first five-year plans, the Second World War, once again, drastically reduced the country's productive potential, even though, in this case, the interruption was shorter-lived. If the first change in the economic system was to involve the loss of several years, the second change seemed to be heading towards a repetition of the experience, though now there was no world war, or civil war, to blame for it. The decline of Soviet GDP since 1989 has been spectacular. Its performance is unmistakably worse than that of central and eastern European countries. Only Estonia seems to be escaping the fate of a plummeting economy. The causes of such conspicuous failure are complex, but there is no doubt that the way the transition to a market economy took place was crucial. The Soviet Union started out by liberalizing the transitions that were easiest to carry out, or those in which it had a greater interest, such as foreign trade. Yet many sectors were not liberalized, and some continue not to be. Liberalization has been extremely lopsided, and produced all sorts of distortions. The creation of a number of markets, when neither the state nor society as a whole was equipped to fully guarantee mutual obligations, opened the door to all types of organized violence; this turns any entrepreneurial

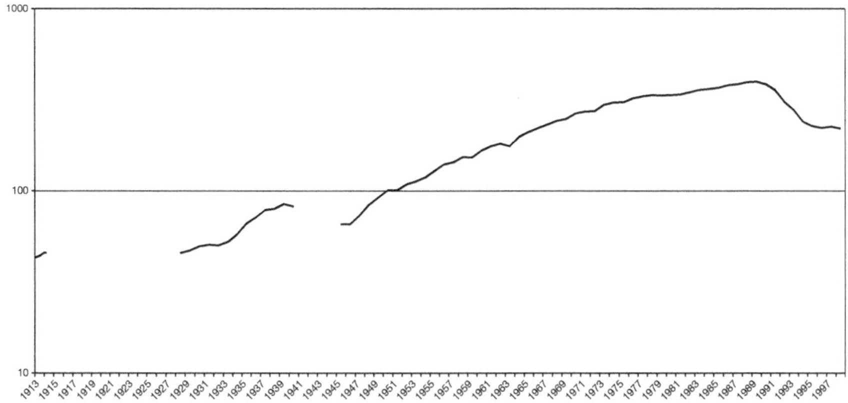

Figure 10.8 Soviet and post-Soviet Russian GDP, 1913–1998 (1950 = 100).

Source: A. Maddison, *Monitoring the World Economy*, Paris, 1995, and *The World Economy. A Millennial Perspective*, Paris, 2001.

activity into a dangerous adventure, and minimizes opportunities for investment. The former Soviet Union has set out on a path of destruction, which strongly resembles the initial phases of the spread of the feudal system in Europe. Hopes of balancing the situation are more remote than in central and eastern Europe, since most Russian economic capacity is inconveniently located, and reflect the plans for autarky that are no longer sustainable. The lack of a period of adaptation to the market system has put an end to any possibility of progressive adjustment to the new price structures, or to the relative scarcities.

The destiny of peripheral countries

The European countries that saw most growth in the twentieth century have one thing in common: they are located in the peripheral areas of western Europe. Some are Scandinavian countries and are the most northerly in Europe, others are Mediterranean and are the most southerly, while others, the most westerly, share features of both. At the beginning of the twentieth century, all these countries were poor relative to those that had already gone some way towards becoming industrialized. Before 1914, only Sweden seemed to have found a short cut.

Sweden and Denmark are two ancient European nations that have long clashed with each other, but they emerged from the Napoleonic wars having spent all their warring energy. Norway gained independence from Sweden at the beginning of the twentieth century, in 1905. Not long afterwards, Finland, which until 1812 had been Swedish, and subsequently Russian, gained its independence from the Soviet Union in 1920. It had already enjoyed considerable autonomy under tsarist Russia, but its real independence came with the dissolution of the tsarist empire.

These four Scandinavian countries had comparable growth patterns and very high, and similar, growth rates. The highest rates were in the three countries that had been the poorest, but none of these was as high as Sweden's. The dominant element of the Scandinavian economic experience of the twentieth century was the rapidity and continuity of growth (see Figure 10.9). Its partial neutrality during the two world wars (Sweden was neutral in both, the other Nordic countries only in one), and the low impact of the 1930s crisis, meant that their economies could enjoy a higher net growth than all the other European countries in the trans-war years. Indeed, the living standards of these countries converged with those of the more advanced countries. Subsequently, growth was maintained, which is not insignificant. The early establishment of the welfare state in Scandinavia, one of its special features, coincides with the 1930s. Scandinavia's (especially Sweden's) way out of the crisis was to favour a 'new social contract', with welfare policies bringing about greater stability on the economic front for all economic operators, and a strong commitment to production on the part of trade unions and managers. High literacy levels, which even then entailed a long period of schooling, enabled all the Scandinavian countries (again Sweden particularly) to specialize in technology-intensive industrial activities and services. Reconstruction after the Second World War and the Golden Age facilitated the access of these countries to expanding markets and the highly favourable international context. The oil crisis hit them all, though some harder than others. With the discovery of oil reserves in the North Sea, Norway managed to become a large exporter of crude oil and, with its high growth rates during the last quarter of the century, surged ahead of all other European countries. These countries were also hit by the European crisis of the early 1990s, although in this case the country that was most affected was Finland, but for different reasons. Finland had been involved in brokerage with the Soviet Union, and the collapse of the USSR, with the consequent liberalization of its trade, meant that Finland lost this lucrative trade. It had to find a new direction for its economy and specialize in other activities, and in the field of electronics and telecommunications Finland has done brilliantly.

Figure 10.9 GDP of Scandinavian countries, 1913–1998 (1950 = 100).

Source: A. Maddison, *Monitoring the World Economy*, Paris, 1995, and *The World Economy. A Millennial Perspective*, Paris, 2001.

In the extreme west of Europe, Ireland and Portugal shared a number of experiences in the twentieth century. For several decades, since its independence in 1920, Ireland grew at the same rate as Great Britain, which during the twentieth century was relatively slow (see Figure 10.10). But Ireland did not enjoy British levels of prosperity. It remained neutral during the Second World War, but was a recipient of Marshall Plan aid. Until the end of the 1950s, Irish economic policy was marked by a degree of autarky, based on agriculture, and Ireland did not join the EEC or EFTA. Its international trading links took place through an agreement with the United Kingdom. It seemed that integration into the European Community, in 1973, might offer Ireland the great opportunity to mobilize and expand all its capacity for growth and convergence. Unfortunately, the international climate was not altogether favourable, and Ireland did not manage to achieve much, in an international economy overshadowed by depression. All it could do was hope for new expansive trends to allow it to fully exploit its potential. This eventually came about, especially after 1993, when the Irish growth rate was being compared with that of the Asian 'tigers'. At the end of the 1980s, Ireland decided to open up to foreign investment. Being an English-speaking country, in a world of enterprise and technology based on the hegemony of the English language, gave it a clear competitive edge. From being a country with high unemployment rates, it became a country that imported labour. The successes of recent years have improved the century-long trend of the Irish economy.

In the first third of the twentieth century, Portugal's political life was convulsive, going from monarchy to republic, and from dictatorship to democracy. The most stable period, a republican dictatorship enforced by Salazar in 1927, was to last until 1974. Portugal confronted the 1930s crisis effectively, and experienced its best moments during the Second World War, when it benefited from neutrality,

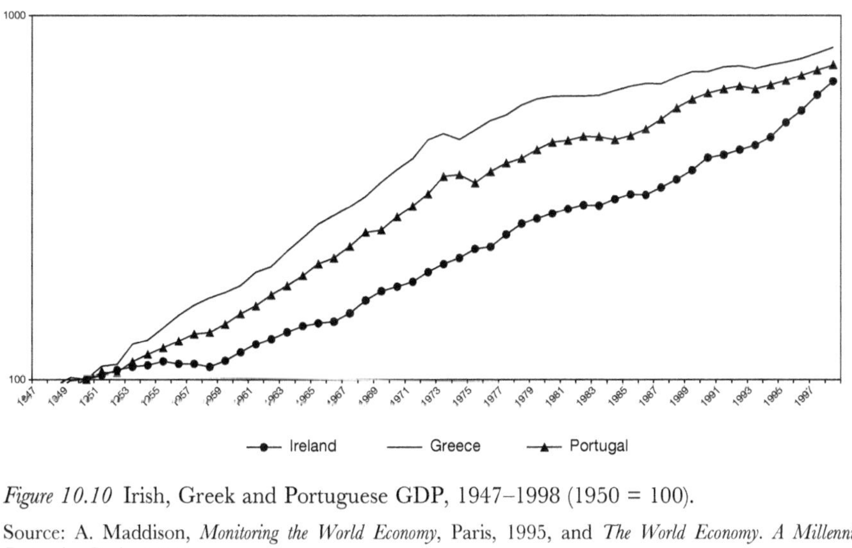

Figure 10.10 Irish, Greek and Portuguese GDP, 1947–1998 (1950 = 100).

Source: A. Maddison, *Monitoring the World Economy*, Paris, 1995, and *The World Economy. A Millennial Perspective*, Paris, 2001.

and in the immediate post-war period, when it was associated with all the initiatives of Western co-operation. Its growth rate was steady. Its policies tended towards a degree of autarky, although in the 1950s and 1960s it belonged to EFTA. Heavy emigration to Europe helped to offset its trade deficit, but in the colonial wars from 1961 to 1974 the country's economic and human resources were drained. The 'carnation revolution', which put an end to the dictatorship of Salazar in April 1974, followed by a rapid decolonization process, created almost a million immigrants from the former colonies, and started a new phase for Portugal. There was a period of social uncertainty, which tended towards an openly pro-Western position about 1980. Since its entry into the EEC in 1986, Portugal has been able to benefit from the opportunities of the great European market, with EC funds channelled into the poorer regions and towards agricultural products. Its excellent growth rate over the century (see Figure 10.10) confirms the success of its efforts at convergence.

Spain remained neutral during the First World War and, as a result, began the 1920s with a much higher level of prosperity than in 1913. Not only had it become much richer, but it had also reduced the gap between itself and the more developed countries of Europe. Thanks to its neutrality, Spain naturalized practically all the investments in foreign hands, and managed to build up the fourth largest gold reserves in the world. It held them until 1936, but dissipated them during the course of the civil war. Although, economically, Spain had enjoyed a peaceful period between the two wars, with strong expansion in the 1920s, and mild depression in the first half of the 1930s, politically and socially it was very turbulent. Ultimately, this sowed the seeds of a long and bloody civil war, lasting from 1936 to 1939. At the end of it, the economy did not manage to find the path to recovery, and sank into a swamp of depression. Unlike the First, the Second World War was not all advantageous for Spain. Its alliance with the Axis powers deprived it of all room for manoeuvre, and made it a prisoner of agreements with Hitler and Mussolini. At the end of the war, it was uncertain whether the allied powers would intervene against Franco. After some hesitation, it was decided not to do so, due to the outbreak of the Cold War. Only when it was clear that the survival of the regime was not in question did economic growth get under way. It took place very rapidly, and to a great extent managed to make up for lost time (see Figure 10.11). During the 1950s, growth took place in a system that was essentially autarkic, but which became more flexible in 1959, when it was realized that opportunities existed in the international economy provided that foreign exchange was liberalized. Tourism, the remittances of emigrants and foreign investment helped to finance the productive restructuring of the Spanish economy, which especially from 1960 to 1973 performed as had been hoped, and showed particularly fast growth. As with so many other European economies, the oil crisis marked the end of the Golden Age for Spain. But the economic depression was also complicated by the delicate political transition to democracy. The new stimulus to Spain's growth has unquestionably been a result of integration both into the EEC and into the international economy.

Of all the peripheral western countries, Greece is the most easterly. Despite its complicated political history in the twentieth century, it is noteworthy that the

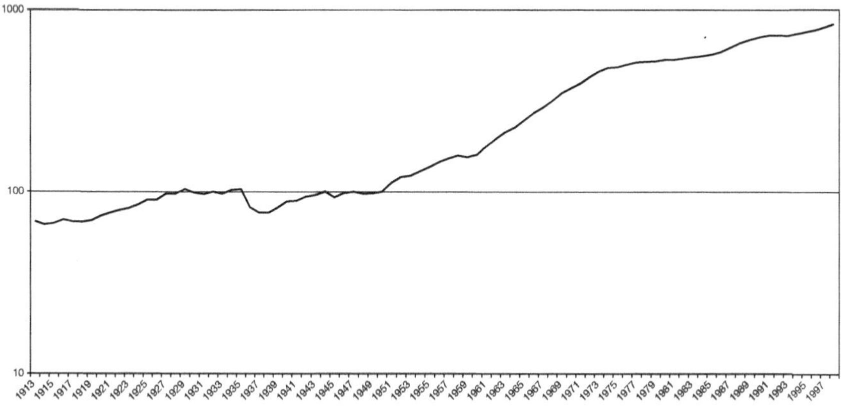

Figure 10.11 Spanish GDP, 1913–1998 (1950 = 100).

Source: A. Maddison, *Monitoring the World Economy*, Paris, 1995, and *The World Economy. A Millennial Perspective*, Paris, 2001.

overall result, in terms of growth, is one of the best (see Figure 10.10). This figure underlines the strong tendency towards convergence when the economy is left free to act. Immediately before and after the First World War, Greece expanded its borders. In the early 1920s, it had to accommodate the two million Greeks fleeing from Turkey as a consequence of massive population resettlement. During the Second World War, Greece suffered serious destruction under the occupation of the Axis troops; this did not end in 1945, but lasted until 1949, because of the outbreak of a ferocious civil war, which foreshadowed the Cold War. Once political life had become stabilized, economic growth followed the pattern of the country's Mediterranean European neighbours. It took advantage of strong western European demand through the remittances of emigrants and the increase in tourism. In 1980, Greece joined the European Community but, unlike Italy, Ireland, Spain and Portugal, has not been able to transform Community resources into a driving force for economic modernization.

In contrast to the comparatively precocious success of the western peripheral countries are the failures of the central-eastern peripheral countries of Europe. We need to remember that in 1913, central and eastern Europe did not exist as such. It was a wholly imprecise geographical expression, when it was not a derogatory way of referring to the Habsburg Empire, the dual Austro-Hungarian monarchy; however, after 1919, the expression became very precise. It corresponded to all the countries created under the peace treaties and that extended between the Soviet Union, Germany and Italy. Their origin was traumatic. They rose from the ashes of four defeated empires: the German, the Russian, the Austro-Hungarian and the Ottoman (which in 1913 had already been defeated in the Balkans), but in particular from the Russian and Austro-Hungarian empires. They had no tradition or resources behind them. The 1920s were spent trying to achieve a minimal state structure, and to build up a national identity. They partially succeeded, thanks to an injection of credit, mainly from North America, but also from France, Britain and Belgium. The economy was neglected, and when the 1930s crisis struck in all its severity, they found themselves at risk from all types of dictators, very often fascist. The countries that remained economically within the German sphere were particularly badly affected by the crisis. The poorest ones, and those that were less integrated into the central European economy, were much better off. But they were all caught in the vortex of the economic expansion of Hitler's Germany. After the Second World War, they nearly all remained under Soviet control, with very few exceptions, notably Finland and Austria. We have already seen the case of Finland, along with the western peripheral countries, and the case of Austria will now be examined.

Austria was probably the western European economy that had the worst of it during the trans-war years. In 1950, GDP (with the same frontiers) was only 9 per cent higher than in 1913 (see Figure 10.12). Germany, which ranked second as regards ill fated trajectories, managed to increase it by 23 per cent. During the First World War, Austria suffered particularly badly. After the collapse of the whole Habsburg imperial structure that had given life to Vienna, the political, economic and financial capital of the empire, its reconstruction was slow and fragile. The dissolution of the empire gave rise to a country whose capital city was out of all proportion to its level of activity. After a modest recovery, in the 1920s, the collapse of the New York stock exchange shook the weak foundations of the new Austrian economy. The prolonged crisis was overcome only during the *Anschluss* (the absorption of Austria into the Nazi economic area), when Hitler assigned it a different role. The 'good years' of the war period (when Austria was completely left out of military involvement) ended abruptly with the allied occupation in 1945, and in a single year GDP fell by almost 60 per cent. Austria, like Germany (and Vienna, like Berlin), was divided into four sectors, each controlled by one of the allied powers. The Austrian miracle was that the allied occupation ended without any territorial division; but the negative aspect was slow reconstruction, which was

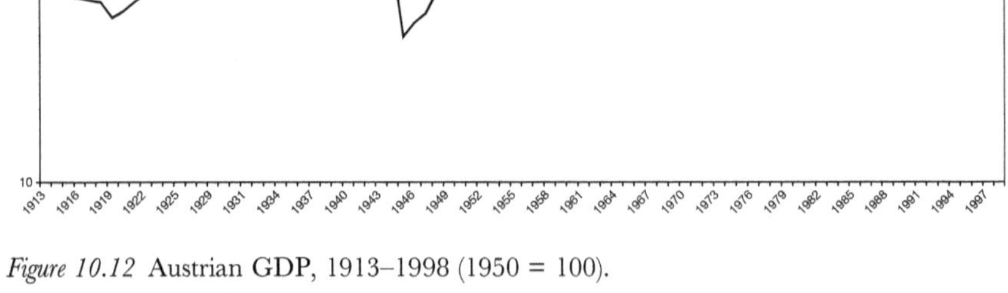

Figure 10.12 Austrian GDP, 1913–1998 (1950 = 100).

Source: A. Maddison, *Monitoring the World Economy*, Paris, 1995, and *The World Economy. A Millennial Perspective*, Paris, 2001.

completed only in 1953. From then on, and with its neutral status established, the Austrian economy began its own 'Golden Age'. There was to be very rapid growth, and the country's geopolitical location would be fully exploited. It was part of the Western economy, but like Finland it was well located, both politically and economically, for intermediating commercially between east and west. Its neutrality from all the blocs was to be a valuable advantage after the oil crisis, and especially with the fall of the Soviet bloc. Unlike Finland, Austria did not have such strong links with the Soviet Union, as it had with the central and eastern European countries. The transition to the market system was to be particularly beneficial to the Austrian economy. All in all, Austria was to catch up after falling behind during the war, and once again took its place among the prosperous countries of Europe.

Between 1945 and 1948, whether they wanted to or not, all the other countries of the central and eastern area became integrated into the Soviet area. They remained in the bloc until 1989, when, in the space of only a few weeks, they experienced a sensational revolution that returned them to democratic life. It involved secessions, bids for independence and, in some cases, extremely brutal wars, as well as a very painful transition to a new economic system. Overall, their evolution has been the most disappointing. In some of the countries, it was even worse than for the Soviet Union itself. As Figure 10.13 shows, the growth of the east European bloc, from 1950 to 1989, was an exact replica of that of the Soviet Union. This was no coincidence, but derived from the fact that they shared the same model, and above all shared the same information strategies and structures. The socialist economies could not afford to spread official information that was negative, and this gave rise to a permanent tendency to manipulate statistical data. Behind the enormous mass of statistics for the Comecon area, it is very difficult to know what is true and what is invented. That the evolution of both eastern Europe and the USSR should be so similar is highly suspect. In any case, the figures reflect strong

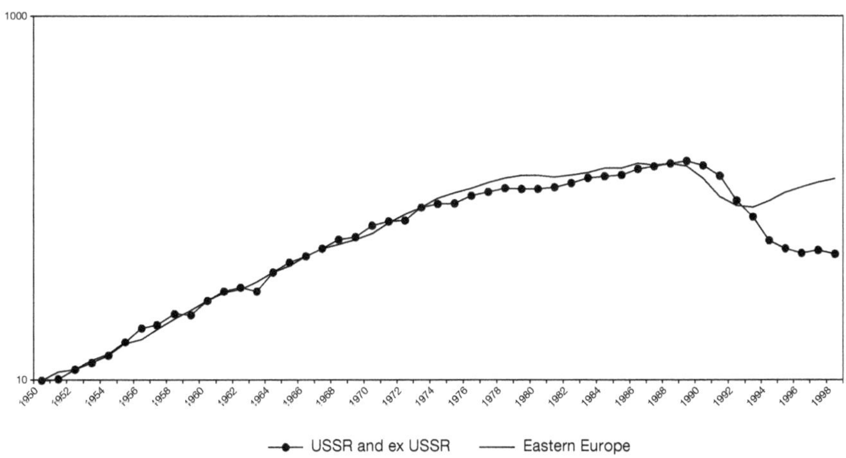

Figure 10.13 GDP of the Soviet Union, eastern Europe and successor states, 1950–1988.

Source: A. Maddison, *Monitoring the World Economy*, Paris, 1995, and *The World Economy. A Millennial Perspective*, Paris, 2001.

growth of what was called 'material output' until the end of the 1970s. Then, somewhat belatedly compared with the west, growth decelerated significantly, and did not cease to decelerate for the whole decade. With the collapse at the end of 1989, like the Soviet Union, eastern Europe plummeted; the only difference is that, on average, the downward trend lasted less in eastern Europe. But the average is deceptive. Some countries did manage to put a rapid stop to the disorganization of production: Poland in 1991, Czechoslovakia between 1992 and 1993 (a little sooner in the Czech Republic than in Slovakia), Hungary in 1993, Bulgaria only in 1997, while Romania seems to have fallen below its 1991 minimum. The former Yugoslavia seemed to have reached its minimum in 1993, but the civil wars upset all predictions. Generally speaking, the three most advanced countries (Poland, Hungary and the former Czechoslovakia, not to mention the former GDR) suffered a severe economic crisis (over 10 per cent of GDP), but experienced growth once again immediately afterwards. On the other hand, the Balkan area suffered a worse initial crisis, with in some cases decreases of 40 per cent (Albania, the former Yugoslavia), from which it rallied weakly, only to fall back before it could raise its head.

Notes

I am very grateful to Fernando Guirao and Xavier Tafunell, who in this and the remaining chapters helped me enormously with their numerous comments and supplementary material, including the unpublished material they allowed me to use. Any errors are my own.

11 The twentieth century – from break with the past to prosperity (II)

The great stages

Albert Carreras

Fluctuations in the economy

The first thing to establish is the time profile of the European economy. The best way to do this is by means of the trend in the GDP. Despite the efforts of specialists, we do not have this combined figure for the whole of the twentieth century. Border changes caused by two world wars, interruptions in the collection of statistical data during the moments of greatest disorganization during, or after, a war or revolution, the lack of compatibility between the national accounts of countries under different economic systems, have all greatly hindered attempts to summarize overall European economic activity throughout the century. Surprisingly, it is easier to achieve this for the nineteenth century.

Maddison has resolved the question for the second half of the twentieth century, and provides data for its complete coverage, including the states that arose after the former Soviet Union was dismembered. However, all this is more complicated for the 1913–1950 period. It is possible to make an approximation for the western countries by aggregating the figures for the main countries. Table 11.1 gives the annual GDP trend for western Europe, from 1913 to 1998. After that, and for the period after 1950, it will be compared with the pattern for eastern Europe.

Table 11.1 is particularly revealing. On the one hand, the overall GDP index enables us to gain a preliminary impression of the phases of the west European economy (see Figure 11.1). On the other hand, the annual growth rates give a better picture of the conjuncture (see Figure 11.2).

The outbreak of the First World War brought about a reduction in GDP. The war years brought ups and downs but the largest fall coincided with the final phase of the war, in 1918, and with the disorganization immediately afterwards. Total recovery came late, and did not become a reality until 1922, with pre-war levels being reached only in 1923. The 1920s saw growing prosperity; starting from the 1921 minimum, it reached a maximum in 1929, with an overall increase of 39 per cent. From 1929 to 1932 the GDP fell continuously, losing just over ten percentage points. From 1933 recovery again began to take place and was to last until 1939, amounting to a 30 per cent increase. But despite appearances, the 1930s would not be at all similar to the 1920s. The economic polices put into effect were not aimed at a return to pre-war normality, but were increasingly autarkic, and focused on preparations for new hostilities. The 1939 peak lasted

Table 11.1 GDP of western Europe, 1913–1998: index numbers (1950 = 100) and annual growth rates (%)

Year	*GDP (1950 = 100)*	*Growth rate*	*Year*	*GDP (1950 = 100)*	*Growth rate*
1913	60.4		1956	135.3	4.5
1914	57.5	–4.8	1957	141.3	4.5
1915	59.0	2.5	1958	144.7	2.4
1916	61.3	3.9	1959	151.6	4.7
1917	59.2	–3.3	1960	161.4	6.4
1918	57.0	–3.8	1961	170.0	5.3
1919	54.4	–4.5	1962	178.2	4.8
1920	55.7	2.3	1963	186.4	4.6
1921	55.2	–0.9	1964	197.4	5.9
1922	59.9	8.5	1965	205.9	4.3
1923	60.1	0.4	1966	214.0	3.9
1924	64.6	7.4	1967	221.5	3.5
1925	67.9	5.1	1968	233.6	5.5
1926	67.8	–0.1	1969	247.4	5.9
1927	71.7	5.7	1970	258.6	4.5
1928	74.4	3.8	1971	267.2	3.4
1929	77.0	3.5	1972	279.1	4.4
1930	74.9	–2.6	1973	294.9	5.7
1931	71.0	–5.2	1974	301.1	2.1
1932	69.2	–2.6	1975	299.2	–0.6
1933	71.8	3.8	1976	311.9	4.2
1934	74.2	3.4	1977	320.6	2.8
1935	77.3	4.0	1978	329.8	2.9
1936	79.6	3.0	1979	341.4	3.5
1937	83.0	4.3	1980	346.8	1.6
1938	84.8	2.2	1981	347.4	0.2
1939	89.7	5.7	1982	350.3	0.8
1940	88.5	–1.3	1983	356.5	1.8
1941	88.8	0.4	1984	365.2	2.4
1942	88.3	–0.6	1985	374.2	2.5
1943	88.2	–0.2	1986	384.7	2.8
1944	84.1	–4.6	1987	395.7	2.9
1945	74.6	–11.2	1988	411.6	4.0
1946	76.3	2.2	1989	425.5	3.4
1947	81.1	6.3	1990	430.4	1.1
1948	86.4	6.6	1991	437.6	1.7
1949	93.0	7.7	1992	442.6	1.2
1950	100.0	7.5	1993	441.1	–0.3
1951	105.9	5.9	1994	453.4	2.8
1952	109.8	3.6	1995	464.2	2.4
1953	115.5	5.2	1996	471.8	1.6
1954	121.8	5.4	1997	483.8	2.5
1955	129.4	6.3	1998	496.6	2.7

Source: Adaptation by the author and Xavier Tafunell, based on data in A. Maddison, *Monitoring the World Economy*, 1995, and *The World Economy*, 2001.

Notes:
From 1913 to 1950 the countries included are: Germany, Austria, Belgium, Denmark, Spain, Finland, France, Great Britain, Holland, Italy, Norway, Sweden and Switzerland. From 1950 all the countries of western Europe, including Greece and Cyprus.

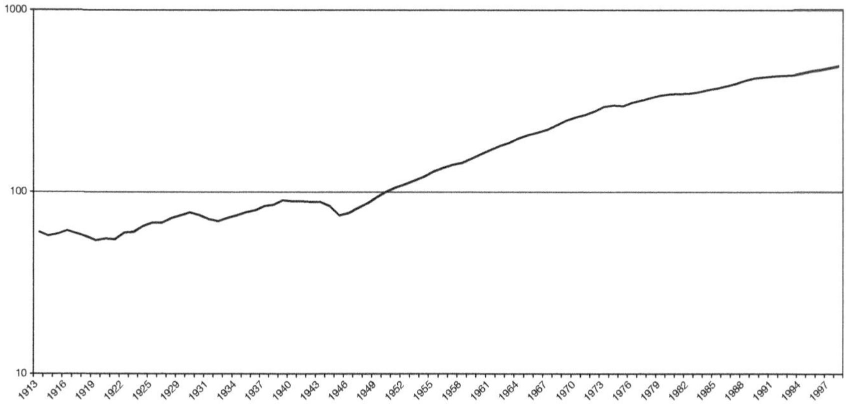

Figure 11.1 Evolution of the GDP of western Europe, 1913–1998 (1950 = 100).
Source: see Table 11.1

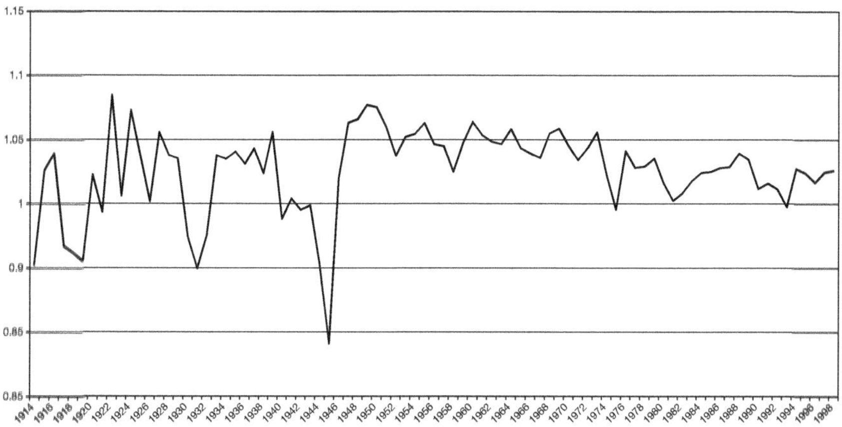

Figure 11.2 Annual fluctuations in the GDP of western Europe, 1914–1998 (1950 = 100).
Source: see Table 11.1

precariously until 1943, then fell dramatically in 1944 and 1945; the 15 per cent drop was to be the sharpest of the century. As the Second World War gradually brought the belligerent countries to a state of exhaustion and confusion spread, production capacity was paralysed. 1946 signalled the start of recovery, but it was very tentative. True recovery would take place only in the years from 1947 to 1950, when the European growth rate remained stable at 7 per cent annually, for four years. In actual fact, recovery was more conspicuous in different national areas, but did not happen simultaneously; nor did it happen everywhere. In 1949, the pre-war maximum had already been reached. This marked the end of the historical period known as the *transwar* years, as opposed to the *inter-war* years. The latter covered the period from 1918 to 1939, while the former began in 1914 and finished in 1945. For purposes of convenience, 1913 is usually chosen as the last complete year of normality, and the duration of the period extends until reconstruction can be considered as concluded, or when pre-war GDP levels are achieved. The strong concern for simplification and rounding off has led to the convention of fixing 1950 as the end of the transwar years.

In any case, the west European GDP started to rise again from the precipice into which it had fallen in 1945. A careful scrutiny of the table shows that, from 1946 until 1975, GDP rose continually. This was the so-called 'Golden Age' of the capitalist economy, or *les trente années glorieuses* as the French like to call it. Where reconstruction was delayed, the estimate is reduced to twenty-five years, but never less than that. These twenty-five years separate the first year of the Marshall Plan (1948) from the last year of definite prosperity (1973). During the years of uninterrupted growth, a number of periods can be distinguished. The first, the years of rapid reconstruction from 1946 to 1950, has already been mentioned. This growth decelerated in 1951 and in 1952, but because of the Korean War and the Cold War, confidence in the western European economy returned, and once again it experienced a stimulus, with the result that growth recovered greater strength for five years, until 1957. However, in 1958, European economies suffered a clear slowdown of growth, due to a combination of crises and uncertainties in exchange rate stability. This uncertainty lasted only briefly, and as early as 1959 growth returned to previous levels. From 1960 to 1964, in the brightest period of the Golden Age – during the Kennedy presidency in the United States – rates returned to levels that seemed impossible to repeat, and there was general optimism. The miracle appeared to lose its brilliance between 1965 and 1967, when there was a slowdown in growth, and there were many who were expecting an end to the capitalist growth model in Europe. But it was a false alarm and when, in 1971, the United States suspended dollar gold conversion, it seemed to be reconfirmed. From 1968 on, a new cycle of expansion began, and would reach its maximum intensity in 1969 and 1973, which would be the last year of tranquillity. The rapid rise in the price of oil was to put an abrupt end to the Golden Age. In 1974, it was still possible to benefit from the state of inertia of the previous period, but the fall in GDP in 1975 was a powerful expression of the change that the oil crisis represented, because of its exceptional nature. After a number of robust adjustments, the western European economies would begin a further growth process, lasting for more than four years, but at a slower rate. The second oil crisis, longer and no less serious, inaugurated a new phase of pessimism. Between 1980 and 1981, growth rates would increasingly fall, though in 1982 they rallied very slightly. There would be a very slow recovery of the rates, which remained in the region of 2–3 per cent and, rather than reflecting true growth, seemed to reflect stagnation. Ultimately, this expression was used for the whole period from 1974 until almost the end of the 1980s. When, in 1988, the growth rate reached 4 per cent – after a phase of slow acceleration – the period of stagnation was thought to be over. The term 'stagnation' has been removed from the vocabulary, ever since a new historical period, marked by the fall of the Soviet bloc, began to dominate the whole panorama of European life after the end of 1989. The recovery of historical data from the pre-1913 period, which has made it possible to compare post-1973 with pre-1913 growth rates, has been of help in this respect. However, the reality is harsh: after the 4.2 per cent of 1976 and the 4.0 per cent of 1988, this was the last moment of rapid growth for western Europe as a whole.

Surprisingly, the dissolution of the Soviet bloc did not involve acceleration in western growth. Between 1990 and 1993, the western European GDP returned to the levels of semi-paralysis that had characterized it in 1980 and 1983. Moreover 1993 was another *annus horribilis* for the post-war European economy, comparable only to 1975. After a loss of vitality, brought about by conflicts between economic policies, greater harmony after 1993 produced a few years of modest, but fairly steady, growth, which continued until 2000.

This was the overall economic configuration of the century. It enables us, at a glance, to establish a number of important stages and some shorter, but very significant, periods. Let us follow them more closely.

The Great War and tentative peace

As the most lucid contemporaries noted, with the outbreak of the Great War in 1914, the world as it had existed until then, that is to say, the era of eighteenth century liberalism, collapsed totally and irredeemably in all its aspects, whether economic, social, political or cultural. Apart from causing upheaval to the models that held economic and social life together, and causing enormous economic turmoil while it lasted, the Great War left in its wake economic and political consequences that were so far-reaching that they conditioned European history for the next quarter of a century. Numerous authors maintain that the causes of the Second World War lie in the outcome of the First. What is more, the latter triggered off the revolution that gave rise to the Soviet model, which was a social system at variance with capitalism. Authors such as Hobsbawm argue that with the collapse of this model, the circle was closed, and the century that started with the first world conflagration was brought to an end.

Concentrating on the purely economic aspects, we can see the significance of the conflict from three different viewpoints: the radical break with the past, the deep transformation in the way national economies and the international economy worked, and finally, the economic consequences of the war itself, or – what amounts to the same thing – its costs.

In August 1914, as soon as the armies of the warring countries joined battle, financial markets plummeted, governments took over control of foreign transactions and put a halt to the conversion of their currencies. In other words, the international monetary system – the gold standard – was swiftly dismantled; the free movement of capital over frontiers was abolished; foreign trade in goods and services was now hampered by obstacles unheard of in the previous century. The unrestricted movement of people from one country to another came to an end, and never resumed again on a wide scale. In reality, the war was an economic revolution in itself. One needs only to see the new role taken on by the state in the warring countries. Governments organized a war economy, with the dual objective of producing the armaments that were being used in huge quantities on the battlefields, and of ensuring the supply of essential goods for armies and civilian populations, as well as for industry, namely food and raw materials. In order to bring about this massive mobilization of economic resources, states deployed systematic dirigistic operations for production and distribution. In the same way, they introduced controls over the income of the main social groups (salaries, profits, leases) and, less successfully, over prices. All this openly contradicted the free market rules that characterized the liberal capitalism that had been in operation until 1914. The war struck economic liberalism a mortal blow. Even if, once the conflict was over, governments made courageous attempts to 'return to normal', and eliminated most of the control mechanisms, it was, in fact, impossible to return to the situation of previously, when there was no state intervention in economic activity, or very little. It was impossible for the state to stand aside from problems of economic reconstruction, or from the struggle between different social sectors in sharing war burdens. A return to the situation of July 1914 was thwarted on the one hand by the financial costs, and on the other by the economic consequences that the war and its conclusion had brought with it, in other words the peace treaties. Before considering these aspects, let us see the macroeconomic impact of the war on the European countries (Table 11.2).

During the war, all the countries generally suffered a decline in their GDP, with the United Kingdom and Italy as two significant exceptions. Italy started by being neutral, and then in 1915 joined the war. It kept military operations outside its frontiers, or away from economically important territories. It worked at full capacity to meet both its own requirements and to offset the void left by the countries

Table 11.2 The impact of the war on the GDP of selected European countries (1913 = 100)

Countries	*1918*	*1919*	*1924*
Central empires and their allies			
Germany	82.0	72.3	92.6
Austria	73.3	61.8	88.5
Hungary	...	...	95.7
Czechoslovakia	...	...	113.7
Yugoslavia	...	...	110.5
Turkey	...	...	73.2
Bulgaria	...	...	69.3
Allied powers			
France	63.9	75.3	116.6
Great Britain	113.2	100.9	98.4
Italy	133.3	111.0	112.4
Belgium	67.8	79.9	110.5
Neutral countries			
Denmark	93.8	105.9	128.5
Spain	99.4	100.9	123.3
Holland	90.7	112.4	142.5
Sweden	84.5	89.4	108.3
Switzerland	89.4	95.3	119.1

Source: A. Maddison, *Monitoring the World Economy*, 1995.

Note: . . . No data.

involved in the fighting. The United Kingdom exploited the fact that the war did not affect its own territory directly, and mobilized all its resources. The remaining countries – including those that were neutral – did not manage any growth in those years, even though some became very rich. After the war, the 1919 figure is especially significant. All the neutral countries were in an optimal situation for benefiting from the return to normality, and they all showed growth. Some (like Denmark and Holland) enjoyed a real boom in output. Among the allied countries, those that had been theatres of war, like Belgium and France, began to recover briskly. On the other hand, the United Kingdom and Italy fell into post-war depression. Their growth had been focused on the requirements of war, and the return to peace would be complicated. Among the central empires, the available figures indicate that at the end of hostilities they were in a state of total chaos, and in 1919 their GDP showed a marked decrease, in the order of 12 per cent (Germany) and 16 per cent (Austria).

The figure for 1924 indicates the end of the period of reconstruction, by which time the great inflations were over. The neutral countries had grown significantly, far surpassing their pre-war maximum. This also applied to the allied countries that had been occupied. On the other hand, the United Kingdom and Italy remained more or less where they had been in 1919, and for them the post-war period was particularly difficult. In Italy it gave rise to Fascism. In the United Kingdom the uncertainty over its decline, after victory, was in sharp contrast to what happened in France. Despite the disgrace over its military incapacity, France was able to pick up again after the occupation. Among the former central empires and their allies, the result, in 1924, was still discouraging. Only countries, such as Czechoslovakia and Yugoslavia, that had not been linked with those that had been defeated and had been able to obtain abundant credit from the victors showed results that confirmed they had overtaken the pre-war maximums. The remainder, Germany, Austria, Turkey, and Bulgaria, did not achieve the 1913 levels, and in some cases were nowhere near them. For these countries, much of the 1920s was spent in efforts at recovery.

According to contemporaries, the main costs of the war lay in the human lives lost. It is understandable they should have thought so, since the number of direct victims could be counted in millions; about 9 million soldiers and 5 million civilians were killed, and the wounded were even more numerous. The human suffering and pain were immense, and obviously cannot be expressed in economic terms. However, what did significantly affect the economies of the countries involved, as well as the international economy, was the exorbitant cost of the goods used and destroyed in military operations and in this respect the war was very costly. The countries that took part in it suffered a considerable loss of wealth and they found their public finances exposed to very severe fiscal crises. Public expenditure plummeted, causing colossal debt. Yet those responsible for policies in the chief belligerent countries took some time before showing any concern about this, since they were determined to demand war reparations from their enemies as soon as they had defeated them. To make matters even worse, the governments of the countries at war, after suspending convertibility, had no hesitation in resorting to the simplest way of providing finance: the printing of money. This policy led to the well known effect of creating high inflation. Public deficit and inflation, the two notorious macroeconomic imbalances, seriously affected economic evolution in the early post-war years.

However, the effects that most upset the world economy were due to what Keynes called the 'economic consequences of the peace'[1]; they were the conditions that the victorious countries imposed in the 1919 Paris peace treaties, the most famous and controversial being the one co-signed with Germany in the palace of Versailles. On the one hand, the decisions entailed redrawing the political map of central and eastern Europe, which brought about serious economic upheavals and acute conflicts; they were also the root cause of the conflicts that have destroyed the Balkans in recent decades. On the other hand, the allies required Germany, and the other enemy powers, to pay astronomical sums to compensate for the economic damage they had suffered. German economic reconstruction, as well as the reconstruction of Europe, was delayed and made more fragile by such demands, besides ruining the spirit of co-operation between countries.

The war generated huge debts between the powers. The allied countries of western Europe (France, Great Britain, Italy, Belgium and others) were considerably indebted to North America and, to a lesser extent, to the neutral countries of Europe. During the conflict, the countries at war needed to import goods they could not produce themselves on a massive scale, since their own production apparatus had been reorganized for the manufacture of war material. Their exporting capacity declined enormously, for the same reason. The result was that they incurred huge deficits in their trade balance, which they met with loans granted mainly by North American banks. By having become the most important supplier to the allies, the United States also acquired the position of being the chief creditor and, once the conflict was over, demanded repayment. But the countries that had received the credits refused to fulfil their obligations, pointing to the fact that, since they had to reconstruct their own economies, they would be able to pay them back only if they were recompensed by the conquered powers.

In this way, the war reparations demanded from Germany became the key issue for the stabilization of the international financial system. Now, in view of the fact that it too had to undertake economic reconstruction and rebalance its public finances, the claim imposed on Germany was excessive, and the country was pushed towards monetary disaster – hyperinflation; thus nothing was gained and everybody lost. The Germans nurtured profound resentment and the allies became bogged down in bitter disputes. The new scheme that the North Americans put forward in 1924 seemed to be an answer to the problem; the settlement of debts among the allies and the reparations were linked by means of a financial circuit, with the United States at either end of it. However, when in 1929 the funds to Germany were no longer being sent, the war debts that had so poisoned international economic relations were laid to rest.

The 'roaring twenties' and the crisis of the 1930s

Return to normality, after the end of the war, was not easy. The year 1919 was economically worse than previous years, except for 1914. The reconversion of war economies to the new requirements of peace was a highly complex task. Moreover, there were millions of refugees. The border changes in central and eastern Europe affected literally half the continent. New state administrations had to be organized out of nothing. Disorganization and the combination of over production or scarcity, which never coincided, explain the economic paralysis of 1919. It took more than two years to normalize the economic apparatus of the countries that had won the war. Recovery was slower in countries that had lost it, or in those that had become the inheritors of former losers. In any case, 1922 was the first year of prosperity, and led to the decade being known as the 'roaring twenties'. The robust growth of 8.5 per cent for Europe as a whole made it reasonable to assume that post-war reconstruction was over. It is true that this was not so for Germany, or for a number of other countries that had been devastated by the war. Germany received special treatment. Initially it was punished very severely with the Treaty of Versailles. Confronted by its inability to pay the reparations that had been stipulated, France, which was counting on them for its own reconstruction, together with Belgium, decided to occupy the rich west German mineral ore deposits, and to recover the German debts in kind. The new German republican state defended itself from this invasion, refusing to work for the occupying powers. It financed the salaries of the workers who went on strike by issuing more money. An inflationary spiral was thus set in motion that in 1923 led to prices multiplying to improbable degrees in only a few months. Money ceased to be used for trading, and Germany became a barter economy. The economic failure was dramatic, despite the fact that anybody who managed to sell goods or services in those circumstances became rich. On the other hand, those dependent on nominally fixed incomes, such as breadwinners, pensioners or salary earners of all types were completely ruined. Germany overcame the chaos of hyperinflation only with American help. The government finally obtained considerable North American credit (through the Dawes Plan), which enabled it to create a new money base, a new currency and to get productive activity working normally again. In exchange, the United States guaranteed the payment of the war reparations, which had been temporarily realigned so that they could be absorbed by the German economy. But, with all these adversities, it was already 1925.

Most of western Europe fared rather better during these years, and between 1921 and 1925 GDP had increased by 23 per cent. The return to normality seemed to be real. The great innovations that had taken place in the United States during the war years were now arriving *en masse* in Europe. In the first place was the motor car. The economic and sturdy Ford Model T was a great sensation and had innumerable imitators. The Ford Motor Company achieved a historical triumph with the innovation of the conveyor belt and the development of efficient marketing networks. Many other products experienced a boom in the early 1920s. Products for the home that made use of electricity – domestic electrical goods – were the other commercial success story of the period.

If normality was a fact, it was time to consecrate it with the last piece of normality that was thought to be missing: the gold standard. The United States, which in 1917 had left the gold standard on entering the war, returned to it in 1919. The Dawes Plan aimed at getting Germany to function again, but it also tried to encourage the European governments to return to the 'gold model', following the German decision in 1924. Great Britain accepted the challenge, and decided to return to the gold standard in 1925. Italy was to follow in 1927 and France in 1928. Great Britain, and Italy, returned to the gold standard at a very optimistic parity, which implied a strong revaluation of the national currency, which was to be offset by reducing labour costs. Swift recession was the immediate effect. In a famous essay Keynes called it 'the economic consequences of Mr Churchill' (the Chancellor of the Exchequer who had imposed the gold standard in Britain)[2], alluding to the fact that it was as great a failure as the Peace of Paris, which he had criticized in a previous article ('The economic consequences of the peace'). The depression, caused by the overvaluation of the pound, triggered off the great coal miners' strike and General Strike in 1926, and would ultimately lead to a great coalition government bringing in the Labour Party for the first time.

After the sharp drop in 1926, the three following years saw a return to normal growth. These were in fact the 'roaring twenties', when the spectre of war had been banished and it seemed that the good old days had returned. The whole of Europe was savouring prosperity. The economies that had been most hit by the war, like those of Germany and Austria, were functioning steadily. After a few years of moderate economic liberalization known as the New Economic Policy (NEP), even the Soviet Union seemed to be following a route that was comprehensible to the Western powers. In 1927, when Stalin adopted a new economic line, marked by economic planning and the socialization of peasant property, all the observers were quite rightly taken by surprise, since it interrupted the promising Soviet recovery of the 1924–1927 period.

Yet, in the midst of all this return to normality, there were still a number of very significant imbalances in the world economy. We will highlight two of these: those that derived from the production restructuring of the international economy, and those that derived from American isolationism. There is much debate about which of these was more important. We shall begin with the consequences of production restructuring, and point to the fact that the war had encouraged an increase in the production capacity of the whole non-European world (non-belligerent countries, to be exact). Europe, shaken up by the war, had mobilized millions of peasants and workers for the military war effort, had also mobilized means of transport (both animal and mechanical) and converted factories from their peacetime uses to new, military uses. Moreover, the war devastated extensive areas of land that had once been fertile. Outside Europe, all these factors led to investments being made to increase areas under cultivation, raise more cattle, produce the traditional manufactures of European industry (textiles, machinery, transport equipment, chemicals, etc.) and in general to replace the markets that had previously been supplied with imports from Europe. Once the war was over, European production capacity returned to normal, both in agriculture and in industry. Since the production capacity of non-European countries had greatly increased, a problem of overproduction emerged that became chronic. Where it caused most damage was among the exporting agricultural producers. Farmers all over the world who exported to Europe, and had to compete with European agricultural products, were badly affected by the return to normality. Industrial products were able to hold out better, by increasing tariff protection, and in this case it was the European industries that were most affected. All these factors created a trend that has been called 'structural deflation', to distinguish it from strictly monetary deflation. Structural deflation supposedly reflected the excessive supply of goods on the markets, and during the 1920s conditioned opportunities for trade, which were scarcer. Some authors, among whom Kindleberger is the best known, argue that the difficulty of reorganizing production is one of the most convincing explanations for the severity of the 1929 crisis. World demand was slowing down because supply was unable to sustain prices; the fall in prices had no beneficial effects, since it was due not to technical progress (new products or new processes) but to continuously selling at knockdown prices.

The second great imbalance, for some the principal one, was the profound North American isolationism which continuously held back the growth of the rest of the world. This isolationism showed itself in different forms. The first, and simplest, was North American lack of interest in the peace treaties and the new world order. The strongest proof of this lack of interest was the negative position of the United States Congress towards joining the League of Nations. The country that had brought about the conclusion of the world war declined to take part in preparing for world peace. A second very worrying forewarning was the sudden closure to immigration. In 1919, after several years without any immigration at all (since wartime mobilization in Europe had prevented emigration), the United States decided that it no longer wanted the sort of immigration it had had before the war, which was largely free and unrestricted. People had been getting used to higher and higher salaries, and the salaried classes of the United States, who were becoming increasingly prosperous, viewed competition from impoverished immigrants with great apprehension. Closure was not total, but was based on the imposition of a quota – the system that has remained in effect until the present day. But in comparison with the magnitude of pre-war immigration, the quota was tantamount to closing the country's borders. This measure meant the end of the most important salary equalizing mechanism on a worldwide scale. Free immigration had attracted millions of Europeans to the New World every year. With the United States more prosperous than ever, and with the impoverishment of Europe owing to the war, there were more reasons than ever for emigrating to America, but now it was far more difficult.

The third element of American isolationism was commercial. In 1913, the United States had voted for the first moderately pro-free-trade customs tariff in its long protectionist history, but the war made it quite impracticable. With the return to normality, which was synonymous with overproduction and saturation of trade, a new tariff was imposed. Around 1928, discussions were started over a reform of the customs tariffs, which became increasingly protectionist as they went through Congress. In 1929, this reform was approved by the study commission, and caused a wave of astonishment throughout the world: the main market of the world was going to close its frontiers. Other countries could have little hope of sustaining their growth by exporting to the US market. Congress was to ratify approval of the proposal in 1930, and the new protectionist tariff would be enforced in 1931.

In this increasingly closed North American environment there was great prosperity. Much of it derived from the enormous profits gained from neutrality[3]. Prices for agricultural, mineral and industrial products were unbeatable, and affluence had spread everywhere. The US market was the most prosperous in the world, and it was there that new fashions and new products spread. The American way of life – or the conveniences of modern life – took hold in this period, and spread with the help of new means of social communication, the cinema being the most dazzling and attractive. In an environment brimming with confidence and prosperity, and in which all kinds of trade functioned, investment on the stock exchange was being significantly increased. During 1928 and 1929, the stock market entered a phase that was decidedly more speculative, attracting more and more funds. The practice of purchasing shares on credit also spread. Underlying everything was confidence that the economy would not stop growing, as had happened in previous years. Yet not everything was going as it should. The increasing disparity between the United States and the rest of the world reduced the size of many markets. The internal market itself became increasingly saturated, and indications began to appear that the growth rate in sales was decelerating. The figures for profits released for the second half of 1929, particularly after the summer, indicated that the economy was slowing down. A run of such figures brought about a change in expectations, and triggered a rush of sales on the New York stock exchange, which, after the Great War, was the world's most important.

At the end of October, in just two sessions – Black Friday and Black Tuesday – quotations plummeted. Everybody wanted to sell and nobody wanted to buy. This episode would have been nothing more than a scare – albeit mortal, for the many who were ruined – if the changed expectations had not continued or become stronger, without anybody being able to do anything about it. The mechanism that poisoned the situation was mainly the question of credit. Many investors had bought shares on credit, and the ensuing insolvency concerned those who had granted loans, mainly the banks. The banks were quick to reclaim the credit that they had granted to customers of all kinds, including credit they would not normally have reclaimed. The contraction of credit started spiralling, in every direction. It annulled the liquidity of solvent companies, who were forced to suspend payments, despite their healthy financial situation. Numerous enterprises were forced to close down, leaving the work force without employment. Furthermore, banks reclaimed credit that had been granted to other European banks or to European enterprises and administrations. This type of action had been frequent with the German and Austrian countries, which had had easy access to North American credit under the Dawes Plan. From the viewpoint of the internal consequences for the United States, it seems astonishing that the Federal Reserve (FED), the US central bank created in 1914, did nothing. FED opinion was that the crisis affected marginal enterprises that had been overrated and banks that had taken excessive risks, and there was no need to intervene. Neutrality only intensified the crisis, since the spiralling destruction of credit was very strong. The FED was much criticized, but was defended by experts and politicians, starting with President Hoover himself, in much the same way as the validity of the gold standard had been defended. As time went by, the critics gradually gained strength and had the effect of influencing

Roosevelt's candidature for the presidency in 1932. With hindsight, the most authoritative criticism came from Friedman and Schwartz, who in their monumental monetary history of the United States, maintained that the FED should have concentrated on defending price stability, which involved the need to fight deflation as well as inflation. In other words, it should have put money into the system. In the meantime, unemployment continued to grow.

What was happening in the United States was also having enormous consequences in Europe, and the change in expectations was instantaneous. The contraction of credit was felt on the Old Continent, and created its first important victims in the spring of 1931, when the Creditanstalt of Vienna and the Darmstadter of Berlin announced the suspension of payments. Many other central and eastern European banks were dealt a mortal blow, and to a lesser extent a large number of western banks as well. The Italian mixed bank collapsed in the crisis, but the prevailing atmosphere of censorship meant it could all happen very discreetly, unlike what happened in Austria.

While the crisis in the stock exchange was turning into a crisis for banking and finance throughout the world, and especially in Europe, a further destructive mechanism had been set in motion. The American protectionist tariff had caused a reaction in numerous countries, which had responded with higher tariffs against American products. The trend towards a trade war gained strength from the loss of economic activity. Both were leading in the same direction, which was a fall in international trade. The confusion with regard to economic prospects opened the way to ideas and policies that contributed to exacerbating trade relations: the internal market was to be reserved for national producers, all the more so if it was in decline. This was how the crisis spread throughout the world; the crisis became globalized, to use a current expression. Every country was dragged into the net of contracting world trade, and month after month for the next four years, international trade decreased, like a contracting spiral.

In an increasingly closed environment, there was no other remedy for escaping this destructive web than to devalue, but in order to devalue it was necessary to sever links with the gold standard. The mere thought of abandoning an institution that best symbolized the stability, normality and affluence of pre-war years, and that had cost so much to reintroduce, created a sense of unease and irritation among experts and politicians, who resisted with all possible means. To general surprise, however, the United Kingdom, the most conservative of all the countries as regards monetary matters, was the first to leave it. In September 1931, the United Kingdom announced it was leaving the gold standard. All the countries of the Commonwealth, and the small European countries that most depended on the British market, followed suit. While it had been difficult to return to the gold standard, it was even more difficult to leave it. Eichengreen has mockingly described the gold standard as being akin to 'golden fetters'. France put up a great resistance (until 1936) and the United States until the winter of 1933. Germany did not leave it *de iure* but rather *de facto* as from 1933. All in all, the countries that left the gold standard earlier were those that performed better, unlike those that insisted on maintaining links with it. The former managed to devalue and recover their competitive power, while the latter lost it.

In general, the crisis lasted from three to four years, from 1929 to 1932 or 1933, as the case may be. Western European GDP decreased by ten percentage points, and in some cases much more. The countries most affected were those that had been defeated in the war, together with their heirs, since the two great mechanisms for spreading the crisis – credit and trade – hit them particularly hard. Table 11.3 shows that the countries most affected by the crisis were Germany at the top, then Austria, Poland and Czechoslovakia. Not even Germany suffered a crisis as deep and long as that of the United States, but it was certainly the most rapid, the one that reached the lowest levels, and the one that managed to surpass the 1929 levels first. Poland took a year longer and Austria three. The scanty data available for Czechoslovakia indicate that recovery took a long time. Other

Table 11.3 The impact of the 1929 crisis on GDP (1929 = 100)

	Minimum		
Countries	*Year*	*GDP*	*Year of recovery of 1929 level*
Pro memoria: United States	1933	71.5	1939
Deep and long-lasting crises			
Germany	1932	76.5	1936
Austria	1933	77.5	1939
Poland	1933	79.3	1937
Czechoslovakia	1935	81.8	. . . .[a]
Intermediate crises			
France	1932	85.3	1939
Yugoslavia	1932	88.1	1936
Holland	1934	90.5	1937
Hungary	1932	90.6	1935
Switzerland	1932	92.0	1937
Belgium	1932	92.1	1936
Slight and/or short crises			
Spain	1931	93.9	1935
Italy	1931	94.5	1935
Greece	1931	93.5	1932
United Kingdom	1931	94.2	1934
Sweden	1932	95.7	1934
Finland	1932	96.0	1933
No crises			
Norway	1931	99.1	1932
Bulgaria	–	–	1930
Denmark	–	–	1930
Romania	–	–	1930
Soviet Union	–	–	1930

Source: A. Maddison, *Monitoring the World Economy*, 1995.

Notes:
. . . No data.
– Not applicable.
[a] Post 1937.

European countries like France, Belgium, Holland and Switzerland, though less tied to Germany's imperial past, partly shared its difficulty, with crises involving falls in GDP of between 8 per cent and 15 per cent. This was also the case with Hungary and Yugoslavia, and by extension with Austria. France is a separate case, however; its decline was not so serious, though its recovery was very slow and short-lived. In 1939, it had just about recovered the 1929 level, but that was not sufficient to resist the impact of German occupation.

Among the countries that suffered the crisis, but not very severely, Great Britain needs to be mentioned first. Unlike what happened when it joined the gold standard, which had been much pondered and in the end badly articulated, Great Britain confronted the crisis very well, at the expense of totally forgetting its economic dogmas. Together with Great Britain, we find a combination of countries that were only slightly affected by the crisis (the Scandinavian countries, with the GDP of Denmark not even decreasing), or only briefly (Spain and Italy). In the Balkan countries (Bulgaria, Greece and Romania), where reconstruction had been a very slow process, the crisis was nothing more than a slowing down of growth. Finally, as we know, the Soviet Union was not affected at all, being completely taken up, as it was, by its experiment in forced industrialization.

There were different ways out of the crisis. The small countries managed to adapt to new models of competitiveness, and discovered considerable niche markets. Some of the great multinationals linked to these countries (Switzerland, Holland, Denmark, Sweden and even Czechoslovakia without German mediation) successfully managed to enter the world market, and consolidate their positions in those years. However, the bigger countries found it more difficult. In all cases, the solution to the problem had elements in common: a certain degree of closure to trade, and greater state intervention. The extreme cases were Germany and the United States, which started out on the path of state intervention almost simultaneously. During the winter of 1933, Roosevelt, who had won the November 1932 presidential election, introduced a package of measures. They included leaving the gold standard, with the aim of sustaining internal demand by means of federal initiative. He fixed minimum prices for agricultural products, facilitated membership of labour unions and the participation of unions in collective bargaining. He also set in motion large-scale public works programmes, came to grips with government deficits and so on, with the aim of reactivating internal consumer demand and investment. A few months later, Hitler carried through measures that were not very different, although in his case they were tinged with a totally different political colour. Heavy investment in public works was a similar aspect but, in contrast, Hitler destroyed the unions and attempted to eliminate all political opposition. Hitler's economic policy was essentially based on rearmament, and huge sums were invested to rearm the army, which created heavy public debt. Another aspect was autarky. Consciously aspiring to retaliation and another war, Hitler inclined towards autarky with regard to all economic decisions. He systematically encouraged the production of goods to replace those that would have had to be imported, and supported closure to trade. Strangely enough, he stayed with the gold standard, but later shifted to systematic intervention in foreign exchange through solutions including import licences and bilateral clearing agreements, with the aim of limiting foreign trade and saving on the use of gold. Some of the new elements of economic policy introduced in the United States and Germany were also adopted in other countries. In Great Britain, public housing was promoted through large-scale state investment programmes. In 1936, in France, the Popular Front government, modelling itself on the Roosevelt measures, was resolute in improving workers' pay, introducing paid holidays and the British forty-four-hour working week, as well as the very innovative and radical measure of nationalizing the railways. In Italy, the move towards autarky and the spread of state intervention in the field of enterprise were typical aspects of Mussolini's government.

The change in economic policies made it easier to find ways out of the crisis, and technological and industrial progress contributed to this objective. During the 1930s, there was a spread of innovations such as the radio, which had taken its first steps in the previous decade, artificial fibres, small automobiles manufactured in Europe, aluminium, new domestic electrical goods and a whole variety of products that were to revive entrepreneurial supply and private demand. From the 1932–1939 minimum, economic expansion started a seven-year period of uninterrupted growth. Spain, which was involved in a destructive civil war between 1936 and 1939, was the main country not to enjoy this expansion. It was on Spanish soil that the new armaments being developed by the German army were tested, and which were to be decisive for Nazi military success all over Europe.

The Second World War and plans for the new international economic order

The Second World War was far more destructive than the First. The more modern armaments that were utilized claimed far more lives (around 16 million soldiers). The hatred between adversaries was much deeper, and gave rise to policies for the systematic annihilation of civilians, which ended the lives of a further 26 million people. The most notorious events involved the concentration camps, forced labour and extermination, thought up by the Nazis, but they were not the only ones. On several occasions, the Nazis themselves carried out *in situ* extermination operations, and noncombatants were totally caught up in the ferocity of the war. Where the war was at its cruellest, loss of life was in millions, and affected as much as 10 per cent of the whole population. (This was the case in the Soviet Union, Poland, Germany and Yugoslavia.)

The conflict gave rise to centralized economic efforts on the lines of those of the First World War, but on a much greater scale. All the great belligerent countries, including Germany, the United Kingdom, Italy and the Soviet Union, but not France, which was very soon occupied by German troops, as well as the United States and Japan outside Europe, attempted to centralize all their operations. They devoted a much higher proportion of their national resources (their GDP) to the war effort than they had in the First World War. The vast military and economic mobilization stretched the production capacity of all the countries involved to the utmost. Indeed, unemployment, which was still lingering as a legacy from the Great Depression, completely disappeared as an effect of war mobilization. The overall GDP of Europe did not grow; but GDP did grow in the countries at war that were not under military occupation. The case of the United States is an extreme example. On the other hand, Nazi occupation involved channelling productive effort into ends defined by the German high command that were usually military ends. Table 11.4 illustrates how the evolution of the belligerents differed from one another.

The Axis powers had carried out much of their preparation for war before it broke out. Germany made great efforts to increase its GDP, but the results were mediocre. Japanese results were even worse, and even the Italian results were disappointing, though in the latter case Italian occupation, from the summer of 1943,

Table 11.4 Evolution of the GDP of belligerent, occupied and neutral countries, 1939–1945 (1939 = 100)

Belligerent countries

Year	*Germany*	*Great Britain*	*Italy*	*USSR*	*Japan*	*USA*
1939	100.0	100.0	100.0	100.0	100.0	100.0
1940	100.7	110.0	100.6	113.9	102.9	107.7
1941	107.1	120.0	99.4	98.1	104.3	127.3
1942	108.5	123.0	98.1	86.9	103.8	152.8
1943	110.7	125.7	88.9	126.8	105.2	183.2
1944	113.5	120.8	72.2	135.2	100.7	198.6
1945	80.7	115.5	56.6	108.2	50.4	190.6

Occupied countries

Year	*France*	*Belgium*	*Holland*	*Denmark*	*Norway*	*Greece*
1939	100.0	100.0	100.0	100.0	100.0	100.0
1940	82.5	88.1	88.1	86.0	91.1	...
1941	65.3	83.5	83.4	77.5	93.3	...
1942	58.5	76.3	76.3	79.2	89.7	61.4
1943	55.5	74.5	74.4	88.0	87.9	...
1944	46.9	78.9	49.9	97.2	83.3	...
1945	50.9	83.6	51.1	89.9	93.3	36.4

Allied countries of the Axis, non-belligerent countries and neutral countries

	Allied countries of the Axis			*Non-belligerent countries*			*Neutral*	
Year	*Austria*	*Bulgaria*	*Hungary*	*Finland*	*Spain*	*Portugal*	*Sweden*	*Switzerland*
1939	100.0	100.0	100.0	100.0	100.0	100.0	100.0	100.0
1940	97.4	97.4	93.2	94.8	108.6	93.5	97.0	101.0
1941	104.4	99.3	93.7	97.9	108.6	102.2	98.7	100.4
1942	99.1	94.5	98.4	98.2	114.7	100.8	104.7	97.8
1943	101.5	97.5	...	109.5	117.7	107.6	109.4	97.0
1944	104.1	90.1	...	109.6	122.9	113.7	113.0	99.3
1945	43.0	70.3	...	103.2	114.2	109.3	116.1	127.8

Source: A. Maddison, *Monitoring the World Economy*, 1995; except Soviet Union: M. Harrison (ed.), *The Economics of World War II. Six Great Powers in International Comparison*, Cambridge, 1998; and Portugal: D. Batista, C. Martins, M. Pinheiro and J. Reis, *New Estimates for Portugal's GDP*, Lisbon, 1997.

Note: . . . No data.

needs to be taken into account. The Nazi war effort has to be considered in conjunction with a further two factors: its pro-Fascist allies and the countries it occupied. Against all odds, the countries that were allied to the Axis managed to maintain their pre-war GDP level. Those closest to Germany, like Austria (which was not in reality an ally, but was annexed to Germany), achieved it in the course of the war, and plummeted only in the last year with the allied occupation. Bulgaria and Hungary, two countries that later joined the allies, were more successful at preventing a fall in their GDP than the occupied countries, whose GDP evolution, shown in the middle section of Table 11.4, was disastrous. Those, like Norway, that were able to attain a better *modus vivendi* with the invader, showed a maximum GDP fall of only 17 per cent. Denmark, Holland and Belgium suffered declines of over 20 per cent. Denmark, which in 1941 fell as much as 22.5 per cent, later managed to recover in so far as it was not in conflict with Hitler. The figures for Holland and Belgium worsened by the year, and by 1943 they were already 25 per cent below the GDP of 1939. In 1944, Belgium, liberated and administered by the allies, started to improve. But Holland was particularly badly affected by the war in 1944, and reached a level that was half its pre-war GDP. For France, each year was worse than the previous one; the occupation and the war plunged the north-eastern part of France into chaos and destruction. As in other countries, occupation brought disorganization, sabotage and the transfer of productive resources (transport equipment, machinery, raw materials, labour) to Germany. Thus, the increase in German GDP was achieved very largely by exploiting the occupied countries. The war effort devoured resources on an enormous scale, and increasingly impoverished growing areas of territory. The scanty figures for Greece show that in some countries exploitation and chaos were far-reaching, with two-thirds of the GDP being eaten away.

The allied countries that were at war started badly. Although it had made concerted preparations for the war between 1938 and 1940, the Soviet Union was unable to put up much resistance to the first German offensive. It lost vast areas of territory, and its GDP decreased by a quarter between 1940 and 1942. The great success of the Soviet Union, and of Stalin, was the capacity to reorganize and prepare for all-out mobilization of its own productive resources. The supreme effort at resistance resulted in a spectacular recovery of GDP of 45 per cent in 1943, as well as of Soviet military capacity. This was an incredibly high rate, which can be explained only in terms of the exceptional circumstances and limited period. In fact, by 1945, once the war had been won, the pressure dropped. After the first months of disorder, Great Britain managed to make its economy more dynamic than Germany did (without overwhelming occupied territories). Great Britain relied heavily on its imperial resources, though these were no longer as abundant as in 1914, having been partially exhausted during the First World War, and on resources loaned to it from the United States. British GDP reached its peak in 1943. Thereafter it dropped, on account of the war now being fought on its own territory; these were the years of the systematic bombing of southern England by the Luftwaffe. Britain would have had grave problems, if it had not had the backing of the United States. This is where the allied 'miracle' of the Second World War has its roots. The United States achieved spectacular success in production. With the fighting a long way from its territory, and enormous productive potential that had been underutilized since the 1929–1933 crisis, the United States managed to practically double its 1939 GDP in only five years. The factors contributing to this success are still being studied today. They lie in the all-out utilization of labour and capital, with particular emphasis on the quantity and quality of labour. North Americans worked far more than they had done previously, and than they were to do subsequently. Moreover, they worked with greater concentration, enthusiasm and commitment.

The neutral countries, Portugal, Sweden and Switzerland, were few in number and small. Finland and Spain did not join the war, but that did not mean they were impartial. They were unable to take part for different reasons. Finland had lost a lightning war against the Soviet Union, to which it had ceded territory in exchange for keeping its independence and neutrality. Spain had only just emerged from a civil war, and despite the fact that he owed much to Hitler and Mussolini, Franco kept the country in a state of non-belligerence, but did authorize volunteer troops to be sent to the Russian front in support of the Germans. Spain was too weak to run the risk of entering the war, and Franco himself would have lost his position of hegemony if it had done so. The countries that were truly neutral did benefit from the war, but in different ways. Portugal, under a corporate-type dictatorship, but linked with England by an alliance that had lasted several centuries, was able to 'have it both ways'. The war years were peaceful, from the economic point of view. Sweden was negatively affected by the initial disorganization of the whole European economy, but being the neutral supplier to the Axis bloc, was able to adapt, and showed a net improvement in its GDP between 1941 and 1945. Switzerland remained on the sidelines of the war, though it was unable to be totally neutral, since it was surrounded by German forces or their allies. It carried out an important role of 'recycling' money between the two opposing blocs, and between 1939 and 1945 lived through the situation as well as possible without any losses or gains. The magic moment arrived in 1945, when Swiss neutrality attracted many Nazis who were fleeing, and who brought huge quantities of gold and currency with them.

Preparing for reconstruction

The horrors and destruction of the Second World War easily surpassed those of the First. On the other hand, in the second post-war period, there was no repeat of the world economic instability and crisis of the inter-war period. On the contrary, after rapid economic reconstruction the world, and not only the Western world, witnessed a drive towards the greatest economic growth ever known. If the Second World War was so much more costly and devastating than the First, how could its consequences have been so unlike those of the First, or precisely the opposite? The paradox is only apparent, and is soon accounted for. Unlike thirty years previously, in the second post-war period governments of the Western countries, chiefly the United States on the one hand and Great Britain on the other, were firmly convinced of the need for economic co-operation.

The outbreak of the Second World War led political leaders of the main Western allied powers to overturn their attitudes on how economic relations between countries should develop in peacetime. The link between the Great Depression and the war conflict shook the consciences of the rulers of the threatened democracies, and in that critical and grave moment they learned the 'lesson of history'. They were not to demand war compensation, so as not to strangle the languishing economies of the belligerent countries. The United States would no longer make the mistake of withdrawing into itself and remaining indifferent to the financial needs of countries undergoing reconstruction. Finally, there would be a need to set rules that everyone could, and would, accept in order to ward off the danger of a repetition of beggar-my-neighbour policies. In the 1930s, the practice had been excessive protectionism, combined with devaluations to increase competitiveness, which had ultimately plunged the world into the worst recession ever known.

This new challenge made it mandatory for the international community to provide itself with a new institutional structure that could guarantee free multilateral trade, and an international payments system that was stable and could absorb the foreign imbalances of different countries. That, at least, is how the United States and Great Britain, the two leaders of the international economy and bastions of the allied bloc, saw it. From 1941, they worked on a model for the post-war economic system. Three years later, they reached agreement on the plan and urged other countries to join. For this purpose, they called an international economic conference; it was held in the North American locality of Bretton Woods, in June 1944. The international institutional framework that was approved at that meeting was of exceptional importance, since from then on international economic relations were to conform to it. Although the new financial and commercial order could not solve the urgent balance of payments problems that the various countries had in the immediate post-war period, it certainly had the merit of defining the environment for the ideal operation of trade, movement of capital and foreign payments. Bretton Woods succeeded in setting up a goal towards which trade and exchange polices should be directed, a goal that, with a number of modifications, still continues to be fully valid today.

The Bretton Woods agreements were based on the creation of three new supranational institutions: the International Trade Organization (ITO), the World Bank (International Bank for Reconstruction and Development, IBRD) and the International Monetary Fund (IMF). The mission of the first was to strengthen free non-discriminatory trade, but this very soon proved to be a titanic task. The ITO did not in fact take off, and the vacuum had to be filled by a more flexible and less comprehensive agreement. This was the General Agreement on Tariffs and Trade (GATT), which continued to exist until the creation of the World Trade Organization (WTO), which supported the progressive liberalization of world trade by means of successive negotiation rounds. The aim of the IBRD, for its part, was to contribute to financing the type of long-term investments that were strategic for economic development, but that were not usually met with private capital. A further aim was to co-operate in the economic reconstruction of countries devastated by war. Its commitment in the latter was invaluable, and at first only modest in the former, though with time it acquired greater importance. However, the essential element of the structure set up at Bretton Woods was the IMF, which set about defending a fixed-rate exchange system, which could be regulated. The Fund was thus able to lend financial assistance, on certain conditions, to countries with foreign payment deficits. This was to prevent simply resorting to changes in the exchange rate in order to gain immediate competitiveness abroad and improve the trade balance and current accounts by increasing exports. Those who created the Bretton Woods institutional structure conceived the IMF as a tool that could best combine discipline (fixed rates and currency convertibility) with flexibility, and thus lead to greater stability and predictability in the international monetary system. The reality did not reflect their predictions, either in the short term or in the very long term (from 1970 onwards), but without the IMF, and without the other institutions mentioned, the world would undoubtedly have experienced lower economic growth during the second half of the twentieth century. International economic relations would have been far more uncertain and unstable, and would have had a negative impact on the international movement of goods, services and production factors.

In the short period, the agreements fixed terms (two years from the actual end of the war) to enable the countries that had been affected by hostilities to reconstruct, reorganize and stabilize their economies, and open them up to the international flow of goods and capital. However, in the memory of contemporary observers, the measures adopted at Bretton Woods paled in comparison with the thrust and publicity devoted to the Marshall Plan.

Post-war reconstruction, division into blocs and regional integration

The first two years after the war were initially dominated by humanitarian aid policy. Help was needed for tens of millions of wounded, prisoners and displaced people, devastated cities and disorganized states. In the territories liberated from Nazi control, the new governments turned their attention to these urgent tasks for survival with the aid of the allied armies and the United Nations Relief and Rehabilitation Administration (UNRRA). The disorganization and chaos were gradually overcome, and 1947 was a particularly dynamic year for reconstruction efforts. Collective life was also slowly normalizing, and European countries managed to hold elections and map out new political prospects. The summer of 1947 was the deadline fixed for putting the Bretton Woods agreements into effect. Instead of applying them, which seemed premature to everyone, the United States launched a proposal for a large-scale aid plan for the reconstruction of Europe.

The economic situation in western Europe was no worse in 1947 than it had been in 1946. Indeed, the rate of recovery accelerated, and the only worrying symptom was the trade balance with the United States. Yet in the first months of 1947, instead of following the model for reducing the 1946 trade deficit, all the European countries launched recklessly into a race to import capital goods from the United States. The whole of Europe had embarked on ambitious production modernization programmes, in order to improve its competitiveness, now that a new international economic order was coming into effect. Since these imports far exceeded the payment capacity of the European countries, the problem lay in how the strong European demand should be adjusted, rapidly and immediately. The reason for the aid plan was the uncertainty that this situation created for the North American economy, and which evoked the much feared post-war recession (as happened in 1920). Washington felt an overriding need to find ways of maintaining the exceptionally high level of exports, and hence of enterprise and employment, that the American economy had achieved thanks to the war.

Between April 1948 and June 1951, the US government provided the countries of western Europe – except Spain (which requested it but did not get it) and Finland (which did not request it) – with aid to the tune of $13,000 million. This aid formed the basis of the European Recovery Program (ERP), which we know as the Marshall Plan, since General George Marshall, the then Secretary of State, was the first to announce the project in its embryonic form, in a speech at Harvard University, on 5 June 1947.

Table 11.5 lists the countries that received aid. They are classified in descending order of the amount they received, with the percentage of their GDP for 1950 that the amount corresponded to, so that its relative impact can be better appreciated. The countries that benefited most were some of the small ones such as Greece, Austria and Holland. The remaining countries (large and small) obtained resources corresponding roughly to a share that varied from 5 per cent to 10 per

Table 11.5 Distribution of European Recovery Programme funds among member countries, April 1948 to June 1951

Countries	*$ millions*	*% of GDP in 1950*
United Kingdom	2,731.6	7.2
France	2,401.0	9.2
Germany (FR)	1,297.3	5.1
Italy	1,297.3	8.5
Holland	977.7	17.2
Austria	560.8	20.3
Belgium and Luxembourg	546.6	9.8
Greece	515.1	27.7
Denmark	256.9	8.5
Norway	231.7	7.8
Ireland	146.2	12.0
Turkey	144.7	...
Sweden	118.5	1.8
Portugal	50.5	2.8
Trieste	33.4	...
Iceland	23.7	...
Total	11,314.7	

Source: Own adaptation based on data in T. Geiger, 'Reconstruction and the Beginnings of European Integration', in M.S. Schulze (ed.), *Western Europe. Economic and Social Change since 1945*, London, 1997, pp. 23–42, and for GDP, P. Bairoch, '*Europe's gross national product*', 1976.

Notes: The total does not include freight, administrative expenses, humanitarian aid given prior to the start of the ERP, funds assigned to multilateral institutions like the UEP. If these data are included, the $13,000 million mentioned above are reached.

... No data.

cent of their 1950 GDP. Ireland is a case apart, despite its neutrality; the same applies to Portugal and Sweden, but precisely because of their neutrality. The aim of the Marshall Plan was to finance, for a maximum of four years, the imports that Europe seemed to need but which exceeded its payment capacity. In exchange, once post-war recovery had been achieved, Europe was committed to starting the process of trade liberalization, to which it was bound under the 1944 Bretton Woods agreement.

With the intention of rapidly bolstering the regional economy, the US government not only financed exports of goods to western Europe, it also carried out two crucial measures for the economic future of Europe as a whole. In the first place, it did away with the upper limit on production that had been imposed on Germany after the war. This measure facilitated the normalization of production for the whole of western European industry, which historically had been very dependent on German exports. However, it involved the division of Germany, and hence of the European continent. In the second place, it allowed European governments temporarily to set up preferential systems in order to strengthen intra-European trade. Discrimination against third countries was only provisional, and would end with the Marshall Plan. If it worked according to the original intention, the result of the Marshall Plan would be a Europe that fully respected the Bretton Woods system, in other words with the opening up of European markets to competition from the most efficient producers of the world: those originating in the dollar area.

The outcome was not in the original plan, however. The Europeans financed the reconstruction policies they had each outlined and agreed on even more generously, preventing the Americans from modifying them, even in the slightest. Moreover, they masterminded a way to continue discriminating against the rest of the world, beyond the duration of the Marshall Plan, indeed until this day. Thus the Marshall Plan not only divided the European continent in two, but also encouraged the west Europeans not to comply with the firm commitment to open up to international competition that they had grudgingly accepted in 1944.

In effect, thanks to the creation of the European Payments Union (EPU) in 1950, Europeans had found the formula, accepted by the United States, for eluding the commitment to fix exchange rates in accordance with the Bretton Woods agreements. The question of the exchange rate – like that of the gold standard during the inter-war period – was the most delicate. In September 1949, in the middle of the reconstruction period, and with the ERP under way, the devaluation of the pound sterling was an extraordinary event, almost on a par with leaving the gold standard in 1931. The United Kingdom, a loyal ally of the United States, had pledged not to touch the pound (in exchange for greater American aid), but it could not, and would not withstand the cost of overevaluation. In the storm that followed the devaluation of the pound, west European countries managed to introduce a plan for intra-European monetary co-operation with the aim of saving dollars and achieving exchange rate stabilization more rapidly. This was the European Payments Union (EPU), which was to end in 1958. The achievement of the EPU, in providing the means of payment for the dynamic intra-European trade, encouraged its members to go one step further when the time came to disband the system of multilateral compensation. The European Economic Community was that step further. Already there had been a number of precedents moving in this direction.

In the first experiment at integration, the key sectors of the first industrialization played the leading role. In May 1950, the French Foreign Affairs Minister, Robert Schuman, proposed that Franco-German production of coal and steel should be placed under a joint High Authority. The fact that France was trying to secure supplies of strategic raw materials for itself does not diminish the historical far-sightedness of the initiative. With the 'Schuman declaration', the French government gave up its sovereignty in a sector that was essential to the economic activity of the period. In the second place, it recognized the government of the newly formed German Federal Republic, heir to those that had violated French territory on three occasions since 1870, as an unrivalled ally. Both gestures proved to be enormously far-sighted for the future of the European economy. Giving up sovereignty meant that supranational structures could be created, whilst linking vital national economic interests, in the heart of Europe itself, and meant that the main source of instability on the continent since 1870 could be rooted out: anchoring Germany to Europe – in other words, constructing a Europe in which to include a strong and free Germany. With the Treaty of Paris in 1951, the creation of the European Coal and Steel Community (ECSC) was formalized.

The positive political outcome of the ECSC, combined with the excellent economic results of the EPU and the challenge of the Bretton Woods exchange convertibility, were decisive in getting Germany (FRG), Belgium, France, Holland, Italy and Luxembourg to overcome their reluctance and agree to the creation of the European Economic Community (EEC). This was the Treaty of Rome, signed in 1957 and in force from early 1958. The EEC wanted to create a solid platform for symbiotic economic growth in the common interests of both Germany and the other Community members. The advantages, which for France, Italy and the Benelux countries (Belgium, Holland and Luxembourg) lay in preferential access to the increasingly dynamic German market, were matched by assurances from the federal government that Germany could fully deploy its growth potential without any need for apprehension on the part of its neighbours. Intra-European trade (the 'common market' was the familiar expression for the EEC), which was the earliest field of interest in the original Community agreements, acted as a driving force for prosperity among Community members.

With the EEC there was a complete change in intra-European balances. First, mention should be made of the western European countries that did not accede to the Rome Treaty, or were not invited to join. In 1959, led by the United Kingdom, they formed the European Free Trade Association (EFTA), made up of Austria, Denmark, Norway, Portugal, Sweden and Switzerland. From 1961, Finland became an associated state. They were all small countries that looked to Great Britain for their trade, or countries that politically could not be integrated into the EEC. Either they did not meet the political requirements (Portugal was not a democracy) or had to remain neutral (Austria and Finland), and thus were not compatible with the more political orientation of the EEC. It should be noted that Ireland did not form part of EFTA, since it had its own trade treaty with the

United Kingdom. Only Spain and Greece ended up by remaining outside the great trade alliances, despite Greece being a member of NATO. Second, we should not forget the impact on the area under Soviet influence of the whole process of European integration, from the Marshall Plan up to the EEC and EFTA.

All the countries under Soviet occupation, as well as those that had accepted Soviet Union leadership, were invited to take part in the Marshall Plan. The Soviet Union advised them to decline the offer, which they did. It was clear that the invitation meant ceding power and control to the benefactor – the United States – and Stalin was in no way inclined to generosity of that sort. At Yalta and Potsdam the world had been divided into spheres of influence that reflected the armies that had advanced on the territories previously occupied by the troops of Hitler. It was not a case of the Soviet Union losing its conquests for a mess of pottage. Moreover, nobody could protest about being tricked: the Marshall Plan was the American response to the pro-Soviet *coup* in Czechoslovakia, which was a sign that democratic evolution in countries within the Soviet orbit would be impossible. The Americans and British, who saw events in the area under Soviet influence as a sign of the world being divided into blocs, counted on victory against the Communists in the elections in France and Italy. The Marshall Plan would greatly help them. Once the danger of electoral defeat had been averted, and after the Communists had lost the civil war in Greece, the countries of the pro-American bloc took the decision to create a military alliance, the North Atlantic Treaty Organization (NATO).

In 1949, the creation of the Council of Mutual Economic Aid (better known as Comecon) was nothing other than the political response of the Soviet Union to the creation of NATO. Comecon grouped together all the countries with a socialist economy in the Soviet sphere of influence. Its activity was very limited while European integration was still at the planning stage. This could hardly be otherwise, considering that in the Soviet area there was nothing that resembled the Marshall Plan; quite the contrary. The Soviet Union recovered war compensation from the occupied countries, especially those that had formed part of Nazi Germany, or had been its military allies. This siphoning of resources towards the Soviet Union – comprising transport equipment, machinery, raw materials and semi-finished products – hindered the possibility of reconstruction in the eastern countries. The process ended only with the creation of Comecon. Talking about 'mutual aid' was incompatible with the recovery of compensation in kind.

The countries that remained under Soviet influence (Albania, Bulgaria, Czechoslovakia, Hungary, Poland, the German Democratic Republic, Romania and Yugoslavia), adopted their own national strategies once the turbulent period of establishing the new regimes was over. In two cases, Albania and Yugoslavia, this meant moving away from the field of Soviet influence. Albania formed closer links with the China of Mao, and Yugoslavia attempted to sit on the fence between Communism and the non-aligned countries of the Third World. In any case, all these countries focused on a similar model for development, which could only be described as 'autarkic'. Links with the rest of the world were limited in three repects. The first originated in the requirements of the Soviet Union, which fixed quantities and prices for products to be traded among the Comecon countries. As a rule, exchanges were to the advantage of the Soviet Union, which continued to claim compensation (with greater discretion) for the damage suffered during the Second World War, though keeping a strong hold on its leadership at the same time. The second was related to the lack of liberty within Comecon. Negotiations among its members always had to be subject to Soviet approval. As a consequence of the first, there was no way of increasing trade among the countries of the same bloc. Comecon ended up as a series of bilateral trade relations between each country and the Soviet Union. The third was related to the lack of product competitiveness within the area, or, possibly even worse, from the inability of knowing what price to fix in order not to lose ground in international trade. The abolition of the market price system in the Soviet area weakened the members of the bloc in the sphere of free trade, which was international trade. There was a constant tendency to oscillate between prohibiting trade and dumping.

The Treaty of Rome, and the creation of the EEC and EFTA, troubled the still waters of the Soviet bloc, and forced those countries to act. Comecon seemed to be the appropriate institution, so much so that it even gave the impression of foreshadowing the efforts at integration in the western countries. Something was done in this direction: within the Comecon area the running of railway wagons was approved, and little else. The growth model was not discussed, and the dynamism of western Europe, which was so attractive to the citizens of the east that they were prompted to emigrate illegally, was condemned. The most conspicuous example of the division of the two halves of Europe was the construction of the Berlin wall in 1961 by the GDR, to prevent people escaping to the west. This marked the climax of the phenomenon known as the Cold War. There was tension between the blocs, which did not cause actual wars between the two opposing sides – the United States and the Soviet Union – but did cause numerous 'hot' wars outside Europe.

The emergence of the Third World; the Golden Age

The expression 'Third World' is an explicit reference to the first two. The first was the capitalist bloc under the United States, with affluent market economies, systems of private ownership and political democracies. The second was Communist, and was led by the Soviet Union, with relatively prosperous economies, central planning, systems of collective ownership, and 'people's' democracies (in actual fact dictatorships). The Third World included all the rest, and above all it was poor. The leaders who were the most apprehensive as regards North American and Soviet control created the movement of non-aligned countries, a subcommittee of the Third World – its politically aware vanguard, to use the language of the period. The countries forming it did not want to be subjected either to the United States or to the Soviet Union, capitalist or socialist, a market or a planned economy, a formal or a people's democracy. Much of the Third World was made up of countries that had been colonized by Western powers, or by Japan. Some, like China, wavered between membership of the Second or Third World but after 1960 sought to create their own sphere of influence at a distance from Moscow.

Decolonization was the main factor unifying the so-called 'Third World' countries; hence the Latin American countries harked back to their emancipation in the early nineteenth century in order to be accepted as members of the 'club' of Third World countries, or, more significantly, the 'club' of non-aligned countries. Besides Japanese decolonization – which took place during the last years of the Second World War, and involved liberating all the countries under Japanese occupation between 1931 (Manchuria) and the first years of the war, and which involved almost the whole of the Far East – the two great decolonization processes were British and French. They took over twenty years, between 1945 and 1965, although the most intense phases were around 1947–1949 with the emancipation of India, Pakistan and Indonesia, and around 1960, when most of French Africa was liberated and the liberation of British Africa was speeded up. It had started in 1957 with Ghana, and was finally completed in 1964. Portuguese decolonization took place much later, between 1974 and 1975.

Independence offered new opportunities for political and social development, which was not always successfully realized. The formulas that seemed to work for western Europe after the war did not work the same way in the new countries that had emerged with emancipation. In addition to cultural and social issues, one problem was the relationship with the metropolitan markets. Although the mother countries granted their former colonies preferential access to their markets, this was not always of great interest. By now the home markets had become less important than previously, and furthermore they were subject to other international agreements (chiefly GATT), which limited their margin for intervention.

For all that, the economic results for the Third World were, on the whole, very positive during the Golden Age. Between 1950 and 1973, Asian GDP grew at a rate of 5.2 per cent (excluding Japan), and African GDP at 4.5 per cent. The economic dynamism was largely negated by the enormous increases in population that occurred precisely during this period (2.2 per cent in Asia, excluding Japan, and 2.3 per cent in Africa).

The global nature of economic growth is in fact one of the distinct and more genuine features of the Golden Age. Between 1950 and 1973, the *per capita* GDP of western Europe grew by 4.1 per cent, and of the Soviet Union and eastern Europe by 3.5 per cent. In the large overseas countries that were formerly British colonies (including the United States) it grew by 2.4 per cent. In Asia, excluding Japan (which grew by an amazing 8.1 per cent), it increased by 3 per cent, in Latin America by 2.5 per cent and in Africa by 2.2 per cent. Though relatively low, the 2.2 per cent of Africa was already a formidable rate, especially if one takes into account that, in the following quarter of a century, the continent's GDP growth *per capita* remained fixed at 0 per cent. In short, everybody did well. The fact that prosperity was general was not always compatible with the revolutions and revolts that proliferated everywhere. With the benefit of hindsight, we can appreciate that growth increased the aspiration to progress, and that the struggle between systems further increased the aspiration, especially the wish for a more equal distribution of property and income.

Despite the homogeneity of growth, its forms were very different. We do not have sufficiently reliable data for the whole world to be able to prove the outline that follows, but some features are sufficiently significant and universal to account for the essence of what happened. The growth figures throw light on the type of development that was pursued.

Table 11.6 summarizes some of the basic patterns of the Golden Age. In the first place, overall growth in GDP was very high and similar for four great areas of the world (the countries with market economies, the countries of the Soviet area, Asian and Latin American countries): it was always above 5 per cent and below 6 per cent. The significance of the fact that the world grew by 5 per cent cannot be overstated. In the west it had not been seen, nor would it be seen again. Only the growth of the Far East, after 1973, has reached such levels for such an enormous population.

Second, the land factor was of very little importance, and of no importance at all in the more developed countries. The other factors, and total productivity factors (TPF), showed very different patterns. The work factor was very significant, oscillating between 35 per cent and 41 per cent in the Soviet bloc countries, in Asia and in Latin America, but only 12 per cent in the OECD countries. From this figure alone, it could be conjectured that it was so because those countries were more capitalist, but nothing could be further from the truth. The less important role of the work factor in the OECD countries simply camouflages the lower population growth, combined with the reduction in working hours per person. The pattern for the factor of capital allows of no simplification whatsoever. As in the OECD area, the Soviet Union mobilized more capital than labour, but with one big difference: the Soviet Union mobilized double the capital of the OECD. The other two continents mobilized rather more capital than the OECD countries,

Table 11.6 Growth accounting, 1950–1973

		Contribution of factor (%)			
Bloc or country	*Growth of GDP*	*Land*	*Labour*	*Capital*	*Contribution of TPF* [a]
OECD [b]	5.4	0	12	26	62
Soviet Union	5.1	3	35	51	10
Asia [c]	5.6	1	41	33	26
Latin America	5.2	3	35	27	34
Japan	9.3	–1	16	26	59
United States	3.7	0	31	28	41
Great Britain	3.0	0	2	33	66
Germany (FR)	5.9	0	2	27	70
France	3.1	0	7	21	72

Source: own adaptation based on data in A. Maddison *The World Economy in the Twentieth Century*, Paris, 1989.

Notes:

[a] *TPF*: Total productivity of factors.

[b] The Organization for Economic Co-operation and Development (OECD) groups the countries with more developed market economies, including all those of western Europe, the United States, Canada, Australia, New Zealand and Japan. In the table 'OECD' is the arithmetical mean of the five countries listed in the same table: Japan, United States, Great Britain, Germany (FR) and France.

[c] The value for Asia also includes the GDP of Japan. Without Japan the Asiatic GDP is 5.2.

27 per cent and 33 per cent. The greatest differences are in the TPF. TPF includes everything that is not measured under the factors of land, labour and capital: it could be that there was improved allocation of resources, improved efficiency, technical progress not involving fresh capital, non-measurable quality of productive factors and so on. These elements as a whole, which are difficult to pin down, account for 62 per cent of the growth of the OECD countries, only 10 per cent in the Soviet Union, 26 per cent in Asia and 34 per cent in Latin America. In short, the more advanced countries grew because of a better integrated use of the factors, rather than because of the addition of other factors. Soviet growth was extensive, while that of the OECD countries was intensive. This in brief was the third feature of Western growth during the Golden Age.

A close look at the last five rows of Table 11.6, which gives figures for some of the OECD countries, shows that the most tangible feature of this institution, namely the great importance of the TPF, is accentuated in the case of the great countries of western Europe. The United States, on the other hand, shows patterns more like those of the Latin American economies as a whole. Japan shares the basic features of the OECD model. Germany, Great Britain and France, on the other hand, are extreme cases of the model itself. Labour contributed very little to growth, while TPF accounted for practically everything.

What lies behind this spectacular growth in TPF of western Europe during the Golden Age? It must lie in the effect of reconstruction, and narrowing the gap between the United States. Once the war was over, the quantity and quality of technologies available to Europeans were astonishing, and all that was needed was to copy them. In such circumstances, a sufficiently skilled population, working hard and efficiently, can produce well. A further requirement is an efficient environment, where effort is not wasted. Contributing factors were, on the one hand, the political and economic system defended tooth and nail by the west European governments, in view of the tension between the two great blocs; on the other, the greater merging of national policies, which, after thirty years of conflict, aimed at increasing political and social cohesion. This in its turn created a solid basis for sustained economic growth.

Furthermore, if Europe developed spectacularly after 1950, it did so thanks to the policy of firmly anchoring the German Federal Republic, one of the future engines of the world economy, to a regionally important structure that had been planned *ad hoc*. Liberalization of intra-European trade, as well as international trade, caused western Europe to grow faster and better, encouraging the emergence of more efficient models of product specialization.

Both the creation of the EEC and the new requirements for stability agreed at Bretton Woods had an impact on the western European economy. 1958 was a year of economic crisis because of the adjustments in production imposed by the onset of a world of fixed parities. Some of the great western countries, like France, were compelled to request aid from the IMF to finance their balance of payments problems during the transition to the new situation. Belgium, Denmark, Ireland, Portugal and Spain were also significantly affected by the difficulties of competing in an economy where trade flows were changing direction, and unilateral modification of exchange rates was limited by international agreements.

In effect, between 1958 and 1971, western Europe and much of the world lived in a world of fixed parities. It was an experiment that had been building up for years, and which was finally realized. After initial adjustment problems, it was a great success. It could be said that these were the real years of the Golden Age. Previous years, though they had enjoyed higher growth rates, were dominated by the effect of reconstruction. Even the 1950s had been a great experience in intra-national and international economic co-operation, but without the essential complement of exchange rate stability. 1958 saw the start of the phase that most closely approached the system of international economic relations envisaged by Bretton Woods (without the International Trade Organization). For the European countries associated with the EEC, stability (political and exchange rate) and the liberalization of trade were important factors in the uninterrupted and spectacular growth of intra-European trade.

The next twelve years, revealingly, witnessed continual British requests to join the EEC. Year after year, between 1958 and 1969 (when he stepped down from power), General de Gaulle of France firmly refused. Without de Gaulle, and with greater British willingness to agree to the whole of the Treaty of Rome, the request of the United Kingdom was rapidly accepted. In 1973, Denmark, Great Britain and Ireland joined the European Community. Now that they had been abandoned by their trade leader, the other EFTA countries hesitated about which route to follow. Some, like Norway, submitted the decision to a referendum, and set off a series of negative responses to the EEC among the population. Ireland seized the opportunity to abandon its permanent trade isolation.

Confirmation that everything was functioning more than satisfactorily during the Golden Age was the strong trend towards convergence in *per capita* income, and the classification of growth rates for this variable – the most significant for economic growth – endorses it. Table 11.7 includes the growth rates for the United States and the world, to show the points of comparison. Since the United States was the leading world economy, a comparison with it is mandatory. All the European countries, except the United Kingdom, grew more than the United

Table 11.7 Growth of *per capita* income, 1950–1973 (%)

Western Europe				*Eastern Europe*	
Greece	6.21	Belgium	3.55	Bulgaria	5.19
Spain	5.79	Holland	3.45	Romania	4.80
Portugal	5.66	Norway	3.19	Yugoslavia	4.49
Italy	4.95	Denmark	3.08	GDR	4.48
Germany (FR)	4.94	Switzerland	3.08	Hungary	3.60
Austria	4.94	Sweden	3.07	Albania	3.59
Finland	4.25	Ireland	3.04	Poland	3.45
France	4.05	United Kingdom	2.44	Soviet Union	3.36
				Czechoslovakia	3.08

Source: A. Maddison, *Monitoring the World Economy*, 1995, for the two Germanies and A. Maddison, *The World Economy*, 2001, for the remainder.

Pro memoria: United States: 2.45; world: 2.93

States. Year after year, many grew more than the North American rate by two percentage points, the convergence rate considered optimal. The growth rate for the world as a whole indicated that the European economy showed better growth than the rest of the world, but that even here there was a certain degree of convergence. In western Europe, the countries that showed most growth were the poorest (with the exception of Ireland), and those that had become poor because of the war, disorganization and subsequent paralysis. Those that grew least were those that were already prosperous, those that had been neutral, and those that had not had direct experience of war on their own territory. Even eastern Europe benefited from an evident process of convergence. The Balkan countries, which were poorer and suffered most during the war, had the opportunity to grow faster than their normally more prosperous northern neighbours.

It is interesting to note that inward-looking and inward-based – in other words autarkic – growth strategies did not produce poor results during the Golden Age. The growth of eastern Europe was remarkable, despite being slightly lower than that of western Europe. The measurement of such growth is always problematic, since the national accounts of the socialist bloc countries differed from those of capitalist countries. The relative concept of GDP was limited to physical output, namely to agriculture and industry. Services were considered not productive, and therefore not calculated. The objective was clearly to maximize industrial production, and the policies applied in all the eastern countries have been defined as 'forced' industrialization. The explanation for the priority given to industry was concern to imitate the Soviet Union, and an urge that was common in all the eastern countries to be able to produce the elements of their own strategic independence (armaments of all types). With all its limitations, Table 11.8 gives the economic result for the whole Soviet bloc (including the Soviet Union).

Taking the figures of this table into consideration, the Golden Age was practically identical on both sides of the Iron Curtain. During the quarter of a century

Table 11.8 Physical product of eastern Europe and the Soviet Union: index numbers (1950 = 100) and growth rates (%), 1950–1975

Year	*1950 = 100*	*%*	*Year*	*1950 = 100*	*%*
1950	100.0		1963	178.2	–0.4
1951	101.9	1.9	1964	197.8	11.0
1952	107.0	5.1	1965	208.3	5.3
1953	112.0	4.6	1966	219.3	5.3
1954	117.3	4.8	1967	228.7	4.3
1955	126.8	8.1	1968	240.8	5.3
1956	136.6	7.7	1969	245.3	1.8
1957	141.3	3.4	1970	261.4	6.6
1958	151.2	7.1	1971	271.5	3.9
1959	152.0	0.5	1972	276.3	1.8
1960	165.1	8.6	1973	296.8	7.5
1961	174.7	5.8	1974	307.9	3.7
1962	179.0	2.4	1975	311.5	1.2

Source: own adaptation based on data in A. Maddison, *The World Economy*, 2001.

between 1950 and 1975, the growth rate is equally high, with an annual rate of 4.8 per cent until 1974. Episodes of lower growth were recorded, as in 1963, or less critical ones (as in 1951, 1959, 1969 and 1972), but generally speaking there was a prevalence of high rates.

Oil crises, stagflation and challenges from outside Europe

The Golden Age did not finish suddenly, though at times it is convenient to think of it as doing so. The internal compromise mechanisms that had led to such good results for guaranteeing social peace and reinvesting profits, and that had reassured entrepreneurs and workers respectively, had gradually started to deteriorate. This, however, was merely due to the passage of time and the emergence of new generations who felt they were less bound to the conventions and attitudes of their parents. At the end of the 1960s and in the early 1970s, trade union unrest increased and reached worrying levels. Moreover, when US President Nixon chose to suspend dollar convertibility, on 15 August 1971, an essential compromise for stability in the post-war economic world – namely exchange rate stability – was lost. Afflicted by public deficits, the outcome of huge and growing military expenditure on the Vietnam War, the United States needed a free hand, so it could implement policies that were more inflationary and allowed for devaluation, in response to balance of trade difficulties. The North American decision meant the end of the period of the Bretton Woods monetary agreements – which had been so painstakingly achieved in 1958 – and inaugurated a period of international monetary instability. Initially, growth rates in the world economy were not affected, but there was new uncertainty on the international economic scene. Mechanisms of co-operation among European currencies were strengthened by adopting what was known as the monetary 'snake', whereby bands of currency fluctuation were fixed. Any shock from outside would produce an effect in a world where the most developed countries had a wider margin (unwanted but real) for implementing their monetary policies.

The shock arrived from where it had been least expected; it was the result of the sudden increase in the price of oil that had been agreed at the end of 1973 by the Organization of Petroleum Exporting Companies (OPEC), apparently in retaliation for the pro-Israel stance of the Western countries during the Yom Kippur War. It marked the end of the era of cheap energy, which had lasted since the Second World War. In a very short space of time (from October 1973 to January 1974), the price of oil increased fourfold, and caused massive trade deficits in all the countries importing liquid fuel. In the majority of countries, oil was already the main import item at pre-OPEC decision prices. It was 'the staple of industry', more so even than coal had been at the beginning of the century. It had continued to replace coal for all energy uses, and was the raw material of the powerful petrochemical industry. The new oil prices meant, quite simply, that the importing countries would become poorer, since they had to pay the producing countries four times as much for their oil. In the short term, there was no way out. In economic terms, the demand for oil was very inelastic.

The world was not only divided into countries exporting or importing oil. Curiously enough, there was also a third category, made up of countries that were mainly self-sufficient; these were the United States and the Soviet Union. The two great world powers were generally shielded from the crisis. They were great producers, with only moderate exposure to foreign trade. The economies that suffered the crisis most were those of western Europe, Japan and the whole of the oil-importing Third World. Thus the oil crisis divided the world along new frontiers. The United States overcame the crisis by making a considerable effort to save energy. The Soviet Union took advantage of the increase in oil prices to boost its export drive, and to achieve great profits on the world market. The OPEC countries became extraordinarily rich. The rulers of the small Arab emirates and the other tiny oil-exporting countries managed to share out the torrent of dollars among family relatives and subjects. The countries with larger populations (Iran, Iraq, Algeria, Venezuela and to a lesser extent Indonesia and Nigeria) implemented ambitious industrialization and social welfare programmes. OPEC's decision was a hard blow to progress in the standard of living in the oil-importing Third World, and the countries involved were able to withstand the crisis only by contracting debts and waiting for better times. Their greatest problem was the reduced purchasing power of the more developed countries, where their exports were directed. For their part, the OECD countries, with the exception of the United States, found themselves greatly impoverished. All these countries went from growth rates that had invariably been high for twenty or twenty-five years to much lower or even negative ones. This new state of affairs was unexpected, and economic actors had difficulty coming to terms with it.

There were different responses to the crisis. The breakdown of the international exchange rate stability agreed at Bretton Woods, but applied only since 1958, brought about a new situation dominated by fluctuating exchange rates, rather than the traditional fixed exchange rates. In this framework of greater uncertainty, governments had greater room for manoeuvre, and were able to adopt different policies. In effect, the Community countries abolished their plans for monetary unification, and put forward others for co-ordinating their monetary policies in order to gain greater freedom of action. Three types of policies can be distinguished.

In some countries, such as Sweden and Spain (despite being different their response was similar), the governments claimed that the crisis was only transitory, and that the loss of purchasing power of the country as a whole could be absorbed through the national budget. Oil prices did not fully affect the population, and the state decided to agree to a reduction in taxation, which was retrieved on the sale of products derived from oil. These countries managed to enjoy slightly higher growth rates than the other OECD countries, particularly during 1974 and part of 1975, but were not able to escape from the overall pattern of depression that the oil shock implied. In the following years, they did not set up any form of energy-saving policy, nor did they prepare the population for any co-operative response to reduced affluence.

The second, and most numerous, group adopted a strategy of transferring the new prices to public spending, and met the crisis forcefully with a clear energy-saving plan. However, incomes policy remained unchanged, and the trade unions, which in recent years had shown their strength and bargaining power, obtained salary increases in line with price increases (including those of oil). In order to try to square the circle, governments had to agree to create more money, and thus financed inflationary policies. These countries (mainly France, Great Britain and Italy) failed to realize that the oil shock had made them worse off, even if they made efforts to reduce their oil consumption.

Finally, the FRG and Japan were ready to accept the idea of a loss of prosperity. Japan immediately implemented steep increases in the price of oil and its derivatives. In 1974 and 1975, it suffered the most serious crisis of all the developed countries, but once the new price structure had been assimilated, it again started to show very rapid growth; it now concentrated on the development of sectors that were less energy-intensive, like electronic consumer goods. The FRG aimed at a similar objective, but through different mechanisms. The Bundesbank maintained the objective of containing inflation (which the Japanese waived) and forced economic operators – families, businesses, trade unions and public administrations – to reduce their income. Germany emerged from the crisis with a stronger currency, with low inflation, gains in competitiveness, and a renewed industrial structure without the dead weight of the sectors consuming most oil.

However, inflation increased in all the OECD countries, and so did unemployment. The combination of economic stagnation and inflation, known as 'stagflation', was the greatest headache for politicians and economists, since it had not been predicted in traditional Keynesian models of economic policy.

Just when all these policies had started to produce results, whether good or bad, and especially now that the price of crude oil had become stabilized, along came the second oil shock. In 1979, the Shah of Persia was deposed in an Islamic-inspired revolution, led by the Ayatollah Khomeini; his anti-Western sentiments, and the tension with the United States, created uncertainty in the oil market. Fear turned into panic when, in the autumn of 1980, war broke out between Iran and Iraq. This not only affected two great oil exporters, but spread to their oil-producing regions. OPEC took advantage, and imposed further increases in crude oil prices (two and a half times more), which again caused a reduction in the prosperity of the importing countries, and a recession between 1981 and 1983.

Responses were now much more uniform. Governments were convinced they had no room for manoeuvre, and everywhere applied similar measures. In Japan and Germany, where robust energy-saving policies had already been implemented, the impact was, in fact, negligible. In countries that had not managed to assimilate reduced national prosperity, but only the reduction in energy, the second shock provided the opportunity to confront the unresolved problem of national agreements, with the aim of a responsible distribution of the burden of energy costs. This is what happened in France, Great Britain and Italy, though their policies were different (respectively left-wing, right-wing and centrist). The countries that had attempted to ignore the first shock, like Spain and Sweden, were very seriously affected by the second, since now they needed to implement readjustments in energy and social systems simultaneously, and without further delay. All EEC governments made great efforts to co-ordinate their policies better, and that is why they reactivated the European Monetary System (EMS), with relatively tight margins of oscillation between the currencies. The principle whereby it was better to join forces in the struggle against inflation was triumphant.

The second oil shock (1979), in conjunction with changes in quotations for the dollar and in interest rates, led to further consequences. The most important of these was the debt crisis. Let us proceed step by step. In the advanced industrial countries (those of the OECD), the oil crisis had a reverse side of the coin, namely the economic surplus in the OPEC countries. The Arab monarchies, with small populations and large quantities of oil, managed to accumulate enormous fortunes, and to spend extravagantly. Dollars from the sale of petroleum, or 'petro-dollars', were earned very easily, and could just as easily be spent. They ended up returning, in large quantities, to Western stock markets and banks in pursuit of opportunities for profitable investment, which were not available in the small monarchies on the Arabian peninsula. This was an unusual phenomenon, since it had always been the norm for rich countries to invest in poor countries; the *nouveaux riches* of the poor countries were now depositing their money in the rich countries, and on a massive scale. The most heavily populated of the OPEC countries (Algeria, Iran, Iraq, Indonesia, Mexico and Venezuela) with independent political regimes set up more ambitious investment strategies aimed at developing their economies. In all cases, they tried to develop oil refining and all the industries associated with it. In some cases, they even dared to launch into heavy industry, like iron or cement. It was always carried out with gigantic investment programmes, to match the urgency of spending resources obtained quickly and in large quantities. In order to complete their projects more rapidly, and thus join the 'club' of industrial countries – and escape from being mere exporters of raw materials – many ran into debt.

These projects went up in smoke when the situation of the international economy changed. The international dollar rate had remained relatively low during the 1970s, but after the suspension of dollar–gold convertibility in August 1971, and with the arrival of Reagan to the US presidency, it started to rise. The change had, in fact, started a little earlier with Volcker at the head of the Federal Reserve. The Federal Reserve started a new policy of money scarcity, coming at the same time as the federal government started another policy of intense rearmament; this entailed the government entering into debt. Since the Federal Reserve was fixing high interest rates in order to sustain the exchange rate of the dollar, Reagan found that investors worldwide were turning to US public debt bonds in view of expectations regarding the reserve value of the dollar and increases in its exchange rate. Any other country would have found such a situation unsustainable. Normally, if a government runs into deficit, and becomes over-indebted, it is expected to meet its own finances by issuing more money; but this undermines confidence in the national currency. However, the United States exploited its position of hegemony, and how the world perceived future prospects for the North American economy, and the strength of its currency, public deficits notwithstanding. The result was an unstoppable rise in the dollar, as well as in the federal government's public deficit. Investors all round the world – starting with the holders of petro-dollars – had no hesitation in counting on an increase in the rate of the dollar. Between 1980 and 1985 the dollar did rise almost unstoppably for five years, which mainly affected all the economic players who had become indebted in dollars. This was the case with some of the large OPEC countries – Mexico, in particular. Many other non-oil-producing countries had contracted debts in dollars, in order to close the deficit in their trade balances, in the hope of better times and cheaper oil. This happened to many countries of the Third World without petroleum resources, in Africa as well as in Latin America. It also happened with countries of the Second World, and this is where the debt crisis arose.

It had a very inconspicuous start in Poland, in 1980. After the take-over by General Jaruzelski, Poland had to acknowledge the massive debt it had incurred in order to meet its current obligations, and that the rise in the price of the dollar had made it impossible to pay back the credit. At the time, the Polish deferral of payments seemed to derive specifically from the great political conflict that had been taking place between the *Solidarnośc* trade union, which was fighting for power, and a government in disarray. However, it was later discovered that the problem was not only Polish, but that all the eastern countries had become indebted during the 1970s. The advantages of the low cost of the dollar, and the credit facilities offered by opening up to east Germany (the *Ostpolitik* of Chancellor Willy Brandt), encouraged the governments of the people's republics to modernize their infrastructure and industrial apparatus, by resorting to Western credit.

In early 1982, the debt crisis broke out openly in Mexico when oil prices had ceased to increase and the dollar continued to rise. The government of President Lopez Portillo, now at the end of its term, had little room for manoeuvre and handled the crisis badly. The Mexican peso rapidly lost value, and thus complicated the problem of debt reduction. The fall of the peso undid all the plans for recovering the resources needed to pay the debt. It seemed to be an unstoppable vicious circle, and generated panic in the international financial community, which realized that its investments in many countries could be put at serious risk. The panic had exactly the same effect as the repeated bank panics in the nineteenth century, or the 1929 Wall Street crash. Apprehensive bankers started to demand repayment of credit, without agreeing to the usual renewals. They needed liquidity in order to neutralize Mexican non-payment. Investors were still far from amortizing credits, and had enough problems with paying the interest on the debt. Pressure from the banks forced many countries to order the suspension of payment of the foreign debt. In absolute terms, the most significant cases were those in Latin America, but probably the most important, in relation to national economies, were those in Africa. For years, discussions on how to renegotiate the debt payment were held. The North Americans were the ones who played the leading role in the bargaining. The main banks involved were American, as was the rule that declared any debt outstanding for over three months a default. The diplomacy that attempted to obtain refinancing agreements was American. The dollar problem was American. It was in Washington that the World Bank and the International Monetary Fund, the two great organizations involved in stabilizing the international economy, were situated. The negative image of them both, which has spread today, originated then. They not only had to deal with financing investments (the IBRD), and financing temporary foreign debts (the IMF), but, as a consequence of actions started unilaterally by the world economic leader, were forced into dealing with the stabilization and development of the international economy.

The first half of 1980 was dominated by numerous efforts to bring about order. The initiatives already mentioned were implemented in Europe (and in Japan), with the aim of controlling macroeconomic imbalances, and, in the first place, inflation. Results came gradually, and from the 1981 minimum until 1988, the European economy experienced a modest, but steady recovery. In the rest of the non-developed world (and in many of the Soviet bloc countries), adjustments were dominated by the criterion of mobilizing resources required for foreign debt payment. In the meantime, the United States had become immersed in liberal-conservative structural reform policies set out by the Reagan presidency.

Between 1985 and 1986, everything changed quite suddenly. All the factors that had marked the previous period, the high cost of oil, the dollar and North American interest rates, reversed their pattern and began to recede. In January 1986, Saudi Arabia broke the OPEC cartel and increased production. In the course of a few months many countries followed suit, and the price of crude oil plummeted, reaching its real level (not its monetary level) before the 1973 crisis. At the same time, the interest rates fixed by the Federal Reserve began to fall, and the dollar with them. The debt crisis became manageable, and gradually disappeared from discussion. A declining dollar made it easier to deal with the payment of interest on foreign debts. Cheap oil ended the balance of payment problems in the majority of countries. The only countries to remain up in arms were those of OPEC.

In this more optimistic climate, made all the more so by Spain and Portugal joining the EEC (from 1 January 1986), the EEC launched the proposal for the Single Act. This meant the *de facto* completion of the unification of the European common market, which had been envisaged since 1957. The Single Act was ratified by all the member states and was gradually applied from July 1987 to January 1993, which was the date set for the completion of the internal market. Meanwhile, the movement towards the liberalization and integration of markets gripped financial operators. In 1986, the City of London began deregulation, and was rapidly imitated by stock exchanges worldwide. European expansion, now based on more solid foundations, started a few years of moderate growth, which culminated in 1988, when western Europe as a whole achieved a growth rate of 4 per cent. Since 1976 such a figure had been unheard of, and seemed almost to belong to the Golden Age. Even the stock market crisis of October 1987, the first crisis of financial globalization, the outcome of greater variability resulting from the newly inaugurated interconnection of all the stock exchanges of the world, was rapidly and robustly overcome, to general surprise and satisfaction. With this renewed optimism, the EEC again revived its plans for economic and monetary integration; initially, this involved the twelve member states adhering to the fluctuating exchange rate of the European Monetary System.

Fall of the Soviet bloc, resumption of European integration and globalization

The year 1989, *annus mirabilis* for Western capitalism, will go down in history as the year when the Berlin Wall fell, and the majority of eastern European dictatorships collapsed. The process was extremely rapid: in a little over six weeks, in November and December 1989, the so-called 'satellite states' of the Soviet Union set out on a new path which brought them closer to the free Western world. The year 1989 was also the last year that high growth could be recorded, with a 3.4 per cent increase in GDP for western Europe as a whole. The next decade would be very different.

Eastern Europe and the Soviet Union had experienced a slow decline since the end of the Golden Age, as Table 11.9 shows. The first oil crisis affected the two halves of Europe in similar ways, and there were no great differences between the Soviet Union and its European allies. The second crisis, between 1979 and 1981, had a greater effect on the eastern countries. The lesson had not been learnt, and as a result the second blow did more damage than the first. For years, the countries under Soviet influence had been able to buy oil from the Soviet Union at lower prices than on the world market, and resell it. This was possible because, within Comecon, transaction costs between its members were set according to a moving average of the previous five years, to prevent temporary fluctuations. In as much as the cost of oil rose during the first shock, it meant the availability of cheap oil for east European countries, and the chance of extra income by reselling it on world markets. Moreover, as we have already said, the generous flow of Western credit had started, and everyone took advantage. With the second shock, there was an overlap between the increases due to costing methods and the new market increases. The situation became unsustainable after 1981. Many countries were forced into debt with the West, in order to meet essential import needs. The credit that had previously been contracted was already generating huge interest, which was now made worse by the increased value of the dollar. After 1981, things went from bad to worse. While the western European countries slowly but steadily recovered their growth rate, those in eastern Europe were not able to stabilize their economies at the level of expansion. After 1985, the contrast was very marked. Even the Soviet Union, which had compared much more favourably with the West

Table 11.9 Growth rates of GDP for the Soviet Union (and former Soviet Union) and eastern Europe, 1975–1998 (%)

Year	*USSR*	*Eastern Europe*	*Year*	*USSR*	*Eastern Europe*
1975	2.8	3.6	1987	1.3	–0.6
1976	4.7	2.6	1988	2.1	0.9
1977	2.4	3.5	1989	1.5	–1.3
1978	2.5	3.2	1990	–2.4	–7.7
1979	–0.5	1.5	1991	–6.3	–10.9
1980	0.1	0.5	1992	–15.6	–5.3
1981	0.9	–1.2	1993	–9.9	–1.6
1982	2.5	0.9	1994	–13.9	3.9
1983	3.2	1.5	1995	–5.4	5.7
1984	1.3	3.1	1996	–2.8	3.8
1985	0.9	0.1	1997	1.7	2.9
1986	4.1	2.8	1998	–2.0	2.3

Source: own adaptation based on data in A. Maddison, *The World Economy*, 2001.

during the early years of the decade, was not able to overcome its difficulties after 1986. Military spending on the war in Afghanistan, combined with the military challenge from the United States, multiplied defence expenditure. The reforms undertaken by Gorbachev did not bring the hoped-for economic results, and the system continued to lose all capacity for manoeuvre. After the pro-democracy revolutions in the autumn of 1989 in eastern Europe, the Soviet Union decided to accelerate the transition to democracy and capitalism, albeit less vigorously. In August 1991, the process suddenly precipitated, as a result of an attempted *coup* aimed at bringing Gorbachev down, and returning to Communist orthodoxy. The *coup* failed, though it did manage to unseat Gorbachev, who was replaced by Yeltsin, the leader of the resistance to the *coup*, who accelerated change. This, effectively, involved the solemn break-up of the Union of Soviet Socialist Republics, its replacement with a Confederation of Independent States and the calling of democratic elections.

Once the dictatorial regimes of eastern Europe had been brought down, the transition from a planned and closed socialist system to an open capitalist market system was extremely traumatic. In terms of GDP, it meant four years of down turn, from 1990 to 1993. The first two years showed falls approaching those following the two world wars and the chaos after defeat: a fall of 18 per cent in two years. In 1992 and 1993 the fall was reduced, and in 1994 there was a return to positive growth rates. What happened in those years? There had been a true economic revolution. Economies opened up to foreign trade and services, and to the movement of people and capital. Such a change, which for many countries might have taken decades, happened almost instantaneously, like a 'big bang'. Planning ceased to function, and markets emerged, though without any controls, without institutions of arbitration or any laws protecting contracts. This second shock was slower, but only slightly. The third great change was the privatization of public property. Since this step towards capitalism had enormous repercussions on public accounts and on private fortunes, it was the one that was discussed most openly, and the one that more than any other defined the positions of the emerging political parties. Of the three great changes, it was the one that took the longest – and in many cases has not been completed. But even so, it has to be recognized that it took place with astonishing rapidity, if we take account of its economic, social and historical significance. On the whole, the countries that decided to accelerate the pace of change have been able to abbreviate the ordeal of the transition phase, and enter a new period of growth. Those that hesitated during the transition phase have remained bogged down between two systems, and have experienced distressing decline. Table 11.10 illustrates the two models.

The different cases that we have indicated can be easily examined. The most successful transition – perhaps the only true success – was that of Poland; during the system change-over, it managed to minimize losses (in terms of fall in GDP, and its duration), and under the new system was able to return to rapid growth, and surpass the 1988 GDP levels, which was the highest under the socialist regime. The former Czechoslovakia did not manage such good results. With the peaceful division into the Czech Republic and Slovakia, it seemed that the former had everything to gain. The Czech Republic completed a rapid transition, almost as rapidly

Table 11.10 Rates of variation of GDP for eastern Europe, 1989–1998 (%)

Country	*1989*	*1990*	*1991*	*1992*	*1993*	*1994*	*1995*	*1996*	*1997*	*1998*	*1998/1989*
Poland	–1.6	–9.7	–7.0	2.6	3.8	5.2	7.0	6.0	6.8	5.0	117.8
Czech Republic	0.8	–2.8	–11.6	–0.5	0.1	2.2	5.9	3.8	0.3	–2.3	96.6
Slovakia			–14.6	–6.5	–3.6	4.8	7.0	6.5	6.6	4.4	
Hungary	–2.2	–6.7	–11.9	–3.1	–0.6	2.9	1.5	1.3	4.5	4.9	90.0
Romania	–3.2	–10.9	–12.9	–8.8	1.6	3.9	7.1	4.0	–6.9	–7.3	69.6
Ex-Yugoslavia	–1.3	–7.3	–13.3	–19.0	–16.7	3.9	5.3	4.9	6.2	2.9	67.1
Bulgaria	–1.8	–10.9	–8.4	–7.3	–1.4	1.8	2.8	–10.2	–7.0	3.6	66.4

Source: own adaptation based on data in A. Maddison, *Monitoring the World Economy*, 1995, and *The World Economy*, 2001.

as Poland, but for years was not able to sustain a good growth rate. The result was that the country experienced an initial cycle of growth and crisis without managing to recover the productive maximum achieved under the former system. Slovakia, which had a worse start, with a political system that seemed closer to the *ancient régime*, little infrastructure, a less educated population and an oppressive legacy of large-scale state enterprise, managed, after prolonging the transition for two years, to show renewed vigorous growth after 1994, and recovered the previous levels. The transition of Hungary was half-way between the Czech Republic and Slovakia, but did not manage real take-off into growth. Whereas these two countries, together with Poland, achieved growth rates of over 5 per cent remarkably quickly, Hungary's growth came much later. On the other hand, its new economic structure was based on more solid foundations. Hungary and the other countries previously mentioned were the ones that were successful in making the transition to capitalism and to the market system, and are therefore candidates for joining the future greater European Union. The other three are cases of failed transition.

In effect, both Romania and Bulgaria, after making their transition at a similar rate to Slovakia, and after achieving positive growth rates, relapsed into a more acute economic quagmire, and are having to completely rethink their systems and policies. The numerous reasons for this situation are inevitably linked with the difficulties of adapting to the market that are encountered by very backward countries, in which the main investments made during the period of Soviet hegemony proved to be completely useless – if not negative – in the new context of an open market. This also happened in the GDR, but absorption by the FRG, with the outlay of enormous resources, resolved the problem. We will come back to that later. In the Balkan countries, unlike their northern neighbours of the Soviet bloc, the tradition of Western practices (in politics and law) was more recent. The most extreme case (not to mention the small country of Albania) was that of the former Yugoslavia. Unlike that of Czechoslovakia, its fragmentation was extremely traumatic, and gave rise to lengthy, devastating and brutal wars, which took up the whole decade, and continued to occupy the start of the next. The fall – or collapse – in GDP between 1989 and 1993 did not so much reflect the transition to the market system, as quite simply the chaos deriving from the violent fragmentation of the Yugoslav state. Conditions for the change-over of system should have been favourable for the Yugoslav economy, which was the one with the highest concentration of internal and external markets of all the eastern European economies. What should have been a strong point in confronting the challenges and opportunities of transition – the existence of numerous private enterprises, more widespread Western market practices, emigration to western Europe, incipient foreign investment, opening up to tourism, more liberal foreign trade and so on – all this was completely and utterly ruined in the *manu militari* dismemberment of the republic. Slovenia, the first to break away, was the one to benefit most during the decade, but it cannot be considered an economic miracle in absolute terms. However, merely by being on the outside of the chaos, it managed to save itself from the quagmire.

The Soviet Union experienced the most traumatic transition. Compared with the other countries of eastern Europe, change started earlier and lasted much longer. Starting in 1985, the government of Gorbachev introduced reforms in an atmosphere of freedom of information (*glasnost*) and political life, but very little or nothing in the economy. In fact, Gorbachev did not touch the system of planning. Only after the failed *coup*, in August 1991, and the subsequent liquidation of the Soviet Union, did an economic transition begin. It took place in a climate of confusion, and without any sense of direction, order or even agreement. Foreign trade was immediately liberalized, while the majority of internal markets continued to be under the control of a central planning office. This brought about the collapse of the state's capacity for collecting revenue, and the dissolution of all the mechanisms for the monopoly of power that are characteristic of a state. From 1990 to 1998, one can speak of an economic disaster, worse than in any other country of the Soviet bloc. Only the degree of the collapse can be measured (see Table 11.11). The republics of Uzbekistan, Estonia and Belarus were able to overcome the economic difficulties, and carry through something like a transition to a new economic system. They have been more successful than the Balkan states: the other countries are worse off.

The GDR is a unique case. The most prosperous of the east European economies enjoyed the good fortune to be absorbed by the FRG, through the process of political and economic unification – a true union of states – which was immediately set in motion after the fall of the Berlin Wall, and legally sanctioned a year later (in October 1990). For the FRG, it was a huge challenge to absorb the impact of the integration of the GDR inside its borders and in its budgets. The population of the GDR was a quarter that of the FRG (16 million inhabitants), and it had to be provided with the economic rights, infrastructure and opportunities equivalent to those in the FRG. All this necessitated heavy investment, which the new unified Germany carried out by incurring debts. Just as Reagan had financed his rearmament programme, Chancellor Kohl exploited the centrality of the mark and the German economy in Europe: all he needed was for the Bundesbank to raise interest rates in order to attract funds from all over the world, and in particular from all over Europe. The problem of financing the reconstruction of the former GDR was thus spread throughout the countries of the European Union. Since the different currencies were restricted within a limited fluctuation band, due to agreements that had led to the EMS, the central banks defended the parity of

Table 11.11 Fall in GDP of the states emerging from the Soviet Union, 1990–1998 (1990 = 100)

European states		*Asiatic states*	
Belarus	80.1	Armenia	61.9
Estonia	86.4	Azerbaijan	49.0
Latvia	57.6	Georgia	36.0
Lithuania	68.5	Kazakstan	61.2
Moldavia	33.6	Kyrgizstan	60.8
Ukraine	40.9	Tajikistan	31.9
Euro-Asiatic states		Turkmenistan	62.7
Russian Federation	57.7	Uzbekistan	90.6

Source: A. Maddison, *The World Economy*, 2001.

their currencies with the EMS as far as possible. But the trend for the Deutschmark to be revalued was inexorable, and ultimately led to a serious exchange crisis in September 1992. The pound sterling and the Italian lira left the exchange rate mechanism of the EMS. Later, in order to prevent the Spanish, Irish and Portuguese currencies from doing the same, agreement was reached to widen the fluctuation bands from more/less 2.5 per cent to more/less 15 per cent, making strong devaluations easier, and effectively legalizing those that were already being implemented. The instability was to last for the whole of 1993. The commitment to monetary integration, agreed in 1991 with the Treaty of Maastricht, which formed the European Union, was broken off due to the lack of co-ordination and co-operation among the countries. The economic decline, which was absolute in western Europe as a whole, and which had previously occurred only in 1975, brought about a redefinition of all the problems. The high interest rates, which all the central banks had misapplied – following the German example – had slowed down the pace of the economy. Devaluations were an unexpected and unwanted response, but they made it necessary to seek a new equilibrium.

The Economic and Monetary Union was the collective response to the conflict that had arisen from the widespread uncertainty over the unification of Germany in 1990, and the German need to give priority to solving internal problems, at least for the time being. The Bundesbank's misguided monetary policy made it clear that monetary policies independent of the German one could not be adopted. By common agreement, Germany raised its monetarism to European level, while its Community partners guaranteed that a common monetary policy would take account of their respective interests, through bodies at the supranational level. Thus, when the European Union officially came into being in 1993, the monetary integration policies were reactivated. The euro would represent the maximum expression of European economic integration. In 1994, the European Monetary Institute was created, and the timetable for fully applying the criteria for joining the single currency was set out, and was to be achieved by the middle of 1998. The criteria, known as the 'Maastricht convergence criteria', were to dominate the economic life of western Europe throughout 1994–1998. They were to consist in not having devalued in the previous two years, not having an inflation rate a point and a half higher than the average of the three lowest, not having long-term interest rates two points higher than the three with lowest inflation, not having a public debt of over 60 per cent of GDP, nor a deficit in the public accounts of more than 3 per cent of GDP. The Maastricht criteria, and the political will to apply them, smoothed the progress towards reducing inflation which had begun at the start of the previous decade but had subsequently been held up. The resolute political commitment to contain expenditure and debt, and to exercise monetary control, contributed to achieving the objectives that had been set out, where it could least be expected: with the confidence of the markets. Effectively, the price of the dollar started to fall throughout western Europe. The economic crisis, in conjunction with the vigour of the monetary policies, brought about a reduction in the cost of money. With *cheaper capital*, it was easier to control public deficits, generally due to over-indebtedness. With lower deficits, it was easier to reduce the volume of debt. This virtuous cycle enabled the European economy to start growing again, and at the same time greatly improve its monetary stability. With the obligations fulfilled by most Community members – whose number had increased to fifteen as from 1 January 1995, when Austria, Finland and Sweden became members – the fixed parities of the euro were approved in May 1998, and the single currency began to be quoted on the money markets as from 1 January 1999. Since then, the fear of losing room for manoeuvre on the part of national governments, which was what lay behind reservations about its adoption, has had no reason to arise. The euro has continued to decline against the dollar, which reflects the fact that European economic conditions, considered collectively, needed a downward adjustment.

Globalization

Globalization could be defined in many ways, but one should always remember that the term refers to the worldwide integration of markets. It is a very old phenomenon, as there have been many 'globalizations' in the history of humanity. Financial markets have integrated far more than goods markets, and these far more than the labour market. This is where many of the current anxieties lie. People face huge obstacles in order to emigrate, goods are subject to considerable limitations, but flows of capital (both in the short and in the long term) are not. The result is that stock markets have integrated far more than any other business activity. Table 11.12 shows how, between 1983 and 1998, aggregate stock market capitalization grew at a rate of 15 per cent annually. This is approximately six times more than world GDP. Growth in the volume of negotiations on the world stock markets has grown even more rapidly.

The integrating factors of the financial markets have been political, economic and technological. They have been technological, since they have made full use of the new information technologies. The interconnection of world stock markets in 1987 was possible thanks to the spread of information by means of personal computers, and thanks to improvements in telecommunications, which facilitated the transfer of data over long distances. However, changes in telecommunications are a partial result of transformations in the structure of the telecommunications

Table 11.12 Growth of stock exchanges, 1983–1998 ($ billion and %)

Year	*Capitalization world exchange*	*Rate of growth*	*Volume negotiated*	*Rate of growth*	*Growth of world GDP*
1983	3,384		1,228		
1986	6,513	24.4	3,574	42.8	3.9
1989	11,713	21.6	7,468	27.8	3.7
1992	10,922	–2.3	4,783	–13.8	1.8
1995	17,782	17.6	10,216	28.8	3.0
1998	26,520	14.3	22,874	30.8	3.4
1983–98		14.7		21.5	3.1

Sources: W.L. Megginson and J.M. Netter, 'From state to market. A survey of empirical studies on privatization', *Journal of Economic Literature*, 3, 2001, pp. 321–89; A. Maddison, *The World Economy*, 2001, and own adaptation.

industry, which went from being a series of national monopolies to becoming liberalized and deregulated in the United States, Great Britain and other countries that were culturally akin. These changes had strong political roots, and were part of the 'conservative revolution' of the 1980s. Moreover, the transition to the euro, with its insistence on rigorous monetary policies, contributed to centralizing the stock markets. With very low interest rates, investment on the stock market is the main refuge for investors.

The 'new economy' (the economy of enterprises connected with the Internet) has had a less explosive development in Europe than in the United States. The stars in the firmament of the European stock exchanges have been the telecommunications companies, which were privatized during the 1990s, generating an enormous thirst for capital, and at the same time exploiting enormous commercial opportunities. Europe had lagged behind the United States as regards the Internet, but not as regards telephones, particularly mobile telephones, whose growth has been extraordinary. Prospects for future trade that could be created by integrating Internet technologies with mobile telephones underlie the latest cycle of the European economy. The topic falls outside the range of this chapter, but what can be said is that it is a good example of the tension that arises between the efforts of countries to create revenue and the difficulty and uncertainty of the development of new technologies and new investments. In 2001, the year the share prices of all the great European telecommunications enterprises fell, weighed down by debt, no economic historian could help recalling the precedents of the cycles of railways and electricity: with regard to technology, the economy, organization and relations with the state they are so like the development of contemporary technological enterprise.

Integration in the goods markets is proceeding much more slowly. International trade transactions are particularly complex and sensitive, especially from the political point of view. The international trade in services – traditionally of very little importance – has been transformed into a dynamic growth area, thanks to the Internet.

Unlike what happened during the Golden Age, the quarter of a century following the oil crisis showed no significant movement towards convergence of growth rates within Europe or between European countries and those, such as the United States, that were more advanced, as Table 11.13 shows.

Table 11.13 Growth rates of *per capita* GNP, 1973–1998 (%)

Ireland	3.97	Denmark	1.86	Czechoslovakia	0.67
Norway	3.02	United Kingdom	1.79	Switzerland	0.64
Portugal	2.29	Holland	1.76	Hungary	0.59
Austria	2.10	France	1.61	Albania	0.26
Italy	2.07	Germany	1.60	Former Yugoslavia	–0.11
Finland	2.03	Greece	1.56	Bulgaria	–0.57
Spain	1.97	Sweden	1.31	Romania	–0.74
Belgium	1.89	Poland	0.94	Former Soviet Union	–1.75

Source: A. Maddison, *The World Economy*, 2001.

Pro memoria: United States: 1.99. World: 1.33.

Very few European countries – only a minority of the smaller ones – outstripped the economic growth of the United States to any significant degree: Ireland by almost two points, and Norway by little more than one. These are both interesting exceptions, but they are statistically insignificant, as they affect only 1 per cent of the European population. This is a European failure. Within Europe, growth was not inversely proportional to the initial income level. This is for two reasons: on the one hand, and mainly because of it, the countries of the former Soviet area, which were generally poorer than the western countries, have grown much less than the western countries. This is the first great discrepancy. Second, and less obviously, the western countries do not appear to have acted according to any logic that can be related to their previous prosperity. Elements beyond the simple model of convergence – as the policies followed might be – must have been more important. A closer look might even lead us to wonder why the two countries that have stubbornly refused to join the European Union – Norway and Switzerland – stand out for opposite reasons. After Ireland, Norway has had the best growth (greatly helped by North Sea oil), while Switzerland has had the worst (though its enterprises have been very successful). In either case, there is a large gap (about seven-tenths) between the next western country. Excluding Ireland, Norway and Switzerland, what remains is a 'club' of countries with very similar growth rates, between 1.3 per cent and 2.3 per cent. The five countries with the largest populations show even lower variation (less than half a percentage point): 2.07 for Italy and 1.60 for Germany. Few circumstances are more emblematic than those shown by European integration: strong similarity in rates of growth but not convergence, and a loss of vigour in comparison with more advanced areas. The world as a whole has grown at rates below the United States (there has been divergence), below western Europe, but above eastern Europe. This is poor consolation, as well as cause for concern: nothing would have been more cheering than to witness the success of the poorer countries in catching up.

Notes

1 J.M. Keynes, *The Economic Consequences of the Peace*, London, 1919, p. 414.
2 J.M. Keynes, *The Economic Consequences of Mr. Churchill*, London, 1925, p. 480.
3 B. Eichengreen, *Golden Fetters: The Gold standard and the Great Depression 1919–1939*, New York – Oxford, 1992, pp. 158–160.

12 The twentieth century – from break with the past to prosperity (III)

Economic and social policies

Albert Carreras

What distinguished the European economy in the twentieth century was the growing role of the state. Compared with the nineteenth century, which had been dominated by less state involvement, and more by markets, the twentieth century experienced the opposite trend: increasingly controlled markets, and increasing state involvement in the economy. This tension between market and state is the consequence of the serious economic and social problems that continued to exist, and that needed to be solved. In this respect, the twentieth century was a permanent laboratory for political experiment, in which economic and social policies played an exceptional role. We shall now examine them, going from the most radical to the most conservative, the most provocative to the most conciliatory, the most statist to the most liberal.

Property rights policies

Until a little over ten years ago, these would have referred exclusively to socialization policies, but after a few decades of privatization policies it is clear that the historical process can go either way, in the direction of state ownership or of privatization.

After a nineteenth century dominated by the liberal notion of private ownership, deemed sacred and inviolable, the twentieth century opened with the 1917 Bolshevik revolution, which led to private property being abolished, and replaced by socialized property, under the control of *soviets*, or revolutionary councils. The widespread expropriation, without compensation, carried out by the Soviet Union was one of the most important economic events of the twentieth century, indeed of the whole contemporary era; it broke with the convention of respect for property rights, and implemented measures that in the nineteenth century had gone no further than attempts at revolution by anarchists or socialists. Its impact on the entire political spectrum was enormous. Conservative sectors were horrified, and immediately mobilized against the Soviet Union and against the slightest hint of a communist policy, wherever it appeared to arise. The political left became fragmented into those who welcomed the Bolshevik revolution and its immediate or potential consequences, and those who repudiated it, and two practically irreconcilable camps were created. The moderate social democratic left, led by the Menshevik Kerenskij, which had supported the 1917 February revolution, broke away completely from Lenin and the Bolsheviks. The admission of social democrats into the government in post-war Germany, and continual conflicts with the communist parties created after 1920 on the same lines as the Communist Party of the Soviet Union, in practically all the countries of Europe, further dampened the enthusiasm of the moderate reformist sector of the socialist movement for the Russian revolution. Many other socialists were, none the less, attracted by revolution, and everywhere formed communist parties to defend and spread the soviet revolution. The anarchists were also enthusiastic, but soon felt defrauded by the powerful statist element of the Bolsheviks. Widespread Bolshevik expropriation affected the private property not only of Russian people, but also of foreigners who had invested massively in Russia in the decades immediately before the First World War. This caused a diplomatic conflict that would block relations between the Soviet Union and the Western countries for several decades.

Outside the Soviet Union, during the inter-war period, the drive towards socialization or state ownership decreased greatly, but did not disappear. Social democracy defended the right to private property, in combination with state subsidization to guarantee other complementary rights, in order to improve people's standard of living. No further socializations took place, but there were certainly take-overs by the state, or nationalizations. These occurred in a great variety of contexts, but dictatorships with fascist leanings were generally those that were more likely to nationalize. In Spain, in 1924, General Primo de Rivera expropriated (without compensation) all the telephone companies, and three years later the enterprises that refined and distributed oil; the aim was to create a monopoly which would subsequently be auctioned off. In Italy, Mussolini nationalized the great investment bank and all its investments immediately after the crisis in the early 1930s. The 'salvage operation' took place secretly in 1931, but it was, in effect, state expropriation of the central structure of Italian capitalism in the first third of the century. In this case, contrary to what happened in Spain, not only was there no compensation, but the Italian state had to refloat the enterprises saved from bankruptcy with public money. Mussolini created the Institute of Industrial Reconstruction (IRI) to group together all the industrial enterprises that remained in his hands. Hitler's Germany also directly intervened in establishing industrial projects, enforcing the merger of companies and setting detailed targets. In other European countries there were other experiences. These were either at the municipal level or, in cases where public services such as the railways, telegraph or telephone required it, with management based on public ownership. Roosevelt's new-style interventionist policies in the United States encouraged the non-communist left wing to view the possibility of nationalization as a plausible element in governmental programmes. The first case of real significance was the nationalization of the French railways in 1936, during the government of the Popular Front. With all political parties (except liberal and conservative) turning to nationalization, the success of these policies was assured. In the very thick of the Second World War, many enterprises were nationalized because of urgent war requirements. Even without being at war, the dictatorship of General Franco was actively nationalizing and creating new enterprises under state ownership, the latter being concentrated under the National Institute of Industry (INI), created along the lines of the Italian IRI.

After the Second World War, there was an authentic wave of nationalization throughout Europe. In the east European countries occupied by Soviet troops, nationalization was one of the fundamental and distinctive policies of the new order. It was carried out resolutely, and in certain cases excluded only small peasant holdings; the right to private ownership was, in fact, practically abolished. In western Europe, great democracies like Great Britain, France and Italy, during the years of left-wing government, also nationalized some of the large industrial companies and services. Public services, and industrial sectors under more concentrated ownership (the coalmining sector, the iron industry, electricity), passed to the state. In all these cases, political considerations were combined with technical arguments – the need to achieve economies of scale or make public services equally available to all citizens. Ultimately, the wide-ranging objectives of nationalization (producing goods or services at politically acceptable costs, making them available to the population as a whole, returning the country to a state of equilibrium, contributing to full employment, adequately sustaining the welfare of workers, and improving technological potential) were their weakness.

On the formal administrative level, there were two types of nationalized enterprises. Some were transformed into enterprises that operated under private management, but its managers were accountable to parliament. This was the British solution, and it attempted to maintain the best of private management flexibility; at the same time it expressly acknowledged that the enterprise belonged to the nation, which was represented by Parliament, and, in accordance with democratic logic, the government appointed its executive. The other model, which was more usual in France and Italy, was the state enterprise accountable to a ministerial department, often through the intermediation of a ministry, or an *ad hoc* public body. At the other extreme, not infrequently, nationalized enterprises were transformed into state dependencies, the same as any other service or ministry. This was the destiny of the railways and public services generally.

However, there were episodes of nationalization in later periods. In 1962, in Italy, after the socialists had entered the government, the electricity industry was nationalized. The most recent episode took place in 1981, in France, when the left-wing coalition, led by Mitterand, came to government. Enthusiasm for more recent nationalizations did not last long. With the oil crisis, and the new phase of economic stagnation and industrial reconversion, state enterprises proved to be far more rigid than privately owned ones. Since they had to meet several mutually incompatible objectives, results went from bad to worse, and by the early 1980s it had become a simple matter to blame them for the poor state of public accounts. They demanded subsidies and transfers that increased more and more, and were less and less easy to justify. Two years after the French nationalizations, Margaret Thatcher was already starting the first privatization processes in the United Kingdom.

As Table 12.1 shows, in 1979, public enterprise had reached its maximum importance in the economies of the United Kingdom, Germany and Italy. France was to reach this maximum after the nationalization process carried out by the first Mitterand government. Spain, like other western European countries, would also nationalize enterprises running at a loss, until 1983; this was not due to any

Table 12.1 The economic weight of public enterprise in western Europe, 1963–1990 (%)

Country	*1963*	*1979*	*1985*	*1990*
France	19	18	24	18
Germany (FR)	11	13	12	10
Italy	12	20	20	19
United Kingdom	10	19	13	4
Spain	12	10	12	10

Source: P.A. Toninelli, 'Il ruolo dello state nell'economia', P.A. Toninelli (ed.), *Lo sviluppo economico moderno. Dalla rivoluzione industriale alla crisi energetica, 1750–1973*, Venice, 1997, pp. 561–96. The 'economic weight' is the arithmetic mean of the percentages of employment, gross investments and added value.

ideological considerations of the first socialist government, but rather to the fact that numerous industrial enterprises had collapsed after the second oil shock. After that date, only nationalizations associated with the liquidation of mineral or industrial reconversion processes took place; privatization processes were carried out, and this was to accelerate after 1989, when the fall of real socialism made wide-scale privatization possible, and justifiable. In fact, since then, privatization has continued to reverse the long process of state ownership that had developed in Europe, for the most part, between 1917 and 1948 (Table 12.2).

The privatization process meant the creation of large numbers of shareholders in private enterprises. This type of people's capitalism, which was at the heart of

Table 12.2 The process of privatization, 1988–1999

Countries	*Sales ($million)*	*GDP 1998 (%)*	*Countries*	*Sales ($ million)*	*GDP 1998 (%)*
Italy	108,762 e	9.3	Switzerland	5,500 e	1.9
Germany	79,691 e	3.8	Bulgaria	3,199 w	31.7
Great Britain	73,898 e	5.8	Norway	2,276 e	1.5
France	66,755 e	4.6	Slovakia	1,979 w	9.9
Spain	41,446 e	7.5	Romania	1,866 w	6.0
Portugal	21,952 e	20.6	Lithuania	1,536 w	17.1
Holland	18,415 e	4.7	Serbia and Montenegro	922 w	6.3
Hungary	13,999 w	30.7	Estonia	778 w	15.9
Sweden	13,235 e	5.8	Latvia	679 w	11.5
Poland	12,172 w	8.1	Slovenia	521 w	2.7
Finland	9,418 e	7.6	Macedonia	491 w	18.9
Greece	9,144 e	7.4	Ukraine	32 w	0.1
Austria	9,087 e	4.2	Albania	29 w	1.1
Belgium	8,065 e	3.1	Moldavia	27 w	1.5
Russian Federation	7,660 e	2.3	Belarus	11 w	0.0
Denmark	7,648 e	4.3	Bosnia-Herzegovina	. . . w	. . .
Czech Republic	5,633 w	10.9	Ireland	. . . w	. . .

Source: 1988–1999: The Economist, *The Economist Pocket Book*, London, 2000 (e) and 1990–1999: World Bank, *World Development Indicators* (w), always taking the highest figure from the two sources. The first usually corresponds to the western countries and the second to the eastern countries.

the Thatcherite, or Reaganite, project, spread all over the world. Privatization had a very strong impact in Latin America and the Far East. The most radical forms naturally occurred in the Soviet Union, and in the other former communist countries of Europe. Some of them (Hungary and Bulgaria) have launched into general privatization. The relatively insignificant figures for the privatization process, during the transition to capitalism in eastern Europe, will come as a surprise. It is noteworthy that this process has been much slower than expected. However, probably what is more important is that expectations of profit from state property were very low, and in many cases this continues to be so. In contrast to the neighbouring western countries, where privatized enterprises held out exceptional expectations of profit, the economic – and especially legal – uncertainty associated with the fall of real socialism has led to a depression, which has reduced the market value of the assets on offer. This underlines still further, if that is possible, how important it is for legislators to define property rights correctly, and for the definition to be acted upon, over the course of time.

State interventionism

From the start of the First World War, the warring countries actively intervened in the way the economy was run, with the aim of ensuring the best conditions for military success. In general, state interventionism in the twentieth century stemmed from the endeavour to achieve non-economic objectives, normally military or strategic. We can distinguish three main types. First, there is the systematic intervention that we know as planning. Second there is selective intervention, which is what underlies the so-called structural policies. Finally, there is ordinary intervention, aimed at some markets.

Planning policies

Almost at the same time as the Soviet revolution, Europe was also witnessing another revolution of far-reaching significance: economic planning. This developed, in the first place, in German ministerial offices. It was then put forward by the British cabinet, and later abandoned after the First World War. In the Soviet Union, in 1927, the Stalin governments revived it again, raising it to extreme levels. Fascist governments made use of it for various purposes, and during the Second World War it gained renewed legitimacy everywhere. In the immediate post-war period, the British Labour Party brought it back again in attenuated form, and shortly afterwards planning crossed the right-wing rubicon when it was adopted by the Gaullists, who qualified it as 'indicative'. At this point, in the 1960s, the Franco government was to adopt it. Tied to the nationalization processes, it took its final steps with the first socialist government of Mitterand.

While 'nationalization' was a policy linked with left-wing politics – with the exceptions already mentioned – 'planning' had a less ideological tinge to it. It was appreciated by the military of whatever orientation, and by engineers conscious of their managerial abilities; many economists toyed with it for decades, convinced of the need to establish great investment projects and macroeconomic objectives from the top. It lost its attraction when it became evident that planning was inadequate to meet changing requirements and tastes, or respond to technologies that did not lend themselves to centralized management. Planning might be suitable for a world of large-scale technology with a low number of production units, as in ironworks or nuclear power stations, but it did not work at all for technologies that were used and managed by individuals, as in the case of the car or the personal computer.

Development or structural policies

Policies for promoting economic growth in backward areas were unknown before 1945. There had been the antecedent of the case of areas designated for regional development put forward by the Fascist regime. But they spread only after the second post-war period, defended by development economists who argued the need for robust state incentives to create infrastructure that would enable poor regions or countries to acquire the physical capital that was essential for their growth. The development of the ruined Balkan countries after the war was the first case that the founder of 'development economics', Paul Rosenstein-Rodan, put forward. The large organizations of economic co-operation, such as the United Nations Organization for European Economic Co-operation initially, the OECD later, and the World Bank, have backed this type of plan. The Marshall Plan was essentially based on a large-scale co-ordinated development programme for almost the whole of western Europe. In 1950, the creation of the Southern Italian Development Fund (Cassa per il Mezzogiorno) was another notable example of state intervention for promoting regional development. This type of policy, which enjoyed great prestige in the 1950s and 1960s, underlies the structural policies of the European Economic Commission and the European Union. Special financing for less developed regions is based on the principle that, if the infrastructure is created, it will allow these regions to catch up, and reach the same level as the wealthier areas. In other words they will converge.

With the crisis and subsequent industrial restructuring in the second half of the 1970s and first half of the 1980s, structural policies were implemented to finance declining regions and sectors, with the aim of facilitating their conversion to new activities with a more promising future. Today these policies have lost much of their initial credibility as a way of promoting economic development, but since they entail the distribution of very large sums of money they cannot be discarded without political consequences. They are usually linked with specific regions, specific sectors or predefined plans, normally for investment in physical or human capital.

Intervention in the market

Between 1914 and 1918, a wide range of instruments of intervention were deployed. Many of them were limited to a specific market, as was the case with the money markets (when gold convertibility was suspended), the production of armaments (which came under firm state control) or rent (which everywhere was blocked to offset higher costs in subsistence goods). During the war, interventionist measures increased in number, though arbitrarily. With the return to peace, many were abolished, but a number managed to survive. During military mobilization before the Second World War, and during the war itself, there was a return to state intervention. The second post-war period did not see them disappear, and many were continued. Indeed, the trend towards increasing state intervention could be seen almost everywhere. It is always wars that justify intervention, but once it has been carried out, it is much more difficult to do away with it.

The most obvious example of temporary intervention in the market was the ration book. Reduced food supplies during and after the wars led many countries to impose rationing. Ration books entailed intervention in the market for food, drinks, tobacco and fuel, which was conditioned by wartime scarcity and deprivation. In Great Britain, after the Second World War, it was also a powerful mechanism for equalizing real income, and exemplifying inter-class solidarity. On the other hand, in Spain after the civil war, the fact that they were kept until 1953 indicated the failure of the reconstruction policy.

Controlled price fixing by state administrations became routine in many countries: controlled rents, minimum wages, controlled rates for many services are now normal aspects of European life, though it is usually forgotten they were originally provisional and associated with the impact of the First World War, or that of the second post-war period. Often, state regulations have even gone as far as to enforce production and trading methods (for example, shop opening hours), and were questioned only when the Reagan and Thatcher revolution began to systematically challenge them.

Expenditure policies

Before the First World War, there was a budgetary orthodoxy that no politician could question, which was that normal state expenditure had to be met by ordinary tax revenue, and there had to be no deficit. Only extraordinary public expenditure, such as wars, could be financed temporarily by means of heterodox mechanisms, such as debt or the right to issue coin, in order to achieve victory, as rapidly as possible. Subsequently, the excess of extraordinary expenditure had to be financed by reducing ordinary expenditure, or by increasing taxes. Containing the size of state administrations was also part of the liberal orthodoxy, and the state had to limit itself to providing those functions that were in the public interest: representative institutions, representation overseas, the armed forces, law and order, justice, taxation and little else. Economic functions were reduced to promoting and administering public goods and services, such as the postal service, lighting and not much more. This tendency gradually disappeared, opening up to more modern conceptions of public goods and services, but it continued to be strong up to the eve of the Great War.

The twentieth century would be marked by an increase in the functions assumed by the state, and by a corresponding increase in public expenditure, and in the revenue required to fund it. In either case, during the century, the tendency was for public intervention to go from strength to strength, with the state becoming increasingly involved in the economy. However, a closer look at the annual figures, summarized in Table 12.3, allows us to modify this statement. The trend did increase, but the wartime conflicts accelerated the process, necessitating sudden increases in public expenditure, which never returned to the normal pre-war situation once the war was over. After the wars, the state retained numerous functions that it had assumed during the war years. The consequence was the constant drive to increase expenditure. Only in recent years has this been challenged, when conservative parties all over Europe argued against the fiscal voraciousness of the state, and called for adjustments in the use of public resources.

Clearly the new programmes of expenditure, in effect what came to be called the 'welfare state', required more and more revenue. A comparison of Tables 12.3 and 12.4 shows that tax revenue and public expenditure did not always grow at the same rate, which caused indebtedness, one of the most frequent problems for European state finance during the century. We will turn to this question again.

As public spending became increasingly directed towards lasting social objectives, it was inevitable that it would be financed by taxing people's permanent income. The introduction, and spread, of income tax was one of the features common to all the countries of western Europe. The more advanced countries, like Great Britain, had already introduced it in the mid-nineteenth century, but the vast majority did so during the twentieth century, as Table 12.5 shows.

Table 12.3 Public expenditure as a percentage of GDP, 1913–1996

Country	*1913*	*1929*	*1938*	*1950*	*1960*	*1973*	*1982*	*1996*
Germany	17.7	30.6	42.4	30.4	32.5	42.2	49.4	49.0
France	8.9	12.0	23.2	27.6	34.6	38.8	50.7	54.5
Holland	8.2	11.2	21.7	26.8	33.7	45.5	63.7	49.9
Italy	17.2	19.5	29.2	30.3	37.4	50.2	54.7	49.2
United Kingdom	13.3	23.8	28.8	34.2	32.6	41.5	47.4	41.9

Source: A. Maddison, *Monitoring the World Economy*, 1995 and V. Zamagni, *Dalla rivoluzione industriale all'integrazione europea*, Bologna, 1999.

Table 12.4 Tax revenue of public administrations, 1910–1992 (% of GDP)

Country	*1910*	*1930*	*1950*	*1970*	*1992*
Germany	5.1	25.6	29.3	37.5	44.3
Spain [a]	8.3	9.8	7.8	20.4	38.5
France [b]	10.7	20.0	26.7	37.2	45.0
Italy	21.3	21.9	20.9	28.4	41.5
United Kingdom	10.0	21.8	41.3	37.4	35.3

Source: F. Comín, *Historia de la hacienda pública, I, Europe*, Barcelona, 1996.

Notes:
After 1970, this is total non-financial revenue.
[a] Until 1950, only state revenue.
[b] 1910, only state revenue.

Table 12.5 Income tax, 1910–1992 (% of taxation by the state)

Country	*1910*	*1930*	*1950*	*1970*	*1992*
Germany [a]	...	25.0	22.5	36.9	43.6
Spain	...	0.3	1.8	1.1	37.6
France [b]	...	18.5	18.8	17.2	38.4
Italy [b]	16.2	23.1	14.0	17.6	51.6
United Kingdom	11.2	43.6	39.1	37.8	38.4

Source: F. Comín, *Historia*, 1996.

Notes:
[a] From 1970: taxes paid by households on income and on assets. Also for the United Kingdom, 1992.
[b] 1992: Taxes on income and on assets for France and Italy.
... No data.

Social welfare policies – the new public expenditure of the twentieth century – were based on general public subsidy programmes for health care, old age pensions, unemployment benefit and compulsory schooling. The Scandinavians were the pioneers in these policies, but their great supporter was Lord Beveridge, at a time when the United Kingdom was still fighting against Hitler. Social welfare policies dominated the political scene in the second post-war period, and are now on the agenda in almost all European countries (see Table 12.6).

Compulsory education programmes were the earliest of these policies, and by the end of the nineteenth century many western European countries already had them. They were often financed by municipal or regional administrations. The first attempt at health insurance and pension cover on a large scale dates back to the 1880s, in the Germany of Chancellor Bismarck. The scheme gradually spread to the Scandinavian countries, and the small countries of central and eastern Europe. The most significant period for its spread was in the years after the Second World War, when the different left-wing parties had a wider share in government, and when the principle of citizens being guaranteed their minimum requirements had become more widely adopted.

Table 12.6 Expenditure on social welfare (% of state expenditure)

Country	*1910*	*1930*	*1950*	*1970*	*1990*
Germany [a]	5.0	26.0	27.1	20.6	40.9
Spain [b]	7.7	5.1	8.1	14.5	33.1
France [c]	3.4	16.4	8.3	15.0	39.1
Italy c	2.0	6.2	13.5	19.2	31.4
United Kingdom [a]	...	21.7	18.4	20.0	32.1

Source: F. Comín, *Historia*, 1996.

Notes:
[a] Public administrations.
[b] State. From 1990: public administrations.
[c] State. From 1980: public administrations.
... No data.

After the Second World War, welfare policies were developed even more enthusiastically in eastern Europe. A range of measures relating to health care, compulsory education from elementary to secondary school level, old age pensions and unemployment benefits were systematically applied in countries under the influence of real socialism. Indeed, these measures formed the most advanced and most questionable element of the people's democracies. The scale of social protection was extremely high, higher even than in the Scandinavian social democracies. One profound consequence of the generalized development of the welfare state in the north and east of Europe was the more equal distribution of income. When the regimes in the Soviet area fell, the financial basis of their welfare policies also collapsed, and the consequence was a decline in the living standards of the sectors of the population most at risk (health, old age, loss of employment), as well as greater inequality.

Public expenditure on welfare tends to be very rigid, since permanent compromises need to be made, whatever state the economy is in. Taxation, on the other hand, is generally a direct function of economic activity. We are thus faced with a significant paradox: public expenditure is constant, whereas tax revenue is cyclical. Trying to accommodate them both brings about phases of deficit and phases of surplus. Liberal orthodoxy had it that surpluses should be used to amortize debts that had been incurred in extraordinary circumstances, while deficits were not allowed. This orthodoxy was attacked on theoretical, as well as political, grounds during the 1930s crisis, when tax revenue and private income plummeted, and nobody could see any apparent end to the crisis. Economists like Keynes, and politicians of different ideological persuasions, in countries like Great Britain, Sweden, Germany and the United States, resorted to deficit spending as a way of increasing economic prospects. They managed this by financing public works projects, housing programmes, unemployment benefit schemes, or rearmament. In each case they injected money into the economy by increasing public demand. As Keynes argued, these policies were justified when the balance of aggregate supply and demand fell below full occupation. The lower this balance, the more essential it was to increase it by injecting state money.

The success of these policies in finding a solution to the economic crisis – as against the failure of those who stuck to the orthodox balance of payments principle – brought them great credit. These were known as Keynesian policies, after the British economist who supported them on theoretical grounds in his many writings, and in particular in his great work *The General Theory of Employment, Interest and Money*. The Second World War reinforced Keynesian ideas, and they permeated political and economic life in the post-war period.

During the barely three decades between the end of the war and the start of the oil crisis, many state expenditure policies were influenced by Keynesianism. A deficit in the national accounts ceased to be a heterodox practice, and was generally accepted, as long as it was justified. The continuing high growth rates meant that the rigorous balance of accounts criteria could be eased to some extent and, furthermore, the fact that increased spending was mainly on social objectives made it politically acceptable. In the short term, Keynesianism was put into effect in the British 'stop–go' policies whereby public expenditure was stopped when growth in the private sector increased, and public expenditure was stepped up when the private sector entered a phase of recession. The more the total revenue and expenditure of the economy were under public sector management, the more efficient was this policy of balancing the business cycle.

When the Golden Age ended, all the Keynesian policies entered a crisis. Keynes's remedies originated in the world of the Depression, and could not have the same importance in a world of full employment. In the Europe of the 1970s, the containment of public expenditure had recessive effects, but increasing it did not have expansive effects. Deficit public expenditure had lost its usefulness in reactivating the economy. It was alleged that businesspeople anticipated what measures the state would take, which meant that those measures lost their effectiveness. The critics of Keynesianism were known as monetarists, since they based most of their arguments on a reinterpretation of the macroeconomic role of money. Their points of view have continued to be influential in the last fifteen years or so. Once again, the relevance of fiscal orthodoxy has returned to favour, and stress has been laid on the need to reduce public expenditure, as well as taxation.

Trade policies

During the entire nineteenth century, the economic policies *par excellence* were trade policies. During the twentieth century there was a much broader range of instruments available, but trade policy was never abandoned. Indeed, all the other policies could be interpreted in terms of trade policy, or at least they all affect trade policy.

Not surprisingly, the First World War led to protectionism being introduced on a wide scale in all national policies. Implicit in the declaration of war was the prohibition of trade with the enemy, and the neutral countries took advantage by conducting a great deal of trade during the war. Submarine warfare worsened the barriers between countries of the same bloc (the allied bloc), since freight and insurance costs increased to exorbitant levels. All seaborne trade – almost all international trade – experienced higher costs, and in many cases they were prohibitive.

With the return to normality, the interests that had been created everywhere, protected from the exceptional circumstances of the war, manifested an absolute need for customs barriers: the years between 1919 and 1921 saw an abrupt trend towards generalized protectionism. Only when economic activity recovered and there was a return to a certain degree of normality could there be any weakening of the pressure from protectionism. However, the seed of protectionism was planted everywhere, and the whole decade was taken up with debate about the appropriate level of protection. The first systematic studies on the comparative level of protectionism stem from those years, carried out under the auspices of the League of Nations. The *coup de grâce* was delivered by the US Congress, when it approved a heavy increase in customs protection with the so-called Smoot-Hawley tariff. The effect was far-reaching. Whereas in 1921 the United States had closed the door to immigration, in 1929 it announced the intention of closing its market. Any hope of exporting to the United States, which was of crucial importance to the economies of half the world, vanished. There was an escalation of reprisals, and international trade was destroyed in the space of a few years. Numerous studies have pointed out that the severity and universality of the crisis, which started in 1929, was mainly due to the Smoot-Hawley customs tariff.

The 1930s were marked by increasingly strict closure to trade. In some countries, the phenomenon even led to autarkic policies being drawn up, or foreign trade being abandoned. At a time when there was still only one model of an autarkic country – the Soviet Union – the Great War had made autarkic positions feasible, given that many countries were forced to manage with very little foreign trade. This was especially so in the case of Germany, and Hitler himself strongly advocated a return to the policy of total closure to trade. Dictatorships of all types, especially fascist ones, favoured the adoption of autarkic policies. They matched well with nationalist ideals, plans for rearmament and preparation for war. Less extremist than autarky, in much of the world the protectionist reaction favoured the implementation of new measures for state intervention in foreign trade. There was an increase in bilateral 'clearing' agreements for the foreign balance of payments, import quotas, importation permits and licences, cash payments, and no end of mechanisms that were specially created in a situation of mutual suspicion and mistrust, and which tended towards the generalization of barter.

Agreements for the period after the Second World War, and more particularly the Bretton Woods agreements of July 1944, arose out of the deep and general conviction that obstacles to trade were bad for the whole world, and that a new economic and international order should guarantee free trade. The Havana declaration of 1948, based on greater liberalization of exchanges, was to become the cornerstone of the new framework regulating international trade. Since there was an awareness of the difficulty of moving from a highly protected trade regime to one of free trade, the agreements that were prepared set out detailed conditions for the gradual liberalization of international trade. The difficulty of finalizing them was so great that one of the pillars of the Bretton Woods agreements – the creation of an International Trade Organization – was a failure. In its place, it was agreed that this function should be entrusted to a permanent office of inter-ministerial conferences for the reduction of tariffs and the liberalization of trade. The agreement was known by its abbreviation GATT (General Agreement on Tariffs and Trade), and it did not become an international organization as such until fifty years later, in 1995, with the name of World Trade Organization (WTO). The conferences, and all the negotiations associated with them, were known as rounds, since they usually decided on relatively modest liberalization measures, but they were always open to new and more significant accords. The most famous – the Kennedy round, in the 1960s – smoothed the progress of customs tariff reduction and freedom of trade for tens of thousands of commercial transactions worldwide. But more important in quantitative terms (the amount of trade affected by liberalization) and in qualitative terms (its different implications) was the Uruguay round, which culminated in the creation of the WTO. The body of regulations had become so great that international negotiations could be measured by the number of transactions, or tariff conditions, that were modified. The complexity of the negotiations, and agreements, ultimately led to language itself becoming confused; in order to reconcile the founding aims of liberalization with national resistance, the mere annulment of a trade prohibition, or the elimination of a non-tariff trade barrier, ended up by being called 'trade liberalization' (which implies that a product can be freely traded). So that when a product, instead of being prohibited in trade between two countries, was permitted, with a customs tariff of 100 per cent, this was considered – and still is considered – a case of 'liberalization'. This is a true contradiction in terms of the late nineteenth century and early twentieth century, when the only barrier to trade was the tariff, and trade liberalization consisted in merely reducing customs duties.

The European Economic Community arose in this context of tariff reductions, resentfully negotiated one by one. The future Community members accepted the idea that it was worth their while to liberalize their trade, since they were trading more and more with each other. The successes achieved by sitting down at the same table as the enemies from two world wars gave enormous significance and popularity to the EEC. So much so that the free trade areas had to organize their own specific regional agreements to show their capacity for reaction. Even the countries of eastern Europe called the Comecon a trading community among equals. The EEC and EFTA did not mean the end of trade policies, quite the contrary. Both organizations, and especially the EEC, devoted enormous effort to outlining and applying their common trade policy (and still do). The EEC has three great areas of development. First there are the relations with the aspiring member countries, at the end of which they may be accepted, and an agenda drawn up for their adjustment to the community tariff. Second, there are the relations with poor countries, which are linked with aid policies and overlap with them. Third, and more important, there is the normal foreign trade policy, which plays the European Union against the United States, Japan and the economies of the Far East, or the great Asian and Latin American countries.

The greatest success of the EEC was to integrate the EFTA countries stage by stage, with the exception of Norway and Switzerland, who have preferred to remain on the outside. Between the creation of the EEC, in 1957, and the entry of Great Britain, Ireland and Denmark, in January 1973, fifteen very important years passed. Almost the same amount of time was to pass until Spain and Portugal joined, in January 1986, and a further nine years until Austria, Finland and Sweden joined, in 1995 (not forgetting Greece in 1980). The good result, as regards the EU 'club' as a whole, has to be interpreted as the triumph of the centrality of its trade policy, likewise its opening up to the eastern European countries. Being in the 'club' means benefiting from a combination of structural policies (essentially, aid for the less developed areas, and for agriculture) and trade policies. Permanent negotiations on the admission of new members mean that trade barriers are undergoing constant selective modification.

Stabilization policies

By stabilization policies we mean those that aim to reduce variability in exchange rates and prices. Both are intimately connected, and stabilization measures entail acting simultaneously on exchange rates, and on the general price level. Stabilization, or monetary, policies are the most classical and conservative of all policies, which is why they are always in the eye of the cyclone. We do not consider them as being at the bottom of the table of economic and social policies – be they the most radical or the most conservative – since international co-operation, and wage bargaining, demand the very highest skill in managing international and national economic policies respectively. There have always been stabilization policies. During the period when the gold standard was in force, stabilization policies were automatic, or almost. Without the gold standard, governments had to commit themselves more openly to achieve the same results.

The First World War meant the immediate abandonment of the gold standard, almost all over the world. Central banks announced they would no longer convert notes into gold, neither their own nor those of other countries. Abandoning convertibility was an expedient that had been used on numerous occasions, especially on the outbreak of a war. All countries, whether at war or not, left the gold standard, even if it was only to control, with an iron fist, the gold in circulation and international transactions of the precious metal. Indeed, without the automatic control over monetary reserves exercised by the gold standard, governments could request the monetary authorities to issue further fiduciary money, guaranteed not by gold but by the signature of the governor of the central bank, guaranteeing that the notes would be accepted under obligation to pay debts, and in return for the sale of goods and services. The suspension of convertibility everywhere led to an increase in monetary reserves that was higher than from trade transactions, and led to inflation. In exchange, governments obtained the right to issue money, and were freed from the servitude of the balance of payments orthodoxy: they could spend more than they produced, but not without consequences. As Table 12.7 shows, after a period of contained inflation at the beginning of the century, with the exit from the gold standard there were much higher levels of inflation throughout Europe. The countries that had been the strictest as regards containing prices were the neutral ones, while among those that had been at war the most rigorous was Great Britain.

With the return to normality, there also came a return to the gold standard. We have already seen in Chapter 11, what a painful process it was. The 1920s were dominated by the slowness of this process, and by the instability of the system that resulted from it. Deflations were frequent. In short, the return of the large countries was completed by 1927 (with Italy), but by 1931 some of the largest countries (Great Britain) had again left the gold standard. In the 1930s, the great decision, which was connected with abandoning the gold standard, was not whether to adopt inflationist policies as after 1914, but to decide whether to devalue or not. The gold standard prevented devaluation. Having abandoned it, governments aspired to devalue their currencies, to recover their competitive edge in international markets, and to limit the volume of imports. There seemed to be no end to the vicious circle of competitive devaluations, defined as the policy of beggar-my-neighbour. The countries that most successfully resisted devaluation, such as Nazi Germany, had to be exceedingly rigorous in their policies of direct intervention in foreign transactions. The countries that devalued most were those least concerned to implement cumbersome controls on foreign trade. Currently, and among the convincing arguments of Eichengreen[1], there is broad agreement over the logic of the stabilization policies applied in the 1930s. Quite simply, and as

Table 12.7 Inflation in Europe, 1913–1998 (cumulative annual growth rates of consumer prices, as %)

Country	*1900–1913*	*1913–1920*	*1920–1929*	*1929–1938*	*1938–1950*	*1950–1973*	*1973–1983*	*1983–1993*	*1994–1998*
Austria	1.8	92.7 [a]	*	–0.7	18.1	4.6	6.0	3.1	1.6
Belgium	0.9	20.0 [b]	7.9 [b]	–0.7	11.5	2.9	8.1	3.1	1.5
Denmark	0.6	15.3	–4.5	0.7	5.1	4.8	10.7	3.7	2.0
Finland	1.1	37.2	2.5	–1.4	22.3	5.6	10.5	4.6	1.0
France	0.9	20.5	5.5	2.9	28.1	5.0	11.2	3.7	1.4
Germany	1.3	39.3	*	–2.2	3.8	2.7	4.9	2.4	1.5
Greece	. . .	23.8 [a]	21.0	1.4	60.6	3.7	18.8	17.5	6.8
Ireland	. . .	8.1 [c]	–0.8 [c]	–0.1	5.3	4.3	15.7	3.8	2.0
Italy	1.4	24.4	2.4	–0.2	38.4	3.9	16.7	6.4	3.1
Holland	1.1	9.9	–3.0	–2.1	7.4	4.1	6.5	1.8	2.0
Norway	1.4	17.4	–6.4	0.4	4.3	4.8	9.7	5.1	2.1
Portugal	0.8	28.4	16.9	–1.6	5.4	2.9	24.2	13.1	3.1
United Kingdom	0.9	13.9	–3.8	–0.6	5.3	4.6	13.5	5.2	3.1
Spain	–0.5	9.8	0.4	0.0 [d]	13.2 [d]	4.6	16.4	6.9	3.0
Sweden	1.1	15.5	–5.0	–0.2a	4.1a	4.7	10.2	6.4	0.8
Switzerland	1.8	12.5	–5.7	–1.8a	4.0a	3.0	4.3	3.2	. . .

Sources: A. Maddison, 'Economic Policy and Performance in Europe, 1913–1970', in C.M. Cipolla (ed.), *The Fontana Economic History of Europe. The Twentieth Century*, Glasgow, vol. 2, 1976, pp. 442–508; A. Maddison, *Dynamic Forces in Capitalist Development*, Oxford, 1991; A. Maddison, *Monitoring the World Economy*, 1995; A. Maddison, *The World Economy*, 2001; 1994–1998, United Nations Economic Commission for Europe, *Economic Survey of Europe*, 1, 2001, p. 253. For Greece, 1900–1950 and for Ireland, 1920–1950, B.R. Mitchell (ed.), *European Historical Statistics, 1750–1988*, New York, 1992. For Portugal, 1900–1993, N. Valério (ed.), *Estatísticas Históricas Portuguesas*, Lisbon, 2001. For Spain, 1900–1936, E. Ballesteros, 'Una estimación del coste de la vida en España, 1861–1932', in *Revista de Historia Económica*, 2, 1997, pp. 363–95; 1936–1950, J. Maluquer de Motes, 'Precios, salarios y beneficios', in A. Carreras (ed.), *Estadísticas Históricas de España. Siglos XIX–XX*, Madrid, 1989, pp. 495–532 (but this is for wholesale prices)

Notes:

[a] 1914–20.

[b] 1913–21 and 1921–29.

[c] 1914–22 and 1922–29.

[d] 1929–36 and 1936–50.

* Hyperinflation makes prices non-comparable.

. . . No data.

his most famous book attempted to underline, the gold standard was no more than 'golden fetters' on the countries that adopted it. The sooner they liberated themselves from those fetters, and recovered their freedom of action, in monetary, trade and fiscal matters, the better. With the hindsight afforded by economic history, and more than half a century of experience, Eichengreen re-established the soundness of Keynes's diagnosis of what happened in the 1930s, and what needed to be done. Numerous governments discovered it for themselves, and faced the crisis better than others which were more anchored to dogmatism and past remedies. In any case, in the 1930s the new gold standard entered an apparently definitive crisis.

The 1930s saw the last period of generalized inflation. During the Second World War there were no stabilization policies. In all countries, as during the First World War, every effort was aimed at winning the war, no other consideration being allowed to hinder the path to victory. It was towards the end, when those who already felt they had won, namely the Allies, began to concern themselves about the stability of the new system. In Chapter 11, we have already outlined the main economic characteristics of those years. The concern for monetary stability bore its fruits, and prevented a repetition of the hyper-inflation of the period after the First World War. In the years after the Second World War there was greater recourse to rationing and there were strict controls over the issue of money instead. Some countries that tended towards inflationist policies, like Italy and France, were pressed into abandoning them by the United States, and Marshall Aid was a powerful incentive in this respect.

With the end of post-war reconstruction, around 1950, a long period of monetary stability began. As Table 12.7 shows, between 1950 and 1973, inflation rates were modest – between a little under 3 per cent and a little over 5 per cent – and very similar throughout western Europe. No country aspired to inflation that was so low as to lead the economy into a depression, but all the monetary authorities kept prices under strict surveillance. Only towards the end of the period were there any symptoms of inflationary pressure escaping the control of the central banks.

With the suspension of the dollar's gold convertibility and the oil crises, strong redistribution conflicts all over Europe led to loss of control over inflation. Practically everywhere experienced a sharp rise to double-figure rates. Only the nucleus of countries that followed the FRG in its commitment to monetary stability – Austria, Switzerland, Belgium and Holland – would manage to keep inflation down to single figures. The other countries were to experience several years of runaway inflation, years which later would only go to show that inflation served no purpose at all. The return to moderate inflation rates – in other words, the recovery of the credibility of stabilization policies – would be slow. In western Europe, it would be very much related to the authority of the prudent and independent monetary policy of the German Federal Bank (the Bundesbank). Plans for European monetary integration would also depend on the high regard for the stability of exchange rates and prices.

The decade after the second oil crisis was to witness a return to the inflation of the Golden Age, but without its being so widespread or homogeneous. Some countries in the south of Europe would lag behind in containing their prices. Only the imminence of complete European monetary integration would be an effective stimulus for motivating governments, and gaining the consensus of the people.

Co-operation policies

The most delicate of all economic and social policies have been left until last: co-operation policies. A distinction between national and international co-operation policies needs to be drawn. National co-operation policies are concerned with arbitration between employers and unions, in order to reach agreement on wages. The early decades of the century were dominated by serious conflict in the field of wage bargaining. The class struggle was the norm for the two opposing sides: the trade unions and the employers' organizations. The more bitter the confrontation, the greater chance there was of revolutionary outbreaks, or fascist *coups*. Both sides tried to resolve the conflict with the victory of one of the sides and/or by banning the conflict itself. Unfortunately, in the inter-war period, there was an abundance of solutions of this type. In this respect, the lessons of history were forceful, and after the Second World War they were taken up by the leaders of the western countries, who realized that the deepening of the conflict over the distribution of capital and labour was very costly, indeed unsustainable.

The experience of strong growth during the Golden Age made it possible to identify the relationship between models of labour relations and the aggregate economic results. It was seen that fragmentation of union representation (and of employers) usually resulted in greater disputes over labour and wages. Strikes were more frequent, nominal salaries generally increased more, the government had to guarantee liquidity for enterprises, and the economy ended by becoming ensnared in a vicious circle of inflation that brought economic stagnation. Countries of the Latin areas and the British Isles suffered the consequences of this model. In these cases, the state was called upon to bring order into wage bargaining. This was the origin of the incomes policies decided centrally by finance ministries, with the two sides more or less agreeing, and involving government leaders in fixing people's net income levels. All the fiscal reforms carried out in Europe, both great and small, had this aim.

On the other hand, those countries that had forms of unified and centralized trade union representation and negotiation, with wide-ranging organizations, normally reached more responsible and sustainable agreements, which brought about virtuous cycles of growth. In general, it was the Scandinavian and Germanic countries that benefited from these systems – often called 'neo-corporatist' since they reproduce (in a strictly democratic context) some of the principles of fascist-style corporatism and in particular recognize the centrality of economic interests, and the imperative national need to reach agreement between the two sides. In effect, in the countries of central, western and northern Europe, and since the Second World War, the formula of negotiating between management and trade unions, with a variable degree of government participation, has been successful. Results have been excellent, with labour conflicts drastically reduced, improvements in income distribution, and greater capacity for adapting to fluctuations in the international economy.

International co-operation policies are the more sophisticated ones. They require more time, involve greater political risk in the short term, but have proved to be extremely effective when it comes to contributing to stabilizing uncertain situations. It is also true that their opposite – international confrontation policies – are extremely powerful. Throughout the whole century, the most frequent image in the mass media has been that of the rulers of the great countries gathered somewhere in the world to discuss ways of resolving their differences. The period between the two wars saw a great increase in these multilateral meetings, not to mention the bilateral meetings, often under the auspices of the League of Nations. International conferences became a kind of meeting place for mobilizing politicians with governmental responsibilities, aided by an important national and international executive, who would do little else but perfect himself in the course of time. As the Second World War drew to a close, the meetings became more and more frequent with a view to preparing the new world order. The international meetings, among which the most famous was Bretton Woods, in July 1944, as we have already seen, culminated in the creation of the United Nations, and with the subsequent deployment of all the international organizations under the United Nations, including the IBRD, the IMF and GATT. The launch of the Marshall Plan reproduced the mechanism on a western European scale. This was a crucial experience, since it formed the basis of co-operation between the leaders and officials of countries that had been enemies, and that were now working side by side under the stimulus of the leadership and support of the United States. The hectic activity of mapping out wider multinational spaces, and which produced among other things the European Office for Economic Co-operation (the future OECD), then the European Payments Union, and the ECSC, in the end created confidence and stable co-operation at the European level. The creation of the EEC was a decisive step, since it gave continuity to the efforts made by the parties of each country involved, as well as to the results they had achieved since the start of the European Recovery Programme (ERP or Marshall Plan). These efforts and results could be measured in terms of growth rates, investment rates, increases in real wages, and finally in terms of greater prosperity and security. According to Milward, the allegiance that leaders could obtain from their electorate that heralded phases of great political stability in numerous European countries has been the main benefit of the Marshall Plan, and of the historic phase that started in Europe[2].

When the international political and economic scene began to deteriorate, as a consequence of the OPEC challenge to the large economically advanced countries and chief oil importers, the structure of international co-operation proved to be inadequate. Neither the great organizations of co-operation such as the World Bank, the International Monetary Fund, the Organization for Economic Co-operation and Development nor international institutions like the United Nations could sufficiently articulate the response of the more advanced countries. It is within this context that the G-7 meetings between the leaders of the most developed countries began, in an attempt to reach agreement that demanded great co-ordination, confidence and commitment.

The whole history of European integration is an extreme case of the significance of international co-operation policies. As we have already seen, the efforts at co-operation that started with the creation of the EEC continued with successive enlargements, and their role extended to all aspects of trade integration with the signing of the Single Europe Act in 1987. With the signing of the Maastricht Treaty, in 1991, the transformation of the European Community into the European Union, and the agenda for monetary integration, were formulated. These negotiating processes were exceedingly complex, but once they were completed they were able to bestow great stability on the Community economies, and offer very clear prospects to those who were still not members of the European Union. In a world of prevailing instability and uncertainty, anything that can be achieved in terms of stability and reduction of risk is a significant contribution to the general well-being.

Notes

1 B. Eichengreen, *Golden Fetters: The Gold standard and the Great Depression 1919–1939*, New York – Oxford, 1992.
2 A.S. Milward, *The Reconstruction of Western Europe 1945–1951*, London, 1984, p. 423.

Bibliography

1 The economy of the fifteenth century: preconditions for European expansion

Bergier, J.F., *Una storia del sale*, Marsilio, Venice, 1982.

Braudel, F., *Civiltà e imperi del Mediterraneo nell'età di Filippo II*, Einaudi, Turin, 1963.

Braudel, F., *Civiltà materiale, economia e capitalismo, secoli XV–XVIII*, vol. I: Le strutture del quotidiano; vol. II: I giochi dello scambio; vol. III: I tempi del mondo, Einaudi, Turin, 1981–82.

Cameron, R., *Storia economica del mondo. Dalla preistoria ad oggi*, il Mulino, Bologna, 1993.

Carpenter, E., 'Autour de la peste noir. Famines et epidemies dans l'histoire du XIV siècle', *Annales E.S.C.*, XVII, 1962.

Cattini, M., *Introduzione alla storia economica moderna e contemporanea del mondo, secoli XV–XX*, Bocconi University, Milan, 2000.

Cipolla, C.M., *Allegro ma non troppo*, il Mulino, Bologna, 1988.

Cipolla, C.M., *Tra due culture. Introduzione alla Storia economica*, il Mulino, Bologna, 1988.

Cipolla, C.M., *Le tre rivoluzioni e altri saggi di storia economica*, il Mulino, Bologna, 1989.

Cipolla, C.M., *Storia economica dell'età preindustriale*, il Mulino, Bologna, 1990.

Crosby, A.W., *Lo scambio colombiano. Conseguenze biologiche e culturali del 1492*, Einaudi, Turin, 1992.

Day, J., *The Medieval Market Economy*, Oxford University Press, Oxford, 1987.

De Rosa, L. and Di Vittorio, A., *Dall'economia feudale all'economia precapitalistica*, D'Anna, Messina and Florence, 1975.

De Rosa, L. and Di Vittorio, A., *L'espansione economica europea, secoli XV–XX*, *Storia universale*, ed. E. Pontieri, Vallardi, Milan, 1977.

Felloni, G., *Moneta, credito e banche in Europa. Un millennio di storia*, Faculty of Economics, Genoa, 1977.

Felloni, G., *Profilo di storia economica dell'Europa dal Medioevo all'età contemporanea*, Giappichelli, Turin, 1997.

Heers, J., *L'Occidente nel XIV e nel XV secolo*, *Mursia*, Milan, 1973.

Kulischer, J.M., *Storia economica del Medio Evo e dell'epoca moderna*, 2 vols, Sansoni, Florence, 1964.

Léon, P., *Storia economica e sociale del mondo, vol. I: Le origini dell'età moderna, 1300–1580*, Laterza, Rome and Bari, 1981.

Lopez, R., *La nascita dell'Europa, secoli V–XIV*, Einaudi, Turin, 1966.

Lopez, R., *La rivoluzione commerciale del Medioevo*, Einaudi, Turin, 1971.

Luzzatto, G., *Storia economica dell'età moderna e contemporanea*, Part I: *L'età moderna*, Cedam, Padua, 1955.

Malanima, P., *Economia preindustriale. Mille anni: dal IX al XVIII secolo*, B. Mondadori, Milan, 1995.

Mauro, F., *L'Europa del XVI secolo. Aspetti economici*, Mursia, Milan, 1974.
Mercanti e viaggiatori per le vie del mondo, ed. G. Motta, F. Angeli, Milan, 2000.
Mokyr, J., *La leva della ricchezza. Creatività tecnologica e progresso economico*, il Mulino, Bologna, 1990.
Palermo, L., *Sviluppo economico e società preindustriali*, Viella, Rome, 1997.
Parry, J.H., *Le grandi scoperte geografiche*, A. Mondadori, Milan, 1991.
Smil, V., *Storia dell'energia*, il Mulino, Bologna, 2000.
Storia d'Europa, vol. III: *Il Medioevo, secoli V–XV*, ed. G. Ortalli, Einaudi, Turin, 1994.
Storia d'Europa, vol. IV: *L'età moderna*, ed. M. Aymard, Einaudi, Turin, 1995.
Storia dell'economia mondiale, vol. I: *Permanenze e mutamenti dall'antichità al Medioevo*, ed. V. Castronovo, Laterza, Rome and Bari, 1996.
Storia dell'economia mondiale, vol. II: *Dalle scoperte geografiche alla crescita degli scambi*, ed. V. Castronovo, Laterza, Rome and Bari, 1996.
Storia economica Cambridge, vols. I–IV, Einaudi, Turin, 1975–82.
Storia economica d'Europa, ed. C.M. Cipolla, vol. I: *Il Medioevo*, Utet, Turin, 1979.
Tangheroni, M., *Commercio e navigazione nel Medioevo*, Laterza, Rome and Bari, 1996.
Verlinden, C., *Le origini della civiltà atlantica*, Avanzino & Torraca, Rome, 1968.

2 European expansion in the sixteenth century

Braudel, F., *Civiltà e imperi del Mediterraneo nell'età di Filippo II*, Einaudi, Turin, 1963.
Braudel, F., *Civiltà materiale, economia e capitalismo, secoli XV–XVIII*, vol. I: *Le strutture del quotidiano*; *vol. II: I giochi dello scambio*; vol. III: *I tempi del mondo*, Einaudi, Turin, 1981–82.
Braudel, F., *Il secondo Rinascimento. Due secoli e tre Italie*, Einaudi, Turin, 1986.
Cameron, R., *Storia economica del mondo. Dalla preistoria ad oggi*, il Mulino, Bologna, 1993.
Cattini, M., *Introduzione alla storia economica moderna e contemporanea del mondo, secoli XV–XX*, Bocconi University, Milan, 2000.
Cipolla, C.M., *Saggi di storia economica e sociale*, il Mulino, Bologna, 1988.
Cipolla, C.M., *Tra due culture. Introduzione alla storia economica*, il Mulino, Bologna, 1988.
Cipolla, C.M., *Tecnica, società e cultura. Alle origini della supremazia tecnologica dell'Europa*, il Mulino, Bologna, 1989.
Cipolla, C.M., *Storia economica dell'età preindustriale*, il Mulino, Bologna, 1990.
Cipolla, C.M., *Conquistadores, pirati, mercatanti. La saga dell'argento spagnuolo*, il Mulino, Bologna, 1996.
De Rosa, L. and Di Vittorio, A., *Dall'economia feudale all'economia precapitalistica*, D'Anna, Messina and Florence, 1975.
De Rosa L. and Di Vittorio, A., *L'espansione economica europea, secoli XV–XX*, in *Storia universale*, ed. E. Pontieri, Vallardi, Milan, 1977.
Doria, G., *Nobiltà e investimenti a Genova in età moderna*, Institute of Economic History, Genoa, 1995.
Felloni, G., *Moneta, credito e banche in Europa. Un millennio di storia*, Faculty of Economics, Genoa, 1977.
Felloni, G., *Profilo di storia economica dell'Europa dal Medioevo all'età contemporanea*, Giappichelli, Turin, 1997.
Koenigsberger, H.G., Mosse, G.L. and Bowler, G.Q., *L'Europa del Cinquecento*, Laterza, Rome and Bari, 1999.
Kulischer, J.M., *Storia economica del Medio Evo e dell'epoca moderna*, 2 vols, Sansoni, Florence, 1964.
Léon, P., *Storia economica e sociale del mondo*, vol. I: *Le origini dell'Età moderna, 1300–1580*, Laterza, Rome and Bari, 1981.
Luzzatto, G., *Storia economica dell'età moderna e contemporanea*, Part I: *L'Età moderna*, Cedam, Padua, 1955.

Malanima, P., *Economia preindustriale. Mille anni: dal IX al XVIII secolo*, B. Mondadori, Milan, 1995.
Mokyr, J., *La leva della ricchezza. Creatività tecnologica e progresso economico*, il Mulino, Bologna, 1990.
Pacioli, L., *Summa de Arithmetica, Geometria, Proportioni et Proportionalità*, Paganino de' Paganini, Venice, 1494.
Palermo, L., *Sviluppo economico e società preindustriali*, Viella, Rome, 1997.
Parker, G., *Un solo re, un solo impero. Filippo II di Spagna*, il Mulino, Bologna, 1985.
Parry, J.H., *Le grandi scoperte geografiche*, A. Mondadori, Milan, 1991.
Smil, V., *Storia dell'energia*, il Mulino, Bologna, 2000.
Storia dell'economia mondiale, vol. II: *Dalle scoperte geografiche alla crescita degli scambi*, ed. V. Castronovo, Laterza, Rome and Bari, 1996.
Storia d'Europa, vol. IV: *L'età moderna*, ed. M. Aymard, Einaudi, Turin, 1995.
Storia economica Cambridge, vols. I–IV, Einaudi, Turin, 1975–82.

3 European expansion in the seventeenth century

General works:

Borelli, G., *Temi e problemi di storia economica europea*, Libreria Universitaria, Verona, 1994.
Braudel, F., *Capitalismo e civiltà materiale*, Einaudi, Turin, 1977.
Braudel, F., *La dinamica del capitalismo*, il Mulino, Bologna, 1981.
Braudel, F., *Espansione europea e capitalismo*, il Mulino, Bologna, 1999.
Cipolla, C.M., *Storia economica dell'Europa preindustriale*, il Mulino, Bologna, 1981.
De Vries, J., *The Economy of Europe in an Age of Crisis, 1500–1750*, Cambridge University Press, Cambridge, 1976.
Felloni, G., *Profilo di storia economica dell'Europa*, Giappichelli, Turin, 1997.
Huppert, G., *Storia sociale dell'Europa nella prima età moderna*, il Mulino, Bologna, 1990.
Léon, P., *Storia economica e sociale del mondo*, Laterza, Rome and Bari, 1981.
Livet, G. and Mousnier, R., *Storia d'Europa. Dallo Stato assoluto all'Illuminismo*, Laterza, Bari, 1982.
Morineau, M. *Pour une histoire economique vraie*, Presses Universitaires de Lille, Lille, 1985
North, D.C., *Istituzioni, cambiamento istituzionale, evoluzione dell'economia*, il Mulino, Bologna, 1994.
Tenenti, A., *L'età moderna*, il Mulino, Bologna, 1980.
Tilly, C., *La formazione degli stati nazionali nell'Europa occidentale*, il Mulino, Bologna, 1984.
Wallerstein, I., *II sistema mondiale dell'economia moderna*, Bologna, 1982.

Demography:

Cipolla, C.M., *Cristofano e la peste*, il Mulino, Bologna, 1981.
Cipolla, C.M., *Uomini, tecniche, economia*, Feltrinelli, Milan, 1990.
Flinn, M.W., *Il sistema demografico europeo*, il Mulino, Bologna, 1983.
Guillaume, P. and Poussou, J.P., *Démographie historique*, Colin, Paris, 1970.

Agriculture:

Bouchard, G., *Le Village immobile*, Plon, Paris, 1972.
De Moor, M., Shaw-Taylor, L. and Warde, P., *The Management of Common Land in North West Europe, c. 1500–1850*, Brepols, Turnhout, 2002.
Hoppenbrouwers, P. and Van Zanden, J.L., *Peasants into Farmers? The Transformation of Rural Economy and Society in the Low Countries, Middle Ages – Nineteenth Century*, Brepols, Turnhout, 2001.
Le Roy Ladurie, E. and Morineau, M., *Paysannerie et croissance*, PUF, Presses Universitaires de France, Paris, 1977

Le Roy Ladurie, E., *I contadini di Linguadoca*, Laterza, Bari, 1984.
Overton, M., *Agricultural Revolution in England. The Transformation of the Agrarian Economy 1500–1850*, Cambridge Universiyt Press, Cambridge, 1996
Poni, C., *Fossi e cavedagne benedicon le campagne*, il Mulino, Bologna, 1982.
Slicher Van Bath, B.H., *Storia agraria dell'Europa occidentale*, 500–1850, Einaudi, Turin, 1972.
Thoen, E. and Van Molle, L., *Rural History in the North Sea area. An Overview of Recent Research, Middle Ages – beginning of the Twentieth Century*, Amsterdam, 2003.
Van Bavel, B. and Thoen, E., *Land Productivity and Agro-system in the North Sea Area, Middle Ages – Twentieth Century*, Amsterdam, 1999

Cities, manufacturing, commerce and finance:

Cipolla, C.M., *Il governo della moneta a Firenze e a Milano nei secoli XIV–XVI*, il Mulino, Bologna, 1990.
Guenzi, A., Massa, P. and Piola Caselli, F. (eds), *Guilds, Markets and Work Regulations in Italy, Sixteenth to Nineteenth Centuries*, Ashgate, Aldershot, 1998.
Israel, J.I., *Gli ebrei d'Europa nell'età moderna*, il Mulino, Bologna, 1991.
Le Goff, J., *La borsa e la vita. Dall'usuraio al banchiere*, Laterza, Bari, 1987.
Lis, C. and Soly, H., *Povertà e capitalismo nell'Europa preindustriale*, il Mulino, Bologna, 1986.

Holland:

Boxer, C.R., *The Dutch Seaborne Empire, 1600–1800*, Hutchinson, London, 1969.
Dash, M., *La febbre dei tulipani*, Rizzoli, Milan, 1999.
Davids, K. and Lucassen, J., *A Miracle Mirrored. The Dutch Republic in European Perspective*, Cambridge University Press, Cambridge, 1995.
Huizinga, J., *La civiltà olandese nel Seicento*, Einaudi, Turin, 1977.

France:

Braudel, F. and Labrousse, E., *Histoire économique et sociale de la France*, Presses Universities de France, Paris, 1970.
Campbell, P.R., *Luigi XIV e la Francia del suo tempo*, il Mulino, Bologna, 1997.
Duby, G. (gen. ed.), *Histoire de la France urbaine*, 5 vols, Seuil, Paris, 1981.
Le Roy Ladurie, E., *L'ancien Régime*, il Mulino, Bologna, 2000.

England:

Campbell, M., *The English Yeoman under Elizabeth and Early Stuarts*, Barnes & Noble, New Haven CT, 1942.
Coleman, D.C., *The Economy of England, 1450–1750*, Oxford University Press, Oxford, 1977.
Hill, C., *La formazione della potenza inglese*, Einaudi, Turin, 1977
Kishlansky, M., *L'età degli Stuart*, il Mulino, Bologna, 1999.

4 The European economies in the eighteenth century

The best and most recent general studies are to be found in the essays from the book edited by V. Castronovo, *Storia dell'economia mondiale*, vol. II: *Dalle scoperte geografiche alla crescita degli scambi*, Laterza, Rome and Bari, 1997. For detailed accounts of the different national or regional economies see also C.M. Cipolla (ed.), *The Fontana Economic History of Europe*, vol. IV: *The Emergence of Industrial Societies*, Collins, Glasgow and London, 1973 (Italian trans.: *Storia economica d'Europa*, Utet, Turin, 1980).

The best general studies on the European economy of the period include:

Berg, M. and Clifford, H. (eds) *Consumers and Luxury: Consumer Culture in Europe, 1650–1850*, Manchester University Press, Manchester, 1999.

Brewer, J. and Porter, R. (eds) *Consumption and the World of Goods*, (London, 1993.)

Cipolla, C.M., *Storia economica dell'Europa preindustriale*, il Mulino, Bologna, 1994.

Crouzet, F., *A History of the European Economy, 1000–2000*, University Press of Virginia, Charlottesville VA, 2001.

De Vries, J., *The Economy of Europe in an Age of Crisis, 1500–1750*, Cambridge University Press, Cambridge, 1976.

De Vries, J. and van der Wande, A., *The First Modern Economy. Success, Failure and Perseverance of the Dutch Economy, 1500–1805*, Cambridge University Press, Cambridge 1997.

Duplessis, R.S., *Transitions to Capitalism in Early Modern Europe*, Cambridge University Press, Cambridge 1997.

Faucci, R., *L'economia politica in Europa dal Cinquecento ai nostri giorni*, Einaudi, Turin, 2000.

Mauro, F., *L'éxpansion européenne 1600–1870*, Presses Universitaires de France, Paris, 1996.

O'Brien, P.K., 'Inseparable connections. Trade, economy, fiscal state and the expansion of empire, 1688–1815', in P.J. Marshall (ed.), *The Oxford History of the British Empire*, vol. II: *The Eighteenth Century*, Oxford University Press, Oxford, 1998.

Ogilvie, S., *The European Economy in the Eighteenth Century*, in T.C.W. Blanning (ed.), *The Oxford Short History of Europe. The Eighteenth Century*, Oxford University Press, Oxford, 2000.

For the industrial revolutions see:

Berg, Maxine and Hudson, Pat `Rethinking the industrial revolution', *Economic History Review*, 45, 1992.

Berg, M., *The Age of Manufactures, 1700–1820*, Routledge, London and New York, 1994.

Hudson, P., *La rivoluzione industriale*, il Mulino, Bologna, 1995 (original edn. 1992).

Mokyr, J., '*Was there a British industrial evolution?*' *Research in Economic History*, Supplement IV, Greenwich CT, 1991.

Mokyr, J., (ed.), *The Economics of the Industrial Revolution*, Rowman & Allanheld, Totowa NJ, 1985.

O'Brien, P., and Quinault, R., *The Industrial Revolution and British Society*, Cambridge University Press, Cambridge, 1991.

Pollard, S., *Peaceful Conquest. The Industrialisation of Europe*, 1760–1970, Oxford University Press, Oxford, 1981 (Italian trans.: *La conquista pacifica. L'industrializzazione in Europa dal 1760 al 1970*, il Mulino, Bologna, 1981).

For the statistical data see:

Bardet, J.P. and Dupaquier, J., *Histoire des populations de l'Europe*, vol. II: *La Révolution démographique, 1750–1914*, Fayard, Paris, 1998.

Wrigley, E.A., *People, Cities and Wealth. The Transformation of Traditional Society*, Blackwell, Oxford, 1987.

Other sources cited in the text include:

Bairoch, P., *Commerce extérieure et développement économique de l'Europe au XIX siécle*, Ecole des hautes études en sciences sociales, Paris, 1976.

Berend, I.T. and Ranki, G., *The European Periphery and Industrialization, 1780–1914*, Cambridge, 1982.

Bergeron, L., *L'Episode napoléonien. Aspects intérieurs, 1799–1815*, Seuil, Paris, 1972.

Crouzet, F., *The Victorian Economy*, Methuen, London, 1982.

Davis, R., *Rise of Atlantic Economies*, Cornell University Press, Ithaca NY, 1973.

De Vries, J., *European Urbanization*, Harvard University Press, Cambridge MA and London, 1984.

Deyon, P. and Guignet, P., 'Royal manufactures and economic progress in France before the industrial revolution, in *Journal of European Economic History*, 9, 1980, pp. 611–32.

Engerman, S. (ed.), *Trade and Industrial Revolution, 1700–1850*, vol. II, Elgar, Cheltenham, 1996.
Geremek, B., *La pietà e la forca. Storia della miseria e della carità in Europa*, Laterza, Rome and Bari, 1986.
Gerschenkron, A., *Economic Backwardness in Historical Perspective*, Harvard University Press, Cambridge MA, 1962. (Italian trans.: *Il problema storico dell'arretratezza economica*, Einaudi, Turin, 1965).
Gutton, J.P., *La Société et les pauvres en Europe, XVI–XVIII siècles*, PUF, Presses Universitaires de France, Paris, 1974.
Hohenberg, P.M. and Lees, L.J., *La città europea dal medioevo ad oggi*, Laterza, Rome and Bari, 1987.
Inkori, J.E. and Engerman, S.L. (ed.), *The Atlantic Slave Trade, Effects on Economics, Societies and People in Europe, Africa and the Americas*, Duke University Press, Durham NC, 1992.
Klein, H.S., *The Middle Passage. Comparative Studies in the Atlantic Slave Trade*, Princeton University Press, Princeton NJ, 1978.
Klima, A., 'Beginning of the machine-building industry in the Czech Lands in the first half of the nineteenth century', *Journal of European Economic History*, 4 (1), 1975.
Kriedte, P., 'Demographic and economic rhythms. Krefeld in the eighteenth century, *Journal of European Economic History*, 15 (2), 1986.
Rostow, W.W., *The Stages of Economic Growth*, MIT Press, Cambridge MA, 1960.
Tracy, J.D. (ed.), *The Rise of the Merchant Empires*, Cambridge University Press, Cambridge, 1990.
Wallerstein, I., *Il sistema mondiale dell'economia moderna*, vol. III: *L'era della seconda grande espansione dell'economia mondo capitalistica, 1730–1840*, il Mulino, Bologna, 1995 (original edn. 1989).
William, J., *British Commercial Policy and Trade Expansion, 1750–1850*, Oxford University Press, Oxford, 1972.
Wilson, C., *England's Apprenticeship 1603–1763*, Longman. London, 1965.
Woolf, S.J., *Napoleon's Integration of Europe*, Routledge, London, 1991.

5–8 The economic development of Europe in the nineteenth century

Editorial requirements and the aims of the book make it necessary to restrict the bibliography to the essential and more general works. Specific texts are indicated in the notes to the text, where numerous essays from collective editions are also cited in the bibliography under the names of the editors.

Arndt, H.W., *Lo sviluppo economico. Storia di un'idea*, il Mulino, Bologna, 1990.
Ashwort, W., *Breve storia dell'economia mondiale dal 1850 ad oggi*, Laterza, Bari, 1976.
Asselain, J.Ch., *Histoire économique. De la révolution industrielle à la première guerre mondiale*, Presses de la Fondation National de Sciences Politiques et Dalloz, Paris, 1985.
Bairoch, P., *Commerce extérieur et développement de l'Europe au XIX siècle*, EHESS, Paris, 1976.
Bairoch, P., 'Europe's gross national product, 1800–1975', *Journal of European Economic History*, 5, 1976.
Bairoch, P., *Economia e storia mondiale. Miti e paradossi*, Garzanti, Milan, 1996.
Bairoch, P. and Hobsbawm, E.J. (eds), *Storia d'Europa*, vol. V: *L'età contemporanea*, Einaudi, Turin, 1996.
Barnett, V., *Kondratiev and the Dynamics of Economic Development. Long Cycles and Industrial Growth in Historical Context*, Macmillan, Basingstoke, 1998.
Barsby, S., 'Economic backwardness and the characteristics of development', *Journal of Economic History*, 29, 1969.

Baryot, O. (ed.), *Industrialisation et sociétés en Europe Occidentale du début des années 1880 à la fin des années 1960. France, Allemagne-RFA, Italie, Royaume-Uni et Bénélux, Sedes*, Paris, 1997.

Berg, M., *The Age of Manufactures, 1700–1820. Industry, Innovation and Work in Britain*, Routledge, London, 1994.

Borelli, G., *Questioni di storia economica europea tra età moderna e contemporanea*, Cedam, Padua, 2001.

Braudel, F., *Civiltà materiale, economia e capitalismo*, Einaudi, Turin, 1982.

Briggs, A., *L'Inghilterra vittoriana*, Editori Riuniti, Rome, 1978.

Brusio, C. and Marchese, C., *Il potere di spendere. Economia e storia della spesa pubblica dall'Unificazione ad oggi*, il Mulino, Bologna, 1986.

Cafagna, L., *Dualismo e sviluppo nella storia d'Italia*, Marsilio, Venice, 1989.

Cameron, R., *Storia economica del mondo. Dalla preistoria ad oggi*, il Mulino, Bologna, 1998.

Carera, A., Trezzi, L. *et al.*, *L'Ottocento economico italiano*, ed. S. Zaninelli, Monduzzi, Bologna, 1993.

Castronovo, V., *Storia economica d'Italia. Dall'Ottocento ai nostri giorni*, Einaudi, Turin, 1995.

Cattini, M., *Introduzione alla storia economica moderna e contemporanea del mondo*, Cà Sanguinetti, Modena, 2000.

Chandler, A.D., *Dimensione e diversificazione. Le dinamiche del capitalismo industriale*, il Mulino, Bologna, 1994.

Ciocca, P.L. and Toniolo, G. (eds), *Storia economica d'Italia*, vol. I: *Interpretazioni*, Cariplo-Laterza, Milan, Rome and Bari, 1998.

Cipolla, C.M. (ed.), *Storia economica d'Europa*, Utet, Turin, 1979–80.

Ciriacono, S., *La rivoluzione industriale. Dalla protoindustrializzazione alla produzione flessibile*, B. Mondadori, Milan, 2000.

Collins, M., *Banks and Industrial Finance in Britain, 1800–1939*, Macmillan, London, 1991.

Collinson, S., *Le migrazioni internazionali e l'Europa. Un profilo storico comparato*, il Mulino, Bologna, 1994.

Crafts, N.F.R., 'Patterns of development in nineteenth-century Europe', *Oxford Economic Papers*, 36, 1984.

Crafts, N.F.R., 'La recente storia quantitativa della rivoluzione industriale', *Rivista di Storia Economica*, 3 (1989).

Crouzet, F., *Histoire de l'économie européenne*, Albin Michel, Paris, 2000.

David, P.A., *Technical Choice, Innovation and Economic Growth*, Cambridge University Press, Cambridge, 1975.

Davis, P.A. and Huttenback, R.A., *Mammon and the Pursuit of Empire. The Economics of British Imperialism*, Cambridge University Press, Cambridge, 1988.

Deane, P., *La prima rivoluzione industriale*, il Mulino, Bologna, 1973.

De Cecco, M., *Moneta e impero. Il sistema finanziario internazionale dal 1890 al 1914*, Einaudi, Turin, 1979.

Drummond, I., *The Gold Standard and the International Monetary System, 1900–1939*, Macmillan, London, 1987.

Eichengreen, B. (ed.), *The Gold Standard in Theory and History*, Methuen, London, 1985.

Elbaum, B. and Lazonick, W. (ed.), *The Decline of the British Economy*, Clarendon Press, Oxford, 1986.

Flinn, M.W., *Il sistema demografico europeo*, il Mulino, Bologna, 1983.

Fontana, G.L. (ed.), *Le vie dell'industrializzazione europea. Sistemi a confronto*, il Mulino, Bologna, 1997.

Gerschenkron, A., *Il problema storico dell'arretratezza economica*, Einaudi, Turin, 1965.

Gille, B., *Storia delle tecniche*, Editori Riuniti, Rome, 1985.

Grigg, D., *Storia dell'agricoltura in Occidente*, il Mulino, Bologna, 1994.

Hajnal, J., 'Modelli europei di matrimonio in prospettiva storica', in M. Barbagli (ed.), *Famiglia e mutamento sociale*, il Mulino, Bologna, 1977.

Hartwell, R.M. (ed,), *La rivoluzione industriale*, Utet, Turin, 1971 (original edn. 1967).

Hartwell, R.M. (ed.), *La rivoluzione industriale inglese*, Laterza, Rome and Bari, 1973 (original edn. 1971).

Heffer, J. and Serman, W., *Il XIX secolo, 1815–1914. Dalle rivoluzioni agli imperialismi*, Italian edn. ed. S. Zaninelli, Led, Milan, 1998.

Hudson, P., *La rivoluzione industriale*, il Mulino, Bologna, 1995.

Kemp, T., *L'industrializzazione in Europa nell'800*, il Mulino, Bologna, 1988.

Kennedy, W.P., *Industrial Structure, Capital Markets and the Origins of British Industrial Decline*, Cambridge University Press, Cambridge, 1987.

Kenwood, A.G. and Lougheed, A.L., *The Growth of the International Economy, 1820–1990*, London and New York, 1992.

Kuznets, S., *Modern Economic Growth. Rate, Structure and Spread*, Yale University Press, New Haven CT, 1966.

Kuznets, S., *Popolazione, tecnologia, sviluppo*, il Mulino, Bologna, 1990.

Landes, D.S., *Prometeo liberato. Trasformazioni tecnologiche e sviluppo industriale nell'Europa Occidentale dal 1750 ai giorni nostri*, Einaudi, Turin, 1978.

Landes, D.S., *La favola del cavallo morto. Ovvero la rivoluzione industriale rivisitata*, Donzelli, Rome, 1994.

Landes, D.S., Mathias P., Mori G., North D.C. *et al.*, *La rivoluzione industriale tra il Settecento e l'Ottocento*, ed. L. Segreto, Mondadori, Milan, 1984.

Leboutte, R., *Vie et mort des bassins industriels en Europe, 1750–2000*, Hachette, Paris, 1997.

Leboutte, R., Puissant, J. and Scuto, D., *Un siècle d'histoire industrielle. Belgique, Luxembourg, Pays-Bas. Industrialisation et sociétés*, Sedes, Paris, 1998.

Léon, P., *Storia economica e sociale del mondo*, vol. IV: *Il capitalismo, 1840–1914*, Laterza, Bari, 1980.

Lesourd, J.A. and Gérard, C., *Storia economica dell'Ottocento e del Novecento*, Italian edn. ed. G. Mori, Isedi, Milan, 1973.

Lévy-Leboyer, M. and Bourguignon, F., *L'Économie française au XIX siècle*, Economica, Paris, 1985.

Lévy-Leboyer, M. (ed.), *Histoire de la France industrielle*, Larousse, Paris, 1996.

Livi Bacci, M., *Popolazione e alimentazione. Saggio sulla storia demografica europea*, il Mulino, Bologna, 1987.

Lloyd-Jones, R., *British Industrial Capitalism since the Industrial Revolution*, UCL Press, London, 1998.

Luzzatto, G., *Storia economica dell'età moderna e contemporanea*, 2 vols, Cedam, Padua, 1955–60.

Macry, P., *La società contemporanea*, il Mulino, Bologna, 1992.

Maddison, A., *Le fasi di sviluppo del capitalismo*, Giuffrè, Milan, 1987.

Maddison, A., *Dynamic Forces in Capitalist Development. A Long-run Comparative View*, Oxford University Press, Oxford, 1991.

Maddison, A., *Monitoring the World Economy*, OECD, Paris, 1995.

Malanima, P., *Economia preindustriale. Mille anni: dal IX al XVIII secolo*, B. Mondadori, Milan, 2000.

Marseille, J. (ed.), *L'industrialisation de l'Europe occidentale, 1880–1970*, ADHE, Paris, 1998.

Mathias, P., 'Riflessioni sul processo di industrializzazione in Europa', in G.L. Fontana (ed.), *Le vie dell'industrializzazione europea. Sistemi a confronto*, il Mulino, Bologna, 1997.

Mathias, P. and Davis, J.A. (eds), *Le prime rivoluzioni industriali*, Cacucci, Bari, 1992.

McCloskey, D.N. and Floud, R. (eds), *The Economic History of Britain since 1700*, 3 vols, Cambridge University Press, Cambridge, 1994.

Mendels, F., 'Protoindustrialization. The first phase of the industrialization process', *Journal of European Economic History*, 32, 1972.

Milward, A.S. and Saul, S.B., *Storia economica dell'Europa continentale, 1780–1870*, il Mulino, Bologna, 1977.

Mitchell, B.R., *European Historical Statistics*, Macmillan, London, 1981.

Mitchell, B.R., *International Historical Statistics of Europe, 1750–1988*, Macmillan, Basingstoke, 1992.

Mori, G. (ed.), *L'industrializzazione in Italia, 1861–1900*, il Mulino, Bologna, 1989.

Mokyr, J., *Twenty-five Centuries of Technological Change*, Harwood Academic, New York, 1993.

Mokyr, J., *La Leva della ricchezza. Creatività tecnologica e progresso economico*, il Mulino, Bologna, 1995.

North, D.C., *Structure and Change in Economic History*, Norton, New York, 1981.

North, D.C., 'Transaction Costs in Economic History', *Journal of European Economic History*, 14, 1985.

North, D.C. and Thomas, R., *L'evoluzione economica del mondo occidentale*, Mondadori, Milan, 1976.

North, D.C. and Weingast, B., 'Constitutions and Commitment. Evolution of Institutions Governing Public Choice in 17th-Century England', *Journal of European Economic History*, 18, 1989.

Parker, W.N. (ed.), *Economia e storia*, Laterza, Rome and Bari, 1998.

Pecorari, P., *Il protezionismo imperfetto. Luigi Luzzatti e la tariffa doganale del 1878*, Istituto Veneto di Scienze, Lettere ed Arti, Venice, 1989.

Pollard, S., *La conquista pacifica. L'industrializzazione in Europa dal 1760 al 1970*, il Mulino, Bologna, 1981.

Pollard, S., *British Prime and British Decline. The British Economy*, Arnold, London, 1989.

Reinhard, C.M., Armengaud, A. and Dupaquier, J., *Storia della popolazione mondiale*, Laterza, Bari, 1971.

Riannetti, R. and Toninelli, P.A. (ed.), *Innovazione, impresa e sviluppo economico*, il Mulino, Bologna, 1991.

Rosenberg, N. and Birdzell, L.B., *Come l'Occidente è diventato ricco. Le trasformazioni economiche del mondo industriale*, il Mulino, Bologna, 1988.

Rostow, W.W., *Gli stadi dello sviluppo economico*, Einaudi, Turin, 1962.

Schumpeter, J.A., *La teoria dello sviluppo economico*, Utet, Turin, 1932.

Schumpeter, J.A., *Il processo capitalistico. Cicli economici*, Boringhieri, Turin, 1977 (partial Italian edn. of *Business Cycles. A Theoretical, Historical and Statistical Analysis of the Capitalist Process*, 2 vols, McGraw-Hill, New York, 1939).

Singer, C.(ed.), *Storia della tecnologia*, 7 vols, Bollati-Boringhieri, Turin, 1961–84.

Sylla, R. and Toniolo, G. (ed.), *Patterns of European Industrialization. The Nineteenth Century*, Routledge, London, 1991.

Storia economica Cambridge, vol. VI: *La rivoluzione industriale e i suoi sviluppi*, ed. H.S. Habakkuk and M.M. Postan, 2 parts, Einaudi, Turin, 1974.

Storia economica Cambridge, vol. VII: *L'età del capitale*, Part I, *Gran Bretagna, Francia, Germania, Scandinavia*; Part II, *Stati Uniti, Giappone, Russia*, ed. M.M. Postan and P. Mathias, Einaudi, Turin, 1980.

Storia economica Cambridge, vol. VIII: *Le economie industriali*, Part I, *Lo sviluppo delle politiche economiche e sociali*; Part II, *I casi nazionali*, ed. P. Mathias and S. Pollard, Einaudi, Turin, 1992.

Tilly, R., 'La banca universale in una prospettiva storica. L'esperienza tedesca', *Banca impresa società*, I, 1990.

Toninelli, P.A. (ed.), *Lo sviluppo economico moderno dalla rivoluzione industriale alla crisi energetica, 1750–1973*, Marsilio, Venice, 1997.

Tortella, G., *El desarrollo de la España contemporánea. Historia economica de los siglos XIX y XX*, Alianza, Madrid, 1994.
Trebilcock, A., *The Industrialization of the Continental Powers, 1780–1914*, Longman, Harlow, 1981.
Wrigley, E.A., *Demografia e storia*, Il Saggiatore, Milan, 1969.
Wrigley, E.A., *La rivoluzione industriale in Inghilterra. Continuità, caso e cambiamento*, il Mulino, Bologna, 1992.
Woronoff, D., *Histoire de l'industrie en France du XVI siècle a nos jours*, Seuil, Paris, 1994.
Zamagni, V., *Dalla periferia al centro. La seconda rinascita economica dell'Italia, 1861–1990*, il Mulino, Bologna, 1993.
Zamagni, V., *Dalla rivoluzione industriale all'integrazione europea*, il Mulino, Bologna, 1999.

10–12 The twentieth century – from break with the past to prosperity

The publications I refer to are essentially texts that offer, totally or partially, an overall view of the European economy of the twentieth century. They do not mention the enormous specialized literature referring to countries or periods.

The great reference works on European economic history, with or without explicit reference to the rest of the world, are:

Storia economica Cambridge, Einaudi, Turin, 1974–1979/80–1992 (but attention to the twentieth century in vols VI, VII and VIII is generally limited to the first third or just after).
Cipolla, C.M. (ed.), *The Fontana Economic History of Europe*, vol. V: *The Twentieth Century*, 2 vols, and vol. VI:, *Contemporary Economies*, 2 vols, Collins Fontana, London, 1976.
Léon, P. (ed.), *Storia economica e sociale del mondo*, vols IV, V and VI, Laterza, Rome and Bari, 1979–81.

The great textbooks that summarize world economic history and that are worth consulting, are:

Cameron, R., *Storia economica del mondo. Dalla preistoria a oggi*, il Mulino, Bologna, 1998, chapters 13–16.
Foreman-Peck, J., *Storia dell'economia internazionale dal 1850 a oggi*, il Mulino, Bologna, 1999.
Toninelli, P.A. (ed.), *Lo sviluppo economico moderno. Dalla rivoluzione industriale alla crisi energetica, 1750–1973*, Marsilio, Venice, 1997.

Recent efforts have been made to renew the reference base, and it is noteworthy that the very high level of effort has been Italian. The following should be noted:

Anderson, P., Aymard, M., Bairoch, P., Barberis, W. and Ginzburg, C. (eds), *Storia d'Europa*, vol. I: *L'Europa oggi*, Einaudi, Turin, 1993.
Bairoch, P. and Hobsbawm, E. (ed.), *Storia d'Europa*, vol. V: *L'età contemporanea, secoli XIX–XX*, Einaudi, Turin, 1996.
Castronovo, V. (ed.), *Storia dell'economia mondiale*, vols IV–VI), Laterza, Rome and Bari, 2000–01.

Very brief but useful, is:

Zamagni, V., *Dalla rivoluzione industriale all'integrazione economica*, il Mulino, Bologna, 1999.

Among the textbooks specifically devoted to the twentieth century I would mention:

Aldcroft, D., *From Versailles to Wall Street, 1919–1929*, London, 1977.
Castronovo, V. (ed.), *Storia dell'economia mondiale del XX secolo*, 5 vols.

These are now classics.

Hardach, G., *La prima guerra mondiale, 1914–1918*, Etas, Milan, 1982.
Kindleberger, C.P., *La grande depressione nel mondo*, Etas, Milan, 1982.
Milward, A., *Guerra, economia e società, 1939–1945*, Etas, Milan, 1983.
Wee, H. van der, *L'economia mondiale tra crisi e benessere, 1945–1980*, Hoepli, Milan, 1989.

The following have appeared more recently:

Asselain, J.C., *Histoire économique du XX siècle*, 2 vols, Presses de Sciences Politiques and Dalloz, Paris, 1995.
Pollard, S. (ed.), *Storia economica del Novecento*, il Mulino, Bologna, 1999.
Thomas, J.P., *Politiques économiques au XX siècle*, Colin, Paris, 1990.

For the post-war world:

Gauthier, A., *L'economia mondiale dal 1945 ad oggi*, il Mulino, Bologna, 1998. The original French edition covers the whole twentieth century: *L'Économie mondiale depuis la fin du XIX siècle*, Bréal, Paris, 1995.

The following cover only Europe:

Aldcroft, D.H., *The European Economy, 1914–2000*, Routledge, London, 2001.
Ambrosius, G. and Hubbard, W.H., *Sozial- und Wirtschaftgeschichte Europas im 20. Jahrhundert*, Beck, Munich, 1986.

The lack of up-to-date material for the period after the Second World War has led to the preparation of specific volumes. The following concentrate on Western Europe:

Crafts, N. and Toniolo, G. (ed.), *Economic Growth in Europe since 1945*, Cambridge University Press, Cambridge, 1996.
Schulze, M.S. (ed.), *Western Europe. Economic and Social Change since 1945*, Longman, London, 1999.

For international economic co-operation in the post-war world see:

James, H., *Rambouillet, 15 novembre 1975. La globalizzazione dell'economia*, il Mulino, Bologna, 1999.

The best synthesis for the period between the two wars, which contains the most recent developments in research, is:

Feinstein, C., Temin, P. and Toniolo, G., *L'economia europea tra le due guerre*, Laterza, Rome and Bari, 1998.

An excellent overview of the European economy at the beginning of the century is given in the last chapter of:

Pounds, N.J.G., *An Historical Geography of Europe, 1800–1914*, Cambridge University Press, Cambridge, 1985.

The great 'data processor and organizer' of the historical national accounts and other macro-economic variables is Angus Maddison. The following works are very useful in themselves, and provide extremely interesting data bases:

Maddison, A., *The World Economy in the Twentieth Century*, OECD, Paris, 1989.
Maddison, A., *Dynamic Force in Capitalist Development. A Long-run Comparative View*, Oxford University Press, Oxford, 1991.
Maddison, A., *Monitoring the World Economy, 1820–1992*, OECD, Paris, 1995.
Maddison, A., *The World Economy: A Millennial Perspective*, OECD, Paris, 2001.

There are many texts that provide the historical context. A very complete and widely praised introduction is:

Hobsbawm, E., *The Age of Extremes. The Short Twentieth Century*, Michael Joseph, London, 1994.

As an interpretative essay of the great political and social problems of the twentieth century in terms of economic history, recommended reading is:

Tortella, G., *La revoluciòn del siglo XX*, Taurus, Madrid, 2000.

A concise and provocative essay on the century as a whole is:

Ciocca, P., *L'economia mondiale nel Novecento. Una sintesi, un dibattito*, il Mulino, Bologna, 1998.

There have been a number of important monographs by Eichengreen and Milward:

Eichengreen, B., *Gabbie d'oro. Il 'gold standard' e la grande depressione, 1919–1939*, Cariplo, Milan, 1994. (original edn. *Golden Fetters. The Gold Standard and the Great Depression, 1919–1939*, Oxford University Press, New York and Oxford, 1992).

Eichengreen, B., *La globalizzazione del capitale. Storia del sistema monetario internazionale*, Baldini & Castoldi, Milan, 1998.

Keynes, J.M., *The Economic Consequences of the Peace*, Macmillan, London, 1919.

Keynes J.M., *The Economic Consequences of Mr Churchill*, Hogarth Press, London, 1925

Milward, A., *The Reconstruction of Western Europe, 1945–1951*, Methuen, London, 1984.

Milward, A., *The European Rescue of the Nation-State*, Routledge, London, 1992.

Index

www.ingramcontent.com/pod-product-compliance
Lightning Source LLC
LaVergne TN
LVHW021117300926
849160LV00010B/757
* 9 7 8 0 4 1 5 3 5 6 2 5 1 *